W9-CRH-198

Praise for The Art of Community, Second Edition

"In recent years, the growth of community management has been noted across a range of industries, and there is no better mentor than Jono Bacon and *The Art of Community* for unraveling this new profession. Jono provides a comprehensive guide to growing and empowering communities and taking the time to cover the many subtleties hidden in the details. Highly recommended."

> —AARON FULKERSON, CEO, MINDTOUCH

"One hundred years ago, there was no such thing as a "product manager" or a discipline of "product management." In *The Art of Community*, Jono Bacon takes the best and boldest step toward showing the emergence of another new discipline in business: community management. This is a non-optional, pragmatic business function that every executive needs to understand and invest in *right now*."

> —SAM RAMJI, VP OF STRATEGY, APIGEE; PRESIDENT OF THE BOARD, OUTERCURVE
> FOUNDATION

"It was a privilege and honor to be asked to provide a testimonial for the second edition of *The Art of Community*, although at first I was a little bemused, as I wondered what he would add to something he'd already covered so well with such insight. Well, after reading the second edition, I certainly see it was time well spent on his part, and even more so for the reader. As someone who has been consulting in open source for almost 15 years, I've seen a lot of what works and what doesn't, as well as lots of trial and especially error. Reading *The Art of Community* WILL make you smarter and at the same time more caring and considerate of your community colleagues and allow you to reduce the number of trials you go through. At the end of the day, we can't all be Jono Bacon, for whom much of this seems effortless, but through a carefully blended combination of theory, practical advice, and illustrative stories, he's managed to provide us with a path to ultimate community nirvana."

> —ANDREW AITKEN, FOUNDER, OLLIANCE GROUP, A BLACK DUCK SOFTWARE COM-
> PANY, AND THE OPEN SOURCE THINK TANK

Praise for the First Edition

"The Internet provides the potential to separate us into a cacophony of discordant voices or to congregate us as purpose-driven communities. Jono Bacon, in his insightful *The Art of Community*, teaches the latter path, detailing the principles of successful community-building in a way that will appeal to both neophyte and expert alike. Given the increasingly critical role of community managers in the technology industry and beyond, *The Art of Community* should find a place on any businessperson's bookshelf, not to mention that of the PTA president, book club organizer, or union activist. Yes, it's that good."

—MATT ASAY, ALFRESCO AND C|NET

"Jono Bacon truly understands communities, and, more importantly, how to build communities that thrive. This is the definitive guidebook to building successful communities—definitive because it is based on Jono's extensive experience as community manager for Ubuntu, a product that inspires an Apple-esque devotion in very large part because of its vast and dedicated community. For developers and entrepreneurs who want to learn how to tap into the power of community, as Ubuntu has done so masterfully, this book is a must-read."

—IAN MURDOCK, FOUNDER OF DEBIAN AND VICE PRESIDENT OF EMERGING PLATFORMS AT SUN

"One thing that's impressed me about Jono Bacon—something one can notice back when he and others were building a community around their pioneering Linux podcast—is that he simply gets the concept of community. It comes out in most everything he says and most every decision he makes. This is the kind of a person you want writing a book on the topic. Open source community building cannot be boiled down to a formula. It's a constant effort, a soft science, an art, and Bacon is an ideal art teacher."

—DAN GOLDSTEIN, PROFESSOR OF MARKETING, LONDON BUSINESS SCHOOL, AND PRINCIPAL RESEARCH SCIENTIST, YAHOO! RESEARCH

"The success of the open source software movement demonstrates that no obstacle is insurmountable when people come together around a shared vision. In *The Art of Community*, Ubuntu Community Manager Jono Bacon gives readers a profound glimpse into his hands-on experience as the orchestrator of one of the movement's most powerful communities. His book offers valuable lessons on effective leadership and community building. Its compelling combination of useful theory, real-world best practices, and instructive personal anecdotes make it a richly comprehensive guide for both aspiring and experienced community leaders."

—RYAN PAUL, ARS TECHNICA

"Communities are very complex ecosystems of human beings. Cultivating, growing, shaping, and guiding the community to make it productive is definitely as much (or even more) art as science. In *The Art of Community*, Bacon does an excellent job of explaining in detail the considerations for managing and cultivating a healthy open source community. He provides a blueprint for developing and maintaining an open source community in a programmatic way, and his attention to detail and understanding of the dynamics of communities make this book an invaluable resource for anyone looking to build and maintain a community. Drawing from his own extensive experience, Bacon does a great job of explaining how to help foster a community, and provides great advice, ranging from choosing infrastructure, measuring growth, and even hiring a community manager. All in all a must-read for any community manager."

—MARK R. HINKLE, VICE PRESIDENT OF COMMUNITY, ZENOSS, INC.

"Jono Bacon has long been an insightful voice for the open source community. Now his artful stories distilling the ethos of organizing people and activities on the Net, at conferences, and in our daily routines provide a framework for successful, community-building strategies."

—PETE KRONOWITT, LINUX AND OPEN SOURCE STRATEGIST, INTEL

"In *The Art of Community*, Jono Bacon once again shows that his nom de guerre is apropos. He breaks down the soft science of community management in a way few others could. With his trademark British humor, he deftly explores the intricacies and subtleties of his trade. The result is both informative and entertaining, and is a must-read for those looking to better understand the soft science that is community management."

—JEREMY GARCIA, FOUNDER OF LINUXQUESTIONS.ORG

"To a soundtrack of heavy metal, free-software geekstar Jono Bacon recounts the story of how he learned to gently yet productively manhandle groups of unruly Internet folks gathered around a common topic or cause. His process and methods are set out in his book, *The Art of Community*, where Jono's non-ego-driven account of community building will aid all manner of bosses, since almost every subject matter these days has a community with hundreds, thousands, tens of thousands, and even (as in the case of World of Warcraft) millions of people clamoring around it. (Even David Hasselhoff!) Be forewarned, capitalist! There is no chapter called 'How to Turn Communities into Dollars,' but following Jono's suggestions may yield you what every leader (even a capitalist) wants: a loyal and passionate community willing to collaborate to achieve a common goal."

—IRINA SLUTSKY, GEEKENTERTAINMENT.TV

"If you listen to open source fans, you might get the idea that the community is elves who come out of the woodwork to fix your broken software while you sleep. In *The Art of Community*, Jono Bacon explains how reality is a little more complicated, and what the community needs in return. This book will help you get started with the diverse skills required to keep a collaborative community on track, including copywriting, social software selection, conflict resolution, and measuring if it's all working."

—DONMARTI, CONFERENCE CHAIR, OPENSOURCEWORLD, AND ORGANIZER,
WINDOWS REFUND DAY, BURN ALL GIFS DAY, FREE DMITRY, AND FREEDOMHEC

"Who would have known, when I first met a scruffy student from Wolverhampton Uni at a LUG meeting all those years ago, that he would end up being the name on the Internet synonymous with the word 'community.' The fact that the Internet's Jono Bacon is now one of the foremost authorities on building and nurturing a community shows that in a volunteer project no one cares about your questionable dress sense, dodgy taste in music, or strange choices in facial hair—all that matters are your contributions, and your ability to get on with, and inspire, others.

"In this book, Jono draws upon a wealth of experience from projects small to big (and when you consider the worldwide phenomenon that was LugRadio, and the worldwide phenomenon that is Ubuntu, you're talking pretty big) to lay out a blueprint for creating and sustaining communities, as well as using real-world examples from prime ministers to celebrity chefs to ground the topics in a wider context. There is a nice balance in that many of the examples are based on success stories, but Jono is brave enough to also illustrate his points with some of his (relatively few) mistakes.

"This book will be useful for anyone looking to build a volunteer community around any kind of project or cause, whether it involves software, open source, raccoons, or none of the above."

—PAUL COOPER, MOBLINUI & APPS ENGINEERING MANAGER, INTEL

"As a rock-solid book, *The Art of Community* is not only about communities, but also management, organization, and even marketing—it is the bible for community leadership. This book should have been out a long time ago, and reading through the chapters made me reflect on almost every important situation I had to face with teams, from conflicts all the way to handling buzz. It would have helped solve some of the issues I was stuck in much faster than I did (although all the issues solved in the end were exactly how Jono described it). I am eager to apply more of this wisdom on the current projects I am involved in."

—SEIF LOTFY, GNOME FOUNDATION, ZEITGEIST COFOUNDER AND TEAM LEADER

"Few people, in my experience, understand how to create, build, and support community better than Jono Bacon. With *The Art of Community*, Jono's taken his experience, his intelligence, as well as his great humor, and has effectively distilled it into an indispensable book for anyone who wants to start a community (whether around software or any other shared interest or endeavor, really) or participate in one in a positive and productive way. Jono understands that communication and authenticity are at the core of effective participation, and goes beyond the theoretical to provide practical guidance on things like governance, process, conflict resolution, and avoiding burnout that is right on the mark. *The Art of Community* is an excellent book!"

—DAVID SCHLESINGER, DIRECTOR, OPEN SOURCE TECHNOLOGIES, ACCESS CO., LTD.;
GNOME FOUNDATION ADVISORY BOARD MEMBER

"Jono Bacon, in *The Art of Community*, takes you on a personal journey to the heart of what it takes to have and become part of a productive and well-oiled community."

—AMBER GRANER, UBUNTU COMMUNITY MEMBER

"Jono Bacon's *The Art of Community* is a wonderful meditation on building communities using modern infrastructure tools and practices gleaned from the Free and Open Source Software movement. Jono's examples, taken from his work on Ubuntu, give a good picture of a working community and how it functions. The fact that the book is backed by a conference (*http:// www. communityleadershipsummit.com/wiki/index.php/Session_Notes*) and an online community (*http://artofcommunityonline.org/*) means this fine effort will potentially continue to grow into the watering hole for community gardeners, leaders, and managers."

—DANESE COOPER, OPEN SOURCE DIVA AND OSI DIRECTOR

SECOND EDITION

The Art of Community

Jono Bacon

Beijing · Cambridge · Farnham · Köln · Sebastopol · Tokyo

The Art of Community, Second Edition

by Jono Bacon

Published by O'Reilly Media, Inc., 1005 Gravenstein Highway North, Sebastopol, CA 95472.

O'Reilly books may be purchased for educational, business, or sales promotional use. Online editions are also available for most titles (*http://my.safaribooksonline.com*). For more information, contact our corporate/institutional sales department: 800-998-9938 or *corporate@oreilly.com*.

Editor: Andy Oram	**Indexer:** BIM Publishing Services
Production Editor: Holly Bauer	**Cover Designer:** Mark Paglietti
Copyeditor: Audrey Doyle	**Interior Designer:** David Futato
Proofreader: BIM Publishing Services	**Illustrator:** Rebecca Demarest

May 2012:   Second Edition.

Revision History for the Second Edition:

2012-05-09   First release

See *http://oreilly.com/catalog/errata.csp?isbn=9781449312060* for release details.

ISBN: 978-1-449-31206-0

[LSI]

1336570586

*For my loving wife, Erica, and all the ways she
continues to make me smile.*

CONTENTS

FOREWORD FROM THE FIRST EDITION

FROM ANTS TO ANTEATERS, bees to beekeepers, community is a fundamental part of our life on the planet. We thrive when we are immersed in it, suffer when deprived of it, and wherever humans go we create it. We define ourselves by our communities: tribe, family, work, clubs, schools, churches and temples, these are who we are. We are born into community, and if we're lucky we'll end our days surrounded by it.

It's no surprise that as soon as humans began to go online, communities formed, but as easy and natural as group formation is for us in real life, we can find it frustrating online. Many of the cues that grease the wheels of human interaction in person are missing online. Gone is the grin that can soften a criticism, the pat on the back that can heal a rift. How can you "hug it out" when your antagonist is a continent away and you know no more about him than his handle and a few lines of signature? Online groups can breed the most vicious of rivalries. The Hatfields and McCoys have nothing on *alt.tv.doctorwho*.

Communities are tough enough to maintain when you're all in the same room; how much harder is it to build, maintain, and nurture a community online? That's why this book is such a boon to those who run communities and the rest of us who participate in them. Jono Bacon has firsthand experience with managing a group of the most bloody-minded and independent people on the planet: open source programmers. The information in this book has been forged in the white-hot crucible of free software. You don't get tougher than that.

My experience with online forums began 25 years ago when I started a bulletin board for Macintosh users called MacQueue. It's not easy to start a flame war with dual 14.4 kbps modems and 20 MB of storage, but the MacQueuers managed. A few years later I joined The Well, a legendary online community based in Sausalito, California, and imbued with the peace and love ethos of the San Francisco hippies. That didn't last long. The Well went through an arc I came to know intimately, one that most online communities seem to follow.

When any affinity group forms online it's a joyous occasion. The founders and early members are wreathed in the cooperative enthusiasm that accompanies most new beginnings. Conversations are civil, helpful, and kind. Posts twinkle with good spirits and bonhomie. All's right with the Web. Then the rot begins to set in. Tempers flare, resentments build, rivalries form. It's a lot like marriage.

Unlike most marriages, however, online members have looser ties to the group and a reduced stake in its success. When trolls become annoying, the flame wars too fiery, members move on, and pretty soon that happy online forum turns into a ghost town, or worse.

But it doesn't have to be that way. With his usual wit and good humor, Jono has written a guide with everything you need to keep your online groups healthy and productive. With proper planning, a modicum of guidance, and the occasional banishment, your community can avoid that seemingly inevitable descent into fear and loathing. We need good community managers because we need healthy communities online. I've started my share of communities online, and killed a few with neglect, too. I'm so grateful to Jono for giving me the tools to do it right from now on. I know we all are.

—Leo Laporte
Broadcaster and Founder of the TWiT Network
Petaluma, California
June 30, 2009

FOREWORD

WHEN I'M NOT RUNNING *WIRED*, I RUN A COMMUNITY CALLED DIY DRONES. Here more than 20,000 members collaborate to make open source unmanned aerial vehicles (UAVs), which are essentially fully autonomous airplanes, helicopters, and other things with spinning propellers that fly all by themselves.

The DIY Drones community has created countless products, but the most successful is ArduPilot, a series of autopilots based on the Arduino computing platform. We're part of the Open Hardware movement, which is to say that there is both a software and a hardware element to the autopilots our community creates, and both are open source. Although I and others also have commercial companies that make and sell this hardware (mine is called 3D Robotics), under the terms of the open source license, anybody, absolutely anybody, can use the designs our community creates and make them to compete with us. It may sound crazy, but such openness can create innovations faster, cheaper, and better than traditional closed source research and design in regular companies. The only risk is that some other company will clone the product and sell it for less, fully within the legal terms of the license.

This is exactly what happened in late 2010. We got word that Chinese copies of our ArduPilot Mega design were for sale on Taobao, eBay, and other online marketplaces. And indeed they were—well-produced, fully functional clones. Not only that, but our English instruction manual had been translated into Chinese, too, along with some of the software.

Our community members reported this blatant "piracy" and asked what we were going to do about it.

Nothing, I said:

> This is both expected and encouraged in open source hardware. Software, which costs nothing to distribute, is free. Hardware, which is expensive to make, is priced at the minimum necessary to ensure the healthy growth of a sustainable business to ensure quality, support, and availability of the products, but the designs are given away free, too. All intellectual property is open, so the community can use it, improve it, make their own variants, etc.
>
> The possibility that others would clone the products is built into the model. It's specifically allowed by our open source license. Ideally, people would change/improve the products ("derivative designs") to address market needs that they perceive and we have not addressed. That's the sort of innovation that open source is designed to promote. But if they only clone the products and sell them at lower prices, that's okay, too. The marketplace will decide.
>
> BTW, the Arduino development boards have gone through exactly the same situation, with many Chinese cloners. The clones were sometimes of lower quality, but even when they were good, most people continued to support the official Arduino products and the developers that created them. Today, clones have a small share of the market, mostly in very price-sensitive markets such as China. And frankly, being able to reach a lower-price market is a form of innovation, too, and that is no bad thing.
>
> Personally, I'm delighted to see this development, for four reasons:
>
> 1. I think it's great that people have translated the wiki into Chinese, which makes it accessible to more people.
> 2. It's a sign of success—you only get cloned if you're making something people want.
> 3. Competition is good.
> 4. What starts as clones may eventually become real innovation and improvements. Remember that our licence requires that any derivative designs must also be open source. Think how great would it be if a Chinese team created a better design than ours. Then we could turn the tables and produce their design, translating the documentation into English and making them available to a market outside China. Everybody wins! (Hey, a guy can dream ;-))

Shortly after I wrote this, a member named "Hazy" responded in the comments that he had been working with the team that had made the boards, and was the one doing the translation. I complimented him on the speed at which it had been done, and then asked him if he'd consider porting the translation to be part of our official manual, which takes the form of a wiki on Google Code, where our repository is. He agreed to do so, and I gave him edit permission to the wiki and otherwise set it up for a parallel Chinese translation that users could select.

At the time, we were using the Subversion version control system (we're now using Git), and Google Code had a relatively basic implementation of it. The wiki pages were just files in the same repository as the source code for our autopilots, and I hadn't investigated the permissions options very well. To let people edit the wiki, I just gave them blanket "commit" access (the ability to create and edit files) to the whole repository.

When I gave community members such access, I usually asked them not to mess with the code by mistake (membership in the code development teams was more exclusive, because the danger of messing things up was higher), but in the case of Hazy, I forgot.

The first thing Hazy did was integrate the Chinese translation of the manual seamlessly, so users could simply click a link to switch easily between the two languages.

Then, because he was an expert in our autopilot (he had, after all, been part of the team that cloned it), he started making corrections in the English manual, as well. I could see all the commits flowing by and approved them all: they were smart, correct, and were written in perfect English.

Then it got interesting: Hazy started fixing bugs in the code itself. The first time this happened, I had assumed he'd made a mistake and pushed a wiki file into the wrong folder. But I checked it out, and it was code, and his fix was not only correct, but properly documented. Who knew that Hazy was a programmer, too?!

I thanked him for the fix, and thought little more of it. But then the code commits kept coming. Hazy was working his way through our Issues list, picking off bugs one after another that the dev team had been too busy to handle themselves.

Today, he is one of our best dev team members. I've still never met him, but after a while I asked him a bit about himself.

His real name is Xiaojiang Huang. He lives in Beijing, and by day he is a PhD student in computer science at Peking University.

He told me his story:

> When I was a kid, I was fascinated by all kinds of models, and I wished I could have a RC plane. Several years later, I was able to afford a RC helicopter when I graduated from college. I also got RC trucks and planes. Sometimes, I am derided as naïve for playing with "toys," but I'm happy because it's my childhood dream. I met ArduPilot by chance when I was surfing the Web, and was attracted by its powerful functions. Some friends of mine were also interested in it, but it felt a little inconvenient because of the English documents. So I tried to translate them into Chinese, hoping to reduce the difficulty of playing with ArduPilot for the Chinese fans. Thank you for the great work of DIYDrones, and I hope it will help more people make their dreams come true.

What happened there is magical. When we first got word of the cloned boards, some in our community initially jumped to the conclusion that this was another case of blatant Chinese piracy and wanted to know when we were going to sue. But by reminding them that this was not a "pirated" version, but instead a "derivative design" fully permitted and even encouraged by our open source license, the tenor changed.

By not demonizing the Chinese team, and instead treating them as part of the community, they acted that way, too. Hazy stepped forward, and rather than just exploiting our work, he contributed to it, too.

So now the "pirates" work for us. Instead of just using our technology, they're working with us to improve the technology for everyone. "Hazy" realized his dreams, and in doing so helped us realize ours, too. That is the power of community.

We all have our different stories of community, and this was just one example of how great communities can touch every one of us. Building a community is a complex business, though. It involves careful planning and consideration, but also the freedom to empower your community members to accomplish things that you never dreamed of.

I can't think of a better guidebook than *The Art of Community* and your fearless tour guide, Jono Bacon, for helping you navigate this journey. In the first edition of the book, Jono created a strong foundation of knowledge for building and empowering communities. The second edition not only refines and extends this body of work, but also shares many other stories of how successful communities have been created and the choices made in doing so. This combination of Jono's experience and insight as well as these real-world stories from other community leaders provides a strong pathway to success in your own communities.

—Chris Anderson

Editor of *Wired Magazine*, author of *The Long Tail* (Hyperion), creator of DIYDrones

Berkeley, California

November 15, 2011

PREFACE

COMMUNITY IS A FUNNY OL' WORD. In recent years our humble nine-letter friend has come to mean many things to many people. No longer merely the domain of charity groups and overtly friendly neighbors, community has gone on to be the talk of technologists, businesspeople, politicians, students, welfare groups, and just about anyone who has connected to the Internet. Throughout this explosive community lovefest, a minor detail has been omitted in all the excitement: how on earth do we build an inspiring, engaging, and enjoyable community in our own walk of life?

Toward the end of summer 2008 I received a phone call from Andy Oram, a well-respected author and editor at O'Reilly. Although at the start of the call Andy was soliciting advice for building community in the educational world, the call ended by sowing the seeds for *The Art of Community*.

Andy's interest in putting together this book was intriguing, but it could not have come at a more complicated time. My days were hectic as the Ubuntu community manager, leading my team to grow, refine, and optimize the global Ubuntu community; I was in the midst of recording a solo metal album as part of a new Creative Commons project called Severed Fifth; I was coorganizing LugRadio Live 2008, recording and producing LugRadio shows every two weeks; and I was making plans to relocate to California. I had written three books before and I was intimately aware of just how incredibly time-consuming the process can be. Writing a book is like having a baby: it requires care and attention, and typically results in late nights, lack of sleep, and heartburn. Consequently, my best friend (who is also an author) and I had struck a no-more-books pact.

Despite all of this, I was intrigued. Community and the skills involved in motivating, building, and inspiring it were rampantly undocumented, and much of my own skills had been developed through trial and error, exposing myself to different communities and observing how they worked. I was fortunate enough to have cut my teeth in community in some compelling environments, and I had always wanted to write a book on the topic.

Fortunately none of these aforementioned challenges made any difference when I talked it through with my best friend, Stuart. He and I have been discussing, debating, and at times arguing about community since 1999, and he knows my views, perspectives, drive, and ambitions about community better than anyone. What's more, he had been wittering on about me writing something down about community, despite our no-more-books pact. Ten minutes with that ginger ball of fury and my mind was made up: it was time to buy some antiheartburn pills and get some coffee in....

Documenting the Undocumented

Part of my initial hesitation in writing a book on community was that I knew it was going to be a tough one to write. In my talks at conferences I often referred to my role as "herding cats." Much of the art of community is subtle, undocumented, and unwritten, and much of my own approach was largely the product of feeling my way around in the dark and learning from what I found. I knew that to write this book I would need to think carefully about not only how to articulate these topics, but also how to handle the more complex challenge of structuring this stream of consciousness into a consistent read that, y'know, actually makes sense.

With this I wrote the first edition and I was proud of the results. The book brought together many of the primary elements involved in building a productive, collaborative community. To do this I distilled my own experiences and insight along with wisdom from others and illustrated these topics using a wealth of examples, stories, and anecdotes. The book started by taking a high-level view of how communities work at a social science level, and then delved straight into topics such as strategic planning, communicating well, building effective and nonbureaucratic processes and infrastructure, creating buzz and excitement, handling conflict and burnout, measuring community, creating and managing governance, organizing events, and even how to hire a community manager.

The Second Edition

When I released the first edition in 2009 I was terrified of how it would be received. The first edition presented a book about a topic that few other books had covered, was a challenge to structure in a logical way (community management topics all intermingle like a spider web), and I wasn't sure if I had hit the right mark with the content. With a nervous twitch I watched it go to press.

Fortunately the book did well. It netted positive reviews and my original worries were alleviated. As the book started to spread I was delighted to see reader feedback, opinions, and ideas shared with me across the various social networks and over email. I continued to push and promote the book, and particularly that the content could be shared freely, and it was wonderful to see various communities and their leaders enjoying the book and finding the content empowering.

Over the next few years I continued doing what I was doing; my Ubuntu community management team grew, Severed Fifth started taking off, I started doing the Shot Of Jaq podcast, and I got the Community Leadership Summit up and running. Across these various projects and spending time with the folks involved I continued to learn more and more about community management and leadership.

As time went on my pride of the first edition was increasingly augmented with a list of things I wanted to add to it—exciting new approaches, ideas, and topics that I had learned and developed that I wanted to share with the readers who had been so generous in their feedback about the first edition. As such, I wrote to Andy Oram to suggest the idea of a second edition. As ever, Andy was supportive and I started putting together content for the book you hold here in your hand (or computer, tablet, or phone).

For this fully revised second edition, I have been through the entire text and added various additional pieces of information, clarified certain points, and refined and updated the content. I have also added a number of new big pieces of content. This includes three new chapters:

Chapter 6, Social Media
> With the advent and popularity of social media this new chapter covers the major social media networks (Twitter, Facebook, and Google+) and the different strategic and day-to-day approaches to harnessing social media for your community.

Chapter 8, Measuring Community
> This entirely new chapter presents approaches and techniques for tracking the work your community or team commits to and methods of keeping this work on track. This is important in delivering value to your community, particularly within the context of volunteers working together effectively to deliver projects.

Chapter 14, Community Case Book
> This book is all about stories and using stories to share experiences and lessons to help you develop your skills as a community manager. This chapter provides a collection of interviews with established community leaders such as Linus Torvalds (creator of Linux), Tim O'Reilly (founder of O'Reilly Media), Mike Shinoda (cofounder of Linkin Park), Mary Colvig (community leader at Mozilla), and many others. I hope you find these stories as inspiring as I did.

There has also been a wealth of additional content draped throughout the existing chapters. This includes:

- A discussion in Chapter 2 of methods for generating revenue to financially support your community
- Additions to Chapter 7 for how to coordinate event attendance, create effective presentations, and deliver great talks
- A discussion in Chapter 8 about how to react to community concerns in a structured and feedback-oriented way
- Several additional conflict and relationship scenarios in Chapter 11 and how to handle them
- A significant addition to Chapter 12 for how to create a community summit, using the Ubuntu Developer Summit as an outline

Of course, there are many additional sidebars, clarifications, notes, and other pieces hidden throughout the book, too.

While this edition provides a solid map for the road ahead, I am a firm believer that the road map will continue to expand and take on color and texture through further editions. Community leadership is still very much a young science, and this book is still very much on that journey.

Where much of this insight will continue to grow is on the book's website at *http://www .artofcommunityonline.org* and at the annual community leadership event that I organize, the Community Leadership Summit (*http://www.communityleadershipsummit.com*). I would like to invite all of you good people to first enjoy *The Art of Community* and to then provide your own feedback, stories, and experiences to guide future editions.

THE COMMUNITY CASE BOOK

We're always watching and learning, and iterating on our designs as the community evolves so we can build a better and more enjoyable experience, and everything we have learned will be applied to our future projects.

—*James Spafford, on Learning*

Read the full interview in Chapter 14.

Who Is This Book For?

This book was written to be open and applicable to a wide range of communities. While O'Reilly is traditionally a computer book publisher, *The Art of Community* is not specifically focused on computing communities, and the vast majority of its content is useful for political groups, digital rights, knitting, and beyond.

Within this wide range of possible communities, this book will be useful for a range of readers:

Professional community managers
    If you work in the area of community management professionally

Volunteers and community leaders
    If you want to build a strong and vibrant community for your volunteer project

Commercial organizations
    If you want to work with, interact with, or build a community around your product or service

Open source developers
    If you want to build a successful project, manage contributors, and build buzz

Marketeers
    If you want to learn about viral marketing and building a following around a product or service

Activists
    If you want to get people excited about your cause

Every chapter in this book is applicable to each of these roles. While technology communities provide many examples throughout the book, understanding these examples requires little technical knowledge.

The Road Ahead

Throughout this book we are going to delve into the wide range of topics that face those of us who want to build and inspire great communities. Page after page we are going to weave an intricate web of the concepts, skills, and approaches involved in energizing a vibrant community and helping the members of that community to energize themselves.

This book is divided into 15 chapters, with each building on what went before. Let's take a quick glance at the road ahead:

Chapter 1, *The Art of Community*
    We begin the book with a bird's-eye view of how communities function at a social science level. We cover the underlying nuts and bolts of how people form communities, what keeps them involved, and the basis and opportunities behind these interactions.

Chapter 2, *Planning Your Community*
    Next we carve out and document a blueprint and strategy for your community and its future growth. Part of this strategy includes the target objectives and goals and how the community can be structured to achieve them.

Chapter 3, *Communicating Clearly*

At the heart of community is communication, and great communicators can have a tremendously positive impact. Here we lay down the communications backbone and the best practices associated with using it.

Chapter 4, *Processes: Simple Is Sustainable*

We then move on to focus on putting the facilities in place for your community to do great things. In this chapter we build simple, effective, and nonbureaucratic processes that enable your community to conduct tasks, work together, and share their successes.

Chapter 5, *Supporting Workflow with Tools and Data*

We continue our discussion of community facilities to build workflows that are driven by accessible, sensible, and rock-solid tools that enable your contributors to do great work quickly and easily.

Chapter 6, *Social Media*

We now take a look at social networking, what it is, how it can help us, how to avoid the hype, and how to harness it in our communities.

Chapter 7, *Building Buzz*

With a solid foundation in place, we move on to build excitement and buzz around your community and encourage and enthuse every man and his dog to get involved and participate.

Chapter 8, *Measuring Community*

Although many consider community touchy-feely and unmeasurable, this chapter confronts the myth and guides you in tracking, monitoring, and otherwise measuring the work going on in the community so that it can be optimized and simplified.

Chapter 9, *Managing and Tracking Work*

Continuing on from measuring our community, we now explore methods by which you can ensure that your community projects and participants stay on track and deliver great results.

Chapter 10, *Governance*

Our next stop is the wide-ranging and seemingly complex topic of governance. We explore what options are available for a low-friction, capable, and representative governance strategy for your community.

Chapter 11, *Handling Conflict and Relationships*

One of the most sensitive topics in community leadership is handling conflict. In this chapter we explore how to identify, handle, and prevent irksome conflict; handle divisive personalities; and unblock problems.

Chapter 12, *Creating and Running Events*

Events offer an excellent opportunity for your community to bond, be productive, and have fun, and this is where we cast our beady eye in this chapter.

Chapter 13, *Hiring a Community Manager*

We now explore some advice and guidance for organizations that want to hire a community manager to conduct and implement the wide range of topics that we have discussed throughout the book.

Chapter 14, *Community Case Book*

Next I present a fascinating collection of interviews from accomplished community builders about how they created their own inspirational communities to help round off your knowledge with the experiences of these leaders.

Chapter 15, *Onward and Upward*

Finally, we close *The Art of Community* with some additional resources and events to continue your journey.

Each of these broad topics is a piece in the jigsaw puzzle, a note in the song, and a letter in the book. Step by step we will discuss these topics using a liberal supply of stories, anecdotes, and examples to illuminate the path ahead. As we continue throughout the book, more and more of the road will become clear, and you will begin to develop your own approaches, patterns, and methods of engaging your own community.

If You Like (or Don't Like) This Book

If you like—or don't like—this book, by all means, please let people know. Amazon reviews are one popular way to share your happiness (or lack of happiness), or you can leave reviews at the site for the book:

http://oreil.ly/art_of_community_2e

There's also a link to errata there. Errata gives readers a way to let us know about typos, errors, and other problems with the book. That errata will be visible on the page immediately, and we'll confirm it after checking it out. O'Reilly can also fix errata in future printings of the book and on Safari Books Online, making for a better reader experience pretty quickly.

License

This book was very carefully licensed to ensure that everyone has access to the content. O'Reilly and I believe that community and the skills that encompass the growth and management of community should be available to everyone. We don't believe that only people who can afford to buy books should have access to this information. With this in mind, *The Art of Community* has been licensed in a way that ensures that everyone has access to the information.

The book is licensed under a *Creative Commons Attribution-NonCommercial-ShareAlike* license.

This license allows you to freely download the book and share it with your friends. The license also allows you to freely copy content from the book and share it with others or in other (noncommercial) documents under the requirement that you credit the work to *The Art of*

Community (O'Reilly) by Jono Bacon. You are not allowed to commercially redistribute the book; if you want to discuss commercial redistribution or commercial opportunities, please contact O'Reilly.

Join Our Community

Since I began working on *The Art of Community*, this book has developed its own community, which is primarily composed of those who are passionate about building strong and compelling communities.

The hub of this activity is at *http://www.artofcommunityonline.org*. The website has a range of features available at the time of this writing, and likely will have many more when you get there:

Download the book
> You can download the full version of the book, available under the Creative Commons Attribution-NonCommercial-ShareAlike license.

Stay up-to-date
> Get updates on the book, and share and read about success stories of communities that are using the book.

Discuss success stories
> The website is filled with resources in which you can chat and talk about great community building with other readers.

Learn more
> Stories, case studies, and other content are regularly published to the site, to help build your knowledge.

Provide feedback
> The website is a great place to leave feedback about the book for future editions.

In addition to the main website, you can also keep up-to-date with news on the book and other community-building stories on Twitter at *http://www.twitter.com/jonobacon*.

Typographical Conventions Used in This Book

The following typographical conventions are used in this book:

Italic
> Indicates new terms, URLs, email addresses, filenames, file extensions, pathnames, and directories.

Safari® Books Online

Safari Books Online (*www.safaribooksonline.com*) is an on-demand digital library that delivers expert content in both book and video form from the world's leading authors in technology and business.

Technology professionals, software developers, web designers, and business and creative professionals use Safari Books Online as their primary resource for research, problem solving, learning, and certification training.

Safari Books Online offers a range of product mixes and pricing programs for organizations, government agencies, and individuals. Subscribers have access to thousands of books, training videos, and prepublication manuscripts in one fully searchable database from publishers like O'Reilly Media, Prentice Hall Professional, Addison-Wesley Professional, Microsoft Press, Sams, Que, Peachpit Press, Focal Press, Cisco Press, John Wiley & Sons, Syngress, Morgan Kaufmann, IBM Redbooks, Packt, Adobe Press, FT Press, Apress, Manning, New Riders, McGraw-Hill, Jones & Bartlett, Course Technology, and dozens more. For more information about Safari Books Online, please visit us online.

How to Contact Us

Please address comments and questions concerning this book to the publisher:

O'Reilly Media, Inc.
1005 Gravenstein Highway North
Sebastopol, CA 95472
800-998-9938 (in the United States or Canada)
707-829-0515 (international or local)
707-829-0104 (fax)

We have a web page for this book, where we list errata, examples, and any additional information. You can access this page at:

http://oreil.ly/art_of_community_2e

To comment or ask technical questions about this book, send email to:

bookquestions@oreilly.com

For more information about our books, courses, conferences, and news, see our website at *http://www.oreilly.com*.

Find us on Facebook: *http://facebook.com/oreilly*

Follow us on Twitter: *http://twitter.com/oreillymedia*

Watch us on YouTube: *http://www.youtube.com/oreillymedia*

Acknowledgments

This book was a long time coming, and I want to thank a number of people who directly and indirectly helped me to make this book a reality. First and foremost I want to thank my incredible family: my wonderful and hugely encouraging wife, Erica; my Mum and Dad; Martin and Simon; Grandad; Joe; Sue; Adam; and Emily. Thanks also to my best pal Aq for bullying me into writing this book; to the horsemen Daniel Holbach, Jorge Castro, David Planella, Michael Hall, and Nicholas Skaggs on my team at Canonical; and to Rick Spencer, Matt Zimmerman, Mark Shuttleworth, and the LugRadio Team (Adam, Chris, Ade, and Matt).

I also want to express huge thanks to the many people who contributed the stories and interview content that is featured in this book. Your contributions have added flesh to the bones and helped to illustrate the book so well. Thanks also to the many people who are featured in the book's stories and examples; those experiences have taught me so much and allowed me to share this knowledge with my readers.

I also want to give my utmost thanks and gratitude to Andy Oram from O'Reilly for making this book happen, and to Simon St. Laurent and Isabel Kunkle for lending their editing prowess. Also, thanks to our fantastic team of review editors: Stephen Walli, Stuart Langridge, Amber Graner, and Erica Bacon.

Finally, huge thanks to everyone who has supported my work and the book on *http://www .artofcommunityonline.org/* and *http://www.jonobacon.org/*, and to the hundreds of people who have spread the word through their blogs, podcasts, Twitter/identi.ca feeds, Facebook, and elsewhere. I appreciate every ounce of your support!

All right, 'nuff chatting. Let's get started....

CHAPTER ONE

The Art of Community

"Great things are not done by impulse, but by a series of small
things brought together."

—*Vincent van Gogh*

As **my watch ticked over to 6 p.m., I knew I was in trouble.** First of all, I was late, and
not fashionably late either. In fact, at the time, I was about as unfashionable as you could get
for someone staring 18 down the barrel. Long hair, Iron Maiden t-shirt, baggy camouflage
trousers, and a thumping-great leather jacket. I left my parents' house and got into my small
van, adorned with oversized speakers and a tree-shaped air freshener. It was time to roll.

"Rolling" was optimistic. Instead, I sat bumper-to-bumper in traffic with half of Southern
England, all joined in curiosity about whether or not that film with Michael Douglas could
become a reality on this cold English day.

This wasn't helping my nerves. As a fairly outgoing, angsty teen, nerves were not usually my
bag, but tonight, I was dining on them.

You see, tonight was different. Tonight I was doing something unusual, something that had
seemed like a great idea…when I wasn't running 30 minutes late, hammering my way down
the motorway, with my *Number of the Beast* cassette ritualistically sacrificed to the gods of hi-fi
just for good measure.

Thankfully, the world's longest mechanical conga line decided to crank it up a notch. Before
I knew it, I found myself on a street I had never been to, in a city I had never been to, about
to head into a room full of people I had never met before, all united by one simple symbol…

A penguin.

An hour before, that penguin had seemed so inviting and friendly. It was a symbol that encompassed everything about the movement it represented, a movement that came together in spirit and mind to build a system that drove a new generation of technology and freedom... a movement that celebrated this drive by forming user groups in unknown streets, in unknown cities, and with unknown people.

But as I stood there, doorbell already pressed, none of that was even close to my conscious thoughts. Instead, the brain of one Jonathan E. J. Bacon was battening down the hatches, preparing for ultimate, unparalleled discomfort as I walked into a place I both did and didn't want to be at the same time.

Then the door opened and a rather nice chap called Neil welcomed me into his home.

Community is a funny beast. Most people—the kind who watch talent shows on television and occasionally dip bread in oil in an expensive restaurant—don't understand people like Neil. Why on earth would this guy decide to open his home, free of charge, to a collection of strangers who met on the Internet? Why would he want to spend an evening drinking tea and making jokes about something called "Emacs"? And why would he fund online resources like fliers, a mailing list, and a website from his own pocket; start a book-lending service for the group—and even shell out for tea and biscuits?

One person who really didn't seem to understand was Neil's wife. Somewhat bemused, and referring to us as his "Internet friends," Neil's significant other decided tonight was the night for visiting a long-lost (or possibly ignored) relative, rather than sticking around and faking interest.

Collaboration-Driven Ethos

But Neil is not unusual. At least, not in the Open Source, Free Software, Libre, and Free Culture world. There are many Neils all over the globe, organizing groups, setting up mailing lists, scheduling meetings, and coming together to share an *ethos*: the combined set of beliefs, customs, and sentiment that flows between like-minded people.

In the past 10 to 15 years, we have seen Free Culture in technology, art, and the media explode into our consciousness. The entire machine is driven by people like Neil; people who volunteer themselves to the concepts of community and togetherness wrapped around such an ethos.

There are Neils outside the Free Culture world, too. They're in church groups, helping the poor and unfortunate; in Neighborhood Watch and Meals on Wheels campaigns, reaching out to those around them; and in public art installations, political groups, and craft fairs. They volunteer, perform, and share their opinions and creativity on anything from aerobics to knitting to yoga.

What intrigued me when I first walked into Neil's living room was the concept of a *collaboration-driven ethos,* although at the time I had no idea what those words meant. What that experience taught, and what that evening inspired in me, was an excitement about what is possible when you get a group of people together who share a common ethos and a commitment to furthering it.

In my world, that ethos has thus far been Free Culture, Free Software, digital rights, and breaking down the digital divide, but it can be as critical as creating world peace or as fanciful as sharing photos of kittens playing guitars on the Internet. The importance of community is not in the crusade, but in how you unify people to march forward together, side by side.

At its heart, *The Art of Community* is a distilled set of approaches and thoughts about how to build community. The book is a collection of experiences, observations, and thoughts from my career and elsewhere. My aim is to bring this grab bag of concepts and curiosities together into one consistent text.

However, it is important that we keep the book in perspective in the wider scheme of your growth as a community leader and organizer. You should mentally frame the content here as a foundation for your own ideas, but remember that practical experience is the real magic that we want to create, with theory merely the glittery jacket and spinning bow tie.

Community is fundamentally a *soft science.* Compare it with, for example, programming. If you want to write a computer software application, you write it in a programming language. These synthetic languages are vessels of logic. They live and breathe in a world where the answer to a question is either *yes* or *no*; there is no *maybe*. In a world where *maybe* does not exist, you can plan ahead for an answer. With community, the importance and diversity of the question is equally essential.

MAPPING OUT THE JOURNEY

In this chapter we are going to be exploring the big-picture attributes that are present in every community. As such, this chapter is filled with a lot of high-level theory that's important to our journey.

It may be tempting to steam ahead and dig into the hands-on content in later chapters, but it is recommended that you read and understand all of the concepts in this chapter first.

This chapter was designed for tea and snacks. Go and grab some, curl up in a chair, and get ready to explore the social schematics of your community.

The Essence of Community

On February 26, 2004, three friends and I released the first episode of a new audio show called LugRadio (*http://www.lugradio.org/*). Although LugRadio will be featured extensively in this book as a source of stories, all you really need to know about it right now is that (a) it was a loose and fun audio show (a podcast) about open source and free culture, (b) on that day it was entirely new, and (c) we had absolutely no idea what on earth we were doing. Radio personalities across the world were not exactly shaking in their boots.

Recorded in a very small room that I called a studio, but was actually a bedroom filled with secondhand recording equipment, LugRadio involved my three compadres and me opining into four precariously balanced microphones that fed into a computer. Episode 1 was around half an hour long, composed of bad jokes and a book review, and totally unpolished. At the time, it was just new and different. Little did we know that four years later we would wrap up the show having achieved over 2 million downloads. Anyway, enough of the self-congratulatory back-patting and back to the story....

With the show out, we did what many of us in the open source world do—we set up forums, wikis, and channels, and tried to get people together around our new project. The forums went online first, and people started joining.

The 22nd member was a guy called Ben Thorp, known as mrben on the forums. An Englishman living in Scotland, mrben was an open source enthusiast who stumbled onto the forums, listened to the show, and liked what he heard. For the four years that LugRadio lasted, mrben was there every single day: in total contributing over 3,000 posts; involving himself in the chat channel, the wiki, and the organization of the live events; running an episode download mirror; and much more. Mrben was there every step of the way, loving every second of it.

The first question is, Why? Why does a 30-something Engli-Scot decide to immerse himself so deeply in a group of people he has never met before? What is it that makes him want to spend time away from his friends and family to contribute to a radio show performed by four strangers in a different country? Why would he want to contribute to something with seemingly no financial, career, or other conventional benefit to him?

A cynic could argue that mrben is some kind of socially challenged nerd who can only communicate with other similarly socially inept nerds. Conventional wisdom sometimes argues that anyone who freely contributes his time to something that could not benefit him financially is weird. This was clearly not the case with Ben. He had a job, a wife, and a child. He went to church regularly. When I had the pleasure of socializing with him, I found him a fun, smart, and entertaining part of the group. In fact, at two of the live events, he was a guest in my home. Social deviation was clearly not the answer, or if it was, he hid it well.

The reason why Ben was so involved in LugRadio, why Neil ran the Linux User Group meeting, and why thousands of other community members around the world get together, comes down to one simple word: *belonging*.

By definition, a community is a collection of people (or animals) who interact with one another in the same environment. Community exists everywhere in nature. From people to penguins, from monkeys to meerkats, the vast majority of organisms exhibit some form of collective grouping. Grouping, however, is a touch simplistic as a means to describe community. It is not merely the group that generates community, but the interactions within it. These interactions, and the feeling of belonging that they produce, are generated from a distinctive kind of economy: a *social economy*.

Building Belonging into the Social Economy

At this point in our journey, it is clear that *belonging* is our goal. It is that nine-letter word that you should write out in large letters and stick on your office wall. It is that word that should be at the forefront of your inspiration behind building strong community. If there is no belonging, there is no community.

From the outset, though, belonging is an abstract concept. We all seemingly understand it, but many of us struggle to describe it in words. I identify belonging pragmatically: as the positive outcome of a positive social economy. In the same way that we judge a strong financial economy by prosperity, wealth, and a quality standard of living, belonging is the reward of a strong social economy.

An economy is a set of shared concepts and processes that grow and change in an effort to generate a form of capital. In a financial economy, participants put goods and services on the market to generate financial capital. The processes and techniques they use include measuring sales, strategic marketing, enabling ease of access, and so forth. A social economy is the same thing—but *we* are the product, and the capital is respect and trust. The processes and techniques here are different—open communication mediums, easy access to tools, and so on—but the basic principles are the same.

OPEN SOURCE IN THE ECONOMY

Stephen Walli, a prominent commentator on open source in business and review editor for *The Art of Community*, drew some interesting connections between the underlying concepts in a financial economy and how they apply to the open source social economy. He presented these thoughts in his piece titled "Free and Open Source Software Developers Working for Free (Economics 101)" (*http://stephesblog.blogs.com/my_weblog/2007/09/free-and-open-1.html*):

> People value their skill sets differently in different contexts, but value them they do. I use writers as an example to explain this to nondevelopers: a technical or marcomm writer may spend 8 hours a day at their paid job, then spend their evenings and weekends teaching ESL classes at the local college, working on a newsletter for their local church/synagogue/neighborhood organization, helping a child with a school project, and writing a sonnet to their significant other (or the next great novel or screenplay). In every case they're using their writing skills; they're just valuing them differently in different contexts.

There's another way to look at it. Not every market involves exchanging money for goods and services. A gem of an economics book (*Reinventing the Bazaar* by John McMillan, 2002, p. 135) points out that well-designed markets, regardless of market type, have a number of things in common:

- Information flows smoothly.
- People can be trusted to live up to their promises.
- Competition is fostered.
- Property rights are protected, but not overprotected.
- Damaging side effects on third parties are curtailed.

Let's look at well-run free and open source project communities in terms of such market dynamics:

- Information flows smoothly—transparency of community, process, code, policy, bugs, discussions.
- People can be trusted to live up to their promises—the project's license is a social contract. Its governance culture is well understood and supported.
- Competition is fostered—what fixes and features are accepted, and which ones don't make it.
- Property rights are protected, but not overprotected—code copyright management and licensing is handled properly in well-run projects.
- Damaging side effects on third parties are curtailed—the point here from the book is that WHEN real damage might be done to third parties, there are ways governments can involve themselves in the market to curtail such effects, whether by defining/enforcing property rights, taxes/incentives, or policy/regulation. The community's license comes to mind.

Individual projects behave as markets from one perspective, and code is currency, the medium of exchange. Just like all economic exchanges, the contributor offers something they value less (a fragment of code solving a particular need) for something they value more (the functioning software package in its entirety). Nobody is working for free in an economic sense.

Social capital is known by us all, but we know it by many different words: *kudos, respect, goodwill, trust, celebrity, influence, supremacy, greatness,* and *leverage,* to name a few.

The first known use of the term *social capital* (referred to in Robert Putnam's *Bowling Alone: The Collapse and Revival of American Community* [Simon & Schuster]) was by L. J. Hanifan, a school supervisor in rural Virginia. Hanifan described social capital as "those tangible substances [that] count for most in the daily lives of people: namely goodwill, fellowship, sympathy, and social intercourse among the individuals and families who make up a social unit...."

Social capital is the collective family of positive interactions between two or more people. When you affect someone positively (this could include being generous, helping someone, sympathizing over a problem, or something else), it has ripple effects on the community you and he are a part of. In addition to creating goodwill for you (increasing your own social capital), it strengthens the other person and the community in ways that ultimately benefit your social capital, too. Hanifan identifies the opportunity behind social capital:

The individual is helpless socially, if left to himself…If he comes into contact with his neighbor, and they with other neighbors, there will be an accumulation of social capital, which may immediately satisfy his social needs and which may bear a social potentiality sufficient to the substantial improvement of living conditions in the whole community. The community as a whole will benefit by the cooperation of all its parts, while the individual will find in his associations the advantages of the help, the sympathy, and the fellowship of his neighbors.

The meat in Hanifan's description is the opportunity for social capital to "bear a social potentiality sufficient to the substantial improvement of living conditions in the whole community." In essence, if a member of your community has a positive approach to another member, her social capital grows, which has a positive impact on that person and the community as a whole. It all sounds a lot like karma, and it is.

Of course, capital, whether monetary or social, is not the end game. People don't make money for the purposes of just having money. They make money because it allows them to do other things.

This is an important aspect of understanding where an economy starts and ends. Most folks riding the financial economy are not purely greedy numbers freaks who just want a big pot of money; most people who work with social capital are not merely air-kissing, hand-waving, superficial animals who simply want to name-drop and be name-dropped in the interests of social acceptance. Of course, the greedy and the socially obsessed do exist, but it is important not to use them as a basis for judgment. The economy is not flawed; those people are flawed.

A final point: for an economy to work, every participant needs to *believe in the economy*. Belief is a critical component in how any group of people or animals functions. This can be belief in God, belief in values, or belief in a new future. Whatever the core belief is, the economy and the community can be successful only if everyone has faith in it.

So let's have a quick recap:

- A sense of belonging is what keeps people in communities. This belonging is the goal of community building. The hallmark of a strong community is when its members feel that they belong.

- Belonging is the measure of a strong social economy. This economy's currency is not the money that you find in your wallet or down the back of your couch, but is *social capital*.

- For an economy and community to be successful, the participants need to believe in it. If no one believes in the community that brings them together, it fails.

- Like any other economy, a social economy is a collection of processes that describe how something works and is shared among those who participate.

- These processes, and the generation of social capital, which in turn generates belonging, need to be effectively communicated.

So far, we have talked extensively about our goals (belonging), the medium of exchange (social capital), and what is at the heart of an economy (processes). We now need to focus on the final component that binds each of these concepts together: communication.

In many ways, an economy is like a flowing river: it never stops, and the flow is critical to its success. Economies never stand still. Every day they change, adjusting to stimuli in the world that affects them. At the heart of how this movement works is *communication*.

The Basis of Communication

Peter Bloch, a consultant on learning, makes an important foundational observation about communication in a social economy: "Community is fundamentally an interdependent human system given form by the conversation it holds with itself." When I first heard that quote, I realized that the mechanism behind communication in a community is *stories*.

Stories are a medium in which we keep the river flowing. They are the vessels not only in which we express ideas ("I was taking the subway to work one day, and I saw this lady on there reading the paper, and it made me think xyz"), but also in how we learn from past experiences ("There was one time when I saw David do xyz and I knew I had to adjust how I myself handle those situations in the future"). Furthermore, when the characters in the stories are people in a community, the stories are self-referencing and give the community a sense of reporting. Communities really feel like communities when there is a newswire, be it formalized or through the grapevine.

Not all stories are cut from the same cloth, though. Communities tend to exchange two very different kinds of story: *tales* and *fables*.

Tales are told for entertainment value and to share experiences. They are individual units of experience that are shared between people, and their primary value is in communicating a given person's experience and adding to the listener's repertoire of stories and experiences.

Fables are different. Fables are stories designed to illustrate an underlying message. The vast majority of us are exposed to fables as children, and these stories are passed down from generation to generation, each one extolling a moral message to the youth of the day.

Let us now take a step back to our earlier story about mrben joining the LugRadio community. This story was itself a tale that shared an experience that encased many of the concepts we have explored.

When mrben joined the LugRadio community he identified with the ethos of the show. Then he began to engage with stories—first hearing them on the show itself, then getting them from the community, and finally sharing them himself. As mrben contributed more and more, his social capital started to rise—the community had a lot of respect for him and his opinions. He, in turn, believed in the community and in his own abilities. This objectivity in his storytelling and his general demeanor contributed to his social capital. As he continued to be a part of the community, his sense of belonging developed. At this point, mrben was living and breathing LugRadio, its community, and its ethos.

The result of this process is a community member with a strong sense of loyalty. Some of the greatest examples of belonging and commitment to an ethos occur when the community is threatened. An interesting example of this was when we released Season 5, Episode 3 of the show and received a rather angry statement from a listener who was clearly agitated at the level of expertise on the show and the generally positive attitude toward Ubuntu (which all of the presenters expressed):

> Nowadays I mostly stick to Dave Yates at lottalinuxlinks who is a genuine Linux obsessive, Chess Griffin at linuxreality who maybe does stuff for noobs but is genuinely knowledgeable about Linux, and the guys at the linuxlinktechshow because they work with Linux and know what the fuck they're talking about.

Mrben, who had spent a few years in the community by then, responded to the criticism using stories to make his point:

> I think you'll find that all of the presenters on LugRadio work with Linux on a daily basis. Whether or not they know wtf they're talking about is, of course, a matter of opinion. But the addition of Chris and Adam to the team, both of whom (IIRC) are professional Linux sysadmins, is an influx of knowledge on that side of things. Jono has a long history of working with Open Source and Linux within the community (bingo!) even if his technical knowledge is not at the same level. Aq is a Free software zealot, but is also experienced in web development and usability. I still think it's a good mix, personally.

> The Ubuntu thing is an issue, admittedly. But then, LugRadio still reflects my experience of LUGs—the majority of people are talking about Ubuntu. It has become the mainstream desktop distro, and the benchmark that most people mark other distros against. But, IMHO, the recent shows haven't shown an overly Ubuntu slant. Look at this show—you've got an interview with Quim Gil, which is about Maemo, not Ubuntu, the finger of God, which is plain silliness, the software vendors and security issue, which applies across the board, and packaging, which was fairly Ubuntu specific, but could easily relate across to other Debian-based distros, and, as Chris said, he would've talked about RPM if it had been possible.

> The "Ubuntu slant" is more about personal usage and experience, rather than a change in the show's direction (which was unashamedly Debian slanted before Ubuntu came out....)

In his three-paragraph response, mrben referred to 12 distinctive points and facts, citing many from existing online material. His response sought not only to convince the original poster of his error, but also to demonstrate to the community that the poster was wrong, thus providing a sense of security. By using objective facts, he also spoke with the voice of the community, not just his own opinion. Mrben's response was driven by belief in the community, formed by familiarity with stories, and legitimized by a wealth of social capital. Subtle, yet inspiring.

Although the underlying social economy infrastructure in community is compelling, it is important to remember that it is merely a structure designed to deliver a far more exhilarating prospect—*opportunity*. And with that, let's spin back in time....

Unwrapping Opportunity

When I first learned about Linux I was running a small bookshop in Milton Keynes, in Southern England, and living at home, having taken a year off before starting university. When Simon, the elder of my two siblings, stayed in our house for a few weeks on his return from the United States, we frequently spent the evenings talking about computers and stand-up comedy.

On one of those evenings, while I was hurling abuse at my computer, Simon expressed surprise that I used a "Mickey Mouse operating system." I was surprised myself. As far as I knew, Windows—Windows 98, at that—was all that existed. Simon told me about something called "Linux," which I could get for free from the back of a book.

Armed with my 10% discount, I eagerly snagged a copy of *Slackware Linux Unleashed*, and Simon set to installing Slackware 96 on my desktop computer. Two weeks later, having used guile, cunning, and a soldering iron (literally), and maintaining the alignment of the planets, I actually got the thing to boot. As I gazed eagerly at the screen, ready to experience the next generation of operating system technology, I was confronted with:

```
darkstar login:
```

It was not exactly *Minority Report*.

Simon, being the kind and sharing brother he was, wrote the username and password down on a piece of paper, stuck it to my screen, and promptly sodded off. The following day he moved out. I was left with a login prompt, some nerves, and absolutely no idea of what to do. So I cracked open the book, threw on a Testament album, and started reading.

It was then that I read about the Free Software community: a worldwide collection of enthusiasts all connected by the Internet, sharing an ethos that software should be free while building a replacement to the Microsoft behemoth that frustrated so many. Piece by piece, this global army provided software alternatives, many of which improved on their commercial counterparts. Back then, Linux was in the dark ages of computing. It was all command-line-driven, devices rarely worked, and to do anything you needed to compile code. Still, this concept of a worldwide community sharing code absolutely fascinated me. This is when I first smelled the sweet aroma of *opportunity*.

Although the reality of open source in 1998 was primitive, the potential within the community is what inspired me to stick with it. To be honest, I was pretty perturbed by the sheer complexity of it all. In those days it was insanely complicated to get a system up and running, and the innards of the operating system were on display for all to see. (These days, as Uncyclopedia [*http://uncyclopedia.wikia.com/*] so eloquently puts it, "Linux distros are so idiot-proof that you can put their install CDs into the floppy drive upside-down and it will still work" [slightly edited for a family audience].) Back then, we all knew that life with Linux was a lot harder than it needed to be, but the strong sense of underlying opportunity helped spark the imagination to put up with that complexity for the potential of a better future.

There is an important connection here in which *imagination* and *opportunity* are close friends. Imagination offers the mind a vision of how things could be. If there is a viable path toward this future, we build a sense of opportunity. If there is no viable path, we enter the world of fantasy.

Linux, and the possibility of it becoming a prominent operating system, was by no means a fantasy. The rails were on the ground. The community just needed freely available tools and communication channels to gather the materials, build the train, and put it on the track. In the case of Linux, this manifested in three primary areas:

Open communication
> With an open community and publicly visible and accessible communication channels, anyone can join the community and meet hundreds of thousands of other community members just like them.

Licensing of work
> Every contribution to the Linux community is licensed in such a way that it benefits the entire community. The fair licensing of all contributions adds a strong sense of confidence to the security of the community.

Open tools
> Anyone with an Internet connection and a computer can contribute. All of the development tools and documentation are entirely free and open to access. This provides a low barrier to entry, and lets new users play with the technology.

Although these elements were essential at the birth of Linux, it is not open communication, licensing, and tools that generate *opportunity*. These elements merely made it possible to build a world-class Free Software operating system. Opportunity is born in a sense of *belief*.

Belief is a critically important human function. Whether your belief is in an all-creating god, in a family member's ability to achieve something for herself, in a better future in your neighborhood, or in the reliability of a restaurant guide, belief is what gives us hope for the world around us. Belief can also make human beings surprisingly resilient in intensely difficult and uncomfortable situations.

One example of this is an incident that occurred a few years back. Every year, as part of LugRadio, we hosted a face-to-face get-together called LugRadio Live (*http://www.lugradio.org/ live/*), which is a very different style of conference. We had worked hard to deliberately make the conference fundamentally a community event. Equality between commercial vendors and the community was a key attribute, and we deliberately set a low cover charge to keep it accessible. In addition to this, we worked to produce a very informal and inclusive atmosphere, inspired largely by music events. (Many referred to LugRadio Live as a "rock conference.")

LugRadio Live has carved out something of a reputation for being different, and each of its participants has been very keen about advocating it and its formula. There was a strong sense of belief in the event—an event that was distinctively community-oriented and -driven, open to participation, and available to all.

With LugRadio Live scheduled for July 22–23, 2006, everything was going to plan. The speakers and exhibitors were sourced, the schedule was in place, the social events were arranged, and the crew and community were ready. Everything was great until the evening of July 18, when I received news of an impending rail strike. The strike was planned for the full weekend of the event, with every rail link going down. The country would be completely inaccessible by train.

I had never experienced such anger and frustration. For about an hour, I transformed into an ultraconservative right-wing anti-union crazy, and I stomped around the house, venting in the direction of my computer screen. We had spent six months of feverish planning and hard work, and this union decided that their problems were more important than anyone else's, and it was entirely reasonable to take the country down. I, for one, was not a happy bunny.

But, as my fellow organizers and I seethed on the phone, the community was already doing its thing. Forum threads appeared instantly to keep people up-to-date on the strike, blog entries were drafted, a nationwide car-sharing scheme kicked into play, and speakers and exhibitors were notified. While all of this was going on, I was on the phone tearing a strip out of both the union and the rail organization for their decision. Fortunately, the strike was called off a few days later.

What stunned me was just how mobilized the LugRadio community was. The community saw a threat to something they felt invested in, and reacted as a team to cover all the bases and try to limit the damage. Without any prodding from us, they made things happen. In a time of such panic and frustration, that community wrapped around each organizer like a comfort blanket. It was one of the most inspiring examples I have ever seen of a community coming together, driven by a belief in something we all shared.

Where belief gets exciting is when it is combined with that friend of ours from a few pages back: opportunity. Belief in a shared crusade—and a sense that the tools and opportunities are available to achieve that goal—is an intensely liberating feeling. People get a sense that they have control over their own destiny.

An example of this was the election of Barack Obama as President of the United States. Building up to his victory, the US was facing difficult times. Led by a president who many lacked faith in, and faced with a global economic crisis and a complex set of foreign affairs, the US had a lot to deal with, including a growing sense of cynicism among its people. Many Americans had lost faith in politics and pride in their country. As Barack Obama stepped up as a candidate for the presidential election, he instilled a sense of belief and opportunity that inspired his followers.

When people feel that they can achieve a dream, it builds an incredible sense of liberation and a willingness to step up to the plate. People become very committed, very quickly. We saw this in droves throughout the presidential election. Thousands of people across the country took to the streets to tell the world about Obama.

Around that time I had kissed chilly England goodbye and relocated to sunny California. The Bay Area was a particularly fascinating place to be—people setting up tables, selling stickers, knocking on doors, and making phone calls. It seemed that one in three people on the street was wearing an Obama t-shirt.

Whether Obama was the right man for the job is the topic of a thousand other books, but he had the ability to define belief, opportunity, and liberation in a language that a nation could understand. His inspiration—and his army of passionate Obamaniacs—sealed his place in the Oval Office. This in itself was an incredible exercise in building, energizing, and inspiring community, and regardless of your political inclination, it was a stunning feat.

A Community Manager: Becoming the Community

So far, we have explored some of the high-level concepts and architecture behind community and how it is structured. It is these concepts, such as social economy, belonging, belief, social capital, and communication, that help to draw the outline of the picture. We will use the rest of the book to color in the details.

Before we move on, though, we should spend some time profiling the artist holding this palette of colors. What are the skills required to draw the picture? What attributes will help us put the right colors in the right places? What do you need to build a really great community?

Metaphor aside, community building is a genuine art form. Like any art, there are attributes and characteristics that define someone as an artist, but every artist has his own "special sauce" that makes him unique and different. Every one of you lucky enough to have your nose buried in this book will have yours. Although I talk about some common characteristics all community managers should have, always strive to find your own approach.

THE COMMUNITY CASE BOOK

If you work hard to improve your craft, and care deeply about the integrity of your art, I think you have a good shot. I believe if you make something good, success will follow.

—*Mike Shinoda, on Success*

Read the full interview in Chapter 14.

Cracking Open the Personality

When exploring the mind of a community manager, we can break the attributes you need into two broad areas: *personality* and *strategic traits*. The latter, strategic traits, are skills, perspectives, and abilities that help you to organize complex problems into logical boxes, develop action points and a plan, and implement those intentions in a controlled way. Strategy is a large and complex subject, and we will discuss it extensively in the next chapter. As such, I will defer exploration of this part of the community manager's brain until later. For now, let's talk about personality.

My wife and I often joke about how I respond when someone asks me what I do for a living. I used to describe my job as "managing a worldwide community of volunteers," which sounded rather accurate and complete to me. My wife was less impressed. She rightly nudged me and suggested that made it sound like I manage a large online forum of very weird Japanese animation fans with a worrying obsession with tentacles. From that discussion onward, I have tried to summarize in one sentence what it is that we community managers do. The best I have come up with is:

> I help to enable a worldwide collection of volunteers to work together to do things that make a difference to them.

I know, it needs work. Send better suggestions to the usual address....

Twenty of those 21 words are really just filler around the word that I *truly* think describes what we do: *enable*.

Our function as community leaders is to enable people to be the best they can be in the community they have chosen to be a part of. Our job is to help our community members achieve their greatest ambitions, and to help them work with other members to realize not only their own personal goals, but also the goals of the community itself.

Trust Is Everything

At the heart of this enablement is *trust*. As we have already discussed, community is fundamentally a social economy, and its participants build up social capital via their contributions. With social capital being, by its very nature, a product of social interaction, trust is critical. If people in a community don't trust you, you will be met with caution and you will struggle to build your social capital.

For community leaders and managers, trust is a critical component in gaining the support and confidence of your community members. Earlier, we explored the example of Barack Obama stepping forward to enthuse a nation in turbulent times. Part of the reason why those times were turbulent was a significant lack of trust in President George W. Bush. When trust vanishes, words and promises lose their meaning. When trust is present, words and promises flourish in a world where they have purpose and potential.

Trust, though, is not something you can learn. Either you are trusted or you are not. As my father-in-law said to my family one evening over dinner, "Live your life honestly—if you don't, you always have to remember to not be yourself." His words teach an important lesson: when trust is implicit in every step you take, you can always be confident in the transparency and openness of your actions. This is the most important aspect of community leadership, and of life itself.

Part of the reason why trust is so critical is that, as a community leader, you want to be emotionally close to everyone in your community. You want everyone in that community to think of you as an accessible, approachable, sensitive person, and trust is required for any of these roles. People will approach you for advice, for guidance, to discuss personal issues, to handle conflict, and more. Many of these situations will be complex, and will require a significant level of sensitivity and confidence.

The Value of Listening

Part of achieving that sense of trust and confidence is having a firm foundation of understanding and patience. You should be aware right now that some people are going to frustrate you. Some people will be too quick to act and opine on a subject, and some will be too timid and reluctant to put their hands up. Some people will obsess about the wrong things and regularly produce what appears to be a tempest in a teacup.

But then again, some people will inspire you with their sense of responsibility, their ability to react to situations with grace and elegance, and their willingness to care for the community. As a community leader you will experience all sides of human nature, from strength and innovation to weakness and uncertainty. Whatever you hear from your community, you should endeavor to be the best *listener* that you can.

When you can demonstrate trust and the ability to listen, your community will develop respect for you. They will be there to listen to you, to work with you, to stand side-by-side with you in your battles and become a large extended family that you can rely on.

This respect has an important function in reinforcing belief in your community. When community members have responsive positive interactions with community leaders, it makes the community feel more inclusive, which generates belief and, importantly, belonging.

Respect is a wonderful gift, and you should cherish it and protect it at all costs. Getting that respect back after you lose it is a near-impossible task.

Avoid Ego, or Others Will Avoid You

Just as the right kind of inspiration can cause lasting effects, wrong decisions and approaches can cause lasting damage.

The biggest risk that can face any community leader is *excessive ego*. Unfortunately, ego is something that plagues a lot of people who assume a form of leadership.

One rather fun side effect of an influential position is *fame*; people know who you are, they read your words, and they listen to your opinions. The growth of the Internet and online communities has made it easier than ever to bolster your ego. Google searches, social networking websites, news feeds, alerts, statistics tracking, and more make it easier than ever to find out how many people love (or loathe) you. While this may seem incredibly flattering at times, strive to put your audience in perspective. The world is a big place, and you have some incredible contributions to add to it, but you should always aim to strike a balance between valuing your contributions and disappearing up your own arse.

Unfortunately, I have seen ego claim too many victims. I have seen community leaders who have commanded incredible respect and adoration from their legions of fans, but have washed it away when they assume a sense of *entitlement*. In any community, entitlement is an enemy: it values the person over the contribution, creating unrealistic expectations about how people should be treated. People with this sense of entitlement typically identify the wider contributions of the community, but see their fame as a red carpet that others don't have access to. You can avoid the wrath of ego by always remembering that in your role as a community leader you are responsible *to* the team, not *for* the team.

One such example of this was a guy (who shall remain nameless) who got very involved in a large open source project. Although not a developer, he became a very public face in the project. He talked very loudly and very enthusiastically about the project and its work, and he actively participated on the mailing lists, in discussion channels, and in blog conversations. His contributions were certainly valid: he acted as a champion and enthusiastic voice in the project, encouraging others and getting people pumped up.

As time went on, his name started to be mentioned more than the project. He started performing speaking engagements around the world, and his blog became filled with in-jokes shared with his well-respected, cool friends. He was very much part of the perceived "cool club," if there is such a thing in ultrahardcore technology circles.

As his fame grew, so did his inbox. He clearly felt that other people, with "less important" tasks, should respond to the email, as the demands on his time were substantial. But he was also riddled with insecurity, and didn't want to loosen his grip on the project. Things stopped getting done. People started getting frustrated, but these frustrations were largely stifled by the community. They didn't really feel like they could speak out or criticize: they felt that if you spoke out, you sounded like the only voice who did not respect and appreciate the contributions of a "rock star." What a pickle.

Of course, this situation could not go on forever. People started to share their frustrations at conferences, in chat channels, and in other arenas. Before long, annoyance and disrespect had become public, and ego had claimed another victim.

The most frustrating part of this tale is that the guy in question was and still is a good guy. At no point did malice or ill will drive any of his decisions or actions. He simply got a little too big for his boots and lost track of how to manage his responsibilities.

I would like to pretend that these cases are rare, but unfortunately they are not. They happen every day, in a range of communities around the world, and you should always have this risk at the forefront of your mind: don't be *that* guy.

Theory Versus Action: Action Wins

A subtler side effect of ego is one that doesn't threaten reputation so much as how you prioritize what is important. The threat is based on a sense that your opinion, approach, and perspective are the only ones with merit. While arrogance is one outcome of these elements, a much subtler risk that can bubble to the surface is becoming *too focused on theory*.

Theory has an important place in community leadership. Heck, I have just spent the past several sections talking about social capital, belonging, economy, belief, and other theoretical dispositions. However, you will note that the hardcore theoretical content is confined to this chapter. The emphasis of our work should be on getting on the front lines and trying out ideas instead of burying our heads in a book. Sure, read and learn, but use reading and theory to help you decide where to focus your practical efforts. The most critical lesson here is that you should never replace practical experience with theory.

Part of the reason why I have filled this book with so many examples is that I believe that the most appropriate and effective form of teaching theory is sharing stories and experiences. I would much rather tell you a story about something that I experienced or heard than fill your mind with social science definitions and terms that would be enormously helpful in a game of Buzzword Bingo but of limited use on the ground.

Unfortunately, some folks have something of a love affair with theory. Many of these people write extensive blog entries, give very generic (although well-meaning) presentations, and often seem to think that their primary role is to impart knowledge to others and sound as wildly academic as possible. But there is no secret ingredient in growing community. What makes a great community leader is experience: trying new ideas and concepts and learning from the successes and mistakes.

Of course, theory does have its place: it can help us to see, analyze, and deconstruct the things that are in front of us. I have absolute respect for people who teach others their art, but the teaching really needs to be secondary to getting out and being there with your community and helping to lead and inspire them. Use theory as a means to see the shapes in the chaos, but always ensure that you focus your primary efforts on making the chaos less chaotic.

Becoming Yourself

Before I wrap up this part of our journey, I want to go back to our earlier discussion about finding your "special sauce." In the past few pages we have talked about many of the admirable traits in a good community leader (trust, patience, respect, ability to listen, etc.) and some of the problematic traits (ego, control freak, theory obsession, etc.), and you may be a little lost in how you can get the balance right. Fortunately, the solution is simple.

Be yourself.

Your "secret sauce" is you. Your personality is the greatest asset that you have. Earlier we talked about how trust is the most critical component in being a great community leader. If you try to become someone who you are not, you will sacrifice that most important of traits. Be yourself. Identify your own traits, celebrate the good, and learn to improve the bad, but always be yourself; it will put you in good stead.

I learned this lesson when we started doing LugRadio. At the time, I was a journalist: I wrote for around 12 magazines and also wrote a number of columns for various publications. As part of my work I would write my articles and features in a text editor, and then have plenty of time to edit, choose my words carefully, refine my language, and perfect my tone. I could perform plenty of research, ensure that my citations were accurate, and pull from a worldwide library of quotes and stories that would illustrate my points effectively. In a nutshell, being a journalist allowed me to take my voice and ensure that it was as refined as possible.

We then started doing LugRadio. From day one, LugRadio was set to be a shoot-from-the-hip, loose, opinionated social exploration of Free Software and Free Culture topics. There was no editing. There was no censorship of opinions. Every word that came out of our mouths was committed to history. It was ballsy, it was controversial, but importantly, it was *us*. It was the honesty of LugRadio that we were all so proud of.

Although my writing and journalistic work was honest and I never painted an inaccurate picture of my voice or viewpoints, the editing phase of writing added a little more sheen and more opportunity to remove any controversial aspects to my work. With LugRadio, every word that would flow out of my mouth into people's ears was much less formalized: it was me in my birthday suit, no holds barred.

For about two days I really worried about this. Was LugRadio going to affect my career as a journalist? Would people think less of me because of my participation in this hugely opinionated tech audio show? Was I closing off potential opportunities if people heard me for who I really am?

One evening, while at my karate training, sweating and performing second kata, I decided I didn't care. I had always promised myself that I would be myself in my professional and personal life. I would never cover up my perspectives, my views, my interests, or my ambitions. I was always keen to be professional and respectful of the situations I was in, be they more formalized occasions or low-key social functions, but fundamentally the heart of my approach would be my own. This was the first test of that approach, and since then I have never looked back.

I believe that this commitment to being who you are is critical to being a great community leader. My father-in-law's statement—"Live your life honestly—if you don't, you always have to remember to not be yourself"—actually goes much deeper. Not only should we aspire to lead a good and principled life, but if we live it in a way that is honest to who we really are, we never need to worry about maintaining the illusion. My father-in-law has taken that approach, and so has my father, and I have learned from them and have incredible respect for their methods.

If you take this approach in your work and manage to do a good job engaging and working with your community, you will never need to worry about trust, transparency, or respect; people will know that the words that come out of your mouth are your own, that your opinions are your own, and that your advice is your own.

This is particularly important when you are a professional community manager. When I started working for Canonical as the Ubuntu community manager, I expected people to worry that Canonical may be pulling the strings that make me dance. It has been very important to me that I demonstrate to any community I am involved in that my commitment to it is genuine, and I am as willing to stand up against the commercial sponsor as I am willing to stand up against the community. Trust and responsibility is a two-way street.

Moving Forward

In this chapter we have grabbed a piece of paper and sketched out the primary outlines of community. We have discussed some of the high-level mechanisms of how a community works, explored why people build community, and analyzed what kind of attributes exist in great community leaders. The aim of this chapter was to build out an overview that we will delve into in more detail throughout the rest of this book.

The next step in our journey is to build a plan for our community. Although a community is a fairly organic collection of people and processes, we can architect a surprising amount of structure around it. This gives us an opportunity to more easily map out the road ahead.

I don't know about you, but I am ready to roll. Let's get to it....

CHAPTER TWO

Planning Your Community

"We must all hang together, or assuredly, we shall all
hang separately."

—*Benjamin Franklin*

MY BEST FRIEND IS A GUY NAMED STUART LANGRIDGE, WHOM I CALL "AQ." (He was nicknamed "Aquarius" in an online user group devoted to a fantasy author, for reasons that make my eyes glaze over when he tries to explain them.) I first met Aq in Wolverhampton in Central England, where I'd moved to go to university. We became fast friends.

With my curiosity initially piqued by Neil's Linux User Group, I was eager to form my own: the cunningly named Wolverhampton Linux User Group. Six months later, Aq wandered into a meeting, complete with now-trademark bombastic personality.

Over the years, Aq and I shared many a pint and a curry, debating and discussing every imaginable topic about Free Software. No subject was out of reach, and we relished in each other's passion for the subject. We also relished in the opportunity to prove each other wrong. These debates inspired many projects. One of them was LugRadio.

Throughout the life of LugRadio, Aq and I debated how we—or more specifically, I—recorded the show. As the resident musician in the fabulous foursome, with a room full of recording equipment, I handled recording and editing, using Mac OS X and the Cubase audio production system.

Yes, folks, you read that right: LugRadio was a show all about Free Software but recorded on a proprietary system, with a proprietary application. Fortunately, the community took good stead to remind me of my alleged "freedom hating" pretty much every day. Lucky me. Unfortunately, I didn't want to spend my life engaged in the rocket science that was Linux audio engineering. I love to play music, not spend my days thinking about which sample size I should set my software to.

The debate raged on, and I was getting increasingly sick of the discussion. Something had to change.

One evening at Aq's house, we were drinking tea and debating open source like normal. One additional area in which my cantankerous friend and I shared a deep interest was interaction design: how to make products and interfaces easier. Thus the topic of Linux audio recording arose.

Our debate was more akin to resounding agreement. We both cited example after example of poor interface decisions: methods of interaction that relied on redundant questions, complex assumed knowledge, and other travesties. My solution was to start from scratch. So we did.

We thought it would be fun to totally rethink audio recording. We sat down with paper and pens, and more cups of tea, discussing and debating until 4 a.m. When I got home and dragged my drained body into bed, my laptop bag contained three pieces of paper outlining an entirely new approach to audio recording.

Despite our brainstorming efforts, I just didn't have the time or knowledge to write an audio editor. I could have used my meager audio programming and development skills to produce a rather crufty attempt, but it would have been of little use, and I was already intensely busy. Despite this lack of time and skill, I didn't want our designs to languish in obscurity, so I drafted some mock-ups and wrote a lengthy blog entry explaining how they worked. I informed the LugRadio community and expected silence: the world moving on, our designs unnoticed.

A few weeks later I wandered onto the LugRadio forums and noticed that some code had been committed to a repository. I downloaded it and it looked like an incredibly simple first cut of the interface that existed in my mock-ups.

I was stunned.

So was Aq.

The author was a rather nice chap called Jason Field who had a passion for coding and Linux. I immediately emailed him to make contact. His simple contribution had inspired me to consider the project further and to see whether the designs were really possible to build. He said yes.

The LugRadio community members were equally intrigued by the story about this new audio editor: they nicknamed it *JonoEdit*. I was flattered, if a little embarrassed.

It was time to get the machine rolling. We set up a code repository, a website, a mailing list, and a bug tracker, and scheduled regular meetings. We organized hack days, bug squashing parties, and online discussions to plan and reach some major architectural decisions. New people joined the team, including Laszlo Pandy, who became the subsequent leader of the project.

A little later in the development, the project got an important name change; I wasn't keen on *JonoEdit*. After asking for suggestions, Steve Parkes, one of the original LugRadio presenters, suggested *Jokosher*. The name was formed from "Jo" and "Kosher," which he claimed as "No Bacon," thus constructing my name. Again, I was flattered. It felt weird, but the team liked the new name, so we stuck with it.

Everyone worked hard. We spent long evenings writing code, debugging, fixing bugs, and writing documentation. Piece by piece we built not only an application but also a community. We developed a sense of unity, and we started to become a team.

Eventually, after months of work, we made a first release. From a few ideas, expressed with my amateur-grade design skills, we built something that people could touch. Today, although I have stepped back to work on other things, Jokosher is a thriving project.

Most Free Software projects form from one person scratching an itch. That person writes code and releases it; if the code scratches other people's itches, collaboration begins. Jokosher was different. It existed entirely on paper before it did in software. The application was rooted in a new approach to interaction design, so having a documented design was essential. The design and accompanying specification of the interface acted as a reference from which to build the software.

What this experience taught me, entirely by chance, was that the speed and success of a community has a direct correlation to strategy, structure, and planning: even a simple set of mock-ups can help drive progress in the right direction. Communities that appear more by accident than by intention tend to be slow to develop and mature. Organized communities thrive because structure provides a sense of worth, conviction, and oversight. A strategy will make things happen for your community.

THE COMMUNITY CASE BOOK

From a product standpoint, we make our users stakeholders. We encourage and enable users to customize Firefox and to take part in test driving and providing feedback on our products.

—*Mary Colvig, on Strategy*

Read the full interview in Chapter 14.

Planning for Success

As you will discover throughout *The Art of Community*, I like to introduce concepts in a very specific way. First I present a high-level discussion of the top priorities and get the basics down. Next I focus on the details and flesh out the subject. This approach makes introducing the subject more akin to lowering yourself into a warm pool on a sunny day, as opposed to hurling yourself into an icy river in Finland.

Our goal in this chapter is to explore how to build a strategy for our communities. We first explore four foundations within community. Each of these houses the underlying details that we explore throughout the rest of the book. Inside these foundations are teams, the vessels of community, which we later crack open to see how they work. Next we define our mission, objectives, and goals and build them into a final strategic plan. We are going to cover a lot of ground in this chapter, so grab a cup of tea (I would also recommend a Hobnob to dip in it) and get comfortable.

With many areas of discussion, we need to pick out the key concepts and have them close at hand. It is easy to forget or skim over some subtle yet important aspects in community growth. To make this simple, we will add them to a TODO list as we uncover them throughout the chapter.

Community TODO List

- Example item.
- Example item.

Later in the book we will revisit this list and use it to form the basis of our strategic plan.

Community: The Bird's-Eye View

Building a strong community is an exhilarating and rewarding prospect, but getting there can be complex. You only need to look at this book's table of contents to see that the subject is hugely diverse and detailed.

We first need to step back and understand our broad aims. When we wake up and decide we want to build a community, what do we want to achieve? Aside from the goals of the community itself, be it building a software project, changing a political system, or whatever else, how do we inspire a collection of people to march forward as one? How exactly do we unite a people? Well, we can explain this using...dots.

Yes, dots.

I know what you are thinking: you are mad, Bacon. Dots seem a little simple. Sure they are, but they're different in many ways. Different colors, different sizes, different shapes. You may not know this, but dots have oodles of personality. Take the three dots shown in Figure 2-1.

FIGURE 2-1. The Dot family. Don't they look cute?

Readers, I would like to introduce you to the Dot family: John, Pauline, and Ken. Although similar looking, each has a very distinctive personality and skills. What brings them together is the same passion: creating a completely new and original social networking website, built for dots, by dots, called…DotBook.

John, Pauline, and Ken contribute in very different ways. John (left) is a programmer, Pauline (middle) loves to write documentation, and Ken (right) is rather fond of drawing. I know, he looks like the arty type.

John, Pauline, and Ken are not alone. There are lots of dots like them out there on the Internet….

The problem, as you can see in Figure 2-2, is that all of the Johns, Paulines, and Kens, and their respective skills, are scattered all over the Internet. They don't really know one another. They are all united by the same goal, but they're not working together.

FIGURE 2-2. The Dot family is not alone.

A community is just like Figure 2-2: a scattered collection of dots. One of our first goals is to bring these connected areas of interest together into well-formed teams. It turns out that when

Johns are able to talk to other Johns, some interesting things can happen. These teams are important containers of expertise and interest inside our wider community (see Figure 2-3).

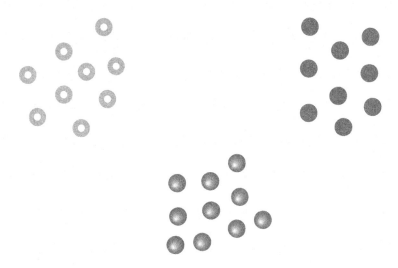

FIGURE 2-3. Uniting people by their interests and passions is an important first step in growing a strong community.

If we think of a community as an interspersed group of dots huddled together over a shared interest (e.g., protesting a ludicrous law, discussing a topic, building an operating system), teams are the smaller subgroups typically based around a primary interest or skill set (e.g., advocacy and documentation) that helps forward that shared interest.

As an example, the Ubuntu community has a shared interest in building a Free Software operating system. To do this there are many smaller groups who perform translations, produce packages, write documentation, test software, advocate Ubuntu, and much more. These are the teams that we seek to build: to break our wider community into smaller, more manageable chunks. Each team is united by solving a part of the grander aim of the community.

Teams are an essential construct in community building: they are not only the containers in which your community grows, but also convenient units of ability that help you to strategically understand and structure your community and find out what it's capable of. When John Dot meets other dots who share his interests and get excited at the same opportunities, teams also become containers of *belonging*.

Although teams have a primary focus (typically a skill, such as art or documentation), you should not be too rigid in that focus. Every team will have members who are interested in this primary function but who will also bring other expertise and insight to the team. As an example, in a software community, it is hugely valuable for the art team to also have members with abilities in programming: they can often expedite getting art contributions implemented in the technical development of the application. As such, encourage and optimize for membership based on the primary focus of the team, but also celebrate and make use of the other skills of your members.

Teams offer a wealth of opportunities and benefits in building a strong community, and we discuss them extensively later in this chapter. Let's first add this goal to our TODO list.

Community TODO List

- Identify how we can divide our community into teams.

Although constructing teams is valuable, it is not enough. As a unit of ability, a team is still part of a wider community that strives for a common goal. We need to ensure that our teams fit together like a completed jigsaw puzzle. Communication, ideas, and stories must flow freely between your teams, as in Figure 2-4.

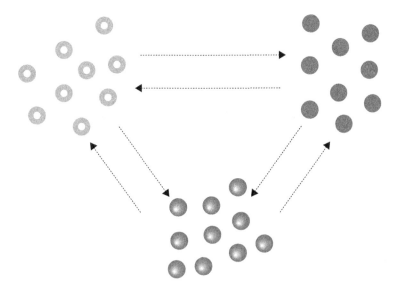

FIGURE 2-4. Communication between teams is essential.

The flow of communication between teams is a lot more complex than you would first imagine. How can you ensure an easy flow of ideas and progress between two teams who focus on different parts of the community? How does your art team communicate well with your development team? This opens up a huge array of questions. Even with the three teams in Figure 2-4, how do they communicate? What mediums do they use? How do they deal with geographic and time zone issues? How do they report their interactions to the wider community? How do they track progress? How do we understand how different teams work together? Not an easy problem to solve.

These questions are not merely about how two or three teams communicate. They get to the heart of the ethos of the community as a whole: the standard for how teams are structured, how they behave, and how they communicate.

As I mentioned earlier, although your teams have a primary focus (such as translations), there will be many other skills present in your teams, and many people will be in multiple teams. We need to not only foster effective communication between teams (such as regular meetings, progress checks, and shared communication mediums) but also make use of people who have their feet in multiple teams. They can be the glue that sticks teams together. These people should absolutely be on your Christmas card list.

This topic is part of *governance*, and is so large and critical to community success that I have dedicated Chapter 10 to it later in this book. Let's ensure that we make a note of team communication on our TODO list, even though we're not looking at how to build this until later, when we discuss governance.

Community TODO List

- Identify how we can divide our community into teams.
- Ensure that teams can communicate clearly and effectively.

The next area to focus on is contributor growth. We like dots like John, Pauline, and Ken, and we want to encourage more of them into our community, as we can see in Figure 2-5.

When it comes to new contributors, we essentially seek to satisfy two primary desires: *capacity* and *diversity*.

With *capacity*, our goal is to provide more hands on deck. More (coordinated) hands generally mean that more things get done. Most communities have somewhat audacious goals (which we will discuss later), and these goals almost always outstrip the resources available to implement them. This bottleneck can cause burnout (a topic we discuss extensively in Chapter 11), but more immediately it generates a need to find more resources.

Attracting members to your community is one task, but attracting a diverse range of contributors is an entirely different ball game. Although not critical in a community, diversity has huge value: different skills, cultures, perspectives, attitudes, and experiences make for a richer community experience.

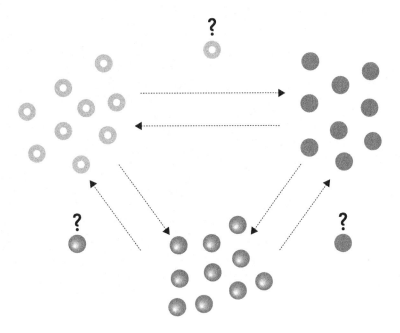

FIGURE 2-5. Bringing in new contributors is an essential task.

Later in this book, in Chapter 7, we explore how to attract members to your community. This requires not only making your community attractive to prospective members but also offering them an effective workflow so that they see their contributions put to use without too much hassle. What challenges do your members face in contributing? How can we make the barriers as low as possible to new blood while still bringing in the right skills? What are the right skills? Let's add this important goal to the TODO list.

Community TODO List

- Identify how we can divide our community into teams.
- Ensure that teams can communicate clearly and effectively.
- Attract a diverse range of contributors to our community to get involved and contribute to our goals.

The final major step in building a strong community is in building a positive environment, as shown in Figure 2-6 (we will focus on building a strong environment in Chapter 4). Your community should feel inspired, engaged, and thrilled by the opportunity to achieve the goals they dream of.

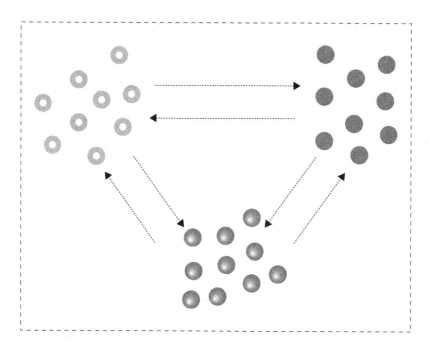

FIGURE 2-6. Build a strong environment, and you will have a strong team.

Environment plays a huge role in everything that we do. Every element of our environment affects our perspectives, emotions, and expectations.

Consider a conventional environment such as a neighborhood. Many environmental attributes can affect perception, with one such example being the feeling of safety. Examples that affect this feeling include the size and style of the houses; the types of cars on the street; the residents, what they wear, and their body language; the lighting of the street at night; the background noise; the amount of traffic; and more. Compare and contrast a seemingly friendly, social neighborhood in which kids are walking around and people are talking in the street, with an unfriendly, closed, and restricted place in which few people are talking and sharing their lives with one another. Money is not the decider here: super-expensive gated communities are often as socially sparse as very poor inner-city tower blocks. Fundamentally, both have the same core pieces—houses, roads, cars, streetlights, residents, and so on—but the environment hugely affects perception. The mental perception of a quaint country town adorned with its small streets, tea shops, and abundance of elderly people playing chess is very different from that of an inner-city block with its square buildings, large gates, and commuters rushing to work.

Environment not only affects perception but opportunity, too. In a neighborhood that is perceived as unsafe, residents are less likely to interact with one another due to fear. In a community that feels safe and welcoming, local groups, ad hoc conversations, and other interactions thrive. These considerations don't just apply to geographical communities; your online environment is equally important.

Let's add environment to the list and take a quick recap of our key issues thus far.

Community TODO List

- Identify how we can divide our community into teams.
- Ensure that teams can communicate clearly and effectively.
- Attract a diverse range of contributors to our community to get involved and contribute to our goals.
- Build an environment conducive to our wider goals.

Teams: The Building Blocks of Belonging

Every goal on our TODO list is key to strong community, and although you may not realize it, every item on that list also has a commonality: *teams*. Let's explore this in more detail.

Teams are the building blocks of community structure; they are the Lego bricks that build an army of volunteers united by a mission. But as building blocks, they fit together in many different ways, with countless variations and possibilities in how they are constructed.

For us to understand community, we need to understand what makes teams tick. We are now going to spend some time focusing on the essential ingredients that should be present in all teams. These ingredients are the best-practice elements that make teams strong, welcoming, and productive. We will explore these foundational ingredients now, and then later in the chapter we will determine which specific teams will comprise our community.

Finding Your Place

Everyone has dreams. We all have ambitions and experiences that we lust after, and we are all guilty of using the opportunity of a rainy day to stare out the window and let our minds take us toward these grand visions, be they flying into space, making millions of dollars, or playing bass guitar in front of thousands of people.

Adam Sweet's dreams were different. He *had* played bass in front of thousands of people. The young, spiky-haired, cigarette-smoking bundle of energy got a band together with his friends and managed to score a record deal at the tender age of 18. Known as Passion Star, the band went on to play the Radio One Roadshow: a UK-wide tour composed of established artists and new talent.

Though it sounded fun, Adam had had enough. He wanted normality. He wanted a house, a girlfriend, and a regular life, not life in a small bus with four hygienically challenged musos. Adam still wanted a passion, though (without the star). He needed an interest to wrap his natural sense of curiosity and exploration around. So he bought a computer.

Even though it was the year 2000 and he was 24, it may surprise you that Adam had never owned a computer before. Immediately puzzled with his new friend, he bought a magazine to understand it better, and said magazine happened to feature the Linux operating system on the cover. Not knowing any better, he jumped in and installed it. Of course, it was an epic disaster, as Linux generally was back then. While trying to find help, Adam stumbled across his first community, which doubled as a team: my Linux user group.

When Adam walked in, he faced the same fears, uncertainties, and curiosities that I shared at the start of the book. However, he was equally as inspired and intrigued by the concept of community. Although he felt weird, he also felt compelled to stick with it.

When Adam first joined the group, he asked a barrage of questions, regularly apologizing when he felt they were "stupid," despite reassurances that there were no stupid questions.

As he built his confidence, he started experimenting. The group had become an excellent place for people to give away old equipment. Adam would take this endless stream of clapped-out gadgets, try new software, and share his experiences with the rest of the group. As new members joined and asked questions, he would answer them and share his experiences. He was fast becoming something of a Linux expert.

He continued to play, continued to grow, studied at university, and, before long, landed a job as a system administrator. Shortly after that he met his girlfriend, Jenny, and soon they moved into their own house, Adam had achieved what he wanted: normality, a sense of security, and a passion.

What I find so endearing about Adam's story is that a Linux user group (a team within the general Linux community) was so instrumental in furthering his ambitions. If Adam had not joined a team, whether my LUG or any other group, I am not sure that the story would have had the same ending.

Teams fill an important role in a strong community: they are small ecosystems with attributes that can be hugely valuable to success on the wider scale of your community. Once we've taken a high-level look at these attributes, we can use this knowledge to build our practical implementation strategy later in this chapter.

Units of Belonging

Teams are units of belonging. Members join, are energized by the team's spirit, and develop a sense of belonging that encourages them to contribute back to the team. This "Circle of Life" philosophy provides the team with a consistent exchange of experiences and value.

If we slice open a team, we can see a number of generations, like rings in a tree trunk. Each generation is a source of stories (already established in the previous chapter as an important source of communication) and also a source of mentorship. Each generation passes down stories, experiences, and life lessons to the new generation.

This is exactly what happened with Adam. When he joined the group, he needed assistance and support. When he received this help, the team provided a sense of value to him. This value inspired Adam to treat the team with respect and to prioritize its importance in his life. As the team opened doors to knowledge, social connections opened and he felt a sense of belonging. This belonging was sealed each time he imparted his own experience to new and existing members of the group; he would duly receive the appreciation and thanks that he delivered to others when he was new.

Part of the reason why Adam had such a positive experience is that he understood the full breadth of the team. In any natural human grouping, *scope* and familiarity of environment play an important role.

Scope defines the breadth and range of something. It is the length of a book, the size of a festival venue, and the comprehensiveness of a project. Scope describes the extent of the mental fishbowl that you are in, be it a book, venue, or initiative. A typical example of scope that is familiar to all of us is the place in which we live.

The world is a pretty big place. Its magnitude is reinforced by the television, websites, books, stories, and photographs that we see every day. For thousands of years, humans and animals have developed a natural inclination to divide the world into more manageable chunks. Society takes the same approach: countries are divided into states and counties; states and counties are divided into cities, towns, and villages; and cities, towns, and villages are divided into streets and, ultimately, houses.

Geographical communities are analogous to digital communities: with both, our perception affects our confidence. Take the example of someone who relocates to an entirely new area. For most people who have just moved, the environment is initially hugely overwhelming. Once this person has explored most parts of her city, town, or village and knows where the grocery store, hospitals, and other key resources are, she starts to develop a sense of confidence. Understanding the scope of the area gives us this confidence.

The reason for this is that we are all raised to be cautious of the unknown. Unfortunately, this makes us afraid of it, too. When we know the full extent of the fishbowl that we live in, as well as the other fish in that bowl, it helps us to build a measured sense of safety. Your sense of scope makes you feel safe when you confirm that you live on a safe street and not in the middle of a gangland.

The scope of the natives also affects our perception. Contrast someone with few friends and seemingly alien neighbors with someone who has lots of friends and very social neighbors. When you start to make recurring personal connections with regular friends, acquaintances, and love interests, a sense of belonging begins to flow through your veins. This is no different in a small face-to-face or online community.

Teams are hugely valuable in providing a manageable scope for your new contributors. If your community has 1,000 people in it in a single team, your community can feel overwhelming. If your community is instead broken down into 10 teams, each with 100 people in it, and each team focuses on a distinctive area, this is far more approachable.

Let's add this important premise of team building to our TODO list.

Community TODO List

- Identify how we can divide our community into teams.
- Ensure that teams can communicate clearly and effectively.
- Attract a diverse range of contributors to our community to get involved and contribute to our goals.
- Build an environment conducive to our wider goals.
- Define the scope of each team, and help team members understand that scope.

Read Versus Write

Communities come in many forms. They surround books, movies, software products, political campaigns, civil rights efforts, hobbies, and more. In all their colorful and varied forms, all communities share one distinctive trait: the unity of people around a shared belief or interest. It is passion that binds these people together.

Read-mostly communities

A great example of this passion is *Star Trek* fans. While I am by no means a member of that community (and only have a basic knowledge of the show), it is clearly far-reaching and maintains an extensive membership. *Trekkies*, as they are known, gather around the world to discuss, debate, and consume *Star Trek* in all of its wild and rather weird glory. Oh, and they wear quite ridiculous and at times bizarre outfits, too.

We can define Trekkies as *fans*—they enjoy a common interest together, either online or at conventions around the world, and their primary role is to share the consumption of that interest with others. As fans, Trekkies rarely have any direct impact on the unifying interest: the average Trekkie could not change the storyline of the show, contribute to the costumes or the digital effects, or improve what already exists. Instead, collaboration in the Trekkie world produces content for other Trekkies: it won't take you long to find wonderfully detailed fan-made costumes, props, tattoos, fan fiction, and other creations.

Although there appears to be a very distinctive collaborative divide between the provider (the show) and the consumer (the fan), there is a middle ground. These communities are becoming increasingly important to providers and never before have artists, musicians, producers, and politicians been so aware of their followers. The Internet has enabled fans to connect more easily with their heroes, and this has developed a kind of collaboration.

There are many examples of this. Stephen Fry, a well-respected British actor, started using the Twitter microblogging service and within months he had 400,000 people following his updates. The Obama administration has made use of blogging and YouTube extensively to distribute content and invite feedback.

One producer who has engaged repeatedly with his fan community is Joss Whedon, the Academy Award-nominated and Hugo Award-winning American writer, director, and executive producer of *Buffy the Vampire Slayer*. Whedon has been known to use a range of online mediums to interact with fans, and has even referenced fan contributions in his work.

One such example was a reference in an episode to a "Polgara demon." The name "Polgara" originally comes from books written by American author David Eddings. Whedon's decision to use the name was inspired by a fan who posted regularly to the official *Buffy the Vampire Slayer* forum with the same name. Whedon and producer David Fury used the name as a tribute to her regular contributions in the community.

Another example of Whedon's commitment to his community bubbled to the surface during a writers' strike. He worked with other writers to write and produce *Dr. Horrible's Sing-Along Blog*, a 45-minute short musical that was released on the Internet. Each episode of the musical went online for only a few days, and Whedon generated interest inside the community using Twitter to interact with the fans.

These are all examples of community building in action. Producers are uniting groups of interested people together, providing communication facilities, and encouraging and enabling those people to collaborate. Even if the extent of that collaboration is a group of fans providing feedback on a forum, collaboration still happens.

This is how most communities work. Collaboration is an unofficial by-product, and although it may not change or improve on the creation of the producer, it is still likely to offer real value. The primary focus in these communities is to ensure that the community (a) always has access to the product and (b) can communicate about it with others. The foundation of these kinds of communities is *access*.

While each community has the characteristic of people gathering around a shared belief or interest, the actual impact of the community on this shared belief or interest varies greatly.

Write-centered communities

For some communities, collaboration goes much further. It becomes much deeper, more intrinsic, and more accessible to all. Instead of merely *enjoying things together*, collaboration goes so far as to help people *create things together*. In these environments, the community also assumes the role of producer of the content.

The typical example here is one of the many Free Culture communities, such as Linux, Wikipedia, OpenStreetMap, Creative Commons, and so on. In these communities, community members have the opportunity to change the very content that brings them together.

The Ubuntu community is one such example. Ubuntu is an entirely free Linux operating system that is designed to provide a complete, free, stable, and secure system for desktops, servers, or mobile devices. Ubuntu is built using hundreds of pieces of preexisting Free Software tools that we refer to as *upstream* applications. Each upstream application has its own community of volunteers and developers. Ubuntu itself has a community of volunteers and developers who take said upstream software and assemble it in an easy-to-install and easy-to-use system.

Ubuntu has spawned a huge community. Over 200 Ubuntu user groups, known as Ubuntu LoCo teams, have formed around the world. Nearly every country has a LoCo team, with a range of users from Linux experts to entirely new users. These people are, in a word, *awesome*. (Maybe I am a little biased....)

Anyone in the Ubuntu community can affect what appears in Ubuntu itself. Every part of the system is open to contribution. This includes the software on the disk, the supporting documentation and resources, art and design, bug reports, and almost anything else. Everyone has the opportunity, through hard work and merit, to make a positive contribution to the Ubuntu system that the community gathers around.

Understanding how our communities collaborate is important to understanding what we want to achieve and what is possible. Let's add this to our TODO list.

Community TODO List

- Identify how we can divide our community into teams.
- Ensure that teams can communicate clearly and effectively.
- Attract a diverse range of contributors to our community to get involved and contribute to our goals.
- Build an environment conducive to our wider goals.
- Define the scope of each team, and help team members understand that scope.
- Understand the extent and range of collaboration between our teams.

Meritocracy

Before we continue to build the blueprint for our community, I want to take a few minutes to digress and talk about an interesting social attribute that applies to many (but not all) communities: *meritocracy*.

A meritocracy is a system of governance in which its members are given responsibilities and recognition based on achievements, merit, and talent. Those who are part of a meritocracy (such as in the Ubuntu and other open source communities) can make tremendous advances in respect and responsibility by simply doing good work. In these communities, money, class, and family connections have little or no impact on the ability to progress and build a reputation.

The magic of meritocracies is that the playing field is level for *everyone*. Those who work hard and show a recurring commitment to the community are rewarded. Those who think that driving a car with a blue neon light underneath it will impress us are going to be sadly disappointed.

Few would argue that a meritocracy is a bad thing. Its fundamental basis is in rewarding hard work. This concept largely maps to the general life lessons that we are all raised with: work hard and you reap the rewards of your efforts.

In these collaborative meritocracies, our primary goal is to ensure that the communication and contribution channels to collaboration are open, well defined, and enforced. These communities are complex: there are many different aspects that affect how simple it is to become involved and collaborate.

Although meritocracies represent the poster child for what many consider great communities, they are *not* a requirement. Some communities absolutely distinguish between members based on who they are, where they come from, and other attributes. This has been particularly applicable for business-oriented communities that maintain a clear hierarchy and members who are by no means considered equal.

Your community needs to decide for itself whether it is a meritocracy. I would, however, tender one piece of advice: if you are involved in a volunteer community that is open to all, I would highly recommend you take a meritocratic approach. It will make your community look and feel more accessible and help to encourage a sense of belonging and equality as opposed to a community divided by classes. From the perspective of new members, the opportunities offered by meritocracies are inspiring. It is hugely attractive to members when anyone can join a community and further themselves and their reputation based on great work and participation.

If your community is currently or has decided to be a meritocracy, you should communicate this extensively to the outside world. Don't use the word *meritocracy*, though: most people have no idea what it means. Instead, talk of equality and provide examples of how your members have built their reputations based on their efforts.

We talk about many of these areas throughout the book, specifically when we talk about *processes* in Chapter 4 and *infrastructure* in Chapter 5. For now, though, we need to focus on the raw material that forms teams—*people*.

Working Together Is Success

Henry Ford was a pretty smart guy. In 1891 he went to work for Edison Illuminating Company, where he started experimenting with the concept of a gasoline engine. After refining his design into what he called the Ford Quadricycle, he resigned in 1899 and founded the Detroit Automobile Company, which would later become the Ford Motor Company.

Although Ford was a brilliant engineer, this is not why I am talking about him. Instead, it's because of this quote that slipped out of him:

> Coming together is a beginning, keeping together is progress, working together is success.

Although many consider Henry Ford the founding father of the motor car, this quote points to his other incredible achievement: understanding and motivating people.

Ford was very firmly a businessman who had his beady eye on the dollar, but in addition to this he was a pioneer of *welfare capitalism*, intended to reduce staff turnover and improve efficiency. To achieve this, he used many methods: he paid his staff a higher salary, improved working conditions, and automated large parts of the process. We can thank Henry Ford for inspiring the modern assembly lines that we see in mass production factories around the world. (Those of you who work on such lines may not be quite so enamored, mind.)

Ford built a business based not only on a core product, but also on an understanding of people. He knew how to divide his workforce into teams and have them work together to produce a single, consistent product. He knew that people driven by a common goal and united in similar skill sets would be productive. And he was right.

One of Ford's most significant and, at the time, controversial initiatives was the introduction of a 40-hour week and a minimum wage. His seemingly generous increase took a daily wage from $2.34 to $5. Back in 1914, this was unheard of, and rocked other industrialists and Wall Street. Ford's reasoning was simple and elegant, though: he wanted his employees to be able to afford the very cars they were building.

Ford knew that if his employees could afford to buy Ford cars, they would value their contributions to the company more. His employees would be able to see, feel, and enjoy the fruits of their labor.

Your teams also need to enjoy the fruits of their labor. Volunteer communities can sometimes feel like production lines. The work is not always enjoyable and not always pleasant. There are times in every community when repetition, housekeeping, and conflict play a role in an otherwise enjoyable merry-go-round. When the community begins to see more bureaucracy and repetition than useful and enjoyable contributions, something is wrong. Very wrong. It is important, in these challenging times, to remind your community members of their crusade and the value of their work in achieving it.

Ford's generous wages did not come without a catch. The increased salary that his workers enjoyed was only available to employees who had been at the company for six months or more, and also demanded that employees lived their lives in a way that the company's "Social Department" approved of: no excessive drinking or gambling. Erk. Unsurprisingly, that scheme was soon abolished, and the company had to accept its staff for who they were. *Diversity* was becoming a hot topic, and continues to be in any community.

Diversity

The building blocks of community are its teams, and the material that makes these blocks are people. When we understand people, we can build humane environments that are energizing and inspiring. Central elements of a healthy environment are respect, diversity, and rewarding people for their efforts, regardless of who they are or where they come from.

Typically, when we talk about diversity, we use familiar examples: gender, race, sexuality, and class. Although important, these poster children of diversity can sometimes focus attention away from subtler and potentially more potent forms of diversity that we can encourage, explore, and celebrate. Diversity descends much deeper than skin color and gender.

George B. Graen, author of *Dealing with Diversity* (Information Age Publishing), argues that not all differences are equally relevant or as important as you would think in all circumstances. He broadly divides diversity into *surface-level* diversity—readily observable characteristics such as race, gender, and age—and *deep-level diversity*, important but less readily transparent traits such as personality, values, and attitudes.

Building deep-level diversity can bring a wealth of goodwill and openness to your community. Often these deeper, hidden kinds of diversity teach us life's most valuable lessons. While all equality is important, we need to grow this sense of deep-level diversity.

At the start of the chapter we identified that we need to build an environment that is conducive to energizing and enabling our community. Deep-level diversity is the open door that welcomes this enablement. When you encourage this deep-level diversity of contributions (e.g., translations, documentation, development) as well as diversity of opinions, values, and experience, your members will feel unrestrained, unrestricted, and energized. This should be a constant consideration throughout your work.

Unfortunately, many communities merely focus on hammering home equality of surface-level diversity, but Graen suggests in *Dealing with Diversity* that it doesn't make a big difference in the effectiveness of the community:

> In a study of 45 teams from electronics divisions of three major corporations, Pelled, Eisenhardt, and Xin (1999) found that the effects of surface-level diversity (age) on emotional conflict diminished as a function of team longevity. Similarly, Chatman and Flynn (2001) found that demographic homogeneity (race and gender) was less predictive of team cooperation as team members interacted with each other.

This insight is interesting when combined with another research study, also discussed in Graen's book, that found that deep-level diversity provides the kinds of benefits we are looking for:

> In a study of 144 student project teams, Harrison, Price, Gavin, and Florey (2002) found that surface-level diversity negatively affected early cohesion in the team. Over the course of a semester working together, surface-level diversity became less predictive, whereas actual deep-level diversity (measured by conscientiousness, task meaningfulness, and outcome importance) and perceptions of deep-level diversity became increasingly important to team social cohesion and performance.

Although this experiment may seem a little abstract, Graen summarizes that "as team members interact, attributions about underlying differences based on race, gender, and age are likely to be minimized; however, the underlying differences in terms of personality, values, and attitudes are likely to have an increasingly negative effect on team cohesion and performance." We need to be cognizant of these underlying deep-level attributes in people and ensure that we encourage and help them thrive in our communities.

Deep-level diversity is further underlined by the sheer extent of diversity in most communities, particularly those online. Diversity is everywhere. We have so many opinions (sometimes it can feel like too many), viewpoints, perspectives, recommendations, and other reactions to stimuli. At every step, we need to foster and encourage open and frank debate. Every communication channel that you construct needs to have a common theme of openness and respect that encourages this kind of diversity.

Although this is an intellectually responsible position, people are people, and people can be irresponsible. For diversity to thrive and prosper, it needs to be built on a foundation of *respect*. When members of a community are respectful and considerate of one another, it encourages an environment in which people feel comfortable bringing their own kind of diversity to the game. It is this respect that affirms Graen's previous acknowledgment of the risks of diversity on team cohesion and performance.

In the Ubuntu community, there is an important document called the "Ubuntu Code of Conduct" that builds this foundation of respect in contributors. I have reproduced the core of the document here, as it not only outlines these core attributes of respect, but also could be useful in a range of communities:

Be considerate

Your work will be used by other people, and you in turn will depend on the work of others. Any decision you make will affect users and colleagues, and we expect you to take those consequences into account when making decisions. For example, when we are in a feature freeze, please don't upload dramatically new versions of critical system software, as other people will be testing the frozen system and will not be expecting big changes.

Be respectful

The Ubuntu community and its members treat one another with respect. Everyone can make a valuable contribution to Ubuntu. We may not always agree, but disagreement is no excuse for poor behavior and poor manners. We might all experience some frustration now and then, but we cannot allow that frustration to turn into a personal attack. It's important to remember that a community where people feel uncomfortable or threatened is not a productive one. We expect members of the Ubuntu community to be respectful when dealing with other contributors as well as with people outside the Ubuntu project, and with users of Ubuntu.

Be collaborative

Ubuntu and Free Software are about collaboration and working together. Collaboration reduces redundancy of work done in the Free Software world, and improves the quality of the software produced. You should aim to collaborate with other Ubuntu maintainers, as well as with the upstream community that is interested in the work you do. Your work should be done transparently and patches from Ubuntu should be given back to the community when they are made, not just when the distribution releases. If you wish to work on new code for existing upstream projects, at least keep those projects informed of your ideas and progress. It may not be possible to get consensus from upstream or even from your colleagues about the correct implementation of an idea, so don't feel obliged to have that agreement before you begin, but at least keep the outside world informed of your work, and publish your work in a way that allows outsiders to test, discuss, and contribute to your efforts.

When you disagree, consult others

Disagreements, both political and technical, happen all the time, and the Ubuntu community is no exception. The important goal is not to avoid disagreements or differing views but to resolve them constructively. You should turn to the community and to the community process to seek advice and to resolve disagreements. We have the Technical Board and the Community Council, both of which will help to decide the right course for Ubuntu. There are also several Project Teams and Team Leaders, who may be able to help you figure out which direction will be most acceptable. If you really want to go a different way, then we encourage you to make a derivative distribution or alternative set of packages available using the Ubuntu Package Management framework, so that the community can try out your changes and ideas for itself and contribute to the discussion.

When you are unsure, ask for help

Nobody knows everything, and nobody is expected to be perfect in the Ubuntu community (except of course the SABDFL [Self-Appointed Benevolent Dictator for Life]). Asking questions avoids many problems down the road, and so questions are encouraged. Those who are asked should be responsive and helpful. However, when asking a question, care must be taken to do so in an appropriate forum. Off-topic questions, such as requests for help on a development mailing list, detract from productive discussion.

Step down considerately

Developers on every project come and go, and Ubuntu is no different. When you leave or disengage from the project, in whole or in part, we ask that you do so in a way that minimizes disruption to the project. This means you should tell people you are leaving and take the proper steps to ensure that others can pick up where you leave off.

NOTE

The "Ubuntu Code of Conduct" is available at *http://www.ubuntu.com/community/ conduct* and licensed under a Creative Commons Attribution-ShareAlike license, which allows you to use it in your own communities. Although a Code of Conduct is not required for a thriving community, it is highly recommended.

Although the "Ubuntu Code of Conduct" draws attention to understanding and respecting a deep level of diversity, it is sometimes misinterpreted as simply "don't be an idiot." It means far more than that: it encourages us to not only take responsibility for our actions and our reactions, but also to use this diversity as an opportunity to learn and grow, turning differences into opportunities for personal development and learning.

Therefore, in addition to adding diversity as a goal to the TODO list, let us also note that we should put in place a Code of Conduct.

Community TODO List

- Identify how we can divide our community into teams.
- Ensure that teams can communicate clearly and effectively.
- Attract a diverse range of contributors to our community to get involved and contribute to our goals.
- Build an environment conducive to our wider goals.
- Define the scope of each team, and help team members understand that scope.
- Understand the extent and range of collaboration between our teams.
- Encourage diversity and opportunity in the community.
- Produce a Code of Conduct.

Every community needs to cherish and respect deep-level diversity. Its importance is not something that can be enforced with actions, bullet points, success criteria, or other organizational devices. Leaders are responsible for modeling the right behavior and encouraging it in others, but ultimately all members are responsible for remembering why your community is doing what it is doing and standing shoulder to shoulder, connected by diversity to grow and take on future challenges. It is diversity and this sense of united openness that will keep your community strong and reactive to any obstacles in its way.

In the previous few pages we have explored some of the core aspects of building community. We have learned that we need to take a cast of dots, bring them together into teams, help them communicate, and create an environment that is conducive to building strong community.

These essential elements of community are the primary goals that we want to achieve in our social economy. There are no specific actions or tasks that can achieve each of these elements; instead, they need to live in the woodwork of your community. They are attributes that we should always strive for, both throughout the rest of this book and throughout our future endeavors.

Now it is time for us to change gears and delve into the specifics of exactly what you want to achieve in your community.

Designing Your Community

At the start of this chapter, I waxed lyrical about strategy. Unfortunately, many community leaders consider strategy as an afterthought: they think of it as a nod toward the bureaucrats, not as something that actually helps their community grow. This view is misplaced, because leaders *can* maintain the flexibility they need while producing plans that can help structure and enable the community. Indulge me....

When your community kicks off, you'll be way ahead if you can get down on paper its primary purpose and core goals. To do this you need 1 tablespoon of aims, 1 mission statement, and 1 cup of objectives and goals; bake for 45 minutes, and allow to cool. The result: a *strategic plan*.

> **NOTE**
> The strategic plan that we develop throughout this chapter is a hugely important tool if you are a company that is likely to hire a community manager. We discuss this in more detail in Chapter 13.

To get started, you first need to answer some simple yet broad questions. Write down a single detailed sentence or a collection of single words that answers the following:

What is the mission?
> We want to understand our primary mission—the bright, shiny prize for which we encourage and inspire our community. What is this eventual outcome that we lust for? Is it a software release, political change, to help a demographic of people, or to produce something?

What are the opportunities and areas of collaboration?
> We want to explore how our community can work together to create and achieve things. What are these areas? How can we work together in different ways?

What are the skills required?
> We want to identify what skills we need in our community so that we can later establish teams to house these skills. What are these skills?

These simple questions are the foundation of a more detailed set of objectives that we will flesh out over the following pages. Let's look at a few example answers.

Earlier in this book, we talked about the Jokosher audio production software project that I kicked off from my mocked-up designs. The project is focused on producing an easy-to-use application to record and mix audio. Let's apply these questions to Jokosher:

> MISSION: To produce an integrated audio production environment for the purposes of recording, mixing, and exporting audio built on the principles of ease of use and simplicity, utilizing open source technology.

OPPORTUNITIES: Easing audio production, rethinking assumed knowledge, and asking questions in an integrated environment, and open and free access to simple audio production technology.

AREAS OF COLLABORATION: Interface design, development, documentation, translations, testing.

SKILLS REQUIRED: Programming (audio, interface), documentation, web design, web content, testing, bug triage, translations.

Note how these answers have been structured. We have used a single, very detailed, and carefully considered sentence for the "MISSION" and "OPPORTUNITIES," and single words or short phrases for the other areas.

Now spend some time thinking carefully about how you distill your answer to the "MISSION." Let's delve into it in a little more detail:

To produce an integrated audio production environment for the purposes of recording, mixing, and exporting audio built on the principles of ease of use and simplicity, utilizing open source technology.

This single sentence communicates all the key aims of the project:

- The kind of tool we wish to produce: audio production environment

- The primary functions of the tool: recording, mixing, and exporting audio

- The principles of the project: ease of use and simplicity

- The scope of its approach: using open source technology

Distilling the broad goals of the project into a single sentence helps you to understand what you really want to achieve. It also gives you a great summary of the project that you can share within minutes. This is called the *elevator pitch* and is useful for attracting new contributors and spreading the word about your community. More on this later.

The "OPPORTUNITIES" answer is the area in which you should identify all the exciting opportunities that are possible if you achieve your goals with the community. Producing revolutionary software? Changing the quality of life for homeless people in your neighborhood? Furthering a particular skill? Helping kids to eat healthy foods? Whatever your dreams, these should be the most important and inspiring opportunities that you are seeking. Remember, we are looking for high-level, essential goals here.

The "AREAS OF COLLABORATION" answer is where you can note the areas in which the community can *work together* on a task. This could include writing documentation, organizing events, performing advocacy, writing software, etc. Some tasks in the project cannot or will not be collaborative (e.g., administering the infrastructure facilities for the community); you obviously should not include these.

The "SKILLS REQUIRED" part is where you should note the skills that are required to make your mission a reality. What types of skills are needed to achieve those goals? Scribble down the full range of skills that you will need. This explicit statement will be handy later when attracting contributors.

Our Jokosher example earlier was a very technical project focused on open source software. Let's explore another: a neighborhood watch community.

> MISSION: To build a sense of safety within the FooVille area of BarTown by creating a sense of community, opening up communication, and building oversight into daily lives.
> OPPORTUNITIES: A safer neighborhood, fewer worries for kids playing outside, more desirable living conditions, more attractive house-buying area, better social interaction between residents, improved relations with the police.
> AREAS OF COLLABORATION: Organizing events, publicity, online discussion, signage.
> SKILLS REQUIRED: Event organization, design, web design, advocacy, writing.

Here we focus on building a sense of safety in a specific region of a specific town.

Go ahead, write the "MISSION," "OPPORTUNITIES," "AREAS OF COLLABORATION," and "SKILLS REQUIRED" for your community.

With a defined, core set of objectives and their characteristics noted, it is now time to flesh them out into a mission statement and form the basis of our strategy.

Baking in Openness

Always remember that, when building your community, transparency and openness are critical considerations. Few open volunteer communities succeed without transparent methods and approaches. As such, you should be open and inclusive with your community as you develop your strategy.

> **NOTE**
> Throughout this book we talk about transparency and the best methods of growing it in your community. It is an important consideration in everything you do, and it should be a top-level priority in how you work.

Your role in building this strategy is in facilitating discussion and helping to bring conclusions from those discussions into a single strategic document. You are not here to make decisions on your community's behalf. You also are not here to dictate direction and decisions. You are here to gather feedback, opinions, and ideas publicly and develop a strategy that meets as many needs and expectations in your community as possible.

There are many approaches to building a strategic document in an open and inclusive way, but here is my recommended approach:

- Have a central place in which the strategic documentation is developed. I recommend a website or wiki. Ensure that everyone in your community has access to this location.

- As you work through the concepts in this chapter, engage in public discussions with your community to make decisions. This could happen in face-to-face meetings or in online mediums, such as mailing lists and forums. Gather this feedback and use it as a basis for additions to the plan.

- Regularly update the documentation and solicit feedback from the wider community on your changes.

This approach ensures that you develop your strategic plan in an open and transparent manner, and that the plan reflects the perspectives and desires of your community. The key is regularity of communication and feedback, and a central document that brings it all together. If you approach your strategy in this manner, your community will feel open and accessible.

One difficult aspect of this process is when people disagree on direction. You may get some people who believe that Approach A makes sense and some who feel that Approach B is more appropriate. Unfortunately, there is no easy solution to this problem.

An example of this problem occurred in a derivative distribution of Ubuntu called Xubuntu. The Xubuntu community took the underlying Ubuntu system and swapped out certain components to make it more lightweight and suitable for lower-powered computers. Some time ago, the community unfortunately hit something of a roadblock when deciding in which direction to move forward. They not only disagreed on the direction of the project, but also disagreed on who should coordinate the strategy.

To resolve this, I stepped in and scheduled a public online meeting and invited the entire Xubuntu community to attend. My first goal was to focus on what the community agreed on. Much of the meeting consisted of gathering everyone's feedback and collating the recurring themes into a broad, high-level direction. After 45 minutes or so of discussion, this was finalized as:

> To produce an easy to use distribution, based on Ubuntu, using Xfce as the graphical desktop, with a focus on integration, usability and performance, with a particular focus on low memory footprint.
>
> The integration in Xubuntu is at a configuration level, a toolkit level, and matching the underlying technology beneath the desktop in Ubuntu. Xubuntu will be built and developed as part of the wider Ubuntu community, based around the ideals and values of Ubuntu.

I managed to converge on this statement by repeatedly refining it based on feedback. This happened over and over again until we got something that virtually everyone agreed on. This agreement is composed of two parts. The first provides a broad mission statement, and the second specifies a broad set of high-level goals that can implement that statement. This dynamic duo could then be used to form the basis for an additional set of discussions to flesh out a full strategic plan.

THE IMPORTANCE OF LEADERSHIP

As this story highlights, leadership is a critical function in building an effective and fulfilling community. We will be discussing leadership throughout this book, but always remember that leadership is a skill that is learned, refined, and improved based on our own experiences and learning the lessons of others. As you work to grow your community management skills, also think carefully how you can become a stronger, more effective, and more empathetic leader.

For this process to happen effectively, it needed a coordinator, and my next job was to get agreement on who this coordinator should be. The community was united in recommending a competent and regular contributor in the form of one Cody Somerville. Cody worked with the community using the approach I recommended and produced a full strategic plan. The Xubuntu community went on to do some great work built around this strategy.

Building a Mission Statement

In the same way the Xubuntu community agreed on their high-level goals, a mission statement holds a lot of value for any kind of collaborative project, be it a commercial product or a volunteer community. These statements emphasize the promise, opportunity, and definition of what your community is seeking to achieve. Their purpose is to articulate ambition with a detailed, succinct, and elegant approach. Mission statements help get everyone in your community on the same page.

Mission statements are intended to be consistent and should rarely change, even if the tasks that achieve that mission change regularly. When building your mission statement, always have its longevity in mind. Remember, your mission statement is your slam-dunking, audacious goal. For many communities these missions can take decades or even longer to achieve. Their purpose is to not only describe the finish line, but also help the community stay on track.

Many of us are more than familiar with mission statements. They are one of the first documents we see when we join a new company. Unfortunately, staff members typically ignore them. These statements are usually written by senior management and often bear no day-to-day resemblance to the work done by the folks on the ground. Don't use these often-pointless examples as a reason to consider mission statements irrelevant: these companies are simply doing it wrong. The mission needs to be at the forefront of every member's mind, and should be a regular driving force that is the justification behind the day-to-day work. Your community members need to be able to draw a connection between the daily work of the community and your mission.

Now sit down and write your mission statement. Take the "MISSION" sentence that you wrote down earlier, break it apart, and illustrate it using descriptive, evocative, and stimulating words. Your mission should define the purpose of your aims, the bigger picture of where they fit in, and the uniqueness of your approach. You should expand on your "MISSION" while also using your "OPPORTUNITIES," "SKILLS," and "AREAS OF COLLABORATION" for inspiration. Although there are no fixed guidelines for the size of a mission statement, keep it detailed yet concise. If you exceed 300 words, you may be babbling a little too much. This, my friends, is a babble-free zone.

When you have completed the statement, you should run it through three rigorous tests:

Test 1

Put yourself in the position of a potential community member. If you had no knowledge of the community or its goals, would the mission statement explain it all within a minute? With every sentence, you risk the reader getting bored and wandering off for a love affair with his PlayStation. If your mission doesn't deliver your aims quickly, efficiently, and compactly, go and improve it.

Test 2

Get someone else to read it. Ask her to tell you what she thinks and how she perceives the aims of your community. Typically this person may be a friend, but friends often skirt around criticism. Make sure your reader is encouraged to criticize where needed, and tell her you won't get in a huff if she says something sucks. If she says something is unclear, fix it.

Test 3

Is this mission statement going to inspire you and your members through the toughest times of the community? In *Organizational Vision, Values and Mission* (Crisp Learning), Cynthia D. Scott et al. describe this perfectly: "A mission evokes a personal response. Work on it until it gets to be so clear that reminding yourself of it will keep you, on a really bad day, from walking out and quitting." Is your mission going to stop you from quitting when the world has climbed onto your shoulders? One day this is going to happen, and you need to be able to look at your mission statement and have "a moment."

When you have successfully navigated through these three tests, you should have a rock-solid and rigorously tested mission. Our mission is our first guiding document for our community. We'll use it now for the next step: building our *strategic plan*.

Building a Strategic Plan

The purpose of a strategic plan is to document your goals and ambitions for a given period of time and to provide a central body of agreement in your organization or community. It should clarify what your objectives are and which goals are part of those objectives; it should also state how progress is measured and who is leading the work. A detailed, realistic strategic plan is hugely valuable for your community. Having a strategy does not mean that you have bent to the gods of bureaucracy.

A strategic plan is broken into objectives that we seek to achieve before a given milestone. This milestone can be measured in either time or a specific achievement. Your choice is entirely dependent on the type of community and project you are involved in.

As an example, some software projects use fixed release cycles, such as Ubuntu with its six-month cycle. Other software projects set their milestones as a given release that will have an agreed amount of functionality. Nonsoftware communities often use other kinds of metrics, such as an amount of money to raise in donations or a date when a particular event or initiative is launched.

FIXED SOFTWARE CYCLES

Many of you reading the *The Art of Community* will be seeking to apply these principles to open source software development. With this in mind, here are a few more words on the merits of fixed release cycles versus the release-when-ready approach.

Fixed release cycles offer many benefits to your users and developers:

- They're predictable and reliable. Your users know when every release will happen.
- It's easier to break the cycle into parts. When the cycle is fixed in length each time, you can divide it into the requisite parts (development, translations, UI freeze, hard freeze, release candidate, etc.) more easily.
- Particularly for open source projects, fixed release cycles make it easier for distributions to factor your release into their road map. This happens with the GNOME and Ubuntu projects, for example.

There is, however, one distinctive disadvantage with a fixed cycle: it makes it harder to develop large new features and changes that take longer than the duration of the cycle to implement. This is something we discovered in the Ubuntu community. Planning longer-term features sometimes needs to be broken into chunks and spread across release cycles. Interestingly, breaking the problem into chunks is often a better approach, regardless of release cycles.

Release cycles are fairly serious beasts. Fortunately, they lead to more fun and exciting prospects: our goals. When you hit these goals, you should let your hair down and celebrate, and when this occurs regularly, it reaffirms a strong sense of community and teamwork by acknowledging that you have all been working your socks off toward your goals. We discuss methods of celebrating releases in Chapter 12.

You should think carefully about what kind of milestone you want to apply to your project. It is far better to choose a milestone that is six months away and achieve less than it is to pick a milestone that is two years away and achieve more. Regular milestone achievements give your community a much-needed dose of excitement and satisfaction.

Choose your milestones now (e.g., using a fixed cycle, a given set of features, a given date, or some other indicator of completion).

Structuring the plan

With your milestones decided, you can focus on the structure of the strategic plan. We will familiarize ourselves with this structure and then begin discussing how we can identify the objectives and goals to fill it. Before we begin, you should remember to fulfill your role as a facilitator and work with your community in a transparent fashion to combine input, feedback, and opinion into a single consistent plan that everyone can follow.

There are many, many ways of structuring a strategic plan. Everyone has his own approach, and countless books have been written on the subject. The technique that I am going to use here is one that I have found particularly effective for the communities that I have been involved in. Unfortunately, many of the books written about strategic design and planning are written with businesses in mind, and some aspects of business strategic planning are unsuitable for community strategy.

This is because business strategic planning typically presumes an organizational structure that provides a more central decision-making function: it is always clear who has the authority and expectation to make decisions. Ironically, this perspective is becoming increasingly old-school in business circles, with many businesses focusing on a more community-oriented collaborative planning approach that helps foster deeper team commitment even when there's a central position of responsibility (not authority).

The challenge here is that there is no cut-and-dried path to community, and the same applies to your strategic planning. As you grow and build your community, you should feel free to experiment, explore, and refine the approach we use here. You should develop a strategic plan that works for you and your specific community.

Our approach here involves defining a number of *objectives*. These are the broad, high-level things that you want to achieve. Each objective is divided into a number of *goals*. Each goal includes three pieces of information.

- The *success criteria* describe a set of measurable methods for evaluating the goal's success. You should be able to look at this statement and determine straightaway whether the goal was achieved (example: 20 new community members).

- The *implementation plan* describes what tasks need to happen to achieve the goal. These are a set of directions that clearly indicate the steps involved in achieving the goal.

- Finally, and this is optional with many communities, we specify the *owner*: the person responsible for the goal. Accountability is an important element in building successful community: when people feel responsible for their work, they ensure that positive outcomes are generated.

Your plan should not live in isolation. Its final home really shouldn't be a piece of paper in your office drawer or a random document on your computer. It should be shared. It should be read. It should become a core document in your community.

To make the plan easy to read, I recommend that you structure each objective and its goals in a consistent manner. Let's look at an example of an objective and one of its goals (remember that most objectives will have many goals):

OBJECTIVE: Build a website for the project.

GOAL: Build a structural design for the website content.

SUCCESS CRITERIA:

>   All areas of the website structure documented in a specification.

>   Community feedback gathered on the proposal.

IMPLEMENTATION PLAN:

>   Identify the needs of the website by liaising with the community.

>   Document the structure of the website on the wiki.

>   Email the core community team with feedback and merge feedback in.

>   Organize an online meeting to propose any changes to the specification.

>   Build a prototype.

OWNER: Jono Bacon.

This example demonstrates a number of subtle points in building a comprehensive strategic plan:

- The OBJECTIVE should be a specific outcome that you would like to achieve. These should be high-level (such as "Build a website for the project") but not too fluffy (such as "Make everyone feel warm and fuzzy").

- Each objective can have a number of GOALS, and each goal should have SUCCESS CRITERIA, IMPLEMENTATION PLAN, and (where appropriate) OWNER items.

- The SUCCESS CRITERIA should be a set of measurable assessment methods. You should be able to look at each SUCCESS CRITERIA point and definitively know whether it was achieved. Each item should clearly state what needs to be achieved to be considered complete. Avoid vague and general statements; instead, use specifics. Success criteria help the wider community reach a consensus on what constitutes success and identify when progress is being made.

- The IMPLEMENTATION PLAN is a set of reasonably granular steps that indicate how you can achieve the goal.

- In some cases it makes sense to assign an OWNER to a goal, even if that owner merely has oversight in getting it done. OWNER does not necessarily map to responsibility for the goal in a community, although it typically does in the business world.

With this consistent structure across your plan, you will be able to effectively document the broad objectives and specific goals and measure and evaluate progress on your action points. Now let us use this structure to add some meat to the bones.

Filling Out the Plan

With a mission statement, strategic plan structure, and some notes about our aims, we have already made some great progress in getting organized. Many communities are built on vague ideas that are barely communicated and shared, and progress is scattershot. Their approach is often uncoordinated and without schedule. Our work so far already has our community off to a rocking start.

But the devil is in the details. We need to use our structure here to flesh out what we want to achieve in our mission statement. We need to take our mission; combine it with our notes about opportunities; and produce a set of objectives, goals, success criteria, and implementation plan items.

Unfortunately, in terms of your community I have no idea what you specifically want to achieve. Some of you will be working on software projects. Some of you will be setting up user groups. Some of you will be traveling to far-flung lands to help poor children. I cannot directly choose your specific objectives and goals, but I can advise you on *how* to choose them.

First, take your mission statement and pick it apart. Now use the high-level aims as a source of discussion for brainstorming sessions. We need to flesh out, discuss, and debate our ideas and their implications and requirements. These sessions will generate this set of ideas that you can merge into the strategic plan.

Brainstorming Ideas

The justification for collaborative brainstorming is twofold. First, no matter how intelligent you are or how worldly you consider yourself, collaborative brainstorming *always* uncovers new ideas, concepts, problems, and techniques that you never considered. This is hugely valuable. Second, collaborative brainstorming is an important step in building transparency and openness in your community. This sense of openness is critical at every step, including strategic development.

Getting people together to share ideas and opinions should be exhilarating. It should open everyone's mind to flow in an environment that encourages the expression of ideas. Great brainstorming sessions inspire their participants: members feel not only that they can contribute, but also that they can control the implementation of the very ideas they propose. Unfortunately, many brainstorming sessions don't quite work that way.

Many sessions comprise one driving force (the leader of the session) moving the discussion forward, backed up by a core group of two or three primary contributors. The rest of the group often sit in silence, observing the melee around them. Many of the ideas from these sessions are often plain and obvious; they fail to uncover core opportunities and issues.

Fortunately, great brainstorming sessions have a core formula:

Define a purpose

Your session should have an aim, a goal, and a purpose. What do you want to achieve in the session? What outcomes would you like to generate? Would you like ideas, work assignments, or other elements? Make sure each of your participants is aware of the session's aim. Remember, an important source of focus for your sessions should be the objectives of your mission statement.

Organize and invite your participants

Make sure the people you want in the session know about it and can attend. If the session is online, be conscious of time zone issues. Allocate enough time to run the session. Usually 1–2 hours is enough time without boring the pants off people.

Get your resources in place

If your session is face-to-face, make sure you have somewhere to jot down ideas. A whiteboard or flip pad is a great resource for this. If the session is online, a wiki or note-taker is a great option. Another great option here is a collaborative text editor, such as the freely available Gobby (*http://gobby.0x539.de/trac/*).

Set some ground rules

Make it clear that everyone is encouraged to participate. Also make it clear that offensive discussion and nonconstructive criticism should be avoided. Ideas should be expressed in high-level detail, but not discussed in overly specific detail due to time constraints.

Help people relax

For many people, a brainstorming session is a social nightmare. Try to make the atmosphere as loose and informal as possible.

With this recipe in place, we can explore some methods of generating the best ideas from the session.

Technique 1: Question assumptions

With every brainstorming session, there is a set of assumptions and perceived norms. Your first point of order should be to tear open those norms and question whether they are effective. If they are not, the road is open to alternatives.

If your session is about improving ease of use in your software, is your current design the best approach? If you are discussing how to lower crime in your area, consider your assumptions: is it as bad as you think? If you want to bring more people to your community, does your target audience read and reside in the areas you think they do? Questioning assumptions can often uncover some great talking points and areas of investigation.

While we are on the subject of questioning the norms, it is also healthy to regularly question your own perspective and approaches. As a community leader, people look to you for guidance. It is hugely valuable to regularly sit back and reconsider the approaches that you ordinarily take for granted.

It might sound a little unusual, but I personally conduct a performance review of myself twice a year. In it, I ask my community for feedback on my approach, language, productivity, responsiveness, and other aspects of my work. On many occasions this review has helped me uncover some great areas in which to improve how I work with my own communities. I recommend you do the same.

Technique 2: Think outside the box

While we are all wrapped up in self-reflective thought, you should also question what you could achieve if you let your imagination run loose. What are the subconscious limitations that you are placing on yourself when thinking of ideas? In other words, if all the barriers are removed, what is possible?

A great example of this is the Nintendo Wii game console. For years, console after console had shipped with a control pad that players used to control the on-screen characters. These pads went through many variations, but they all shared one common characteristic: the buttons controlled the action.

Of course, there were attempts at alternatives: light guns, dance mats, plastic guitars and drums. Most still had the assumed knowledge that the player controlled the action by pressing buttons. These alternative approaches were never a core part of the systems. They were novelty add-ons that often had limited appeal.

The Wii changed all of that. Shigeru Miyamoto, a renowned video game designer and cocreator of many games, including Super Mario Brothers, Donkey Kong, and The Legend of Zelda, sat down with other designers and questioned whether they should be limited to the existing norms of the game interface.

The result was one of the most significant developments in video game history: the Wii Remote, which allowed gamers to control the action by moving the unit itself. This enabled all manner of physical interactions, from 10-pin bowling to boxing to ski-jumping. The Wii changed how we think about video games, and is clearly having an effect on the design of other consumer products as well.

Thinking outside the box takes time and focus to master. The trick is in questioning everything around you. A great exercise for this is to spend an hour noticing the details in your world and questioning why they work the way they do. Try to find faults. Try to find justification for the way things are. Importantly, when you ask these questions, try to think of solutions. If you question why the heater control in your car is labeled the way it is, what would be a better label? If you question why you always need to pay your rent check manually, how could it be automated for both you and your landlord? These are great opportunities to enjoy being a cantankerous consumer but with the added benefit of expanding your own problem-solving skills. Meaningless buzzword fans may want to refer to this as *Cantankerized Consumer Problem Assessment* (CCPA).

Technique 3: Let's make it suck

A great technique for questioning everything and uncovering new ideas is one that I tried first at the Ubuntu Developer Summit (UDS) in Cambridge, Massachusetts, in early 2008. The idea is simple: reverse the aims of what you want to achieve.

As an example, imagine you wanted to design a cell phone. Traditionally, you would brainstorm the attributes of a great cell phone. Instead, turn everything on its head. What would make the worst possible cell phone? Maybe it ignores all calls? Or maybe it only accepts calls from telemarketing companies? Maybe the buttons are too small? How about really short battery life?

When you ask these kinds of questions in a brainstorming session, it almost always breaks the ice and gets people talking. Such ridiculous questions generate a lot of fun discussion, laughter, and ludicrous ideas. Make sure you write down every one of these nuggets of madness.

After your group has exhausted their initial pool of ideas, you should invert each idea again. How do we make sure that our phone accepts all calls? How can it avoid calls from telemarketing companies? How can we make sure the buttons are the right size and not too small? How can we improve battery life?

Aside from the benefits of getting your group brainstorming, this approach is an excellent method in building defenses against the infuriation of normal life. It helps to identify frustrating attributes and protect against them, and this will in turn provide better results. I have used this technique for brainstorming websites, processes, products, and more, and it has always been fun, productive, and useful.

Pulling Together the Threads

At this point in our journey into the depths of strategy you have four very important assets. Each of these was developed from our structured approach to thinking throughout the chapter:

- A set of TODO list items: essential concepts that are important throughout all aspects of your community building
- An initial set of MISSION, OPPORTUNITIES, AREAS OF COLLABORATION, and SKILLS REQUIRED notes that flesh out a set of aims for your community
- A more complete mission statement that helps determine high-level goals and ambitions and serves as a source of inspiration for brainstorming
- A set of ideas generated from your brainstorming sessions

Our task is now to convert these assets into a strategic plan structure that can be shared with the rest of your community.

First, produce a set of objectives from the high-level goals in your mission statement and the list of ideas from your brainstorming sessions. Create objectives that you feel you can achieve within a reasonable time frame. Again, the choice of time frame is dependent on your project, but I would recommend it not exceed 6–12 months.

Now put this list of objectives into the strategic plan and apply the consistent structure we discussed earlier. Here is a quick recap of this structure:

OBJECTIVE:

GOAL:

SUCCESS CRITERIA:

    Item

    Item

IMPLEMENTATION PLAN:

    Item

    Item

OWNER:

GOAL:

SUCCESS CRITERIA:

    Item

    Item

IMPLEMENTATION PLAN:

    Item

    Item

OWNER:

For each objective that you have decided on, divide it into goals and assign each the SUCCESS CRITERIA, IMPLEMENTATION PLAN, and (optionally) OWNER items. You should now go and flesh out each of these items for each of your goals.

Let's now take a look at our TODO list.

Community TODO List

- Identify how we can divide our community into teams.
- Ensure that teams can communicate clearly and effectively.
- Attract a diverse range of contributors to our community to get involved and contribute to our goals.
- Build an environment conducive to our wider goals.

- Define the scope of each team, and help team members understand that scope.
- Understand the extent and range of collaboration between our teams.
- Encourage diversity and opportunity in the community.
- Produce a Code of Conduct.

Each item on this list is critical in building a strong, proactive, effective community. They are all important attributes that need attention when building a healthy environment for our contributors.

Some of these items are discussed later in this book. We will defer discussion of how to "build an environment conducive to our wider goals" and "encourage diversity and opportunity in the community" until our chapters on processes (Chapter 4) and building buzz (Chapter 7), respectively.

We have already added "produce a Code of Conduct" to our list of objectives. This leaves us with some outstanding TODO list items, all of which relate to dividing our community into teams.

Teams: Divide and Conquer

Earlier in this chapter, we rambled on about the importance of teams. We explored how meritocracy, diversity, and working together can help us build these units of belonging.

Since that discussion, we have identified a set of objectives, each with related goals. It is now time to divide our community into a set of healthy, motivated teams.

Although we are going to strategically develop a set of teams to form our community, you should encourage free-form team creation. Giving your community the ability to build its own teams without prior approval can produce incredibly diverse and productive results. We have seen this in droves in the Ubuntu community, with many seemingly random teams doing great work in areas we never envisaged.

Although the door should be open to form new teams, a primary set of teams will perform much of the work in the community. Our four remaining Community TODO List items provide a set of guidelines for forming these core teams.

Identify how we can divide our community into teams

Earlier in this chapter we fleshed out some initial notes about our community and what general considerations we think about in terms of a mission, skills, and objectives. If you followed my advice earlier, you will have worked in an open and transparent manner with your community to flesh out this direction into a strategic plan. Your objectives and the work necessary to achieve them should be no surprise to your primary community members who were involved in constructing this strategy. To achieve our strategic goals, we need to form these teams that are so important to our community.

There are many approaches to setting up teams, and there is no standard recipe for how to do this. It varies among different types of community, and it varies among the experience and expectations of your existing members. When deciding on teams, consult again with your existing community. Have a discussion about which teams make sense. You can't build teams out of nothing, and as such, your first set of teams will almost certainly map to regularly contributing community members who want to engage in certain types of work. As an example, if you have contributors who want to work on documentation, they would be a great foundation for a documentation team.

When most communities set up teams, the approach is almost always based on what similar communities have done. As an example, most open source projects will have development, documentation, and translation teams. This is largely because these teams are what we are familiar with in those communities. I highly recommend that you look into these existing communities and learn from their approach. This can offer valuable insight about the most suitable solution for you.

For most communities, it seems that teams typically map very well to primary skills. Earlier on when we built our initial notes about our community, we created our own list of these SKILLS REQUIRED. Many of these skills often map well to teams.

As an example, a software project will typically require these skills:

- Programming
- Writing documentation
- Testing
- Bug triage
- Advocacy
- Website development

Each of these skills could map to the following teams:

- Programming→Development Team
- Writing documentation→Documentation Team
- Testing→QA Team
- Bug triage→QA Team
- Advocacy→Marketing Team
- Website development→Web Team

Some skills (such as testing and bug triage) naturally map to the same teams. This is perfectly normal, and should be encouraged. Although you want to ensure that a good range of teams cover the different types of contributions, you don't want to overload your community. Form new teams only when existing teams cannot sufficiently cater to new needs and requirements.

It is important that your teams have the ability to expand their mandate, adjusting their focus as they mature. As an example, a documentation team may expand to include general communications and education. As such, try to foresee this growth while keeping the team focused.

Define the scope of each team, and help team members understand that scope

Earlier we created a mission statement for the wider community, but mission statements can be useful for specific teams, too.

For each team you should produce a mission statement that outlines the specific work that the team performs. With this statement available for each team, you will better understand how your teams fit together, and so will prospective contributors: this statement will help you articulate the purpose of the team and help new contributors know which team to join.

As before, your definition should explain the typical activities that the team will do. As an example, the following could be used to describe a documentation team:

> The documentation team identifies and prioritizes areas in which documentation is required, builds processes for producing high-quality documentation and best practice, and produces said documentation.

As a continued effort in transparency and openness, when writing team mission statements I recommend that you work together with other members of your community who are on those teams, in order to come to an agreement on them.

Understand the extent and range of collaboration among our teams

Teams are not insulated from one another. Every team needs to work with other teams, and some will have more crossover than others. Identify how your teams will interact in different ways, and try to optimize for those teams that cross over the most.

Identifying these collaborative crossovers typically requires a significant amount of day-to-day experience in how the community functions. With this in mind, you should regularly observe how your community's teams collaborate.

For example, in the Ubuntu community, the bug squad (who triages and organizes bugs) works very closely with the development team. By observing how the teams work, we were able to optimize the lines of communication, how both teams work together on the bug list, how meetings and events intersect, and other initiatives.

Ensure that teams can communicate clearly and effectively

You should always be cognizant of how your teams communicate with one another. How can the documentation team communicate effectively with the marketing team? How can the QA team work well with the development team?

The answer to these questions is complex and multifaceted. My recommended approach is to identify how you communicate tasks, issues, and goodwill:

Tasks

> Enable teams to share and report what they are working on. When teams are able to identify who is working on what, this avoids duplication and confusion. Great approaches to this are regular meetings, notes, and articles (such as blog entries). This will be discussed in more detail later in this book, when we refine our communication facilities and processes.

Issues

> Have regular, open opportunities for teams to communicate. Every team will have questions, concerns, queries, opportunities, and other topics to communicate to other teams. We need to ensure that these lines of communication are open. Again, regular, published meetings are the perfect opportunity to cover these kinds of issues.

Goodwill

> Encourage and inspire strong and positive relations between teams. Always remember that your teams are part of the same mission. As such, they should celebrate victories together and console one another in hard times. If you don't focus enough on ensuring that teams feel part of the same machine working together in the right direction, the community will feel fragmented. This all boils down to bonding. Different teams should regularly bond together, either online, at physical meetings, and/or during other occasions. We will discuss this in more detail in Chapter 12, when we discuss events. In the Ubuntu community, this occurs at every Ubuntu Developer Summit: different teams bond together, which helps the project as a whole.

As mentioned, we can achieve each of these methods of communication by producing a set of processes and events that every team makes use of. Reporting can help with tasks, regular meetings can help with issues, and social interaction and bonding can help with goodwill. We will talk later in this book about these different elements and how to implement them.

Setting expectations is critical in building community. When expectations are unrealistic or misaligned, the community forms its own theories. This can be a rocky road. The problem is that of Chinese Whispers (also known as Telephone, to some)—the game where a message passes from one person to another and changes at each step until the original meaning is garbled. When an expectation is surprising, often guesses and assumption are communicated as fact. This causes misinformation, concern, and typically negative outcomes.

The goal of this chapter is partly to clearly define these expectations. Your strategy is a means to get everyone in your community on the same page. If aspects of the strategy are unclear, there is the potential for mismatched expectations.

Again, this is an area in which experience plays a valuable role. After a short time working with your community, you will begin to better understand how they and you perceive the work that your community performs. This understanding will help you build a better strategy that will be more effective in achieving your objectives and goals.

Documenting Your Strategy

By now, a number of chunks of our strategy are in place. These include:

- A mission statement
- A set of objectives and goals, each with success criteria, an implementation plan, and owner details
- A list of skills and how those skills map to teams
- A list of teams, each with a definition of its scope
- A set of TODO list items that we can utilize throughout our community-building activities

Our final task in this chapter is to put the fruits of our labor somewhere that is accessible, easy to read, and easy to update. We need to communicate our strategy with the wider community and ensure that it can be referenced and updated when required.

At a bare minimum, your strategy should be available online, and at least available in the most common language that your community speaks. Multiple languages would be beneficial under the condition that every translation covers the full strategic documentation. Half-complete translations are not useful to anyone; the strategy must be complete.

The strategy that you publish should be made available in full and should not omit any sections. The purpose of this strategy is to unite the community behind one set of documentation and to form agreement around the objectives and goals outlined in that documentation.

There are a number of options available when it comes to publishing online, from a simple web page to a full content management system. The specifics of how you put your strategy online generally are not important; instead, open access to the content is the primary focus.

Many communities are using wikis as a method of publishing strategy online. A wiki is a website whose content anyone can update, the most significant example being Wikipedia. The idea is simple: a community sets up a wiki to use as a general area for collaboration, and so it makes sense to put the strategic plan on there.

With anyone able to edit the content on a wiki, your community needs to decide how changes to this content are handled. You may welcome cosmetic changes such as spelling and grammar, but you should discourage random changes to the core agreement that is your strategic plan.

Remember, the devil is in the details in strategic documents. To handle the tension between maintaining continuity and allowing fresh input, you have several options, some of which include:

- Putting up the strategic plan as a static web page that changes only after a rigorous process of internal discussion and voting. New goals and other changes can be emailed to project leaders or brought up in meetings.

- Putting up the mission statement and other rarely changing documents as a web page, but using a wiki or other malleable document for objectives and goals, so they can be rapidly updated by anyone involved.

- Putting everything on a wiki, but making sure you subscribe to all changes through email, an RSS feed, or whatever other medium on which you like to receive news.

Other options will certainly arise as new online mediums are developed.

Whichever approach you take, if the ability to change content is restricted, you need to be able to justify why those who have access do and why others don't. "I created the content" is not enough of a justification.

When some members of your community are given elevated responsibilities and privilege, it automatically puts a hierarchy in place in your community. The outcome is that those with this access are seen as leaders and governors. The production and development of these strategic documents is part of the responsibility of governing the community, and as such this governance may need to be formalized into a recognized body, such as a Community Council. We will discuss governance in detail later, in Chapter 10 of this book.

As a final note, always remember that documentation and strategy do not solve every problem. Many people will be unaware that your strategy exists, and many who are aware will simply not read it. A strong and well-documented strategy does not replace the culture of communication and unity that we seek to grow throughout this book.

Financially Supporting Your Community

Another consideration to think about when planning your community is the level of financial resources you are going to need to operate.

For some communities this will be negligible. As an example, if you are running a local book club that meets once a week in a coffee shop, most of the costs (e.g., gas for your members to get to the meetings) is likely to be absorbed by the members themselves. Other communities may have more extensive financial requirements. As an example, a community that is creating software for a particular device will likely need financial support to purchase the hardware so that the community can do their work.

The first question you should ask yourself is, What equipment and facilities are *required* for *the community* to be successful? Now, when I say *required*, I really do mean *required*. There are lots of things that would be nice to have—branded underwear, therapeutic spa sessions for hard-working contributors, ivory back-scratchers—but we are talking about the *essentials here.*

Here some possible requirements to think about:

Infrastructure

What resources do you need in order to do your work and represent the project? Fortunately, in terms of online resources such as web or code/bug/translation hosting for software projects, there are many free services available that you can use. There are also many services available for creating and hosting websites (many of which can be set up with a few clicks and no coding experience). You should also assess which commercial services or infrastructure you may require that have no free alternatives. Also remember that one of the benefits of free services over most commercial services is that your community members can use them freely, too; we always want our community members to be able to participate without reaching into their pockets.

Equipment

What equipment is required for participation that would be unreasonable to expect a community member to possess? As an example, for a software community we can reasonably expect our community members to have a computer and Internet access (we should not pay for these from the community organization's pockets). Continuing the example, custom hardware may have to be loaned to a community member for him to do his work. For local communities other equipment, such as tools and materials for a DIY group or facilities for a music group, may be required.

Travel

One of the most common costs in communities is travel; this can be difficult to do on a shoestring, but it is possible. Before you decide you need a travel budget, you should assess whether you can be represented at the event by asking friends for help (e.g., asking community members local to the event to attend).

Events

Of course, you may want to put on your own events and feel you need funds to either run the event and/or fund travel and accommodation for some of your community members. Events can be expensive to run, but it is possible to do a lot with a little money.

You should put together this list of requirements and ask for feedback from other community members to see if they feel like it represents the community's needs accurately. You can then use this as a requirements list to outline things for which you need to find funding.

Before we talk about potential areas of revenue, I strongly encourage you to try to satisfy these requirements in a *grassroots* kind of way. As an example, each year I organize the Community Leadership Summit (you can read more about the event in "The Community Leadership Summit" on page 523). While the event definitely requires some funding (as an example, we are required to purchase the coffee from the conference center vendor, and this is heavily marked up and costs around $3,000), we also try to run the rest of the event in a very cost-efficient way. We have volunteers who staff it, we are loaned much of the equipment, the venue space is donated, and other areas are handled in a very communal fashion.

There are two reasons why I strongly encourage you to think creatively about how you can satisfy these requirements:

Asking friends is easier than asking strangers
> Asking friends, colleagues, and community members to loan equipment, contribute time, and volunteer in other ways is much easier than asking someone for money to pay for these things. In tough economic climates it is increasingly difficult to have people pledge money to communities.

Less paperwork is a good thing
> As soon as you bring money into your community you then have to engage in all the paperwork and policy that surrounds it. This includes accounts, taxes, setting up foundations (if applicable), and other such fluff and nonsense. I don't know if I am in the minority here, but I *hate* this kind of work, and it sucks the fun out of working with community. If you can avoid handling money and thus avoid the paperwork this can often make life much easier.

The general rule of thumb I recommend is to run your community in as grassroots a way as possible and then get funding for the areas that you can't support in this way.

Revenue Opportunities

If you do decide that you need to find some money to cover the requirements you outlined earlier for your community, there are a number of different options available. Fortunately, setting up and delivering these options is fairly straightforward. Let's look into each of them.

Online advertising

Everyone hates ads, right? Why would I want to return to the 1998 era of banner ads obnoxiously draped across my community's website?

Well, fortunately it is not as bad as that. In recent years online advertising has become a valuable service that not only provides a revenue opportunity for communities (as well as individuals, businesses, and anyone else), but also has been tuned to better integrate these ads into websites and to display ads that are relevant to your visitors.

At the time of this writing, the big player in online advertising is Google with its AdSense service. The concept is pretty simple: when you sign up for the service Google provides a small chunk of code that you embed into your website that will read in the content on each page and display ads that are relevant to that page. As an example, if you write a blog entry about horses, you will likely see equestrian-related ads.

Each time someone clicks on the ad, the company that placed the ad will pay a small fee to you and to Google. This fee is calculated using some kind of mystical formula that you can learn about elsewhere, but the practical result is that when you display ads and people click on them you get paid.

What is nice about the AdSense service is that you can choose different ways in which the ads are displayed (e.g., different sized ad blocks, different numbers of ads, whether images or just text links are displayed, etc.). Using the service is really simple; just sign up at *https://www.google.com/adsense/*.

Another nice feature specific to AdSense is that you can provide ads on your YouTube videos. This opens up another channel in which revenue could be generated, and if you have a viral video on your hands, you can cash in on quite a chunk of change.

Selling

Another avenue for generating money is to sell items at a profit. Examples of this could include selling branded t-shirts, mugs, and other merchandise. Many communities have used this approach with varying levels of success.

The first step in using this method is to think about what you could sell. Brainstorm a list of potential items and then prioritize that list into the kind of things that people might actually want to purchase. Much as a thong with your logo on it might sound cool, is anyone really going to want that (apart from you)?

When you have this list you can look at different supplier options.

Many of you will be interested in producing wearables (e.g., t-shirts, hoodies, caps, vests) and promo items (e.g., mugs, stickers, key chains, etc.). For these kinds of products you have two broad options:

Bulk production
> You could choose an item (such as a t-shirt) and bulk-produce it, such as getting 300 made. This is by far the cheapest approach, and the higher the quantity the more the cost per unit goes down. The problem with this approach is that you will need to fund this up front, you will have stock to get rid of, and you will need to fulfill the orders (package them up and send them out). You will also need to be able to handle payments (although this is not that challenging when using a service such as PayPal).

On-demand production
> An alternative approach is to use a service such as CafePress (*http://www.cafepress.com*), Spreadshirt (*http://www.spreadshirt.com*), or Zazzle (*http://www.zazzle.com*) to create an online store, upload your logos, and then have people purchase their items from there. Each item will be made on a one-by-one basis, and unfortunately this means the price for these items is often much higher. The benefits are that these companies will handle all the production, sales, and fulfillment, and there are no up-front costs or stock required.

Both of these approaches can work well for different communities. The former is definitely the most cost-effective in terms of making profit on the items you sell, but the latter is definitely more convenient. Unfortunately, for the latter I have traditionally found it harder to sell items than with the former approach.

Donations

Severed Fifth is a project that I set up to see how far a band could take its music by giving the music away and building a community around the band that could help grow and support the band in different ways. I set up the band, wrote an album, and recorded a demo in my home studio, and then we started a campaign to raise funds to record an album professionally.

What started next was a busy period of blogging, releasing videos, and raising awareness around the goal of funding the production of the album. After around four months of campaigning, I raised $4,000 from community donations to take to the studio to record the album.

Lots of communities have started donation drives of this kind, and many have been successful. Unfortunately, many others have been unsuccessful. Here are some tips that might help you improve your chances of success:

Make donating easy

Be sure to make donating a piece of cake. Most people will want to donate online with a credit or debit card or with PayPal. For Severed Fifth we used PayPal to gather the donations, but you can also use a service such as KickStarter (*http://www.kickstarter.com*), which rallies prospective donors around a target figure. Regardless of the service you choose, make sure that donating is a breeze and only takes a few minutes.

Pick a goal

A donation drive should have a target and focus and not just be a case of "give us money, please!" Whether it is a target outcome (e.g., the recording in the previous Severed Fifth example), a target amount, or anything else, be sure to have a goal that people feel passionate about supporting with their wallet.

Message extensively

Donation drives need a lot of messaging. Be sure to keep banging the drum about how people can help your effort and why their contributions are important, and regularly updating people on the progress of the donation drive and how close you are to the goal.

Provide incentives

Another useful approach is to provide incentives for different types of donations. As an example, with Severed Fifth we provided different rewards for different amounts (e.g., $50 gets you a t-shirt, $60 gets you a t-shirt and CD, etc.). This had great results.

If you can create a campaign around something that people are passionate about and keep the messaging going, it is incredible what is possible when people are willing to support a shared goal.

Sponsorship

Sponsorship is another useful area for funding. This will be more complex for smaller, newer communities, and much of the sponsorship game is about knowing the right people who can present your case for sponsorship to the respective companies.

While sponsorship is often considered within the context of providing checks for a chunk of money, you should also investigate sponsorship for the provision of goods and services. As an example, a company called Bytemark Hosting (*http://www.bytemark.co.uk*) provides sponsorship to run the Severed Fifth website and hosting. In many cases these requests for sponsorship are easier for the company than cutting a check.

When applying to different companies for sponsorship you should produce a sponsorship pack that outlines some key pieces of information:

About you
> Describe the community, your goals, and the progress you have made, and word this in a way that is sympathetic to the company's goals.

What you require
> Outline the specifics of what you are asking the company to provide. Is it money? If so, how much? Is it equipment? If so, what equipment and how many units? When making these requirements, base them on what you are likely to get (e.g., don't ask a small start-up for a huge amount of money it probably doesn't have).

What they will get
> Explain what they will get in return for their sponsorship. In most cases the company wants branding on your website and on promotional materials. Describe what sponsoring companies will get in return (e.g., their logo on your website, mentions in your social media feed and newsletter, their logo on your event t-shirts, etc.).

Wrapping Up

In this chapter, we have made some great progress in our journey. We have laid the foundation for an organized, well-planned strategy that will unite your community behind the same set of objectives and goals. With this foundation in place, we can expand and refine it as we progress through the book and explore the many other concepts farther down the road. If you have followed through with each exercise in this chapter, it will have helped you to think structurally about your community and its goals, and share the fruits of this structured thinking with everyone involved. By definition, this will help your community rock and roll that little bit harder.

When we started our journey into community, we talked about the social economy as a collection of processes to achieve social capital. These processes are essential in a simple, effective, and nonbureaucratic community. They affect how people join your community, how they collaborate, how ideas are communicated, how problems are communicated, and more. These processes can be the difference between success and failure.

The first set of processes that we need to consider is how we communicate effectively in our community. With this in mind, let's dive into the next chapter. All set? Let's go....

CHAPTER THREE

Communicating Clearly

"Before I speak, I have something important to say."

—*Groucho Marx*

WHEN I WAS 11 YEARS OLD, MY FRIEND SOMEHOW OBTAINED AN LP HE HAD "BORROWED WITHOUT ASKING" FROM HIS BROTHER. He handed me the large disc adorned with cardboard sleeve, all carefully buried in a white plastic bag. As I retrieved said sleeve from said bag, my eyes widened and I skipped a breath: it was the first time I witnessed the sheer brilliance of an Iron Maiden record.

I listened to that LP until it damaged the pin in my record player. I loved the energy, I loved the look (including the spandex…I am not kidding), and I just wanted to be them. Unfortunately, I had neither talent nor spandex, but merely a bowl haircut and large white socks.

Inspired, I decided I was going to learn to play the guitar. My parents bought me an old acoustic guitar and I parked myself on my bed night after night trying to sound like my rock and roll heroes. Of course, I instead sounded like an incompetent 11-year-old with an acoustic guitar. I sucked, but I stuck at it.

As the years rumbled on, so did my guitar playing. Fortunately, my skills were improving and I was reading more and more about music, guitarists, and the bands I loved. While flipping through a copy of *Guitarist* magazine, I came across a quote that I seem to remember was from Eric Clapton, but I'm not quite sure. Whoever it was, his words really resonated with me (pun intended):

It's not the notes you play, it's the notes you don't play.

While I am still making oodles of music today, this quote didn't really take hold of me until five years later when I started writing. What the little nugget of wisdom implies is that, although we may obsess over the obvious components in an art form (such as the notes in music), it is often the hidden and underlying messages that offer the most value (such as not playing certain notes).

This is a strong and relevant message for building communities. Community is absolutely about understanding the ether. Our notes are the processes, governance, tools, and methods in which we work together. The notes we don't play are the subtle nuances in how we pull these notes together and share them with one another. The space between the notes is *communication*.

He Said, She Said

Communication is essential in community. It is the metaphorical highway that connects the many towns and people in your world. Effective communication brings together your community members in a manner that is free-flowing, productive, and accessible.

You may spend hours putting together elegant and sleek processes, infrastructure, and governance, but if members of your community can't communicate well with one another, you may as well pack up your bags and go and pursue a career in cabaret on *The Love Boat*.

Our analogy with highways and towns maps eerily well to how we wire up our community with the communication channels it needs. To ensure that our towns can work together, we have two primary tasks on our hands:

Create the highways
> First, your community needs to build a set of resources to facilitate communication, discussion, and the sharing of ideas and best practices. In many cases these resources are online facilities, such as mailing lists, forums, and discussion channels.

Encourage great driving
> Once your communication channels are in place, they can be used in all manner of ways. There will, of course, be some good drivers and some bad drivers; some will communicate exceptionally well, and some will irritate and agitate anyone who crosses their path. You want to inspire and encourage a baseline quality of communication. This is not about excluding people who are imperfect writers or speakers, but rather about providing a consistent example of simple approaches to communication that make the community easier to understand and more pleasurable for everyone involved.

In this chapter we are going to cast our sights on both of these topics, discuss a range of mediums for building the free flow of communication, make good use of those facilities, incorporate transparency, and avoid the common problem of a community preferring to speak rather than do.

So, let's get started by laying down the highways and putting some cars on the road. Now is the time to build our community's communication backbone....

Building Your Communication Channels

Earlier we created our TODO list of key aims and ambitions for building a strong community. We are now going to dig up that list and cast our sights on one very specific item.

Community TODO List

- Ensure that teams can communicate clearly and effectively.

Good communication serves many purposes in a community. It is the foundation of how your members work together, share goals and ambitions, and build social relationships with one another. It is communication that ensures that everyone is on the same page, heading in the same direction, marching to the same beat.

Good communication is also a powerful security blanket. When communication breaks down in community, it can cause havoc. Volunteer communities are driven by members with a set of values that reflect themselves and the values of the wider community. These values are important to regularly reinforce in your community: they are the metabolism that fights off the threats and problems that can undermine the goals of the community. When your members feel like they are disconnected from the community, they lose their sense of value.

Communication can be divided into three primary areas:

Incoming

Receiving and processing feedback and viewpoints for the purpose of improvement. An example of this could include surveys to determine how well a part of your community is working.

Outgoing

Sharing news, stories, and achievements from the community with the rest of the world. An example of this could be showing off something your community has created.

Internal

Internal discussions and meetings in the community to discuss objectives, goals, conflict, and other issues. An example of this could include meetings that are designed to decide how your community will work together toward its goals.

Each of these forms of communication is essential for a strong community. All communities need open and objective feedback. They should all share their achievements and what they have produced. Finally, all communities need to have regular internal discussions and meetings to ensure that everyone is interacting smoothly. Great communication should be a goal for the many different parts of your community, as opposed to one specific area. When we get great communication right, community feels vibrant, thriving, and accessible.

We are going to cover all three of these topics in this book. We will discuss incoming communication in Chapter 8, outgoing communication in Chapter 7, and internal communication here.

Striving for Clarity

As communication is critical to the success of your community, it is stunning how many communities just get it plain wrong. Many are plagued with long-winded, overly complex, and difficult-to-use communication channels, and it seems you need a degree in rocket science to understand how to join these channels. Then, it seems you need to go back to school to get a degree in computational linguistics to fit into the culture and expectations of these communication channels. Many have an unwritten rule book stapled to the side of the channel, and if you are unfamiliar with its scriptures, the response can be terse, forthright, and sometimes outright rude. This is the last thing you want. Instead, you want to create simple, efficient, welcoming, and enjoyable methods of keeping in touch with other members of the project.

The greatest form of communication is always going to be sitting in a room with a real person, face to face. In this setting you can speak freely, your words flowing as quickly as your brain conjures them up, with body language, gestures, and facial expressions further augmenting the flow of conversation. Any technological form of communication is going to compromise some of these attributes. Of course, many who are socially uncomfortable in face-to-face situations will hail the muting of these additional attributes in conversation as a victory for accessibility and openness.

When laying down the lines of communication for our community, our goal is to strive for *clarity*. Imagine, if you will, a world in which every communication is clear, accessible, and well understood by your community. You need to think carefully about the culture in which your community communicates and strive to build a highway and driving style that achieves that culture. You first need to lay the foundation, which can be found in clarity and transparency. Your members want to be able to hear, read, or experience each communication and understand it straightaway. When clarity is in place, contributions will begin to flow shortly afterward. When confusion, misunderstanding, and opacity set in, your members will either spend their days seeking clarification or move on, confused and frustrated.

Clarity and transparency are also important in attracting new members. For example, most online communities' communication channels are indexed by search engines. How many times have you typed something into Google and some of the results that appear are mailing lists, forums, or other online discussions that are happening inside a community? Potential new community members will read these discussions and it will affect their desire and willingness to join your community. If the communications are complex, socially fraught, or otherwise suboptimal, potential members may prefer to spend their valuable spare time playing Guitar Hero rather than joining you and your band of merry men and women.

Achieving clarity requires attention to two areas. First, a sensible choice of communication medium is required (mailing list, IRC, forum, etc.). This is relatively straightforward and actually fairly uninteresting. We will make some decisions about this over the following pages. The second, more complex part is picking communication channels that match the needs of the users while maximizing clarity. Let's spend some time talking about that.

Choices, Choices

Your community has oodles of communication channels to choose from, each with qualities that make sense in different scenarios and to different people. The goal is to match the right medium to your community and to understand the pros and cons of that medium to help the pros bubble to the surface and keep the cons well away from the kitchen.

Picking an appropriate medium is largely about understanding your contributors and their workflow. Each type of contributor will have different preferences. Software developers generally prefer content to be delivered directly to them. They are typically most comfortable with mailing lists and RSS feeds (updated content from websites and online resources) and don't like to have to refresh a browser to see if new content exists. This is part of why many (typically Western) developers don't get on very well with forums. Some communities have bridged this divide by providing gateways so that a mailing list post goes to a forum and vice versa (an example of this is the Banshee project at *http://banshee-project.org/support/*).

> ### NOTE
> Of course, many developers do love forums. The last statement was based on general experience with developers over a range of projects and development cultures, largely in Western countries. If you know developers who love forums, don't be alarmed: we are all friends here.

Users are (typically) different. Users often love forums for their accessibility and simplicity. The conversation flow is clear, the interface is friendly, and the web browser is a familiar window to that world. Users are used to having to refresh their browser to see if updates exist. They are used to visiting many websites to find content, and they generally feel uncomfortable about technical barriers to these discussions and content. Users just don't like to jump through hoops, particularly technical hoops that can easily trip them up.

Believe it or not, these roles are fairly set in stone. Trying to persuade a developer to use a forum can be like persuading a cat to chase after a stick. A developer may agree to give it a shot, but I can almost guarantee you that it won't work out. Communication channels are highways of habit: people have their preferences and they generally stick to them.

At the beginning of a community you need to know which roles and personalities are most comfortable with which communication mediums; this is the very first step in building great communication. You can then make informed choices. We will explore some of these common mediums and some notes that can help inform these choices in just a moment.

Communication fetishism

Another key consideration when building effective communication channels is keeping discussion focused. This is a two-part process in avoiding *communication fetishism* and also *keeping all your eyeballs in one place*.

Communication fetishism is particularly prevalent in online and technical communities and points to the problem of new communities wanting to provide every possible communication channel under the sun. They set up mailing lists, forums, IRC channels, Second Life worlds, and more. This is the *wrong* thing to do. You should instead identify the key roles and personalities in your project and choose mediums that make the most sense to those roles. Let's look at an example.

When I set up the Jokosher project, I knew that the primary roles in the community were going to be users and developers. I wanted to ensure that the project had communication channels for technical discussion about the development of the application, but also a place for musicians to discuss Jokosher, share tips, and show off their compositions. I decided to set up a mailing list for the developers and a forum for the users. These mediums reflected the respective developer and user roles well. The only other medium I set up was a #jokosher IRC channel for real-time discussion and meetings for the developers. Although the channel exists, we never point regular users to that channel; the forum is far more appropriate.

The second part of the process is "keeping all your eyeballs in one place." One of the mistakes a lot of new communities make is to fragment individual communication mediums too heavily. Let's look at another example.

When we started LugRadio, I wanted us to provide a place for listeners to talk about the show and the topics in each episode. Forums were the best choice, so I set them up.

In most discussion forums you can have a number of subforums. As an example, if you had a software project, you could have subforums for General Discussion, Development, Documentation, and so on. When I set up the LugRadio forums I created three subforums: General Discussion, Ideas for the Show, and Mirrors. Each subforum had a clear purpose for discussion.

In contrast to many other forums, we had a tiny number of subforums. Many new forums have 10 or more subforums, and we had 3. This was deliberate. When you set up a new community, you want to generate discussion quickly. You want to initiate the discussion but encourage and inspire others to participate and get involved. If you have a forum with too many subforums, you will fragment the discussion: you will get many tiny bits of discussion across the subforums, and little consistency. Keep the discussion in just a few places, and conversation will flow.

This happens because people waste time choosing the right forum instead of just posting. What is worse, some get confused and just don't post at all. Discussion gets going faster when you have fewer choices.

The Mediums

With some general best practices under our belts, let's now roll up our sleeves and take a look at the nitty-gritty of the range of mediums available to us. Over the following few pages I am going to provide a quick-shot summary of these mediums and many of their behavioral elements.

Before we begin, we need to discuss a key consideration in choosing an effective medium: how easy it is to record and retrieve conversations that have occurred in the past. When communicating with others online, each medium places different opportunities in the hands of others to find these conversations. This attribute can dramatically adjust how people behave and converse in a given medium.

As an example, it is well known in many communities that mailing lists have their conversations archived and publicly available on a website. This website is then archived and retrievable by search engines, such as Google. With this in mind, participants in mailing lists often act in a more formalized and "professional" capacity: you never know when that conversation on a mailing list will show up when a prospective employer is Googling you for a job interview.

On the flip side, there is the real-time IRC chat medium. While many IRC channels can and are logged, it is far harder to find the logs and find relevant discussion in the reams of chatter that happen each day on an IRC channel. As such, the medium feels less recorded, and many of the participants feel more comfortable in communicating more socially.

You should consider these implications when building out your communication facilities, and ensure that your participants are fully aware of where they stand. No one wants a situation where someone says something, assuming it is not archived, and then finds (to his chagrin) that it appears in a Google search.

Mailing lists

Mailing lists are an excellent medium for discussion. They are low-bandwidth, a familiar interface (email), and fairly accessible, and conversation is delivered directly to your email client. The delivery of the conversation reduces the chance of new contributors forgetting about your community: each time they check their email, they are reminded that your community exists, and they may actually read the messages and respond.

Mailing lists are typically preferred by software developers, and of common interest in the open source world. Many nonprogramming contributors often use and enjoy mailing lists.

Mailing lists are not all sweetness and light, though. Joining a mailing list is a little complex. It requires people to know how to join, sign up with an email address, respond to the mail, and know where to send messages. Also, unforgiving spam filters can make the whole process icky.

Mailing lists also assume that you are interested in all discussions, and when you join, all discussions come to you. This makes mailing lists implicitly of most interest to those who plan a serious contribution or interest in a community.

Another issue to bear in mind with mailing lists is their lack of immediacy. As an example, if you are a community software developer working at 10 p.m. on a Saturday and you have a problem, you could post a question to the mailing list, but you may not get an answer until Monday or Tuesday and are thus stymied. If more immediate results are needed, real-time communication channels such as IRC are better (of course, assuming people are on the channel: silence sucks on all mediums).

Normal end-user and consumer reaction to mailing lists is mixed. Many users have single-shot queries and questions, and the requirement to battle through the somewhat complex sign-up process and then receive all conversations can be off-putting.

> **NOTE**
>
> **An important consideration to make when setting up a mailing list is whether the list is archived on the Internet. If you want the conversations to be private (such as if the mailing list is for a governance body), you should close off the archives. We discuss governance in detail in Chapter 10.**

Discussion forums

Forums are a very popular, low-barrier-to-entry medium. They manifest in the form of websites that allow you to create an identity and have a discussion using that identity.

Forums have exploded in popularity in recent years, and some huge forums have developed across the Internet. At the time of this writing, the biggest in the world is an anime role-playing community with over 15 million members and over 1 billion posts. Now that is a lot of tentacles and oversized eyes. Even the far smaller LugRadio forum has over 1,000 members and 40,000+ posts. A common use for forums has been as a support channel for your community. Many software projects (including Jokosher) have found this useful.

Forums are a popular choice among less-technical users. They are easy to join and easy to use, and many forums allow users to inject personality into their profiles with avatar pictures, personal details, and signatures. Many forums also encourage discussion via the use of ranks—special community descriptions based around the number of posts that a member makes. Many forum users cherish these rankings and take great pride in making many posts to achieve them.

NOTE

Be careful with these ranks as a means of measuring community; they are often not all that insightful. We will discuss this in Chapter 8.

Due to the user-focused nature of forums, discussion is often from the perspective of new users, and often those who are less familiar with netiquette. As such, you may attract some immature behavior and spam on forums. With this in mind, you should ensure that you have a number of moderators who can tend to this kind of behavior. The best approach to moderation is to anoint a handful of well-respected and trustworthy contributors who use your forum.

NOTE

Many social media sites, such as LinkedIn and Facebook, provide forum-like functionality built into their sites. These can be useful for some communities.

Social media

Social media is a large and comprehensive medium for many different types of communication, so much so that all of Chapter 6 in the book is devoted to it.

IRC

IRC is a real-time chat medium that has become increasingly popular for communities. There are IRC providers all over the world, and many IRC networks cater to specific purposes. As an example, the Freenode network (*irc.freenode.net*) is specifically aimed at providing IRC channels and conversation for open source projects. Although an entirely open and accessible medium, IRC is still very much populated by technology-related channels.

The value of IRC is in real-time discussion, and there are many benefits:

Bonding
> Communities bond effectively in real time. It provides a chance for people to have general day-to-day conversations that would be out of place on a more formalized medium such as a mailing list. Many people use IRC for socializing and often spend time chitchatting: this all helps for bonding.

Speed
> Discussions can often occur faster on IRC. It provides an excellent medium for discussing and debating, and it is smoother and easier to debate on IRC than on a mailing list or forum.

Meetings

IRC offers an excellent opportunity for real-time meetings. We will discuss this later in this chapter and in Chapter 12.

Logs

IRC channels can be logged, which provides an excellent means of documenting discussions and meetings.

If you are setting up a community that is focused on technology or the Internet, an IRC channel could be a useful addition. It is important that your IRC channel is open, accessible, and well publicized. You should ensure that it is listed on your community's website.

NOTE

Many IRC services are blocked from commercial work environments, and some of your members may therefore not be able to take a sneaky IRC break while at work.

There are some web-based IRC clients that may solve this problem for those users, and you may want to list some of these alternatives on your community's website.

As with any medium, IRC attracts its own kind of personalities, but the IRC personality profile is fairly mixed. On the one hand, we see many developers making use of IRC every day to keep in touch with their communities. On the other hand, we also see many new users joining IRC. You should ensure that your IRC channel(s) cater to these different types of users. If you are running a development project, it is best to have separate channels for developers and users (such as *#myproject-dev* and *#myproject-users*, respectively).

An interesting personality trait in IRC that you should be aware of is the desire for power. Many communities have discovered that a lot of importance is placed on IRC channel moderation and control. IRC allows people to become channel operators, and these privileges allow people to be kicked out and banned from channels. Many communities have experienced power struggles, arguments, and bickering over these privileges: being an operator is a badge of honor for many people. You should give out channel privileges sparingly, to those who will treat those privileges with care.

NOT SHOWING POWER

In all IRC channels, some people can be operators and have the power to kick out or ban people from the channel. By default, an icon appears next to the operators in your channel. Many channels decide not to have the operators display their privileges in general.

On the one hand, this makes sense: if there are no visible operators, the channel feels very equal. On the other hand, having visible ops can be self-policing because it can ensure that people behave properly. My recommendation: if someone is an operator, ask her not to display the icon, but if someone needs to be kicked out of the channel, have the operator switch on her privileges and firmly plant that boot in the offending user.

Leading by Example

However you decide to lay down the lines of communication and whichever tools and mediums you decide to use, you should strive for communication in your community to be friendly, clear, and productive. You want your community's members to not only feel engaged, excited, and enabled, but also to enjoy their interactions with the rest of the community.

This may not be quite as easy as it sounds, however. Communities are, by definition, groups of people, and those people have different personalities, habits, opinions, and approaches. These nuances can sometimes complicate how we communicate.

People can and do get frustrated with one another, have mismatched expectations, engage in unclear and tense discussions, and indulge in other agitating agendas. Not only that, but people sometimes just get out of bed on the wrong side. Everyone has bad days. Confusion happens. Life will get in the way, and people get busy.

Many of these causes are entirely innocent and simply the nature of being human. With people being the catalyst of community, you could be forgiven for thinking that there is nothing we can do about these problems in communication.

Not so.

Communities are vessels of culture: every community has its own norms, and these norms are defined by community leaders—community leaders such as *you*. You can avoid many of these potential issues in communication by not only setting a strong example, but also inspiring the wider community to follow a positive example in how they communicate with one another.

YOU ARE ALWAYS LEARNING

Some time ago I was at an Ubuntu Developer Summit and busily running from session to session, coordinating discussions, planning work for the release, and handling other related tasks. One afternoon, Amber, a friend of mine and a community member (and proofreader of *The Art of Community*), asked if she could have a quiet word with me.

Of course, this was never going to be a good word, and probably not all that quiet, either. I braced myself for impact.

Amber then shared that she had noticed that I had been a little too directional and focused in some of the sessions. She felt I was pushing too fast for outcomes and conclusions, and racing through debates to find solutions in a sometimes fairly abrupt way. I thanked her for the feedback (which was surprising to me, as I felt I had been pretty balanced in my communication), and we discussed what might be the cause. Was I stressed? Was I being impatient? Amber was keen to stress that I was not rude, just a little too focused at times. As we discussed this we then hit on the cause.

Canonical, like many start-ups, is a very intense and focused environment. There are lots of meetings, and no one wants to sit around wasting time; everyone is focused on solutions and getting there as quickly as possible. I realized when Amber shared her feedback that I had been communicating with our community members at the event in the same way I would communicate with colleagues. Importantly, the pace of many volunteer community members is different from the pace of Canonical staff members who have work items, deliverables, metrics, and other pressing matters to deal with.

It was a salient and memorable experience, and it taught me not only how I should moderate my approach to communication with different environments, but also that we are always learning each day about how to be great communicators and feedback is the key to learning and refining how we do it.

To lead by example, we can break down the problem into the following two bite-sized chunks:

Daily communication
> The day-to-day discussions, ideas, and debates that are expressed across your range of mediums

Longer writing
> Longer, more thoughtful, written forms of communication that are often used to inspire, advise, and direct your community

Let's now take a spin through both of these areas and explore some best practices, tips, and tricks for communicating well.

Daily Communication

Leading by example means communicating in a way that you feel is representative and appropriate for you and your community. It is about inspiring your community to get behind an ethic of good communication and ensuring that your community is exposed to that ethic on a daily basis. Life has taught us that consistent exposure to high-quality content can engender a high-quality response among onlookers. Great music often inspires great musicians; great art inspires great artists; and great community inspires great community members.

To lead by example, you need to be the living incarnation of the advice you offer to your community. As community leaders, we often settle ourselves happily into the role of *Chief Advisor of Doing Things the Right Way*, and it is hugely important that we practice what we preach and get intimately familiar with the taste of our own dog food.

Being a great daily communicator is not about being an incredible writer, being a proficient speaker, or using words reserved for a Scrabble-winning smackdown. Great communication instead focuses on clarity, detail, objective thought, and a consistently high quality of interaction.

Teaching great communication is complex, and many books have been written on the subject. Fortunately, becoming a great communicator doesn't require an exercise in academically satisfying hand waving or an attempt to sound like a monocle-wearing intellectual, but to simply be clear, friendly, and straightforward in your communications.

To achieve this, there are two stages involved. First, you should familiarize yourself with some simple recommended rules of engagement. These are:

Be clear

> Always try to communicate as clearly and transparently as possible. Speak frankly and use language familiar to your recipient. Try not to blind people with science, but don't patronize them either. Always try to craft your communications to your audience.

Be concise

> Keep to the point, and don't weigh your communications down with babble. Don't use 1,000 words to say what could be said in 100. With many of us receiving so many emails, messages, phone calls, and other distractions every day, don't burden your community with unnecessary rambling. If an email takes longer than five minutes to type, you may be doing something wrong (or you are a really, really slow typist).

Be responsive

> You don't have to be wedded to your computer, but try to get back to people within a few days of them getting in touch with you. If you are drowning in emails and work, just let people know you might be a little delayed, so their expectations are set correctly. This issue is applicable not just to personal communication directed to you and other community leaders, but also to mailing lists, forums, IRC, and other public channels. Put yourself in the sender's position: it is impossible to tell the difference between "nobody is answering my question because nobody knows the answer, meaning that what I'm trying to do is impossible and I should try something else" and "nobody is answering my question even though everyone knows the answer, because everybody is too busy, meaning that I should sit and wait longer rather than abandoning this approach." It helps to make your community seem friendlier to new members and outsiders if they can tell the difference between these two things.

Be fun

> One of the biggest mistakes that people make when they become well respected in a community is to hide their personality in the interests of "looking professional." Let your personality shine through. Make jokes and witty comments, and be sarcastic. Communities are supposed to be fun, and this is an important part of leading by example.

Be human

> We are all human, and we all make mistakes. If you screw up, say so and apologize. People will cherish your honesty and your integrity to hold your hands up when you get it wrong. This is a critically important part of leading by example: you want your community to also accept when they get it wrong. What we want to avoid is defensiveness, because it causes people to enter into a game of rebounding defensive statements, which is frustrating and damaging. If your hands are tied in being frank and open about your mistakes (such as if your employer would be less than thrilled), identify what went wrong and try to secure confidence in your community that it won't happen again in the future.

The second step is to learn from others. Observe email, chat conversations, phone discussions, and other interactions, and deconstruct them in your mind to find nuggets of wisdom and inspiration. You are sure to find some people who are always clear, concise, and detailed in their communications, and these are excellent role models for you.

Netiquette

In many online communities there are often localized technical cultural norms that are in play. These are small conventions and methods of communicating that are typically localized to a community, be it online or physical. Respect for these conventions and (often unwritten) rules is known as *netiquette*.

Although most of you will be familiar with some of the common conventions of communicating well on the Internet, you should be familiar with some of the local conventions in your specific community.

As an example, many communities use mailing lists as a primary method of communication. In many technical communities, some members can get rather agitated when new members unwittingly use an approach called *top posting*. Let's illustrate this with an example. Imagine you are subscribed to a public mailing list. You get the following simple email:

> Hey All,
> I just wanted to ask what is the answer to Foo?
> Thanks!
>   Bob

Top posting is when you reply above the quotes message. As an example:

> Hi Bob,
> The answer is Bar.
>   Jono
> > Hey All,
> > I just wanted to ask what is the answer to Foo?
> > Thanks!
> >   Bob

This is often frowned upon. The reason is that in online discussion threads with a series of messages replying to pieces of previous messages, top posting makes this thread of discussion difficult to follow. Here is an example of when someone replies to a top-posted message, but below the message:

```
> Hi Bob,
> The answer is Bar.
>   Jono
>> Hey All,
>> I just wanted to ask what is the answer to Foo?
>> Thanks!
>>    Bob
OK, thanks for the reply, Jono!
   Bob
```

The conversation is already a pain in the nether regions to follow. If everyone responds below the quoted text, the conversation would instead look like the following at this point (particularly when cutting out the bits of unneeded conversation):

```
>> Hey All,
>> I just wanted to ask what is the answer to Foo?
> The answer is Bar
OK, thanks for the reply, Jono!
   Bob
```

Though this might seem like a minor detail, many online communities get surprisingly frustrated at these kinds of mistakes. Unfortunately, communities often fail to document these expectations around discussion, and many innocent bystanders get short shrift when they accidentally get it wrong.

You should always try to document these expectations around communication on your community's website. If you are new to a community, it is recommended that you first observe the communication for a few days before you participate. This will help you to get a firm idea of these social conventions.

Avoiding bikeshedding

Almost every technical community I have seen makes the same two common mistakes: obsessing over resources and discussing topics to death. The latter of these two problems is rather excitingly called *bikeshedding*.[1]

In many collaborative communities, one of the first communication resources to be set up is a mailing list or forum. As with any new community, excitement is high, and the thrill of communicating with your new community members from all over the world gets everyone pumped up and fills these communication channels with discussion.

With the communication lines open and an unbridled sense of excitement around the shared goal of the community, plans get made posthaste. Ideas, thoughts, commitments, and other agreements get discussed. The community gets its first opportunity to dream together, and it feels like the world is your oyster. The result of this exciting brainstorming period is a stack of

---

1. To learn why, visit *http://en.wikipedia.org/wiki/Parkinson%27s_Law_of_Triviality*.

incredibly exciting plans and ideas. All that needs to happen now is to turn those dreams into reality, right?

Unfortunately, it's not quite that simple.

Talking is always easier than doing. It is far easier to discuss a great idea (often in exhaustive detail) than to implement a great idea. Reams and reams of discussion from many interested parties can explode on your mailing list, but this in itself can be a blocker to producing the very projects you discuss. While up-front specifications can help communities build something, overspecification and information overflow can have the inverse effect.

Part of the problem is that many communities focus a little too much on having every "i" dotted and every "t" crossed before work begins. The issue here is twofold. First, too much discussion will typically result in a hugely complex plan that is difficult to keep track of if not well documented. This can be off-putting for volunteers who just want to get started with something fun and manageable. When you overdiscuss and overengineer an idea, the complexity can be daunting.

The second problem, particularly in the early stages of your community, is that your new members need to see results or they will grow bored and leave. A great community is often built by a small set of capable and fast-moving contributors right at the beginning of its evolution. If a community spends three months discussing an idea yet produces little or nothing, many potential contributors will grow impatient with the discussion and develop a sense that the community is nothing more than a talking shop. This is exactly what we want to avoid.

There are two approaches that can help prevent this problem from occurring. First, you should not discuss topics in too much detail without connecting them to specific plans. Ask who is going to work on what, when the work is likely to be completed, and how you can help. As an example, if you are working on a software project, you should aim to have some code written within a week of the project starting. Always keep your eyes on the prize: reaching the goals of the community, be it software, an event, a campaign, or whatever else.

Another solution is to build a culture of experiments in which your members channel their energy into a specific project that can be proposed to your community at a later date. This has been a popular approach in the open source GNOME desktop community. Many developers have worked on their own pet projects that involve a handful of developers. These projects are created, enhanced, and refined, and when they are mature enough, they are proposed for inclusion in the main GNOME desktop. This is an excellent, productive, and engaging approach to creating things together.

BUILDING A "CAN DO" CULTURE

It is also important to set your own expectations correctly when it comes to your new community members.

The vast majority of people who join your community will be passive and contribute little more than opinion and commentary. This is perfectly normal. You should go into your community and expect bikeshedding to be a very real threat. You should expect that most of your new community members will contribute little in the way of practical results.

You instead need to build a culture around doing things. You need to inspire your contributors to make things happen. You should speak positively about your goals and encourage everyone to contribute to their implementation, no matter how small the contribution.

Longer Writing

In addition to day-to-day discussion, email conversations, online chats, and other elements, great communication often calls for longer, more considered pieces and articles. These longer chunks of writing are often required in a number of different places, including:

Blogs
> With the continued growth of blogs as not only a personal publishing medium but also a community publishing medium, you may need to write articles, stories, and features about your community.

Emails
> Many community leaders send out longer, more considered, and more strategic emails that help to guide the community in its direction.

Magazine articles/web articles
> Your community may get the opportunity to be featured in a magazine or website, and you will need to be able to present your thoughts well.

Documents
> Your community will produce documents, guides, specifications, help, and more, and these should be clearly written and easy to read.

Writing well happens at both a mechanical and a stylistic level: you first need to produce properly written language and then build on this with words, expressions, phrases, and approaches that are interesting to read. Let's explore some of these topics now.

The mechanics of writing

The first step in being a good writer is to learn the mechanics of great writing. At this level we are absolutely focused on the nuts and bolts of writing: spelling, grammar, and punctuation.

For some people this is the be-all and end-all of communication: producing "perfect writing" that follows strong editorial guidelines. Using our previous "It's not the notes you play, it's the notes you don't play" quote with which I opened this chapter, the mechanics of writing are our metaphorical notes. Though it is absolutely not the be-all and end-all, writing in a "correct" way does offer a baseline that all writers should build on. Producing fantastically literate, illustrative, and textured writing just doesn't work if your spelling and grammar suck.

To achieve this baseline, I recommend grabbing a good book on the topic. There are plenty to choose from, but don't feel you need to devote your life to it: pick a short book that covers the main points, digest it, and use some of the advice it presents. A great read that I recommend for those of you who want to brush up on this is Strunk and White's classic *The Elements of Style* (Longman). While you read and learn the topics, also look at other people's writing and try to learn what makes their writing structurally interesting and simple to read.

If there is one piece of advice I would recommend more than any other, it is to proofread your work extensively. Proofreading offers an excellent chance to read the piece and ensure that it structurally fits together.

Let's use this chapter as an example. If you take a look at the range of content that is covered, it has been laid out in a very specific way. The content has been structured to discuss different topics, each building on what went before. As I write these words right now, I have already written a significant chunk of content for the chapter, and although I could proofread this specific section on "The mechanics of writing," I need to proofread the entire chapter to ensure that this section fits in and flows correctly.

When many people write, they first create the main chunk of text and then read the whole piece again as their proofreading pass. This is fine, but I would encourage one more step before the proofread: read the entire piece aloud. Although this may sound a little crazy for a piece that is intended to be read silently, reading your content aloud can be hugely valuable in finding badly written sentences that don't flow well.

CULTURAL DIFFERENCES IN WRITING

One additional element you should be aware of is just how much writing varies around the world, even within the same language. Aside from some of the spelling differences (e.g., color and colour, prioritise and prioritize), there are also changes in language use itself.

One example of this is how active the voice is. Some countries speak in a very passive voice (e.g., "Today this was done by the group"), whereas some use a more active voice (e.g., "Today the group did this").

You should ensure that you write in the manner that most suitably targets your audience. If it is an open-ended audience, simply pick one approach and use it consistently.

Don't write like an institution

When I was at university, I used to write articles about Linux and technology. The work was great for furthering my career while also funding my somewhat ludicrous lifestyle of working and partying.

I eventually went on to make writing my career when I graduated. Each day I would write countless articles for various magazines, and throughout this time I focused my radar on all manner of different topics. While most of my research was performed online or on the phone, much of my in-person research time was spent in press conferences.

Press conferences and engagements were interesting beasts, mostly following the same formula. We the press would represent the cynics of the world, and the marketing folk would represent the optimists of the world. They fed the press not only coffee and small sausage rolls, but also a diet of unparalleled marketing nonsense.

Throughout my career as a journalist I witnessed example after example in which concepts and topics were dressed up with buzzword-laden diatribes that were often so jam-packed with marketing fluff that it would be barely understandable for us tech media hacks, let alone the average Joe.

One of the finest (read: most disturbing) examples of this happened when an organization (that shall remain nameless) sent me one of its new press releases. As I sat there one morning sipping my coffee, desperately trying to wake up, I was presented with this humdinger of a no-nonsense buzzfest:

> Program Focuses On Helping The Open Source Ecosystem Grow Sustainable Businesses By Implementing A Community-Leveraged Model

Unfortunately, the literary smackdown didn't end there. It went on to say:

> XXXXXXXXXX, a leading provider of commercial open source middleware solutions for database high availability, today announced XXXXXXXXXX. The program is focused on creating a rising tide for the broader open source ecosystem, and is focused on leveraging community-driven development and frictionless distribution to extend the ecosystem.

The language in this press release was by no means unusual. Plenty of companies would send paragraph after paragraph of overcooked verbiage pouring into my inbox across press releases, briefings, product announcements, and other material.

Of course, there was a lot of sense in targeting writing to a specific audience and using language and references that are meaningful to that demographic (many of which were businesses and buyers). Unfortunately, in many of these cases the abundance of completely meaningless bluster manufactured in marketing meetings with the intention of sounding professional merely complicated as opposed to clarifying the matter.

You should be careful to not fall into this trap. If you bring out the big literary guns with your community, you face the risk of not only confusing people but also agitating them. Remember, communities thrive on clarity and transparency: if you start talking like a slick-haired marketing copywriter, some members of your community are likely to interpret your words as dressed-up claptrap. Speak with your own voice and you avoid this problem. If you are a community manager who reports to a marketing department, this may seem like quite a challenge. Instead, see it as part of your responsibility and talent in helping to translate between these two sets of language so that you can deliver the message in the right way.

One of the widest-respected writing teachers, William Zinsser, speaks extensively on this topic in his seminal *On Writing Well* (Harper Perennial), a book devoted to writing clearly. When I started writing for O'Reilly, the nice folks there kindly sent me a copy of the book. As I sat curled up on my couch reading it one afternoon, one paragraph in particular on this topic leaped out at me:

> Just because people work for an institution, they don't have to write like one. Institutions can be warmed up. Administrators can be turned into human beings. Information can be imparted clearly and without pomposity. You only have to remember that readers identify with people, not with abstractions like "profitability," or with Latinate nouns like "utilization" and "implementation," or with inert constructions in which nobody can be visualized doing something: "pre-feasibility studies are in the paperwork stage."

Zinsser is a staunch advocate of clear writing. He believes the enemy of great writing is the modern expectation that writing must be laced with buzzwords and meaningless terms to make it sound "more professional." Earlier, when we discussed that "it's not the notes you play, it's the notes you don't play," the professionalism that many seek to achieve in writing is absolutely the notes you don't play. These meaningless buzzwords are the equivalent of slamming your hands on the piano to get attention.

Untwisting the tail

As I step down from my high horse, I have to acknowledge that distilling complex processes and concepts into simple language without blinding people with science or meaningless words is really quite hard. It takes skill to explain these topics in a way that is clear, easy to read, and devilishly simple to understand. While I am eager not to turn *The Art of Community* into a creative writing textbook, let's look at one quick example in which complex issues are communicated easily and effectively, in a world intimately familiar with verbosity: *licensing*.

Creative Commons is an organization that produces a set of free licenses that allows content producers to freely license their work. Founded by highly respected law professor Lawrence

Lessig, Creative Commons has gone on to achieve remarkable success, and thousands of artists are licensing a range of music, video, art, and other creative endeavors under its range of licenses. Each of its licenses promotes and encourages a so-called Free Culture—that is, the freedom to share, remix, and derive from existing work. Its range of licenses provides different levels of these freedoms depending on the desires of the artist.

The creation and free availability of these licenses is a wonderful gift from Creative Commons, but an even more impressive contribution is the ease with which the licenses can be understood. An example of this is the Creative Commons Attribution-NonCommercial-ShareAlike license. This is the very license under which *The Art of Community* is published. Figure 3-1 shows what the license looks like.

You are free:

 to Share — to copy, distribute and transmit the work

 to Remix — to adapt the work

Under the following conditions:

 Attribution. You must attribute the work in the manner specified by the author or licensor (but not in any way that suggests that they endorse you or your use of the work).

 Noncommercial. You may not use this work for commercial purposes.

 Share Alike. If you alter, transform, or build upon this work, you may distribute the resulting work only under the same or similar license to this one.

- For any reuse or distribution, you must make clear to others the license terms of this work. The best way to do this is with a link to this web page.
- Any of the above conditions can be waived if you get permission from the copyright holder.
- Nothing in this license impairs or restricts the author's moral rights.

FIGURE 3-1. Creative Commons provides this simplified summary of how the license works.

Traditionally, licenses have been ugly beasts. They haven't evolved far toward readability, and they include reams and reams of complicated legal mumbo jumbo to confuse the poor artist.

Creative Commons developed the concept of the Commons Deed, shown in the figure, which showcases the primary features of the license in a simple, easy-to-read, and visual way. It managed to transpose these attributes of a license in such a way that is simple for an artist to learn and apply to his work. It made perfect sense: if the licenses were too complicated to understand and use, artists will either (a) not use the licenses or (b) more worryingly, pick a license that they don't understand and suffer negative consequences around the use of their work in the future.

To help improve the accessibility of its licenses, Creative Commons produces two documents for each one. First is the full-blown legal document with the nitty-gritty of how the whole deal works. If a case ever got to court, this legal smörgåsbord would be the primary point of reference. That document is great for the legal eagles, but not for artists. As such, Creative Commons then went on to convert this 3,000-plus-word document into the simple Commons Deed shown in Figure 3-1. Creative Commons realized that licensing simply needed to be easier to understand for the real consumers and propagators of the licenses: an exercise in clear and targeted writing.

Zinsser's earlier observation about not writing like an institution is an important lesson when documenting all aspects of your community, but particularly processes. When producing documents that you want your community to read and act on, don't be lured into filling them with meaningless buzzwords, overly complex descriptions, and other fluff. Take Zinsser's advice and try to write and produce documents that are simple, easy to read, and designed for the audience who should read them. Simplicity in writing will ensure that your community can do great work easily.

ME, MYSELF, AND I

A useful tip for writing clearly and humanly is to write as if you're talking to a colleague or friend sitting next to you. That kind of clear but informal banter makes the reader feel comfortable and cared for. This, combined with proofreading aloud, as we discussed earlier, is an excellent way to bring a conversational finesse to your writing.

Setting tone

Tone is an important element in all writing. Tone is the impression and "feel" that you take away from a piece based on how it is written. Tone can often be subtle and entirely subjective in how it is interpreted. Let's look at an example. Here are two different ways of writing a piece asking people to write reports about their work, each with a very different approach to the tone:

Way 1

Hi, everyone! As our community continues to grow and rock the world, it is difficult to keep track of what we are all working on. As such, I think it would be awesome to produce reports that can help us all to know what we are doing. It should only take a few minutes, but it could be a great contribution and well worth the time. Thoughts? :)

Way 2

> Hello. Could everyone please produce a series of reports for their work to facilitate the community in understanding which work is being tended to? Thank you.

With the first piece the tone is very open, friendly, and participatory. The language is loose, and the writing openly asks for comments and feedback. The second piece is far more formal, and a little more demanding in asking people to provide reports. Although both are clearly written, the choice of words and structure affects the tone.

Tone is hugely important when writing content for your community. Following on with our "notes you play" quote, it is tone that is the finest example of "the notes you don't play." The tone you choose can hugely affect how the piece is interpreted.

There are two different elements to consider when thinking about the tone of your writing:

General tone

> One of the most important considerations to make with your writing is the general tone that you use throughout your communications. For most of us this is baked in: your tone is expressed each time you write, and it largely reflects your general personality. You should endeavor for your tone to be loose, open, friendly, and inviting. You should feel entirely comfortable about mixing in humor, and you should write in a way that makes your community feel like equals.

Context-specific tone

> Depending on the context, you will need to adjust your tone to be appropriate. The choice of tone varies significantly between contexts that involve conflict, getting people excited, and governance topics.

Your choice of tone and how you apply it will significantly affect how you are perceived in the community. This choice does require balance, though: being too happy-go-lucky can have the same effect as being a grumpy curmudgeon.

Imagine a line drawn in the sand in front of you. On the far left of the line is an overly chirpy, overly friendly, and potentially disingenuous level of bright smiles and happy thoughts. On the far right side of the line is a grumpy, monotonic, miserable, and snappy approach. Although it is easy to see how those on the far right will rattle people's cages, those on the far left create not only potential annoyance and frustration, but also mistrust: if someone is over-the-top happy in his communication to everyone, it could be interpreted that the person is doing it for effect and not being honest with the community. As ever, a balance is needed. Be yourself: err to the left side of the line, as we like friendly people, but use your best judgment to determine how far toward Happyville you edge.

Within the realm of tone, many different people take different approaches; some work well and some don't. Compare and contrast the frankness and pointed tone used by a New York investment banker and the friendly and submissive tone of a San Francisco charity worker.

Let's now look at some ingredients that can be used when considering your tone and how they can affect your community:

Seriousness

> Communities react very differently to seriousness in different scenarios. As a general rule, you should keep your community loose and informal, but at times you will need to be serious and focused. You should fully expect a more serious tone when discussing conflict, governance topics, or personal problems with a specific community member.

Humor

> Humor is a huge boon when used correctly with community. If you are funny, your community will likely take to you, but your humor needs to (a) actually work (yes, you need to actually be funny) and (b) not distract the audience from the topic. You need to always ensure that your humor matches the context. For example, humor in an emergency meeting will probably go down like a lead balloon.

Wit

> Closely related to humor is wit. If you are quick-witted, particularly in an amusing way, it can bring a loose and fun atmosphere to your community. One risk you should be aware of, though, is to not use your lightning-fast wit to embarrass or show up a fellow community member. Also, wit is typically not very welcome in contentious or argumentative scenarios, so tread carefully there.

Frankness

> Being frank and to the point can be received in many different ways. Some people who receive this kind of to-the-point approach will respond with a very defensive and confrontational tone, whereas others will relish your frankness. Take the pulse of the people you are talking to, and adjust this element of tone based on how well you think they will react.

Your choices and approach to tone will adjust, grow, and mature over time. As with everything else when working on your communication, it is always valuable to look below the surface of other people's communications to learn how they have approached situations. As an example, if you are dealing with a contentious situation, look at the tone of how others have responded and learn from them. You may also want to directly ask people who have been there before for advice. We will be looking into conflict resolution situations extensively in Chapter 11.

SOMETIMES WE ALL SUCK

One attribute of tone that I have always found compelling is those who are willing to be slightly self-deprecating. This is a particularly welcome trait in leaders: when a leader is willing to joke about herself or her situation, it can often help warm her reception to others.

Naturally, you should do this only if you feel comfortable doing so. Faking self-deprecation just sounds patronizing.

Inspiring your community

One of the most fundamental qualities that a community leader can bring to a community is inspiration. At their heart, communities are collections of people united by a shared ethos and most typically by a shared opportunity and goal. Not only does inspiration bolster everyone's commitment and excitement around that goal, but it can also build a sense of unity and togetherness that is essential for a thriving community.

Unfortunately, there is no recipe or formula that teaches you how to inspire. Inspiration is a hugely complex topic to teach, because it is heavily dependent on your approach and the kind of community that you have. Part of the reason for this is that your approach is, in itself, also highly dependent on you as a human being.

Being able to inspire is based heavily on whether you are believable as an inspirational figure, and your approach needs to reflect you as a person. As an example, if you are a generally fun, jovial person but try to deliver a Winston Churchill monologue, it will be laughable at best and seen as a desperate attempt for validation at worst. On the flip side, if you are a serious and forthright person and you deliver a George Carlin-style comedic slap-down, your audience will probably feel the same way they do when they see their dads edging toward the dance floor at a wedding. You need to match the approach to inspiration with what qualities and attributes you as a person already have. When you make inspiration your own, it becomes other people's inspiration.

The best advice I have for writing inspirationally is to discover who and what inspires you and learn from it. Everyone has his own individual answer to this question. Some are inspired by musicians, authors, politicians, and people related to their field of interest or expertise. For me, one of my most significant inspirations is the unique combination of Aaron Sorkin and Martin Sheen.

Sorkin was the writing genius behind *The West Wing*, a show written about the goings-on of an American administration in the West Wing of the White House. Every time I watch the show, I feel inspired by the dialogue. I love the way the characters speak to one another. I love how their directness of conversation is underlined with humility and humor. Being the ultra *West Wing* nerd that I am, I have every episode on DVD, and those shiny little discs are littered with incredible examples of inspiring writing and the masterful delivery of that writing by Martin Sheen as the president. Whenever I watch the show, my own use of language changes a little and my own approach to writing adjusts a little more. It inspires me.

We should, though, keep things in perspective: *The West Wing* was written by a skilled team of writers who spent every day working to make those little hairs on the back of your neck stand on end. It is important not to judge yourself too heavily in what you produce. When you find your inspiration, pick it apart and try to discover what about it inspires you, but ensure that you merely use it as a guide. Don't expect to become the next Aaron Sorkin overnight. Just focus on the most immediate goal of learning, sharing your thoughts using what you have learned, and seeing how your community reacts.

FINDING YOUR INSPIRATION

You should spend some time trying to figure out where you find yourself thinking and writing inspirational thoughts and ideas. For some it is in the shower, when taking a walk, or while lounging around in bed. Everyone is different. All people have times when they feel inspired and creative.

The next time you feel inspired, note what you were doing when it happened. It is likely you will see a correlation. When you know what the magic scenario is, you can trigger it and get some more quality inspiration time!

Summary

Throughout this chapter we have explored some of the many topics involved in building a culture of simple, powerful, and effective communication. While all of the topics covered in this chapter are firmly seated in the "communication best practices" category, it should be noted that effective communication is something we should exercise across all of our community-building efforts.

With this solid chunk of great communication best practice under our belts, let's continue our application of simplicity to community by applying it to an area often bastardized by utter complexity: building *processes*. Fasten those seat belts, friends.

CHAPTER FOUR

Processes: Simple Is Sustainable

"Light is the task where many share the toil."

—Homer

RAY KROC WAS A FAIRLY SIMPLE GUY. As a small-time salesman in the 1950s, he had moved on from the thrill-seeking paper cup world to selling multimixer drink machines to restaurants across the US. His machines allowed anyone with rudimentary operating abilities to create a delicious, creamy milkshake that was so thick it required the power of a thousand vacuum cleaners to suck it up the straw.

Kroc's machines were a hit, and it wasn't long before his path crossed with that of Dick and Mac McDonald, owners of a small restaurant chain called McDonald's. A partnership was born, but Kroc's ambitions went way beyond milkshake-making machines. His ambitions also went way beyond those of Dick and Mac. Before long, Kroc purchased the chain and started growing his empire.

From these humble beginnings McDonald's continued to grow, and now serves over 47 million people every day. Kroc, starting with his inventive approach to milkshakes, died with a fortune of over $500 million. Boy, that is a lot of milkshakes.

Love it or hate it, McDonald's has been hugely successful. Its food is cheap, readily accessible, efficient (in an increasingly busy world), and typically of acceptable quality. Of course, some of you will disagree with that last part, but let's put any gripes to one side for a moment. I am more interested in the mechanics behind the meals.

With 31,000+ restaurants in over 119 countries, McDonald's has an average of 1,500+ customers every day in each of its establishments. Its menu is packed with products, each of which has its own preparation method, ingredients, and form of presentation. But let's be honest: the average McDonald's employee is not exactly a master chef. Most of the people who work at McDonald's are untrained, and the training they do get is rudimentary. McDonald's low cost in terms of staff is a key area in which it competes effectively—but how does it do it?

Like Henry Ford before it, McDonald's has broken complex processes into sets of steps that almost anyone can replicate. If you were going to cook fries at home, you'd have to consider a lot of variables: the time it takes to heat the oil, how small you need to cut the potatoes, cooking time, how much salt to sprinkle on top of the fries, and how to avoid inadvertently plunging your hand in the oil (an ever-present risk when I am in the kitchen). McDonald's has eliminated the need for this range of knowledge by converting the cooking process into a series of simpler steps: unpacking boxes, filling containers, pressing buttons, and so on. McDonald's has perfected process simplification.

The inverse of simplification is complexity, and we don't like complexity around these parts. Complex processes are ugly beasts, and their effect is to merely build *bureaucracy*.

You need to avoid this 11-letter word at all costs. Bureaucracy is the enemy in this chapter: it is the vitriol that breaks down the opportunity, potential, and belief that we celebrated so strongly earlier in this book. Great processes blend into the background, functioning as required and as expected. Great processes let people get on with doing real, human, interesting things. Bad processes serve as nothing more than a dartboard for your contributors to throw their frustration at.

Great processes are our aim in this chapter. We are going to assess the many and varied processes involved in your community, break them down into steps, and make them as simple and effective as possible. Processes are everywhere in communities, determining how:

- New people join
- People submit contributions
- People collaborate with one another
- People deal with conflict, and so on

It is no coincidence that the word *people* is in each of those examples. People are the foundation of community, and for us to ensure that these people can work well together, we need to focus on people as the foundation of our processes.

When we (a) know which processes we need to create and (b) make these processes delightfully simple, our community members can get on with enjoying the community that they signed up for.

Eyes on the Prize

One of the challenges of writing a chapter about processes is that they are so abstract. The word *process* is unspecific: it describes a set of steps that achieves something. For newcomers to the subject, this is difficult to get your head around without specific examples of processes. This could include the examples we just spoke of: how new people join your community, submit contributions, collaborate, and deal with conflict.

When thinking of how to approach this chapter, as well as the wider book, I am keen to not merely provide you with answers to specific problems. This reminds me of the old Chinese proverb:

> Give a man a fish and you feed him for a day. Teach a man to fish and you feed him for a lifetime.

I want to teach you all how to fish. I want the content in this book to help you grow and build best practices that can be applied in a range of scenarios. This absolutely applies to processes.

But this brings us back to our original conundrum: processes can be a little abstract and difficult to understand if not accompanied by an example. As such, as you read this chapter always consider how you can apply the content to the examples we discussed earlier, such as encouraging new members into your project.

Throughout this chapter we will discuss how to build processes that are smooth and effective, explore what is important to consider when building them, identify our needs, and document and communicate them in our community.

Keeping Things in Perspective

Right now I can imagine that some of you are not exactly exhilarated at the idea of reading a chapter all about processes. I admit that even I, while planning this book, was initially hesitant about devoting a chapter to processes. Some of you may see processes as a waste of time, an overly formal mind game that makes life less fun for everyone involved. Some of you may even go so far as suggesting that to define processes is to limit community and entangle its members in rules. But just invert this oversimplification and you will be closer to the truth: well-thought-out, simple, and well-documented processes enable your community members to do their real work easily and effectively.

Here is the crux of how we frame this perspective: processes are useful when they become a means to an end. I don't want to overplay the importance of constructing processes, but I do want to stress the importance of the activities that they implement. In other words, making it easy for new members to join your project is really important, but the process that makes this happen should never overshadow the end goal. A consciousness of processes is good; obsessing over them is bad and breeds bureaucracy. We always need to keep our eyes on the prize.

I raise this distinction for an important reason: building processes is a core activity in governing a group of people. Unfortunately, all too often the act of governing can overtake the goals of the governance. Always bear this in mind when building your processes, and always ensure that you are not building processes for the sake of building processes. Not all problems can be solved with documentation and rules.

The Impact of Processes

Shortly after I joined Canonical in 2006 I underwent an experience that changed the way I saw my role as a community manager and how I build effective processes.

I was working at home one day when I got an email that told a stunning story. The sender was a kid (unfortunately, I can't remember his name) who was living with his family in a remote region of Africa. Some time ago some visitors had come to his village and these visitors had laptops that were running Ubuntu (the software we produce at Canonical).

When the kid asked these people what was on their computers and they mentioned Ubuntu, it immediately resonated: the word *ubuntu* is an ancient African word meaning *"humanity to others."* This piqued the kid's interest and he asked for more information about the software. They then told him how the software was entirely open and created by a global community who worked together to create software that people could share with one another. Although the kid had spent little time in front of computers (he didn't own one and had no access to the Internet), he was absolutely fascinated by the premise of Ubuntu and open source and this culture of sharing. He felt compelled to participate.

He told me that, to earn money, on weekdays he would do odd jobs and bits of work around his village when he was not at school, and then on the weekends he would walk three hours to the nearest town and spend his money in an Internet café, where he would pay for an hour's worth of Internet time and use it to contribute to Ubuntu. After his hour was up he would walk three hours back to his village, excited about his contributions. He did this every weekend and told me that all week he would look forward to the weekend to contribute to Ubuntu.

I was moved by this email. Not only did it demonstrate the sheer humanity and good nature of this kid, but it also demonstrated how powerful inspiration and community can move people.

Importantly, though, and related to this chapter, it gave me a new way to define and assess my work. My job was simple: to help that kid get the most out of his hour. If he was spending his week earning money to contribute to Ubuntu, and was willing to walk six hours in one day to contribute to our community, it was my responsibility to help him not only enjoy his hour, but also have few, if any, obstacles and barriers to overcome in order to participate. This meant ensuring that the processes that were part of Ubuntu were slim, efficient, and designed to help our contributors achieve great things.

Building Great Processes

Processes are everywhere. There is a process to withdraw money from your bank account. There is a process to change the oil in your car. And of course, any interaction with the government…well, I am sure you can end that sentence yourself. Unfortunately, many people who interact with processes experience little reward for a lot of frustration.

Processes are like television news: we only ever hear the negative stories. Television news favors accounts of murders and accidents over local charity success stories and animal rescues. In the same manner, the only processes we ever hear about are often problematic ones: people queuing for two hours to mail a package, piles of forms we have to fill out to file taxes, and the hoops we have to jump through to buy insurance. Believe me, even though I have written this chapter, I hate bad processes just as much as you do.

Processes that don't work, suck, plain and simple. Some process failures are far more dramatic than others, though, and can have very severe human ramifications. One such example is the product recall. In *Process Improvement Essentials* (O'Reilly), author James R. Persse talks up product recalls and the insights they offer:

> As a rule, corporations like to keep their troubles quiet. They prefer to keep their problems from showing up on the street. It can be embarrassing. And it takes a lot of explanation to a lot of people who probably aren't prepared to appreciate that these things happen. Nobody's perfect. Defects happen.

We are all familiar with product recalls, those little notices in supermarkets and newspapers that indicate that something went horribly wrong when the product was created. Recalls are bad for business because they say, very clearly, that the manufacturer's quality assurance processes don't work. Whether nuts contaminated a nut-free zone, pieces of glass broke into a large vat of baby food, or a batch of eggs was exposed to salmonella, product recalls point the giant finger of blame in the general direction of the manufacturing process. These recalls not only destroy faith in brands, but also cause concern in customers, and sometimes even panic.

Bad processes are one thing, but a process that nearly costs people their fingers is something entirely different. Persse shares with us the curious case of the Chevrolet Venture minivan debacle:

> Take the Chevrolet Venture for example. This popular minivan ran into something of a quality problem in the late 1990s. At issue was the questionable design of its passenger seat latch. The company received data that indicated maybe the latch had an operational defect. After some study, Chevrolet determined that a general recall of the 1997 Venture was in order. Here is an excerpt from the text of that recall notice: "RECALL NOTICE (1997 Chevrolet Venture): Passenger's fingers could be severed by latch mechanism that moves seat fore and aft (Consumer Reports 2005)."

Now, as a general rule, severed fingers should not be a part of anyone's driving experience. What manufacturer would want that picture etched into the brand image of their minivans? Chevrolet no doubt brought its forces to bear. That latch was probably redesigned and re-manufactured against the highest standards, with inordinate attention to detail: test after test, exhausting verification runs, complete assurance of unquestionable integrity. It wouldn't surprise me if that latch today—almost 10 years later—stands as the world-class epitome of efficiency and safety in seat latch technology.

This was a pretty serious problem, to say the least. The outcome of a bad process (quality control) could have been disastrous. Aside from the obvious safety problems with many recalls, the nightmare goes much further. Products are expensive to replace. Advertising the recall is expensive, too. Legal issues are likely to arise from embittered customers. Whether they involve a thousand and one tax forms to fill in or a latch that may sever your fingers, bad processes cause significant harm.

Similar risk applies to communities. When we take a laissez-faire approach to processes, we put confidence in our community at risk. Processes are the conceptual buttons that your community members push to make things happen, and when those buttons don't work as expected, people get bored and frustrated and move on. On the other hand, if we craft smooth, efficient, and effective processes, our community feels nimble, responsive, and great to be part of.

Breaking Up the Puzzle

Building a quality process is like taking a road trip. You know where you want to go. You want to take the shortest route, and you want to avoid as many bottlenecks and problems as possible. When you plan your perfect route, you are careful to take the fewest number of roads, take advantage of available freeways/motorways, avoid rush hour, regularly check on current road conditions, and ensure that an In-N-Out Burger restaurant is on the route at regular points (that's just my personal criterion...).

You should take the same approach to efficiency with your processes. How can you achieve what you want as quickly and efficiently as possible? How can you communicate the journey as easily as possible to new members? How can you ensure that your processes are always amenable to current conditions?

Great processes are beautiful creatures, but they need care and feeding to thrive. Our goal in this chapter is to identify these needs and produce processes that exhibit the following criteria:

The goal of the process is achieved as quickly as possible
> The quicker a process ends, the quicker your community can get on with more interesting things.

The fewest possible steps can achieve the goal

Redundant steps merely make the process feel long and drawn out; let's avoid that.

Each step is simple, well documented, and clearly communicated

Each step should be absolutely necessary, and performing it should be simple. A quick technical example: if you need someone to type something in, don't demand case-sensitivity; it only complicates that step.

The process is as friction-free as possible

We want to avoid confusion and annoyance, not only with each step in the process, but also in the process as a whole.

Quality is maintained at every step

We need to identify and maintain the different types of quality involved in a process: its accuracy at achieving the outcome, how efficient it is, how well documented it is, how current it is, and how open to change and improvement it is.

Although we will talk about it shortly, *simplicity* is the foundation of all good processes. As an example, consider how members join your community. How can you develop a process that is as easy as possible to follow and simple to explain to others? Put yourself in the position of a new community member who has no idea how to join your community. How can you learn how to get involved and get there in as few steps as possible? When this is as efficient as possible, you have a much better chance of recruiting new members.

Continuing the example, some communities have incredibly elaborate processes for how people join. They require applications, supporting evidence, membership council votes, signed documentation, agreement to terms and conditions, and more. Some communities are far simpler, merely requiring someone to participate in a discussion. Your community will be somewhere between these two points, and although only your community can really decide where this is, our discussion throughout this chapter should help you determine this.

Building a process

Earlier in this book we created our strategic plan. In it we produced a set of *objectives* and *goals*, each of which we broke into steps and documented. This approach is also excellent for building processes, albeit with a different set of criteria.

When you need to build a process for something (such as how members join your community), note the following criteria:

Goal

What is the goal of the process? What does it seek to achieve? What is the outcome when the process has been followed?

Target participants

Who is the process designed for? Is it intended for a particular kind of contributor, such as a developer, documentation writer, translator, or advocate?

Requirements

> What tools, knowledge, and experience must the contributor have in order to follow through with the process? If she does not possess these requirements, how can she obtain them easily? Are these requirements a barrier to entry (such as entry fees or limited availability)?

Steps involved

> What are the chronological steps involved in achieving the goal? What could go wrong? Is it possible for people to accidentally fail to complete a step? How is feedback provided about each step? Who provides the feedback?

Verification

> Who decides when a process has been completed successfully? Also, how is successful completion of the process communicated to the contributor?

Let us now apply these criteria to our previous example of a contributor joining a community.

In our example we are the members of a small open source project that is working on a video game that pits open source community managers against one another with the stylings of Street Fighter II. Naturally I would expect my own representation to be somewhat more muscular and toned than the sad example of my real body.

As this is an open source project, we want to encourage people to contribute code (such as a patch to crank up my muscles). For developers to contribute, though, they need to have access to the code repository. Before we give them this access, we need a process that helps them contribute some code that we can assess first, so we can ensure that only capable developers can contribute directly to the repository.

Let's now apply to this example the set of questions we discussed earlier. Here are some answers:

> Goal: To assess developer contributions, and if approved, permit direct access to the repository.

> Audience: Developers with some experience in the project.

> Requirements: Development experience, interaction with the community with regard to software development.

> Steps Involved:

>> Developer can email patches to existing developers or attach them to bugs.

>> Developer creates an application page on the contributor wiki with:

>>> Name.

>>> Email address.

>>> List of patches contributed and a link to their commit email.

>>> Any additional notes.

Applicant waits for a decision within one week.

Verification: The core development team.

If you are not technically savvy, don't be thrown off by terms like *patch* and *commit email*; they're not really important. The value in this example is how it outlines the core structure behind a typical process. Also note that this process does not cover specifically how the existing development team assesses these applications from new developers: that would be its own separate process.

> **NOTE**
> **Later in this chapter, we are going to dig into more detail about how to make it as simple as possible for contributors to join your community.**

In a few pages we will determine what process needs you have for your community and then apply this formula to those needs. First, though, I want to talk through a few additional important best-practice considerations when thinking about processes in general.

Process Considerations

The art of building effective processes is in not forgetting the big picture when fleshing out the details. Processes get very granular very quickly. It is easy to sometimes get lost in the details and forget some of our wider ambitions.

To complement our approach to fleshing out process criteria, let us now explore some of the key themes that make good processes. These key themes should be at the forefront of our minds while we work.

Simplicity is key

Life is pretty complex, and modern technology seems to exacerbate as much as relieve that complexity. Take the now-somewhat-archaic example of the VCR. For years, thousands tried to set their VCR to achieve a seemingly simple task: tape a show at a specific time. Unfortunately, many of us failed. We heard endless horror stories of missed tapings of *Falcon Crest*, *Days of Our Lives*, and other such travesties (sounds like a blessing in disguise to me). VCRs seemed to just confuse the heck out of many of us. There are similar examples: car entertainment systems, computer software, automated ticketing machines in parking garages, and online banking, to name a few.

Part of the problem is that design and engineering have traditionally not been particularly good bedfellows. This is not a new problem. Way back in 1847, Sir Henry Cole, one of the forefathers of industrial design, expressed his concerns over this problem to The Society of Arts:

> Of high art in this country there is abundance, of mechanical industry and invention an unparalleled profusion. The thing still remaining to be done is to effect the combination of the two, to wed high art with mechanical skill. The union of the artist and the workman, the improvement of the general taste of our artificers, and of the workmen in general; this is a task worthy of The Society of Arts and directly in its path of duty.

Cole was suggesting that we approach mechanical inventions with the mind of an artist and vice versa. He understood that artists and designers have a fresh approach to how we think and interact with things. He also understood that engineers can build reliable and useful inventions. When we combine this understanding of the human psyche with the ability to build devices, machines become easier to operate and invariably look less like something that I myself would bodge together in my garage.

Examples of simplicity are everywhere. Andy Oram, who has lovingly edited this book alongside Simon St. Laurent, shared one such example of this with me. Andy had a conversation once with a user interface expert about a quiz program he had developed. His interface was good, but could have been better. It worked like this: first he had people create an account and then create and save a quiz. Andy's user interface mentor suggested he let people create the quiz right off the bat on the first screen. This meant the user could sign up for an account if she decided the quiz was worth saving. This suggested change was a simple example of optimizing a process and removing a barrier to participation. This is exactly what we want to achieve.

Avoiding bureaucracy

While writing this book, I experienced something of a disaster. As I was talking to my wife one evening about some Ubuntu work I was doing, I was gesticulating and inadvertently threw wine all over my laptop. Seemingly not satisfied with my quota of laptop abuse, a few days later I managed to also throw tea all over the poor blighter. I, my friends, am a clod. Said laptop complained and refused to switch on. As such, a replacement was needed, so I hopped online and ordered myself a snazzy new machine. And thus the pain began....

In the space of the following week, I was tortured by customer support. Issues with a credit card payment, and need to use another credit card? Problem. I need to register a card and wait 24 hours. Entirely incompetent staff. Want to speak to a supervisor straightaway? Problem. I am entered into a queue, and will get a call in 24 hours. Laptop arrives and fails to switch on.... Can a replacement be ordered automatically? Problem. I have to first wait for a refund, manually reorder the laptop, and wait for it to be built and dispatched. I was not a happy boy.

I am sure all of you can report similar experiences. Each of these frustrations was caused by bad processes. We learn from such experiences that an organization must not only create a simple process, but also set up ancillary processes that kick into action when something goes wrong. The problem during my laptop order sprang from a company that was thinking like a company and not like a human; in other words, it set up processes that were convenient for its organizational structure and resources, not responsive to customers.

Many of these problems could have been avoided with feedback. The most important ingredient when building processes is an understanding of people and their expectations. And this understanding requires you to solicit feedback, along with a culture devoted to always improving and refining your processes. When we understand and react to participants' expectations, processes behave as participants expect them to. Part of the reason why feedback is so important is that it prevents bureaucracy: rules that are maintained because *they are the rules."*

Spread the message in your community that tomorrow may always bring a better way to carry out a current process. Processes provide an excellent opportunity to simplify tasks, tend to needs, and help your community focus on innovating more easily.

Encourage and enthuse your community to question your processes. This feedback will keep your processes on their toes and protected from the dreaded B-word.

Transparency

Another distinctive benefit of feedback is to bring an air of transparency and openness into your community. When people can contribute their thoughts and opinions, and those views get rolled back into community processes, openness is achieved.

All volunteer communities thrive on a sense of openness, because they are *associative*. These communities are built by people who choose to live their lives there. People who participate in a volunteer community do so because they enjoy it: it is not a job or a requirement. As such, to keep them involved, there needs to be a sense that their input is valuable, and this absolutely applies to their input on how well community processes are working. Ask yourself this question: would you rather live in a community where you can have an impact on the governing rules, or a community in which other people decide?

Unfortunately, not all communities get this right. Back in March 2003, the xFree86 project was struggling with transparency. xFree86 was a free implementation of X, the core windowing system that many Linux, BSD, and Unix systems relied on. Everyone with a graphical interface on those systems was almost certainly using xFree86.

Back then, the processes and procedures that outlined how developers joined the project were minimal, undocumented (or unknown), and restrictive. The directors of the xFree86 Corporation dictated these processes, even though the technical direction and leadership of the project had traditionally been governed by the xFree86 Core Team (composed of the main xFree86 developers).

One person who was deeply unhappy with this was Keith Packard, a core X developer who was working at Hewlett-Packard at the time (see *http://www.xfree86.org/pipermail/forum/2003 -March/002165.htm*):

> While the xFree86 Board of Directors is nominally in charge of xFree86, they have absented themselves from governing the project and left that to the xFree86 Core Team. The community is left wondering who is actually in charge of xFree86. As a result, community trust in xFree86

leadership has suffered. Decisions appear to be arbitrary and are not seen to reflect the will of the community. The leadership has no accountability to the community: thus community members have no ability to change project direction and the Board has little incentive to do so. In addition, the lack of clear formal policies has made it difficult to resolve disputes when the usual consensus breaks down.

This breakdown in governance and lack of clear, community-led processes had very real ramifications for the project. Fewer developers were able to join. xFree86 development was slower than expected. Those projects that depended on xFree86 could not progress further due to technical limitations in X, so free operating systems were failing to benefit from the features and performance offered by new generations of graphics hardware. As a critical component in the Linux desktop, xFree86 was holding everyone back. It was a real mess.

Unfortunately, the bylaws of the community stated that any changes in governance had to be initiated by the directors of the xFree86 Corporation. This was a problem. The board members were evidently not particularly responsive or reactive to the concerns of the community, as Packard noted (see *http://www.xfree86.org/pipermail/forum/2003-March/002165.html*):

> xFree86 has the trappings of democracy, but the community has no voting rights and no elections are held.

Ultimately, the desire for openness and transparency won out. On January 22, 2004, the X.org Foundation was formed. The new foundation brought the open governance and open processes that are common in open source to X. Since then, the X Window System produced by the X.org community has thrived.

These risks with transparency can happen to any volunteer community. The solution to this is simple: involve your community at every step of your community growth. Involve them in the strategy, the processes, the governance, the execution of these decisions, and more. Have public communication channels and public meetings, and instead of questioning whether something should be public, question whether it should be private. When we work together, the world feels like a very open place.

Assessing Needs

Earlier in this book we explored many of the best-practice aspects of community building and compiled a TODO list of these elements. One of these items rather conveniently relates to our current discussion of processes.

Community TODO List

- Build an environment conducive to our wider goals.

Effective environments are built on effective processes. As a community leader, your goal is to build an environment that offers rich opportunities and is simple to engage with. So you need to figure out which processes you require in your community and apply your recipe and best-practice concepts from earlier in the chapter.

Processes can be broadly divided into three primary categories:

Environment and strategy
> This is a continuation of the strategy that we built earlier: the general concepts that apply to everyone in your community, such as milestones, direction, processes that define how people collaborate, and external feedback.

Infrastructure
> The technical nuts and bolts and tools of your community: the day-to-day facilities that your community members require to get things done.

Governance
> The governing bodies, legislation, rules of engagement, and other, more political components required to organize and govern your community.

Each of these areas is of significant importance in building a strong community, and in this book I have devoted a chapter each to infrastructure (Chapter 5) and governance (Chapter 10). Each of those chapters helps you build effective processes in those respective areas using the best practices described in this chapter.

So let's now talk through some of the environment-related concepts that are important in our community. This will give you some handy examples that you can apply to your own community.

Community Cycles

Most communities, particularly collaborative ones, require some kind of planning cycle. Whether you are working toward a software release, a conference, a local event, or something else, planning is key.

Many of these objectives are reoccurring. Software regularly has releases. Events regularly occur. In addition to this regularity, there are regular milestones that need to be completed to achieve the objectives.

One such example is software. Most software releases adhere to the following broad set of milestones:

1. Development begins.
2. Feature freeze.
3. User interface freeze.
4. Beta freeze.

5. Beta release.

6. Translations freeze.

7. Release candidate.

8. Final release.

Another example consists of the milestones involved in planning a local community conference:

1. Planning begins.

2. Call for papers/exhibitors opens.

3. Final speaker list is chosen.

4. Final exhibitor list is chosen.

5. Schedule is published.

6. Venue equipment is finalized.

7. Event begins.

For both of these examples, the milestones combine in chronological order to define a cycle. If you have similar milestone-leading-to-goals requirements, I recommend that you produce your own cycle.

Leading by example: Ubuntu

Ubuntu releases a new version every six months. Each release cycle involves a number of tasks: updating the toolchain, syncing and merging with the Debian release upon which Ubuntu is built, deciding on a direction at the Ubuntu Developer Summit, scheduling freezes, releasing alphas and betas, and other elements.

At the beginning of every release cycle, our release team documents the release cycle on the Ubuntu wiki. As an example, the 9.04 Jaunty Jackalope release cycle was documented at *https://wiki.ubuntu.com/JauntyReleaseSchedule*.

The release team broke down the cycle into a number of weeks, dividing the weeks into sections by month. Each week is placed into a table that has "Week number," "Date," "Status," and "Notes" columns. Here is a snippet from the March part of the Jaunty plan.

March 2009			
Week number	Date	Status	Notes
18	March 5	User Interface Freeze Artwork Deadline Two	
19	March 12		Alpha 6
20	March 19	Beta Freeze Final Artwork Freeze	Rebuild Test
21	March 26	Beta Release Docs String Freeze	Beta

An important component that enables the planning cycle is knowing how long each task should take to complete. When you build your own cycle with your community, make a fair assessment of how long your tasks should take, and build in some redundancy for delays.

When your cycle is complete, you should ensure that it is published and available to all your community members. An excellent way to do this is to place it on a wiki.

The Gates of Your Community

Now let's take a look at another item on our TODO list.

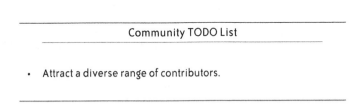

Community TODO List

• Attract a diverse range of contributors.

Attracting new contributors is an essential part of any community. Earlier we used this item as an example in fleshing out a description of our process. I want to now explore this important item in more detail.

In attracting contributors, our goal is not merely to get the word out; it is about getting the word out to the *right people* and ensuring that they can join us in achieving our goals.

In this work we have two primary outcomes that we want to achieve:

• To ensure that the on-ramp from consumer of buzz to full-fledged community member is as smooth as possible

• To attract community members who will demonstrate commitment and a willingness to work toward the goals of the community

The first point may seem obvious, but the second is subtler. What we want to avoid are drive-by contributors. These are people who join a community for a few weeks, you help them get up and running, and they then get bored and move on.

Drive-by contributors are expensive, not necessarily financially, but in terms of time. Contributors often require a certain level of (wo)manpower. The community responds to their questions and provides the help, guidance, training, and mentorship needed to get them on their feet. If these contributors receive this assistance and fail to deliver anything of value, they become expensive propositions.

Animal welfare communities have dealt with this for years. Cristina Verduzco is the volunteer/ outreach manager for the East Bay and Tri-Valley SPCA (*http://www.eastbayspca.org/*). Cristina is responsible for recruiting, training, and managing volunteers. She is responsible for all facets of the volunteer program, coordination and planning of multiple events, and coordination of mobile adoptions.

Retention is important for animal welfare communities. Not only do volunteers need to be trained in how to care for the animals, but they also develop bonds with the animals they care for. It is in the interest of the animals to maintain sustained contributions: they feel more comfortable around familiar faces. Cristina told me she is fully aware of the biggest risk to retention:

> Retaining volunteers will always be a problem for any animal welfare organization. While the work is rewarding, it can also be difficult. We are fortunate that our euthanasia rates are lower than almost all other shelters, as we don't euthanize animals for lack of space. While it is common that issues around euthanasia tend to be a big reason for people not to return, we don't see that quite as often at our shelter.

Every community is strained by push and pull forces that will affect your ability to retain volunteers. This will apply equally in your community. For the SPCA, euthanasia is clearly a blocker for many to get involved. What is your equivalent blocker? This could be difficult personalities, suboptimal working conditions, hugely complex processes and technical procedures, or anything else.

You should identify these blockers and ensure that you have resources to help people over the hump. Importantly, you should not downplay or cover up the difficulties in your community, but until you can fix the problems (which you should seek to do as a matter of priority), it is entirely reasonable to make those difficulties as pleasant to navigate as possible.

You should also focus on the attracting forces that bring people to your community while again ensuring that you communicate a balanced perspective. At the SPCA, the clear attracting force was kittens and puppies, but Cristina is keen to balance this with the reality:

> Let's face it—playing with kittens and puppies sounds fun until you realize there's cleaning and training involved, and sometimes that deters volunteers. Sometimes people have every intention to commit, and down the line realize their schedules don't work out.

These long-term contributors are the real rock stars in your community. Cristina and her colleagues rely on their "angels" heavily:

> Fortunately, there are always those people who come in, fall in love with the work, and stay for the long haul. Some of our volunteers have been with us over ten years, and they come every week without fail. We refer to them as our "angels". Our volunteers are the reason shelter animals don't go crazy in confinement, and for that reason we are indebted to them.

You have an enormous opportunity to find your own "angels" if you offer enough enthusiasm and excitement to pique interest in your community, give them a realistic set of expectations about the work involved, and ensure that their experience is positive.

Before we move on, I want to be entirely clear when I say "long-term contributors" here. You should not expect your contributors to be working full-time for your community. Your focus should be on sustained contributions, no matter how long each contribution lasts. If your contributors put in three hours a week every week, that is an excellent gift to your community. This gift is also far better than two days of frenetic full-time contribution and then nothing else.

Retaining contributors sounds complex, but is thankfully pretty simple. If you want people to stick around, you need to offer them *a regular sense of achievement*. Your community members need to feel (a) that they are productive, (b) that their contributions are appreciated, and (c) that (a) and (b) happen repeatedly.

This is particularly important for new contributors. When someone first expresses interest in joining your community, she needs to follow what I call the *contributor ramp*:

- Identify an area in which she can contribute
- Learn the skills required to contribute
- Know which specific task to work on
- Know how to submit her work

When you start attracting people to your community, you are encouraging them to begin interfacing with this process. As such, you need to make sure you have all of the above in order before you even make a peep. The most logical home for this information is your website.

Assessing Contributors

Many collaborative projects embody some kind of access control. In a typical open source project, those who can contribute code are restricted, and developers are assigned a username and password to contribute code to the repository. The reason is simple: you don't want just anyone changing the project. The integrity of the code base is essential. You always want your code to run, be as error-free as possible, and maintain consistent coding guidelines. If access were entirely open, those with malicious intentions or error-prone (in)abilities could introduce bugs, defects, and security flaws to your project. Having a vetting process is important to ensure that your developers can be trusted and will demonstrate this level of quality.

As we briefly discussed earlier in this chapter, it is important for us to figure out how new potential developers can gain access to the project. If I want to contribute to an open source project and am unknown, how do I prove my abilities?

The first task is to assess what your expectations of quality are. For many open source projects, they are relatively simple:

- A reasonable knowledge of programming; the contributor should not be making the obvious mistakes that new developers make.
- A familiarity with the code base and coding conventions.
- A regularity of contribution.

Although the implementation of these expectations involves infrastructure technology (bug trackers, source control systems, etc.), which we defer discussion of until later in this book, we can take a high-level view of how some of these processes work.

THE ELEVATOR PITCH

Before we continue, again remember that simplicity is key to good processes. One of the most effective methods of determining whether your processes are really as simple as you think they are is the "elevator pitch." This is easy to test.

Imagine you are out having a drink with some friends and talking about your community. One of them asks how he can get involved. To pass the test, you should be able to recite your process and have him understand it within a minute.

If the person you are speaking to stumbles on any part of the process or needs it reexplained, your process needs some work.

Reviewing new developers: In depth

Ad Hoc Peer Review is common in the open source world. Here is how it works: you have an existing member of the community review a new contributor's proposed contribution, and if it is acceptable, the existing member will commit it on the new contributor's behalf.

As an example, imagine Adam would like to fix a bug in the OpenOffice.org project. He grabs the code, programs a solution to the bug, and then sends an existing OpenOffice.org developer the fix. That developer (let's call him Michael) then reviews the fix, and if it is suitable, he commits the fix to the main OpenOffice.org code base.

Typically this process would be repeated until each proposed contribution from Adam is almost certainly going to be accepted by Michael. At this point, Adam would be given direct developer access to the source code repository.

A range of projects use this approach. One such project is Jokosher, which was mentioned earlier in Chapter 2. When the project first started, a new contributor called Laszlo Pandy wanted to get involved. He joined the IRC chat channel to express his interest and was asked to submit some patches (small bundles of code changes). To make this as easy as possible for new contributors, we had written a web page that explained how this worked.

I reviewed some of his patches. With each one, I provided him technical feedback: areas that worked, elements that needed fixing, and so on. When Laszlo's patches were of sufficient quality (which required only minor adjustments), I committed them for him. After three or four patches, every one was excellent. At this point we gave him direct access to the Jokosher repository. As a bonus piece of Jokosher trivia, Laszlo went on to become the leader of the Jokosher project.

There are a number of requirements for this process to work:

- You need to clearly explain in what form new contributors provide a contribution. Should this be a patch? An email? A document? Explain what is required.

- Where do new contributors send their contribution? Post it to a mailing list? Mention it on IRC? Email a specific person? Attach it to a bug report?

- Your community must be able to access these new contributions and have existing, experienced contributors provide feedback. It is important that this feedback is not held up due to having only a limited set of contributors who are able to provide it. Every contribution should be seen as a gift, and as such should rightly expect feedback, even if this feedback is just "This is excellent work, I have committed this."

- There needs to be a method of tracking these recurring contributions. If a new contributor has contributed three or four excellent patches that have been committed with few or no changes, you need a means of identifying this recurring quality. This could be as informal as some core contributors keeping a mental note of the new contributions, or as formal as maintaining a written log of contributions.

Although this approach has been described here within the context of providing code contributions, this could equally apply to other types of contributions, such as documentation, art, and translations.

For nontechnical projects, a similar approach can involve simply reviewing prior work by the contributor. If you are organizing a local community event and you want a contributor to do the art for the brochure, you could ask him to produce some initial drafts, make sure they're acceptable, and then accept the contributor as the brochure artist.

Unfortunately, for some larger communities (particularly large open source projects), the previous approach is unsuitable. This can be due to a number of reasons:

- The technical requirements involved for the new contributor are too complex to be assessed in a loose and ad hoc way.

- There are too many new contributors submitting content for the existing developers to assess in a timely manner.

- The project is hugely popular, touching thousands or even millions of users, and as such, granted access needs to be more rigorously assessed.

Although the core technique of reviewing proposed contributions does not change with a more formalized approach (having people check a contribution before it is committed), what does change is how you track and review those contributions.

Let's look at an example. In the Ubuntu community, we have a little more formality in how new contributors can gain access to one of our key repositories, Universe. Our guiding policy has always been that new contributors should demonstrate a *significant and sustained contribution*. That is what we seek to assess in new contributors.

The Universe repository is a large collection of applications that are packaged by volunteers. These applications are not officially supported by the Canonical technical support service, and they don't receive security updates. The members who work on these packages are called MOTUs (short for Masters of the Universe). The MOTU community is led by the MOTU Council, a small group of well-respected MOTU contributors.

Although more formalized, the process is still relatively simple:

1. New contributors make their contribution by attaching a patch to a bug report. They then subscribe the ubuntu-universe-sponsors team to the bug report. The collection of bugs subscribed to that team is called the Sponsorship Queue.

2. The team looks at each patch, reviews them, offers feedback, and, where suitable, uploads the changes.

3. This process repeats a number of times to demonstrate the sustainability of contributions from a given contributor.

4. After a number of contributions have been made, an existing MOTU will often recommend that the contributor apply for MOTU approval.

5. Candidates prepare a wiki page outlining the contributions they have made to the project and also some endorsement statements from existing MOTUs to approve their application.

6. The application is reviewed by the MOTU Council and then approved where appropriate.

The MOTU community's approach has been refined over the years. At its heart, new contributors add their contribution to a queue, go through review, and then apply to the MOTU Council. The only differences are the sponsorship queue and the approval process, which make the approach more formalized.

Managing Feedback

Gathering feedback from the outside world is an often-overlooked but important facet of a strong and healthy community. Feedback is important for providing you with others' perspectives, and these perspectives can help identify opportunities, problems, and areas that need renewed focus. It is this feedback that tells you what people outside your community think of your goals, ambitions, and progress. As such, feedback is a positive double-edged sword: not only does it provide pleasant confirmation of things we're doing right, but it also reveals and focuses our minds on areas to improve. Finally, a good process for handling feedback can improve all your other processes, as I explained earlier in this chapter.

Unfortunately, many community leaders view feedback as a nuisance, and disregard it if it challenges their work and the norms of the community. This is the wrong perspective to take. Feedback instead offers us an incredible opportunity to improve how our community functions.

None of us is perfect. None of us gets things right every time. Even the greatest community leaders in the world—and the most intelligent and hard-working community members—get it wrong sometimes. But being wrong is not black and white. In many cases we craft interesting and inspiring initiatives, but we sometimes focus on the wrong things or overcomplicate matters. Feedback helps zone our minds in on which elements to fix.

This happened to me a few years ago. Back in February 2008, my team and I were thinking of methods to improve how we handle our list of bugs in Ubuntu. As Ubuntu has grown and is now used on millions of computers around the world, the list of reported bugs has grown, too.

After fleshing out a number of different possible approaches and plans, we announced a new scheme called 5-A-Day. The idea was inspired by the popular meme of eating five portions of fruit or vegetables every day to stay healthy. I wanted to apply this concept to software bugs: encouraging everyone in the Ubuntu community to work on five bugs every day. This would make our bug list, and resultantly Ubuntu, healthier, too.

The response was stunning. Many contributors got involved, and thousands of bugs received attention. Many of our contributors didn't stop at five bugs, though; they were often nailing upward of 20 or 30 a day. Some were even hitting 100 a day. These people were bug-squashing machines.

Ten months later, at the Ubuntu Developer Summit in California, I scheduled a session to review 5-A-Day. I was keen to gather feedback and opinions about the initiative and how we could improve it. In the session, a friend of mine called Robert Collins raised a valid point: in measuring 5-A-Day, we were measuring the wrong things.

Robert argued that 5-A-Day should not be recognizing those who were smashing past the five-bug target for each day and hitting the high bug numbers. He felt that in keeping with the Ubuntu ethos of *significant and sustained contributions*, 5-A-Day should instead cap the number of bugs at five per day and track *how long* people were maintaining their daily 5-A-Day. Robert felt that it was more valuable if we knew that a contributor had consistently worked on five bugs a day for a month, instead of doing 155 bugs in a day. He was right. Sustainability is an essential component in community: more bugs get fixed, people consistently set a good example for others, and we build a long-term contributor base that is regularly working on bugs as opposed to localized spikes of interest.

In this example, our request for feedback at the Ubuntu Developer Summit resulted in a valuable piece of insight, one that may never have occurred to my immediate colleagues or to me.

Gathering feedback

Feedback can be collected in many ways. The simplest and often most effective way is to set up an email address that forwards email to a number of core community members. A simplification of this approach is to set up an account with a free email service and give each of your core members access to the account. This approach is excellent for gathering general thoughts, concerns, and opinions about the community that often reflect on processes.

Another alternative is to set up a public mailing list that people can submit feedback to. This solution is not the most suitable for single-shot chunks of feedback from someone. Mailing lists are designed for discussion, so you should really use mailing lists only if you want people to submit feedback and have a discussion afterward. Another downside of mailing lists is that they require people to sign up, and these members will also receive all email to the list. Someone who just wants to give you a quick chunk of feedback likely won't want to see what everyone else is submitting to the list.

Another possibility is to use a blog. You could post entries to the blog to request feedback and allow readers to provide their feedback in the comments. Remember that all feedback here will be public. You may not want to have everyone and her dog see this feedback (although it is an impressive message of transparency if you do). What's more, remember that search engines will index this potentially negative feedback, showing it to everyone who searches on your project name, even if you've since addressed the problems.

The most productive approaches I've used for gathering feedback have been surveys and one-on-one discussions. We cover surveys in more detail in Chapter 8; they are an excellent means of gathering focused feedback around specific areas of interest. I have used them extensively in my work, particularly online surveys, and they have always gathered excellent results.

Whichever of these techniques you decide to use, you should always augment them with some direct one-on-one discussions. Find people who have an opinion about the process you are investigating, and get them on the phone, send them some specific questions through email, or get together to discuss their views over a coffee. This direct feedback is often very valuable; just remember that feedback will always be tinged with opinion and potential exaggeration, and one-on-one discussions are the most likely candidate for this.

PUTTING CRITICISM IN CONTEXT

One final note about feedback is related to expectations. You should prepare yourself to receive more criticism than praise. This is simply the nature of community and human interaction: we often feel compelled to write an email to criticize, but we rarely get an urge to send an email to praise. As such, if you receive what appears to be a large amount of criticism, it may not be reflective of your community. It is likely that there are a lot of silent yet happy members out there.

Getting Buy-In for Your Processes

So far we have discussed many of the best practices for building simple yet effective processes. We have talked about simplicity, transparency, avoiding bureaucracy, assessing needs, and more. Processes don't mean anything, though, unless your community (a) knows about them, (b) understands them, and (c) uses them.

At the beginning of this chapter, we likened processes to machines and waxed lyrical about how interface design and industrial design have made devices easier to implement. We noted that we should apply the same logic to our processes. We can continue our analogy beyond the development of processes (akin to the devices) and also apply it to their packaging and distribution. How can we make our processes as easy to understand, discover, and use as possible?

Document Them

The first step in making a process work for your community is to ensure that it is documented. The goal here is efficiency. Sure, anyone can write a detailed list of steps outlining how a process works, but who wants to read paragraphs and paragraphs of text? The documentation behind a process should be as close as possible to a cooking recipe: do this...do that...get this result. The emphasis here is on quick, clear, straight-to-the-point directions.

Processes are fundamentally a collection of steps with an outcome. Documenting them is similar to Ikea's instructions for putting together a shelving unit. How can you tell the user how to achieve the outcome as easily and effectively as possible?

When Ikea does this, it uses only pictures, presumably to avoid translating instructions into multiple languages. Although I would recommend using text for most communities' processes, the Ikea model is cathartic and helps focus your mind on the right goal of reducing clutter.

To get you started, let's get introspective for a while and document your own steps for writing a process:

1. First, write down the end goal of your process. What does it achieve?

2. Now, in numerical and chronological order, write down each step in your process, using a single word to describe each step.

3. Finally, for each word, write a single sentence that clearly explains what is involved in the step.

As an example, the following could be used to develop a process for a new developer contributing a patch to a project:

GOAL: Achieving contributor access in the FooBar project.
PRODUCE: Produce a patch with a new feature or bug fix that can apply to the latest development version of the code.
SUBMIT: Send the patch to the FooBar project mailing list outlining what it does.
WAIT: Wait for feedback on the patch and, if required, make adjustments. Otherwise, the patch will be submitted.
REPEAT: Repeat the above steps until a developer considers your contributions consistent enough to offer you direct access to the repository.

When following through with this approach, always read and reread each step, and assess how easy it is to understand. Is it written concisely? Does it use too much jargon? Would it be suitable as an elevator pitch?

Make Them Easy to Find

Processes don't have any value when no one knows that they exist. In addition to ensuring that your processes are clearly written, you should work hard to ensure that they are discoverable. Our goal here is to ensure that community members can find our documented processes easily.

This is a two-step approach:

1. You need to put your documentation somewhere online that people can refer to.

2. You need to inform your community about additions and changes to the documentation when they happen.

The first step involves putting your process somewhere accessible. If it makes sense, you should put it with the rest of the strategic documentation that we discussed earlier in the book. Discoverability is the key here, though.

As an example, if you have a process that new contributors should use to gain repository access, you should make sure new contributors can find it. This kind of documentation should not be buried in a wiki somewhere. You should assess where your potential contributors are reading documentation and where they are likely to look to find your processes. Again, plenty of feedback can ensure that you make the best decision here.

LINKING FOREVER

When putting process documentation online, you should ensure that its location never changes. The link to the location will be referenced extensively, particularly in online communities.

If you need to move your documentation, you should ensure that the old link redirects to the new documentation. The referenceable integrity of your documentation is something you should always endeavor to maintain, even if your documentation moves.

The next step is to announce the new process documentation to your community. Earlier in this book, we discussed communication channels within your community, and you should use these channels to announce this documentation and encourage your community to make use of it.

When you announce your processes, you should include the following details:

- The problem you sought to solve
- A single paragraph overview of the process and how it works
- A link to the online documentation that explains how the process works
- A final paragraph that strongly encourages the community to make use of the process

When announcing new processes, you should tread carefully. You should expect that your members, suffering from the same fear of rigidity and rules I mentioned at the beginning of this chapter, will roll their eyes at the concept of a new process being announced. Your goal is to have them entirely on board by the end of the announcement. Use loose and friendly language, and make them understand that the process is really necessary and not merely an exercise in bureaucracy.

Using Your Processes

With the process documented and announced, the final step is to encourage your community to make use of it. Documentation and announcements are no guarantee your community will make use of a process. In my experience, every process needs a certain amount of manual pushing and poking to become the norm.

Communities generally follow by example: members look toward other people to engage with processes before they do it themselves. You need to put a few examples of successful use of each process in place as a head start to get the community to accept the processes.

A useful approach is to pick four or five key community members and ensure that they are fully behind the process you have announced. You should regularly check in with these members to ensure that they are making use of the process, and when they are not, you should check why and remind them where needed. You should also encourage these key members to spread their best practices throughout the community.

You should also identify incidents that act as opportunities to reaffirm the purpose of the process. This could be handled in two ways. On the one hand, you should find success stories: examples that used the process with very positive results. These examples are always fantastic to show off. On the other hand, when someone doesn't follow the process and things go wrong, you can use it as a chance to remind your community about the purpose of the process. Do tread this line with caution: you should absolutely *not* show up your community members in front of others, and you should try not to climb up on your high horse and send out an "I told you so!" message.

The On-Ramp: Creating Collaborative Processes

Throughout this chapter we have discussed how to build great processes that are focused on accomplishing things effectively and reducing the level of bureaucracy involved in the community (screw you, bureaucracy). These processes can be applied to anything that involves any kind of structure or deliverable outcome, but I want to spend a little time focusing on a very specific family of processes that you will want to get right: the *on-ramp*.

The on-ramp is the set of steps and processes that are involved in helping someone to get up and running participating in your community. While the term *on-ramp* has been used for some time, there is little consistency or best practice when it comes to what actually constitutes an on-ramp.

Over the years I have developed my own approach to the on-ramp and a set of steps and processes that not only help people to participate, but to also gain the skills they need and to feel accomplished and celebrated in their contributions. As I have developed this standard approach I have applied it to a range of different communities with good results.

I define the on-ramp as shown in Figure 4-1.

In my on-ramp there are four steps, each of which is important in the community member collaboration experience. They can be summarized as follows:

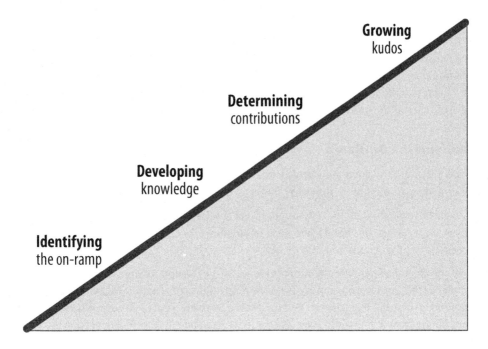

FIGURE 4-1. An on-ramp is a useful means of defining the different milestones in how a community member learns how to participate in your community.

Identifying the on-ramp

> For a community member to be able to participate, he needs to know he *can* participate. We need to be able to reach out and make it clear that collaboration and contributions are not only possible, but also actively encouraged.

Developing knowledge

> With any kind of collaboration a set of skills and knowledge is required in order for people to take part. As an example, if you want to write documentation, you need to know how to write the documentation, how the tools work, and how to contribute your work to the community. We want to make this skills acquisition process as simple as possible.

Determining contributions

> When you know you can participate and have the knowledge to do so, you then need to know what to work on. Which areas need participation and contributions? Which problems need fixing? We want to have a solid set of things that people can pick up and do.

Growing kudos

> Finally, when a community member has contributed something to the community, you want to ensure that he feels a sense of appreciation (what I call *kudos*) for his contribution.

These four steps in the on-ramp not only cover the timeline of the contributor experience (learning that you can participate, gaining the knowledge to do so, knowing what to work on, and having your contribution celebrated), but also tend to happen chronologically in that order…hence the premise of it being a ramp.

Just having knowledge of these four steps in the contributor process is useful in itself to be able to identify the kind of processes you need to put in place to serve the collaborative experience well. I want to build on these steps and take a quick spin through each of them to give you some examples of the processes I have put in place in the communities I have worked with.

Identifying the On-Ramp

It doesn't matter how great your processes are farther up the on-ramp; if people don't know they can take part in your community, they will never get involved.

Although this sounds obvious, it is easy to forget this important first component of the on-ramp when we are so busy and knee-deep in building processes, tracking their effectiveness, and dealing with problems and other work.

Part of the challenge here are the different levels of abstraction in your community. As an example, in the Ubuntu community we have many different teams: documentation writers, translators, packagers, bug triagers, and more. At a team level we have generally had the bases covered here; each team would have a website which made it clear that everyone is welcome to participate in her respective team. We went to great lengths to ensure that all the major teams had these pages in place and that new folks who would express an interest in a team would know their participation is desired and encouraged.

While this served us well at the team level, it was also important for us to do this at the higher general community level for people who were literally brand-new to Ubuntu and had no idea how the community works. In these cases people had typically tried Ubuntu and were curious about it, and we needed to inform them about how Ubuntu is a collaborative community and anyone can participate. This work was best done by highlighting the many different types of contributions and how these contributions typically map to teams, which then connects the prospective contributor to the team's on-ramping process.

To do this we created a web page that highlighted these different types of contributions and then handed people off to different teams where a team member could continue the on-ramping of that person. We found this worked pretty effectively, but the high-level web page needed a lot of user testing, feedback, and changes to serve these needs well. We discovered that in creating this page we naturally presumed some knowledge that prospective members actually didn't have; the user testing helped us to weed out these presumptions and bring more clarity.

We performed this user testing by putting together a page and asking a range of different types of users with different levels of experience to provide feedback on the page. We then reviewed the feedback, applied some changes to the page, and went through another round of user testing. This was hugely valuable in identifying the assumptions and errors in the page.

Developing Knowledge

Skills acquisition is a critical piece in encouraging successful participation in community. If we want people to contribute to our community, they need to have the appropriate skills to be able to deliver good work.

Skills acquisition involves two broad challenges:

- How do we provide all the facilities required to help new community members learn what they need to contribute?
- How do we help give them the confidence to participate?

The former is the big, obvious challenge. Fortunately in the current age of the (mostly) ubiquitous Internet, self-learning is common. Most Internet users have used various websites and facilities and learned how to do something, be it using web email, using a piece of technology, or something else. The Internet is awash with varying quality levels of help and guidance for almost anything, and people around the world are used to performing research and self-teaching. As such, we want to try to produce processes and resources for learning these skills in our communities.

It is important to remember, though, that skills acquisition is not just about producing tutorials and documentation and putting them online. While this documentation does help, the pure availability of it does not necessarily mean people will read it. Also, when people read it they will likely have questions, problems and issues with their learning, and other areas in which they need help and guidance. As such, when building your solution here you want to strive to produce (a) core knowledge transfer material (e.g., documentation), (b) methods of encouraging the consumption of that material, and (c) support facilities to provide help and guidance.

In the Ubuntu community we served these kinds of needs in a few different ways. First we encouraged the community to document help and guidance that could be useful to others. This included the creation of a knowledge base of content and an actively communicated ethos that the knowledge base should be added to and extended when someone noticed that a key piece of information or guidance was missing. This would result in a growing resource of help and guidance.

We augmented this work with a set of Ubuntu training weeks. These events would produce a week-long set of tutorial sessions, many of which referenced this preexisting documentation, but these sessions also actively focused on teaching a particular skill or approach in the community (e.g., how to create documentation, how to fix a bug, etc.).

Finally, we provided a number of resources for getting help and guidance. This includes a web-based question and answer service, real-time IRC discussion channels, mailing lists, and more. This collection of resources would help provide all the necessary steps for prospective community members to up-skill themselves to contribute effectively.

In our two broad challenges earlier, I also highlighted the challenge of *how do we help give them the confidence to participate?*

This challenge is less about providing documentation resources and more about giving people the motivational support and encouragement that they really *can* learn the skills and contribute great things to the community. In many cases new prospective community members feel a little nervous and self-conscious about whether they can contribute, often because they see so many other smart and active contributors and feel unsure about whether they can match their abilities.

You should make a point of breaking down this self-doubt and replacing it with confidence and support from the community to help grow confidence in contributing. Achieving this usually involves plenty of positive messaging, positive reenforcement, and one-on-one encouragement.

Determining Contributions

While in most communities the previous two steps on the on-ramp get plenty of focus, the determining contributions component often gets less attention.

Part of the reason for this is that making people aware of the on-ramp and helping people to up-skill themselves is often a largely single-shot chunk of work that, when completed, we can forget about. The challenge of giving people something to work on requires more attention to detail as the tasks that need to be completed at any given time change from day to day.

The other challenge here is that different community members with different levels of experience are better suited to different types of work. As an example, an experienced programmer can dig into a code base and get started right away. On the other hand, someone who is very new to a project and programming language will need something much simpler to get started with. Now fold into the mix the many different types of contributions in a community (e.g., advocacy, documentation, translations) and it can be difficult to segment available tasks in ways that are best suited for different community members with different skills and competence levels.

The simple reality here is that for anything other than a small community, you won't have the time to have an overview of all open tasks to be completed and ensure that they are assigned to people with a suitable expertise and skill level. What we instead need to focus our efforts on is ensuring that *new starters* can find something to do, and importantly, that they can feel a *sense of accomplishment.*

The sense of accomplishment of contributing something of value to the community is the secret recipe for success here. If a new community member can join a community, and have a small task to do that is performed and then accepted by the community, it provides a real sense of euphoria. We want to provide opportunities for these new members who can go from zero to hero and do something that is valued by the community.

Some years ago I trialled an approach in the Ubuntu community that has served us well in this regard. The idea was simple: identify a set of bug reports that don't require extensive knowledge to fix and can be fixed within an hour, and put these bug reports in a *bite-size* category. We would then offer these bite-size bug reports to new members of the community who would be able to fix them within their skill level and thus feel a strong sense of accomplishment when they got accepted shortly afterward. This sense of accomplishment would fuel an energy and enthusiasm to fix another bug report, and build a sturdiness to learning more complex skills and contributing to more complex tasks.

To help disseminate these bite-size bugs I asked each member of my team to write weekly blog posts highlighting bugs that need to be resolved, and inviting prospective community members to take a look at these bugs. In each of these blog entries there would also be links to our up-skilling resources, support channels, and more. As such, these blog entries would provide a set of simple issues that need fixing, thank people who fixed the issues from the previous week (which grows the kudos part of the on-ramp), and also highlight a standard set of resources that can be used to learn the skills to fix those issues. We found these weekly posts to be successful in driving more participation in different teams.

Growing Kudos

When you get to this final component on the on-ramp, your community members have already committed extensively to your community; they have been inspired to participate, learned the skills they need, and contributed to a task that needed completing. In any typical case of one human being helping another with something, we say *thanks*; you should find ways to do the same thing in your community.

In small communities this is less of a problem: it is easy to see a contribution and thank the person who performed it. In bigger communities this can be more challenging; when there are hundreds or thousands of things going on every week or month it is impractical to be able to say thanks for everything. This is an important challenge to scale, though; validation is a key piece in helping to maintain a sense of belonging and appreciation for your community members.

I have traditionally focused on encouraging an *appreciation culture* in two core forms:

Broadcast appreciation
> Broadcasting out to the wider community appreciation for work and accomplishments made by particular teams or people

Contextual appreciation
> Saying thanks for work and accomplishments to the people who did them at a one-to-one level

Both of these approaches are important within collaborative communities. From the perspective of the community member being thanked, the broadcast approach is nice to see as you feel a sense of appreciation disseminated across the wider community; the wider community see that you did a great job. The contextual approach is nice to see to provide a general sense of appreciation in your day-to-day activities; you do something and someone says thanks and it makes the community feel positive and fun.

For the *broadcast appreciation* approach you should encourage your community to write blog entries and articles that highlight great work and thank people. This is particularly important for community leaders to do. Communities are social groupings and inspirational leaders thanking and highlighting great work is incredibly motivating.

In Ubuntu we have tackled this approach by encouraging a culture of thankful blogging and I have worked with our community leaders to encourage them to do this. In many cases this would involve me reaching out to a leader and asking this person to blog. In most cases the leader was happy to do this and the recipient of the kudos felt great when seeing it.

For the *contextual appreciation* approach this is more of a cultural norm that you want to build; you want to grow a culture in which it is normal to say thanks when someone does something for or contributes to the community. In Ubuntu we have approached this by regularly reminding people of and encouraging this behavior and highlighting the positivity it generates. We tend to repeat this message at every Ubuntu Developer Summit to keep it fresh.

WHEN THE RAMP IS TOO STEEP

Sometimes, despite your best efforts, the on-ramp that you build for your community will perplex and challenge people in ways you don't expect. Some people will misunderstand components of how they get involved and likely will step on some toes in the process.

This can be frustrating, but hang in there. If the person is taking her time to bungle her way through your on-ramp, she is likely worth the investment of time to help her make the right steps instead of fat-footing it. This will require some patience and mentorship, and it is recommended that you have some community members who you can rely on to help provide this support.

When providing this guidance always try to find a means of tracking and assessing the person's progress. This could mean observing her contributions, getting feedback from others, having regular calls, or something else. This will help you ensure that the progress is on track, and if the person is genuinely not able to contribute, you can start scaling the guidance back at the right point.

Process Reassessment

Processes are living, breathing organisms. They are typically based on current conditions: the current level of contribution, demand, expectations, and goals. They are the clear plastic film that wraps around the assets and members of your community. As the assets and members adjust, so should the processes.

At the start of this chapter, we firmly established that unchanging processes cause bureaucracy. Processes that no longer map effectively to the people who need to use them cause bureaucracy. Our whirlwind tour of process best practices would not be complete if we didn't discuss how we can best evaluate our processes and make changes where appropriate, thus avoiding the dreaded claw of bureaucracy.

Process reassessment has become a staple part of each Ubuntu release. The Ubuntu community has a huge range of processes, initiatives, governance structures, and more. Each of these facilities was developed to serve a specific purpose, but as the community has grown and changed, these purposes and processes have needed to change, too.

An example of this was a change in how Ubuntu members have traditionally been approved. Anyone can be a member under the premise that he has demonstrated a significant and sustained contribution to open source. Traditionally, the way this assessment was made was that the candidate would first produce a wiki page outlining these contributions. The next step would be to attend a Community Council meeting online in which the council would discuss the application and vote. A majority vote would approve the member.

As the Ubuntu community continued to grow, this process became increasingly overstretched. The vast majority of Community Council meetings were devoted to approving members, and meetings were dragging on for nearly three hours. At an Ubuntu Developer Summit we identified the problem and proposed that we set up a series of regional subcouncils. We planned to set up a council in the Americas, Europe, and Australasia, and these would take over the task of approving members.

The new councils were formed, and subsequent membership applications have been uniformly more efficient. This not only has benefited prospective members, but also has meant that Community Council meetings have been more focused on governance issues than merely approving members.

These kinds of process reviews used to occur on an ad hoc basis in the Ubuntu world, but we have since tied them to a regular timeline. We now reassess all processes at the beginning of a cycle, and many of these reassessments occur at our biannual Ubuntu Developer Summit. This provides an excellent opportunity to gather feedback (of which we identified the importance earlier in this chapter) and discuss better alternatives.

The problem of overwork and delegating that work to other bodies in your community is part of governance, and we discuss this in detail in Chapter 10.

Building Regularity

With your community, you should schedule regular process reassessments. You should schedule a time in which your community can come together to determine how to improve on these underlying structures and processes.

How you do this is really dependent on your community. For a small local community, why not organize a series of meetings in a coffee shop or at someone's house? For an online community, a series of scheduled sessions on an online chat network such as IRC is often effective. Alternatively, you could organize a more formalized event for your community, akin to what we do with our Ubuntu Developer Summit.

However you choose to organize this reassessment, you should ensure the following:

- The events should be accessible to your community members. They should preferably incur as little cost as possible, and be within reasonable reach. Organizing a reassessment in Jamaica when your community is based in Northern England is not practical.

- The events should be open to all of your community members, and you should explicitly state this when promoting them. You should clearly communicate that everyone is welcome to join in and provide feedback about how to improve how the community runs.

- Ensure a sensible level of representation. Feedback sessions with 2 or 200 people are not valuable. Sessions with 10–30 people offer real opportunity to achieve some conclusions.

- Ensure that you begin organizing these sessions with plenty of notice, particularly for physical meetings.

When advertising these sessions, you should make them as attractive and practical as possible for your members. Don't describe the session as a "governance and process review," but rather as "how to improve our community." Make sure your announcement welcomes everyone, and ensure that it underlines how everyone can have an impact. Here is an example:

Improving Our FooBar Community
1st–3rd Sep 2009 – 5pm–7pm UTC – #foobar on Freenode IRC
Ever since the beginning of the FooBar project, we have all worked hard to produce a rock-solid implementation of Bar, and we have seen many new contributors join our stunning community.
This range of sessions is designed for us to come together, share experiences and feedback on our processes and methods of working in our community, and see how we can make improvements that benefit everyone. Everyone's participation is not only welcome, but encouraged!

When you have scheduled these reassessment sessions, you can build an action plan of what to discuss and how you discuss it. In many of these sessions there is a potential for the discussion to wander off on a tangent. It is therefore important to have a firm idea of what to discuss and what the core issues are.

I recommend following these steps to carve out a method of handling these sessions:

1. Make a list of all the processes that are involved in your community. This should cover topics such as how people get involved, how you work together, how teams work, and so on. I recommend you do this in an online document, such as a wiki page.

2. For each process, include bullet points outlining the feedback you have heard, both good and bad.

3. Look at the full list and reorganize it into what you consider priority order. This is most typically driven by which processes are causing bottlenecks and problems in your community.

4. Inform the wider community of the list and ask people to either edit the list directly (if they can, such as with a wiki) or submit feedback for you to add to the list. You should ask for feedback about the processes and which processes they consider the most important to discuss. Give them a deadline for feedback that is before the reassessment sessions. Merge this feedback into the document and reprioritize the list based on the consensus.

This list is your agenda for the meetings. When you get together with the community, pick the top processes and discuss them in turn. Communicate the good and bad feedback with the community, and focus the discussion on coming up with modifications to the processes that may be an improvement. Always keep these discussions focused on achieving outcomes; they can quickly degenerate into fruitless conversations.

When you reach consensus on changes to these processes, you should ensure that the changes are noted down in the session. These notes provide a TODO list of changes to your process documentation. Remember that each time a process changes, you should announce it to the wider community, just as you did with new processes.

Moving On

At this point, we are making some real progress on our journey through community. We have a strategy and a direction, and we have identified how to build strong processes for many aspects of our community. Now it is time for us to get the tools of collaboration in our community's hands. We need to put the foundations in the ground that our community can use to build great things. It is time to talk infrastructure....

CHAPTER FIVE

Supporting Workflow with Tools and Data

"We shall neither fail nor falter, we shall not weaken or tire...
give us the tools and we will finish the job."

—*Winston Churchill*

WHEN I WAS 16, I KNEW I WANTED TO PLAY WITH COMPUTERS. To access this world of exploration, though, I needed a bundle of what I had precious little of: *money*. One option was to save, but like many 16-year-olds I was more likely to fly to the moon on a potato than save any lucre.

It wasn't just hardware that was at the mercy of money; it was also the Internet. Back in those dim, distant days, dial-up Internet access in England cost 10 pence a minute. As a blossoming Net junkie, I had a (seemingly reasonable) proposal for my parents. For each minute of Internet access, I would put the requisite 10 pence in a cardboard box next to the computer. At the end of the month when the phone bill came in, the money in the box could cover my usage. Simple. Well, at the end of the month a bill for £190 arrived, and there was six quid in the box. The philosophy of "it's easier to ask for forgiveness than permission" didn't wash with my parents.

Over in the US, things were different. Many parts of the country had flat-rate local access and established Internet access at universities. The growth of these cheap networks made it easy for online communities to form. Early on, these communities shared knowledge as text files, packed with ideas, techniques, and recipes to make things. Each text file was shared freely, and people could add new content, modifications, and changes. Eventually, it seemed like information covering every conceivable subject was available online. I myself contributed, writing guitar lessons and putting them on my website.

This global body of knowledge was in many ways the great grandfather of Wikipedia. The Internet not only enabled the sharing of information, but also enabled the sharing of tools to create this content. A new era of collaboration was bubbling to the surface. As that collaboration became more widespread, however, new challenges arose. While the cost of computing and the Internet declined, coordinating people across the Internet proved more difficult than just opening the doors.

THE COMMUNITY CASE BOOK

Lots of online communities can be very competitive, especially between different fan sites and groups, and I wanted to try and have the spirit of sharing be the overwhelming feeling. We tried to always be as inclusive as possible, and work to make people feel like they were part of one big group of friends.

—James Spafford, on Collaboration

Read the full interview in Chapter 14.

Understanding Your Workflow

Tools are a means to an end. They are used to produce an item that is more interesting than the raw materials and devices used to manipulate it. To select the right tools for a job, we first need to understand what we are trying to achieve. We need to know what our *workflow* is.

I am a firm believer that every brain is different. Each interprets the world in a slightly different way, and each defines our differences and individuality. Take music as an example. For some, the purest definition of beautiful music is blues, for some it is rock, and for some it is crushing death metal. Each style has the same instruments and core ingredients, but we all perceive those styles in very different ways.

The same happens, for example, with programming languages. My brain just works with Python. When I started to learn Python, it felt natural. I was productive almost immediately. Other languages, such as Perl, just confuse the heck out of me. No matter how much I try, the square Perl block just doesn't fit into the circular hole in my head. Programming languages are curious vessels of logic and workflow. Each one has a set of semantics, rules, and procedures that must be learned and executed with perfect precision for it to work. In addition to this, different programming languages have different technical approaches, cultures, and expectations. Each attribute must be learned and mastered for the programming language to be a useful tool in helping you to create something. The reason why Python works with my brain is because the workflow and semantics of Python help me to be productive quickly.

These differences are everywhere, and become more important as people work together. It's not just programming languages, though. We see differences in how we keep TODO lists, how we manage email, and how we organize our important documents. Our methods of working and our organization styles vary. A successful workflow requires understanding what you want to achieve and making the steps in which you achieve it as simple as possible for as many people as possible.

One of the reasons why the Firefox browser has been so popular has been its extensibility. A large and growing collection of Firefox add-ons is available. These small bundles of functionality, basically small pieces of software, integrate tightly into the browser and can do anything from block ads to allow web developers to dynamically adjust the layout of web pages. Traditionally, installing software has been possible using a variety of approaches: installers, package archives, compiling code, and more. The Firefox team made it as simple as selecting an add-on and clicking Install. Firefox takes care of the rest. Workflow and usability are close companions.

Another successful workflow example comes from Bytemark Hosting (*http://www.bytemark.co .uk/*). This small company provides virtual hosting machines that run Linux. If my machine was unresponsive for some reason, it offered a command-line-driven administration console that I could log in to. That console let me restart the machine and gather diagnostic information. Although it might have seemed complex and technical to the average Firefox user, the console was fast, efficient, and intuitive for most Linux users. If a machine was down, I could be into the console within minutes and have it back up again, all from my familiar command-line interface.

The connection between both of these examples is the first task in understanding workflow: know your audience.

Roles

People always have expectations. Our job is to understand, predict, and cater to fair expectations in our target audience. To understand these expectations, we need to understand our audience. Although communities are a breeding ground for diversity of personality, experience, and background, we can often see similarities in expectations, skills, experience, and approaches between people who have a shared interest in a particular type of work, be it programming, documentation, testing, advocacy, or whatever else.

Consider programmers as an example. We know we can assume a certain amount of technical knowledge: programmers indulge in a technical art form. They spend their days engaging in technical conversations and manipulating technology to their needs. You can't push these assumptions too far, though. A Windows power user and a low-level assembly device driver writer are both "technically trained," but in different ways. Technical experience comes in many forms. It is important for us to see the correlations, but also to keep track of subcategories.

Roles are critical in identifying preconceptions and experience. Using programmers again as an example, it is reasonable to assume that a programmer will know how to use an operating system reasonably well, know much of the jargon associated with computers, and be fairly self-sufficient in solving technical problems. Each attribute is common in programmers. We draw these parallels from two primary methods: *observation* and *experience*.

Understanding the audience requires observing them in their natural environment. If you want to make bug triage as simple as possible, sit down and watch someone triage a number of bugs. In fact, watch a range of people triage bugs. If you want to understand how to run a booth at a conference efficiently, watch how people set up booths and how they talk to people. As you observe your community engaging in their workflow, ask them to comment on it, telling you what frustrates and annoys them and what works well. This feedback is always valuable. Identify the parallels between the multiple people who perform the same type of task (such as programming), and you begin to build a mental picture of their expectations and experience.

Your own experience will also guide how you build strong community and identify with these different roles. Repeated experiences in particular can be critical for understanding what is going on.

I had a colleague who made sales to big companies. On his first big deal, he went through an intense set of emotions. He first built confidence while the client was excited about the product. As the negotiations moved forward, he was cautious but confident. All was going well until he hit a roadblock in the negotiations. It was an emotionally difficult time: he was about to close a big deal, he was excited but stressed, and he was losing sleep and was constantly anxious to check email. What my colleague didn't know at the time was that this was part of practically every deal: every deal hit a roadblock and every deal had moments of doubt. After a few more deals, his experience taught him what was the norm in his world. From then on he knew how to manage his expectations. Your own experience will uncover similar secrets about the roles you are seeking to understand.

Importantly, your community members can help you to understand these roles, too, but you really need to figure out their current workflow and ask them for specific feedback about its different parts. Have a series of frank and honest conversations about the overall workflow. This provides community members with an opportunity to share how the workflow benefits their lives and how it complicates them. You should also get to know their general perspectives and opinions that surround the workflow. As an example, if you are talking to a programmer, ask for her opinions on related topics such as testing, bugs and triage, translations, code commenting, documentation, and other topics; this will help you build a better sense of her views and expectations. While having these conversations, take copious notes: the devil is almost always in the details, and you don't want to lose anything.

Building a Simple Workflow

After establishing roles, we now need to sit down and flesh out a workflow. In this chapter our focus is on technical, tool-based workflow, so we will assess the technical steps involved in achieving a goal. To do this we will identify an "OBJECTIVE," the "AUDIENCE," and then a number of "OUTCOME" steps that can achieve the objective. An example will best illustrate how that works.

When I was involved in Jokosher, we wanted people to test the application and provide feedback. We wanted to take a snapshot of the application for members of our community to test and tell us when things went wrong. This would give us an opportunity to fix remaining bugs. That helps us produce the first item in our workflow specification, the objective that you want to achieve:

> OBJECTIVE: To have more users install and test a development snapshot of Jokosher and provide feedback on bugs.

The next step is to identify the audience. We did not want developers to test Jokosher; we wanted real users to test it. We wanted people to use Jokosher for real music production and make assumptions based on real use cases.

THE RISKS OF AUTOPILOT

A common problem that can occur when observing how people use software is when the user knows of a particular quirk in a product and works to naturally avoid triggering the quirk. This is common with software developers, and before release, the software typically is not used in the same manner as it is by normal users after release.

A good antidote to this problem is to simply put new users in front of the software who are entirely unaware of the quirks and oddities. They can often present the most valuable feedback.

Let's now add our audience to our spec:

> AUDIENCE: Musicians or audiophiles who have basic computer knowledge.

The next step is in describing the primary pieces in the workflow. At this point we're just identifying the major steps; we'll add the details later. Add these as a series of OUTCOME items. For example:

> OUTCOME: Install a current snapshot of Jokosher and all required dependencies.
> OUTCOME: Use and test primary features in Jokosher.
> OUTCOME: Provide feedback about bugs.

These three outcomes are the major steps involved in achieving our OBJECTIVE. The next step is to combine our AUDIENCE with each OUTCOME.

This is the most important part of the process, where we assess how to make our workflow as simple and attuned to our audience as possible. Let's look at our first OUTCOME in the preceding list as an example. We need to combine this with our audience of new users. How can we make it as easy as possible to install Jokosher for a user base that is not technically sophisticated?

When we were faced with this challenge, we considered a range of options. We heard some suggestions to provide simple documentation that would show people how to compile code and install dependencies. That was too technical and complex as an option. There were also suggestions to make packages available for each distribution. That required skills that were not present in the team, and would involve sourcing external help.

The ideal scenario was that someone could simply download a file and Jokosher would run: this matched our audience profile. It would be simple, easy, and efficient, perfect for our users. Stuart Langridge produced a script that downloaded the Jokosher code, installed the relevant dependencies on the user's system, and ran Jokosher with a click of the mouse. The script checked to see whether the dependencies were already installed, and skipped their installation if they were. The user could use the same script for the first run and subsequent runs, and not even think about the concept of installation. Simple.

In the workflow spec, you should document each step from the perspective of your AUDIENCE. For the Jokosher installation example:

OUTCOME: Install a current snapshot of Jokosher and all required dependencies.

Download a script from jokosher.org.

Make the script executable (explained with documentation).

Double-click the icon to run the script and install Jokosher.

To rerun, double-click the icon again.

This process was as simple as we could make it for the user. The hardest part was making the script executable, and there is no safe technical solution to automate that process. Our solution also required few resources to develop, just the time for one person to produce the script instead of lots of packagers to package Jokosher for every conceivable Linux distribution.

Once you have written your workflow steps into your functional spec, you should go through each step and ask the following questions of it:

- Is this step really required?
- How easy is this step to understand? Could it be simplified?
- Are the requirements easy to obtain or access?

When you have applied these questions to each step, you can apply these questions to the entire workflow:

- Is this workflow as efficient as it could be?
- Is this the most intuitive approach to the workflow?
- Is this workflow scalable?

If you have satisfied each question, you should have a pretty rock-solid workflow in place.

The Mechanics of Collaboration

Earlier in the book we added a critically important item to our Community TODO List.

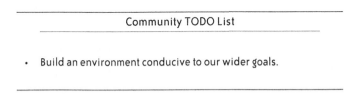

Community TODO List

- Build an environment conducive to our wider goals.

The operative word here is *conducive*. What does that mean, though? How exactly do we optimize our environment for the purpose of achieving our goals?

Collaboration is all about working together for a common purpose, opening up a channel in which content can flow between interested parties for the purpose of building something interesting. This content and the tools that make it flow are the *mechanics of collaboration*.

Collaboration is a form of conversation, a reciprocal back-and-forth of communication around a common topic. At the heart of all conversations are at least two people and a:

- Shared language
- Shared topic
- Communication channel

Imagine a normal spoken debate taking place in a London pub. The shared language may be English, the topic could be how effective the prime minister is, and the communication channel is the spoken word (lubricated with a pint of something cold). These simple attributes combine to create a thread of responses, each building on the previous statement. This combination of responses comprises a conversation.

An Example: Ubuntu Bug Workflow

Technical collaboration has similar components and similar results. The mechanics of collaboration are so important because when you understand what conversations occur, you can optimize how people converse. Take bugs, for example. Every piece of software ever written has bugs. Software is written by people, people make mistakes, and bugs are human mistakes formed as bits and bytes.

Most software projects use a special piece of software called a bug tracker to have a bug conversation. Someone files a bug. Someone else asks for more information on the bug. Those who are affected by the bug offer clues and information. Someone else may propose a fix. People try the fix and provide feedback. The essence of conversation is the same: a shared language (English), a shared topic (exploring and fixing the bug), and a communication channel (the Web).

When considering how to build your community's infrastructure and tools, you need to identify what these mechanics of collaboration are. You need to think carefully about how people have conversations, both in natural language (such as discussions) and in technical language (such as with bugs). When you understand the driving forces behind how conversations occur, you can make some really interesting things happen.

Awhile back my team spent some time working on optimizing the conversation around bugs. Before I explain the solution, let's take the problem for a spin.

In the open source world, bugs are a complex topic, and they are particularly complicated for Linux distributions. Consider the problem. Erica is using Ubuntu and experiences a problem in the text editor: when she tries to spellcheck, the editor crashes.

As an experienced open source citizen, she is familiar with the mantra that when something goes wrong, you should report it. She clicks the Help menu in the text editor and clicks on "Report a problem..." to report the bug. At this point she now expects someone in Ubuntu to tend to the bug report and hopefully fix it. So far, so good.

Now it gets a little more complicated. The text editor in Ubuntu is actually called GEdit. It is an open source project that is part of the GNOME (*http://www.gnome.org/*) desktop. The GNOME project is an independent project that produces software, and the open source parlance for this kind of project refers to it as an *upstream* project.

Ubuntu developers take the upstream GNOME source code (including GEdit) and build packages to ship it in Ubuntu. When this code is built, some modifications are made to make GNOME (and as such, GEdit) integrate well in Ubuntu. This includes consistent themes, file dialog boxes, folder locations, and more. In a nutshell, Ubuntu takes the original upstream source code, adds some changes, builds it, and ships the final product as part of Ubuntu.

This raises our first question: who is responsible for the bug? Was the bug present in the original upstream code from GNOME? Was it in the changes made by Ubuntu developers? Does the bug exist outside GNOME and GEdit? Does the bug even exist at all? Fortunately, this is a fairly simple question to answer: some quick checking of the upstream code can usually identify the source of the bug.

The second question is the one that is pertinent to our bug conversation. How do we deal with the bug report? Erica rightly reported the bug, but should she report it in the Ubuntu bug tracker (called Launchpad) or the GNOME bug tracker? In addition to this, many other people may have experienced the bug. Some will report it in their distribution's bug tracker and some will report it in the upstream bug tracker. It is not entirely inconceivable that there is a bug report in each distribution's bug tracker and one in the upstream bug tracker all pointing to the same bug. This is hugely wasteful.

Regardless of all this duplication of effort, if the bug exists upstream and the distribution ships it, the bug *does* still exist in the distribution and it *does* exist upstream. The challenge is to bring these different bug conversations together so that everyone who experiences the bug can share his experience to fix it. The solution to this problem is to identify how the flow of conversation and collaboration happens between these different bug reports and to optimize it.

Fortunately, software can address these issues. Launchpad, the web service that Ubuntu uses as a bug tracker, already had the ability to link bugs, whether they're in the same tracker or a different one. When Erica filed her bug, she or someone else could connect her bug to an existing bug in an upstream bug tracker. It works like this:

1. If the developer knows the bug is an upstream bug but does not know which bug it is in the upstream bug tracker, he can add an *upstream task* to the bug report. This upstream task indicates that the bug should be linked to an upstream bug when it is found.

2. If the developer knows the bug in the upstream bug tracker matches the Ubuntu bug, he can link the two bugs. This involves finding the Ubuntu bug and using the Link feature in Launchpad to enter the URL of the upstream bug.

When a bug is linked, any changes made to the upstream bug are synchronized in Launchpad and vice versa. This feature connects the two separate conversations.

Getting to know the problem

Although this is a hugely useful and valuable feature, we got the impression that not enough bugs were getting linked. The problem I wanted my team to solve was to explore why these bugs were not being linked, and to help increase the linkages.

Although we had a hunch that not that many people were linking bugs, we really had no idea. We had no concrete statistics to back up our assumptions. Our first task was to learn more about the problem.

To do this we produced a tool called the Ubuntu Upstream Report. The report mined the Launchpad bug tracker to show the top 100 upstreams shipped in Ubuntu ordered by the greatest number of open bugs. We knew that these 100 upstreams were likely to be the largest and most significant projects: more bugs in the open source world typically means larger projects with more users using the software and therefore filing more bugs.

For each upstream in the report, we showed which bugs were open, which had been triaged to determine they were actually bugs, which were known to be upstream bugs (marked as upstream tasks), and which had linkages associated with those tasks.

The differences between the numbers generated interesting conclusions. As an example, if a project had a significant difference between the number of *open* bugs and the number of *triaged* bugs, we knew which projects needed more help with bug triage.

A key conclusion that we discovered was the difference in many projects between the *upstream tasks* and the *linked bugs* numbers. As an example, one project had 229 bugs with upstream tasks but only 101 of those bugs had upstream links. This left a total of 128 bugs that were known to be upstream bugs that didn't have linkages. This told us the project was not linking bugs well and needed help. It also told us which specific bugs were known to be upstream bugs without linkages. We could use these bugs as a target for our community to make those linkages.

Breaking down the conversation

The raw data in the upstream report was the foundation of not only exploring the problem, but also solving it. The data confirmed our suspicion that a lot of bugs weren't being linked. On a practical level, it helped us to understand which upstreams needed help, and therefore which contributors to speak to.

To raise the number of linked bugs, we needed to identify the three key aspects of the bug-handling process (reporting, triage, and linking) and improve them. Our first area to focus on was linking, as it was the most immediate goal. We examined and optimized each step in the process of linking a bug. We discovered, for example, that finding bugs in the upstream bug tracker took the most time, so we explored methods of syncing bug data across the Launchpad and upstream bug reports automatically, automating duplication searches, and simplifying the user interface for the whole shebang.

Our next step was to optimize the reporting and triage process. This was an area in which we had already poured extensive work, and our workflow here was generally pretty good. Where there appeared to be a disconnect, though, was with documentation and people reading and making use of that documented best practice. Although there was plenty of documentation, it was scattered all over the Ubuntu wiki, difficult to navigate, and complex to read. We reorganized and improved it, dividing it into better sections and making it easier to understand. We organized documentation days; encouraged community participation; celebrated the improvements; and encouraged our bug triagers to review, expand, and make use of the new documentation that was produced.

Lessons learned

This example reflects a useful approach to help you "build an environment conducive to our wider goals." Its key themes likely apply to your community:

1. Identify the primary ways in which you collaborate. These are the areas in which your tools and workflow should be as flawless and intuitive as possible. In our example, we identified bugs as a key area.

2. Understand the problem. How does your community understand and engage in the process you are exploring? Which parts of the problem are more problematic than others? What do you want to achieve? In our example, we knew that linking was a problem, and focused on it.

3. Break down the workflow. When you understand your areas of focus, examine the process and ask whether each step is entirely necessary or could be improved.

These three simple steps are all based on the principles of understanding the problem and making a solution that is as simple as possible. *Simplicity* is a key goal in everything we do with community.

Building Great Infrastructure

Consider the humble can opener. Years ago, to use a can opener you had to place a very small cutting blade on the lip of the can, ensure that it hooked over correctly, and then twist the handle, invariably making your fingers ache. As you twisted the handle, the blade often slipped off the can. Even when you had managed to get the lid off the can, you might cut your finger on the lid or the sharp top of the can. We now have electric can openers in which you simply press a button and the lid is cut and taken off for you. Even manual can openers are effortless and go so far as to blunt the lid and the top of the can. Manufacturers were well aware of the problems and explored the workflow and potential solutions to evolve their tools.

Collaborative online projects need a diverse set of supporting tools to flourish. Even the simplest community will use tools for communicating, storing work, and sharing information. Many communities build on top of these staples with a variety of tools and facilities for different functions in the community. Different contributors have different needs for their types of contribution. Developers need bug trackers, patch systems, and version control; documentation writers need wikis, text processing tools, and editors; translators need translation tools; testers need test suites; and everyone needs to communicate with everyone else.

It's tempting to go out and set up a wide range of tools, but think carefully about how your tools integrate. An efficient and integrated set of tools will be far more pleasurable to work with than a completely disconnected set of tools.

For years I have been playing music, and writing and recording my own songs in my home studio. As a strong believer in a Free Culture music industry, Severed Fifth (*http://www .severedfifth.com*) was my contribution. This was a project I set up to change perceptions of the music industry while writing and playing music. I wrote, produced, and recorded an entire solo metal album and released it under a Creative Commons Attribution-ShareAlike license. I set out to build a community around the project and the music, incorporating many features into the site: news, a blog, forums, static web pages, and more. I wanted the entire site to feel as integrated as possible. My friend Stuart implemented a single user account that worked with all features on the site. Although the site consisted of two WordPress blogs, a Vanilla forum, and some static web pages, having an integrated account and an integrated look and feel made all of the separate components feel like a single well-oiled machine.

Integration offers a range of opportunities for collaborative projects. Workflow is the foundation for identifying these avenues of integration. Workflow is a larger process that can contain many individual components.

Take, for example, the workflow to fix a bug. A simplified process could involve finding a bug in the bug tracker, checking out the code, writing a patch to fix it, attaching the patch to the bug report, and informing the developers of the fix. This workflow involves three separate tools: the bug tracker, the source repository, and the mailing list. It could arguably involve additional tools, such as those required to produce the fix and generate the patch. There are many areas in which the tools could be integrated:

- The bug tracker and source control system could use the same login credentials.
- The bug tracker could display recent branches in the source control system that refer to a specific bug number in the changelog.
- When a patch is attached to a bug report or a bug status changes, that could generate an automatic email to the project mailing list to inform the community that a fix has been made available.
- When a fix is sent to the mailing list with a bug number, additional information from the bug tracker could be automatically added to the message.

Every project has the opportunity to draw similar integration opportunities between the different tools in the workflow. The key is in identifying how different tools can talk to each other in useful ways.

The first time I experienced this firsthand was with Jokosher. When the project started, we needed the following facilities:

- Source control
- Online commit log history
- Source viewing
- Bug tracking
- Wiki

One approach was to set up a number of separate tools to provide these facilities. We could have set up Bazaar, WebCVS, Bugzilla, MediaWiki, and other tools. Each tool would be largely insulated from the others, and each would have a separate account. Our final solution was to use a system called Trac (*http://trac.edgewall.org/*).

Trac is a popular project management and software development system that provides an easy-to-use and integrated system for source control, issue tracking, commit logs, and a wiki. We used a hosting company called Python-Hosting (now WebFaction; *http://www.webfaction.com/*) that offered a free Trac instance for open source projects. Trac was simple, integrated, and hugely productive.

Trac was by no means the only option. Systems like SourceForge (*http://sourceforge.net/*) existed, but with Jokosher development so new, SourceForge felt like a very large hammer to crack a very small nut. Integration can go too far, and some software development solutions can include oodles of features and facilities that simply distract from what is important. Back then, SourceForge was vexed with this problem. Eventually Jokosher outgrew Python-Hosting and settled on Launchpad (*https://launchpad.net/*).

Software As a Service

The Jokosher example raises an important question when it comes to integration. Do you want to run the toolchain facilities yourself or use an existing online system?

Integration has always been a challenge in IT, and subsequently many companies have sprung up to provide solutions. I have already mentioned Sourceforge and Launchpad, but there are many more. These solutions put integration at the center of their offering: they can give you most of the tools that you need in a single integrated system. These online services are often referred to as the *cloud* or *Software as a Service* (SaaS).

Many new projects make the mistake of setting up their own tools for the sake of just controlling the tools themselves. This is a shortsighted perspective. But it's equally shortsighted to simply use an existing online service without thinking through your needs now and for the immediate life cycle of the project. Let's think through some of these choices right now.

We should first look through the different attributes of both approaches. Let's start with benefits. Self-hosted systems offer a number of benefits and disadvantages, listed in Table 5-1.

TABLE 5-1. Benefits and disadvantages of self-hosted systems

Benefits	Disadvantages
Control—you have complete control of the toolchain. You can always add features, facilities, and additional software where you see fit.	Maintenance—having control is a double-edged sword. It requires care and feeding, security updates, and the installation of additional software.
Choice—you can choose which tools you want to use in your community.	Cost—if you host your own tools, you need to provide the hosting and bandwidth.

Now let's look at the benefits and disadvantages of a cloud-based solution, listed in Table 5-2.

TABLE 5-2. Benefits and disadvantages of SaaS-based solutions

Benefits	Disadvantages
Ease—setting up your entire toolchain could be as simple as registering with a SaaS solution.	Data—when you use a SaaS solution, you put your data on someone else's system. You have to continually back up your data outside the cloud, in case that provider goes away intermittently or permanently.
Maintenance—in the cloud, someone else looks after security and updates, so you don't have to.	Bandwidth limitations—some cloud providers limit disk space, bandwidth, and other attributes in a project. You may hit these limitations.
Potential reliability—SaaS solutions are typically hosted on high-bandwidth networks with a powerful backbone. This could potentially offer improved reliability over a self-hosted solution.	Tool choice—if you pick a SaaS provider, it may provide 80% of the tool choice that you want, but may choose a different tool for another part of your workflow. This could potentially limit what you want to do.

At this point your head is probably spinning with options, and you may be unsure of what to choose. My recommendation is almost always to choose a SaaS-based solution.

SaaS-based solutions offer one major benefit: lower maintenance. The last thing you want to be doing in your community is spending time fiddling with tools. You should instead be focusing your efforts on growing community, building a team, and achieving the objectives and goals you outlined in your strategic plan. Online resources such as Launchpad and Sourceforge are excellent solutions to this problem. They give you everything you need, and they put the maintenance and bandwidth responsibility in someone else's hands.

This recommendation comes with a caveat, however. We are still in the early days of the cloud, and it's difficult to know how stable the cloud will prove to be in future years. Many of the Internet companies that were prominent five years ago are either no longer around, have been acquired, or have otherwise faded into obscurity. When you put your data in the cloud, you face the risk that your provider may suffer these consequences.

I also worry about SaaS security perceptions. Storing data on a third-party service requires trust: trust in the provider and trust in the concept of the cloud. When that trust is compromised, the entire industry suffers. The airline industry has experienced this. When the attacks on the World Trade Center happened on September 11, 2001, all air travel felt unsafe. People avoided flying like the plague. The entire industry suffered due to a perception that air travel was no longer safe.

If one of the large cloud providers faces privacy or security issues, the concept of the cloud will feel unsafe and the industry will suffer. The risk to you is that if the cloud industry suffers and your data is on the cloud, your data could potentially go away. You need to assess the current industry and keep abreast of the risks involved.

BACK UP THE CLOUD

If you do decide to go with a third-party online SaaS provider, I again strongly recommend that you have a backup solution in place, just in case you face these problems. Always ensure that if your provider goes away, it still can be business as usual in your community.

Avoiding Resource Fetishism

Before we move on to look at some of the technical specifics of different tools, I just want to spend a little time talking about a problem that faces a range of new collaborative communities.

The problem looks a little like this:

1. A new community is born around a goal. This goal could be to produce software, change the political landscape, or anything else.

2. The founders of the community set up the communication channels, and some early members join.

3. Additional tools are required. This could involve a website, blogging tools, technical development facilities, or anything else.

4. Using a website as an example, a discussion kicks off asking which content management system should be used. A long and drawn-out debate starts over which system to use. These debates can drag on for a long time.

I have seen this same scenario happen over and over again. There is nothing wrong with wanting to choose the best tools for your community, but you need to get your priorities straight.

When you set up a new community, one priority is more important than all others: *building a team*. Your #1 goal is to get people involved. You need to get people inspired to join your crusade. If you don't attract people and get them up and running and productive as soon as possible, your community will feel like it is treading water.

Debates over which tool to use should be kept as short and sweet as possible. You should seek to establish requirements and gain consensus around a chosen tool as quickly as you can. Always remember that these discussions will garner strong opinions for different tools. You will never make everyone happy, so you need to identify the requirements and pick something as soon as viably possible. The sooner you get your tools up and running and get people focused on doing useful work, the better.

Technical Considerations

Most of this chapter has focused on best practices for assessing optimal workflow for a project, staying detached enough from specific technologies so that the information can apply to any kind of community and workflow. The next few pages delve into some technical specifics of particular interest to software projects, such as bug tracking, source control, and collaborative editing.

As we cover these topics I am going to deliberately avoid recommending specific solutions or pieces of software. This is because software changes a lot more quickly than books do, and the last thing I want to do is recommend a piece of software that has since become unsuitable for your requirements. Instead, the following pages will advise you of some key considerations that you should keep in mind when evaluating which tools you want to use to solve a particular problem.

When evaluating specific software solutions, you should meld the advice here with your current requirements. You should also factor in predicted requirements for the next three years. If you can find a solution that will keep your project productive for three years, you have hit the jackpot. Our goal here is to keep migration to new systems to a minimum: migration is disruptive, complex, and time-consuming.

Bug Tracking

Bug tracking is a critical part of any software project, particularly open source projects. It is one of the core mechanics of how your project works. It should be a central part of your development process and a daily component for each of your developers.

A range of bug-tracking solutions are available, from those your project hosts (such as Bugzilla) to third-party-hosted systems (such as Launchpad). Bug trackers vary hugely in terms of features. Some are simple, designed for small projects with a small number of developers. Some are hugely complex, infinitely customizable behemoths of functionality.

Before you choose a bug tracker, you should evaluate your requirements. Do you need a simple bug tracker to merely maintain a list of defects in your software, or do you need a complex solution with custom fields, multiple projects, teams, automation, and other features?

A common temptation for new open source projects is to install the most feature-packed bug tracker available. The reasoning behind this is usually "just in case we need those features."

Whatever your needs, always keep usability as a key requirement in picking a bug tracker. If you use a solution that is too complex, it will annoy potential bug reporters and most certainly annoy those performing triage.

TRANSPARENCY IN BUG TRACKING

You should ensure that your project's bug tracker is publicly available and that anyone and everyone can access it. As such, you should not restrict viewing the bug tracker to username and password access.

There are many reasons for this:

- There is no need to restrict bug information if it affects a collaborative community project.
- Users who are experiencing problems can search quickly and easily for information that might help them fix the problem.
- Eric Raymond, a well-known open source proponent, once uttered, "Given enough eyeballs, all bugs are shallow." Open bug tracking provides an excellent opportunity for community members who are blighted by the same bug to explore, share notes, and possibly even fix the bug together.

The only time I consider a closed bug tracker or private bug reports to be suitable for community projects is when Non-Disclosure Agreement (NDA) work for a specific vendor is occurring, but in a manner that does not compromise the wider project. Bugs that affect the wider project should never be private.

Bug reporting

You should make every effort to make bug reporting as easy as possible. Some projects (such as Ubuntu) embed a link into an application that simplifies this process. Ubuntu also uses a special tool called Apport to bundle up debugging information to send to the bug tracker automatically when something crashes. This is a useful feature, as traditionally many developers doing triage would ask bug reporters to enter a series of commands that gather debugging information and add it to the report. Apport (*https://wiki.ubuntu.com/Apport*) automates this process.

Other projects make the act of reporting the bug on the bug tracker as easy as possible. An example of this is Jokosher, which only asks for a Subject and Description of the bug, leaving it up to the Jokosher triage team to manage the rest of the information. It is important to remember that your bug reporters are unlikely to know most of the requirements for a bug report.

Another project that has taken an interesting approach is GNOME. GNOME produced a simplified frontend to its Bugzilla (*http://www.bugzilla.org/*) bug tracker, and the tracker asks only a few simple questions. It is recommended that you keep your own bug reporting frontend as simple as possible.

Bug triage

For each bug that comes into your bug tracker, various decisions need to be made. This includes confirming whether it is actually a bug, asking for additional information from the reporter, assigning the bug to people or teams, and classifying the urgency of the bug.

Triage is a process that your developers will typically need to engage in, and few developers want to spend any more time on it than is absolutely necessary. As such, triage should be as straightforward and painless as possible. Understanding bug workflow, ensuring that it is simple and effective, and picking a suitable bug tracker is a critical part of this process.

As your project grows, you likely will become inundated with bug reports. As the bug reports flow in, it is also likely that your developers simply won't have time to triage the bugs as well as fix them. As such, you may need to consider setting up a dedicated triage team. This, my friends, is a path that you should tread carefully.

Triagers straddle a delicate middle ground in your community. On the far left are your users who have been gracious enough to report a bug in the interests of it being fixed and benefiting the wider community. This is a generous gift on their part, and this gift should be rewarded with the attention it deserves. On the far right are your developers who have only so many hours in the day to fix bugs. If the developers don't have enough time to triage the bugs, a triage team is expected to sit in the middle and help ensure that the reported bugs are assessed and then routed to the right developers. If this process is successful, all bugs get triaged and the most critical and important bugs get fixed promptly by the developers who have the most appropriate experience in that part of the code base. If the process is *not* successful, the original users will grow resentful that their bug was "ignored," and the developers will either drown in bugs (not enough triage), never see bugs (lack of visibility in triage), or focus on the wrong bugs (wrong triage).

The process of setting up a triage team needs extensive work and resources to be successful:

Documentation

You'll need extensive documentation about how to triage, what is involved, where to find help, how to respond to users to gather more information, and so on.

Mentoring

New triagers need to learn the ropes, and mentoring can help ensure that these new contributors get up and running as quickly as possible.

Events

You should organize bug days, meetings, triage events, and other methods of inspiring participation.

Communication

Your triagers should never become an island. They need to be in regular contact with the developers and ensure that communication is flowing.

Although it is certainly not impossible to set up a triaging team, and it seems like a fantastic method of contributing, many people often start with triage and grow bored. You should expect this: it is part and parcel of this kind of contribution. Have faith, though, because there will be some people who will join, enjoy, and stick with triage, and you should cherish these contributors and help them to inspire others to get involved.

Source Control

Source control has become an increasingly hot topic in the software development world. Once upon a time, the only real option was a tool called Concurrent Versions System (CVS). We then had an "easier CVS" come along in the form of Subversion. Since then, we have seen the birth of the Distributed Version Control System (DVCS), which adds even more functionality to source control. The DVCS makes it easier than ever for new contributors to produce features and fixes that can be merged into the main branch.

I don't want to get into a debate about which version control system to use; other resources can provide a far better assessment of that. One piece of advice I do offer, however, is that you should strongly consider some of the integrated tools that exist around these systems. As an example, the Launchpad system integrates tightly with the Bazaar DVCS and makes tasks such as reviewing merges and viewing changes a point-and-click affair. These kinds of features can be hugely useful with such an important component in the software development toolchain.

Collaborative Editing

Back in the early days of open source, we all lied to the world about documentation. *"Want to get involved in open source but can't write code?* Sure you can help! Write documentation!"

Back then, if you wanted to write documentation you needed to install a complex menagerie of text processing tools, write your documentation in a markup language, ensure that the document properly validated, and then convert the documentation into something the user could read. In a nutshell, it was way too complex.

Most people who write documentation for open source software projects would fall into the category of "power user." They are technology enthusiasts who are not interested in the super-technical avenues of programming, but want to help out. Many of these people have good writing skills and a good knowledge of using the software, so the documentation fit is natural.

With Jokosher we wanted to acknowledge this profile of user. As such, instead of focusing on complex text processing tools, we encouraged our documentation contributors to use a wiki. Those who did not know the wiki markup would use the graphical wiki editor. We got some great contributions because we identified the workflow with the type of contributor.

Building and Maintaining Transparency

Transparency is a key theme not only throughout this book, but also throughout community building in general. Openness is an important ingredient in healthy communities, and your community needs to feel that there is transparency throughout its governance, processes, communication, and workflow.

In terms of workflow, transparency can be divided roughly into three areas:

Tool access
> How open and accessible are the tools that form the foundation of your community and workflow?

Communication
> How open and accessible are the communication channels in your community?

Reporting
> How well do you report what your community is doing?

Each of these areas is important for a healthy community. Let's now spend some time looking into them, and cover some of the key points in keeping your community open and accessible.

TRANSPARENCY FOR NEW CONTRIBUTORS

An important area in terms of transparency is how people who are not yet trusted contributors can contribute to the project to gain trust. This is covered in Chapter 4.

Tool Access

You should always ensure that the tools you choose to use for your community are easy to access, well documented, and freely available.

This has historically been an important factor for most open source projects. If you look at the majority of open source projects, the tools and dependencies they use are also entirely free and open source. An example of this is the GNOME desktop environment. Not only is GNOME free and open, but the tools used to build it also are free and open. This includes the toolkit (Gtk), C compiler (gcc), debugger (gdb), GUI designer (glade), and more.

Although most open source projects use free tools, many projects do use proprietary tools. Some years back I spoke at a Microsoft DeveloperDeveloperDeveloper! Day in the United Kingdom. As an open source guy, I was expecting to be greeted with a healthy dose of suspicion. Not only was everyone incredibly welcoming, but there also was a surprisingly strong sense of community. There were a number of user groups and communities based around Microsoft technology, and in addition to this, many Microsoft fans released open source software, but they used proprietary Microsoft products to produce the code.

Although this is fine, I recommend using freely available tools. Contributing to a community where you can download the tool immediately for free is far easier than having to spend $300 on a tool before you can participate.

When you have decided on your toolchain, you should ensure that it is well documented on your community's website. You should specify:

- The tools that are used in your project
- Where you can obtain the tools required
- Instructions for how to use these tools to obtain the work your community produces (such as the source code for an application) and how to run it

Another useful goal to aim for, particularly with regard to software development, is to ensure that each contribution is documented. Ideally, you want any contributor to be able to point to any of her contributions by referencing a URL on the Internet. If every contribution can be referenced, your community will be transparent by definition.

An example of this is how many open source projects have mailing lists that get posted to automatically with each new commit to the source control system. This simple solution ensures that anyone can subscribe to a list of source code updates. One alternative to a mailing list is an RSS feed of updates.

Communications

Openness in communication is essential. Your communication channels are the very lifeblood of how ideas, problems, and solutions flow between the different members of your community. The golden rule here is to ensure that anyone (including those who are not currently part of your community) can reference every communication online after it has occurred. I would like to be able to go to any community and read conversations that I was not a part of so that I can evaluate the decisions that were made.

This is happening today in most open source projects. Most projects have open mailing lists, and these lists have publicly visible archives that are automatically made available on the Web. Many communities also have small programs called *bots* that log IRC conversations and make the discussions available on the Web.

I would highly recommend making these kinds of archives and logs available. In many cases, doing so is as simple as switching on a configuration option. The only time I consider it reasonable to have private archives is when a communication channel is being run by a Community Council. For many communities, sensitive and private discussions, particularly those around conflict, are taken to the council. There are also conversations that pertain to an individual, such as if a contributor has had some complaints made about him. These kinds of discussions need honest input from the council members, and if archives of the conversation are available, many council members will feel uncomfortable making statements they would otherwise make in private. Just compare and contrast the statements you make in public and in private.

Transparency in communications is not purely about the free availability of archives, though. It is also about ensuring that everyone in your community is welcome to participate and communicate in an open manner. There is one enemy to this kind of participation—*cliques*.

Cliques exist everywhere. Some of them are pronounced, such as the thousands of invitation-only clubs and associations across the world. Some of them are less pronounced, such as the informal, unwritten, yet obvious groupings that occur when we are all at school. There is nothing wrong with groups; they are natural functions of human social interaction. But they can be destructive in communities that are explicit about their openness to new contributors.

I noticed this for the first time years ago when I set up my Linux User Group in Wolverhampton. As the group grew and regular members attended, a sense of familiarity set in. There were insider jokes, everyone knew the regulars, and the group was generally bonding. Although we welcomed new members, we occasionally heard of people being put off due to "cliquishness." Although you should not have overt cliques in your community, you also should not inhibit the ability for people to bond and form personal relationships.

As you continue to engage with your community, there are some members who will naturally group together due to similar perspectives, senses of humor, or other attributions. Encourage and welcome these groups, but always be cognizant of the risk that these groups will be off-putting to new users. Everyone knows what it feels like to feel unwelcome, but not everyone knows what it feels like to be a possible cause of that feeling.

Reporting

The final aspect of transparency with regard to workflow is keeping everyone on the same page. This is all about reporting.

Some time ago, we wanted to improve how different parts of the Ubuntu community communicate what they are working on. We have hundreds of contributors all over the world, each working on different teams, and I was keen to see a single web page from each team with bullet points containing what they had achieved that month.

This was something of a challenge. Reporting is not a natural by-product of community, and most communities struggle at producing metadata such as this. Communities are great at doing the work that interests them, but activity reports and additional information does not flow naturally. The only chance of making this work was to make the process as simple as possible, and to encourage as many people to engage in the process as possible.

The process I developed was about as simple as I could get. I had a set template on the Ubuntu wiki, and each template was named for the given month. I asked all teams to get their feedback in by the 20th of every month. This would leave a few days to tidy up any missing pieces of the report and announce it on the 22nd of each month. For each team, I asked someone to be a team reports contact, and every month I would nag the contact person to get her content in. Some teams would be as reliable as you could imagine. Some less so. In general, though, the team-reporting framework generated some useful content.

The value of the team reports was obvious. They were well received, and it was fascinating and inspiring to see what everyone was working on. The approach I fleshed out could easily be rolled out to your own community. You should seriously consider it.

Another little story I will share about reporting was one that we faced at our Ubuntu Developer Summits (UDS). At every UDS we would have a large number of discussion sessions, and we had some facilities in which people could listen in on the sessions through an audio stream and communicate with us via IRC. Despite these methods of engagement, we still wanted to release a set of proceedings from the summit. This would be a summary of decisions made at the UDS that would affect the development of the next version of Ubuntu.

Our first shot at this was to produce a wiki page for each track at the UDS and ask attendees to update the page at the end of each session. It was a simple process, but it got limited uptake. There simply was not time at the end of the sessions for people to summarize the agreements. As such, we got relatively sparse proceedings for each track.

For the next UDS, we had a different idea. In recent years microblogging platforms such as Twitter and identi.ca (*http://identi.ca*) had become a common part of many people's workflow. It was not uncommon to send out a quick "tweet" or "dent" to let the world know what you are doing. We figured this could be an interesting approach for our proceedings at the UDS.

To do this, we conducted an interesting experiment that worked rather well. Using identi.ca we registered an account for each track at the UDS. In each track room we had the login details for the account on the whiteboard. We would then encourage everyone to microblog as the sessions continued. The final part of the process was to write a script that took each microblog entry and divided the messages into the relevant sessions. As an example, all the messages on the community track between 1 p.m. and 2 p.m. would be automatically grouped under the heading "Making LoCo Teams Rock," the name of the session at that time on the community track.

The moral of this story is that to get effective reports, the method needs to be as low-friction as possible. People were already used to microblogging, so asking people to microblog sessions was entirely natural for many people. This is the essence of effective reporting.

COLLABORATIVE TEXT EDITING

Another useful tool that has been a common staple at the UDS is a collaborative and cross-platform text editor called Gobby (*http://gobby.0x539.de/trac/*).

In the Gobby text editor, multiple people can edit the same document at the same time. You see the changes that other people make in real time in your instance of Gobby. It is a clever little tool.

Gobby is useful when multiple people are working together to record notes for a session or working together on a specification or strategic document.

Regular Workflow Assessment

Like any process, structure, governance, or other agreed method of working, workflow should always be subject to change. Your workflow and the tools that are crystallized in it should always reflect the optimal way in which your community can work. If the tools become too complex and too laborious, you should consider adjusting your workflow, and possibly your tools as well.

An example of this occurred when I was involved in Jokosher. When the project started, we wanted a simple means of tracking issues and problems, and so we used the issue tracker that was part of our Trac development forge. We used the issue tracker for a variety of purposes, and it was simple and effective.

As the project grew, we were building up to shipping a major release. The project had more than doubled in size, and there was a significant chunk of functionality built into the application. When our community was reporting problems in the issue tracker, they had to manually enter a lot of information, and tracking and prioritizing this increasing number of issues was becoming a problem.

After a short discussion on IRC, we decided to move to a full-fledged bug tracker. We chose Launchpad as our solution, and we never looked back. Launchpad was more suitable, more flexible, and the right choice at that point in the Jokosher history.

One of the most useful lessons that I have learned in my community work is that you should regularly reassess everything: your workflow, processes, governance, and anything else. A community is built on a set of rapidly changing people, needs, and requirements. Regular reassessment is important to ensure that your workflow is matching the day-to-day work of your community.

I recommend that you set this regularity now. The length of time before reassessments is really up to you and your needs, although I would make sure to do a reassessment at least once a year.

Gathering Structured Feedback

When performing your reassessment, your aim is to find solid feedback about the good and bad aspects of your current workflow. The real value that you should be seeking is constructive, objective feedback from those who really dig into the workflow. Those community members who are using the workflow day in, day out will have the most valuable feedback for you. Before you consider changing any aspects of your workflow, you should gather an extensive level of feedback and use it to identify correlations in aspects that work and don't work.

A useful technique for getting good feedback is to produce an online survey. There are a number of free survey sites that enable you to produce a set of questions and have anyone fill in the survey. Many surveys also allow you to choose between invitation-only responders and a free-for-all public survey. This is an important decision when running the survey. There are benefits and disadvantages to both. For open public surveys, there is always a risk of getting a lot of inexperienced feedback that is not particularly useful, and this noise can skew the results. On the other hand, public surveys feel more community-spirited: they are open and accessible, and anyone can participate. Invitation-only surveys allow you to choose who responds, and if you choose wisely (read: not just people who will give you good feedback), you can get some great objective and practical results. On the flip side, invitation-only surveys feel closed, cliquey, and restrictive.

I recommend you do both. Start out with an invitation-only survey with at least 10 respondents. When you have this feedback gathered, open up the survey to anyone. Keep the public survey open for a set period (a month is a good amount of time), and promote the survey in places where your community reads and resides. You can then use both sets of results to draw conclusions. I would recommend that you put more faith in the invitation-only survey results, as they come from your key community members, but the public survey will undoubtedly uncover some useful results.

When you have performed your surveys, you should schedule some meetings with your community to discuss the results, propose solutions, and share more experiences. As with normal meetings, these meetings should be very focused on driving to a conclusion: finding solutions to the problems.

Moving On

Building effective workflows is complex. It involves a combination of understanding people, technology, and usability. As is a common theme throughout this book, you should look to simplicity as your inspiration. At every step of the way, you need to ask questions: Is this more complicated than it needs to be? Is this the most effective way to do this? Is my community going to be able to follow this workflow every day and not get frustrated?

Although we covered a range of concepts in this chapter, don't push yourself too hard. Experience and learning from your successes and mistakes is all part and parcel of being a great community leader. Some of the concepts in this chapter will take a little while to settle into your flow.

We are now going to move on to an essential part of leading a community: getting people fired up! We have some great structure in place so far. Now it's time to assemble an army....

CHAPTER SIX

Social Media

"In labouring to be concise, I become obscure."

—*Horace*

YOU ARE ALL WONDERFUL PEOPLE. Every last one of you; even you, Peter in Boston.[1] You are all so smart, so intelligent, and…have you lost weight?

Astute readers may have detected a hint of ass-kissing. Well, guilty as charged. This is not without good reason, though; unfortunately, I am going to say something that might not sit well with some of you. I would be remiss, though, if I wasn't honest and frank with you lovely, intelligent, attractive…forgiving…people.

Social media is completely overrated.

OK, now that we have that gristly chunk out on the table, I can try to claw back your respect and explain exactly what I mean.

Back in May 2008 I sat in a hotel in Prague in the Czech Republic at the twice annual Ubuntu Developer Summit. On the sleepy Sunday afternoon before the event started I was working in the lobby with a group of colleagues and community members. One of those community members was Alan "popey" Pope, a friend of mine who I got to know through LugRadio and who was an active member of the Ubuntu community.

---

1. That should freak at least one guy out…"*the book is talking to me!*"

That afternoon, Alan and a few others were raving about Twitter, which at the time was starting to build momentum but was still largely the forte of geeks and computer nerds. For those of you who are unfamiliar with Twitter, it is a website in which people can send short messages and follow one another's messages.

Alan had become a big fan of Twitter and extolled the many benefits, uses, and general good times of being on Twitter. I, however, stubbornly resisted. Back then, when asked about my views on Twitter, I used the often-trundled-out response of "Why would I want to read about people buying milk and other such nonsense?"

Fast-forward to today and I am a very active user of Twitter. Alan won this one, but not by any conventional means.

Clearly knowing how stubborn I was being (who'd of thunk it, eh?), Alan decided to secretly register a Twitter account in my name (*@jonobacon*) and start tweeting, pretending to be me. Alan and his cohort, Dave Walker, trumped out tweets about me sleeping, thinking about community while in the shower, *communitizing the community with community tools*, and other such high jinks. I discovered their tomfoolery, was amused at their mutiny, yet demanded the login credentials. Now I was stuck with a Twitter account, but I had no milk to buy and no one to tell. Although I didn't want it, I figured I might as well play with it. I am glad I did. It has been an invaluable tool both professionally and socially.

Don't Be That Guy/Girl

In light of my conversion to Twitter use, some of you may be a little confused about why I earlier referred to social media, the umbrella term for Twitter, Facebook, Google+, and other services, as being *completely overrated*. Let me explain. You'd better sit down.

With the advent of social media, the tools that have surfaced as a result of this more social approach to computing have certainly had an impact on the world. Facebook, Twitter, and others have percolated into our lives in different ways and opened up interesting opportunities. Social media has raised the visibility of many campaigns, from the media and movies to those resulting in significant political change in many countries.

They are, however, just *tools*. There are many useful tools in the world that have become new and disruptive to our behavior, but few have been immersed in the sheer amount of hype, nonsensical ramblings, and just pure, unfiltered, salty bull that social media has.

In every industry there have always been *hangers-on*: people who join an industry and just want to be seen, respected, and included in their definition of the "cool-kids club." Typically these people are riddled with insecurities about what value they bring, so they try to accomplish value via association. They try to get invited to the cool parties, attend the cool conferences, and talk about and share articles about cool topics and buzzwords. Of course, let's not forget that *cool* is entirely subjective in this context (often about as cool as a blazing furnace). But you know what? It's fine…these folks exist everywhere, and no harm, no foul.

Unfortunately, social media has been a magnet for some of these hangers-on. In the wake of this new technology, a generation of people have formed who bring little value other than getting into philosophical debates and theoretical hand waving about the who, why, and what of social media without bringing any practical application to those findings.

Now, I get it. I am English, and some of us English folk can be a tad cynical at times. But friends, I have tried to resist taking a cynical view. Oh, I have tried. I have engaged with some of these folks with the hope of understanding the importance of this philosophical layer of discussion, and to hear some substance and practical application of such discourse and ultimately be proven wrong. I would love to be proven wrong. While there are definitely people who have an interest, talent, and value in social media and who use it for real, practical purposes, there is still far too little signal to the sheer amount of noisy, rambling, ethereal nonsense that clogs up the Internet.

Social media really is a *genuinely valuable tool*, but it is *just a tool*. While social media has certainly opened up new opportunities for community and user engagement, the tools are really not the interesting ingredient in the mixing bowl; what is really interesting is how the tools shine a spotlight on the social values, needs, and opportunities that are implicit in humans. These social values have been around since humans started walking (or slithering, depending on your view); the tools are just a means of bubbling these attributes to the surface.

There is a balance to be struck, though. Sure, the tools are just tools, but the philosophy of what social media opens up for us is just philosophy, too. Philosophical hand waving and tool obsession will not grow you a productive, fun, and empowered community; day-to-day application of these tools and an understanding of what lights our social fires will.

I was debating with myself whether I should even share these views in the book, but my responsibility throughout this book is to help you all become successful community leaders and managers. Part of this goal involves sharing skills that you can use in your work, but part of it is seeing some of the social norms and dysfunctions that can form around the work of community leaders and managers. One of these social norms, particularly in the formative years of the profession of community management, is that you will see some of these folks with little practical substance who are more interested in playing debate club than building real value in community. Don't get dragged into that; many of these folks do this to prove their abilities, knowledge, and intellect…but the real proof is not in the academia that can be cited; rather, it is in the community that you build.

In this chapter we are going to focus on the substance of how social media can help you grow and build your community.

THE COMMUNITY CASE BOOK

I'm not convinced that the current generation of social media sites have helped communities to prosper in the way that earlier technologies like mailing lists or even Usenet did. They create a social graph centered on the individual rather than the community. The development of tools to support communities is still an untapped opportunity.

—Tim O'Reilly, on Social Media

Read the full interview in Chapter 14.

Being Social

One of the challenges of talking about technology in books is that technology changes so rapidly that the content can quickly become outdated. This is a particular challenge for a topic such as social media, as we need to talk about specific tools to really understand how social media works. As such, we are going to talk about tools that are prevalent at the time of this writing in 2012, but if you are reading this in 2025 while commuting to work on your jetpack, with your hoverboard under your arm, there are likely to be similar services to which you can apply the same approaches.

Today, in the disappointingly *lacking-in-jetpacks* year of 2012, the following social media networks are the most common:

Twitter

A devilishly simple concept that has taken the world by storm, Twitter allows people to register on the site and send messages of no more than 140 characters in length. (The size limit comes about because Twitter was designed to be convenient for users of SMS text messaging, which had an arbitrary size limit by design.) The site allows you to follow people, see their messages, and even republish the messages. The concept may seem strange to those of you who have never used Twitter, but it has become an invaluable tool for connecting to people and keeping up-to-date with what they are doing and their interests.

Facebook

Another runaway success story, Facebook offers a place for people to provide updates on what they are doing, post pictures, share their interests, and keep up-to-date with what is going on in their friends' lives. Facebook also provides tools for organizing events, creating campaigns, and more.

Google+

While still very new at the time of this writing, Google+ is gaining momentum and provides many similar features to Facebook but in an arguably nicer and more refined way—the *same great social networking taste, just in a Google can*. The major difference seems to be that Google+ is designed for sharing among a plethora of selected groups ("circles") whereas Facebook is still more commonly used for sharing one's life with the world.

Each of these tools can help us with three primary functions that we commonly have in our communities. These are:

Broadcasting
> Social media is useful for sharing events, developments, content, and other things going on in our community. Well-crafted social media channels can communicate our news and ideas to a significant number of people. What's key is not just the volume of content or the number of people who see it, but communicating *interesting* content to the *right kinds of people*.

Feedback
> Social media can be a tremendous tool for getting better feedback on what our community members, users, customers, and other people think about us and our community. Seeing and understanding our work and its effect is a key part of understanding how to do better, and social media can be hugely helpful here.

Collaboration
> Social media can also be a useful tool for collaborating with others, planning events and projects, and more. In addition, it is a useful means of encouraging others to participate in collaborative campaigns and efforts.

Later in this chapter we are going to explore each of these areas and how you can use social media in your communities with some solid examples. First, though, let's take a quick spin through each service and get started using them.

Social Media Services in a Nutshell

There are a great many social media networks around the world, and many of them are focused on specific countries and regions. Here we will take a look at some of the most recognizable social networks.

Twitter

Back in 2006, a little-known podcasting company, Odeo, had a daylong meeting with its board members. Jack Dorsey, one of the members, presented an interesting idea he had been working on: a text message–oriented service for sharing messages between groups. Originally called *twttr*, following the trend of picking a word and removing vowels (which I bet frustrates the Dutch), this is the service through which Dorsey published the first of what would later be known as a *tweet* in March 2006.

Shortly after the first prototype was working, the service was launched publicly. After some modest initial success, the service started to skyrocket in 2007 at the popular *South By Southwest* festival; there the number of daily tweets *tripled*. As Twitter awareness grew, celebrities joined it, as they so often do, and Twitter became referenced commonly in magazines, on television, and on websites. In June 2010, around 65 million tweets were being sent each day. To a cynic, that is a lot of pints of milk being talked about.

Like many technologies, Twitter started out life as a technical curiosity with those who were technically savvy enough to discover such curiosities, but has since become a global phenomenon. Celebrities, politicians, business leaders, community members, and many companies are using Twitter as a primary method of communicating with people. It is not a fad, either; these folks wouldn't use it unless they saw real value in it.

With the so-called Web 2.0 revolution (when the Web became more interactive and dynamic) many start-ups and products tried to become ubiquitous, but Twitter didn't only succeed at bringing a technology to the masses, it created an entirely new medium that is a common part of how many of us communicate online. You don't often see whole new mediums of communication being taken on by everyone and his dog.

As such, Twitter is a service you should definitely be using in your community, even if you are the least technical, most online-adverse group. Twitter is a tremendous fishing net for you to attract community members, as well as communicating to others things that are going on in your world.

WHY TWITTER IS INTERESTING

Twitter is interesting for a few reasons. First, it has become a truly ubiquitous means of communicating with others. Its sheer popularity has become a common reason to use the service, particularly if you want to raise the awareness of your community and get other people involved.

Twitter is also a wonderful medium for encouraging the viral dissemination of information; that is, broadcasting news about your community and encouraging it to be shared again and again as the audience grows. This is largely due to the ease of sharing tweets by *retweeting* (Twitter users sharing their messages with their own followers) and the ease and low friction involved in following a user on Twitter.

Getting started with Twitter

To get started, we first need to understand how Twitter works. Let me explain, using myself as an example.

Through the unusual path I explained earlier, I have an account with Twitter under the username *@jonobacon* (all Twitter accounts have an "@" at the beginning). Using Twitter, I can post messages that are no more than 140 characters long (called *tweets*) to the website. The website tells me how many characters I have left as I type, so I don't have do any counting on my own. As an example, I could write:

Been a long week this week, I am ready for the weekend and ready to relax!

Each message that a Twitter users posts appears on his Twitter feed page, which is at *http://www.twitter.com/<username>*. As an example, my Twitter feed is at *http://www.twitter.com/jonobacon*.

People who have an account on Twitter and who visit my page can click the Follow button there, after which all of my tweets will appear in their *timeline*. The timeline is a chronological list of tweets from everyone you follow. As an example, here are the three most recent tweets on my timeline:

> @Anthrax (Anthrax (Band)) SOLD OUT Anthrax show and Metal Master's Clinic this Monday, Sept. 12! Watch the entire show LIVE on... fb.me/GcVvxr5B 1 minute ago

> @CNN (Breaking News) cnnbrk CNN Breaking News Protesters in Egypt breach wall, enter Israeli Embassy on.cnn.com/r1ZCC8 3 minutes ago

> @sil Getting locked out of my house sucks. It particularly sucks at 4am. 4 minutes ago

Here you can see that I am following the metal band Anthrax, the CNN news service, and a frustrated call for help from a friend. You may have also noticed that there are some short web links in there (*fb.me/GcVvxr5B* and *on.cnn.com/r1ZCC8*); many people use Twitter to share interesting links to different websites and content online.

Importantly, many people don't actually use the main Twitter site to send their tweets, but install a program that helps them manage their tweets from their desktop computer, tablet, or cell phone. There is also Twitter support built into many websites that makes it easier to share interesting links and content on Twitter. We will discuss these tools in more detail later in this chapter.

The first step you should take when signing up for Twitter is to find interesting Twitter feeds and follow them, so they will appear in your timeline and you can start to get used to the culture and style of tweets.

When you see an interesting tweet and feel a burning urge to tell the person who posted it what you think about the tweet or something related to it, you can *reply* to it. To do this, click the Reply link next to the tweet and type in a message (again, no longer than 140 characters). That message will be sent directly, but still publicly, to the person who wrote the original tweet. Inside everyone's Twitter account is a link called Mentions that will show you all of the tweets that highlight your username (e.g., *@jonobacon* for me). You can also send someone a message by just mentioning her username somewhere in the tweet. For example:

> Looking forward to seeing @Anthrax this weekend playing live in San Francisco.

This will make my tweet appear in Anthrax's list of Mentions.

This reply feature is one of the coolest features of Twitter. It means you can follow your friends and your favorite celebrities and send a message that they will likely see. Do bear in mind, though, that as people get more followers, they also typically get more replies, and for celebrities with millions of followers your reply may get lost with a thousand other replies. So you can tell Tom Cruise how much you love him, but he might not see it.

Another useful feature in Twitter is *retweeting*. Each tweet from people you follow in your timeline will have a Retweet link next to it. Clicking this will send that tweet to your followers via your account. This is a great way to share interesting tweets that others may not have seen.

There are, of course, many other features included in Twitter, such as lists, photo sharing, and so on, but here we are covering the key features that are useful for our communities. If you want to find out more, be sure to check out *The Twitter Book* by Tim O'Reilly and Sarah Milstein (O'Reilly).

NOTE

One notable alternative to Twitter (under the general category known as *microblogging*) exists: identi.ca. It works a lot like Twitter, but its main selling point is that it is open source code and encourages other companies to set up other sites running the same software. Identi.ca is popular among proponents of Free Software and open culture. As a start to its goal of open data sharing, it lets you set up an automatic feed so that your postings to identi.ca get reposted immediately to Twitter.

Facebook

Back in October 2003, a young Mark Zuckerberg, who is now known as the baby-faced founder of Facebook, wrote Facemash while at Harvard University. Although the site was initially a hot-or-not type of voting site where you could rate things as being *hot* or *not*, Zuckerberg expanded it and created a social study tool for his art history project. With it he would upload photos and provide a means for his classmates to leave comments on the photos. Zuckerberg then started thinking a lot about how social experiences could work with technology, and created a first cut of these ideas called thefacebook.com.

While thefacebook.com was initially limited to Harvard students, it soon expanded to MIT, Columbia, Boston University, New York University, Stanford, and Yale. As the site grew in popularity, it was expanded to a high school version and then eventually was opened up to everyone over the age of 13 in 2006.

In 2008 Facebook was rocking out with around 100 million active users, but that grew to 750 million active users by mid-2011. Subsequently, Facebook has continued to be a huge success and has developed intense ubiquity as a place where most people can find their friends, interact with them, see status updates, share photos and videos, organize events, and more.

Facebook has also become popular for various campaigns and awareness groups to get involved. Facebook has often been used as a vehicle for showing support for, or outrage toward, a particular perspective. Politically it was used by advocates of same-sex marriage to rally support for marriage equality around the time Proposition 8 in California was in the news. Facebook was used in a more comedic setting with the "Can this pickle get more fans than Nickleback" page. The pickle won (I would have hated to be Nickleback's manager, breaking that news to the band). There are countless other examples of where Facebook was used as a central tool to unite opinion or even coordinate events.

WHY FACEBOOK IS INTERESTING

Facebook provides a number of interesting features for communities. First, it is a great networking tool for meeting other people, and meeting their friends by association. This will expand your personal network and provide a useful means to meet other people who could be interested in being part of your community.

Facebook also provides useful community growth features such as Pages, Events, and Groups. Pages are particularly useful for representing your community online and Groups can be an effective communication tool for communities. Events are a useful and simple means to provide exposure for your community events.

Getting started with Facebook

Compared to Twitter, Facebook is a far more comprehensive platform and has a lot more functionality built into it. Here we are going to cover some of the basics, and there is plenty of help and documentation online for you to discover the rest. First, though, you should head over to *http://www.facebook.com* and register.

On Facebook, every user has a *Profile*, which is basically a web page that describes you. This can include things such as:

Employment
> Places you have worked and where you work right now. When you add a company, you can often click on the company name to see other folks who work there, too.

Beliefs
> Your political and religious viewpoints.

Places
> Places you have lived and where you live now.

Relationships
> Other people on Facebook whom you would characterize as your spouse/girlfriend/ boyfriend, or your family members.

Photos/videos

> Pictures and videos that you want to share with others. You can say who is in these photos/videos through a feature called *tagging*. When someone is tagged in a photo/video, the photo/video appears in that person's own list of photos/videos on his profile page.

A key part of your Facebook Profile is your *Wall*; this is a place where you can post messages about what you are doing. Interestingly, other people can post replies to your messages, and they can post their own messages on your Wall, too. This makes Facebook a lot more social and interesting than some of the other social networking offerings.

With your Facebook Profile all set you can now find and add friends. When you add friends you can see their updates and activity on your *Facebook Home*, which is a rolling list of updates. Let's say, for example, that your old schoolfriend Adam Hoffert is on Facebook. You can search for him using the Search box, and when you find him you can add him as a friend. If he accepts your friend request he will see updates from your Facebook Home and vice versa. You can then look at his friend list and see if it contains people you know, and then invite them to be friends with you; this is a great way to keep in touch with folks.

While most Facebook users primarily just set up and use their own profile to share updates and interact with their friends, Facebook does have some other useful features:

Events

> Alerting people and inviting them to events is simple and effective on Facebook. You can create the event, specify the location, date, and description, and then invite people to the event. Everyone who is invited gets a Facebook message and can specify whether she is coming, maybe coming, or not planning to attend. Facebook Events are a useful tool for organizing community events and getting a rough idea of attendance.

Pages

> Facebook Pages allow you to create a profile page for something (e.g., your community, product, etc.). With each page you can post information, pictures, videos, and more, and people can mark themselves as *liking* the page. When they like a page, status updates sent to the page will appear in the Facebook Home timeline. Pages are similar to groups but are far more viral; I highly recommend that you set one up for your community.

Groups

> Groups provide a means for creating a place for people to join the group and interact with other group members. A Group functions basically like a shared Wall and provides a place for adding group-related content. Groups are useful if you want to build a small community whose members can keep in touch.

Applications

> Facebook also supports a wide range of custom applications, and you have probably seen all the games and other apps that are available there. The Facebook app system is pretty flexible, so if you want to create a highly customized application for your community, this could be another option.

Each of these features can be useful in different community building campaigns. We will discuss this in more detail later.

Google+

A later player to the game, Google+ was launched in June 2011 as Google's offering in the increasingly popular and competitive social networking space. Thanks to the huge success of Twitter and Facebook, Google was no stranger to competing with them. Google had tried to claim the social networking crown previously with its failed Google Wave and Google Buzz efforts, and at its launch you could not help but feel that Google+ was going to be Google's final stab at the social networking crown jewels.

The site provides a service that is somewhat similar to Facebook: Profile with a means to group friends in different ways, post photos and videos, and see one another's status updates. Many initial reviews called Google+ a "slightly more pleasant-to-use Facebook." Where Google+ did get very favorable reviews was in its *Hangouts* video conferencing functionality, which has had very positive praise and active use.

Google has an uphill climb, though. With Facebook sporting so many profiles from a wide variety of demographics, many potential users were uninterested in Google+ because their friends were already on Facebook. Early adopters and tech enthusiasts naturally flocked to Google+ right away, and fortunately for Google the growth continued. Within a month, membership had reached 10 million. At the time of this writing, it is too early to tell whether Google's investment will ultimately pay off and unseat the Facebook king.

WHY GOOGLE+ IS INTERESTING

Google+ provides another social network in which to share and broadcast information about your community, and a means for people to potentially join your community. Today, Google+ is primarily useful as another avenue of growth in addition to Twitter and Facebook.

In my mind, currently the most useful feature in Google+ for community building is its excellent *Hangouts* capability; this is an invaluable tool for community meetings and conflict/dispute resolution sessions.

Getting started with Google+

Google+ works in a similar way to Facebook; you can register a profile and add information about yourself, add photos, and more. Unlike Facebook, though, in which you have one big friend list, Google+ lets you group your friends in logical buckets.

Google+ uses the concept of a *circle*, which is a group of friends with a description. As an example, I have a circle for my team at work, a circle for my management team, one for my closest friends, one for Ubuntu users, and others. Although users can see your friends, they can't see which circles they are in, and this feature provides a nice means of grouping together friends in a way that will not offend anyone. Circles are also useful for gathering groups together for hangouts and other discussions.

Possibly the most innovative and useful feature in Google+ is Hangouts. A Hangout is an audio and video chat feature that lets you chat with either a person or a group of people. Unlike other videoconferencing tools, the Hangout feature feels particularly well designed. When you join a hangout, you see the other people's webcams in a row, and when someone talks, a larger video view shows that person speaking. This provides a particularly immersive and interactive experience. I use a hangout for my team meetings (which includes participants from the US, Germany, Spain, and Egypt) and my meetings now feel far more realistic and "in person" than they did before.

Google+ also includes some other features, such as *Huddles* (instant messaging within circles) and *Sparks* (a means of sharing search topics with others), but it currently lacks many of the features in Facebook (although these may be present by the time you read this).

GOOGLE+ PAGES

Google+ also includes a feature similar to Facebook Pages that allows you to create profiles about a product, community, topic, or otherwise and post content there. I recommend that your community has representation across both Facebook and Google Pages.

Harnessing Social Media

With a better idea of the social networking services available to us and the basics down in terms of how they work, let's now start talking about how you can harness these services for your community. To start, I want to share a few lessons that I have learned about when and how you use your social media resources. Remember, this is *social*, and as such we want to avoid making some social faux pas, which is definitely possible.

One particular social faux pas is not distinguishing enough between your work and social habits and where the lines are drawn. Let me share a little story about this.

I have always done things in my spare time outside of work. In 2010 I was kicking off the Severed Fifth music project, had formed a band, and wanted to see how we could influence the music industry around openness and Free Culture. I got Severed Fifth onto Twitter, Facebook, YouTube, ReverbNation, and others, and I became a content producing machine. I was writing blog entries every day with the tiniest of updates and sharing these updates across the social networks.

While excited about Severed Fifth, I was also keen to ensure that this work did not eat into my day job. So I would never do any Severed Fifth work or post on the Severed Fifth social network accounts until I had finished work at 7 p.m. At 7 p.m. all bets were off, and I would blast content left, right, and center.

A few months later I was at a work event and heard from a colleague that a few community members were concerned that I was working on Severed Fifth content during the day when I should have been working in the Ubuntu community. I knew that I wasn't and I defended my honor vigorously. But then the reality set in.

How were folks supposed to know I was off the clock?

First, how would they know what time I finish work (many were unclear which time zone I was in, too), and would they really notice the timestamp and date of the messages I sent out on the social networks? I soon realized that the social media world doesn't really have a concept of *off the clock*; it is too easy to confuse when you are working with when you are not.

The moral of this story is that as a community leader and manager, and particularly if you work for a company that employs you to work with community, you should ensure that your community has the right impression about when you are and are not working. Although it may seem like a small detail, the community misinterpreting when you are and are not working can affect your credibility in the community.

A useful technique for avoiding this confusion is to write a blog post or article about the topic, get it out on the table, and explain when you will be working and when you are indulging in spare-time hobbies.

NOTE

Don't use your community social media resources for unrelated content. For example, if you are the community leader for the FooBar community and you use the FooBar Twitter and Facebook accounts to talk about your newfound interest in DIY, you are going to frustrate a lot of your community members. Never abuse community social media networks to bring attention to yourself.

Remember, social networks are filled with different types of people from different cultures and with different opinions. When you start working with social media, you will find yourself dashing off messages quickly at a heartbeat's notice, and sometimes a throwaway tweet or message can embody a tone that you didn't intend and give your community members the wrong idea.

In "Being Social" on page 162 we discussed the three primary areas in which social media can be useful: broadcasting, feedback, and collaboration. Let's take a look at each of these now.

Broadcasting

Social media is a hugely useful tool for sharing and broadcasting information about your community. Through social media networks, you have the ability not only to inform and update your existing community about things that are going on, but also to attract and interest entirely new community members. Social media also makes it devilishly simple for people to share your news across their social networks, thus continuing to expand your reach.

For you to effectively broadcast things using social media, you are going to need interesting things to broadcast. This may seem obvious, but it is all too often forgotten. That doesn't mean you need to limit yourself to broadcasting groundbreaking news. Quite the opposite: small details and updates can be wonderfully interesting and provide juicy nuggets that your community and onlookers want to read about.

Here are a few prime pieces of social media meat that you may want to consider sharing:

News

> Your community will thirst after every drop of news they can find. Be sure to have a blog, post plenty of news to it, and share links to the news across your social networks.

Progress updates

> If your community is building something (such as a piece of software, a product, or a service) be sure to share plenty of updates about what new features you are bringing to it. Visual things such as photos, screenshots, and videos are always very popular.

Events

> Be sure to broadcast not only community events, but also the details of how these events are coming together (e.g., the call for papers, the final schedule, the attendee lists, etc.).

Meetings

> Whether you have online or face-to-face meetings, share announcements about them so that people know to attend. Also broadcast the meeting notes/summary.

Accomplishments

> If your community enjoys some achievement (X number of users/downloads, press reviews, testimonials, etc.), be sure to share it.

Statements

> If you need to make a formal statement (e.g., in response to criticism), be sure to broadcast the statement or a link to a web page containing the statement.

Kudos

> It is nice to specifically highlight people or groups in your community for their good work and to broadcast a short message celebrating their work. Kudos goes a long way toward building goodwill.

Each of these types of information is an ideal candidate for broadcasting outward and is something your community is likely to be interested in. Many of the topics you share across your social networks will point to content that exists somewhere else. As an example, you may have a blog for your community with official news and updates, and share messages on your social networks with a link to each blog entry. Another example could be videos that you produce and post to YouTube, or press articles that refer to your community.

Messages that reference these blog posts, videos, articles, and so on are typically a lot more popular than simple thoughts and opinions shared via your social networks. I strongly encourage you to produce and reference plenty of this more substantial content. To provide content reflecting what's important to you, you may want to look into creating resources such as a blog, video feed, or other resources if they don't exist already.

Twitter is an ideal service for this kind of broadcasting. It is useful for a number of reasons:

Ubiquitous

> Twitter is hugely popular. It is almost expected that most communities, companies, and people have Twitter accounts that can be followed by users. You should definitely make the most of this ubiquity and get as many eyeballs on your content as possible.

Flowing

> One of the reasons why Twitter is so popular is that it transiently fits into our lives; we can easily dip in and out of Twitter and it doesn't have to be a huge time sink. Twitter provides a means of keeping up with what is going on in a low-bandwidth way throughout your day.

Easy to follow

> The perfect tweet is one that will encourage the reader to follow you on Twitter and thus see all your future tweets in his timeline. Fortunately, Twitter makes following your content stream as easy as a single click. This simplicity means that it is not uncommon for users to follow many feeds, yours being one of them. The more followers you have, the more eyeballs will see your content.

Insanely shareable

> Another wonderful benefit of Twitter is how easy it makes it to share updates. If one of your followers sees a tweet she likes, she can share it with all her followers with a single click. This not only disseminates your content to even more people, but also improves the likelihood of them following you. Sometimes a single retweet from someone with a large number of followers can bring you a huge number of new followers, who then see all your new messages.

Responsive

> Twitter feeds are conversations: people can respond and reply to your tweets and offer their feedback and opinion. This is useful for expanding your own worldview, hearing new ideas, and responding to critiques. It is also useful if you want to use Twitter to ask for feedback or opinion; people are often very responsive.

To get started, register a Twitter account for your community. You can register multiple accounts if you want (such as a personal account and community accounts). Set your profile picture to your community logo, and add details about the community in the description. You can also add a web link to your community's home page, pointing to the Twitter feed. Configure a theme on your Twitter page to match the look and feel of your community: Twitter offers a lot of flexibility for colors, the background image, and more.

Getting more eyeballs

With your account set up, start posting the types of information and topics discussed in the previous section. I recommend that you strive to send out at least one interesting piece of news each day, preferably more. Our core goal with a new Twitter account is to distribute plenty of content and focus on increasing the number of followers. Regularity of content is what is going to encourage people to follow you, so keep it coming, and keep the tone and grammar professional.

It won't be long before someone will send a reply to one of your tweets. Another effective way to encourage people to follow you, and particularly to retweet your messages, is to be responsive to their replies. When someone replies, send a response as soon as possible and again be polite and respectful. Some replies you get may be positive and motivational, and you can reply to those with thanks and encouragement. Some may be critical or even disrespectful, and you should reply to those with poise and clarifications (or apologies where required).

Another useful tool for getting more eyes on your tweets is to use *hashtags*. A hashtag is any word or phrase you add to a tweet that starts with a hash symbol (#). As an example, here is a tweet from me with a hashtag:

> @jonobacon Be sure to check out The Art of Community! #community

The #community part of that message is a little like a category that you make up on the spot for you to put your tweet in. When people read the tweets on your timeline, they can click on the hashtag and see all tweets (not just yours) that use the same hashtag. Because Twitter messages must be short, people get used to even more compressed uses of tags:

> @jonobacon Be sure to check out The Art of #community

The primary benefit of using hashtags is that when a given hashtag becomes popular, it opens up your tweets to many more eyes from people looking at that particular search term. People who don't know who *@jonobacon* is may be interested in communities and may search for the #community hashtag.

Twitter also has a pointer to *trending topics*, which are essentially hugely popular hashtags. If your tweet fits into one of those topics (don't spam the trending topics, though), it can put thousands or even millions of eyeballs on it. Mind you, when a topic is trending, your tweet will appear on that search term's timeline for only a minute or so before being knocked off by 50 other tweets with that hashtag from the same minute.

While my discussion of broadcasting has focused on Twitter, other sites such as Facebook and Google+ support similar features for sharing messages on their respective profiles. While those are useful, Twitter has thus far been the most effective medium for raising the sheer number of eyeballs on your content. It is recommended, though, that you cross-post to multiple social networks, and we discuss this later in this chapter.

Tuning up your messages

Although all social networks place a limit on the size of each message, Twitter imposes the most conservative limit: 140 characters for each tweet. While you can certainly stretch your metaphorical legs out on Facebook and Google+ and share longer messages, the 140-character limit is actually a rather nice discipline to get used to. As such, I recommend that you take some time getting used to writing short, cohesive, professional messages.

Writing these short messages, complete with the links and hashtags that you may want to include, can be tough. It definitely takes a little bit of practice. Some folks go so far as to use txtspeak to shorten messages (e.g., "chk out my gr8 new articl on my wbsite"), and although it is efficient, it makes you come across like a gangly, angsty 14-year-old. Always strive to ensure that your tone is professional, and not that you live with your mom and play Pokemon alone at night.

There is a useful trick you can use to provide a link to a web address in your message. Although Twitter also provides this service built in, a range of link-shortening services take a long web address and generate a shorter address for use in your social media messages. As an example, the bit.ly (*http://www.bit.ly*) service will take an address such as this blog post from my blog:

> http://www.jonobacon.org/2011/09/13/community-management-crib-notes-conflict-resolution/

and convert it to:

> bit.ly/nN97va

If the user clicks on *bit.ly/nN97va*, it will link to *http://www.jonobacon.org/2011/09/13/community-management-crib-notes-conflict-resolution/*. Your user will still see the same content, but the link won't eat up your tweet. A nice feature of bit.ly is the ability to see metrics about how many people accessed and shared the link.

Avoiding social media overkill

As I mentioned earlier, when I formed the Severed Fifth project, I became something of a social media maniac. I registered accounts across almost all of the different social media networks and posted a lot of content. In my earlier story highlighting *when* you should post, I didn't discuss just *how much* you should post.

Surely this should be simple; I mentioned earlier how you should post a lot of content and post it regularly, so we should post as much as we can, right?

Well, *kind of.*

Although getting a community up and running always requires a certain amount of momentum, there is definitely a risk of *social media overkill.* Unfortunately, I fell into this trap with Severed Fifth.

When I kicked off the project, not only did I post four or five pieces of content in a day, but I had also connected my social media services together (more on this later) to ensure that the same message went out to all the networks. The result of a lot of content cascading across a lot of networks was a bombardment of Severed Fifth information, in epic proportions. While it demonstrated the sheer level of activity going in the Severed Fifth camp, it ended up weakening my messaging to some extent because some folks switched it off due to the sheer quantity of material.

This was communicated to me when I went to an event and a number of people joked about the Severed Fifth Propaganda Machine being dialed up to 11. While they were kidding, I could tell that there was an underlying nugget of frustration buried in the humor. The attitude was news to me, but it was an important lesson; social media is a means to an end, and the means was impacting the effectiveness of the end.

Getting this balance right is difficult. While you should keep the momentum moving with enough content, sometimes a *less is more* restraint is most appropriate.

Key Points About Broadcasting

- Post good content regularly, particularly in the beginning when you want to get your follower count up.
- Proofread your messages.
- Use web address shortening services to squeeze as much text out of your messages as possible.
- Use hashtags to get more exposure to your messages.

- Don't overdo it and bombard people with content; too much can have the same effect as too little: people will stop following you.

- Be careful not to accidentally send out a tweet publicly if it was intended for just one person, or accidentally send an SMS from your phone to Twitter (it has been done in the past with often hilarious yet disastrous results).

Feedback

Having great visibility and the ability to take the temperature of your community is critically important. As we discuss elsewhere in the book, you can track many different types of metrics to give you insights into specific projects, campaigns, and efforts, but getting a feel for the general perception of the community can be difficult. There is no single method or approach that can provide this insight; you instead need to pull from a variety of sources and develop a picture from this data.

Social media can help present a useful set of sources for providing this insight. Social media environments are filled with everyday people, different perspectives, different expectations, and radically varying viewpoints. Social media is likely to be filled with the very people your community touches or could touch. These melting pots of opinion and viewpoints are great places to observe feedback and reactions to your community.

In April 2011 we released a controversial new version of Ubuntu: Ubuntu 11.04. The reason for the controversy was that the desktop edition of Ubuntu was shipping an entirely new user interface that had been created and led by Canonical (my employer). Without boring you with the details, the controversy was largely born out of the view that this new user interface, known as Unity, was not ready for prime time and that it was inappropriate to replace the previous solution, known as GNOME, with this young upstart.

Opinion was deeply divided in the buildup to the release, and the debates were emotionally charged and passionate. On release day (Thursday, April 28, 2011) I was bracing myself for the response. My view was simple: I was fine with critiques and with people not liking the release, but I just wanted folks to give it a try and see what they thought for themselves, instead of reading a blogger's regurgitated bias (whether positive or negative). It was never more important in my career for me to have my finger on the pulse of public opinion.

I tracked a variety of different sources to see this opinion; Ubuntu blogs, press articles, discussion forums, responses to me via email, and more. For most of these resources I had to wait as journalists needed to download the new release (which went slowly because *everyone* was downloading it at the same time). There I sat with all of these different sites open in my browser, rabidly refreshing to see the perspective and opinion.

While I was waiting for the journalists and bloggers to do their thing, the social networks were already ablaze. Instead of waiting and writing one big review, the social media users were commenting on every step of their Ubuntu 11.04 experience in *real time*.

Their feedback started right at the beginning of the chain, with comments about how to find the Ubuntu 11.04 software to download, how the site looked, and the download speed, and then moving on to running the installer, commenting on the different elements of the installation process, and booting the system and taking it for a spin, tweeting every step of the way. It was fascinating, and I sat there drinking coffee after coffee late into the night, glued to the screen, watching this controversial product of six months of hard work being consumed and experienced before my very eyes.

This real-time feedback was invaluable to see. It gave me a new set of perspectives on the Ubuntu experience, perspectives that I shared with my colleagues to help us improve our community and product. Social media is a useful tool for not only this blow-by-blow accounting, but also general feedback, perspectives, and viewpoints among those in your community and the policies, processes, output, and approaches your community encompasses.

Where to look

The current social media networks provide a useful range of resources you can employ to get a better feel for what is going on in your community.

Let's start with Twitter. A natural way in which you can take the initial pulse of public opinion is by looking at the reaction from the folks you follow and the replies they send you regarding topics of discussion in your community. While this will provide a limited set of data, primarily from people you know, it can get you off on the right foot in terms of gathering an idea of what people think.

An invaluable data gathering tool in Twitter, though, is its Search function. With it you can search for anything on Twitter and see real-time results as those searches are updated. As an example, if you type "The Art of Community" into the Twitter Search box while I am writing a tweet that includes those words, you will see that tweet almost immediately after I send it. There are also a host of other services online for analyzing Twitter searches, statistics, and more.

There are two distinct uses for Twitter searches:

Context-specific search
> If the context, and particularly the real-time nature, of an incident is important (such as seeing opinion from attendees watching a presentation), it can be useful to conduct a real-time search for a particular term. For many of these incidents, organizers choose a hashtag and people share their views using the same hashtag so that they can easily see one another's results.

General searches of interest

Inside Twitter you can set up and save searches. It is useful to set up a search for terms that are of general interest to you, and that you will take a look at each day. As an example, I have searches set up for "The Art of Community", "#artofcommunity", "Ubuntu", "community", and "Jono Bacon". Each day I take a quick spin through these searches to get an idea of what people are tweeting about that is related to the work I am doing.

While the context-specific search is useful for keeping an eye on individual incidents or topics, the repeated general search is typically very useful for following topics important to you. This approach helps provide not only visibility onto the Twittersphere, but also an opportunity to reply to comments and inaccuracies where they occur, especially if they take place outside your immediate group of associates, friends, and followers.

Facebook also provides a useful search feature that will show all Facebook comments or posts that contain a given term (especially if that term has a page on Facebook). As an example, there is an Ubuntu page on Facebook, and if I search for that term, it will show the Ubuntu page and another option for seeing references to Ubuntu throughout Facebook. Unfortunately, at the time of this writing it is a little confusing to differentiate between the page and the search results.

NOTE
Another useful data point is to look at which tweets get retweeted and which messages are liked on Facebook and Google+. This can provide some insight into popular topics or decisions.

Debates

Back in early 2010 a debate was raging in the Ubuntu community. The Unity team, who I mentioned earlier, had made the design decision to move the window buttons (icons that close, minimize, and maximize windows) from the righthand side of the window border to the lefthand side.

Now, many of you may not see the big deal with this change, but some members of the community were incensed. In fact, a storm of Chuck Norris–like strength kicked into play. While I certainly don't wish to denigrate the views of those who believed this was a genuine usability regression, much of the carping online seemed to spring from a fear of change. There was some wonderfully reasoned, well-communicated, and evidence-driven discussion, alongside a pretty hefty chunk of argumentative, thoughtless rhetoric.

As I mentioned earlier, my view about these kinds of discussions has always been simple. I like to encourage a culture and environment of different ideas and opinions, and the polite exchange of those ideas and opinions, and I never set out to persuade people to change their perspectives. I do, though, strive to correct and debunk misinformation, presumptions, and in some rare cases, outright lies about the work we do. As such, I always look for where the debates are happening in public so that I can participate and bring some clarity when misinformation or misrepresentation would occur.

Social media was a key tool in helping me to see these debates. In many cases I would often be referenced in a debate (e.g., "Not sure about that, you should check with @jonobacon to see what he thinks"), but in some situations I would see fragments of the debate occurring in my own Twitter timeline or in one of my searches.

With this visibility, I could then get involved in the debate and discussion. This was useful not only for ensuring that we reduced misinformation, but also for learning about new perspectives, feedback, concerns, and positive reinforcement from different members of the community who had shared their views.

Asking for feedback

Everything we have discussed so far in this section has concerned learning about discussions and feedback that are already occurring, often with people whom you don't know or are not within your immediate sphere of influence.

Sometimes, being more up-front and frank is a useful way to get your questions answered. As an example, if you are curious to see what your community (or the wider community of onlookers and enthusiasts) thinks about a particular topic, it can often be useful to just ask them on your social networks (or using a particular Twitter hashtag) and see how they respond. Asking such questions can often result in your community having a very positive impression of you because your openness and willingness to seek feedback from the community tells them you care about them as a community manager and leader.

Before asking for feedback, though, make sure you have a way in which you can see the responses. For Facebook and Google+ this is simple: each message you post also has a commenting feature for people to leave their responses neatly connected to your message. For Twitter, though, you should either explicitly ask people to direct their feedback to you, or even better, use a hashtag. The benefit of a hashtag is that everyone can see the responses, not just you.

Key Points About Feedback

- Set up a series of search feeds in the different social media networks to keep an eye on what is happening.
- Always encourage the use of hashtags to improve visibility of discussions.
- Pick standard hashtags for certain topics (e.g., a specific hashtag for an event).

- Seeing the messages is only part of the challenge; look for the patterns and commonalities buried in the messages and the trends that form.
- Don't just look at social media; augment it with news feeds, blogs, and other mediums.
- Be careful to not accidentally send out a tweet publicly if it was intended for just one person, or accidentally send an SMS from your phone to Twitter.

Collaboration

In March 2011 I had a *brainwave*. Shocking, I know.

Back then, my wife, Erica, was about to turn 30 and I wanted to do something special for her. Using a combination of guile and cunning I organized a surprise party for her at our house. The party, while fun, is not the interesting point of this story; social media is what makes this relevant.

Putting together the party was more challenging than you would think. I needed to do a number of things:

- Invite a bunch of our friends to the party.
- Invite people who are friends with Erica but for whom I didn't have contact details.
- Get an idea of who was coming and who couldn't make it.
- Coordinate with others about who wanted to bring food, who was bringing booze, who wanted to help put up decorations, and other elements.
- Provide a means for attendees to communicate with one another so that they could coordinate a carpool, crash space, and so on.

What's more, I needed to do all of this in secret so that Erica would not get a hint of what was going on. Given that we both work from home, this was going to be challenging; it made phone calls and face-to-face discussions with coconspirators difficult.

To achieve this, I used Facebook for everything. First I created a private event (private events don't show up in the search results) and invited all the friends I could think of who I knew she would want there. Then I looked through Erica's friend list and friended the folks for whom I did not have contact details so that I could invite them, too.

With the Facebook event having a communication area (the Wall), this provided a great means for us to collaborate as a group around the event. People volunteered to bring food, and could ask me what pots and pans we had, how many plates we needed, when everyone should arrive, and other questions.

Every day the full group collaborated around the event, and everyone played a part in making it a tremendous night to remember for Erica. She had absolutely no idea beforehand and was flabbergasted when she found out, and everyone had a great time at the party.

This was a case of a small community forming around a goal (making the party fun for Erica and everyone else), with social media providing the perfect engine to make it happen, along with the tools we needed to accomplish a great outcome. Social media made it simple for me to bring people into our little community, and there was no learning curve required as everyone already knew how to use Facebook. It was a great example of focused collaboration.

Of course, there are many different forms of collaboration, and when assessing what collaborative opportunities are available to us in our communities, we often need to assess what tools we have available because these affect what we can do. Collaboration is difficult to kick-start if people don't have the tools they require to participate. We discussed this more in Chapter 5.

Social media is heavily optimized toward some forms of collaboration and not others. As an example, social networks are fantastic for communication, but at the time of this writing they lack tools for collaborating around art and media, around code and software, and around documents. Of course, by the time you read this, the situation may well have changed, but today I see three primary opportunities for collaboration using social media:

Communication

> The vast majority of content that occurs in social networks involves communication between individuals and among groups. Using my example of Erica's party, all of the collaboration there was focused on planning who would work on what and disseminating information to the group. Social networks are excellent resources for this.

Campaigns and awareness

> Social networks are energized by your connecting to people you want to be connected to, as well as opening up the potential to connect to many others you don't know. Campaigns and growing awareness are fueled by hitting momentum with a message, and social media is ideal for this kind of work.

Events

> As I discussed earlier, social media is also ideal for collaborating around events.

Let's now look in more detail at each of these areas.

Communication

When many people think of collaboration, they often assume it means working together on content. This content could be documents, images, computer code, or anything else. A significant sphere of collaboration, however, involves just keeping in touch with others.

I did some consultancy work for a contracting association that wanted to build a community for its members. When I joined the project, they talked a lot about collaboration and creating a community that could "solve problems together." When I considered their high-level needs, I visualized them in my mind based on my collaborative experiences of working online with folks: identifying what tools are needed, putting those tools in place, training community members in their use, and creating a means of allowing the community to share content so that they could build on it together.

In reality, though, their definition of collaboration was much simpler. Their community was populated by many separate businesses and organizations spread all over the US, and they wanted to see different members of these businesses sharing their experience, knowledge, and insight where it made sense to solve problems, thus providing a useful and valuable resource for everyone.

This didn't require any fancy tools. It didn't need special methods of sharing content. It just needed a private social environment in which people could communicate safely and openly with one another. We used a social network for that, and the results were well received by the members.

What is wonderful about most social media networks (e.g., Facebook, LinkedIn, Google+) is that they not only provide excellent tools for you and your colleagues to communicate with one another, but also allow you to pick and choose how these discussions are presented and to whom. As an example, the Ubuntu community wants their discussions to be accessible and open to all, but the contracting association example I just described needed a by-invitation-only policy and a private environment. Social media provides this flexibility.

Facebook has a feature called Facebook Groups that is particularly useful for these kinds of communication-oriented communities. I recommend you take a look.

NOTE
Google and Yahoo! also provide similar group services. These includes facilities for controlling membership, having discussions, and other features.

Campaigns and awareness

In October 2011 I saw a tweet that was retweeted by someone I follow, about a missing girl in Los Angeles. The previous day the girl had gone to work and never came back. Her parents and friends tried calling her, tried emailing her, and asked around, and they could not get in touch with her. Naturally, they were terrified for her safety, and they notified the police. A missing persons report was drafted and the family hoped and prayed she would come home soon, safe and sound.

One of the family members, desperate for options to find her, reached out on social media right away. She created a Facebook page for the missing girl and posted the missing persons poster from the police to the page. She then notified all of her friends and encouraged her friends to notify their friends, too. The Facebook page soon started getting more and more attention from more people. Not only did the page disseminate information and keep the flame burning to

SOCIAL MEDIA   **183**

find the girl, but it also provided a means for viewers to share their concern and support with the family, thus providing a sense of unity and comfort.

The family member who set up the Facebook page then started sending messages to celebrities in the Los Angeles area asking them to raise awareness about the girl who had gone missing. The celebrities, and folks who followed the celebrities, started retweeting the message one by one, each tweet pointing to the Facebook page with the missing persons poster.

After a few days, the family member who kicked off this social media machine reported that they had located the girl, safe and sound. She could not divulge what had happened to her for legal reasons, but everyone felt a unified sense of relief that she was safe.

Social media played a key role here in providing not only the tools to coordinate such a campaign, but also a simple and effective means of spreading the message. These capabilities make social media the perfect vehicle for raising public awareness of certain issues.

> **NOTE**
>
> Unfortunately, social media can also be used in negative ways, as was the case in the London Riots in 2011 when social media was used to coordinate looting and other violence. As such, be aware how social media could potentially be used in a negative capacity that may impact your work and your local community.

If you want to use social media for a campaign or awareness effort, the key is to build a compelling message quickly, to encourage everyone you know to participate, and to have them encourage others to participate as well. When crafting your message, put together an effective elevator pitch that gets across the goals of the campaign or awareness effort right away and makes it clear how other people's participation can help accomplish the highlighted goals. Most people will need to feel a sense of empowerment to feel motivated enough to support you.

In growing awareness and getting people involved, be careful to not spam or bully people into joining or following this work. The greatest social media awareness campaigns become viral quickly, but don't overstep the bounds of soliciting participation. By all means, encourage people to join and spread the word, but don't spam email inboxes, websites, social media feeds, or other places with your message. That will have the opposite effect and will put people off.

Of course, when you do have a popular campaign on a social media network, be sure to use it for a useful purpose. Unfortunately, many community leaders build all this momentum for people to join and then don't provide opportunities for them to work on. When people take part, be sure there is a clear on-ramp of things they can participate in and be sure to celebrate their accomplishments with the rest of the group.

Facebook pages, combined with Twitter and Google+ to spread the word, are excellent tools for organizing these campaigns and awareness goals.

Events

As we discussed in the earlier example, social media is useful for coordinating different kinds of events, and particularly for grassroots events in your local area.

Some years ago, when some colleagues and I used to do the LugRadio podcast, we organized an annual event where we had guest presenters, arranged an exhibition, and put on a live show of a LugRadio podcast. It was a popular event and we loved putting it together. This all happened largely before the social media phenomenon kicked off, and it was much more complex to organize the event back then.

The reason for this is that LugRadio Live was fueled by the time and resources contributed by community members on their own to help the event be successful. People would loan us projectors, PA systems, and funding for the event. They would come and help form the crew to construct the stage, set up the chairs, help the presenters, and more. Such a collaborative community event hinged on how all these moving parts worked together, and before social media we coordinated this work with literally hundreds of emails going out to a set of core contributors.

These days, you can create a Facebook event and coordinate everything there. Facebook events are not useful for gauging attendance, but they are useful for providing a sense that everyone can participate in his own way, and you will find people contributing their time and services in pleasantly surprising and unexpected ways. You can then extend your reach by spreading the word using Twitter, Google+, and other resources to encourage folks to join you and others.

Key Points About Collaboration

- Social media is great for some collaborations, but not all; consider the best ways it can be used for your community.

- Communicating effectively is a form of collaboration, and social media is a wonderful tool for that.

- Campaigns can be ramped up quickly, but make the elevator pitch quick, effective, and inclusive.

- When people join a social media resource, ensure that they have something to do or collaborate on right away.

- Use all the social media networks together to extend the reach of your collaboration.

- Always be careful to not spam or pressure people into joining your social media campaigns and resources.

Social Media on Your Terms

Those of you who have used social media at all as part of your general day-to-day life or as part of a community will have probably discovered that it can become something of an unwieldy beast. When you have your Twitter, Facebook, and Google+ accounts set up and you have started following, friending, and connecting to people you know and people you are interested in, it is incredible how much time all this social media can take up.

I would go one step further and say that social media can be a *complete time sink*.

As we have discussed throughout this chapter, social media offers a lot of opportunity, but if you are not smart about using it, it can end up running your life and getting in the way of other valuable work and community building. Let's now look at some ways in which you can use social media as efficiently as possible.

Controlling the Fire Hose

If we look at just Twitter as an example, it is possible that you will end up following over a few hundred people. These folks will probably be a mixture of people in your communities, friends, people who you admire, and a few celebrities thrown in for good measure. As you use Twitter more, and if you are particularly interesting, you may end up getting quite a few people following you.

As you start following more people and more people follow you, Twitter can become increasingly hectic. Not only do you want to see the interesting content of the people you follow, but as your own follower count grows, so will the number of responses you get to your tweets. Also factor in all the different hashtags, search terms, and other elements that you want to keep track of.

And the worst thing is that this covers *just Twitter*. You have the same challenges with the other social networks.

Fortunately, there a number of applications that provide better interfaces to the social networks. These applications offer desktop, phone, and tablet integration of the networks and tools to optimize your use.

These tools offer a number of benefits. First, you don't have to continually visit the different social media websites and refresh them to see whether there is new content; each time you refresh a site and there is nothing of interest you waste your time. Second, many of these apps build these social networking features into your desktop, phone, or tablet and provide notifications, updates, and more.

As an example, I just installed a tool called Gwibber that integrates social media into my Ubuntu desktop and provides features for displaying notification bubbles containing messages. It supports posting to multiple social media networks at once, and has an interface for easily performing searches and seeing the content I care about. There are countless other such applications available; I won't list them here because the list will become outdated, but a quick search online will turn up the most popular options.

I recommend that you pick one of these tools and take some time getting to know it and configuring it for your needs. One of the most beneficial elements of these apps is that they typically can be configured to show you the information you care about. As an example, I have Gwibber configured to pop up notification bubbles only for messages that are directed to me (so I don't get a constant stream of irrelevant tweets from people I follow). This means I will take breaks to check tweets posted by others, but outside of these Twitter breaks, I can continue with my normal community management work. If I see a notification bubble with a message, I know it is something directed at me and something I might need to respond to. This prevents me from having to break my workflow to check for messages, particularly ones that don't relate to me or require a response.

Optimizing How You Post

Considering all the social media networks available today, it's likely that a certain subset of people are on all the networks, while others are on only one or two. You will probably want to reach out to as many people as possible, and writing a message and posting it individually to each network can quickly become a real pain.

For instance, when I started using social media, I would create a message on Twitter and then cut and paste it to identi.ca and then also to Facebook. With the addition of Google+, Diaspora, ReverbNation, MySpace, and others, this took a lot of time.

The glorious dream for many of us is to write our message once and see it posted automatically to each network. Fortunately, there are some tools and methods for doing this. In general, they can be categorized as *client-side* or *server-side* solutions.

On the client side, you can install an application that allows you to post to multiple networks. As an example, the Gwibber client that I use in Ubuntu allows me to post to Twitter, Facebook, identi.ca, and many other networks. This means that not only can I type in a message once and it gets posted to each service, but also the replies are collated into a single list.

Many applications offer this functionality, and I recommend that you see which works best for you.

The server-side approach involves finding applications or features available on the social networks themselves that can provide this kind of cross-posting. As an example, I use a Facebook app that automatically posts Twitter updates as status updates to Facebook. This means that I only need to use the standard Twitter website or a Twitter client and my posts automatically go to Facebook, too.

Being Socially Responsible

Throughout this chapter we have talked a lot about technology, but social media at its heart is about the sharing and communication of language, ideas, comments, opinions, and viewpoints. The social media wannabes that I so delicately derided at the beginning of the chapter often obsess about the technology, but speak less about the social rules of engagement that come into play when using these resources.

In our position as community leaders and managers we often have to be particularly socially savvy, and this is especially true when using social media. While the 140-character limit in Twitter is useful for keeping messages concise, it also brings some challenges in how we communicate, particularly on sensitive topics. Here are a few tips for overcoming these challenges:

Be mindful of your tone

Remember that when you are using social media many different people are reading your content. This includes people from different walks of life and different countries and cultures, people who know you at different levels, and people who have differing opinions of you and your community. As such, mind the tone you use, and try to be loose and social, yet professional.

Be appropriate

One of the challenges I have faced over the years is that of striving to always be appropriate, yet breaking the ice enough that people can relax around me. A stiff, formal community manager is a bore, but a lewd, offensive community manager won't last long in a community. I always try to be professional and respectful, but also show my social side, posting messages about music, my life, and my family, as well as various amusing duck-related photos. Being appropriate does not mean being boring, it just means being mindful of not causing undue offense.

Don't always wear the flame suit

Your community, your members, and you are likely to be the victims of flaming, bickering, and trolling at some point. I have seen many community managers feel the need to respond to every message and have the last word. Don't succumb to this temptation. I recommend that you always strive to correct misinformation, but remember that they are just words on the Internet and if you try to debate everyone down, you will probably go mad.

Be careful with mobile

A friend (who was a community manager at the time) told me a particularly amusing story of how he sat on a plane one time with the doors about to close and was exchanging some rather fruity text messages with his girlfriend. Just as the steward asked him to switch off his phone he sent one last message to her to give her something to think about while he was flying, and inadvertently texted it to Twitter. All 800 of his followers got the message in their timelines. Fortunately, he had time to call his brother and ask him to delete it. I don't think I need to outline the lesson in this story. Suffice it to say that if I had seen that tweet, I might have "accidentally" retweeted it. Just kidding....

Don't overdo it

As I mentioned earlier in the chapter, always be mindful of not broadcasting too much material. Social media is awesome, but a constant stream of content from you promoting your community or your projects will likely turn off some folks. Always strive to get a good balance of building buzz without building bile.

Remember also that using social media effectively is a learning experience, and you will build your expertise by using it as well as by observing how other folks use it. You don't have to be a social media expert at the beginning of this adventure. Play with the technology, send out some messages, and learn as you go. You will pick it up in next to no time.

Organizing a Community Event

The year 2008 was a busy one for me. Not only was I in the process of moving to the Untied States to live with my wife, but also I was settling into a new life, was meeting new friends, had just released an album, and had just signed the contract to write *The Art of Community*.

I wanted to write *The Art of Community* to share my thesis on how to build and grow a productive and inspiring community, and I wanted to use the book to trigger more discussion about community management ideas, best practices, and approaches. As I settled into the brutal writing schedule, I was excited about the book, but I still felt like something was missing. Seemingly being someone who prefers to replace sleep with heartburn, I decided there was one additional thing I wanted to work on: a central event and meeting place for community managers.

Like many community managers, I had traveled around the world, trudging from conference to conference to talk up my communities, but I had little opportunity to sit down with other community managers, including those from competing companies, to discuss our craft. Back then, community management was still very much in its infancy, so I assumed the attendance would be fairly small, and an intimate event could generate some really great discussion.

And thus was born the *Community Leadership Summit*, which is now an annual event that attracts over 200 community managers each year. Be sure to put it in your calendar; find out more at *http://www.communityleadershipsummit.com/*.

When creating the event I used social media extensively; what follows are details of how I used social media at the most recent incarnation of the event at the time of this writing, the Community Leadership Summit 2011.

The buildup

For the 2011 summit, which marked the third year of the event, I had nearly all of the organizational elements down pat; the venue, A/V equipment, room layout, scheduling facilities, catering, sponsorship, and other components were a piece of cake to put together. I now had the skeleton of the event and I needed to excite and motivate community leaders from around the world to join us in Portland, Oregon.

To do this I set up a series of social media resources in addition to the event's home page. First, I created a Facebook Event for the event. In it I added all the logistical details of when and where the event was to take place, links to the website, links to travel and hotel details, and so on. I also created a vibrant image for the Facebook Event to attract people to click on it (I included the dates of the event in the picture to really drill the information into people's minds).

In addition to adding the boilerplate details, I posted some content to the Wall to provide a sense that the event was already active. I posted some links to content on the website, details about the focus of the event, attendee details, and more.

Having created the event, I then invited all of my friends on Facebook who would likely be interested or available to attend. When you create a Facebook Event you get an indication of whether people can attend, may attend, or won't attend. This was a useful indicator of likely attendance, although for a free event like the Community Leadership Summit, it is normal for people to say they will attend and then not show up. (In my experience, 50% of the people who say they will attend free events actually do show up.)

At this point I was waiting for people to see the invitation on Facebook and hopefully mark the event in their calendars. Now I needed to expand the publicity of the event across other social networks and resources.

So next I wrote a blog post about the focus of the event, highlighted the dates and location (making them boldface so that they stood out in the blog post), and included some pictures to show how dynamic and people-focused the event is. I posted this on my blog first because it is aggregated across a number of other resources (e.g., some news sites related to the communities I manage). Another benefit of posting the blog entry was that my publicity of the event across social media circles would give me something to point people to in case they wanted to read more about it. It is far more effective when announcing an event to provide a link to a blog entry with all the details and an inspirational and encouraging tone than it is to just post the dates and location of the event.

I then started sending out a regular stream of messages to Twitter (which would be automatically posted to Facebook) talking about different elements of the event as it unfolded. This effort included the following activities:

- I regularly updated the list of confirmed attendees and announced it to encourage folks to see all the cool people who would be at the event.
- I posted about new features in the event as they were confirmed.
- With each sponsor confirmed, I posted about the sponsor, what they were providing, and other related content. This clearly pleased the sponsors as well as giving potential attendees a sense that important companies considered the event significant.

- As the social events were finalized, I posted about the venues, times, and what was going on.
- For this event, some sessions were coordinated online among many attendees, and I posted about cool sessions that were forming.
- I also posted countdown messages (e.g., "Only a week until the Community Leadership Summit!").

From the beginning of this series of tweets, I also picked a hashtag to use (#cls11). This would provide a means for people to meet other participants by sending content to the same hashtag. This also was a useful tool for me to see all tweets to that hashtag to get a general feel for people's views of the event.

Finally, I used one of the Twitter boxes that you can get from the Twitter website and embedded it on the event's website. This provided a rolling list of tweets to the #cls11 hashtag, and also provided a feel that the event was attracting a lot of activity and interest.

At the event

In terms of the event itself, as people arrived, social media also played a key role. Before the event even started, people were using the #cls11 hashtag to coordinate travel, hotels, crash space, meeting points and times, and more. As the main organizer, I was also continually checking the hashtag feed to ensure that everything was fine and people had all the information they needed.

When the event started, Twitter became a particularly useful resource. Many folks tweeted continually throughout the event. They shared notable quotes and comments from sessions, along with takeaways and lessons learned. They interacted with one another and retweeted one another's comments. When I did the opening keynote on the first day, I used the Twitter client on my phone to read a series of reviews about how well I did. I tell you, having a phone with a means of sending and receiving Twitter messaging is really handy at events.

Twitter was also a useful way for people to collaborate throughout the event and share further information. Photos were taken and uploaded online. People shared links to reports, comments, and photos, and used Twitter to get in touch with me and the other organizers.

Running a Campaign

As I've mentioned earlier, outside of my passion for community, my other main passion is heavy metal, and playing heavy metal in bands and solo projects. I have been a huge metal fan since I was but a wee lad, and I have been playing in bands since I was 16.

One of those bands is Severed Fifth. The goal of the project was simple: build a community around the premise of giving the music away for free. We encouraged listeners and fans to participate in spreading the word about the band and the project.

When I started Severed Fifth, it was just a solo project. I wrote my first album, *Denied By Reign*, and released it online for free. Shortly after I moved to the US I started writing the second album but also formed a live band to get out and play the music. With the second album ready, I recorded a demo myself (I played all the instruments and recorded it in my home studio). Then we decided as a band that we wanted to record the full album-length demo professionally.

Doing this was going to require some serious coin, but I came up with a cunning plan: let's see whether our community would support us and help fund the recording of an album. This album could then become a good example of a Free Culture-supported project, thus demonstrating the potential of this new music industry model. And thus the Severed Fifth Recording Campaign started.

The preparation

To get things off the ground, first I set up a PayPal account to receive the funds. Then I created a page on the Severed Fifth website where people could make a donation. Originally I simply wrote some text on the page to encourage people to contribute, but then I had the idea of doing something more visual; namely, a video.

Using a small video camera, I filmed myself speaking to the camera. I explained how we planned to influence the music industry via our new model, and how contributing to the recording of the album could help us contribute to moving the industry along. I embedded the video on the page and put the donation box next to the video. The method of receiving payments was now good to go.

In addition, I ensured that I had social media accounts registered across a range of networks. I set up accounts on Twitter and identi.ca, created a page on Facebook, and created accounts on more music-centric sites such as MySpace, ReverbNation, Last.fm, and libre.fm.

ReverbNation was a particularly useful resource here. It allowed me to enter a message and then it would send that message to all connected accounts, which included Twitter, Facebook, and MySpace. This provided a simple and effective means for me to maximize the outreach of the content.

The buildup

I then started an intensive campaign to raise awareness of the Severed Fifth Recording Campaign across the different social media resources. As the donations rolled in, I regularly updated followers about how we were edging closer to our goal. I also highlighted those who gave particularly impressive donations; we had a few $300 donations come in, and I specifically highlighted and wrote a blog post about their tremendous generosity.

As the weeks rolled on, I regularly provided a series of blog updates that I pointed to across the social networks. I also used video continually. I put together a few update videos summarizing much of the great work and contributions going on in the community, and I also released a video highlighting all of the contributors as well as the countries they were from. This not only gave the contributors a pleasant surprise for being included in the video, but it also showed the sheer number of folks who donated and the truly global source of the donations.

In the end we raised over $4,000 to fund the album. It was another example of the power of community and the generosity and belief that people can have in projects that resonate with them. Many thanks to everyone who contributed!

Providing Community Updates

One of the most effective uses of social media is to disseminate news and information about what is going on in your community. This is something we have used extensively in Ubuntu and I want to share a few tips and tricks here.

You should make a point of ensuring that your community is well represented across the social media networks. Be sure to register a Twitter account for your community, a page for it on Facebook, and information on other networks where appropriate.

The Ubuntu community is a large one, distributed across a number of different teams, so we registered a series of different Twitter and Facebook pages to represent each team. Likewise, we have many different websites for these different teams, and have integrated boxes with recent tweets across those pages as well. When a piece of news is ready to share we make a point of sharing it over the most relevant resources, and often cross-posting to all where it makes sense.

CHAPTER SEVEN

Building Buzz

"A wise man will make more opportunities than he finds."

—*Sir Francis Bacon* [1]

ON FEBRUARY 17, 2000, BEN, MY PAL FROM UNIVERSITY, PICKED ME UP FROM MY STUDENT HALLS OF RESIDENCE IN WOLVERHAMPTON. Delicately held under my arm was a large cardboard penguin and a spindle of Linux CDs. This was a special day: Microsoft Windows 2000 was released.

Just a few weeks before, on the other side of the world in Arizona, Deepak Saxena had an idea. With the looming release of Windows 2000, Deepak wanted to see Linux user groups and open source enthusiasts take to the streets to spread the word of open source. Deepak saw the opportunity, and was determined to make it count. He decided to convert a major milestone for Windows into a "Linux Demo Day" when thousands of Linux supporters would evangelize their love of free software.

Within a few weeks, Deepak had persuaded many of the companies in the Linux space—including Caldera, EST, Linuxcare, Linux Central, Linux Mall, Red Hat, SGI, SuSE, Turbo Linux, and TuxTops—to contribute to his cause. He had publicity from some of the largest online tech news sites, and over 150 Linux user groups interested in joining in. Deepak's little idea had become a coordinated worldwide effort.

1. No, he is not my uncle.

195

My group was one cog in this global machine. Five of us climbed into Ben's car, which he drove at a disturbing speed to nearby Birmingham. We proceeded to visit computer and software retailers, bookshops, and libraries, and in some cases, walk up and talk to complete strangers. Unlike those strangers, we were unfazed.

Throughout the day, we explained and reexplained why open source was important. We talked about the ethos, the belief, and the community. We applied our enthusiasm to the slightly bemused subjects before us. It was a long day, but as we drove back to our native Wolverhampton, we were proud of our efforts. Our unity warmed us on that cold day in England.

Deepak's Linux Demo Day demonstrates the potential of community advocacy. Driven by a compelling reason to get out of bed and fueled by a combination of simple tools and elbow grease, the result was stunning. Whether or not the actions of February 17, 2000 had any impact on Microsoft is irrelevant. What was fascinating was the mechanics: the way in which a volunteer community rallied together behind a shared ethos on the same day, all around the world.

Deepak created *buzz*. He generated interest, excitement, and a willingness to contribute to a shared campaign.

This chapter dissects the science of buzz. Buzz is an important part of our community, and it is important that we get it right because missteps can often be problematic. As such, we will first discuss the key attributes of great buzz, what to avoid, and how to articulate ourselves. We will then move on to discuss the *buzz cycle* and the practical implications for different methods of building buzz around your project.

Mindshare

Every year without fail, an article bubbles its way to the surface claiming that this is the *"year of the Linux desktop."* Each time, a new journalist steps up to the plate, and each time the journalist gets it wrong. Although once an exciting and testy headline, today it is one big cliché.

The so-called "year of the Linux desktop" is commonly understood to indicate when Linux seriously threatens the market share of Microsoft and Apple. Year after year, we see these claims, and to be honest, I don't blame the journalists. We are bombarded with articles claiming huge growth in Linux. We hear about people migrating; new deals; large companies and governments switching over; and Linux features in magazines, books, and even television shows. It is easy to feel like those of us on the Linux side of the fence are rocking the world.

In our scramble to find party hats and shot glasses, it seems the analysts want to rain on our parade. Some cite 1% market share, some 5%, and some 20%. Whichever you choose to believe, the analysts are far more conservative. This rather predictably sets off a lengthy debate about whether you can count software that can be freely copied, over and over again.

You know what? In the end it doesn't matter.

Some vector within the great mythic noosphere, the "sphere of human thought," probably knows exactly how many Linux desktops there are in the world, but actual usage doesn't mean a bean in the scheme of things. What really matters is *mindshare*.

Mindshare is perception. It is a global gut feeling. Mindshare and perception is the magic that wins hearts and minds. It is also the explosive, seductive substance that clears the path for change, and it is mindshare that enables communities to have a voice.

The Mindshare Opportunity

Jamie Oliver is a television chef. Known in England for his young and fresh approach to cooking, he has always been popular with foodies and amateur cooks alike. Despite career success, Jamie was not content. He wanted to change something very specific: school meals.

The United Kingdom faced serious health problems in school kids. Obesity had doubled. Eighty percent of kids predominantly ate junk food, and the food parents were giving them was not exactly healthy. In a typical lunchbox, 55% of kids got potato crisps, 40% got a chocolate bar, and 33% got a carton of a sugary drink.

A significant part of the problem had to do with the meals served to kids each lunchtime in school cafeterias across the country. Every day, 3.2 million kids were served on a budget of merely 68p. Unfortunately, that 68p was seemingly funding fried food and other junk.

Jamie wanted change. Although he had a television show about the topic and a reputation, he knew he couldn't change this alone. He worked hard to make the issue one that the nation cared about. Articles, blogs, radio shows, and other mediums were behind Jamie's campaign. After a few months, it seemed that healthy school meals were the hot topic all over England. Jamie achieved mindshare.

With mindshare came change: meetings with the prime minister, new government guidelines, and better school meals for kids. Jamie got the entire country behind his crusade, and kids now have a better shot at a healthier lifestyle.

Mindshare has two potential outcomes, depending on which side of the topic you sit. If you agree with the campaign, it reinforces and strengthens your will and perspective. For those who are not on board, mindshare often causes them to reevaluate.

This harks back to our earlier example of Linux. In recent years, Linux has generated tremendous mindshare. The software and its formation have inspired a generation of technologists, who have in turn inspired others. This mindshare has caused many to reevaluate their choices in computing.

This was particularly the case around the time Windows Vista was released and a new buying cycle opened. Many organizations faced stiff hardware requirements for Vista, so it was a great time to evaluate alternatives, and both Linux and Apple prospered.

The Building Blocks of Buzz

In this chapter we want to build excitement and mindshare around our communities. We want to motivate, inspire, and encourage people to join us and achieve our goals together. If we get this right, we have the opportunity to build a great team and make some incredible things happen.

While some of you reading this book may have a marketing background, it is important to stress that traditional marketing strategies probably won't wash with your community. You can't rely on press releases and advertising; you can't depend on buzzwords and slogans; and often you can't easily measure the impact of your message. Whereas marketing traditionally requires a budget, no budget is required here. Buzz in this world is subtler and more organic.

While we are making comparisons to traditional marketing, it is also important to note that the process of building buzz in community does not need to be centralized. You don't need to appoint a marketing manager for the community and have everything go through him. You should instead encourage everyone in your community to learn the skills behind building great buzz.

This harks back to business expert Peter Drucker's often-cited lesson that great customers help create great customers. You should likewise help your contributors encourage and enthuse other contributors to join the community. I would highly recommend that you send this chapter to your contributors in your project to help them learn the building blocks of buzz.

The Mission

Every community has a mission. Back in Chapter 2, we kicked off our strategic plan with our mission statement. In it we documented what we are setting out to achieve with our community. Your mission is critical to building buzz. First of all, you can't expect to generate excitement around an idea you can't articulate, so by developing a mission statement you sow the seeds of buzz. Second, developing a mission statement trains you to describe your goals and excitement succinctly. The mission is what will pique the interest of your next generation of community members.

The ideal mission statement is concise, specific, and functional; we worship vigorously at the altar of conciseness. Unfortunately, being concise, specific, and functional is not going to excite your potential community members. They are not going to get excited about strategic plans either. They are not going to get excited about governance, and they are most certainly not going to get excited about processes. Our mission needs to dim the lights, throw on some Barry White, and get...sexy...

Uniting Together

Buzz is all about excitement, and excitement is about dreams. We need to present a dream so compelling that it will inspire people to join you to make it happen. Let's begin by taking some inspiration from politics.

I know what you are thinking. Politics? Sexy?

Although too many politicians focus on themselves, politics is an activity engaged in by communities. Political parties in democratic countries cannot achieve their goals without widespread support from those they govern. They gather this support by presenting a dream of the future that appeals to the electorate. Each of these activities has parallels with community building.

The similarities go further. Politics is, in essence, not all that interesting. Political parties spend their days arguing over policies, manifestos, taxes, inflation, and the other details of government. Around election time they have to transform these eye-glazingly mundane concepts into exciting statements that inspire a nation.

An interesting example of this happened in 1996. Putting political persuasions to one side, let's explore how the New Labour party built momentum around its political initiatives. It all started when a rather young and grinning Tony Blair became the leader of the opposition party in the United Kingdom.

Back then the country was deeply dissatisfied with the ruling Conservative Party. Prime Minister John Major had failed to enthuse the country, and the party was riddled with allegations of sleaze and political unrest. But despite multiple attempts to gain power, the Labour party had failed to unseat the ruling Tories for 18 years. Labour was branded by many with a "second-prize" political reputation.

Then, Tony Blair gave birth to his concept of New Labour. He was personable and different, an instant antithesis to the plain and stuffy political norms of the day. Blair formed his team and came bounding into visibility with his mantra of "New Labour: Because Britain Deserves Better."

Blair wanted to enthuse the electorate. Reams of inspiring, motivational language were unleashed on an unsuspecting British public. Consider these examples from the 1997 election manifesto (see *http://australianpolitics.com/uk/labour/97-labour-manifesto.shtml*):

> I believe in Britain. It is a great country with a great history. The British people are a great people. But I believe Britain can and must be better: better schools, better hospitals, better ways of tackling crime, of building a modern welfare state, of equipping ourselves for a new world economy.

> I want a Britain that is one nation, with shared values and purpose, where merit comes before privilege, run for the many not the few, strong and sure of itself at home and abroad.

> I want a Britain that does not shuffle into the new millennium afraid of the future, but strides into it with confidence.

Pretty stunning stuff.

Although younger than his opposition, Blair was a savvy political player. He knew that the British public had lost faith not only in the Tories, but also in politics itself. He knew that the first time people read, watched, or heard about New Labour, he had only seconds to grab them and build their support. He needed to build buzz, quickly and efficiently.

As part of this, he developed what Labour called a "Pledge Card." This small card was carried by politicians and listed five concrete promises. Back then, the combination of "concrete promises" and "politicians" was not typical in British politics. Blair's approach was honest and frank, and the nation responded. On May 1, 1997, Tony Blair's New Labour party was elected into government in a landslide victory. Labour achieved the highest number of seats in the party's history. I remember when it happened. I had a bowl haircut. The country felt invigorated and full of hope for a bright new future.

Inspired Words

A critical component in Labour's victory was its ability to inspire. Words were carefully chosen to be visionary but not tacky. However, these words would have meant nothing if it were not for the underlying message and confidence in Tony Blair that promised a brighter new future.

Labour's words offered huge hope for many who were disillusioned with politics. They spoke of "renew[ing] our country's faith," they talked of "our contract with the people," and Blair dreamed of "a Britain which we all feel part of, in whose future we all have a stake, in which what I want for my own children I want for yours." Blair's ability to level himself with the rest of the country and inspire a joint feeling of change was a work of genius.

When delivered well, this kind of motivational writing can make those little hairs on the back of your neck stand on end. The use of words such as *vision*, *faith*, and *future* helps to paint the dream of freedom, opportunity, and in some cases, healing old wounds. This is the language that will inspire your future community members, and you should endeavor to use it where appropriate.

The greatest inspirational writers are those who have been exposed to great inspirational writing. There have been many great orators throughout history: Winston Churchill and Martin Luther King, Jr. to name just two. Many websites have recordings and transcripts of their speeches. I highly recommend listening to or reading them and identifying the parts that you find most inspiring. Watch out for that tingly feeling up your spine. It is that feeling that we want to create.

Inspiration is not limited to real politics. Many movies, TV shows, and books include powerful, inspired speeches written by hugely talented writers. I recommend watching Martin Sheen as President of the United States in *The West Wing*. He delivers some exceptional neck-hair-raising monologues.

There is no secret recipe for creating community enthusiasm. There is no blueprint. It is as organic and unique as the very community you wish to grow. The most important tip to remember about inspirational messaging is that it must be genuine. Whatever path we follow to build our communities, our leaders must instill a sense of trust and representation. The enemy here is in appearing contrived and disingenuous. Our inspiration must be natural and genuine. If you are real, your community will see that.

Unfortunately, it's easy to risk being seen as a fake. The word *community* has been twisted and contorted to mean many things over the years, some of which don't exactly fall in line with what many of us would consider a community.

The reason for this is that the word *community* almost always conjures up a positive mental image. It alludes to togetherness, compassion, and equality. As such, it has been a target of hype and hot air. If an organization, company, or individual wants to be seen in a positive and engaging light, liberal use of the word *community* makes sense.

There will always be a natural tension between the inspiring speaker and the audience. The speaker will always have a goal or agenda of her own, but needs to strike a balance between honesty around her personal ambitions and an assurance that she takes the wider values of the community to heart.

If your definition of community does not extend to the common expectation of volunteer environments, you will receive short shrift quickly. Readers seeking to build communities around commercial products should be particularly cognizant of this risk. Always remember that whatever their focus, communities are organic units of interest and collaboration. They live and breathe on an understanding that community efforts benefit the community as a whole. Anyone who tampers with that ethos will face problems. This is a critically important point, and I recommend that you read this paragraph again twice. Go on, I will wait.

Becoming the Advocate

When we build buzz, we enter into a relationship with the audience. Advocates and salespeople each enter the same approximation of the relationship, but the rules of engagement vary. Both of these different roles encourage adoption of a product, technology, or lifestyle via positive messaging and reinforcement. How they differ is in how the person who is performing the messaging is perceived.

I have always considered myself an advocate. I define advocacy as the putting forward of a positive message and investing one's personal reputation in that message. Advocates recommend only products, technologies, and lifestyles that they personally subscribe to. Those people on street corners who want to talk your ear off about human rights are advocates. They may be annoying, but they genuinely live their message. For them it is not a job; it is a lifestyle.

Sales are different. Some (not all) salespeople exemplify the philosophy of "I could sell ice to Eskimos." In other words, they take pride in their ability to make the sale. The pride is in being convincing and charismatic. As such, salespeople are often able to detach themselves from the product they are selling. They can effectively work for any company that sells something.

I used to work at OpenAdvantage, a government-funded organization tasked with spreading open source software in the West Midlands region of England. Every year my colleagues and I worked with hundreds of businesses, charities, educational and governmental institutions, and individuals. OpenAdvantage was a vendor-neutral playground. We could recommend whatever solutions we liked to our clients. This became a trial by fire. In my two years there, I tested hundreds of different tools, systems, and applications. In that time we developed preferences that were personal and not mandated by any other agreement or contention. Like any government-funded project, it had a time limit. We had two years. Around six months before the sand was due to empty out of the hourglass, I started looking at other opportunities.

At this point I discovered I was really an advocate: I found it near impossible to consider working for a company that made something that I did not 100% choose, believe in, and make part of my life. I did some stringent analyses on the products I used every day, and this is how I came to work at Canonical: Ubuntu was my choice of operating system.

This makes life tough for an advocate. It means that in your heart of hearts, you can get out there and shout from the rooftops only about what you truly believe in. It also requires that implicit honesty in both directions: if your product sucks, you don't cover it up but instead try to fix it.

The upside is that when people know you are an advocate, and know this is how you tick, your opinion *really* counts to them. Advocacy requires trust: you are putting your belief behind your words. If people like you and trust you, they are likely to trust and like what you are advocating.

Getting It Right by Not Getting It Wrong

Trust is complex to achieve and easy to lose. Months of positive moves are required to gain it, and one misstep can shatter it. With trust comes responsibility, and you have a responsibility to approach your buzz in the way that you would want others to approach you.

Making a lot of noise is easy. Spammers do it. They send out millions of emails advertising a product without any concern for whether the recipient might be interested. The last time I checked, I really didn't need Viagra. Out of the millions of emails that they send, some tiny proportion of people will buy spammers' products. With email's low cost to send, the cost of annoying the world is relatively cheap and the financial rewards are real. Unfortunately, becoming the scourge of the Internet is a price some people are willing to pay.

Of course, the major problem with spam is that it is unsolicited. I don't choose to receive emails about Viagra and Cialis. I never signed up for an announcements mailing list. I never informed anyone that I wanted to receive that email. I received the email purely because I have an email address. Spammers don't care who receives the spam, and anyone who can, will.

To avoid the disgust that this provokes, we need to always ensure that our buzz is relevant. When we seek to excite and inspire people to join our community, we must target the right demographic. Our buzz always needs to be honest.

We are all human, and we will all be tempted at some point to target those outside our demographic. Don't. Sending unsolicited messages to people, no matter how you do it, will not only frustrate many people, but could harm your community. Who would want to join a community with a reputation for spamming? I certainly wouldn't.

Honesty

Unfortunately, honesty is more complicated than you may think. It is not just about the black-and-white approach of not lying. Even the kindest hearts can sometimes get a little carried away with buzz building and promote an image and a culture that is not entirely representative of the reality. It is tempting to lavish a more exciting spin on your community.

Don't be tempted into building a false prophecy: it never works. There is nothing wrong with getting excited and enthusiastic. Tell the world your community has grand ambitions, and inspire people to join. Just don't sell your prospective contributors a story that doesn't exist. Don't tell them you have achieved things you haven't. Don't tell them you have more people involved than you do.

Community is all about transparency and openness. In such a frank and unclouded environment, such exaggerations and fibs will be outed sooner than you think. When such nonsense is revealed, it causes a lack of faith in you and your community. Remember, *trust is a non-negotiable requirement of community leaders*. Don't risk it.

DON'T BUILD YOURSELF UP BY TEARING OTHERS DOWN

Buzz is a great thing. It's all about the glass being half full. It is about celebrating opportunity, and identifying what collaboration can achieve when we all share the same passion.

Unfortunately, some communities and leaders feel that spreading negative energy is an acceptable way to further their own communities. Second to fibbing about your community, disparaging another community for your own benefit is about the worst thing you can do. It makes you and your community appear petty and indignant. Unfortunately, particularly in online communities, this happens more often than not.

As members of your community get more and more well known (and this could include you), a sense of representation often sets in. People begin to feel that they need to not only defend the community at all costs, but also to do it publicly. We then see disagreements and spats played out in embarrassing detail, making the participants look like overopinionated teenagers.

Setting Up Your Base

Many see buzz as a one-way street, analogous to television. They see it as a broadcasted message that people consume. They also see our primary goal as producing a message to be consumed. This is really only half of the goal.

When building buzz, we need to understand what we want. Our buzz is about our community and what our community achieves. When people experience our carefully crafted messages, what do we want them to do? What is *their* next step? What is *our* next step?

A website is *essential* to achieve this. Whether your community is focused around technology, knitting, animal welfare, supporting the poor, or otherwise, a website is a critical resource that you should build and maintain. The ubiquity of the Internet and the low cost of equipment to view it have made an online presence the storefront for your community. If someone hears about your community, the first step he will take is to search for it.

Whether someone hits your website because he stumbled upon it or whether he read about it as part of your buzz, now is the time to grab his attention. You need to enthuse him and pump him up, and while he is engaged, get him up the ramp to be a contributor as easily as possible. Unfortunately, many communities don't do this very well.

Some still see the Web as a largely static medium. You put up a web page, and once it is up, it never changes. These folks see websites merely as electronic information leaflets. My brother Martin used to be like this.

Martin is heavily involved in conservation, and he runs an organization in Northern England called Rotters (*http://www.rotters.org/*). He and his family worked hard to secure land and set up facilities to perform community composting, train ex-prisoners and unemployed members of the local area, and run events. One such event is his woodland festival: a cornucopia of rural attractions, including metalwork, chainsaw tree sculpture, performance art, and live music.

Martin is an outdoorsy guy. He spends all day every day outside with his work. He is the kind of guy who just enjoys being knee-deep in mud and soaked to the skin on a cold English day. Yes, he is mad. Martin was never much of a computer guy. His organization's website was a fairly boring-looking page with information that was once current but never got updated.

But computers became more intrinsic to his life and his organization. He started keeping accounts there, printing fliers and other publicity material, and using eBay to buy and sell equipment. Before long, he and his team rebuilt the website into a vibrant resource about the organization. It had pictures, stories, news, and more. Since the website has been refreshed, Rotters has received more publicity, members, and interest.

Your website is your community's Embassy of Buzz. Make it rock.

Aims

Building a great website may seem like a daunting process. The foundation, though, is simple. Your website should seek to satisfy the following aim:

> Provide a current resource that answers questions and maintains a relationship with the reader.

Write this down and stick it on your wall. Tattoo your children with it if you need to. Let's break this down into key areas. Keep these aspects in mind when considering how to build your site:

Great overview
> If I visit your website, I want to be able to get an overview of the community, its goals, and how to get involved, all within the space of a few minutes. This information should be up-front, easy to access, and easy to read, and should have a simple web address that you can point people to (e.g., *www.myproject.com/overview*).

Great documentation
> Your website should provide documentation and guidance for all aspects of your community. This will always be an ongoing process, but you should consider which aspects of your community are most important and need to be documented. As an example, the process that new members follow to join your community should be a priority.

Great communication
> You should ensure that it is really easy for people to get in touch with you with questions, suggestions, and feedback. I recommend that at a minimum you have an email address that is easy to access. This is a notable problem with many blogs. Many blogging tools (such as WordPress at the time of this writing) do not provide an easy-to-access contact link, and this can make it impossible to get in touch with the author of the blog.

Building a website is a little like painting a picture or writing a song: it is never finished. Creative types always want to add a last fleck of paint or final flourish on the guitar. With a seemingly endless stream of possibility with your website, you need to prioritize. To do this, write down a list of everything you want to achieve, and then order it by what you consider most critical. Naturally, elements such as the contributor ramp should be near the top of the list.

Staying Current

The most important element in any website is content, and the most important golden rule with content is that it needs to be *current* and *accurate*. Of course, those two terms are somewhat intermingled: content about your community that is on your website from 1998 is probably not going to be all that accurate anymore.

Creating current content is a two-part process. First, your community processes and methodologies need to be up-to-date. There is nothing more frustrating than joining a community, following the published guidelines to get involved, and then being told that the guidelines are out of date and that you need to adjust your work. That is a surefire way to annoy new contributors.

The second area, and the area that fits in neatly with buzz, is news and updates. Your site needs to be a window to exciting content about the community, and this window needs to be updated regularly. If you want people to keep coming back to your website, you need to give them a reason. That reason is fresh content.

You should build a strategy for publishing news. This in itself may seem like a simple task. I know what you are thinking: "Jono, I will just regularly post something new to the website. Simple!" Not quite.

Many communities struggle with regular updates. People simply get busy. People get distracted. Other priorities in the community take over. If all of your news gets posted by one person, and that person decides to spend evenings redecorating a house instead, you lose. When people get busy, they tend to drop nonessential and nonfun tasks. News updates are often one of these first casualties.

So divide this work among a number of contributors. Find three or four people who are happy to update the news site, and talk to one another about what news you are going to post.

GREAT CONTRIBUTORS CREATE GREAT CONTENT

It is always important to build out a set of contributors who can bring real value to your website. As an example, O'Reilly's Radar site started out as Tim O'Reilly's personal pulpit, but then expanded as he found other people inside the company who had interesting things to say along the same lines, and eventually people outside the company, too. A lot of people are posting to Radar now, but each is personally chosen and vetted.

Naturally, they don't all have the same opinions and viewpoints, but each one in a way conveys a message that technology is interesting and should be approached with enthusiasm, along with care and a willingness to challenge. We want to try to accomplish the same goals with our community websites, too.

Building Conversation

Posting news is one way to keep a website current. There is, however, another approach to keeping your site alive: *conversation*. The Internet has become an incredible place to have conversations. Countless forums, websites, and blogs have provided a medium in which anything and everything can be discussed. You should ensure that your website is in on the action.

Conversation and commenting facilities are an incredible way to make visitors feel that they have input into the community. These facilities are typically fairly simple: a blog or news entry is posted, and readers can leave a comment underneath the content to share their thoughts. This has two benefits:

Regular content
> Conversation is content that other people provide to your website. Your visitors will come back to participate in the conversation, and your website will always be fresh and full of new and interesting things to read.

Engagement
> Allowing any visitor to the website to post an opinion or comment is an incredible statement about engagement. Providing this facility says to all of your visitors that your site is open and always welcoming comments.

These two features in themselves are justification enough for having these facilities on your website, but there is one reason that is even more important: *community*.

If you allow people to participate on your website, building a reputation tied to their name, community will thrive on your website. Community growth is our end game, and growth happens around conversations.

I have experienced this in a number of places, with the most personal being my own website at *http://www.jonobacon.org/*. For a number of years I have had comment facilities on my site, and over the years I have developed a regular readership that comes back to contribute to the topics of the posts. If this is possible on an individual's website, just imagine what is possible on a community's website!

KEEPING THE CONVERSATION FLOWING

Providing commenting facilities is only the beginning of growing community on your website. To do this you will need to be more proactive than normal in encouraging conversation. Here are some quick tips:

- Be responsive. View every comment to your website as seeking a response. Respond and ask questions to keep the comments coming in.

- Write news that generates discussion. In your news items, you should explicitly ask for feedback and responses.

- Be thankful. Regularly thank your contributors for great comments and feedback.

- Reward the regulars. You should think carefully about how to reward your regular contributors. One approach I have taken with my own blog is to give the top three contributors a gift, such as a DVD or book. This shows people that you really care about their participation.

At the beginning of growing your community, you will need to be proactive, but as conversation within the community grows, you can take a step back.

Getting Online

Fortunately, you don't need to have super-technical skills to get a great website with conversation facilities up and running. There are a number of preexisting tools that will do the job perfectly. The easiest method of getting going is to use a *blogging engine*.

A blogging engine is a software tool that lives on a website and provides a simple interface for you to publish an article. You can use an editor to format the article in different ways (make parts bold, italic, or underlined, provide different headings, links, or images, etc.), and you can also split the posts into different categories. These systems do not require any programming abilities.

There are many free online services for setting up blogs, and with them you can get up and running quickly. They allow you to publish your blog entries and ensure that they are indexed by popular search engines, such as Google. Unfortunately, many of these services don't allow you to have your blog at your own web address.

If you would prefer the blog to be on the same domain as your website, you can install your own blogging engine. There are many free and commercial blogging engines available, but I recommend WordPress (*http://wordpress.org/*). WordPress offers an excellent, easy-to-use, and powerful framework for publishing content easily. To install your own WordPress website, you will need to have your own server, which you can purchase from a hosting company. The company will provide a place to install the software, and you can set it up. Many hosting companies also offer preinstalled WordPress, Drupal, and other systems.

ROLLING YOUR OWN VERSUS USING A PREEXISTING ENGINE

When the need for a new website arises, some people prefer to install an engine such as WordPress, and some prefer to write a site from scratch.

I highly recommend that, where possible, you use a preexisting engine. Years ago I wrote my own website engine, and it just wasn't as good as something such as WordPress. It's fairly simple to see why: a project such as WordPress has hundreds of developers creating new features and fixing problems. This nets more functionality and a more stable experience in general.

If you really feel the need to have your own custom website, ensure that you have the resources to maintain it for a long time. When you invest in that website today, you will need to be able to still invest in its maintenance in a year, in two years, or more. Think carefully about this decision: if you go with a preexisting engine such as WordPress, that maintenance is done for you.

Syndication

In the past five years there has been a change in how people access content on the Internet. Traditionally, the only way you could get updates from a website was to repeatedly visit the website to check for new content or features. This meant having a number of bookmarks in your web browser and cycling through them hunting for updates. Fortunately, a solution to this problem has been developed, known as *syndicated feeds*. Once the forte of the techie, they are now popular across the Internet.

When you use a blogging website engine (such as WordPress), each time you add a new entry, a special feed will be updated with the content. This feed sits on the same website. Your readers can then use a piece of software called a *feed reader* to subscribe to the feed.

As an example, on my website at *http://www.jonobacon.org/*, I have a feed available at *http://www.jonobacon.org/feed/*. This is a Really Simple Syndication (RSS) feed.

NOTE

A good introduction to these feeds is on the BBC website at *http://news.bbc.co.uk/1/hi/help/3223484.stm*.

With most websites providing these feeds, you can subscribe to a number of your favorite websites in your feed reader. Each time you load the reader, it will check each feed for updates and indicate if there is new content. Not only is this a hugely efficient way to read lots of websites, but also the feeds typically don't include all of the website imagery and design. This means you just get the content and don't have to download all the other fluff.

You should ensure that your website provides these feeds. Most engines (such as WordPress, Drupal, Joomla!, and others) provide support for these feeds by default, making it really easy to include this functionality on your website.

Syndication feeds also allow people to take your content and merge it into their own website. This has been happening more and more in recent years. Tools can easily embed feeds into the sidebar of a website, for example.

There is also a new kind of website appearing called a *planet*. These websites take a number of syndication feeds about related subjects and show the posts in the correct order. This produces a rolling collection of interesting content: readers simply visit the planet and then read a large number of related websites that they were probably unaware of. A great example of this is Planet Ubuntu (*http://planet.ubuntu.com*).

You should seek to get your feed syndicated to these other sites. It can drive some incredible traffic to your site and get your words out farther afield.

SEARCH ENGINE OPTIMIZATION

A popular buzzword in the online world is *search engine optimization* (SEO). It is the science of how to ensure that your website appears at the top of search engines. It is a large and complex science, but I want to give you just a few quick tips that will get you started:

- Using preexisting engines can make this easier. When you use a blogging engine, the creators of the engine have likely already thought about optimizing for search engines. This will automatically get you higher rankings.

- Make sure titles and headings (which factor heavily in searches) are meaningful and contain the words people will look for. It's OK to have a cutesy title like "Why I'm tired this morning," but also include some meaningful indicator of the content, such as "...because I finished the Bike for MS research fundraiser."

- When posting images inside your news/blog posts, ensure that you specify some text to describe the image. This is done in the `alt` attribute of the image tag. For example:

  ```
  <img alt="My Dog" src="dog.jpg">
  ```

- Comment and conversation facilities will increase your SEO by bringing regular traffic to your website and encouraging links.

The key to SEO is to have great content that attracts regular traffic. Focus your efforts on getting more people to your website, and your SEO rating will flourish.

The Buzz Cycle

So far in this chapter we have explored many of the wider considerations for building buzz. Before we move on to look at some specific examples, we need to learn the final piece of buzz theory: the *buzz cycle*.

Whenever you build buzz, you execute a set of procedures. When combined, this set of procedures ensures that you plan effectively, get as much anticipation for your announcement, and learn from the experience. These steps help frame the best practice involved in buzz making, and they will help you to better plan and structure how you get people excited about your community.

The four stages are:

Plan

At this stage you sit down and build a recipe for what you want to achieve, how you can achieve it, and what is involved.

Build up

Instead of going straight to the main course, why not start with an appetizer? Build up some excitement and mystery before the main event kicks in.

Announce

The core of our buzz, this is where we kick it out there.

Review

This includes a postmortem of what we did, and an assessment of what worked, what didn't, and how we can improve next time.

Many newcomers to the buzz-building business jump straight to the announcement, with a marginal level of planning. I strongly recommend against this. Buzz is an art form that can net incredible results for your community when executed correctly, but it can also cause lasting damage if you get it wrong. Planning and feedback will keep you with the former. To explain how each stage is important, I am going to use the 5-A-Day example that we talked about back in Chapter 4 that illustrates the buzz cycle well.

5-A-Day was a project I conceived while watching a program about healthy eating. In many countries it is recommended that you eat five portions of fruit or vegetables as part of a healthy diet. It makes healthy eating an easy-to-remember metric that people can factor into their routine, which is a compelling concept.

Around that time, we were very conscious of how we handled our bug list. As Ubuntu grew as a project, the number of users grew; as such, so did the number of reported bugs. Inspired by five portions of fruit and vegetables a day, we formed the 5-A-Day initiative to encourage our community to triage or comment on five bugs a day. The project started and made some incredible progress. Now let's look at the different buzz stages with this example as an illustration.

Planning

The reason buzz requires planning is that, to excite people, you need to know your goals, what tools and resources you need, and how to roll out your plan. You want to squeeze as much juice out of your efforts as possible and get as much focus and attention on your community as possible. You want maximum return for your investment in time.

First, it is time to sit down and consider the different attributes and elements in your buzz initiative. Here are some questions you should have answers for:

- What outcome do you want to achieve?
- What medium(s) are you going to use to achieve it?
- What preparation work needs to occur before you can begin the buildup phase?
- What other people are involved in the buzz and what are their tasks?
- What is the timeline for the entire buzz cycle?

The answers to these questions will give you a firm idea of your goals and how you can achieve them. For plans that involve only you, an awareness of the answers to these questions is enough. If you are going to be working with other people, however, you should document the answers. This will ensure that everyone is on the same page.

In the case of 5-A-Day, I was working with my team, Daniel Holbach and Jorge Castro. The preparation work involved the development of some technical facilities and tools, some documentation, and a timeline. We had a number of conference calls to build the plan, ensure that the requirements were in place, and specify deadlines for each buzz cycle phase.

DEADLINES KEEP YOU ALIVE

Many people hate deadlines. They commit us to specifics. For many, and particularly those who enjoy the free-form nature of community, deadlines are unwelcome.

Stick with them, though. Deadlines are critical to achieve goals. In this chapter our goal is effective buzz. When you have multiple people involved in a buzz-building exercise, you need to ensure that all participants deliver their contributions to the project on time.

When you apply deadlines, ensure that they are documented somewhere. For my team, we plan the deadlines up front and put them on our shared calendar. This is a useful means of reminding you when deadlines are near. The key is to ensure that deadlines are in a place where you will look. If they are buried away in a file or notebook, they are of no use to anyone.

Buildup

The next step is when things start to get exciting. This phase brings to mind the often-trumpeted statement, "Some things are better left to the imagination." It's true.

In this phase we want to tease people with a taste of what is to come. We want to pique their curiosity, tempt their senses, and get people chattering about what we are up to. When done right, this phase can deliver some riveting and memorable buzz, before you even announce what you are doing.

I also used this technique to announce that I was working on *The Art of Community (http://www .jonobacon.org/2009/01/13/announcement/)*. A few days before I announced the project and the website, I took a screenshot of the website and motion-blurred it. I deliberately blurred it so that you could not see what was on the site, but you could just make out the word *Community*. Underneath the screenshot I simply wrote, "*Wednesday 14th January 2009 @ jonobacon.org.*" A flurry of over 35 comments then appeared, each musing on what the project could be. Many even tried to unblur the screenshot to see what was there. An hour before I posted the main announcement, a reader called Kyran managed to unblur the image and provided a link to the new website.

On the 5-A-Day campaign, too, we had an interesting idea. Over the week building up to the announcement, Daniel; Daniel's girlfriend, Mimi; Jorge; and I each posted photos to our blogs that had us showing symbols with the number 5 in them.

My first blog post included the photo in Figure 7-1.

FIGURE 7-1. I designed this photo to build anticipation in the 5-A-Day buzz campaign.

(Although I was clearly trying to look cool in the photo, the world and his dog seemed to be mostly amused at the fact that I was watching *Along Came Polly* on my TV in the background. Buzz can sometimes backfire.)

Underneath the photo, I also pulled some text from Wikipedia about the number 5 and put it underneath the photograph:

5 (five) is a number, numeral, and glyph. It is the natural number following 4 and preceding 6.

Five is between 4 and 6 and is the third prime number, after 2 and 3, and before 7. Because it can be written as $2^{(2^1)}+1$, five is classified as a Fermat prime. 5 is the third Sophie Germain prime, the first safe prime, and the third Mersenne prime exponent. Five is the first Wilson prime and the third factorial prime, also an alternating factorial. It is an Eisenstein prime with no imaginary part and real part of the form 3n − 1. It is also the only number that is part of more than one pair of twin primes.

Five is conjectured to be the only odd untouchable number.

When viewed together, particularly on Planet Ubuntu, the blog posts were clearly connected. This started a flurry of discussion about what we could be up to.

NOTE
Buildup should only be used on genuinely interesting initiatives. Don't bother using buildup on things that will fail to excite people. As an example, buildup would be great for a new project or initiative, but awful for a change in policy in how your community is governed.

Announce

At this point in the cycle, there should be some rampant speculation regarding the hints you have been dropping in the buildup. You should be seeing suggestions from the sublime to the ridiculous. Don't go too far with the buildup, though. Allow just a few weeks before you reveal your mystery with an announcement.

When announcing you need to ensure that you answer all of the most immediate questions the speculators have. If after all the buildup you don't come through with a smörgåsbord of answers, it will simply cause frustration. You want those riddled with curiosity to be delighted to have their curiosity quenched when they hear the news.

The first step when announcing is to point people to a place where they can read, hear, or watch your announcement. You should have a single location to direct people to. For most communities, this is a website. Your goal now is to make the page easy to read.

Most announcements that communities make tend to be posted on their website, but there is an important consideration to bear in mind with web announcements: computer screens are hard to read. Jakob Nielsen, one of the world's highest regarded usability gurus, wrote about the impact of screen text on readers (*http://www.useit.com/alertbox/whyscanning.html*):

> Reading from computer screens is tiring for the eyes and about 25 percent slower than reading from paper. No wonder people attempt to minimize the number of words they read. To the extent this reason explains users' behavior, they should read more when we get high-resolution, high-scanrate monitors in five years since lab studies have shown such screens to have the same readability as paper.

With reading on screens known to be more tiring, this behavior naturally translates to people wanting to read less and scan more. As such, we need to deliver our announcement quickly and effectively.

It's important that we put our announcement in the proper perspective: it will be one of hundreds of things the person will read on the Internet that day. We need to stand out. We need to grab the reader's attention and deliver our content.

Nielsen's solution to this problem is simple: write half as much. In his excellent article "Be Succinct! (Writing for the Web)" (*http://www.useit.com/alertbox/9703b.html*), Nielsen recommends three guidelines that can help:

- Be *succinct*: write no more than 50% of the text you would have used in a hardcopy publication.
- Write for *scannability*: don't require users to read long, continuous blocks of text.
- Use *hypertext to split up* long information into multiple pages.

We are trying to avoid swathes of text. We need to architect our announcement so that our readers can skip over parts and get straight to the meat.

Let's look at an example. Imagine we are writing an announcement to solicit papers for a conference on renewable energy. Let's start with a high suck factor and write an announcement we can tear apart afterward:

> Call for Papers Open
> Cranfield Green Alliance is a renewable energy conference that takes place in Cranfield, Bedfordshire. The conference is located at Cranfield University and runs from 10–12 November 2009. The conference covers a range of topics including renewable energy, alternative lifestyles, green cooking, ecological trends, and more. We are now opening up our call for papers and encourage a variety of environmental professionals to submit presentations in their area of expertise. Papers on a range of subjects are welcome and we would encourage you all to submit something soon. The conference attracts a wide range of attendees and exhibitions, and we welcome your involvement in this important event. Your contributions as a visitor or a speaker will be valuable. To submit your paper you should email *papers@cranfieldgreenalliance.co.uk* no later than 1st October 2009. We look forward to your submissions!

Friends, what we have just experienced is unremarkable, flat, and about as exciting as a paint-drying competition. I am sorry I subjected you to that paragraph: I realize you will never get those minutes back. Consider it a sacrifice for your community.

OK, let's apply some of the guidance we have discussed so far. Let's make the language exciting and inspirational, break up the paragraph so that it is easier to read and scan, and make it succinct and clear. Tighten your seat belts. Here we go:

> Cranfield Green Alliance Call For Papers Open!
>
> 10–12 November 2009: Cranfield University, Cranfield, Bedfordshire, England.
> Leading the way to define a new future fueled by renewable energy.
>
> Including exciting and industry-relevant topics such as renewable energy, alternative lifestyles,

green cooking, ecological trends, and more. Leaders of the field bring a great opportunity to learn from the finest minds in the industry.

PLAY YOUR PART IN THE REVOLUTION

Do you want to get your voice heard? Do you want to help inspire and encourage a new generation of renewable energy? We thought so. It's time to submit a paper....

Submit a paper on any relevant green topic and deliver it to an audience of over 500 attendees.

HOW TO SUBMIT: Send papers to *papers@cranfieldgreenalliance.co.uk* no later than October 1, 2009!!

Good luck!

In this example we performed a number of steps to brighten our announcement. This included:

- Separating the key parts of the message into separate headings and paragraphs
- Converting the language to be more rabble-rousing and inspiring
- Engaging in a rhetorical dialog with the reader by asking questions and clearly showing that the answer was to submit a paper, which is the very aim of the announcement

Your announcement page should pass the elevator test: it should get the reader up to speed with what you are announcing within a minute.

Let's get back to our 5-A-Day example. When we were constructing the 5-A-Day announcement, we produced a page that identified the primary concept of 5-A-Day, how people could get involved, and what they needed to do. Each different piece of information had individual headings, and emphasis was used extensively. View the page at *https://wiki .ubuntu.com/5-A-Day* to see the principles in this section in action—and with a successful outcome.

Review

Postmortems are hugely valuable in any kind of work, and if you don't perform them, you *never learn how to improve*. Whether you are evaluating how well you handled a discussion, cooked a meal, taught your kids how to play football, or built community buzz, a review can uncover great opportunities for improvement:

Efficiency
> When you review your work, it gives you an opportunity to identify areas that are inefficient and redundant. You can use these as a basis for improvement.

Feedback
> Gathering feedback from the people who consumed your buzz is a great way to see what they felt worked and what didn't. This is a great opportunity to get feedback on your writing, structure, and the other concepts throughout this chapter.

Ideas

When any kind of postmortem of an approach occurs, it almost always generates new ideas. These will help future buzz cycles to be more effective.

In the review phase, revisit the questions you asked in the planning phase and compare the plan with what happened:

- Did you stick to your aim and communicate it well to others?
- Did you identify the right outcomes to achieve?
- Were your chosen mediums the most suitable?
- Did you prepare effectively?
- Did you communicate well to others involved in the buzz about what needed to be done?
- Was your timeline for the buzz cycle accurate? Did you hit your deadlines?

To make this process effective, you should gather feedback from members of your community. Seek to gather responses from those who will provide you with constructive advice of what worked and what didn't. Remember, much of the goal here is to identify flaws in your approach. Flaws are nothing to be embarrassed about: they are opportunities to do even better next time.

Later in the book, we are going to talk about measuring community, and we will be able to use many of the techniques there to help us review our work.

Buzz Targets

Buzz needs a target, and that target is the topic you are focusing on. Each time you steal someone's attention, she needs to know that it was worth it. You want to ensure that when she looks in your direction, she feels it was worthwhile.

To do this, you need to decide what you want to promote. Of course, buzz is an ongoing process: you will need to bring attention and focus to your community many, many times. Each time you need to ensure that there is a purpose. Whether the purpose is announcing the community, attracting new members, or anything else, you should ensure that your goals and intentions are clear.

Two kinds of buzz campaigns are useful in virtually all communities:

- The initial announcement
- Ongoing efforts to attract members

We are going to explore both of these, looking at the four elements of the buzz cycle.

Announcing Your Community

The first time you need buzz is when you announce your community. The goal is to get the message out among people who can contribute to your community, pique people's interest, and get them to learn more.

Your announcement should appear fresh and exciting, and an effective buildup phase is particularly important. Earlier I gave examples of the approach to announcing *The Art of Community* and 5-A-Day; you should consider similar approaches.

Multimedia can make an announcement more exciting and memorable. Lawrence Lessig launched his Change Congress (*http://change-congress.org/*) campaign on his blog (*http://www .lessig.org/blog/2008/03/change_congress_launched.html*) by recording a short online presentation in which he narrated the goals of the project. I used a similar technique when I announced my Severed Fifth (*http://www.severedfifth.com/*) project. I recorded an announcement (*http:// www.severedfifth.com/news/2008/06/severed-fifth-launched/*) and put it online on the day of release. These approaches really help captivate the viewer.

The desired outcome with this kind of buzz is to have people visit your website and to spread awareness of your community.

Applying the buzz cycle

Preparation

Ensure that you have your website in place, and that all of the key information about your community and how to get involved is available. You should also ensure that syndication feeds are available. Decide where it's important to get mentioned (websites, magazines, personal blogs by leaders in the field, etc.). You can often source a list of places by asking your community and identifying related websites and magazines.

Buildup

If you have a preexisting blog or other site where you can post content, you could post "Coming Soon..." messages. If you are setting up a local community, you could put up fliers with the date of the announcement and a web address.

Announcement

On the day of the announcement, you should publicize in all the communication channels that make sense. You should provide a short blurb that inspires people to learn about your community and encourage them to visit your website.

Review

You can see where your announcement spreads to and whether you were publicized in all the places you hoped. There's also qualitative feedback: did comments and questions show that you described your project clearly? Did the types of people you want respond?

Attracting Contributors

Contributors are at the forefront of what makes a great community. Not only are they on the front line, furthering your community in the direction of its goals, but they are also your representatives and spokespeople.

Although buzz campaigns can be started to attract contributors, this activity should be seen as an always-present and ongoing promotional effort. Your goal here is to constantly communicate the positive message of your community, its achievements, and how people can get involved.

The greatest communicators of this message are your existing members: you want to turn their satisfaction into active promotion for your community. To achieve this, your members need to feel proud to be in your community. They should feel a drive and passion for your goals and objectives, and they should feel that they want to spread the word so that others can enjoy the community, too. A positive community will always generate a positive message and be a magnet for new contributors.

The first step in achieving this is to build a sense of enjoyment, ease of contribution, and pride in your members. You build this by combining the elements discussed in this book: simple processes, effective governance, transparency, and so on. When you get these core attributes right, your members will thrive on the opportunities and direction your community offers them. You now need to encourage them to share their happiness and drive with others.

Their own resources and social network are an excellent communication channel for this outreach. Your job is to identify methods via which you can help them use these resources to spread the word about (a) the good work your community performs and (b) why they enjoy being part of it.

For the former, give them buttons for their websites and blogs. Give them posters to print out and put in libraries, in stores, and on lampposts. Provide them with email signatures that they can use. Encourage them to set up Facebook/MySpace pages and more. Each of these resources should direct people back to the community's website.

To encourage your members to share their joy of being a part of the community, the key is that the communication focuses on the personal story: you need to encourage your members to share what they specifically enjoy about the project. In doing this you resort to the essence of community that we discussed back at the beginning of the book: *stories*.

Stories are a fantastic viral marketing asset. A great story is never told once; it is shared again and again. If your community members share great stories about their involvement in the community, the stories will travel far and wide and encourage new and unknown people to dip their feet into your waters.

You should talk about the importance of sharing stories with your members. Help them to understand that on any given day they could talk to someone online, in a coffee shop, or on a train or plane and potentially inspire that person to join the community. This can provide your members with a powerful sense of opportunity for bringing people in and will get them involved. You should now augment this discussion with some specific recommendations of viral approaches of getting the word out there:

Blogging

Blog entries get read, linked, and passed on across the Internet. They are easy to create, accessible to all, and permanently archived in search engines and often crop up in random searches. Blog entries are also very gratifying for the author, particularly if the readers leave comments.

Social media

In Chapter 6 we discussed tools such as Twitter and Facebook as excellent methods of sharing experiences. Encourage your members to use these facilities as they do their work.

Word of mouth

Encourage your members to strike up conversations about your community in every possible scenario. Glorify the most insane and ridiculous cases in which a story is told and the recipient joins the community. As an example, one time I met a guy on the London Underground and told him about Ubuntu. He visited the website and eventually joined and participated in the community. This was incredibly satisfying. Share these experiences, and encourage and celebrate them.

Interviews

Some of your community members may have the opportunity to be interviewed on websites, on podcasts, on videocasts, or in magazines. Interview opportunities are harder to come by, but encourage your members to ask these publications if they can be interviewed. If you don't ask, you don't get!

Conference presentations

If you have members who are keen to speak at conferences, encourage them to submit papers. If you have some experience with this process, you should offer them help and advice on putting together a submission.

Meetings/events/open days

Encourage your members to organize meetings and events in which they can tell their story about the community. When I first got involved in open source, I organized presentations and open events at my university to help others understand how fun and satisfying our community is. All I needed was a room and a projector. Planting the idea in the minds of your members is sure to inspire someone to organize an event.

An important element in building buzz to attract contributors is to showcase great work. I used many of these techniques when I started Severed Fifth and provided a range of website buttons and Severed Fifth posters (many of which were produced by the community). To generate buzz, I organized a campaign for fans to put the posters and stickers up in their local area. As part of the campaign, I encouraged typical destinations for the posters such as music shops, notice boards, and lampposts, but also showcased some of the wackier places. I saw examples of Severed Fifth stickers and posters in fish and chip shops, on the London Underground, in railway stations, toilet stalls, concert venues, and buses, and even stuck to someone who was sleeping. As I heard these stories, I blogged them and encouraged fans to send me photos that I could put on the blog. The viral nature of the campaign encouraged more people to participate.

This viral marketing approach to building buzz has become the new way to do business on the Internet. The idea is simple: you build buzz and encourage the consumers of your buzz to also build their buzz on the same topic. With this approach, when you unleash something on this network of viral volunteers, it spreads like wildfire. The key here is to have this network available, and building that network can require a tremendous amount of energy in helping people to feel engaged, but when they do it will pay dividends in buzz. The key is in making people feel a sense of empowerment and responsibility to spread the message.

BUILDING YOUR BUZZ ARMY

As you grow your community, always be on the lookout for those who have a personality that is attuned to getting people excited about the community and the work it does. While you are taking on a responsibility to build buzz, if you can create a team of people who can also build buzz you will develop a much more scalable resource for building awareness and excitement about your community.

People who can build buzz and excitement in a way that is natural and not obnoxious are few and far between, so keep your eyes open and your ear to the ground for these folks and grab 'em when you can.

An interesting project that really set the standard for this kind of outreach was the Mozilla Firefox promotional campaign, Spread Firefox (*http://www.spreadfirefox.com/*).

Back in November 2004, the SilverOrange Canadian web firm was commissioned to build Mozilla's website. As part of its work the company produced an evangelist application on its intranet to manage the structure and content of the site.

Blake Ross (one of the forefathers of Firefox) conceived the idea that Mozilla should encourage and inspire the global Firefox community to lead the marketing for the launch of the popular browser. One of the people involved in this work was Chris Messina. At the time, Chris was a Firefox community member, keen to see the project get better recognition and more widespread focus. Eventually he would go on to lead the Spread Firefox community marketing project in raising over $220,000 in microdonations to launch Firefox to a worldwide audience with an ad in the *New York Times*. As Chris explained to me, he remembers the formation of the project well:

Originally there were probably about 30 of us in this private intranet, but maybe only 10 of us participated in any regular capacity. For me, this kind of work was all new to me—both open source and this kind of semi-anonymous Internet collaboration. It's not like I'd met anyone on the project personally—in fact, I only happened to find out about it because Steven Garrity had blogged that Mozilla was looking for volunteer designers.

After hearing about the project, Chris joined and applied his passion for Firefox to the campaign. At the heart of buzz is the ability to think outside the box to spread the word, and Chris intimately remembers the approaches they used:

> I think there were a number of important elements of this, and that was that we made it fun to get involved. There was both a spirit of camaraderie and of shared purpose (fighting Microsoft), and with that in mind, people came up with some pretty clever ideas in the forums, contributing concepts, strategies, designs...telling the story of how Firefox made a difference to them. We worked hard to promote these efforts through things like the leaderboard (which measured the week-to-week growth in downloads from different affiliate links) and had, I believe, weekly contests or initiatives. Probably the most effective tool was the cumulative download counter... every time we hit a new milestone I would design new artwork to commemorate our success— with each design getting more and more insane.

The efforts of the Spread Firefox team were exceptional: Firefox 3 was downloaded over 28 million times in 24 hours when it was released. The project has gone on to secure a global user base and a reputation for quality, and a thriving and active community that surrounds it.

NOTE

Part of the responsibility of finding members is also going to involve finding leaders. We will discuss this in Chapter 10.

Applying the buzz cycle

Preparation

You should fully research which mediums you want to spread your buzz to. Your aim here is to identify the kind of personality that will be interested in joining your community, and to target the media that they read.

Buildup

I do not recommend any buildup to this target. You want to get straight out there and grab contributors.

Announcement

The announcement should take place in a variety of media. Your aim here is to share and inspire people in the achievements and accessibility of your community. Sell them on the evidence: show them third-party statements and material that firmly demonstrates that your community is a fun and rewarding place to be.

Review

Naturally, one measure of success is how many new people sign up or start helping out on committees. You can also try to see how many existing members helped the buzz with their personal statements, and why they were or were not comfortable doing so.

THE COMMUNITY CASE BOOK

Oh, we've had several times when we've had some really bad growing pains. It's seldom so much about the code not working, as the flow of development not working, and something (often *somebody*) holding things up. And yes, that somebody has sometimes been me, and we've had to figure out how to change how we do things so that no single person ends up being that kind of bottleneck.

—*Linus Torvalds, on Growth*

Read the full interview in Chapter 14.

Building Alliances

Good communication resources and contacts are critical for promotional ideas and concepts to flow from you to the outside world. If you are going to build some great buzz, you need to know how to communicate effectively in different channels. This requires two skills, which must be mastered separately for each channel:

- Find the opportunity to make use of that channel. As an example, if you want to be featured in a particular magazine, you need to create an opportunity in which you can get your content there. This almost always involves building contacts. You should get to know the editors of the magazine and build a relationship that could allow you to feature some content in their channel.

- Ensure that your buzz in that channel is appropriate. The norms of communication between different mediums vary, but the differences can often be subtle and unwritten. If you act outside the expected boundaries (particularly in volunteer channels), it can impact negatively on your community.

NOTE
Also don't forget the old saying, "It's not what you know, it's who you know." If you have contacts who can help get your message out there or who can put you in touch with those who can help, go ahead and ask.

Buzz is designed to be consumed by lots of people. You want as much focus and attention on your community as possible. The more relevant eyeballs there are, the better.

As part of your planning stage for a buzz campaign, you should weigh the amount of effort involved with the number of relevant eyeballs. You want to ensure that your time and effort preparing materials and content is worthwhile and that a reasonable number of people see your work.

Much of this boils down to readership, and readership varies tremendously. Sometimes you can ask for this information, such as with magazines, but sometimes it is more of a guess. There will be some resources that you will assume have a large audience (such as a very popular website) and some not so large (such as a blog).

An important consideration in this area is how the growth of the Internet has changed audience figures. It used to be general wisdom that paper publications were always the source of high audience figures. This is often no longer the case, as many websites—even a number of blogs—have hundreds of thousands of regular visitors.

The Professional Press

The professional press is a large and extensive channel. It encompasses magazines, websites, journals, videos, multimedia content, and more. Each publication has professional paid staff who have a responsibility to publish quality content.

The professional press has three primary concerns at the forefront of its mind:

Quality content
> First and foremost, the professional press wants to produce leading content. It wants well-produced content that is of interest to its audience.

Readership/audience
> Professional publications rely on readership numbers. It is these numbers that largely justify the continuation of the publication. Having high audience numbers depends on getting the previous item in place: quality content.

Advertising opportunities
> Most publications make a significant chunk of their revenue from advertising, and advertising does have an impact on content. Although many publications would deny it, advertising deals are often struck based on relationships between the publication and the company. These relationships need to be maintained to continue to bring in revenue. In many cases the content in a publication may be heavily critical of a company, product, or initiative. Although this *should* never matter, for many publications it does, and the producer of the content is advised to either change the content or focus on other topics.

You should factor these attributes into your plan for building buzz. You want to target the most appropriate publications that are relevant to your community. You will need to provide them with quality content that is of interest to their audience and consider any potential advertising conflict.

You will need to build a relationship with the publication. With these publications largely staffed by paid personnel, it is entirely reasonable to formally contact them via email or phone and ask them if you can contribute some content. A great first step would be to ask if they could feature your community in their news section. In some cases you may have the chance to build some relationships that you can return to when opportunity strikes later.

The first time I experienced this was years back at the start of my career. It was my first time at the Linux Expo in London. I was there running an exhibition stand for the first time for the KDE project. While there, I went to an after-show party, and the editors from *Linux Format* magazine were there. I got to chatting with them, had more than a few drinks, and a little while later asked them if they would consider publishing something by me. Nick Veitch, editor at the time, responded with, "Sure, write something, but if it is rubbish we won't publish it." I wrote my article, it got published, and so started my journalism career.

Linux Format opened many doors for me, but most importantly, it gave me a platform to talk about things I considered interesting. It opened up a set of opportunities that have since helped with building buzz and promotion in the open source projects I have been involved in.

Though it's been some years since my days writing for *Linux Format*, I got in touch with then staff writer and now editor-in-chief Paul Hudson to gather some insight from the perspective of an editor to share with you all. Paul is a firm believer of the have-a-go approach to getting content in:

> Both of us got into the world of free software journalism by saying, "Hey, why don't I write for you?" and I think that same situation occurs a lot—people don't realize how much they can contribute until they just ask.

> I think people imagine some sort of incredible vetting process must take place in order to write for magazines—as if only people in smoking jackets with Ph.D.s from the School of Ignorant Snobbery are able to get stuck into writing, but that's simply not true. Well, not *always* true, at least! Technical magazines and websites are crying out for people to get involved and just share what's cool and what's new in their world.

Paul regularly handles a slew of wannabe writers and passionate community members keen to get their projects featured in the magazine. With this in mind, he offers some useful guidance for improving the likelihood of getting coverage in magazines:

> Don't use email. We get stacks of emails, and most of them remain unread. The reason for this is that PR agencies blast us with all sorts of emails about things whether they are relevant to the magazine or not, so inevitably some important emails get lost in the mess.

> Instead, call first, ask to speak to the news editor or someone else on the team, and just have a chat with them. They want good contacts as much as you do, so if you're someone who

represents a project that's on their radar, they would love to be in touch with you. They are also much more likely to read your emails if you've already made contact by phone.

When you write release announcements, make it really clear what's new. This is something the GNOME project, as one such example, does well (*http://library.gnome.org/misc/release-notes/2.24/ #rnusers*). They list the new features with pictures so that someone can decide at a glance whether it's worth looking into.

If you are a software project, provide at least one screenshot that shows off the best feature you've got to offer. Remember, these guys are looking for "wow" things to print, and if you can send them a shot of your software looking awesome, they are much more inclined to run it as a news story.

Remember that even in technical magazines, some people are still journalists first and geeks second. Put your documentation online and link to all the technical information you like, but when you're trying to get a journalist interested in what you have to say, it's much more important to say, "MyProject 2.0 uses 25% less RAM than MyProject 1.0" than to say, "The switch to the xyz toolkit blah blah blah please send me straight to your Trash folder." Sure, drop in all the technical information you want later on, but you need to win them over in the first two sentences by focusing on what really kicks ass in your software.

If you're not producing software, getting into magazines is slightly trickier, because magazines rarely want to print a story if it's similar to something else they ran recently. So if your user group wants to get featured, you need to step outside the installfest (unless it's *big*) and do something pretty darn special. Whatever you do, take a photo and make it available under a Creative Commons license that allows commercial use.

The rules change with nontechnical magazines because once you enter the mainstream, you need to focus more on people. The *New York Times* won't find the Gecko web rendering engine interesting, but it will find Spread Firefox interesting because grassroots marketing really is changing the browser landscape.

While Paul offers some useful advice on the best-practice methods of getting content in the hands of editors, he is keen to emphasize that many communities simply don't get out and try, and this makes for a huge opportunity for printed nirvana:

> Let me try to make this a bit clearer with a specific example from *Linux Format*. We run a page of LUG information every month, and we have to email people to try to get content to fill those pages, despite printing an open plea every issue asking people to get in touch.
>
> So it's not that community members are struggling to get their information in—it's more that many of them just aren't trying. Perhaps they think we're not interested. Perhaps they think we won't print it. But as they so rarely try, most of them will never know.
>
> Maybe they're just targeting magazines that are just a little bit out of their reach, but that's another schoolboy error—Editor X is much more likely to print an article about your community if Editors Y and Z already have. So start small; find a magazine that fits your niche closely and get yourself covered in there. Then use that to help get coverage in other places, building it up bit by bit.

The professional press can seem a bit unnerving. Professional journalists often feel like a live-by-the-seat-of-your-pants collection of hard-working, focused, and unrelenting writers. Don't let this worry you. Journalists are good people and they get asked for content opportunities all the time. Just go out there and ask.

When I started doing this, I would ask everyone. I would email 10 or 15 magazines to see if I could contribute content. I would not spam them: each email would be focused on that specific publication, and each would be relevant to my topic.

I recommend that you email a list of topics you can write about and ask if you could write something about those topics. Alternatively, write an article and submit it. The benefit of the latter is that the journo has direct access to content, which is often an attractive proposition. Just go out there and ask; there really is no harm.

The Amateur Press

In the past five years, the amateur press world has exploded. The Internet has provided an incredible medium in which anyone can write about anything and have the chance to grow an audience. Technology and open access to information have provided an incredible opportunity to be heard, and many have built new reputations out of these opportunities. Consequently, millions of blogs and thousands of podcasts have sprung up around the world.

The amateur press is a world largely fueled by volunteers. The authors write their words not to claim a paycheck, but to share their ideas, perspectives, and opinions. Although the amateur press is populated by amateur scribes, this does not necessarily equate to a lack of quality. Some of the greatest work I have ever read has shown up on a blog. This could be the musings of Lessig on the copyright wars (*http://www.lessig.org/blog/*) or the deeply amusing yet incredibly well-written and inspired political blather of Flyingrodent (*http://flyingrodent.blogspot.com/*). Both are inspired works, yet very different in content and presentation.

The timeline of the amateur press revolution largely matched that of the professional press revolution many years earlier. The publishing world exploded onto the scene and thousands of books, newspapers, and journals sprung up. Each of these publications had its own perspective on its respective topic, and it became very difficult for readers to identify where the real quality was. The solution to this was the launch of other publications that read, reviewed, and collated this content (a great example being *The Week*).

We have started to see much of this in recent years with blogs and podcasts. Websites such as Technorati (*http://technorati.com/*) have been sifting through the blogosphere and identifying the most popular and interesting blogs. Well-respected members of given communities will also often provide their *blogroll*, which lists the blogs they enjoy reading. These resources all provide an excellent opportunity to identify which blogs you should be focusing on.

The amateur press is hugely important for buzz. The professional press is far more complicated and restricted in terms of getting heard, whereas often a few emails exchanged with the amateur press will net great results.

It's not surprising why:

- The amateur press has a shared appreciation for volunteer community. They understand your reasons and intentions and will often want to promote them.

- There is no advertising conflict in most of the amateur press: they can write about whatever they want.

- There is typically no limitation on content. On a blog you can write as many posts as you like. This opens up more opportunities for you to get in on the content.

The most significant mediums in the amateur press arena are blogs, podcasts, and videos. Let's take a quick look at all three and explore their cultures.

Blogs

Weblogs (typically known as blogs) started out life as online diaries. In them people would share what they were doing, what they were thinking, and what interested them. When blogging started, there were few blogs, and most were devoted to deeply technical topics.

Alan Cox was one of the earliest bloggers that I am aware of. Living in Swansea in Wales, Alan developed his celebrity among early Linux fans due to his work on the Linux kernel. Alan worked on incredibly low-level deep and dirty programming. It was about as unrelentingly hardcore as you could get.

When I first started reading his diary, I was fascinated. This was not the work of Alan Cox communicated through a journalist's eyes. What I was reading were the direct thoughts of the man himself. Without wishing to sound like an overenthusiastic psychology major, I felt like I was actually closer to the person I was reading about. It gave a direct line to his world, and it pretty much rocked mine.

Since then, blogging has expanded somewhat. In addition to blogs being used as personal diaries, many are now referred to as *personal publishing systems*. Many people, myself included, instead use blogs as a means of writing articles that are of interest to them. I use my blog to write about community, music, technology, usability, and more. I also use it as a medium to express achievements, goals, and more.

It is entirely conceivable that both your existing community members and the people you want to have as friends have blogs. With this in mind, blogging should be a critical component in your buzz building.

The first task is to know which blogs to build buzz with. Look for relevant blogs and strike up a relationship with the authors. Explain what your community is doing, and what your goals are. Try to get the author on board with your mission. You can then ask whether the author would be interested in sharing your work on his blog. If you have your own blog, you could offer to provide a link to his blog in exchange.

Blog wars. Although blogging has had a hugely positive impact on how people can articulate and share opinions and perspectives, there has been a dark side. Blogging has also become a medium in which much overzealous opinion can sometimes be expressed a little *too* quickly. Unfortunately, I have a rather embarrassing example of someone who fell into this trap: yours truly.

First, a bit of background. There used to be a company called Lindows that made a version of Linux that shared many visual and operational similarities to Windows. Microsoft frowned at the name "Lindows," and a fight started between the companies to change the name. Lindows initially resisted, but after mounting pressure, it changed its name to Linspire.

Now to the issue. Let me take the liberty to explain in the words of the article (*http://onlamp .com/pub/wlg/7723?page=last*):

> Recently a chap named Andrew Betts decided to take the non-free elements out of Linspire and release the free parts as another Linspire-derived distribution called Freespire. This act of rereleasing distributions or code is certainly nothing new and is fully within the ethos of open source. In fact, many of the distributions we use today were derived from existing tools. Unfortunately, Linspire saw this as a problem and asked for the Freespire name to be changed.
>
> Reading through the notice of the change, the language and flow of the words screams marketing to me. I am certainly not insinuating that Betts has been forced into writing the page, or that the Linspire marketing drones have written it and appended his name, but it certainly doesn't sound quite right to me. I would have expected something along the lines of "Freespire has been changed to Squiggle to avoid confusion with the Linspire product", but this is not the case. Instead we are treated to choice marketing cuts such as "To help alleviate any confusion, I contacted Linspire and they made an extremely generous offer to us all". Wow. What is this one-chance-in-a-lifetime-not-sold-in-stores offer? Luckily, he continues, "they want everyone who has been following my project to experience 'the real' Linspire, FOR FREE!!!". Now, pray tell, how do we get this "real" version of the software "FOR FREE!!!"?
>
> "For a limited time, they are making available a coupon code called 'FREESPIRE' that will give you a free digital copy of Linspire! Please visit *http://linspire.com/freespire* for details." Oh...thanks.

I gave Linspire a pretty full-throated kick in the wedding vegetables in my blog entry. I told the story, objected to what I considered hypocrisy given their own battle with similar-sounding trademarks, and vented. I wish Guitar Hero had existed back then. It would have been a better use of my time.

I was wrong to jump to conclusions and write so preemptively. Shortly after the article was published, then-CEO Kevin Carmony emailed me. He was not a happy bunny. His objection, and it was valid, was that I flew off the handle without checking in with him first. My blog entry was my first reaction. The happy conclusion to this story is that I apologized to Kevin and admitted to being a bit of an arse, and we have remained friends. In fact, a little while later

I joined the Linspire Advisory Board shortly before I joined Canonical to work on Ubuntu. It's funny how things work out.

PRACTICE WHAT YOU PREACH

In this chapter we have discussed the important attributes in setting up a website and blog for your project, and also how to build buzz using other people's blogs.

Importantly, *you personally* should have a blog. Use it as an opportunity to discuss your personal interests and to talk about your community.

Podcasts

Podcasts are audio shows that are distributed on the Internet. They typically have between one and four presenters, and they are often based on fairly specific topics. Many listeners use a special piece of software called a *podcatcher* to subscribe to a podcast so that when new episodes of a podcast are released, they are automatically downloaded to a media player such as an iPod. This is a fantastic way to keep listeners updated with new content.

A significant reason behind the success of podcasts is that they deliver interesting specialist content to the listener to fill those dull minutes while traveling to work. Many podcasts include interviews, reviews, features, debates, and other content. They vary hugely in both audio and content quality, and some podcasts have netted thousands of listeners.

As I mentioned earlier in this book, I cofounded a podcast with some friends called LugRadio. The show was very specifically focused on open source and digital rights. It took a lighthearted and irreverent approach to the content, and we deliberately focused on making the content social, fun, and amusing. Each show presented a range of topics for discussion, and each of us would weigh in and share our thoughts, often resulting in raucous debate and discussion.

Podcasts are always looking for pointers to interesting content and announcements. You should email the presenters and explain what you are working on, and see if they would be interested in featuring your community on the show. If you manage to get a spot on a popular podcast, it could bring a wealth of new blood to your community. Although you may feel a little funny about emailing the presenters out of the blue, go ahead! If you don't ask, you don't get.

When pitching to a podcast, the most important tip is that your tone should match that of the podcast. When we were doing LugRadio, we would frequently get offers for interviews and features, but often the tone would be right out of a Marketing 101 textbook. Not only did this demonstrate that the person making the offer had not listened to the show, but it also was a red flag for boring, emotionless content that had no place on LugRadio. On the other hand, we also got offers of content that was fun, loose, and insightful, and these were snapped up instantly.

If you get accepted for an interview or to have your community featured, listen to a number of episodes of the podcast to get a feel for the tone. Use it as a guide, but don't be afraid to share your own personality: you have the opportunity to inspire people to join your community, so just be yourself within the context of the podcast.

Finally, always ensure that you have a web address to point the listeners to. This will provide an option to feed them more information, and the link can be listed in the podcast's show notes. Ensure that the website the link points to is packed with content that's ready when the episode of the podcast is published.

> ### NOTE
> As a gesture to the makers of the podcast, it is highly recommended that you spread the word about the podcast episode that your community is featured in. You could do this on your website, in your community's communication channels, and on blogs. This will help build a strong relationship with the podcast, leaving the door open for future content and interviews.

Videos

Online video has become increasingly popular as the Internet has become faster and more accessible. Although a hefty Internet connection is required to suck said videos down onto your computer for viewing, the sheer popularity of services such as YouTube (*http://www .youtube.com*) and blip.tv (*http://blip.tv/*) has demonstrated that many do indulge in such audiovisual delights on the Internet.

While some of us may reminisce about the dark days of dial-up Internet access, it is important to remember that many parts of the world still rely on slower dial-up connections. For these folks, videos are simply not an option. As such, before you get too excited to step into the shoes of Steven Spielberg, you should consider how accessible videos are for your community. As an example, if you are reaching out to a community in a remote part of Africa, you may want to rely on another lower-bandwidth medium. In general, my recommendation is to make use of video, but not as a primary medium. Instead, use it to complement your other, more widely accessible resources.

By far the most popular video service at the time of this writing is YouTube. The idea is simple: anyone can upload a video and anyone with a web browser equipped with Macromedia Flash can view it. YouTube opened the doors for anyone with a webcam or a cheap video camera to be able to create and publish online video. This has resulted in thousands of hours of freely accessible video hitting the Internet.

This is only part of the value of YouTube, though. Videos on YouTube are hugely discoverable: it is possible to upload a video and have thousands of people stumble across it. This happens because each video on YouTube also displays a list of videos that are related to the one being viewed. This feature alone hugely increases the likelihood of people finding your videos. To do this you need to ensure that you name and add keywords to describe the content of your video in a way that enhances the chances of a certain demographic of user being able to find it. As an example, if you are part of a mapping community, you might want to tag your video with the words *map, geography, geo, location*, and any specific regions that were featured in the video. It is stunning how many people will find your videos, and this is further bolstered by word of mouth and the simplicity of embedding videos in web pages.

Another hugely useful feature of YouTube are *channels*. These are home pages on YouTube that contain videos from a certain provider (such as an artist, actor, or your community). There are different types of channels on YouTube designed for different types of providers that have additional facilities such as custom logos, blog entries, and tour dates. A huge benefit of a channel is that people can subscribe to it and will be notified when you add a new video. This is an excellent way to keep people hooked into your videos.

YouTube channels are something we have used extensively in the Ubuntu community. As part of our ongoing efforts to educate and train developers in how to contribute to Ubuntu, we created the Ubuntu Developer Channel on YouTube (*http://www.youtube.com/ ubuntudevelopers*). On the site, we uploaded tuition videos, developer interviews, and more. At each Ubuntu Developer Summit, we would interview attendees to get updates about their work on the next release and perform question and answer sessions with key community members. These videos were hugely successful, and many of them gathered thousands of views within weeks of going online. The channel has over 1,800 subscribers at the time of this writing. YouTube is an excellent resource for delivering education and best practice, and I highly recommend that you make use of it if you have the resources and time.

Another interesting option for video is live streaming. This is where you produce a live videocast that people can view as it is being recorded at a scheduled time. Traditionally, live streaming has always been off-limits for most of us: the bandwidth requirements are so epic that it makes it too costly and impractical.

Fortunately, there is another option in the form of Ustream (*http://www.ustream.tv*). The concept is neat: the video you record on your computer with your lower-bandwidth Internet connection is streamed to the Ustream server, and then your viewers connect there with Ustream's oodles of bandwidth to show your video. This means your viewers don't hammer your Internet connection, and it puts streaming in the hands of us all.

Ustream not only provides a simple means of streaming video, but also includes other features, such as a live chat channel for the show, and recording, tagging, and syndication facilities. The live chat channel is particularly interesting: it provides an opportunity for viewers to interact with the presenter as the broadcast is happening. This means a viewer could tune in and comment on the content, and the presenter can read the comment and repeat it in the broadcast.

This is something I first tried around the time I was wrapping up this book. While experimenting with Ustream, I tested it by broadcasting live from my living room and posting the link to the videocast on Twitter and identi.ca. Within minutes I had 24 people viewing my entirely ad hoc and off-the-cuff broadcast. With my interest piqued, I decided to start performing a regular show called *At Home with Jono Bacon (http://www.ustream.tv/channel/at-home -with-jono-bacon)*.

Whether you make use of prerecorded or live video, there are some nuggets of best practice that are useful to keep your viewers engaged in your content:

- Do your best to keep production values high. As an example, if you are recording the video with your laptop's webcam, consider buying an external microphone. Many of the built-in mics in laptops sound awful and distort easily. Ensure that the location the camera points at looks clean, uncluttered, and professional, and wear clothes that don't distract the viewer.

- Before you produce your video, make some notes about what you will discuss. The easiest way do this is to make a series of bullet points with the topics you want to feature. If you are nervous, you may want to write a script, but I highly recommend that you don't. Unscripted content that is delivered well is far more natural and engaging.

- If possible, have more than one presenter. Multiple presenters always make for more interesting shows because there is an opportunity to bounce off each other with conversation, spark up debate, or play specific roles (e.g., the teacher and the learner).

- When creating an educational program (such as a tuition video), consider embedding in the video the focal point of the tuition (e.g., the computer screen if a programming video) or slides. There are many free tools that can capture computer screen content to video to help with this, such as Screencast-O-Matic (*http://www.screencast-o-matic.com/*), Wink (*http://www.debugmode.com/wink/*), and recordMyDesktop (*http://recordmydesktop.sourceforge .net/*).

- YouTube and Ustream allow you to put notes next to your video. This is an excellent place to list the topics you are covering in the video, provide links to websites, and credit those involved in the content and creation of the video.

- Consider the licensing of your content before you release it. I always recommend that you license your video under a Creative Commons license (*http://www.creativecommons.org/*). You should also consider the licensing of third-party content. As an example, if you want to use the latest U2 tune in your video, you might not be able to legally use it, or if you can, you may need to cough up some royalties. Be very careful here: although it is tempting to just go ahead and use the song, many online video producers have been busted for copyright infringement. I always recommend that you play it safe and only use properly licensed content for your needs.

- Finally, you should be aware that at the time of this writing the Macromedia Flash plug-in that many video websites use (including YouTube and Ustream) is closed source. Some proponents of software freedom and open source may refuse to view those videos for this reason. If this is likely to be problematic, it is recommended that you also provide access to your videos in an entirely free format, such as Ogg Theora (*http://theora.org/*).

We only have space here to delve into a few tasty morsels of best practice, so if you are interested in making videos it is recommended that you buy a dedicated book on the topic. This will help you get up and running quickly.

THE COMMUNITY CASE BOOK

There's definitely an oversaturation of content on the Internet and on YouTube now, so it's harder than ever to get noticed and break out. I would recommend ignoring all "overnight successes"—you can't predict that or what will go viral; there's nothing to learn there.

—Mark Bussler, on Content

Read the full interview in Chapter 14.

Events and Conferences

Events and conferences can be really valuable targets for growing buzz and excitement about your community. Depending on what kind of community you are part of, there are often events happening locally and farther afield that are related to your community and the wider topic your community is interested in. As an example, from my career, open source has taken me to events all over the world, ranging from formal business conventions to open source and science fiction crossover events (and *believe me*, the latter is to be seen to be believed).

Aside from being useful, events are just a whole lot of fun, too. You get to meet interesting people, further your community, and maybe even see a new part of the world. Many of us love to travel, so it makes perfect sense to get out there on the road and not only further your community, but also have a great time doing it.

Unfortunately, this fun comes at a cost. While online buzz building is pretty cost-effective, going to events can get expensive, particularly if you don't have a company paying for it. Conference tickets, hotel rooms, plane tickets, food and drinks, and other costs all add up. Before you know it, that $50 conference ticket can easily balloon to $500 or more when you add in all the other costs of getting there and back home. Things can also get pretty costly when you are surrounded by many people who are there courtesy of their company and you need to pay out of your own pocket to join them at nice restaurants, bars, lunch spots, and more.

Even if you have a company sponsoring your attendance, events are costly when it comes to your time. As we discuss in "Be Wary of Too Much Travel" on page 478, the cost of your time away from your community while you go to the conference or event can add up, and if you are traveling a lot, the impact of the travel on your personal life can also cause stress. I have been in the position of traveling too much, and believe me, while it may be fun for you for a while, it will wear you down at some point, particularly if you have a partner or family.

You definitely want to get out there and visit some events, but you also want to ensure that you pick your events carefully and get the most out of the ones you do attend.

Choosing Events

In 2011 I moved a member of my team to focus on a different kind of community. Traditionally, Jorge had been coordinating relationships with other open source projects and how they interfaced with Ubuntu, but there was an increased focus on a new Ubuntu technology called *Juju*. We wanted to build some community growth and outreach around it, and with this in mind I moved Jorge into a new position as our cloud community liaison.

Part of this role was going to involve getting Jorge out to events to speak about Juju, explain what it is, how it works, how to use it, and how attendees of those events can create *Charms* (technical contributions that make different cloud services work with Juju).

With this change I was first faced with a resourcing challenge. At the time, the cloud was an incredibly hot technology and there were literally hundreds of events happening every year in the cloud space. Obviously we could not send Jorge to them all; even if we had the travel resources to send him, we would break his gentle soul with such a brutal and constant stream of airplanes, hotels, and those small bags of peanuts airline staff give you. As such, we needed to pick which events we wanted him to attend, and pick wisely.

With this in mind I asked Jorge to put together a spreadsheet that listed all the events that could be interesting for us to attend. The focus of this list was clear: these need to be cloud events and oriented around technology (as opposed to business events) and DevOps (the audience we were focusing on). I asked Jorge to gather this list of events and to determine the following characteristics for each one:

- Location and venue
- Date(s) of the event
- Typical attendance size
- Number of sessions and average talk audience size
- Team priority

Each of these pieces of information helped to provide an overview of each event and its respective details. The location and dates were useful in terms of logistical planning (e.g., it is cheaper to fly to certain locations). The audience and session size gave us an idea of how many people we could reach out to, and if Jorge got a speaking slot, how many people were likely to be in the audience.

The team priority was a general perspective of how the other members of the Juju team saw the priority of the different events. Even though I was going to be approving and rejecting these events from a resourcing perspective, I knew I didn't have the best insight into the value of many of these events (as I had not attended most of them). This is why I wanted an idea of team priority; it would help us to consolidate the team's expertise into the resourcing process.

The next step was to discuss each event and determine how well it served our needs in the following areas:

Buzz opportunity

> How much opportunity is there to spread the word about Juju? Is the audience likely to be interested? Are there social events that we can spread our message to in addition to the conference? Are there cobranding and sponsorship opportunities? What talks, panels, lighting talks, and other events can we be a part of?

Networking

> Who is going to be there and are there people going who we want to have conversations with? Are there strategic networking goals that we can achieve at this event?

Education

> Which presentations and tutorials are at the event that could be useful for skills acquisition and growth?

The final step was to apply each of these elements to our list of events and balance this with our budget. This gave us a solid prioritized list of events from which we could get the most value.

I recommend that you use the same process when assessing events for your community. Have a clear idea of your resources (whether it is $50 or $5,000) and identify which events make the most sense to attend and where you will get the most value.

One temptation to resist is to pick events because they are "cool"; many so-called "cool" events don't offer a lot of value for you and your community. Instead, focus on what you can use to enhance and grow your community and how much return you can get for the money you invest in getting there.

DETERMINING THE VALUE OF AN EVENT

The *value* of an event can vary tremendously based on the kind of community you are building and whether you work for a company.

As an example, the value derived from a local book club attending an event could be getting more members involved and more books donated. As such, the level of financial investment in attending the event would need to be low due to the grassroots nature of the group. For a larger funded community (such as a nonprofit) the required value may be more demanding to justify the investment of communal funds.

For a company wanting to work with a community there is sometimes a temptation from senior management to judge the value of an event based on lead generation. As a community manager, you may need to articulate the benefits of the event that aren't related to lead generation in a way that the senior execs will understand better. This can be a complex task. Ultimately, though, the value in a company is typically defined in terms of edging the success of the company forward; just think how you can define the benefits of event attendance in this way (e.g., networking, relationships, outreach, comarketing etc.).

Submitting your paper

With your list of target events finalized, you should now see which events you can speak at. Each event should have a website, and on each site there should be a *Call for Papers*; this is event-speak for a period of time during which you can propose a presentation at the event. There is usually a form on the website or an email address where you can send your proposal.

You may be thinking, "I guess I just fill in the form and I am good to go, right?" Hold your horses for one second, my friend....

Regardless of how good your presentation might be, if your presentation proposal is subpar, it will never get accepted. I have served on some paper review boards at various events and I want to share a few tips regarding what can increase your chances of getting accepted. Just like interviewing for a job, there are some good things you can do to improve your chances and some horrible mistakes you can make that will make you screw the pooch.

The first thing you should do is to ensure that you have all the information you need for the submission. You are going to need the following:

Presentation title

> Your presentation title should be short, snappy, and interesting. Many people will never read your summary, so the title should get their attention. As an example, instead of "An Overview of Community Governance Processes," try "Governance: Cat Herding for Fun and Profit." Make sure your title, while fun, still actually communicates what the talk is about (e.g., "Raising the Waterfowl Revolution" would not be a good bet, despite my love of ducks).

Presentation summary

> Your summary should explain the key points your presentation will share. Don't drown the reader in detail; instead, share the core areas your presentation will cover, and present it like you are telling a story. Also be careful to not big yourself up too much; arrogantly written summaries can be off-putting.

Biography

You should include a speaker biography that is written in the third person (e.g. "Bob Smith is a community manager..."). Try to keep this short but impressive. Think of this as your elevator pitch about you; what are your main accomplishments, experience, and credentials? Your bio should be read by a potential audience member to affirm confidence that you know your subject well. Keep it positive, but again, don't be arrogant or egocentric.

Speaking requirements

You should outline what you need for your presentation. Although this may be obvious, if you are delivering slides, be sure to specify that you will need a projector and microphone. If you have any A/V requirements (e.g., sound from your laptop), a whiteboard, or other needs, be sure to specify them. Try to ensure that your speaker requirements just cover the essentials; white doves backstage and your own trailer should be avoided in your requirements list.[2]

Photos

Include some photos of yourself, taken by a professional photographer. These photos should be at a really high resolution so that they can be included in printed material if required. I recommend that you get some portrait shots of you looking smart and professional.

Once you've gathered these things, you should write your submission and have a friend or colleague review it before you hit the Submit button. Always ensure that you try to get your submissions in before the deadline.

With your presentation submitted, now hold your fire and keep your fingers crossed, and wait for the event organizers to get back to you. Whatever you do, don't pester the event organizers for a decision; wait for them to get back to you.

> **NOTE**
>
> When submitting presentations to events and conferences, be sure you can actually attend the event if you get accepted. You should not presume that accommodation and travel sponsorship is available, unless outlined on the website (and even then you should specify it as a requirement if you can't afford to pay your own way there). Never submit a presentation if you can't guarantee you can join the event if your presentation is accepted; for conference organizers this can be frustrating, and you don't want to tarnish your reputation in the eyes of the event planners.

---

2. For an example of inflated speaking requirements, see Richard Stallman's at *https://secure.mysociety.org/admin/lists/pipermail/developers-public/2011-October/007647.html*.

Promoting your talk

Once you get a presentation accepted for an event, the real work begins. Unfortunately, many speakers at events get their acceptance email for a presentation submission and then never do anything to promote and encourage people to actually attend their session.

At many events there are multiple presentations going on simultaneously. You not only want to encourage people to attend the general event, but also want to encourage people to go to your presentation. A packed presentation room is a great thing, and that is what we are aiming for here.

As such, you should start performing some buzz and outreach about your presentation in the buildup to the event. Be sure to blog about it in your community, use social media to spread the word, mention it in interviews, reach out to local user groups where the event is held to encourage them to join, and perform other types of outreach.

One technique I have found useful is to provide teaser updates and snippets in the weeks before the event that outline some of the topics you will be discussing. Publicize these over social media and blogging resources, and keep a regular flow of these little snippets coming to generate excitement and momentum around the presentation.

Delivering Presentations

When I was 17 I gave my very first presentation. It took place at the Linux User Group event that I used to kick off Chapter 1. I came armed with a StarOffice presentation that I had obsessed over ever since I rather stupidly volunteered to give a presentation. I had no idea what a presentation was supposed to look like; it wasn't like there was a YouTube back then where I could pick up tips...hell, there was barely even an Internet.

Somewhat limited in options, I asked my dad for help. A man of many vocations (who should really have a book written about him), he was currently working in a senior role at a large car sales organization. He was at one with the presentation mojo, but his presentations were designed for businesspeople; laden with bullet points, overlapping circles, complex diagrams and other such fluff. This was a different crowd, but I had no idea what they wanted to see.

I put together my deck and delivered it to the Linux User Group. I wasn't so much worried about the delivery (I was a fairly outgoing teen) but more the structure, story, and design of my slides. I really wanted people to *enjoy* my presentation; I didn't want it to feel like a dorky presentation done by a pimply teenager (which of course it was). Fortunately, it went pretty well.

This kick-started years of trial and error in developing my own presentation mojo. Over the course of my career, I have seen some brutally awful presentations and some stunningly entertaining and thoughtful ones. I have always wanted to be in the latter category, and while I don't consider myself an expert in presentation magic, I have come away with some tips I want to share with you all. Given that this book is called *The Art of Community* and not *The Art of Presenting* I don't want to sidetrack us too far from the community path, but delivering great presentations can really excite and motivate people to join your community.

Of course, everyone has his own style, and you should take time to develop yours, but here are some tips that I recommend you apply to your presentations to make them as fun and interesting as possible:

Tell a story

> Bad presentations feel like a rattled-off collection of random thoughts and good presentations take you on a journey and tell a story. Before you write your presentation, think about how you can weave your points together into a logical story. Remember, all stories have a beginning, a middle, and an end; think about how this can apply to the things you want to talk about.

Build tension

> The greatest stories in the world have tension in them; you build up the tension in your audience and then relieve it. You should do the same in your presentations. In many of my presentations I tell a story about how I got somewhere, and often the tension is created when I share how I made some bad decisions and how I got back on the right path. Think about where your tension occurs and make sure you build up to it.

Plan first, design second

> Many people start creating a presentation by getting right into slide design. Don't do this; you will obsess over the design before you know the structure of your presentation, and this is a huge time sink. Instead, grab a pen and a pad (or a text editor on your computer) and start noting the key points your want to cover and how they map to slides. When you have a few words describing each slide and they're in the order you would present the slides, you can use this as a guide for creating your slide deck.

Keep slide content to a minimum

> When you give a presentation your audience should focus primarily on what you are saying, not what you are showing in the deck. Slides full of content, detail, bullet points, and other fluff will merely distract your audience from what you are saying. As such, keep the content on the slides to a minimum.

Know your comedic limitations

> This is a tough pill to swallow for some, but know your comic limitations. A not-particularly funny person trying to be funny is nothing short of embarrassing. I am not saying jokes are off-limits, but do what feels natural to your personality.

Practice, practice, practice

> No matter how many presentations you have given, practice is always the key to a well-executed and delivered presentation. Always run through your presentation a few times, time it to make sure it is the right length, and get it down pat. A great tip here is to video yourself delivering your presentation; you can then observe your body language and delivery better.

Prepare the presentation essentials

Before you deliver the presentation, always ensure that you have available a glass of water and a sheet of paper with a list of your slides. One of these days you will have a dry mouth and a brain fart; make sure you are prepared for both.

Creating attractive slides

By far the most important aspect of delivering a great presentation is in the way the speaker structures and communicates the content. We have all sat through dry, boring, monotonous talks, and many of you will have seen fun, interesting, and vibrant talks.

What is also important in delivering a great presentation is creating slides that support what you are saying effectively. Unfortunately, over the years many presenters have treated their slides almost like an entirely different entity to the content they are talking about. Remember, though, that the purpose of the slides is to visualize and simplify the understanding of the content you are discussing. In other words, what you say and the slides you show should knit together like those mittens your grandma used to give you when you were six years old and had a bowl haircut.

As we discussed earlier, your presentation should tell a story, and your slides should be used like the pictures in a storybook to outline and illustrate your story as it progresses. Unfortunately, some presenters only ever illustrate their presentations with diagrams, overlapping circles, bar charts, and other output from the yawn factory.

Everyone has her own slide design style, but I want to recommend an approach that I strongly suggest you all use. Here it is…get ready for it and fasten your seatbelts:

Your slides can only contain either (1) a picture, or (2) no more than 10 words.

The world has seen enough slides filled with bullet points, overly complex diagrams, arrows, overlapping circles, hundreds of logos, and other presentation horrors.

As you can see with one of my slides, shown in Figure 7-2, I prefer to use only a few words or just an image; it makes the slide less distracting and more visually interesting.

Keep your slides simple and use them as a means to offer a visual cue to indicate where you are in the story. It will distract your audience less (they can't read all those bullets and listen to what you are saying at the same time), it will look attractive, and it will just result in a more interesting experience.

FIGURE 7-2. This simple slide design consists of only a few words and a simple graphic.

Long versus short presentations

In July 2011, I gave one of the opening keynotes at OSCON, a large open source conference in Portland, Oregon. The talk was 15 minutes long, and it was OK. While I didn't consider it a bad talk, it wasn't what I considered my best work.

Immediately after the presentation I gave my second talk, which was 40 minutes long, and I was very happy with the results. A filled room of folks seemed to find the talk useful and there were plenty of questions. I did consider that to be some of my better work.

So, in a nutshell, my 15-minute keynote felt OK and my 40-minute talk felt solid.

Something was bothering me for much of the day about why this was. My dissatisfaction was not with the execution of the keynote; I felt I was reasonably vibrant and articulate in the way I presented it. But I was less happy with the content and the structure. It felt to me that not enough of the rubber hit the road.

I had been giving talks at conferences around the world for over 12 years. I had taken pride in striving to deliver useful content, but wrapping it up in a loose and entertaining style, and providing plenty of anecdotes to identify with the audience. Twelve years in, I felt pretty confident that I had this presentation business down pat. I felt like I had cut my teeth, paid my dues, and made all the mistakes I needed to make to perfect the art of delivering a solid presentation.

Well, I was (and probably still am) an idiot.

When I started preparing the content for my keynote, I really battled with the content and the structure. This was a different type of keynote; it was more along the lines of a lightning talk in terms of duration, but it had the gravitas of a keynote. It needed to be thought-provoking and set the stage for discussions elsewhere at OSCON. But I needed to do this in a short burst of time, and make it feel like an experience that people could identify with. I had my message; I believed we were at the beginning of a renaissance in community management, but I found the shorter nature of the presentation and its position as a keynote more challenging than I expected it to be.

After delivering the keynote and thinking about why it didn't feel as right as it should have, I came to some conclusions, which I want to share. If you are a presenter some of these thoughts might be useful in terms of how you think about your presentations, too.

First, my presentation style has always been story-oriented; I build up a context, provide some tension in that context, and then deliver an outcome that strives to relieve the tension and provide insight. As such, there is a certain amount of setup and context building that gets the audience up the curve; then I deliver the outcome and bring the audience back down over the curve and provide conclusions. This storytelling component takes time...valuable time in a short presentation.

Second, Steph Walli (a friend of mine and proofreader of the first edition of this book) observed that while there is a very real skill in writing novels, there is also a real but very different skill in writing short stories. This observation was insightful to me. Short stories by definition need the storytelling to be more compact, and the finesse and skill is in delivering the same smooth setup and transition of events, but with fewer keyframes thrown into the mix.

As such, I came to the conclusion that I like to tell stories in my presentations, but my career thus far had been from the perspective of a novelist as opposed to a short-story writer. This was illustrated when my longer talk felt more natural and *more me*, yet the keynote felt personally more awkward and *less me*. While I was confident in my skills in delivering a 30- or 40-minute presentation, I discovered that delivering a shorter presentation that needs to have the same or a greater level of gravitas required a very different and distinctive set of skills, which I then wanted to acquire.

Summary

Buzz is a complex and wide-ranging topic and one that can be exercised in many different ways. Fundamentally, the art of building buzz varies from person to person. Some will keep the game simple and use email and blogs to build excitement, and others will organize more grandiose campaigns and events; some will even cut crop circles in the ground in the shape of a logo to get the word out. The extravagance of the buzz campaign is often directly linked to the extravagance of the personality behind it, but this is not a closed-door club in which only those born with a sense of adventure can build great buzz. Anyone can develop this sense for thinking outside the box.

At the heart of these approaches is thinking of ways in which you can point eyeballs in your direction and then deliver a message. It is important to get the balance right here: buzz without substance is *hype*, and you should avoid that like the plague. Always ensure that the message you send is just as compelling as the buzz approach you used.

One last note about thinking outside the box: it is a risky business. You are going to make mistakes and end up frustrating some folks. When you do screw up, see it as a learning process. Pick yourself up and objectively review what you did. All mistakes are acceptable under the premise that you learn from them. As you continue to build more and more buzz, you will make fewer mistakes and create more successes as you bring people to your community.

CHAPTER EIGHT

Measuring Community

"Learning without thought is labor lost."

—*Confucius*

GREAT COMMUNITY LEADERSHIP REQUIRES ACCEPTING THE VOLATILITY OF COMMUNITY.
Volunteer communities are a bubbling pot of varying personalities, commitments, skills, and experiences. This is why I often refer to the work of community leaders as "herding cats." But as leaders we are here not only to lead and inspire our cats, but also to learn to see the patterns in the chaos that is community.

There are many patterns out there: common personality traits, techniques for getting people excited about something, methods of handling conflict, common opinions, and more. It is these patterns, correlations, and structures that help us to better manage our own communities, as well as share our experiences with others. When I see a pattern, I want to share it so that you can use it in your communities. Unfortunately, the randomness of the chaos can sometimes hide these patterns from common view, and many perceive "community measurement" as something of an oxymoron.

Earlier in this book we contrasted logical vessels such as programming languages with more randomized entities such as community:

> [Programming languages] live and breathe in a world where the answer to a question is *yes* or *no*; there is no *maybe*. In a world where *maybe* does not exist, you can plan ahead for an answer. With community, the importance and diversity of the question is equally essential.

You could be forgiven for thinking that community is unpredictable and immeasurable, but let's not overemphasize the challenges of "maybe." Community may not be as straightforward as "yes" and "no," but that doesn't mean we can't see the patterns, learn them, and share them.

Our strategic plan has helped us lay out a blueprint for what our community can achieve. But a plan is just that: a plan. It is a statement of work that we *intend* to do. It is not enough to simply provide your community with a strategic plan, even if it was collaboratively produced. Your community is going to need help, support, and some gentle nudging to achieve these goals.

Great community leadership requires regular and consistent feedback. When we originally produced our strategy, we were conscious of creating a feedback loop to gather input from our community. We now need to enforce the same feedback loop when it comes to executing the items in that plan. To really know we are achieving our goals, we need to be able to *measure* our community effectively.

Community Self-Reflection

People can be broadly divided into three groups that define their approach to tasks.

The first group believes they know best. They go after their goals with little or no input from anyone else. They have a clear idea in their minds of what needs to be done, and they do it. They don't solicit feedback, because they don't need feedback: they know best. They are confident, if a little cocky at times.

The second group wouldn't know a decision if it hit them in the face. They need extensive help and guidance to determine how to achieve their goals, and they need coaching in the individual steps involved. If they had their way, they would ask you to do it for them. In the absence of delegation they instead want you to advise, make decisions, and generally think for them.

I am a fan of neither cocky nor procrastinating people. I am, however, a *huge* fan of the third category of people: those who are confident in their approach, but who reinforce and improve said approach with feedback, mentoring, and guidance. Interestingly, many of the members of the first group shun this approach as a perceived admission of imperfection. Well, I hate to break this to you, folks, but none of us are perfect. The American singer and actress Eartha Kitt described it perfectly: "I am learning all the time. The tombstone will be my diploma."

The greatest leaders are always willing to listen and learn, and the most inspiring people I have worked with have taken this approach. This is what I personally strive for, and I encourage you to do the same.

As we discussed earlier, community is very much a soft science. It is an art form that is improved and extended by sharing stories and experiences. It is these tales that extend our knowledge and offer us insight. The greatest gift you can offer to a community is the willingness to listen. When leaders listen, their community talks and everyone feels engaged.

The Foundations of Feedback

There are lots of easy ways to measure communities—the number of members on a forum, the number of contributions to a shared project, and so forth—but it's not so easy to find *meaningful* measurements. We want our measurements to feed into our interpretations of what we're doing and to trigger changes that can further improve our work.

Unfortunately, many community leaders obsess a little too much over the act of *gathering information* as opposed to gathering *meaningful* information. The goal here is not to construct an enormous vacuum cleaner to suck every tiny detail of your community into a graph. The goal is instead to identify what we don't know about our community and to use measurements as a means to understand those things better.

Measurements without meaning are simply annoying. Randomly sucking in statistics is intensely time-consuming—not only for you, but also for the people who provide you with the input. Most of us reading this book will be building volunteer communities in which time is a precious substance. Don't waste it.

Each time you engage with your contributors to gather feedback, there is an unwritten yet implicit social contract: as a result of the feedback they expect change—hopefully positive change. When positive change does not happen, frustration sets in. If your measurements have purpose and you are willing to make a change based on those measurements, your community will be satisfied.

Defining Purpose

Earlier in this book we constructed our strategic plan, which included a vocabulary identifying the key features of our strategy. Let's have a quick recap:

- We first created a *mission statement* that outlined the broad aims of the community.
- Based on this statement we produced a set of high-level *objectives*. These are the major achievements that together form our mission statement.
- For each objective we have a set of *goals*. Each goal is a near-term outcome that we want to achieve. When we complete all the goals in an objective, we can consider the objective achieved.
- For each goal we have a set of *actions*. When we complete all of the actions in a goal, we can consider the goal achieved.

As you can see, the different parts of the strategy are nested inside one another. They look something like this:

```
Mission Statement
    Objective
        Goal
            Actions
            Actions
            Actions
        Goal
            Actions
            Actions
    Objective
        Goal
            Actions
            Actions
```

Our goals are the target of our feedback. They are what we want to measure. They are the purpose and the reason for our work throughout this chapter.

Inside these goals we are going to build extra features into this hierarchy: *hooks* and *data*. These features will help us gather important feedback on how well we are achieving the goal.

With a clear set of goals, each containing meaningful measurement facilities, we will be able to take a snapshot of the internals of our community that shows us how our strategic plan is proceeding. If the measurements show a lack of progress, we may have to alter actions, goals, or even objectives.

Hooks 'n' Data

So far we've discussed the importance of gathering feedback and measurements from our community, and that the focal point is the goals we decided on in our strategic plan. The next step is to build into each goal a feedback loop that can deliver information about our progress on the goal.

This feedback loop is composed of two components—*hooks* and *data*:

Hooks

A hook is a medium or resource in which we can slurp out useful information about our goal. As an example, if our goal was to reduce crime in a neighborhood, a hook could be local crime reports from the police. The reason I call them hooks is that they are the protruding access points in which we can display interesting information.

Data

If a hook is the medium that provides useful information, data is the information itself. Using our previous example of a goal to reduce crime in a neighborhood, the hook (local crime reports) could provide data such as "10 crimes this month." The data is composed of two attributes, the data itself and the measurement unit. Again, the kind of unit can be used to feed a display (e.g., numerical units are great for graphs).

To help understand this further, let's look at an example. In the Ubuntu community, my team has worked to help increase the number of people who become new developers. In our strategic plan we created an objective to increase the number of community developers and fleshed it out with goals for improving developer documentation, awareness, and education. Each goal had the expected set of actions. For us to effectively track progress on the objective, we needed data about developer growth.

Fortunately, we have access to a system called Launchpad (*http://www.launchpad.net*), which is where all Ubuntu developers do their work. This system was an enormous hook that we could use to extract data. To do this we gathered a range of data types:

- The current number of developers (e.g., 50 developers)
- How long new contributions from prospective developers took to be mentored by existing developers (e.g., 1.4 weeks)
- How many of these new contributions are outstanding for mentoring (e.g., 23 contributions)

Launchpad had all of this information available. Using some computer programs created by Daniel Holbach, we could extract the data. This allowed us to track not only the current number of developers, but also how quickly progress was being made: we knew that if the number of developers was regularly growing, we were making progress.

We could also use this data to assess the primary tool that new developers use to participate in Ubuntu: the queue of new contributions to be mentored. When a new developer wants to contribute, she adds her contribution to this queue. Our existing developers then review the item, provide feedback, and if it is suitable, commit it.

By having data on the average time something sits on that queue as well as the number of outstanding items, we could (a) set reasonable expectations and (b) ensure that the facility was working as well as possible.

In this example, Launchpad was a hook. Using it involved some specific knowledge of how to physically grab the data we needed from it. This required specialist knowledge: a script was written in Python that used the Launchpad API to gather the data, and then it was formatted in HTML to be viewed.

Launchpad was an obvious hook, but not the only one. Although Launchpad could provide excellent numbers, it could not give us personal perspectives and opinions. What were the thoughts, praise, concerns, and other views about our developer processes and how well they worked? More specifically, how easy was it to get approved as an Ubuntu developer?

To gather this feedback, our hook was a developer survey designed for prospective and new developers. We could direct this survey to another hook: the list of the most recently approved developers and their contact details. This group of people would be an excellent source of feedback, as they had just been through the developer approval process and it would be fresh in their minds.

With so many hooks available to communities, I obviously cannot cover the specific details of how to use them. This would turn *The Art of Community* into *War and Peace*—complete with tragic outcome (at least for me). Fortunately, the specifics are not of interest, as all hooks can be broadly divided into three categories:

Statistics and automated data
> Hooks in this category primarily deal with *numbers,* and numbers can be automatically manipulated into statistics.

Surveys and structured feedback
> These hooks primarily deal with *words and sentences* and methods of gathering them.

Observational tests
> These hooks are *visual observations* that can provide insight into how people use things.

Let's take a walk through the neighborhood of each of these hooks and learn a little more about them.

Statistics and Automated Data

People have a love/hate relationship with statistics. Gregg Easterbrook in *The New Republic* said, "Torture numbers, and they'll confess to anything." Despite the cynicism that surrounds statistics, they turn up insistently on television, in newspapers, on websites, and even in general pub and restaurant chitchat. The problem with the general presentation of statistics is that the numbers are often used to make the point itself instead of being an indicator of a wider conclusion.

Statistics are merely indicators. They are the metaphorical equivalent of the numbers and gauges on the dashboard of a car. No single reading can advise on the health of the car; the gauges, along with the sound of the car itself, how it handles, its look and feel, and the smell of burning oil all combine to give you an indication that your beloved motor may be under the weather.

Despite the butchered reputation of statistics, they *can* offer us valuable insight into the status quo of our community. Statistics can provide hard evidence of how aspects of your community are functioning.

Many hooks can deliver numerical data. Here are a few examples:

- Forums and mailing lists can deliver the number of posts and number of members.
- Your website can deliver the number of visitors and number of downloads.
- Your meeting notes can deliver the number of participants and number of topics discussed.
- Your development tools can deliver the number of lines of code written, number of commits made to the source repository, and number of developers.
- Your wiki can deliver the number of users and number of pages.

For us to get the most out of statistics, we need to understand the mechanics of our community and which hooks can deliver data from those mechanics. We will discuss how to find hooks from these mechanics later in this chapter.

The risks of interpretation

Although statistics can provide compelling documentation of the current status quo of your community, they require skill to be interpreted properly. A great example of this is forum posts. Many online communities use *discussion forums*, the online message boards in which you can post messages to a common topic (known in forum parlance as a *thread*). Within most forums there is one statistic that everyone seems to have something of a love affair with: the total number of posts made by each user.

It's easy to see how people draw this conclusion. If you have three users, one with 2 posts, one with 200 posts, and one with 2,000 posts, it's tempting to believe the user with 2,000 posts has more insight, experience, and wisdom. Many forums latch onto this perspective and provide labels based on the number of posts. As an example, a forum could have these labels:

0–100 posts: New to the Forum
101–500 posts: On the Road to Greatness
501–1,500 posts: Regular Hero
1,501–3,000 posts: Dependable Legend
3,001+ posts: Expert Ninja

As an example, if I had 493 posts, this would give me the "On the Road to Greatness" label, but if I had 2,101 posts, I would have the "Dependable Legend" label. These labels and the number of posts statistic are great for pumping up the members, but they offer little insight in terms of quality.

Quantity is rarely an indicator of quality; if it were, spammers would be the definition of email quality. When you are gathering statistics, you will be regularly faced with a quantity versus quality issue, but always bear in mind that quality is determined by the specifics of an individual contribution as opposed to the amalgamated set of contributions. What quantity really teaches us is experience. No one can deny that someone with 1,000 forum posts has keen experience in the forum, but it doesn't necessarily reflect the quality of his opinion and insight.

Plugging your stats into graphs

Stats with no presentation are merely a list of numbers. When articulated effectively, though, statistics can exhibit the meaning that we strive for. This is where graphs come into play.

Graphs are an excellent method of displaying lots of numerical information and avoiding boring the pants off either (a) yourself or (b) other people. Let's look at an example. Earlier we talked about a project to increase the number of community developers in Ubuntu, and one piece of data we gathered was the current number of community developers who had been approved. This is, of course, a useful piece of information, and as the number climbs it helps indicate that we are achieving our goal. What that single number does not teach us, though, is how *quickly* we are achieving our goal.

Imagine that we had 50 developers right now and we wanted to increase that figure by 20% a year. This would mean we would need to find five developers in the next six months. This works out to approximately one developer per month. If we want to encourage this consistency of growth, we need not only to look at the number of current developers once, but also to track it over time so that we can see if we are on track to achieve our 20% target. Using this example in the Ubuntu world, we could use Launchpad to take a regular snapshot of the number of current developers, plot it on a graph, and draw a line between the dots. This could give us a growth curve of new developers joining the project.

Another handy benefit of graphs is to show the impact of specific campaigns on your community. On my team at Canonical we have a graph that shows the current number of bugs in Ubuntu. On the graph is a line that shows the current number of bugs for each week. As you can imagine, the line that connects these numbers shows a general curve of our bug performance. This line is generally fairly consistent.

Each cycle, we have a special event called the Ubuntu Global Jam (*http://wiki.ubuntu.com/ UbuntuGlobalJam*) in which our community comes together to work on bugs. Our local user groups organize bug-squashing parties, and there are online events and other activities that are all based around fixing bugs. Interestingly, each time we do the event, we see a drop in the number of bugs on our graph for the days that the Global Jam happens. This is an excellent method of assessing the impact of the event on our bug numbers.

TECHNICAL TIP

You may be wondering how you can gather data from various hooks and display them in a graph automatically. I just wanted to share a few tips. If this seems like rocket science to you, I recommend that you seek advice from someone who is familiar with these technologies.

Gathering data from hooks is hugely dependent on the hook. Fortunately, many online services offer an application programming interface (API) that a program can use to gather the data. This will require knowledge of programming. Many programming languages, such as Python and Perl, make it simple to get data through the API.

Another approach with hooks is to screen-scrape. This is the act of downloading a web page and figuring out what text on the page has the data. This is useful if an API is not available.

For graphing, many tools are available that can ease graphing if the data is available. One such tool is Cricket (*http://cricket.sourceforge.net/*), and of course, you could load data into a spreadsheet with a comma-separated value (CSV) file if required.

Surveys and Structured Feedback

Surveys are an excellent method of taking the pulse of your community. For us, they are simple to set up, and for our audience, they are simple to use. I have used surveys extensively in my career, and each time they have provided me and my teams with excellent feedback. Over the next few pages I want to share some of the experience I have picked up in delivering effective surveys.

The first step is to determine the purpose of the survey. What do you want to achieve with it? What do you need to know? Every survey needs to have a purpose, and it is this purpose that will help you craft a useful set of questions that should generate an even more useful set of data.

> **NOTE**
>
> **You should avoid surveys just for the purpose of creating a survey. Only ever create a survey if there is a question in your head that is unanswered. Surveys are tools to help you understand your community better: use them only when there is a purpose. Examples of this could include understanding the perception of a specific process, identifying common patterns in behavior in communication channels, and learning which resources are used more than others.**

Again, your goals from your strategic plan are a key source of purpose for your surveys. As an example, if your goal is "increase the number of contributors in the community," you should break down the workflow of how people join your community, and produce a set of questions that test each step in this workflow. You can use the feedback from the answers to gauge whether your workflow is effective and use the data as a basis for improvements.

Choosing questions

When deciding on questions, you should be conscious of one simple fact: everyone hates filling out surveys. When someone has considered participating in your survey, you need to be able to gather that person's feedback as quickly and easily as possible. This should take no longer than five minutes. As such, I recommend that you use no more than 10 questions. This will give the respondent an average of 30 seconds to answer each question.

The vast majority of surveys have questions with multiple-choice ratings for satisfaction. Most of you will be familiar with these: you are provided with a satisfaction scale between 1 (awful) and 5 (excellent), and are then expected to select the appropriate satisfaction grade for that question. Surveys like this are simple and effective.

THE VARIANCE OF THE VOTE

Ratings are a funny beast, and everyone interprets them differently.

A great example of this is the employee performance review that so many of us are familiar with. In one organization I worked at, the scale ranged from 1 (unacceptable) to 5 (outstanding). I did a small straw poll of how different people interpreted the grading system, and the views varied tremendously:

- Some felt that if 1 is unacceptable and 5 is outstanding, 3 would be considered acceptable, and if staff members completed their work as contractually expected, a 3 would be a reasonable score.

- Others felt that meeting contractually agreed-upon standards would merit a 5 on the scale, and that 3 would indicate significant, if tolerable, lapses.

- Interestingly, some people informed me that they would never provide a 5, as they felt there was *always* room for improvement.

When people fill in your survey, you will get an equally varied set of expectations around the ratings. You should factor this variation of responses into your assessment of the results. One way to do this is to add up the responses from each person and increase or reduce them proportionally so that each person's total adds up to the same points. But this may not be valid if someone legitimately had a wonderful or horrific experience across the board.

When writing your questions, you need to ensure that they are simple, short, and specific enough that your audience will not have any uncertainty about what you are asking. When people are confronted with unclear questions in surveys, they tend to simply give up or pick a random answer. Obviously both of these are less-than-stellar outcomes. Let's look at an example of a bad question:

Do you like our community?

Wow, how incredibly unspecific. Which aspect of the community are we asking about? What exactly does "like" mean? Here is an example of a much better question:

Did you receive enough help and assistance from the mailing list to help you join the community successfully?

This is more detailed, easier to understand, and therefore easier to answer. It's no coincidence that the results are more immediately applicable to making useful changes in the community.

Using the previous example of a survey to track progress on the goal of increasing the number of contributors, here are some additional example questions:

How clear was the New Contributor Process to you?
How suitable do you feel the requirements are to join the community?
How useful was the available documentation for joining the community?
How efficiently do you feel your application was tended to?

Each of these asks a specific question about your community and the different processes involved.

Showing off your survey reports

Earlier, when we talked about statistics, we also explored the benefits of using graphs for plotting numerical feedback. We could feed the data directly into the graph, and the findings are automatically generated. This makes the entire process of gathering statistics easy: we can automate the collection of the data from the hook (such as regularly sucking out the data) and then the presentation of the data (regularly generating the graph).

Unfortunately, this is impossible when dealing with feedback provided in words, sentences, and paragraphs. A person has to read and assess the findings and then present them in a report. It is this report that we can present to our community as a source for improving how we work.

Readers have priorities when picking up your report. They don't want to read through reams and reams of text to find a conclusion: they want to read the conclusion up front and optionally read the details later. I recommend that you structure your survey findings reports as follows:

1. Present a broad conclusion, a paragraph that outlines the primary revelation that we can take away from the entire survey. For example, this could be "Developer growth is slower than expected and needs to improve." It is this broad conclusion that will inspire people to read the survey. Do keep one important thing in mind, though: don't turn the conclusion into an inaccurate, feisty headline just for the purpose of encouraging people to read the survey. That will just annoy your readers and could lead to inaccurate buzz that spirals out of your control, both within and outside your community.

2. Document the primary findings as a series of bullet points. These findings don't necessarily need to be the findings for each question, but instead the primary lessons to be learned from the entire survey. It is these findings that your community will take as the meat of the survey. They should be clear, accurate, and concise.

3. Present a list of recommended actions that will improve on each finding. Each action should have a clear correlation with the findings that your survey presented. The reader should be able to clearly identify how an action will improve the current situation. One

caveat, though: not all reports can present action items. Sometimes a factual finding does not automatically suggest an action item; it may take negotiation and discussion for leaders to figure out the right action.

4. Finally, in the interest of completeness, present the entire set of data that you received in the survey. This is often useful as an addendum or appendix to the preceding information. This is a particularly useful place to present nonmultiple-choice answers (written responses).

When you have completed your survey and documented these results, you should ensure that they are available to the rest of your community. Sharing these results with the community is (a) a valuable engagement in transparency, (b) a way to share the current status quo of the community with everyone, and (c) an opportunity to encourage others to fix the problems or seek the opportunities that the survey uncovers.

To do this, you should put the report on your website. Ensure that you clearly note the date on which the results were taken. This will make it apparent to your readers that the results were a snapshot of that point in the history of your community. If you don't provide a date, your community will assume the results are from today.

When you put the results online, you should notify your community through whatever communication channels are in place, such as mailing lists, online chat channels, forums, websites, and more.

DOCUMENTED RESULTS ARE FOREVER

Before we move on, I just want to ensure that we are on the same page (pun intended) about documenting your results.

When you put the results of your survey online, you should never go back and change them. Even if you work hard to improve the community, the results should be seen as a snapshot of your community.

You should ensure that you include with the results the date that they were taken so that this is clear.

Observational Tests

When trying to measure the effectiveness of a process, an observational test can be one of the most valuable approaches. This is where you simply sit down and watch someone interact with something and take notes on what the person does. Often this can uncover nuances that can be improved or refined.

This is something that my team at Canonical has engaged in a number of times. As part of our work in refining how the community can connect bugs in Ubuntu to bugs that live upstream, I wanted to get a firm idea of the mechanics of how a user links one bug to another. I was specifically keen to learn if there were any quirks in the process that we could ease. If we could flatten out the process a little, we could make it easier for the community to participate.

To do this, we sat down and watched a contributor working with bugs. We noted how he interacted with the bug tracker, what content he added, where he made mistakes, and other elements. This data gave us a solid idea of areas of redundancy in how he interacted with a community facility.

What Jorge on my team did here was user-based testing, more commonly known as *usability testing*. This is a user-centered design method that helps developers evaluate software by having real people use it and provide feedback. By simply sitting a few people in front of your software and having them try it out, you can obtain valuable feedback for a design before too much is invested in coding a bad solution.

Usability testing is important for two reasons. The most obvious is that it gets us feedback from a lot of real users, all doing the same thing. Even though we aren't necessarily looking for statistical significance, recognizing usage patterns can help the designer or developer begin to think about how to solve the problem in a more usable way.

The second reason is that usability testing, when done early in the development cycle, can save a lot of community resources. Catching usability problems in the design phase can save development time normally lost to rewriting a bad component. Catching usability problems early in a release cycle can preempt bug submissions and save time triaging. This is on top of the added benefit that many users may never experience such usability issues because they are caught and fixed so early.

Open source is a naturally user-centered community. We rely on user feedback to help test software and influence future development directions. A weakness of traditional usability testing is that it takes a lot of time to plan and conduct a formal laboratory test. With the highly iterative and aggressive release cycles some open source projects follow, it is sometimes difficult to provide a timely report on usability testing results. Some examples of projects that overcame problems in timing and cost appear in the accompanying sidebar ("Examples of Low-Budget, Rigorous Usability Tests") by Celeste Lyn Paul, a senior interaction architect at User-Centered Design, Inc. She helps make software easier to use by understanding users' work processes and designing interactive systems to fit their needs. She is also involved in open source software and leads the KDE Usability Project, mentors the OpenUsability Season of Usability program, and serves on the Kubuntu Council.

EXAMPLES OF LOW-BUDGET, RIGOROUS USABILITY TESTS

There are some ways you can make usability testing work in the open source community. Throughout my career in open source, I have run a number of usability tests, and not all have been the conventional laboratory-based testing you often think of when you hear "usability test." These three examples help describe the different ways usability testing can be conducted and how it can fit into the open source community.

My first example is the usability testing of the Kubuntu version of Ubiquity, the Ubuntu installer. This usability test was organized as a graduate class activity at the University of Baltimore. I worked with the students to design a research plan, recruit participants, run the test, and analyze the results. Finally, all of the project reports were collated into a single report, which was presented to the Ubuntu community. The timing of the test was aligned with a recent release and development summit, and so even though the logistics of the usability test spanned several weeks, the results provided to the Ubuntu community were timely and relevant.

Although this is the more rare case of how to organize open source usability testing, involving university students in open source usability testing provides three key benefits. The open source project benefits from a more formal usability test, which is otherwise difficult to obtain; the university students get experience testing a real product, which looks good on a curriculum vitae; and the university students get exposure to open source, which could potentially lead to interest in further contribution in the future.

My second example involves guerilla-style usability testing over IRC. I was working with Konstantinos Smanis on the design and development of KGRUBEditor. Unlike most software, which usually is in the maintenance phase, we had the opportunity to design the application from scratch. While we were designing certain interactive components, we were unsure which of the two design options was the most intuitive. Konstantinos coded and packaged dummy prototypes of the two interactive methods while I recruited and interviewed several people on IRC, guiding them through the test scenario and recording their actions and feedback. The results we gathered from the impromptu testing helped us make a decision about which design to use.

The IRC testing provided a quick and dirty way of testing interface design ideas in an interactive prototype. However, this method was limited in the type of testing we could do and the amount of feedback we could collect. Remote usability testing provides the benefit of anytime, anywhere, anyone at the cost of high-bandwidth communication with the participant and control over the testing environment.

My final example is the case of usability testing with the DC Ubuntu Local Community (LoCo). I developed a short usability testing plan that had participants complete a small task that would take approximately 15 minutes to complete. LoCo members brought a friend or family member to the LoCo's Ubuntu lab at a local library. Before the testing sessions, I worked with the LoCo members and gave them some tips on how to take their guest through the test scenario. Then, each LoCo member led their guest through the scenario while I took notes about what the participant said and did. Afterward, the LoCo members discussed what they saw in testing, and with assistance, came up with a few key problems they found in the software.

The LoCo-based usability test was a great way to involve nontechnical members of the Ubuntu community and provide them an avenue to directly contribute. The drawback to this method is that it takes a lot of planning and coordination: I had to develop a testing plan that was short but provided enough task to get useful data, find a place to test (we were lucky enough to already have an Ubuntu lab), and get enough LoCo members involved to make testing worthwhile.

—Celeste Lyn Paul
Senior Interaction Architect
User-Centered Design, Inc.

Although Celeste was largely testing end-user software, her approach was very community-focused. The heart of her approach involved community collaboration, not only to highlight problems in the interface but also to identify better ways to approach the same task.

These same tests should be made against your own community facilities. Consider some of the following topics for these kinds of observational tests:

- Ask a member to find something on your website.
- Ask a prospective contributor to join the community and find the resources he needs.
- Ask a member to find a piece of information, such as a bug, a message on a mailing list, or another resource.
- Ask a member to escalate an issue to a governance council.

Each of these tasks will be interpreted and executed in different ways. By sitting down and watching your community performing these tasks, you will invariably find areas for improvement.

Measuring Mechanics

The lifeblood of communities, and particularly collaborative ones, is communication. It is the flow of conversation that builds healthy communities, but these conversations can and do stretch well beyond mere words and sentences. All communities have collaborative mechanics that define how people do things together. An example of this in software development communities is bugs. Bugs are the defects, problems, and other it-really-shouldn't-work-that-way annoyances that tend to infiltrate the software development process.

Every *mechanic* (method of collaborating) in your community is like a conveyor belt. There is a set of steps and elements that comprise the conversation. When we understand these steps in the conversation, we can often identify hooks that we can use to get data. With this data we can then make improvements to optimize the flow of conversation.

Let's look at our example of bugs to illustrate this.

Every bug has a lifeline, and that lifeline is broadly divided into three areas: *reporting*, *triaging*, and *fixing*. Each area has a series of steps involved. Let's look at reporting as an example. These are the steps:

1. The user experiences a problem with a piece of software.
2. The user visits a bug tracker in her web browser to report that problem.
3. The user enters several pieces of information: a summary, description, name of the software product, and other criteria.
4. When the bug is filed, the user can subscribe to the bug report and be notified of the changes to the bug.

Now let's look at each step again, see which hooks are available, and identify what data we could pull out:

1. There are no hooks in this step.
2. When the user visits the bug tracker in her web browser, the bug tracker could provide data about the number of visitors, what browsers they are using, which operating systems they are on, and other web statistics.
3. We could query the bug tracker for anything that is present in a bug report: how many bugs are in the tracker, how many bugs are in each product, how many bugs are new, and so on.
4. We could gather statistics about the number of subscribers for each and which bugs have the most subscribers.

So there's a huge range of possible hooks in just the bug reporting part of the bug conveyor belt. Let's now follow the example through with the remaining two areas and their steps and hooks.

The following are the triaging steps:

1. A triager looks at a bug and changes the bug status.
2. The triager may need to ask for additional information about the bug.
3. Other triagers add their comments and additional information to help identify the cause of the bug.

Here are the triaging hooks:

1. We could use the bug tracker to tell us how many bugs fall into each type of status. This could give us an excellent idea of not only how many bugs need fixing, but also, when we plot these figures on a graph, how quickly bugs are being fixed.

2. Here we can see how often triagers need to ask for further details. We could also perform a search of what kind of information is typically missing from bug reports so that we can improve our bug reporting documentation.

3. The bug tracker can tell us many things here: how many typical responses are needed to fix a bug, which people are involved in the bug, and which organizations they are from (often shown in the email address; e.g., *billg@microsoft.com*).

The following are the fixing steps:

1. A community member chooses a bug report in the system and fixes it. This involves changing and testing the code and generating a patch.

2. If the contributor has direct access to the source repository, he commits the patch. Otherwise, the patch is attached to the bug report.

3. The status of the bug is set to FIXED.

And here are the fixing hooks:

1. There are no hooks in this step.

2. A useful data point is to count the number of patches either committed or attached to bug reports. Having the delta between these two figures is also useful: if you have many more attached patches, there may be a problem with how easily contributors can get commit access to the source repository.

3. When the status is changed, we can again assess the number of changes and plot them on a timeline to identify the rate of bug fixes that are occurring.

In your community, you should break down the conveyor belt of each mechanic that forms your community. These could be bugs, patches, document collaboration, or otherwise. When you break down the process and identify the steps in the process and the hooks, this helps you take a peek inside your community.

Gathering General Perceptions

Psychologically speaking, perception is the process in which awareness is generated as a result of sensory information. When you walk into a room and your nose tells you something, your ears tell you something, and your eyes tell you still more, your brain puts the evidence together to produce a perception.

Perception occurs in community, too, but instead of physical senses providing the evidence, the day-to-day happenings of the community provide the input. When this evidence is gathered together, it can have a dramatic impact on how engaged and enabled people feel in that community.

Even in the closed and frightening world of a prison community, with its constant threat of random violence and tyranny, there are shared perceptions, interestingly between staff members and prisoners. Professor Alison Liebling, a world expert on prisons, discovered common cause between staff members and prisoners in her "Measuring the Quality of Prison Life" study, which took place between 2000 and 2001. Liebling invited staff members and prisoners to reflect on their best rather than worst experiences and identified broad agreement between both groups on "what matters" in prison life. She discovered that "staff and prisoners produced the same set of dimensions, suggesting a moral consensus or shared vision of social order and how it might be achieved." Her work provided a model that described and monitored that which previously appeared impossible to measure: "respect, humanity, support, relationships, trust, and fairness," which had remained hidden under the traditional radar of government accountability.

Perception plays a role in many communities, particularly those online. Some years back I was playing with a piece of software (that shall remain nameless). I spent quite some time setting it up and was more than aware of some of the quirks that were involved in its installation. In the interest of being a good citizen, I thought it could be useful take notes on some of the quirks, what I expected, and how the software did and did not meet my expectations. I thought this would provide some useful real-world feedback about a genuine user installing and using the software.

I carefully gathered my notes, and when I was done I sent them via email to the software community's mailing list. I strived to be as constructive and proactive in my comments as possible: my aim here was not to annoy or insult, but to share and suggest.

And thus the onslaught began....

Email after email of short-tempered, antagonistic, and impatient responses came flowing in my general direction. It seemed that I struck a nerve. I was criticized for providing feedback on the most recent stable release and not the unreleased development code in the repository(!), many of my proposed solutions were shot down because they would "make the software too easy" (like that is a bad thing!), and the tone was generally defensive.

Strangely, I was not perturbed, and I still took an interest in the software and the community, but as I dug deeper I found more issues. The developer source repository was very restrictive; the comments in bug reports were equally defensive and antagonistic; the website provided limited (and overtly terse) information; and the documentation had statements such as, "If you don't understand this, maybe you should go somewhere else." Well, I did.

When all the pieces of evidence combined in my brain, I developed a somewhat negative perception of the community. I felt it was rude, restrictive, cliquey, and unable to handle reasonably communicated constructive criticism.

It was perception that drove me to this conclusion, and it was perception that caused me to focus on another community in which my contributions would be more welcome and my life there would be generally happier.

Throughout the experience there was no explicit statement that the community was "rude, restrictive, cliquey, and unable to handle reasonably communicated constructive criticism." This was never written, spoken of, or otherwise shared.

Measuring perception involves two focus points. On the one hand you want to understand the perception of the people inside your community, but on the other hand you also want to explore the perception of your community from the outside. This is particularly important for attracting new contributors.

To measure both kinds of perception, our hooks are people, and we need to have a series of conversations with different people inside and outside our projects to really understand how they feel. As an example, imagine you are a small software project and you have a development team, a documentation team, and a user community. You should spend some time having a social chitchat with a few members in each team. This will help paint a picture for you.

Some of the most valuable feedback about perception can happen with so-called "corridor conversations." These are informal, social, ad hoc conversations that often occur in bars, restaurants, and the corridors of conferences. These conversations typically have no agenda, there are no meeting notes, and they are not recorded. The informal nature of the conversation helps the community member to relax and share her thoughts with you.

Perception of you

Another important measurement criterion is the perception of you as a person. As a leader you are there to work with and represent your community. Your community will have a perception of you that will be shared with its members. You want to understand that perception and ensure that it fairly reflects your efforts.

Perception of community leaders is complex, particularly when a leader works for a company to lead the community. As an example, as part of my current role at Canonical as the Ubuntu community manager I work extensively with our community in public, running public projects. There are, however, some internal activities that I focus on. I help the wider company work with the community. I work on Canonical projects that are currently under a Non-Disclosure Agreement (NDA). There is also the work I do with my own team, such as building strategy, reviewing objectives, conducting performance reviews, making weekly calls, and more. Many of these internal activities are never seen by the wider community, and as such the community may not be privy to the genuine work that helps the community but is not publicized.

Gathering feedback about your performance is hard work. It is difficult to gather constructive, honest, and frank feedback, because most people find it impossible to deliver that content to someone directly. Even if you are entirely open to feedback, you need to ensure that the people who are speaking to you feel there will be no repercussions if they offer criticism. You need to work hard to foster an atmosphere of "I welcome your thoughts on how I can improve."

Due to the difficulty of gathering frank feedback, you may want to rely on email to gather it. When we have physical conversations or even discussions on the phone, body language, vocal tone, and enunciation make those conversations feel much more personal. The visceral connection may make it intimidating for your respondent to provide frank and honest feedback (particularly if that involves criticism). Email removes these attributes in the conversation, and this can make gathering this feedback easier.

TRANSPARENCY IN PERSONAL FEEDBACK

In the continuing interest of building transparency, an excellent method is to be entirely public in letting your community share their feedback about you.

As an example, you could write a blog entry asking for feedback and encouraging people to leave comments on the entry, and allow anonymous comments.

This is a tremendously open gesture toward your community. It could also be viewed as a tremendously risky gesture. There is a reasonable likelihood that someone could share some negative thoughts about you there, and others may agree. (But that's also feedback you need to collect!)

Anonymity and Privacy

The act of measuring community is an exercise in gathering information about other people and drawing conclusions. Some of this data will be generic to the community as a whole (such as statistics about mailing lists or forums) and some will be specific to an individual (such as a response to a survey). When data can be directly linked to an individual, the subject of anonymity and privacy steps into view. Although at first these two topics may seem like they could potentially cause problems if you put your foot down wrong, their guidelines are simple. Let's talk about them both now.

Anonymity

Anonymity is a valuable tool when gathering feedback, especially around contentious topics. If you are gathering feedback about a particular governance body in your community, many people may feel uncomfortable associating their views with their identity. For this reason, anonymous feedback can be a useful option.

There is a dark side to anonymity, though. The Internet has long proved that when identity can be hidden or obscured, all manner of whack jobs and nutcases want to be your friends or, rather, your enemies. In the world of the Internet, the quote from the 1988 movie *The Dead*

Pool really resonates: "Opinions are like assholes. Everybody's got one and everyone thinks everyone else's stinks." If you open an avenue for people to share their views online, expect anything and everything.

Anonymity creates two major risks. First, when identity is hidden, some jump at the opportunity to be rude, arrogant, and sometimes outright offensive. These people are often referred to as *trolls* in online communities. The second, subtler problem is that anonymity will sometimes cause people to overstate their concern with an issue: they will often dial up the annoyance factor to 11. This means you get a misrepresented perspective, and this can skew your aim of getting genuinely representative views from the community.

With this we have a difficult balance: there is value in anonymous feedback, but there is a significant risk of trolling and overstated unrepresentative perspectives. How do we find a balance? A simple solution is to welcome anonymous data, but be cognizant of what it could represent. Therefore, when conducting your research, you should encourage a combination of feedback with identity attached in addition to anonymous feedback.

Consider the example of running a survey to assess the quality of experience of a contributor joining your community. I recommend that you have two identical surveys: one directed to the 10 most recent people who have joined your community, and the other open to anyone. When evaluating the results, treat the survey that you directed to particular people as the most valuable input, but still consider highly the results of your other survey. Combining the results of both surveys is likely to produce a balanced perspective.

Before we move on, I want to dispel the myth of anonymity on the Internet. This all boils down to a simple rule:

> No one is anonymous on the Internet.
> No one.
> (Yes, that includes you super-elite hacker types, too.)

In the online world it's tempting to believe you are anonymous, but so-called "anonymity" is merely a carefully constructed set of abstractions that ultimately puts most people off trying to discover your identity. These barriers always have a trail, though, and if someone tried hard enough, he could break down the barriers of anonymity.

The value and risk of anonymity is hugely dependent on what kind of community you are building. If you are building a small local knitting community to meet, share patterns, and enjoy one another's company, it is unlikely that anyone is going to work too hard to break anonymity. If you are involved in a technical community based around security and hacking, some will see your anonymity as a challenge. In more technical communities, as well as communities dealing with sensitive issues in politics or health, you may have a harder time soliciting anonymous feedback for fear of others finding out.

Privacy

The middle ground between anonymity and full public disclosure is feedback provided with an identity under the proviso that it is kept private. Maintaining this level of privacy is an important consideration when handling anyone's information, and particularly important when handling sensitive information around conflict.

Privacy is sacred. It should never be compromised, and when you engage with someone who shares private information, you become responsible for that information. As such, you should ensure that you have a suitable means of securing that privacy. This does not need to include super-technical encrypted emails and retina scans to get into your laptop, but simple processes that will ensure that your respondents have confidence in you keeping their information to yourself.

The most fundamental underlying principle here is that people trust you. It doesn't matter what procedures you put in place to stop leaks; if people don't trust you as a warm body, they will not entrust their thoughts to you. As we discussed earlier, you should always build a sense of trust and confidence in your community. You should then build on this trust with methods of gathering feedback that are secure.

As an example, I was once performing an assessment of a governance body and wanted to gather feedback from each member of the group. I was keen for this feedback to be brutally blunt and honest, and to do this I made a few conscious decisions:

- To ensure privacy, I did not use a public resource such as a wiki or forum to ask for the feedback, but instead requested that it be sent to my private email address. This meant that all submissions came directly to me.

- I was explicit in the email that the information provided should be frank and honest and that the answers would be subject to absolute privacy. I made it clear that the feedback would not be shared either publicly, with the other members, or with other third parties.

- I sent the email to private email addresses, not an email address associated with the commercial sponsor. This would remove any conspiracy-theory worries of someone snooping on email on a mail server (which would be inconceivable in a practical sense, but I just wanted to assuage any possible worries).

- I emailed the questions to each member individually, as opposed to using either CC or BCC to send them. This ensured that there would be no accidental Reply-All gaffe in which one member's feedback would go out to the other members.

All of these steps were subtle but important: they helped to secure confidence among the respondents so that they could provide me with the honest feedback that I required. It worked, and I got some excellent feedback in that assessment.

The last bullet on the previous list was all about reducing the possibility of a gaffe. These accidents and mistakes have happened to us all: accidental emails, phone calls, and messages sent to the wrong people with sometimes embarrassing consequences. These gaffes are bad enough in nonsensitive situations, but when we are dealing with private data, they can be very serious. As such, you need to ensure that you are aware of possible gaffes and try at all costs to avoid them.

As a starting point, here is a list of what not to do:

Email

> In an email discussion about private topics, always check who is receiving the email. This is particularly risky these days with auto-completion. Believe me, I speak from experience....

Mailing lists

> Always double-check that when having a private conversation, someone hasn't included a mailing list address. This happens a lot more often than you would imagine.

Blogging

> When you hear that exciting piece of news that someone tells you, ask if you can blog it. Many have fallen foul of blogging private information. That never ends well.

Phone calls

> When discussing private topics, check who is around you. Members of your community whom you don't know may be listening to every word.

Online chat networks

> Before you talk to "jon_c" online about some private topics, double-check that you're not actually talking to "jon_o" or "ron_c". That could get you in quite a pickle.

By carefully considering the expectations and risks surrounding privacy, it is likely that you can gather your feedback with no ill consequences. The key thing here is to *think before you act*. Checking that list of email addresses once more may take 10 seconds, but it could prevent years of potential embarrassment.

THE COMMUNITY CASE BOOK

We balance visibility and privacy in the same way we've always done, with social norms. We don't keep people from peering into our homes at night by living in windowless buildings. We have lightweight privacy mechanisms like curtains, and we stigmatize (and penalize) people who peek through them.

—Tim O'Reilly, on Privacy

Read the full interview in Chapter 14.

Moving On

In this chapter we have explored many of the methods with which we can open up our community to take a peek inside. We have discussed the opportunities and pitfalls associated with measuring community, and this chapter should have provided you with a firm foundation on which to gather data that can help you optimize your community and make it more efficient, pleasurable, and productive.

Now we are going to move on to discuss how we can ensure that our projects stay on track and our contributors are able to keep on top of their commitments to your community. It is time to learn how to manage and track our work.

CHAPTER NINE

Managing and Tracking Work

"Without deviation from the norm, progress is not possible."

—*Frank Zappa*

WHEN I JOINED CANONICAL BACK IN 2006, THE PROFESSION OF COMMUNITY MANAGEMENT DIDN'T REALLY EXIST. Coming from a journalism and consultancy background, I never set out to be a community manager. No one did. Like many, I ended up falling into community management basically by talking myself into it and getting lucky.

On the morning of my first day on the job, I made a cup of PG Tips tea, sat down at my laptop, and logged on. Two weeks later, when I was done jumping up and down while high on the fumes of landing the new gig, said new deal had become very real very quickly. Surrounded by my heroes and directly working for the founder of Ubuntu, I started to feel the crushing sense of responsibility for what I had taken on.

Erk.

I had asked for this job because, in my mind, Ubuntu was (and still is) critical to the success of bringing Free Software, openness, and choice to technology. I saw it as a vehicle for change, and the only way to keep that vehicle moving forward was to grow, excite, and motivate a community. My passion for being the guy who helps make that happen got me through the interviews and kept my nerves under control, but now my nerves were dining out on paranoia. If I was going to be on the hook for driving this vehicle, which direction was I going to take it in?

Credibility and the Need to Track Progress

Aside from working with my heroes, reporting to one of the most well-known people in open source, and not knowing exactly where to start, I faced one other glorious wrinkle in the cheek of my new job: *limited credibility*.

Credibility is the respect you earn from different stakeholders, be they community members, management, founders, press, or others. Gaining credibility is critical if you want to be successful. Consequently, a lack of credibility can be rather damning.

Unfortunately, today gaining credibility is a challenge for community managers. The profession of community management is still very young, and as it continues to evolve, we are surrounded by those who don't understand what we do, express cynicism about what we can achieve, or choose to assume we're doing something entirely different from the reality, and likely far less flattering. I am sure some of you have heard the ol' chestnut of "Oh, you folks just write blog entries all day and spew out headlines to nerds on Twitter, right?"

When I started in my new job, I did have *some* credibility, but it was in a more general, transient sense. I had been writing for years about open source and technology and talking about it on LugRadio, and one of the small perks of such ramblings was that some people remembered my name from my articles, blogs, and podcasts. While this boosted my ego as an opinionated and hungry young journalist, none of that mattered a dime when I started as the Ubuntu community manager. I had limited credibility in the Ubuntu community outside of the faint flickers of a reputation in the wider yet tiny open source fishbowl.

It wasn't that I had negativity stapled to my reputation; but credibility is *context-sensitive* and my name just didn't resonate with the wider Ubuntu community. Ubuntu is a *meritocracy* and it thrives on rewarding those who add significant and sustained contributions with the respect they deserve. Now look at what happened: here was this English guy, with few direct contributions to Ubuntu and a new job title of "Ubuntu community manager," who was tasked with growing and optimizing the community. I am pretty surprised that this didn't result in pitchforks and fires; it just goes to show how pleasant and understanding the Ubuntu community is.

Credibility makes great things possible. Your community is inspired by you and seeks your leadership, your management entrusts some of the organization's most delicate resources to you, and you are considered an invaluable resource to all stakeholders.

Fortunately, gaining credibility is devilishly simple, albeit with hard work as a prerequisite. You need to *prove yourself*. It is as simple as that.

This world is full of talkers: people who chalk their game up on a board, try to sell their abilities, and espouse their accomplishments. Moreover, the young profession of community management has already attracted a subset of *all-talk-and-no-trousers* kinds of people. If you want to get a taste of this, just type "social media" into Google. The social media space has unfortunately been infested with poseurs and wannabes who try to climb to the top of their ladder, churning out the same old nonsense, often with little substance. While talking a big game may get you far, real accomplishments and the demonstration of such abilities will get you much farther.

Therefore, this chapter is all about tracking the progress of our work. Doing so serves two quite different purposes.

First, we'll talk from a communal perspective about how to transform the strategic focus we developed earlier in the book into a project plan, which in turn gives us the basis for tracking our work and resources in order to deliver great results. By structuring our work effectively and executing it in a predictable manner, we can better communicate outward the success of that work and the value it brings.

Second, from a slightly more selfish perspective, all of this project management, tracking, and transparency is going to help us to develop the credibility we need to be successful. This is a *no poseur zone*, my friends.

As such, this chapter is a valuable and important part of our journey. Unfortunately, I have seen many community leaders and managers go about their business without structuring or tracking their work, and who consequently struggle to demonstrate the value they bring. It is these folks who often get pigeonholed as "Oh, you folks just write blog entries all day and spew out headlines to nerds on Twitter, right?" Unlike the poseurs who try to convince people of their credibility, this chapter will help you to *demonstrate* it via real, practical results.

The Importance of Tracking Our Work

In the middle of 2009 an ambitious new open source project started. In the interests of protecting the innocent, we will kindly refer to this project as *Plectrum*. The project had big ideas and was not just planning to create a Free Software implementation of something that had previously existed, but instead wanted to entirely rethink the approach, assumptions, and workflow encased in the problem. Consequently, the founders' ideas were multilayered; they needed to prepare the foundations first and then build up from there.

In announcing their plans for Plectrum, the founders created incredible mindshare with their audience; the planned goals really captured the imagination of onlookers. Those of you who are not distracted and noodling around on Facebook will remember that we talked about *mindshare* back in Chapter 7. We said this in the context of Linux desktop marketshare:

> Some vector within the great mythic noosphere, the "sphere of human thought," probably knows exactly how many Linux desktops there are in the world, but actual usage doesn't mean a bean in the scheme of things. What really matters is *mindshare*.

> Mindshare is perception. It is a global gut feeling. Mindshare and perception is the magic that wins hearts and minds. It is also the explosive, seductive substance that clears the path for change, and it is mindshare that enables communities to have a voice.

While mindshare is what really matters, it has to have *substance*. Mindshare with little substance is nothing more than hype. Thus, in building buzz and excitement you need to ensure that the mindshare is broadly commensurate with the practical value you are able to build within a reasonable time frame.

With such a significant journey ahead of them and much of it down in the weeds in the low-level parts of their plan, the Plectrum founders discovered that attracting contributors was more difficult than they expected, but they plodded on. As the months rolled by, the project continued to chalk up its big ideas, release video interviews, and continue work on the lower layers. Months turned into years, and while the founders of the project were still working solidly on these lower-level pieces, they hit troubled waters when they decided to ask for donations to fund the continuation of the project.

The issue here was not in asking for money (although money is often contentious in Free Software communities), but that this appeal for donations suddenly brought the credibility of the project and its founders crashing into view. A blogger then posted a somewhat cynical post outlining concerns about the ability of the project to deliver on its promises, and a swathe of commentators lined the corridor of conversation, many in raging agreement about such concerns. The vocal cynics had a shared opinion: Plectrum had made more promises than real, practical releases of its wider vision.

Naturally, the Plectrum founders were crestfallen. They had poured months of their lives into their project, had written Free Software for the good of the wider community, and had battled significant technical challenges in delivering their revolutionary solution. I know the founders. They are good people with sincere intentions, but unfortunately they had made one fatal mistake: while they had inspired a vision, they had failed to effectively showcase the steps they had taken in delivering that vision. People can run on a platform of promises for only so long before faith erodes and cynicism and suspicion set in.

This is precisely what we want to avoid. Whether you are running a community, a project, a department in your company, or anything else, you want to build a culture of *delivery*. The greatest contributors in any community or company start with a vision, break it down into pieces, and deliver the results. While many such contributors make great plans and even execute them well, too many people fail to track and articulate this progress to others; this is exactly what this chapter will discuss. Successfully hot-rodding your work to track such progress and then clearly articulating your results will give you a reputation for bringing great value and will build your credibility.

This work is important not only to build credibility, but also to reduce risk for your community and its ability to make decisions and deliver value.

Tracking the Right Things

I was once in Chicago doing some consultancy work with an organization that wanted to grow a community within its membership. This was a familiar gig for me: the company was flying me out to its annual conference where I would talk about the opportunity of community and how we could harness it in the organization. I would deliver the presentation, and then talk more about the specifics of what kind of community the company needed and how to grow it.

The evening before I was due to deliver my presentation there was a cocktail reception. Everyone else seemed to know everyone, whereas I only knew one guy: the guy who had arranged for me to be flown out. He was very much the practical and inspirational leader of the organization, so at the reception he was inundated with people who wanted to schmooze with him. I didn't want to get in his way, so I mingled around the room and got to know some of the other folks in the organization.

Soon I got to chatting with a gentleman who was on the board of the organization. In his early 60s, he was soft-spoken, confident, yet humble; he was one of those people who you could tell had studied at the University of Hard Knocks. He had been there, done that, paid his dues, and survived to tell the tale.

It turned out that he was quite interested in community building and was familiar with some of my work. We had a long and interesting conversation about growing and building teams who want to work together. We talked for around an hour that night and took a variety of topics for a spin, but one thing he said particularly stuck in my mind:

> You know what, Jono, if you are not keeping score, and counting the right things, it doesn't count.

It seemed like such obvious advice, but it resonated with me. For years I had been working to find interesting and effective methods of building community, and had measured and tracked this work in some of the more obvious ways, but his statement got me thinking more about how we decide *which* particular scores count.

For the next few days, I thought about what I keep score of, how I gather those scores, how those scores influence my future decision making, and to what extent I prioritize keeping score in the scheme of my general work responsibilities.

What's important is that the act of keeping score allows you to *do better work*; it helps you to identify opportunities and improve problematic areas. My friend's primary lesson was to avoid being lured down rabbit holes in which you track things that have no tangible benefits or outcomes. In other words, always ensure that you track your progress, but make sure the things you track will shed more light on areas in which you can drive improvements forward. We are not interested in just collecting numbers here; we are interested in collecting indicators of success and failure to help us map out the best possible path forward in our work.

Since that conversation, I developed some general focus points for shaping how we identify these areas to track:

Understand outcomes, not numbers

As we just discussed, always look for the outcome that you want to achieve as opposed to only the numbers; the numbers are just evidence to help you understand something better (e.g., the number of Twitter followers is just a number, no matter how big it is, but what does this number tell us about our success within the scheme of other community metrics?). When thinking about what you want to track, think about what you want to understand as opposed to purely which numbers you want to see.

Know what not to track

Some community managers fall into the trap of tracking things that don't bring a better understanding or that simply bring raw data that means nothing by itself. As an example, tracking the number of posts on a forum does not tell us anything about the quality of the content or participation, it merely indicates traffic. If you want to determine quality you would instead want to look at the content that was posted. Knowing which data is uninteresting, even if other stakeholders consider it important (e.g., managers often consider unintelligent numbers such as the number of forum posts as indicative of growth and therefore success), is a useful skill to develop.

Avoid data porn

There are countless analytics, statistical tracking, visualization, and other tools available. Many companies are making money on the fact that people like *data porn*; that is, an overload of information that makes you feel secure that you have all the available information at hand. Again, try to identify the outcomes on which you seek better visibility, but don't get overloaded in the figures. We want to know how well the car performs, and we don't need to see every number on every dial to accomplish that.

Know how to read your scores

When you're tracking progress, success or failure is determined by combining multiple data points together. Just having the data available is one thing, but being able to (a) read it effectively, (b) combine it with other data to get better outcomes, and (c) communicate these outcomes to others are valuable skills. These skills will develop over time; remember, understanding data and getting outcomes out of it will not happen overnight.

These golden rules are a general best-practice blanket that you should wrap around your work. We will get into the specifics of how you track your projects, growth and decline, and community health later in this chapter.

Within the Context of a Company

Tracking progress and the effectiveness of your work is critically important if you work professionally as a community manager. As I mentioned earlier, community management is still very much a misunderstood art and science, and we need not only to build credibility but also to demonstrate the ways we bring value to both the community and the company that employs us.

At the 2011 gathering of the Community Leadership Summit event I organize each year, I scheduled a session to discuss how we effectively communicate our accomplishments and progress to different stakeholders in our companies. Interestingly, the types of measurements reported by attendees were massively diverse. Some attendees were expected to show pure growth figures (e.g., the number of Twitter followers, forum posts, etc.), some were expected to transpose community into a dollar figure (e.g., how many leads from the community result in sales), and some had no accountability for their work at all.

It is clear that no consistent requirements or formats for demonstrating progress span across all companies. Every company has different needs, expectations, and approaches to how it assesses and justifies its various investments. One thing is fairly certain, though: while you may not need to provide any kind of progress reporting right now, as your company grows, you almost certainly will need to. As such, even if this is not a challenge for you today, I recommend that you start thinking about the solution; it is only a matter of time before you will need to provide this visibility.

Defining value

When demonstrating to your company that its investment in its community and in you as a community manager (and your team, if appropriate) is worthwhile, it is easy to get sidetracked by what I referred to earlier as *unintelligent numbers*. If we all sit down for a few minutes and think about things we can count, we can concoct all kinds of figures: Twitter/Facebook/Google+ connections, mailing list posts, forum users, forums posts, website hits, search engine results, YouTube comments, and more. Numbers don't really tell us anything, though. The challenge here is not in identifying what numbers can represent our work best, but in how we bring *value* to the company and to the community.

Value.

Write it down on a sticky note. Stick it to your monitor. Stick it to your cat. Stick it to your shower head. Wherever you focus your attention, stick that word there: *Value.*

Every company that invests in something seeks to derive value from its investment. If a company invests in programmers, it expects to get valuable code from them. If it invests in designers, it expects to get valuable designs out of them. Likewise, when investing in you as a community manager, a company expects to get a valuable community relationship out of you. Unfortunately, as described earlier, because community management is such a new and unknown art and science, it is often unclear to companies how they define the actual value that they get.

This is why many corporate managers (who are already confused about how the hell to manage a community manager) look for these unintelligent numbers as a justification for the investment. Although those figures may translate well initially, they won't bring *real* value to the company. We instead need to identify where the company wishes to grow value so that we can see how we can apply our efforts to derive value in our work that also meets these wider company needs. In other words, if your work aligns with the company's general goals, it will be easier to justify the value you and your team bring to the company.

When I started at Canonical and reported directly to the founder, Mark Shuttleworth, I had pretty much free reign in terms of where I directed my efforts. Mark trusted my judgment and I worked to bring value to those areas. While this happy-go-lucky, free-form approach worked well back then, the company has since grown significantly, there are many more stakeholders now, and our strategic focus is far wider. As the company and my career progressed, I raised the importance of identifying the company focus and goals so that I could ensure that my team would bring value to these needs as well as the needs of the community.

As an example, at Canonical we started a project to strategically see growth in the number of people creating applications for the Ubuntu platform, as well as growing a wider awareness of the company. I can break this into two broad areas:

Platform maturity
> We needed to make the platform easier to use, create more documentation, do a better job of disseminating news, encourage developers to write more applications, grow the awareness of those applications, and communicate required improvements back to the engineers.

Brand recognition
> We needed to get more people talking about the brand, improve our presence at conferences and developer events, garner more online discussions of the company, and create a better awareness of who works at the company via interviews and other features.

All of these tasks are things we can work on with the community. Together we can improve how the platform functions, improve the documentation, raise company and brand awareness, and more. Likewise, as a community we can better raise the visibility of the company while performing this work.

By identifying where the company as a whole (which typically means where the senior execs see the company going) wishes to build value, your team can architect a set of projects that bring value to those areas. As a result, the execs will automatically get a sense that you are singing from the same hymn sheet as everyone else.

Communicating up and down

When you start working as a community manager for a company, you feel like you just hit the jackpot. Big time. Did they really just hire me and they really are willing to pay me to spend time working with an awesome community? Wow.

So you start your exciting new job and identify a set of projects that you feel will bring value to the community and the company. As we discussed earlier in the book, you put together your mission statement, create your strategic plan, and identify your success criteria. With all this in place and a rocking community to get out there and work with, you start making the magic happen.

Before we continue through this chapter and get into the specifics, I want to ensure that you don't make a mistake that a lot of new community managers at companies make. While we have clearly articulated the importance of tracking and demonstrating progress in your work, it is important to remember that you need to report both down (to your team and the community) as well as up (to your manager and, if applicable, his manager). The mistake is in thinking that the same level of detail is required both up and down the chain.

Your community and your team love detail. They love it because detail demonstrates the openness and transparency of your community and the opportunity for the community to see what work is going on. Your manager and his manager don't need that level of detail; they have so many other, bigger fish to fry that excessive detail will feel like a tremendous inconvenience. You could provide this detail, but they probably won't read it. So you need to provide an effective summary of accomplishments to build confidence and credibility without blinding them with science.

As you read this chapter, always think about how you can track and report progress at these two levels of detail; additional detail for the community and your team, and summarized detail for management and other key stakeholders. We will discuss one useful approach for doing this later in the chapter.

BE CAREFUL WITH SPECIFICS

For those of you who are quite new to working professionally as a community manager, I want to share a quick tip before we move on.

Community is a living, breathing organism. Things change in a fluid manner; people join, people leave, and people who start out as incredibly committed contributors get busy and move on. In all this flux you should be wary of committing too hard to specific metrics or figures.

I made this mistake once, early in my career. Our developer community was doing well and growing quickly. In the heat of the moment, while talking with the founder of the company, I committed to deliver 300 new developers within a year. This, my friends, was a bonkers thing to commit to. It seemed possible when I said it, but it was nothing more than a reflection of my naiveté at the time. We saw growth, but of course, not the level of growth that could achieve such an ambitious goal.

In some cases such numbers may be required of you, but in my experience, trying to play a numbers game does not make your work more effective; it just brings stress and pressure in delivering numbers as opposed to delivering value.

Now, this can be a challenge. You may well get a senior exec up in your face about delivering a specific number. In these cases I recommend that you push back on the number but strive to identify another way to give the exec confidence in what you can deliver. This is one of the trickiest components of *managing up* and setting accurate expectations, but it is a skill that will serve you well.

What We Need to Manage

Now that we have established the importance of managing and tracking the different components of our community, let's get down to the details of what we should be tracking and some techniques we can use to do this well.

In every community there are three broad areas in which you should have a solid workflow in place for tracking the work performed. They are:

Projects

A project is a unit of work that results in a particular outcome. Each project has a collection of steps that must be executed to achieve that outcome, and these steps are typically distributed across lots of different people, many of whom may be volunteers. Examples of projects include creating a website for a community team, building team reporting into your community, creating a new product feature, and forming a governance council.

Growth and decline

Communities are composed of many different moving parts. Examples include teams, processes for contributing work, governance boards, and more. For each moving part we want to track the growth and decline of content and people to ensure that they are working effectively.

General health

Outside of our projects and the mechanics of how our community operates, we also want to get a feel for the general health of the community, where we are seeing positive work, and where there are issues that need to be resolved.

For the rest of this chapter, we will explore these three areas. Each requires a slightly different approach and operates under different constraints. I am going to present some approaches and examples that you can apply to your own communities to get better visibility on your work and that of the community.

Tracking Projects

Projects are a key piece of furniture in every community. Without a clearly defined set of projects to keep your community members occupied and feeling like there is a sense of focus and direction, your community will feel limp and ineffective. *No one* likes limp and ineffective.

Take a moment and cast your mind way back to the dim, distant depths of "Baking in Openness" on page 46 (you can cheat if you want and flip back to that section), and you might remember that we created a strategic plan for our community. This strategic plan was essentially a clearly defined set of goals. Goals are basically projects that we want to coordinate and run to meet the needs of the community.

As a quick recap, we used this format to structure these projects:

OBJECTIVE:

GOAL:

SUCCESS CRITERIA:

  Item

  Item

IMPLEMENTATION PLAN:

  Item

  Item

OWNER:

GOAL:

SUCCESS CRITERIA:

  Item

  Item

IMPLEMENTATION PLAN:

  Item

  Item

OWNER:

To illustrate what one of these OBJECTIVE blocks looks like, here is the same example used back in "Structuring the plan" on page 51 for creating a website:

OBJECTIVE: Build a website for the project.

GOAL: Build a structural design for the website content.

SUCCESS CRITERIA:

  All areas of the website structure documented in a specification.

  Community feedback gathered on the proposal.

IMPLEMENTATION PLAN:

  Identify the needs of the website by liaising with the community.

  Document the structure of the website on the wiki.

  Email the core community team with feedback and merge feedback in.

Organize an online meeting to propose any changes to the specification.

Build a prototype.

OWNER: Jono Bacon.

The trick in managing projects is to understand how different people are interested in different levels of visibility in your projects. When we can conceptualize these layers it helps us to better construct and manage our projects so that different people can see the projects with different lenses that expose different levels of detail.

These three layers are:

The Project level

> The Project level is the highest level of abstraction, where we just need to know whether the project is on track or not. The SUCCESS CRITERIA in our strategic plan help us to ask a definitive question about whether we succeeded in delivering the requirements of the project. For projects that are not yet complete, we also need to be able to take an acid test at any time to determine whether the project is generally on track.

The Work Unit level

> In our strategic plan, the OBJECTIVE defines the high-level project and each GOAL specifies individual pieces of work that need to be completed to deliver the wider project goal. Each GOAL component may be owned and assigned to different people, and we need a means to identify whether work is succeeding at this slightly lower level.

The Work Item level

> Each work unit is divided into a collection of work items that document individual tasks, each assigned to one person and taking no longer than half a day to complete. This is the highest level of detail required, and most people would only see this level of detail for projects they are actively involved in (and for which they have work items assigned to them). In a perfect world we would see all work items from all units and be able to see progress on each (we will talk about how to do this later in the chapter).

For each layer we want to provide visibility on progress made toward achieving eventual outcomes. Each layer maps reasonably well to the visibility required for different people interested in our projects.

As an example, your manager is likely to be interested only in the Project level; she is going to be so busy with her own work that she doesn't want to be swamped with the details. Other active stakeholders and participants (and more curious managers) may want to delve into the Work Unit level. Finally, the people who are actually involved in each work unit will want to get down and dirty with the details of the work items.

Now that you have a clear idea of the different levels of abstraction and the people who are likely to be interested in them, don't make the mistake of only providing these levels of detail to those respective roles (e.g., less detail for managers, more detail for community members). As an example, as a manager for my team I want lots of detail on some projects, and less on others, and in many cases I can't preempt when I require more detail (it could be related to a temporary situation or discussion).

We want to create visibility on our projects that is available to all stakeholders and is updated regularly, preferably in an automated way. This means anyone who wants can see the work, thus resolving the issue of the weekly email updates and, importantly, giving transparency to our work.

> **NOTE**
>
> **Of course, some of you may feel uncomfortable about working so out in the open and with so much visibility into your work. For projects that don't involve sensitive or confidential information, I recommend that you work as openly as possible. It will be a little unusual at first, but it gets easier and will raise your credibility in a very practical and visible way. For sensitive projects, keep as much out in the open as possible, but obviously respect confidences where appropriate.**

When I started working at Canonical as the Ubuntu community manager, my work was far more unstructured in terms of visibility on projects. I would choose areas in which I felt the community needed focus, decide on a set of projects that needed to happen to see improvements, and work on those projects in a fairly ad hoc way. Progress would be made and the projects would typically succeed, but they were *hiding in plain sight*; while the projects were open and transparent, finding details on their progress was difficult for those who were not directly involved.

Today things are quite different. We track projects in Ubuntu at a much more granular level and provide the three levels of visibility outlined earlier (Project, Work Unit, and Work Item). While our approach uses tools specific to Ubuntu, the approach can be customized to other tools; the tools are not what is important, the structure is where the value is.

Structuring Your Projects

This approach to managing projects hinges on the concept of a *blueprint*. In Chapter 2 we created our strategic plan for our different goals. For each goal we should have a blueprint.

A blueprint is a document that captures the current state of a project. The Ubuntu project placed such a high value on these documents that we built a special blueprints feature into the Launchpad system that we use to build Ubuntu, but you can store blueprints in whatever way is most convenient for your community. This could be wiki pages, text files, items in a database, or somewhere else. Please note that you will need a means of pulling information out of blueprints later, so storing blueprints in plain text somewhere online makes the most sense.

The aim of these blueprints is to build visibility and transparency into the system. As such, all data—be it the blueprint, the work items, or the visualization of that data—is completely open and accessible.

A blueprint contains the following information:

Title

A brief description for the work unit, such as "Build social networking support into the website."

Description

A few paragraphs outlining the goals for the work unit and any constraints and requirements in place. This should get the reader up to speed on the focus of the work.

Status

The current status of the work encompassed in the blueprint. Typical status values are Not Started, In Progress, Slow Progress, Blocked, Completed, and Postponed. This field should always be kept up-to-date and should provide a singular overview of the current state of the blueprint.

Priority

The blueprint's priority within the range of projects you are working on. This should be Essential, High, Medium, or Low. Be sure to distribute the projects you are working on among all four status options; having all projects set to High doesn't say anything useful.

Owner

The person who is responsible for delivering the blueprint. This should match the OWNER set for the OBJECTIVE in your strategic plan. This person should be expected to oversee completion of the blueprint. This person may not complete the blueprint himself, but is responsible for guiding those who have work items on that blueprint to deliver them to completion, thus accomplishing the blueprint.

Milestone target

The target completion date for the blueprint. It is called a *milestone target* because communities often have common milestones that adjust with each release iteration (e.g., Feature Freeze, Beta).

These six pieces of information provide high-level visibility of the project; a manager or third party can easily identify whether the project is on track. Of course, the data is only as accurate as the reality it represents, so be sure to keep these details up-to-date. I recommend reviewing all your blueprints on a weekly basis and checking that everything is current and accurate.

> **NOTE**
>
> **An even better approach is to automate updates for some of the details. As an example, the Status field could be updated by counting how many work items are completed, how quickly progress is being made, and so on.**

A descriptive blueprint documents your range of projects and work units at a high level. Now you need to define your work items.

Managing Work Items

Back when I was a freshly minted manager, the company organized some management training sessions to help develop skills among the managers and build best practices in the company. We were told to be at the office at precisely 8:30 a.m., ready for our instructor, whom I will refer to as Irene to protect the innocent. Short and stocky, with a smile like a banana and a pleasingly bubbly personality, Irene was welcomed to the group. There we sat, looking forward to a brisk day of management training.

About 20 minutes in we wanted to kill ourselves. Although only a scrooge would knock Irene for her happy-go-lucky approach to the world, she was steadily beginning to get on our nerves. The issue was not her bubbly nature, it was what she was trying to teach us.

She would pick topics that seemed obvious and simple, even to a teenager, and then would thoroughly teach each of our grandmothers how to suck eggs, one by one, in slow, excruciating detail. We dutifully sat there, exchanging looks with one another as if to say, "I can't believe we have to sit through this. Is she going to teach us how to use a spoon next?"

As the day progressed, Irene continued to waffle on, and our eyelids struggled to stay open from the crushing weight of boredom. Eventually the session came to a close. We thanked Irene heartily, she seemed happy with her work, and we left to drown our sorrows at our usual watering hole. That night we all sat there as new managers, thinking we knew how all this worked, thinking we knew the answers and feeling somewhat smug that so-called *management trainers* tried to teach us what we already knew.

Five years on I realize how wrong we were. While the topics seemed obvious at the outset, painting a picture seems obvious at the outset, too; you just grab a canvas and a paintbrush, right? What the following years of experience taught us was that while some topics may appear simple, they actually uncover some surprisingly complex lessons that are often difficult to teach, but that we can learn through experience. Irene tried to teach me, and I smiled and nodded, but ultimately life itself has taught me to not assume that something is simple just because I perceive it to be simple.

Work items. Actions. Tasks. TODOs. Whatever you call them (in this book we refer to them as *work items*), they also seem fairly simple on the outside, but the devil is in the detail. Irene spent much of her time with us covering how to formulate work items, and in retrospect I now understand why she covered them in such detail. Don't make the same mistake we did. There is a certain art and finesse in deciding, assigning, defining, and documenting work items, which while seemingly simple, actually requires some deeper considerations and skill. I wish I had learned this earlier in my career, when Irene came in to help us.

I can't assure you that I have learned all there is to know about writing great work items, but I want to share some tips that can help you get up and running. If you are tempted to skip this section, don't; this is really important.

Structuring work items

The whole point of a work item is that it documents a specific task that someone needs to complete by a certain date. As an example, imagine that my wife, Erica, and I are going to cook a meal for some friends who are coming over for dinner. Erica is a stunning cook with a great love of food. I am a terrible cook with a great love of eating Erica's food. As such, Erica and I both have clearly defined roles; she is the cook and I try to do all the other fairly unintelligent things that only someone with terrible cooking skills can be trusted to do.

This includes things such as:

- Go to the store and buy the ingredients.
- Chop the cilantro and parsley.
- Juice and zest the lemons.
- Make the salads.
- Pour the chef a few glasses of wine.

These seem like reasonable work items, but looks can be deceiving. While "Chop the cilantro and parsley" seems straightforward, it assumes that I know how much cilantro and parsley are required for the dish. If the work item read "Finely chop 1/2 cup of cilantro and 1 cup of parsley" the expectations would be much clearer.

The "Go to the store and buy the ingredients" work item is even worse. The only way I could successfully achieve it is if I knew which ingredients are required for the dish and which store I need to get them from. It would be better if that specific item were broken into a series of other work items, such as:

- Buy 1 lb of imported prosciutto from Lunardi's.
- Buy 1 gallon of low-fat milk from Safeway.
- Buy one bunch of parsley from Safeway.

Here the work items are much more specific; they indicate the ingredients required, the amount needed, and where they can be purchased. This example demonstrates two key points: work items need to be *small and specific*, and the *scope* of the work required should be clear.

The golden rule for creating work items is that the items should be able to be accomplished by anyone with the requisite skills, and this person should understand what needs to be done by just reading the list of work items. In other words, we want to avoid the situation where people need to ask questions about details of a given work item and the specifics of how it should be executed.

To achieve this, here are some guidelines that should apply to each of your work items:

Be specific
> As we discussed earlier, each work item should be specific and detailed in what it should accomplish. Each work item should accomplish a clear deliverable outcome. Focus on

things such as "Create this" and "Deliver that," and avoid generic items such as "Find out about foo" and "Reach out to bar." Aside from generating a lot of questions and unclear steps, unspecific work items are difficult to complete because their outcome is not clearly known. As an example, if I have to "Find out about foo," is the learning part considered completion of the work item, and if so, how much did I need to learn and to what degree? Should I share the knowledge or write it down? Being specific avoids these uncertainties.

Be tight

I have a general rule that no work item should require more than half a day's work, and at most a full day's work. Items that are too big or feel like too much of a time sink will almost always be left to the last minute to complete, and then will often be forgotten. Smaller, more achievable items require less of an up-front mental and time investment and have a higher likelihood of succeeding.

Assign the work

Every work item should have someone who is responsible for owning and delivering it. Work items that are unassigned rarely get completed because everyone has plenty of work to do. When working with community volunteers, you may feel it is difficult to ask someone to take on a work item and that it would be better to allow people to just pick and choose what they want to do. But from my experience, community members are often more than happy to participate when you request specific commitments to specific work items; it gives them a sense of participation and team spirit in the community. I think many people would also be surprised how many community members also deliver on their commitments.

Define a deadline

Every work item should have a clear deadline for completion. This could be either a specific date (e.g., July 1, 2012) or a milestone (e.g., Feature Freeze). Regardless, the deadline should be clear and agreed upon with the assignee. You also need to keep the deadline up front in the assignee's mind so that she remembers to complete the work. Later in the chapter we will discuss a technique for accomplishing this with burndown charts.

Be able to pass a success test

Every work item should be able to answer the question, "Was this task accomplished?" with a positive response. This is why work items should be specific and clear in what should be delivered, when it should be completed, and by whom. If you can read any work item and confidently answer whether it was completed, you are in good shape.

Let's look at a few examples of some well-defined actions. Here is a simple example:

Produce a first draft of a Code of Conduct (assigned to Tom Araya, deadline of September 22, 2012)

In this example the outcome of the action should be a draft document of a Code of Conduct. It is clear who the work item is assigned to and when it should be complete. Of course, the work item does not delve into what should go into the Code of Conduct. There are other areas where that discussion can happen; the work item's purpose is to document the deliverable, when it is due, and who is responsible.

Here is another example:

> Sign a contract for a $1,000 sponsor for Developer Summit Friday party (assigned to Kerry King, deadline of September 22, 2012)

In this example the outcome is a signed contract for a sponsor who will provide $1,000 for the Developer Summit Friday party. This is also clearly assigned with a deadline.

In both of these examples we can run the *success test* and identify whether the outcomes were successfully achieved; if we are holding a Code of Conduct in one hand and a signed contract in the other, we are feeling pretty awesome right now.

Documenting work items

Alrighty. We defined our project, we talked about how to write great work items, and now we need to write them down. Actually, writing down work items serves a few useful purposes, in addition to just helping us to not forget the work items.

First, we always want to ensure that the hard work we put into defining our work items is captured in such a way that everyone can get a copy. I always recommend that work items be stored online somewhere, be it a wiki, website, formalized work item tracker, or something else. This will ensure that everyone who has a work item (and even those who don't, but are curious to see how well the project is running) can see who is assigned what and when it should be delivered.

Storing work items in a public place also has another subtle benefit. Project management theory has taught us that when you provide the list of work items in a public place where your peers can see that you have work assigned to you, it significantly increases the likelihood of you completing the action for the simple reason that you don't want to look like a lazy slacker in front of your peers. In a world where we strive for transparency in our communities, we can use transparency as an excellent reason to ensure that these work items are public. ;-).

> ### NOTE
> A useful feature built into the Launchpad system that we use for Ubuntu is that people can *subscribe* to a blueprint and will be emailed whenever a change occurs to the work items. One of the major benefits of this is that you can then see updates and changes to the details and work items of a given project, and the information comes to you automatically.

The final consideration when documenting work items is to ensure that each item also communicates how close it is to completion. This is important for two reasons:

- We can iterate over each item and see how far along it is toward completion.

- We can suck these work items and their statuses into a visualization tool, such as a burndown chart.

For each of these you would imagine that the process of documenting the work items is going to be a bureaucratic nightmare. Well, remember our continual take on bureaucracy throughout this book (it is not our friend), so we are going to use a system that is lightweight and gives us flexibility. All we need to do is to be consistent in how we describe each work item. Here is our earlier example, now in this new format:

[tomaraya] Produce a first draft of a Code of Conduct: TODO

The format is simple. On the left, in square brackets, is the name of the person the work item is assigned to (in the Ubuntu world we use the person's username). This is followed by a description of the work item, and finally a colon followed by a status description in uppercase letters.

We use four different types of status:

TODO
The item has not been started.

INPROGRESS
The item is currently being worked on.

DONE
The item has been successfully completed.

POSTPONED
The item was put on hold for some reason (e.g., the assignee left the community, there is a lack of time or resources, etc.).

Because each work item bears one of these status descriptions, it is easy to check the current status of a given item. These simple, consistent descriptions also enable us to write software tools to read in these actions and generate graphs, as we will discuss later.

Eagle-eyed readers will have noticed that our snazzy work item format does not include the deadlines we discussed earlier as being oh-so-important. This is because it makes better sense to group your work items based on their deadlines as opposed to cluttering up each work item with its deadline date.

As such, I use this format:

Work items for 09-22-2012:

[tomaraya] Produce a first draft of a Code of Conduct: TODO

[kerryking] Sign a contract for a $1,000 sponsor for Developer Summit Friday party: INPROGRESS

Here we are specifying the date in a slightly dorkier, more computer friendly way so that if we want, we can read this content in with a program to display the data in interesting ways.

Visualizing Data with Burndown Charts

About three years ago I felt I was pretty organized when it came to managing my team's work and the work of the community projects I was involved in. As described throughout this book, I would identify a *mission statement*, and then build a *strategic plan*. Back then I tracked actions in my own TODO list tracker and things seemed to work rather well. Part of the reason I had become more organized was because my team was growing, the community was growing, and I needed better visibility on the projects and initiatives I was involved in.

Things were getting busier, though, and I knew that would only continue. I needed to handle this growth and expansion while adhering to my stubborn resistance to overtly bureaucratic project management techniques. I was and still am entirely in favor of being on top of my projects, but there is too much *fashion* in the project management world, and I was reluctant to change my team's workflow to use the latest project management gimmick that people were talking about at conferences.

Around that time, Rick Spencer joined Canonical. Rick joined as a colleague in the Ubuntu Engineering Management team and we started to work together. We became fast friends as well as colleagues. While at a company conference, Rick delivered a presentation explaining burndown charts. I sat in the audience, curious but unconvinced. It sounded like another project management fad, so I ignored it and carried on with my work.

However, Rick's presentation resonated with the other engineering managers. One by one their teams started using the burndown charts that he had presented. This approach not only meant documenting and tracking actions as described in this chapter, but also meant tracking this work very publicly, which the burndown charts made easy to do. In retrospect, I think the transparency and visibility these charts lent to my team's contributions also contributed to my reluctance to use burndown charts. This was not because I was not proud of their work, but because I was insecure about my management abilities.

Eventually, *all* the other engineering managers were using burndown charts and I was the last man standing. I knew I had to give the approach a whirl, and boy, I am glad I did. Burndown charts have become a tremendous tool for how I manage projects and coordinate work among a group of people, including both paid team members and volunteer community members.

Using burndown charts

So how do these burndown charts work? Well, fortunately, they are dead simple to understand.

Let's assume you have identified your projects in your *strategic plan*, created your *blueprints*, and documented your *work items* across those blueprints. If you total up all the work items, you typically find anywhere from 21 to 210 work items assigned across a range of different people. Your goal as the community leader is twofold. First, you want to help everyone who has an assigned work item deliver it on time. Second, you want to communicate the progress of this work effectively to onlookers (and, if relevant, to management at your company).

Burndown charts help you do this. Figure 9-1 shows an example chart.

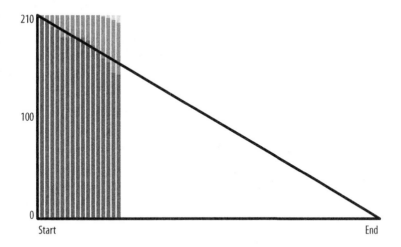

FIGURE 9-1. Burndown charts are an effective tool for visualizing progress.

The burndown chart is essentially a bar chart. Along the y-axis are the total number of *work items*. Along the x-axis is the total length of time allocated for all the work items to be completed. As an example, in the Ubuntu community we release every six months; therefore, I target all work to a six-month release cycle and we have a six-month burndown chart.

The way the chart works is that each day a new bar is drawn on the chart from the left to the right of the x-axis. This bar is broken into three different sections:

Lower, darker color
> The number of work items that are still marked as TODO and therefore have not been started.

Middle, lighter color
> The number of work items that have been marked as DONE and therefore are complete.

Top, lightest color (where appropriate)
> The number of work items marked as POSTPONED, so we do not count them against our completion status. This color may not appear in all bars or even all burndown charts.

Each bar that is rendered on the graph basically shows the proportion of TODO, DONE, and POSTPONED items. Every day a new bar is plotted on the graph to the right of the one from the day before.

From the top-lefthand side of the chart to the bottom-righthand side of the chart is a thick black line. This is called the *trend line*. The goal of people generating the burndown chart is to keep the darkest TODO area underneath the trend line. If regular and consistent progress is made in completing work items throughout the period that the burndown chart represents, you will make steady progress in completing all documented work items in time.

Some burndown charts (such as the ones we use in the Ubuntu project) plot another status, INPROGRESS, in between the TODO and DONE bars. This area generally hugs the trend line to reflect that people are actively working on their work items—unless, of course, the team is ahead or behind schedule.

GENERATING YOUR BURNDOWN CHARTS

In all of this discussion about documenting work items and generating burndown charts, we have not yet covered the all-important question of how you get your work items to generate one of these lovely charts.

Fortunately, a range of options are available, including generating charts in Basecamp, Microsoft Excel, and other tools. I am not going to provide a list of links that probably will be outdated by the time you read this; instead, go to your favorite search engine and do a search for "generating burndown charts," and you will get a slew of results.

To generate burndown charts for the Ubuntu project, we actually wrote a few custom Python scripts. We keep our work items in Launchpad and the Python script just pulls out the work items and generates a graph on a web page. We built this into a community-founded project that became *status.ubuntu.com*.

There are two primary benefits of using burndown charts. First, if you have a small piece of software that reads in the work items automatically and generates the graph, the only work your community will need to do to keep on top of their work is to ensure that they update the status of the work items as DONE, INPROGRESS, or POSTPONED. This provides a simple, nonbureaucratic method of tracking and visualizing progress.

The second benefit is that burndown charts are a great way to demonstrate progress to different stakeholders. When someone understands how a burndown chart works, it is possible to see progress at a few different layers. Here are some examples:

Your team

> For the teams carrying out work items, the chart is a great way to show that everyone is on track. There is also no reason why a burndown chart could not be generated for a specific individual. We found this really useful in the Ubuntu project. Furthermore, there

is additional data that you can present to augment the burndown chart (we discuss this more later).

Managers and supervisors

Managers, supervisors, and other folks who either are in charge or have a level of investment in your work will be keen to see how well the projects are progressing without wanting to know the details. One of the hardest skills when learning to be a manager is knowing how to differentiate between managing down (maintaining visibility into the details for the team) and managing up (not drowning your own manager/supervisor in detail, but just providing the key takeaways). When managers know how a burndown chart works, they can get a status update within seconds of looking at the chart. They are also able to check on status without asking for it, which is a huge boon for a supervisory position.

The community

Another category of folks who can get value from the burndown chart are the general community who are not actively involved in the work encompassed by the chart. The major benefit here is in building confidence in you as a community leader for coordinating this work, and a sense that active, vibrant work is going on and being accomplished. This builds a phenomenal sense of transparency, community spirit, and confidence.

So burndown charts provide a valuable means of empowering different groups of stakeholders to all feel connected to the progress of the project. As a nice side effect, I have also noticed that when a community and team understand how the burndown chart system works, it really raises the sense of team spirit and morale. I have found with my team that the completed burndown chart at the end of a cycle is something of a *shared trophy* that we all feel proud of.

Observing burndown patterns

Although we have covered the basics of how a burndown chart works, special values turn up over time as you get more familiar with it. One of the most valuable benefits a burndown chart provides is a way to look over the duration of the work period and identify patterns that can help you to build on and improve your work.

As an example, Figure 9-2 shows the burndown chart that we looked at earlier. We can pull out a few interesting observations from the chart.

First, we can see that the completed work items are generally under the trend line, so the team is progressing well through the projects. There is no reason for us to be concerned about the completed work items being delivered on time. If the TODO items were flowing far over the trend line, it would indicate that the team was behind.

Another interesting pattern is in the middle of the graph, where five of the bars have the same proportions. This indicates that no progress was made on those days. Five bars would indicate a week (assuming the burndown chart renders one bar for each workday). Take a look at what was going on when this happened. This period could be a holiday season (e.g., Christmas or

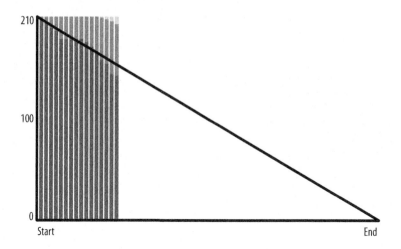

FIGURE 9-2. Burndown charts are useful for both showing progress as a summary (e.g., for managers) and in detail (e.g., for your teams).

Thanksgiving), in which case such a lull in progress is understandable. I have seen similar lulls when teams are attending conferences and other work-related events and are offline and away from their usual daily work. If you are a manager, however, and you are using a burndown chart for your team's work, as I do at Canonical, if you see that you go on vacation for a week and the same kind of lull happens, your team may be slacking off while you are away.

Another interesting pattern is what happens after the lull; you can see a significant burst of progress. Again, identify what occurred at that time. Causes for this can be leaders and managers encouraging folks to ratchet up the progress after a lull, events such as sprints or hackfests in which teams get together to burst through work items, or particular milestones such as the final days before a feature freeze or release. Each possibility teaches you something about your team's productivity and how to improve it.

Finally, another hugely useful pattern to observe is the proportion and pattern of POSTPONED items. In Figure 9-2, a small proportion of POSTPONED items appears in the bars on the righthand side of the chart. This tells us a few things. First, seeing a growing trend of postponed items at this point in the chart (just over a quarter of the way through) is a concern. This would signal to me to keep an eye on how many work items get postponed and what the cause could be. Another interesting indicator is the proportion of postponed items when the chart is completed. The number of postponed items often gives you an idea of whether you are agreeing to too much work in the set time period. For burndown charts specific to an individual and his own work items, this is a useful way to see if he is overstretching himself or if you are asking too much of him.

Generating additional information

Ever since I started using burndown charts, I have found them to be invaluable in helping me to deliver value and results in the projects I am coordinating. Equally useful is some of the other information you may want to pull out of the actions list. You will need to ensure that whatever software you are using to generate your burndown chart can also summarize this information.

The first piece of information is a summary of the different statuses for each person who has actions assigned to him. This could be rendered as a table that looks like this:

Name	TODO	INPROGRESS	DONE	POSTPONED
James Hetfield	3	6	8	1
Steve Harris	2	3	6	2
Ronnie James Dio	2	2	3	2

You may also want to include a *Percentage Completed* field for each person to compare how everyone is doing relative to the whole schedule and relative to the other team members. For example, if you are about halfway through the chart, you should reasonably expect that each person should have completed around 50% of his work items.

Another useful piece of data is to show the percentage complete for each blueprint (indicated by the total completion of its respective actions). This again provides a quick means of assessing whether the project is on track.

Building burndown charts into your workflow

Now that we have a fairly decent understanding of burndown charts, let's talk more about how you can build them into your own community leadership and management workflow. No tool or management approach is going to succeed unless you integrate it properly into the way you and the community work.

The first thing you need to do is get everyone on board in using burndown charts. Although burndown charts are devilishly simple when you understand them, at the outset they do look like big, scary, bureaucratic graphs. Furthermore, they require people to document their actions and keep them updated with current statuses.

I am going to assume here that you have decided on your *strategic plan*, filed your *blueprints*, and defined your *work items*. Each community had different approaches to defining work items; some do it online in meetings, while some, like Ubuntu, do it face-to-face at a community summit. Choose which way works for you, and then you can start building this into your workflow.

Here are some tips:

Organize weekly review meetings

Each week you should get together for a quick call or meeting with the primary assignees of work items and review progress. These meetings are useful for identifying blockers or problems and keep progress moving along smoothly. If there are too many assignees in the list, you could always ask some trusted colleagues or community members to also run meetings and break up the group a little.

Burndowns are breakfast reading

At the start of your day, take a look at your burndown chart and review what needs to be done next, to edge the progress along. Look for folks who seem to be a little bit behind on their progress and encourage them to take a look at their work items.

Look for low-hanging fruit

Every day you should look for low-hanging fruit that can keep the chart on track. It is always better to provide some "buffer" in the chart and get a stack of low-hanging fruit completed, which will then free up some time for delving into the more challenging or problematic areas.

Try to preempt complex work items

Some work items that are supposedly small—requiring only a half day or a day of work, as I have recommended—will turn out to be more complex. It might require other work to be completed first, have other needs that must be met, or otherwise not be as simple as just getting on and doing the work. Try to preempt these topics earlier so that you don't need to put the success of the chart over the line if you discover them at the last minute.

Burndown charts are a hugely useful technique for tracking large collections of work at a granular level and sharing progress at a high level. We took a spin through the core topics here, but there is plenty of additional information online if you want to find out more.

Tracking Growth and Decline

With every *write* community in which participants can actively contribute, there is an on-ramp in which people learn the skills and knowledge they need to take part, and then a participation process in which their first contributions are made. These new contributors are the lifeblood of your community; they keep the train rolling forward and usher in new generations of participants who can bring value to your community. It is always important to keep an eye on the growth and decline of these folks, and the critical systems they use.

As community leaders, it is often tempting for us to focus heavily on creating new things as opposed to effectively maintaining existing things. We like to create new initiatives and new events, generate fresh ideas, and inspire new thinking. While we always want to encourage this creativity, we also need to ensure that we are keeping an eye on our existing initiatives to make sure they are working, effective, and helping to deliver results in your community.

This is particularly important when you work professionally as a community manager. As we have already discussed throughout this chapter, your management and, if applicable, senior management are likely to want to dig in here and there and get an idea of how productive the community is and how effective you are. Earlier we talked about delivering results at a project level, in which you are coordinating a team and community members to work together to bring value, but you should also strive to present an idea of how your community is growing, and how effectively your community-facing processes are working.

The first challenge is to know what to track. As we discussed earlier in the book, generating statistics for the purpose of generating statistics is a bad thing to do. Our goal here is instead to identify how we determine value in our community, and to track those figures to give us an idea of where value is being created and where value is being lost.

Although I wish I could write a big list of areas in which you should create metrics, this is heavily dependent on your community. One approach that I have developed that can help, though, is a set of questions you can ask to help you determine this set of key value judgments. Let's look at these three questions, and then I will provide an example afterward:

Who contributes?
> Summarize the primary classifications of the primary contributors to your community. Divide these by the types of value they bring, primarily in terms of different skills.

How do they participate?
> For each type of contributor that you just wrote down, also note how each interacts with your community to make those contributions. These should primarily be the processes and infrastructure they use to participate.

What do they deliver?
> For each group, write down what value they bring in a practical and measurable form.

Let's now look at an example. The Ubuntu community is a large one, so I am going to look at three primary groups to keep this example lean:

- Who contributes?
  - Developers
  - Advocates
  - Translators
- How do they participate?
  - Developers
    - Sponsorship queue
    - Developer approval process
    - Bug Tracker

> Advocates
>> LoCo teams
>> loco.ubuntu.com
> Translators
>> Translations interface
What do they deliver?
> Developers
>> Packages
>> Bug fixes
> Advocates
>> Materials
>> Ubuntu events
> Translators
>> Complete language translations
>> Individual translated strings

To reiterate, this is a simplified view of Ubuntu in the interest of keeping the example concise. This technique teases out of your community the areas in which you define value. You should be tracking growth and decline for each area.

Visibility Is Key

Back in 2010 my team faced an interesting challenge with regard to growth. This experience helped us to continue to shape our approach in how we track community growth and gain better visibility on what is going on.

Each quarter I would ask my team to prepare a summary of key community metrics for the senior management team. These metrics would include things such as developer growth (folks who build Ubuntu packages and fix bugs), forum growth, the number of local user group events being organized, active levels of participation, and so on. Each quarter we would prepare the statistics, and generally they were on the uptick. For this particular quarter in 2010 I noticed something slightly disconcerting: our developer growth statistics were beginning to flatten out a little. They were not declining, but I saw this as a warning shot.

I immediately got on the phone with Daniel Holbach, who has the job on my team of growing the developer community. We discussed the possible reasons for this flattening effect. Were people less interested in participating in Ubuntu? Was our documentation too complex or sparse? Were there too few opportunities to participate? Were we not inspiring the community enough to take part? While we could hypothesize about what it could be, we realized we didn't have any solid data to determine the cause for this decline.

To get better visibility, I asked Daniel to put together a survey that would go out to all current developers to get a better idea of their perspectives. This survey did give us some solid indicators of where we could focus. Daniel and I talked more and reviewed the results, but a related topic caught our attention: how do we support new developers wishing to get approved as official developers?

In Ubuntu you need to get approval before you can upload changes to the archives, so we have many contributors who perform various contributions to build trust so that they can get approved. In my discussion with Daniel, I realized I had very little visibility on (a) who these folks are, (b) their contributions, and (c) how we can better support them to get through the developer process.

I asked Daniel to help me get this visibility. I asked him to determine a way we could generate a series of graphs of the same time period, with each graph showing spikes of when and to what extent a community developer contributed to Ubuntu. This would help give us an idea of who was performing *significant and sustained contributions*, which is the basic criterion for getting approval as a developer.

Daniel went away and figured out that he could generate these graphs by processing messages sent to the commit mailing list (a mailing list that automatically gets emailed whenever a new update is made). Daniel would read in all these commits, weed out the approved developers, and generate graphs for everyone else. Figure 9-3 shows some examples of these graphs (the names have been removed to protect privacy).

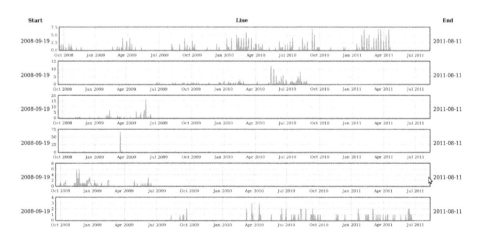

FIGURE 9-3. *Visualizing the quantity and cadence of community contributions is a useful way to spot patterns and activity in your community members.*

Each graph is plotted from September 19, 2008 to August 11, 2011. Each graph represents a single contributor, with the y-axis showing the number of successful contributions they got into Ubuntu. As such, these graphs show real, practical contributions made to Ubuntu and when they occurred.

In the figure, you can see that the person represented in the top graph is very active. This person has made regular, significant and sustained contributions to Ubuntu throughout the timeline. Therefore, this person would be a strong candidate for developer approval; the regularity of contributions certainly shows promise. Interestingly, though, the person's contributions stop abruptly in April 2011. This could be for a variety of reasons: vacation, family issues, busy with the day job, having a child, and so on. For this particular contributor I asked Daniel to reach out and check that everything was OK, and to suggest that the person consider applying to be an approved developer.

The second graph down in the figure shows a different story. This person started contributing in June 2009, then started in April 2010 to contribute really heavily until about September 2010, whereupon the activity just stopped. In fact, this person's activity has remained dormant for much longer than the time shown in the graph. Given that the person contributed consistently for over a year, this behavior is also worth checking into.

These graphs gave us considerably more insight into the different experiences of community members. Importantly, though, having the graphs is only part of the story; if you don't interpret the data to continue to improve your community processes and on-ramps, you are not using the information wisely.

When I saw these graphs, I put together a mentoring campaign to distribute a mentoring facility across the wider Ubuntu team. In the Ubuntu engineering team we have many subteams (Desktop, Server, Foundations, Kernel, etc.). I assigned a member of my team to each subteam, and asked for a member of each subteam to act as a community representative. With these pairs defined, we looked at the list of timeline graphs, identified strong candidates for developer approval, and distributed these folks across the teams so that Ubuntu engineers could reach out to them and provide support. The community representative and paired member of my team would keep on top of this work and report. The result of these efforts saw a significant growth in our developer numbers.

Ensuring Effective Processes

Earlier I talked about when I discovered that Ubuntu's developer growth was flattening a little. Our first response was to perform a survey to gather opinion from our approved developer community (which comprises both employees and community developers) to get a better idea of problematic areas.

The survey provided fascinating insight into the different perspectives on our developer processes. Like any project, we have a set of processes defined for how you contribute changes to Ubuntu, both as an approved and nonapproved developer, how you apply to get approved, how to get security updates out for stable releases, and more. Many of these processes have been in place for many years and the survey gave us a strong idea of the processes that were challenges to our community of developers.

In the survey we asked the developers what was the most challenging and frustrating element of working on Ubuntu. In other words, what should we focus our death ray on first?

The results came in and there was a clear, unanimous answer to this question: *bottlenecks*.

Our developers felt they were feeding information into some processes that were inserting a significant delay in returning a response or other output. These developers would contribute in good faith to Ubuntu and then be met with a frustrating delay. Not good.

Fortunately, we also asked the developers what they felt these bottlenecks were. We also saw some unanimous feedback in answer to this question, with one specific winner: the *Ubuntu Sponsorship Queue*.

The Ubuntu Sponsorship Queue is a facility we have in which unapproved developers (those who can't contribute changes to Ubuntu itself) can fix bugs, create functionality, and get their contributions reviewed by an approved Ubuntu developer. It works like this:

1. Joe Bloggs finds a bug that is frustrating him. He downloads the package source code and fixes the bug. The bug no longer exists on his system and he wants to share his fix and add it to the main Ubuntu system.

2. Joe is not yet an approved developer and as such doesn't have upload rights to contribute the bug fix directly. To submit his fix, he generates a patch for it (a file with the key code changes that fix the bug) and adds the patch to the bug report. He then adds the bug to the Ubuntu Sponsorship Queue; this is a big list of bug reports with fixes attached from nonapproved developers.

3. Sarah, who is an approved Ubuntu developer, wakes up one morning and takes a look at the sponsorship queue. She sees Joe's fix and reviews his patch. It looks good and she uploads it to Ubuntu on Joe's behalf. Now Joe's fix is in Ubuntu and he has made a successful contribution.

This process relies on two key pieces to work successfully: it needs to be clear and easy to use for prospective developers, and it requires our existing approved developer base to actually go and review these contributions.

The feedback from the survey indicated that approved developers were not reviewing the sponsorship queue. I can understand why: these developers are typically very busy with their own work, and did not have time to review other people's work, too. While this is understandable, it is also important that we tend to the sponsorship queue; it is the place where new generations of Ubuntu developers make their first contributions. It doesn't matter how fun or attractive we paint the picture of Ubuntu development; if someone participates and it takes two months to get his contributions reviewed, he will get bored and move on.

To get some better visibility on this, I again asked the graph-making machine, Daniel Holbach, to put together some graphs to show (a) the number of items on the queue and (b) how long it takes to get each item tended to.

The graphs didn't look good. The former contained a lot of items, some of which had been on there for quite some time. The sheer age of some of these items was a tip-off that the latter graph would also tell a grim story: 600 hours on average. Yikes! To be fair, this figure was not entirely representative of the day-to-day experiences of developers, as there were so many old items that skewed the figures, but there was clearly quite a delay in getting many of these items reviewed.

It was clear that we needed to grow the capacity of developers who were able to review the content on the queue, but how could we do this when our approved developers were already so busy?

To accomplish this, we started to focus on the Canonical staff members who work on Ubuntu. We started there because we pay these people and therefore have some pull when it comes to how they spend their time. We basically put together a calendar each month, and every day two staff members would spend half a day each reviewing content on the queue. We made it very clear that their responsibility was to provide an outcome for each item, even if this meant not reviewing it themselves (because they may not have the domain experience) but ensuring that someone else reviews it. This approach would mean that each staff member would need to spend only a half-day a month contributing.

We shared this plan, known as the Patch Pilot plan, with others, and the progress was significant. Figure 9-4 shows the average number of hours that it took sponsorship queue items to be reviewed during the time we were running the Patch Pilot plan.

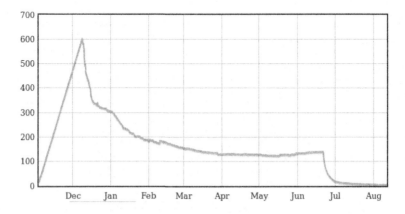

FIGURE 9-4. Tracking the hours until something is reviewed is useful for ensuring that your community contributors get quick responses to their work.

Back in December 2010 the average item would take 600 hours to be reviewed (again, skewed because of the sheer age of some items on the queue). A month later this went down to 300 hours per item, and at the time of this writing the average is around 5 hours.

This has created a significant improvement in how this community process now operates, but what made this possible was getting better visibility on how well the process was functioning and feedback from the people who use it. This helped us to tease the problem apart a little more, put some measurements in place, apply a scheme to repair these issues, and track progress.

HIDING IN PLAIN SIGHT

A key lesson I learned from this experience was to not assume that as a community manager you will know where the bottlenecks and challenges in your community may lurk. Often these challenges are hiding in plain sight, and while you may hear grumblings here and there, it is often only when you hear a chorus of complaints that the problem becomes a priority.

This is exactly what happened with the Ubuntu Sponsorship Queue. I had heard some complaints here and there about it, but when we saw a chorus of opinion shared from folks with strong credibility (our developers), the problem took on a new light.

The lesson here is to regularly reach out to your community and get their feedback on areas that are working well and not-so-well. This will equip you with knowledge of the problem, and then you can shine a light on it and raise the visibility to resolve the issues.

Tracking Health

So far in this chapter we have explored how we can keep track of the very measurable components of community. Tracking projects and work items and keeping an eye on contributor growth and participation is useful for filling in some of the blanks, but some parts of our communities are less structured and less measurable. Unfortunately, many community leaders often ignore these areas and see dire consequences down the road.

This section looks at the general health of your community. You may be tracking your projects well and seeing growth in your participants, but are these participants happy and satisfied with their contributions? Do they feel confident in you and, where appropriate, the company that is investing so heavily in the community? These are some tough questions to answer, and keeping track of this health typically can't be achieved by generating graphs.

One key lesson that I have learned over the years is that no matter how open and approachable you strive to be, your community will not always feel entirely comfortable sharing some of their concerns with you.

I have always tried to be very approachable and open to feedback in my work. Back when I started out as a manager I remember thinking to myself how I wanted to be a different kind of boss. I wanted to be someone who could bring leadership and support to the table, but also be loose and fun to hang out with. As the years have gone by, I have generally been satisfied with the way I have managed the team, and having such a wonderful group of reports has significantly helped with this. Sure, there have been some times when I have had to crack the whip or discipline members of the team (or they have had to discipline me), but these cases have been few and far between.

As my career with community leadership has continued, I have tried to take a similar approach to community management. I have always strived to help our community be successful, help resolve problems and concerns, and hang out and socialize with the community as friends. In my mind it is just as important to shoot the crap with the community as it is to interact with them around projects and work items, and create positive outcomes. I have always tried to encase this work with a very frank and honest approach so that the community can trust me as a friend as well as a community leader.

At one point I started getting a little too complacent in this approach. I felt I was being nice and friendly and open, always keen to hear the community's thoughts, and always being receptive to feedback, and this led me to the false sense of security that if there was a problem, someone would tell me about it for sure. I am just another one of the guys and girls, right? Someone will just drop me an email and we will be good to go? Not quite.

Writing this paragraph is tough, and I almost feel embarrassed to write it. Let me put it this way: in all communities, community leaders are often seen as having a certain amount of… celebrity. Now let's put this in perspective. This is typically celebrity in a *very small fishbowl*. Being well known in a small community does not transpose to general celebrity, nor does it legitimize acting like you have general celebrity. I find it nauseating when people say that I am a "celebrity" or "famous," because that isn't true. What I do acknowledge is that I am well known within a certain community of people.

Now, some of you will like the idea of this. Feeling like a celebrity has to be fun, right? There is no doubt that the *Cheers* effect of "everybody knows your name" is nice, but always keep this in perspective. Unfortunately, I have met far too many community leaders who don't keep it in perspective and they walk around with a smug attitude to their work. No one likes that, particularly your community members. Remember, folks, being known in a small fishbowl is not "celebrity" or "fame."

Regardless of how it should be, many of your community members will unfortunately see you as a celebrity. This will almost always have the effect of making you slightly less approachable, no matter how open you are. Some members of your community simply won't entirely relax around you, and there is nothing wrong with that. What is important to remember is that issues and problems may be happening in the community and someone may not tell you.

So the challenge is, how do we get the visibility on areas of community health even if people feel uncomfortable telling us?

Promoting a Feedback Culture

One of my biggest fears is that a set of opinions or concerns about my work are circulating and no one has the confidence to tell me. My fear is that these concerns and opinions would continue to flow and be shared with people and I would be none the wiser, and as such unable to show a receptivity to the feedback and to try to resolve the concerns where appropriate.

In some of our relationships, providing this kind of feedback is expected. I expect my manager to tell me when he thinks I can do a better job. Likewise, my team should expect that I will tell them when they should be doing a better job. But what about me telling my manager how to improve? How about my team telling me? What about the feedback from my manager's manager about me; should he censor it before it comes to me? How should I communicate concerns from my management peers about my team?

Things get even more complicated when it comes to community. How should community members express feedback to you? How do they express feedback about your team or your manager? How do you handle feedback from community members about another member?

I have always taken a very simple approach to my relationship with others: if there is ever *any* concern about my work, I want to know. If I don't know about it I simply can't fix it.

The first day I work for a new manager or a new member joins my team, I always emphasize this point. My wife and I even have this agreement with each other; we call it our *full disclosure* policy. I make it clear to all of these people that I don't want the feedback censored or deflected, I don't want to be protected from feedback outside of my pay grade; I want to hear the details so that I can react and resolve the problem appropriately. Of course, this is all entirely selfish: I need to know that my peers are being frank with me; otherwise, I would descend into my biggest fear and become a paranoid wreck.

It is important to communicate this policy not just to your managers, teams, and partners, but also to the community. I have gone to great lengths in the past in my work to make it expressly clear that feedback is always welcome, but just saying this is not enough. It is important to demonstrate your receptivity to feedback. A community, like any group of people, is always prone to sharing stories and gossiping about other people. As a community leader you are going to be the prime rib in that particular meal, and you want to ensure that your community has a strong set of positive stories that they can share with one another about you.

As such, you need to demonstrate openness to feedback. Here are some tips:

Document the feedback loop

Write a full and frank article (such as a blog entry) about how you are entirely open to feedback, suggestions, and criticism. When you document your attitude, the community can share the article among themselves. It also provides you with a definitive way to say that you are open to feedback.

Respect privacy

Nothing kills a feedback process like people entrusting their concerns to you and then you breaking that confidence with someone else. Such breaches will become well known quickly, so always respect privacy as the highest priority.

Admit when you are wrong

This may be the hardest element to handle for some of you. The purest definition of proving you are open to feedback is admitting that you are wrong, both on a personal and a public level. Unfortunately, some see a public admittance to a mistake as a weakness; most, however, recognize a measure of maturity and decency in such statements. Of course, don't issue a fake apology to generate this effect; your community will see right through that. Make sure your apology is real and you mean it. Also, when you do admit when you are wrong, credit the community for raising the issue where appropriate; this is another way to prove that you are open to feedback.

Make change happen

Another subtle but key point is that if concerns are shared about something in the community, be sure to be responsive and bring a solution to the table. If your community continually provides feedback and nothing ever changes, they will stop providing feedback at some point.

If you take a very open, responsive, and reactive approach to feedback, your community will not only give you more feedback about their experiences in the community, but also respect you more for your attitude and honesty in accepting and resolving issues where they occur.

IDENTIFYING AREAS OF VISIBILITY

Some of you may be asking which particular areas you should be looking at when it comes to general community health.

Unfortunately, in much the same way as it is difficult for me to advise you on areas to track for growth and decline, the same applies to community health; it is largely dependent on your specific community. You should look at the primary ways your community operates, assess how you would describe a healthy community, and focus on those points.

One piece of advice I would tender, though, is that you focus on getting visibility on the primary areas you feel in the dark about right now. As an example, you may never spend any time with the documentation team, so this means you don't have a decent sense of how healthy the team is. Sit down and think of all the teams and areas where you feel like you don't have a good handle on how well things are working.

Drilling into these areas will help spread your radar around your community and augment the knowledge you have about the parts of the community into which you have visibility, giving you a more complete picture.

Building a Set of Generals

In 2008 I moved to California. When I moved there my entire schedule turned around. In England I would typically be on the phone in the afternoons with folks in the United States and have a few calls earlier in the afternoon with UK and European folks. Upon moving to California that all changed. I was now up every morning at 7 a.m. or 7:30 a.m. to start calls with Europe.

As my job got more complex and my team grew, my calls grew, too. I was getting to a point where I was on the phone for 22 hours a week. Like many folks who get into a similar situation, I tried to cull many of these calls that could be accomplished over email. Unfortunately, this didn't cut it down very much. I needed a weekly call with each member of my team, a general team call, a weekly call with my manager, my management call, and regular calls with key strategic teams and community members. Even when I culled the calls down, I was still clocking up at least 17 hours a week on the phone.

This time on the phone meant that my inbox started ballooning, too. As soon as I was finished with calls I would hit the email, and then finally I could get on with the work I had to accomplish. The net result of all of this activity was that my week became far more compressed and time became a precious commodity.

All of this had one unfortunate impact: I found it harder to get a feel for the general health of the community. I was spending so much time on the damn phone and in email that I didn't have as much time to talk to the community, and there were important projects I felt we needed to move forward on that I just didn't have time to participate in. With little time available, I was stuck between a rock and a hard place; how on earth do I get more things done with no time available?

To help resolve this, I tried a new approach which has become an invaluable way of providing me with a better feel for the challenges in the community and of giving certain community teams more of my support. I refer to this as *building a set of generals*.

The idea is simple: you just identify the teams you wish you could spend more time with and identify leaders in those teams who you can have regular calls with.

As an example, the Ubuntu LoCo Team community is filled with advocates who form local user groups to go out and spread the word about Ubuntu. I believe these teams are critically important in our success; they are our troops on the ground. With this in mind, I could see that Laura Czajkowski, a member of the LoCo Council governance board, was doing some excellent work, so I invited her to have a regular call with me. This gave me some incredible insight into what was going on in the LoCo community at a governance level, and Laura would often expose blockers and issues in moving forward on which I could provide some guidance. The relationship was very positive and it brought real value to both of us.

As time went on, we expanded the call to include some other LoCo leaders who work on the infrastructure side of the LoCo community. As a team we would agree on a set of goals, and the participants on the call would be doing much of the work. My primary function was to keep our eyes on the prize and ensure that the train would move forward. As a result of this work, some great value was brought to the LoCo teams from these community members.

I have set up these calls with a variety of different teams and have found that each time this approach has been really successful. In many ways it is almost as if the community member I am on the call with is an extended member of the team I manage at the company, and many of the similarities in terms of how I work with my team are applied to the community calls: identifying opportunities and problems, defining work items, unblocking issues, and so on.

> **NOTE**
>
> One word of caution in putting together these calls: some community members may see a regular call with the community leader or manager as something of a *status symbol* with other members. This can also arise if you extend your calls to include additional participants; there may be some blowback if a community member feels the presence of additional folks indicates the pure one-on-one calls are of lower value.
>
> On the flip side, those folks who do not have regular calls with you may exhibit some jealousy or frustration over this. Just be a little careful when communicating how and with whom you have these calls; try to be as inclusive as possible.

Reacting to Community Concerns

At some point in your community leadership adventure you are going to face the equivalent of villagers with pitchforks. This will typically happen at a time of stress, uncertainty, or concern, but you may find members of your community expressing frustrations about the structure or operation of the community. Sometimes these concerns can be expressed loudly, as a result of unspoken frustration, and sometimes with a severity that outweighs the issue in question. In other words, you may find yourself getting a kicking from your community because they are unhappy about something.

Unless you are noncommunicative with your community, these expressions of frustration typically arise from a small group of people and are not necessarily reflective of the wider community; you will likely pick up strong undercurrents of problems. Regardless, you should treat these concerns and frustrations with seriousness, dignity, and respect.

Now, astute readers that you are, you may be wondering why I am discussing what seems like conflict resolution in this chapter, and not leaving it until Chapter 11. This section is less about the process of handling conflict than it is about a structured approach to responding to concerns, which involves gathering and measuring data and is therefore pertinent to this chapter.

The rule of thumb here is that, in times of distress, you should be respectful and responsive and strive to find the problems so that you can provide solutions and reassurance. Let me give you an example.

Some time ago I was quietly working one day when my chat program lit up like a Christmas tree. There was a community meeting going on at the time and a small group of people were complaining about some elements of how the community was functioning. Someone asked if these concerns had been raised with Jono, hence the activity on my chat program. So I joined the discussion to learn more about the concerns.

From reading the discussion thus far, the concerns expressed were vague and unspecific. There were clearly frustrations, but the group didn't provide specifics that I could act on to remedy ("The damn car doesn't work and this really sucks" as opposed to "The car engine won't turn over").

My first instinct was to ask the group lots of questions to learn more. I have always been conscious that, as a community leader, I won't know the full extent of what's annoying your community, just as a team may not express certain concerns to their manager. I was also aware that a community leader often has a different perspective and community experience from that of a regular community member, and the last thing I wanted to do was to presume what the problem was. As such, I threw out a stack of questions in the meeting.

This was a mistake.

Throwing out these questions at a time of frustration sounded more like an inquisition than the receptive information gathering I intended it to be. Sensing the building frustration, I assured the group that I was taking their concerns seriously and I would follow up with further action soon. This would give them the reassurance that I cared, along with some time for those who were frustrated to cool down before I reached out for more information.

I was now in a position where I had a vague set of concerns that were clearly frustrating some members of the community, but I had no idea to what extent the community was feeling these concerns (was it a small minority or a wider issue?) and what the specific causes of the concerns were. Without this information I could not build solutions to the problems.

I needed more information, but knew it needed to come from good sources, not be a poll open to everyone and his dog. One of the challenges with surveys is that the data needs to be credible; a survey filled in by random opinionated people on the Internet is not as valuable as one filled in by trusted and established community members. As such, I prepared a survey that asked about some of the concerns raised in the meeting and sent the survey to all officially recognized members of the community. I deliberately kept as many of the questions open-ended as possible (as opposed to multiple choice) to give the respondents the most freedom of expression; the last thing I wanted to do was to limit their feedback.

I sent out the survey and waited a few weeks for the community to respond. I assured the community that I would publish a report in full and that together as a community we could use the survey as a solid chunk of data to help us build solutions to these issues. Throughout this process I blogged about my receptivity to the concerns, the issuing of the survey, and my encouragement to all community members to provide their input and to be as full and frank as possible.

When the survey was complete, I summarized each question into a report, and for the open-ended questions (e.g., "What motivates you about the community?"), I summarized the common patterns and themes in the responses. I was conscious of providing solid data and to not massage or influence the perception of the results. I also included the full responses to all the questions, anonymized to ensure that people could be fully open in their responses.

The survey results were fascinating. Not only did they identify that many of the concerns were indeed not particularly representative of the wider community, which was reassuring, but also they highlighted other areas of growing concern and other areas in which people particularly enjoy participating or find the community motivating.

This was good, solid data, and I published it immediately.

The community started reviewing and presenting their own views on how to read the data and what potential solutions we could create. I joined in those conversations and could tell that the tone had changed from frustration to a shared sense of ownership of the challenges. The atmosphere became more empowering and was positive about fixing the issues outlined; the visibility of the issues clearly provided a sense of having the problem in our sights so that we could understand and solve them.

Building on this momentum, we held a face-to-face community event in the following few weeks and I organized a series of discussion sessions to review the content in the survey, discuss the topics there, and put together solutions. Over the following weeks we started to see many of the issues fading away and the community feeling more involved and empowered.

To be honest, this whole experience was stressful as hell. As a community leader, you always want to feel accomplished in your work and tend to feel a very personal sense of responsibility for your community's happiness. I take any concerns like this (even if they were from a small group such as this) very personally. I became very reflective of myself, did some soul-searching, reviewed how I approached my work and the community, and what presumptions I made. I basically questioned everything I was doing, and while stressful, I am glad it happened; it helped me to take a fresh perspective and recalibrate some elements of our community.

Moving On

This chapter has been all about how to track and measure our work. Many of the skills and experiences highlighted here are things that I have learned over the years as I have faced new challenges and opportunities, and learned better ways of solving some problems that I faced in my work. The chapter provides a good grounding for getting started, but always be open to your own context and how you meet the needs of that context. You will find your own approaches and techniques that will build on and in some cases replace the approaches here. This chapter is a start, not an end to this process.

CHAPTER TEN

Governance

"Which is the best government? That which teaches us to govern
ourselves."

—*Johann Wolfgang von Goethe*

MIKE BASINGER IS A NICE GUY. Some would say a little too nice for his own good: he is one
of those people who are impossible to dislike, no matter how much you try. Quiet,
conscientious, considerate, and understated, Mike is the epitome of the open source
community. Few would imagine that he helps to govern the worldwide Ubuntu community
at the highest level. At the same time, many of the people who know that don't realize that
Mike has never worked for Canonical Ltd., Ubuntu's commercial sponsor; he has always
remained a volunteer.

Back in 2005, Mike joined the Ubuntu community by throwing himself into the bustling
Ubuntu Forums soon after switching to Ubuntu. The forums were a good fit for him. Mike has
a passion for helping people with technical problems. He loves the thrill of the chase: hunting
down those pesky issues and helping to fix them for appreciative community members. As a
good community citizen, Mike was on the front line helping new Ubuntu users get acclimated
to their new waters.

The forums became stunningly popular. Thousands and thousands of excitable community
members joined, and each day pages of conversation on all manner of topics would flow
throughout the site. Interestingly, unlike most other Linux distribution forums, the Ubuntu
Forums were not created by the commercial sponsor (in this case Canonical Ltd.). Instead, the

Ubuntu Forums were created by Ryan Troy, a passionate user who wanted to build an environment in which any Ubuntu user could ask for help and talk to other users.

As the forums grew, their popularity generated a few bumps in the road, and they needed increasing organizational focus. New moderators needed to be appointed, frustrating conflict issues were becoming more common due to the size and diversity of the forum membership, administrators needed to distribute maintenance matters, and there was increasing demand for the forums to integrate with other parts of the Ubuntu community. The forums needed governing, and who should be one of the people to step up to the plate? One Mike Basinger.

Over the following months, the Forums Council was designed, documented, and ultimately approved by the main Ubuntu Community Council. Alongside his peers on the Forums Council, Mike took the lead to govern. He and they did an excellent job, and Mike continued to contribute throughout the community.

In March 2007, the highest governing body in the Ubuntu community, the Community Council, was preparing to elect a new board of governing members. Clearly impressed with Mike's contributions to the Forums Council and elsewhere, Mark Shuttleworth (the leader of the Ubuntu project) asked Mike if he would consider a nomination to the Community Council. Somewhat stunned yet flattered, Mike considered Mark's suggestion and then agreed to be put forth as a nomination.

Just before the Ubuntu Developer Summit in Seville in southern Spain, Mark announced the nominees for the Community Council. The four nominees were put before a Yes/No vote by all approved Ubuntu Members, and Mike was elected to the Community Council in May 2007. It was a good day for Ubuntu, and it was a good day for Mike.

From his beginnings as a volunteer contributor like any other, Mike had risen to one of the most powerful roles in the Ubuntu community. This is entirely due to his hard and careful work and his commitment and devotion to the spirit and community of Ubuntu. When I asked him what kept him excited about Ubuntu throughout this period, he shared his clear passion for Ubuntu and the opportunities it has opened up for him:

> What excites me about the community governance is the sense that Ubuntu is a community of thousands of people from every country, race, sex, and religion who have gotten together and said, "We want computing to be this way." Linux and open source have enabled this as opposed to what Microsoft or Apple tells you. It is the sense that our community's governance is open and anyone who wants to contribute can and has a say in the direction of Ubuntu. It is that the community's main focus is to help each other, whether that means writing code, creating documentation, or answering questions from our users.

I am intensely proud of Mike's experience. Stories like this illustrate the power and opportunity of community to build methods of collaboration and governance that are empowering and rewarding. Stories like this make community leaders feel all warm and fuzzy. They also make us community leaders unusually generous in a bar. If a community manager offers to buy you a pint some day, it's likely that something such as this has just happened....

Accountability

A significant contributing factor in Mike's success is that he feels a genuine and very real sense of accountability and responsibility for his work and for Ubuntu as a whole.

In volunteer environments, participation is optional. Some of your volunteers will spend every day plugged into your community, and some will contribute whenever they please. Unfortunately, the latter form of drive-by contributors can't support many of the responsibilities and leadership components in a community. If you want to release a software product and commit publicly to a release date, you want to ensure that whatever happens, your volunteers feel a very personal sense of commitment to achieving that goal. Likewise, if your community appoints members to lead and govern the community, they must feel and exhibit a strong sense of responsibility and commitment. In short, you want people to feel accountable for their actions: you want them to *make time* when the community is under the gun to achieve something.

Accountability is a valuable asset. It is as close to a declaration of commitment that you will get in a community. Some of your members will feel this sense of accountability and some won't. Those who do are a valuable resource; you should entrust them with responsibility, but don't take advantage of their sense of accountability.

As community leaders, we should be laden with a sense of accountability. We are trusted to guide and inspire the community to move forward, and we should feel that responsibility in a very real way. With that sense of accountability is a responsibility to listen and learn. Our communities seek not only leadership from us, but also substance when it comes to governance. A great community makes it simple and enjoyable for a member to contribute to its tasks, and to contribute to this governance. This is the goal of this chapter.

Governance Does Not Suck

Of all the topics that fall under the umbrella of community leadership, governance is one of the most important yet most misunderstood. In the traditional sense, we are all intimately familiar with governance: it is exemplified by the government of your country. Your government is the representative body that manages the nation's resources and deals with its problems, opportunities, and current affairs. For most of us, our experience of government is the legislation, processes, and laws that define our daily lives, and those who perform this governance are the suited and booted politicians who populate our newspapers, television news shows, and radio broadcasts. We are all familiar with our governments, and we all have an opinion about them.

Unfortunately, opinion often points south, and governments get something of a bad reputation. It is easy to see why: the media is littered with stories of incompetence, sleaze, and self-interest, largely defended by toadying policymakers who refuse to provide a straight answer to a straight question. When government leaders are queried by journalists, TV anchors, and researchers, it is not uncommon for the subjects of the governance (the citizens) to view the whole shebang with an air of suspicion: a government seen as fundamentally disconnected from the people. In a manner of speaking, it can be easy to draw the conclusion that all governments essentially suck.

Unfortunately, many citizens are so frustrated and disappointed by the incompetence in their government that they see the very concept of government as fatally flawed, as a system that fails to engage with its people with a raft of promises, few of which are faithfully kept.

Of course, this view is nonsense. The concept of selecting a few to effectively govern the many works, and we should not allow the incompetence of specific individuals to tarnish the potential of the system. In many cases we never get to hear about the amazing work of government, just the scandals and failed initiatives.

For years many governments have successfully delivered radical change and improvements to their people. Consider the rebuilding of Europe after World Wars I and II, expanding the right to vote, equal access to public accommodations, reducing disease, reducing workplace discrimination, legislation around safe food and drinking water, the nationwide construction of highways, financial security in retirement, scientific funding and technical research, reducing hunger and improving nutrition, space exploration, and more. It is government that helped forward these worthy achievements. When the system works, beautiful things can happen.

THE COMMUNITY CASE BOOK

The Drupal community uses a do-ocracy model, meaning people work on what they want to work on, instead of being told what to work on. Decisions are usually made through consensus building and based on technical merit, trust, and respect. As the project lead, and with the help of my co-maintainers, I help guide the community in strategic directions.

—*Dries Buytaert, on Governance*

Read the full interview in Chapter 14.

Governance and Community

In the same way that the government of a country is tasked with improving infrastructure, living conditions, and the welfare of its nation, the governance body of a community is similarly tasked with the welfare of those it governs. Instead of ensuring clean drinking water, community governance ensures transparency in our deadlines. Instead of readily available health care, we strive for robust resources to do our work. Instead of building that freeway, we build effective and open communication processes. The issues may differ, but the primary function of representing and maintaining the interests of those you govern remains.

Of course, governance is an epic and often academic topic. Thousands of books, research papers, and understudies have sought to understand, rationalize, and quantify what makes great governance. As a result, much of the available teaching is outrageously complex and written for those who have devoted their lives to understanding the subject.

I have *not* committed my life to governance, I have never served a professorship in governance, and I don't plan to do so. I am a community manager, not a governor, and I would rather spend my time helping my community be effective than reading a library full of theory on governance.

Like many of you, what I seek to understand is how I can ensure that my community will be governed well. I want to cut to the chase: what are the important elements to focus on in building a smooth and efficient governance structure?

In this chapter, we are going to uncover these elements. We are going to explore the aims and intentions of great governance, look at different approaches, and then discuss how to produce your own governance bodies. To seal the deal I am going to provide an extensive case study of how the Ubuntu governance structure works: this can be an excellent basis in which to roll out your own approach.

Let's roll....

The Case for Governance

Although I may appear to be a lighthearted guy on the outside, inside burns a cynical Englishman. Like many others, I have a blacklist of irritants in life. Hovering near the bottom of the list are bad customer salespeople, above that are those objects that attract the full velocity of my little toe when I walk barefoot in my house, then sycophantic reality TV imbeciles, and, bobbing around the top of the list, people who jump too quickly to governance.

Governance is not a rite of passage for community. It is not an expected norm, and its absence is not something that is perceived as immaturity. Before we begin exploring the nuances of governance, we need to determine if you need governance in the first place.

At the end of the day, only your community should judge whether governance is required and what form it will take. There are, however, some indicators that suggest that a governing body could be useful to have in place:

Size of the community
> One of the first indicators that governance may be required is that your community grows extensively. If you have a community of around 10 people, governance is probably not required. If you have a community of 100 contributors (not users/consumers/onlookers)

or more, it becomes a more pressing consideration. If you exceed the 1,000 mark, you should strongly consider governance, and possibly muscle relaxants, too.

Increasing conflict

Conflict resolution is a primary responsibility in governance. You should be careful about what you consider real conflict, though. People disagreeing on a few things is not conflict. People having full arguments in which multiple people are involved and factions develop is a far more serious issue. When this happens, sometimes the different sides hit an impasse and can't move forward. Governance can really help here, under the proviso that the community respects the conclusions of the governance body.

Extensive resources

If you find that your community requires significant resources and some of these resources are donated, you may require a governing body to oversee the stewardship of these resources. An example of this could include a software project such as the Debian (*http:// www.debian.org/*) project, which requires extensive resources such as servers, hosting, build farms, and more.

Commercial interests

When there are commercial interests in a community, a governance body can be useful to ensure that the community is "kept honest." The governance body should be tasked with the responsibility of always maintaining and defending the primary values of the community and standing up against any improper requests that may result from commercial sponsors.

If some of these elements apply to your community, it would be worth considering governance in more detail. Let's now expand on this introduction and explore some of the responsibilities that governing bodies can provide, and consider how this could apply to your own community.

To ensure that we focus our minds on these important topics, I am going to revisit the approach from earlier in the book when we built a Community TODO List to remember which items were important in growing strong community. Our list will look a little like this:

Governance TODO List

- *Item.*
- *Item.*
- ....

Follow the Leader

The primary responsibility of a governance body is to lead. It is there to initiate and engage in a conversation about topics that affect the community as a whole and represent the best interests of that community. A governing body seeks to understand and make decisions that are representative of the community, its goals, and its culture.

For many communities, leadership is broken into a few different threads that pull in the same direction to form a diversely detailed governing body. Just as a conventional government will have leaders and departments that focus on specific areas (e.g., Department of Health, Department of Employment), many communities divide their leadership, too.

For most communities, this leadership is divided as follows:

General governance
> Decisions that need to be made around general topics that apply to the community as a whole. This could include things such as how people join the community, resources and infrastructure, community-wide policies and procedures, governance changes, and so on.

Direction
> Decisions about the goals, ambitions, and focus of the community. As an example, with a software project, this kind of leadership would decide which features to aim for in the next release. In a local civil rights group, this could be how the group is planning to raise awareness and which campaigns will be organized.

Specialist governance
> This really applies only to larger communities. Specialized governance may be required in specific areas of expertise. As an example, in a software community the developer community may require its own governance, and so may the discussion forums.

For many communities, each type of leadership falls together inside a single governance body. This is particularly common in smaller communities.

For example, many user groups have a known collection of leaders who advise and govern around all manner of topics, including how people can join the group, how the group should focus their efforts, which campaigns should be worked on, how money and assets are handled, and more. It is often the same small set of people who advise on these issues, and the expertise and more general focus of a user group makes this kind of simple approach a perfect solution.

For larger or more specialized communities, these separate leadership roles are often divided into different governance bodies. As an example, in the Ubuntu community we have the following governance bodies:

- Community Council→General Governance
- Technical Board→Direction (technical direction and processes)
- Team Councils→Specialist Governance (e.g., the Forums Council governs the Ubuntu Forums)

If this approach piques your interest, you should be tickled pink to learn that I will be providing a detailed summary of how Ubuntu is governed later in this chapter. We will look at the structure of its governance, crack it open, and see how it works. Let's now add our first item to our Governance TODO List.

Governance TODO List

- Ensure that your community is governed in terms of General Governance, Direction, and (if applicable) Specialist Governance.

Engage the People

Governments are, fundamentally, representatives of the people, and for this representation to be fair and accurate, the government needs to engage with the people. A government that lowers itself into a silo and rarely interacts with its people is doomed to a future riddled with problems. If a government fails to communicate with its people, the people will not only lose faith in those who govern, but also lose faith in the confidence of being governed in the first place.

George Burns, the famous American comedian, replete with arched eyebrow and cigar smoke punctuation, had a lot to say about government. In a 1979 issue of *Life* magazine, Burns shared a nugget of insight that resonated with many people:

> Too bad that all the people who know how to run the country are busy driving taxicabs and cutting hair.

He isn't wrong. When I started my career in community management, I spent a lot of time traveling. At OpenAdvantage I would hurl myself across Europe from conference to conference, and my move to Canonical expanded my travel to the worldwide stage. As I moved from plane to plane, and ate miniature bag after miniature bag of salted peanuts, I went to meet and greet the various members of my community. While en route, I had my own opportunity to meet a battalion of taxi drivers, each with his own carefully considered manifesto of what his government had screwed up and the rather obvious solution to the problem. I heard views on Chinese politics in San Francisco, opinions of US trade treaties in Prague, and just about everyone had a view on George W. Bush. I suspect that that man doesn't get as many Christmas cards as he used to....

Virtually all of these taxi drivers had one thing in common: they all felt their voice was rarely heard by their governments. Their right to vote was always cherished, but it was seen as a binary decision around favor or rejection. These always-entertaining cabbies weren't asking for much, they just wanted to be able to have a conversation with their governments, and so they should.

Great communities always have a close connection between the governing bodies and the members of the community. This relationship requires more than a communication channel with the governance body; that part is simple. Real engagement is when government and community enter into a two-way conversation. Gone should be the days in which the government dictates to the people. Today governance should focus its heart on engaging in conversation with its members. Whether you call it shooting the breeze, having a good ol' chin-wag, or anything else, you need to be having it with the people who govern you.

It is likely you are going to be governing others, and as such we need to ensure that we are cognizant of engaging in conversation with our communities. Let's put this on our list.

Governance TODO List

- Ensure that your community is governed in terms of General Governance, Direction, and (if applicable) Specialist Governance.
- Build communication channels between the governance body and those whom they govern.
- Foster a culture in which the members of the community can engage in conversation, debate, and discussion with their governing bodies.

Aspire to Inspire

Every community looks to its governing members for direction and advice, and leadership helps to ensure that the community is on the right path and feeling productive and nimble. A very close cousin of leadership is inspiration. Your members will also look to you to inspire, motivate, and enthuse them. If you make the hairs on the backs of their necks stand on end when you lay out your vision and what you want accomplished, your community will succeed.

Inspiration is an important responsibility for leaders. Earlier in this book we spent some time discussing how to write inspiring words for your community. Unfortunately, some community leaders who work to build governance bodies seem to forget that governance is seen as leadership and leaders are expected to inspire. Don't fall into the trap of assuming that governance is merely about decision making. There is no reason why you can't constrict it in this way, but you will be missing out on a wealth of opportunities to excite and energize your community.

You can see the divergence in this approach in conventional government. Compare and contrast how some presidential figures have approached inspiration. A recent example of an inspirational orator is Barack Obama. Regardless of where you stand on his politics, Obama has inspired a significant chunk of the electorate behind a rhetoric of pumped-up, energized, forward-looking narrative, and the promise of a bright future. I am sure you can think of many presidents who merely took office and started legislating.

Obama primarily inspired people with the promise of a brighter future, and you should do the same for your own community. However, there is another important and more focused responsibility that your governance bodies should shoot for: inspiring your members based on the values of your communities.

Governance is almost entirely based around values. When a government appears open, transparent, and honest, it generates trust, respect, and faith in its leaders. When a government throws values out of the window and replaces them with self-interest and sleaze, your community may as well pack up its bags and go home.

You need to not only understand your values, but celebrate them. It is these values that will continue to make your community feel open and engaging. When you learn to inspire based on values and the promise of the future, it will stand you in good stead and stand your community in even better stead.

Let's ensure that we make a note of this important topic on our TODO list.

Governance TODO List

- Ensure that your community is governed in terms of General Governance, Direction, and (if applicable) Specialist Governance.
- Build communication channels between the governance body and those whom they govern.
- Foster a culture in which the members of the community can engage in conversation, debate, and discussion with their governing bodies.
- Seek to inspire, motivate, and enthuse your community based on future opportunities and the honesty and openness of your governance.

To Bring Peace

A final topic that is an essential function of governance is the ability to bring peace to your community. We all look to our leaders to resolve and calm conflict, and your community will be no different.

Every community faces conflict. Communities attract different personalities, goals, approaches, attitudes, ambitions, and opinions, and some of them are going to rub us the wrong way. In the worst of these situations, conflict can cause deadlocks, and the community will look to its governors to unblock it. We need to expect conflict, acknowledge it, and react to it elegantly.

Conflict resolution is a large and complex topic, and with this in mind I have devoted Chapter 11 to it. As such, we will revisit this topic in that chapter. For now, you should simply ensure that inside the box in your mind that says "Governance" is a smaller box with "Conflict Resolution" written on the front. Let's also add it to our TODO list.

Governance TODO List

- Ensure that your community is governed in terms of General Governance, Direction, and (if applicable) Specialist Governance.
- Build communication channels between the governance body and those whom they govern.
- Foster a culture in which the members of the community can engage in conversation, debate, and discussion with their governing bodies.
- Seek to inspire, motivate, and enthuse your community based on future opportunities and the honesty and openness of your governance.
- Provide a clear, objective, and mature approach to solving conflict and contentious issues and for providing a decision when faced with deadlocks.

Learning from the Leaders

With a firm understanding of the needs and aspiration behind governance, let's now take a few minutes to look at some of the approaches to governance that some communities have taken.

Of course, there are thousands of communities around the world, with varying governance approaches. Fortunately, there are patterns in the chaos, and there are three prevalent themes in many communities. These are:

Dictatorial charismatic leadership
    Governance and decision making that is largely driven and controlled by a single person

Enlightened dictatorship
    Governance that effectively has no formal leader but in which leadership is determined by reputation in the community

Delegated governance
    Governance that is delegated to a series of smaller units that all fit together to form a single governing body

Let's take a quick spin through these different themes and see how they apply to our communities. This can provide us with an idea of how we want to structure our own governance.

Dictatorial Charismatic Leadership

People hate the word *dictator*. It typically gets something of a bad reputation in polite conversation. Unfortunately, history has taught us that many of the most famous "dictators" were mass-murdering psychopaths who foisted their attitudes onto their people. I am sure this is why some of you may have been a little surprised to read that there is a type of acceptable governance that is driven by dictators. Fortunately, mass murder is not a common practice in these communities. Dictator-led communities work just like they say on the tin: they are communities in which a single person calls the shots. This person will often set direction and focus, approve what is acceptable in the community, and in technical communities will be the arbiter of what gets included in the project. If you still can't stomach the word *dictator*, substitute *charismatic leader* in your mind each time I use it.

Now, I know what you are thinking: this doesn't sound very community-spirited. A community in which one person acts as the funnel through which everyone else must flow? Surely that can't actually work! You would be surprised.

There are many dictator-led communities that are popular and attract large numbers of people. Two very prominent technical examples of this are Linux and Python. Within these communities exist two highly visible leaders: Linus Torvalds and Guido van Rossum, respectively. Linus and Guido are the people who have traditionally decided on direction, set focus, and accepted or rejected contributions.

In the Free Software world, one of the most notable cases of dictatorship was the choice of the third version of the GNU General Public License, perhaps the software license in most widespread use by Free Software projects (including Linux). Years of discussion went into this license, including intense meetings and negotiations with representatives of companies and software projects of all sizes. Yet in the end, someone had to make a decision, and that person was the illustrious president of the Free Software Foundation, Richard Stallman.

Although the dictators in these communities are typically the original founders of the community, this does not mean they don't lean on the community for help and support in judging contributions to the project. Typically these leaders will handpick trusted and reliable members to lend a hand. In these communities there is often no open governance, no elections, and no community-discussed focus and direction.

Despite these communities' restrictive nature, time and time again contributors join up and enjoy their involvement. Despite this, however, I recommend against a dictator-led community, for a few reasons:

Lack of transparency
> Earlier I went into detail about why openness and transparency are important in volunteer communities. Dictatorial communities are something of an antithesis to this approach, and their leaders always face the risk of not representing the views of the wider community.

Bus factor
> Communities that have a single, strongly focused leader face considerable risk if that leader gets hit by a bus. Other, more openly governed communities are often able to transition to other leaders more efficiently.

Direction
> Communities with a single leader who decides what direction the community takes can have difficulty expanding their focus. As an example, if your community is building a website, the leader may stick with outdated ideas of how it should be structured and behave after the rest of the world has moved to new technologies and architectures. There is a very real risk of "It's my ball and we are playing my game" with this approach.

Of course, if you are the founder of your community, only you can decide whether the dictatorial approach is suitable. In almost all scenarios I recommend against it, and if you are keen to have a strong level of control, at least delegate some control to councils (as we will discuss in the section "Delegated Governance" on page 325).

Technical communities who have successfully implemented the dictatorial model often refer to their primary leader as a *benevolent dictator*. This term is inspired by historical leaders such as Mihailo Obrenović III, Prince of Serbia; Maria Theresa of Austria, Queen of Bohemia; and Frederick II of Prussia, King of Germany, who led and governed their people as dictators but applied rationality to their approaches.

In historical terms, this rationality was manifested as religious toleration, freedom of speech and the press, and the right to hold private property. In the technical space, benevolent dictators apply the same sense of rationality to toleration, and freedom of speech and press, but also often inspire open contributions, delegated responsibilities, and more.

Enlightened Dictatorship

In contrast to dictatorship and benevolent dictators, a popular form of community that has grown in both online and offline communities is *enlightened dictatorship*. With this approach the concept is simple: there is essentially no leader.

Confused? Don't be.

Not all collaborative communities need leaders; they just need a general ad hoc agreement of what is not acceptable. When your community knows what is "not cool," it means all other contributions are, by definition, "cool."

While this may sound like an environment driven by chaos and mismatched focus, many communities have been productive with this approach. Although there is no formal leader, the sense of leadership naturally grows out of reputations that are developed and matured within the community.

At its heart, this is a pure form of meritocracy: when people do great work, they become thought leaders. Although some communities may enable people to climb the ladder based on meritocracy, in an enlightened dictatorship there simply is no ladder.

An interesting example of this approach is the KDE project. Founded by Matthias Ettrich, KDE set out to build an easy-to-use desktop environment, and it has become popular among Linux and other Free Software enthusiasts.

I was one such enthusiast. Back in 2001 I joined the project, attracted not only by its purpose and direction, but also by the apparent openness in the community. To participate back then involved learning a fairly stiff set of programming tools that was commanded by the Aladdin's Cave of complexity that is the C++ programming language.

My C++ skills were, frankly, pants. I tried my best to learn. I bought books, read websites, took courses, and even watched tuition videos hosted by a man with a kipper tie. Despite my bumbling attempts at C++, one magical opportunity existed: I knew that if I could gain those skills, I was welcome in that community. Of course, these days a more diverse menu of opportunities is available for those who want to participate in KDE, but even in the dark age of when I was involved, openness was always present.

Although KDE has hundreds of contributors from around the word, there is no formalized leader that exists beyond the limited set of developers who look after the different chunks of code (called modules) and the release manager. It is the many developers involved in KDE who are the arbiters of which bugs get fixed and what features are added. This makes for an interesting dynamic when interacting within the group and how the group is perceived by the outside community. This dynamic has created something of a mantra of "those who code get their way," a position that some cherish as a pure approach to open source community and some believe makes a community less approachable. Whichever position you take, the KDE project has made great strides in productivity.

One of the most evident places this mantra is exercised is within the KHTML portion of the project, which produces technology for displaying web pages. As WebKit (an alternative technology originally based on KHTML) has gained traction within the embedded and desktop markets, many people from outside the community have questioned why KHTML is still maintained at all and not been abandoned in favor of WebKit.

As Ian Reinhart Geiser, a longtime KDE contributor and member of the KHTML project, explained to me:

> Technical arguments aside, it is the choice of the maintainers of KHTML to keep maintaining their code base and continuing its life. There is no active movement against WebKit and in fact there is a smaller group of developers who are working on a KDE version of WebKit. The will of the KHTML developers is what decides the technical direction of progress in the KDE project.

It is the presence of enlightened dictatorship that Geiser arguably believes has enabled the KHTML developers to push forward with their own approaches that they feel happy with. Although it may not make sense to some, it exemplifies the freedom in this project for raw technical contributions to define direction—a freedom that has helped the project maintain its flexibility and its momentum.

Delegated Governance

Our final approach to governance is the one I find most appropriate, open, transparent, and conducive to robust community. In essence, it puts governance in the hands of an openly nominated and elected group of people who have respected and recognized expertise.

Many powerful examples of this approach to governance are in place, and it is an approach that we have used extensively in the Ubuntu project. We are not alone, though; each major Linux distribution takes the same approach, including Debian, Fedora, and OpenSuSE.

In delegated governance, the founders of the project nominate a diverse body of leaders to represent the best interests of the community. This governing body has a mandate and a set of responsibilities, along with a transparent procedure for electing or otherwise replacing members, and these members are typically chosen for their well-respected contributions to the community. Although the approach is very open and transparent, it does have one distinctive risk: *complexity*.

Building an open yet responsible governance body is not a particularly simple task. You need to know what you want to achieve, how to structure the governance, what are the requirements of your members, and how to ensure that your community is fully supportive of the authority put in the hands of the resultant Community Council.

That can appear complicated to put in place, and can also seem overly complex to your community. As such, we need to work hard not only to craft an effective governance body, but also to communicate to the whole community the way governance works and get them on board. Again, we can do this. We just need to pay keen attention to detail and ensure that we tick all the right boxes.

THE UGLY B-WORD: STILL UGLY

Here I need to throw out another quick reminder of the importance of avoiding *bureaucracy*.

Always remember that most people view governance as neither cool nor interesting. Our goal is to keep the amount of governance infrastructure and documentation to an absolute minimum while still maintaining the quality and objectivity that we strive for.

Setting Up a Community Council

If you follow my advice and choose delegated governance—or at least some elements of it—you need to build a governance body. For many communities this means forming a *council*. A council is a group of selected members in a community who govern collectively. Issues and topics can be presented to this council, and they will come to a united opinion that is typically concluded in a vote. As an example, if the council has seven members, they may allocate 20 minutes to discussing a proposal and let it go forward if four members support it. (In practice, if your council is deciding a lot of issues on the basis of a bare majority, the community is not well governed and there is likely to be destructive conflict—but we're just covering the basic principle here.)

Many communities form a *Community Council,* a single council that governs the entire community. For most communities this is a great solution, but larger communities benefit from delegating some authority from the Community Council to additional subcouncils. For now, though, we are going to explore what is involved in setting up a single Community Council to govern your community.

COUNCILS VERSUS TEAMS

This chapter discusses long-term forms of governance, which are basically invested in *councils* or *boards*. This is different from groups that form more organically and naturally to handle particular objectives or goals in your strategic plan. The less formal groups are usually called *teams* or *committees.* I talked about teams in Chapter 2, and they are certainly the basis for effective community work. But teams or committees focus on getting some concrete task done, not on governance, so I don't cover them in this chapter.

Certainly, a council can form a team to handle a specific task related to governance, such as writing one of the documents I describe in this chapter or nominating members for councils.

Designing a Council

Our first task is to understand what you want to achieve with your Community Council and document the full extent of its responsibilities. Governance bodies are fundamentally institutions with an authority the community agrees on, so we need to understand where that authority begins and ends. This agreement is also important for your community: they will want to have confidence in what the Community Council can help with, and also will want to understand what areas are beyond their control. Obviously, the limits are even more important for subcouncils so that they don't make decisions at cross-purposes.

Designing and documenting your council is important for three reasons:

- Explicitly discussing the council's responsibilities will help you as a community leader understand the full rationale behind the council and how it should work.
- Clear expectations also help all council members know how to handle their responsibilities and will make them more willing to serve.
- A well-designed and -documented council will protect your community from accusations of corruption. If the remit and extent of the council are well known and the members are known to act within those expectations, accusations of favoritism or misuse of authority will be rare.

The building blocks of a council are your decisions regarding:

- Responsibilities
- Structure
- Membership
- Communication

The next few sections of this chapter look at the choices you have for each of these building blocks, and some of the criteria that help you make your choice. Along the way, I'll show you how to document your decision—a crucial aspect of governance. Like anything else you want your members to learn about, a council requires documentation.

To make this as simple to understand as possible, it's easiest to describe an example fictional council. So, friends, for the next few pages we are all members of an exciting new open source project that has produced a Frequently Asked Questions content management system called Tobe (named after "To be or not to be, that is the question"). Actually, trivia fans, this was an old project I worked on many moons ago when I was a web developer, so it seems like an apt choice for an example.

The Tobe project is no longer running, so don't get too excited if you are looking for something similar. I still think a FAQ management system would be an incredible resource for many communities, though, so if you produce one, do let me know!

Our fictional Tobe system is a complete web application for maintaining FAQs. It is written using the PHP language and MySQL database. Because it's fictional, let's say it has an excellent user interface, wonderfully written code, and legions of fans around the world (including Johnny Depp and Nicole Kidman). As such, Tobe has a large and bustling contributor community, so large that we are feeling the need for a Community Council to help guide the project forward and ensure that the community is always open and accessible.

Responsibilities

The primary purpose of a council is to provide fair governance and feedback on an agreed set of responsibilities in the community. What you choose as these responsibilities will vary: it is highly dependent on your community. But your community needs to be united in agreement about what these responsibilities are. We need the community to be fully aware of what purpose the council serves.

Choosing this set of responsibilities may be more complicated than you imagine. What we are shooting for here is a council that members need to consult relatively rarely and only when there's no way around it. What we don't want to do is to build an environment in which someone can't scratch her leg without consulting the council. If we assign too much responsibility to the council, it will annoy the community and make it feel restrictive, and I can guarantee that the council will also become an impediment to getting things done. For communities, I heartily endorse the old aphorism, "That government is best which governs least."

On the other hand, we don't want to provide the council with too little responsibility: it does need to have the power to resolve disputes and set direction firmly when the community needs that guidance. In a nutshell, we need to strike a balance.

The common responsibilities that you may want to consider for your council are:

Membership approval/rejection
A council is often a useful body for approving or rejecting members who want to join your project. You need to decide what kind of members these should be—general members, developers, other contributors, and so on. We will discuss this in more detail shortly.

Conflict resolution

Many councils act as an objective third party in dealing with conflict. In this case, members of the community will schedule a conflict discussion with the council, and the council members decide on an appropriate outcome. This has occurred in the Ubuntu community many times, and the Community Council typically has been successful in bringing closure to conflict issues.

Project values

Many councils act as an arbiter over the core values of a community. As an example, in the Ubuntu community there is a set of core values around freedom that the project always seeks to maintain. If anyone feels these core values should be adjusted, or if they have not been met, the member is advised to raise this with the Community Council. Note that upholding core values is key to conflict resolution, but it's not quite the same thing, because communities also sometimes drift away from their values unintentionally and just need a reminder.

Community process changes

Councils can drive changes to processes in your community and get those changes accepted. If you have a Community Council that is known to fairly represent the community and they approve a process change, your community will feel like the process is now considered "official." As an example, in the Ubuntu community we changed the process in which developers applied to be a member of the project, and the Community Council needed to approve it. When it was approved, the community unequivocally accepted it.

Ordaining governance bodies

If your community is large and requires multiple governance councils, your primary Community Council should be the body to make a proposed subcouncil official. As an example, Ubuntu's Community Council approved and officially nominated members for subcouncils such as the Forums Council and IRC Council.

Direction

Councils often determine, or at least weigh in on, the long-term direction of a project. As an example, if you are a software project, your council may decide on the feature goals for a given release targeting a given release date. This is a controversial topic in governance, and many communities vary in whether they allow a governing body to dictate features or their timing. In the Ubuntu community, a separate body called the Technical Board acts as an arbiter over debates concerning feature direction.

While you are considering which responsibilities your council should take on, ask yourself how much impact these topics are going have on the day-to-day work in your community. As we said earlier, you want to achieve a state in which your community has to interact with a governing body only on limited occasions.

Let's look at a few examples of what not to do:

- As I mentioned, leaders may decide to grant councils the right to set feature direction when there's no need for it. If you have excellent contributors who are not on the council, the right features may simply arise from their work and discussions.

- The council does not act as a bottleneck to choose people for small, straightforward roles such as mailing list moderator. Making the moderators go before the council to approve a new moderator is a waste of everybody's time, as long as the moderators are happy with their own decision.

- The council should not have to approve the formation of a new team. Let people set up their own teams as they see a need. This will result in more teams and more diversity in your project. But the council could set up a special category of *approved teams* who have additional responsibility and need to be vetted by the council. An example of a useful role for an approved team is the Approved LoCo Teams (local user groups) in the Ubuntu community. While anyone can set up a local Ubuntu LoCo team, those teams who have demonstrated consistent good work can be approved and will have better access to merchandise, content, and resources. This is a useful way to reduce waste of resources because approved LoCo teams are generally a lot more responsible.

After deciding on these responsibilities, you should put together a document that outlines each responsibility in detail. This can be the basis for forming the council.

Let's apply this to our Community Council for the Tobe project example. I think this would be a suitable selection of privileges.

TOBE COMMUNITY COUNCIL RESPONSIBILITIES

The Tobe Community Council (TCC) will govern the Tobe project by exercising the following responsibilities:

- Developer Approval—The TCC will judge applications for project developer positions. A prospective developer should present a wiki page that outlines his work in the Tobe project and lists at least two endorsements from current developers. The TCC will vote on the application.

- Process Changes—Any significant changes to community-wide processes should be approved by the TCC.

- Governance Changes—Any changes to community governance (including the formation of new governance bodies) should be approved by the TCC.

- Conflict Resolution—If a member of the community has a conflict with other members that is hampering work and cannot be resolved, this issue can be raised to the TCC. The notice can either be given publicly in a meeting or be privately posted to the TCC mailing list. Any case put before the TCC should have as much externally referenced evidence as possible to demonstrate the conflict.

(You may notice that I have not included "Direction" in these responsibilities. I don't believe that governed feature direction is necessary for a small community such as Tobe, because it could inhibit innovation.)

Structure

With our responsibilities in place, we now need to plan our council's structure. While a council may seem like fairly straightforward structure—a group of cooperating members—we need to consider some important details.

The first decision is how many members should be on the council. For most of the councils I have been involved in, a good number is five to seven. This provides a good range of opinion on topics while building in enough redundancy to handle absences (such as when members are on vacation).

Base the number of council members on the number of good candidates you actually have available. Don't pick seven members for the sake of a large size if you only have two or three existing contributors who would make suitable council members. We will discuss how to assess quality members later in this chapter.

The next decision is whether one of your council members has a tie breaking privilege. If you have a meeting attended by six council members and three vote on each side of an issue, you have reached a deadlock that cannot move forward. So seriously consider appointing a member with the privilege to cast a tie breaking vote in a deadlock situation. In the Ubuntu community, Mark Shuttleworth has this privilege. The Fedora and OpenSuSE Linux distributions have similar roles in place.

If you decide to include a tie-breaking role, ensure that the person in this role is the very model of objectivity and responsibility. The privilege confers great power, and you must ensure that it is always exerted with the best interests of the community at heart. We will discuss membership requirements in the next section, and your tie breaker should excel in demonstrating the attributes covered in that section.

> **NOTE**
> Of course, you may consider yourself for this privilege. But before you do, look at yourself in the mirror and ask whether you deserve it. Although by reading this book you evidently have the interests of community at heart, can you really offer an entirely objective opinion?

The next consideration when deciding on the membership structure of the council is how long each member serves. There are, of course, varying opinions on this. Some believe that one year is a suitable term, particularly given the fast-changing nature of community. Others believe two years is more appropriate because it provides a better sense of stability and focus for the council, and it lets your community get used to the same names and expectations. Some people, after serving on councils, say, "It took me a year to figure out how the council works."

I believe that term length is largely dependent on (a) the type of council you are building and (b) the maturity of the membership you have available. For general Community Councils that oversee process changes, conflicts, and other similar elements from our list of responsibilities a few pages back, it is reasonable to have a two-year term. This has been used in many existing councils and has worked out well. For technical and direction-focused councils, I feel a one-year term is often more appropriate. A shorter term always ensures that your council has fresh perspective, and if the current council is serving well, simply allow the members to continue their term.

Term length is related to the decision of whether existing council members can (a) serve repeat terms and (b) be on multiple councils simultaneously in your community.

I am personally against term limits. If you have excellent governing community members, you should allow them to continue doing great work. However, you should also have a fair and representative system in place to ensure that your community does not develop an "old boys' club" with ineffective governing members who may not be especially forward-thinking. In other words, excellence should not be capped by term length, but you should ensure that your community can kick out ineffective members.

ALWAYS MAINTAIN QUALITY

Remember that if you have problems with an "old boys' club" nesting in your council, your governance structure *can* be changed to prevent it.

In some communities, if the selection process for governing members repeatedly nets ineffective officers the general feeling can be, "Well, that's the way the community works and we just have to deal with it."

Don't just deal with it. If your community governance is not working, change it so that it can work. In doing this, it's important not to single out and excoriate problematic members. A proposed modification to council nomination or election should not be "David Foo is doing a terrible job, so he should be banned from applying to the council in the future." Instead, you should build a system that weeds out ineffective members quickly and averts their nomination in the first place. You can base the system on experiences with current bad council members, but think in general terms.

Criteria for excluding and removing council members could include a required level of participation, audits of how well the council works, and an agreed manifesto listing what members will work on.

Each of these initiatives can help your community judge whether a member is effective. Finally, institute a process to review whether members should still be on the council.

Of course, you need to temper these considerations with moderation: you do not want council members to feel like Big Brother is constantly checking in on them.

Commercial sponsorship

Before we move on, I want to raise a sensitive consideration when it comes to the structure of your council: commercial investment and sponsorship.

Many communities have commercial sponsors and investors. These sponsors often have a staff of developers and contributors who work within the community to make contributions that benefit the investor. Sometimes the community has a single sponsor, who perhaps founded the community in the first place.

Examples of this situation include the major Linux distributions: Ubuntu was founded and is mostly funded by Canonical Ltd., Fedora by Red Hat, and OpenSuSE by Novell. With such significant investment in these communities, what impact should these investors have in the governance of the project? At what point is investment in a community considered a reasonable justification for governance?

Let's take a look at the impact of these sponsors on the governance of those projects:

Ubuntu (sponsored by Canonical Ltd.)
> Of the seven places in the Ubuntu Community Council, only one seat is appointed—that of Canonical founder Mark Shuttleworth, who has tie breaking power. The other six seats are open to anyone, from Canonical or otherwise.

Fedora (sponsored by Red Hat)
> The Fedora Board (its Community Council) has a Red Hat-appointed chairperson with tie breaking power and nine seats. Of those nine seats, four are appointed to Red Hat staff members and the other five are openly elected. This means at least half of the board must be working at Red Hat, one of whom has a tie breaking vote.

OpenSuSE (sponsored by Novell)
> The OpenSuSE Board (its Community Council) has a chairperson who works for Novell and who has tie breaking privileges. There are four other seats, two of which must be occupied by Novell staff members.

Although the numbers are different, the Fedora and OpenSuSE approaches produce essentially the same effect: a board in which 50% of the seats are reserved for the sponsor, one of whom is the chairperson with a tie breaking vote. This means that, conceivably, the sponsor could push through any issue they want: in OpenSuSE, the Novell staff could vote their majority, while in Fedora, there would be a deadlock of votes down the middle, allowing the chairperson to cast the deciding vote.

The Ubuntu approach is different: Mark Shuttleworth has the only reserved seat. Even with his tie-breaking privilege, it would be difficult to push something through unless it got to a deadlock, and Canonical has no way to engineer a deadlock internally, as all other seats are equally available to non-Canonical contributors. In fact, at the time of this writing the majority of members on the Community Council don't work for Canonical.

I believe that for general volunteer communities such as open source projects, sponsorship and investment should never buy you a place in a governance body. I say this not because these commercial sponsors cannot be trusted, but because volunteer associative communities are often based on the contributions of all members, and these members give of themselves in exchange for the assurance that their hard work will go toward their fellow members and the community's future.

Let us now apply some of this thinking to our Tobe example council.

TOBE COMMUNITY COUNCIL STRUCTURE

The Tobe Community Council (TCC) will have five membership seats, one of which is held by the founder of the project and has a tie breaker privilege.

Commercial sponsorship does not guarantee representation by employees of the sponsor on the council.

Membership

With a clear idea of your requirements and structure, the next step is to figure out what you are looking for in your council's members.

A council is nothing more than a collection of dependable people with a set of responsibilities. You need to depend on the members of your council to demonstrate maturity, competence, objectivity, and sensitivity. Good council members are there not just for their personal contributions and abilities, but because they can represent the needs of the community.

After I gave a keynote on governance at the SoCal Linux Expo in Los Angeles, a chap came over and asked me what appeared to be a devilishly simple question:

What kind of people should I look for to be on my community's council?

This got me thinking. Can we build a recipe for an excellent governing community member, and list the ingredients to look out for when choosing these members?

Well, kind of. In my experience, community members come in many shapes and sizes. There is absolutely no commonality in terms of gender, race, career choice, technical experience, or age. You simply can't look at someone on the street and determine that she is a great council member. As we discussed earlier in the book, these checkboxes of surface-level diversity items will not help you to build a great council. We instead need to look for deep-level attributes that point to maturity and capability in governance.

Fortunately, there is a common set of traits that you should be looking for. These ingredients will indicate that someone has the chops for governing your community:

Willing to listen

Great governors are always willing to listen. You will rely on your council members to listen to your community and make sensible decisions based on hearing the full story. This is particularly important in cases of conflict resolution. A useful method of identifying this trait is to listen to a prospective council member in a normal conversation and make a mental note of just how much he listens as opposed to speaks. See how much he contributes to the discussion, see how often he chips in or interrupts, and see how much he queries the information he hears. This will help you determine whether he is a good listener.

Unbiased and objective

Your council members need to ensure that they don't demonstrate any apparent sense of bias. Of course, everyone is biased in one way or another, but you need to shoot for council members who can do their best to put their biases to one side. A good test of this is if a prospective council member is open to changing her views based on further information. Another good sign is whether she is able to agree on a topic with someone whom she typically disagrees with. Watch her debate, and observe if she adjusts her argument as the debate progresses: this is a great attribute to have in a governing member.

Detail-oriented

Great governors pay serious attention to detail. They understand that the devil is in the details, so they pick up on the hidden details in a discussion and ensure that these details get covered. Watch how they communicate to see how they raise and react to details.

Reliable

One of the most significant considerations with community-based governance is simply having people show up and fulfill their responsibilities on the council. If you have a governing body that has members who should attend meetings, don't be surprised if some members don't show up. You need to find people who are willing to put that PlayStation controller down, willing to get out of bed early if a meeting is scheduled to cater to another part of the world, and willing to *make time* for your community. Of course, life happens and people cannot always make meetings, but you can assess how reliable your prospective members are by seeing how often they attend your community over an extended period of time. Don't assess them for the few months building up to nominations for the council, as they may try harder than normal to demonstrate reliability. Instead, observe them over a wider period of time without them knowing. This will help you get a more objective view on their reliability and attendance.

A fair fighter

This is a rare trait. You really want to look out for people who will fight for the right thing, but put the integrity of the council and the community above the outcome of a fight. The ideal person here is relaxed and calm, but when required, will put his head above water to do the right thing. The only way you can assess this is to look at this person's experience since he has joined the community and balance the times he stood up for different things, whether it was justified, and how he handled losing an argument.

With these expectations in mind, you should properly document the expectations of council members so that prospective candidates have a clear idea of what is involved. Let's apply this to our Tobe example.

TOBE COMMUNITY COUNCIL MEMBERSHIP EXPECTATIONS

Each seat on the Tobe Community Council (TCC) is for a period of two (2) years and has the following expectations:

- Engagement—Each member of the TCC is expected to engage with the community politely and fairly and to refrain from using bad language, offensive statements, or insulting comments.

- Fairness—Each member of the TCC is expected to consider each case brought to it; listen to all the evidence and perspectives from the people involved; and pass a fair, unbiased, and objective decision based on the evidence provided, the goals of the Tobe project, and the best interests of the community.

- Reliability—The TCC has a defined set of required meetings and responsibilities. Each member is expected to be responsive and receptive to these responsibilities. Each member is also expected to notify the TCC concerning any prolonged periods of absence. If a member of the TCC cannot fulfill his or her responsibilities, lacks the time to participate effectively, or otherwise cannot tend to the requirements of the TCC, he or she is expected to step down gracefully. It is also preferable but not required that the member who has stepped down help his or her replacement transition into the role easily.

This rather juicy statement combined with the *Responsibilities* and *Structure* statements earlier provide a comprehensive set of expectations around the role of a governing member and its scope.

Before we move on, I want to share a few thoughts about your own expectations. If this is your first time working to set up a governance body, it can often be difficult to figure out which people have the right requirements. If you are anything like I was when I first did this, you will be terrified that you have missed an important piece of fine print when documenting the council, and that you are going to unwittingly recruit a destructive idiot.

First, don't worry. This is your first time. Everyone makes mistakes, and you are going to as well. The best medicine for avoiding mistakes is experience, and I would highly recommend you find someone who has worked on governance before and ask that person to take a look at your work and pass comment. Take a quick look online at some of the existing governance bodies in communities that you follow, see who was involved in setting them up, and drop him an email to see whether he would be willing to offer some advice and thoughts.

NOTE

Of course, by saying this I know I am about to get deluged in email! I am certainly willing to help, but when the deluge occurs, I might not be able to help all of you, so don't be offended if I don't have time.

In this section we have focused our efforts primarily on the attributes that we are looking for in our council members, but not how we actually elect them. We will discuss this a little later.

Communication

With a design in place that has firm responsibilities, structure, and membership expectations, we now need to decide how our council members will communicate with one another. Here we need to decide (a) which resources they will use to communicate and (b) the requirements we make on their time for activities such as meetings.

Let's start with resources. You first need to ensure that you have a primary communication channel in place. Earlier in this book we discussed some of the resources that are available, so we won't cover that ground again; instead, let's look at a suitable approach that many communities have used: a single mailing list and online chat channel.

A mailing list is an excellent method of having general discussion inside the council. It is simple and low-bandwidth, and you can ensure that people's access to it is restricted to their term on the council. Mailing lists are also useful for documenting discussion that may need to be revisited later.

I highly recommend setting up a mailing list, whatever your community. Before you rush out and do this, though, you need to make a few important decisions about its use:

Focus

Mailing lists are excellent for general discussion. Although they can also be used for voting on an issue, I instead recommend real-time discussion such as a phone call or IRC channel for that. Many communities have found that voting on mailing lists can take weeks to finalize. With real-time discussion, the voting is much quicker.

Membership

Provide access to your mailing list only to members of the council. Make it clear that when they leave the council or their membership expires, their subscriptions to the mailing list will also expire.

Privacy

Mailing list software packages provide the option to have public archives of the discussion. I strongly recommend that you have private, nonpublic archives. While this may surprise you, I recommend this because when public archives are available, your members will not be as blunt or honest in their feedback. When your council deals with a conflict issue or a membership request, you rely on honest opinions from your members about the individual(s) concerned. This can be tricky if the mailing list is public and a council member wants to share some critical views of that person with the rest of the members. If the list archives are private, you will get a better quality of feedback from your members.

On the other hand, some organizations require open meetings by law. In this case, provide two mailing lists: a public one for most community issues and a private one for personnel issues, which includes the conflict and membership situations just mentioned. This is comparable to physical meetings where councils ask visitors to leave, and go into "executive session" for personnel issues.

The problem with a mailing list (particularly one with limited membership and closed archives) is that it lacks the transparency and access that your community will rightfully expect. So I highly recommend that you augment your mailing list with regular real-time meetings, preferably using IRC or possibly even an open conference call on the phone. These meetings should be publicized as an opportunity for your community to raise topics with the council.

The choice between IRC and the phone depends on the habits of your community members. From a pure features perspective, IRC is better: it is cheaper, easier to log, and accommodates more simultaneous participants than the phone. The problem with IRC is that only technical communities tend to know much about it. If your community has no idea what IRC is, getting them to use it is akin to trying to make a cat bark. As such, the phone could be a better bet.

NOTE

Of course, if your community is small and local, there is no reason that meetings can't occur face-to-face in a local coffee shop or somewhere similar. Look at your community and make a decision based on the norms of how it communicates.

Whatever you decide, you should have regular meetings for your council. The purpose of these meetings is to provide an opportunity for your community to engage with the body that governs it. As such, you should make it explicitly clear to your council members that they should attend every meeting.

A final note on communication is to make sure your community can add items to the council meeting agenda in a simple and organized way. Your community needs to feel that they can raise topics on the council. I recommend having a public agenda visible so that (a) people can add items to it and (b) others can see what items are planned for discussion and join in if it interests them.

A useful way to do this is to set up a wiki and simply ask people to update the agenda page when they want to discuss a topic.

Let's now put a policy regarding communications in place for our Tobe Community Council.

TOBE COMMUNITY COUNCIL COMMUNICATIONS

The Tobe Community Council (TCC) has two primary resources for internal communication and interaction with the community:

- tobe-community-council Mailing List—This mailing list, which is by invitation only, is available to all council members but to no one else. Council members are removed from the list when their role on the council ends. It can be used to raise any issue in private within the TCC. Discussions occur only among TCC members and are not archived or shared elsewhere.

- #tobe-meeting—On the first Tuesday of every month at 18:00 UTC, the TCC has a public meeting that the full community is welcome to attend. The agenda, available at *http:// www.exampleproject.org/tobe/wiki/MeetingAgenda*, will be discussed in each meeting. If you want to add an agenda item to the meeting, update that page and ensure that you attend. All meetings are logged and available at *http://www.exampleproject.org/tobe/meetinglogs*.

Codifying Your Council

We are now a-rocking and a-rolling with a good idea of how our council is going to look. Throughout our discussion we have documented our decisions for our Tobe example, and you should do the same for your own community. You can then gather these notes together and combine them all into the same document. This process is known as *codifying* the council.

When you have this document together, make it publicly visible. You can then use it as a starting point to gather feedback from your community about the proposed council. Notify your community and provide a simple way for them to provide feedback (such as updating a wiki page).

This feedback provides an excellent opportunity to clarify any elements that are vague or incomplete in the document. It will also help you to engage with the community to ensure that the governance structure is really supported and reflective of the needs of the wider community. If you develop a Community Council plan in secret and in closed quarters, you will find it incredibly difficult to push it through, and rightfully so. This proposed governance body is a social contract about how your community is run, and the community must not only agree to it but also feel as contented about it as they do about that lovely old pair of comfortable shoes that we all have.

To help illustrate council codification, I'll present the codification document we used when forming the Ubuntu Forums Council. This was a council that was put in place in 2006 to help govern the hugely popular Ubuntu Forums. Our codification document received extensive review and refinements, and when most people were happy with it, it was approved by the Ubuntu Community Council and put in place. Here it is.

FORUMS COMMUNITY GOVERNANCE CODIFICATION

The forums represent many people's first meeting with Ubuntu and are an important resource for support and social interactions and have become one of the most important subprojects within Ubuntu. They are the single largest GNU/Linux support forums and one of the most important venues for community support and interaction. Started independently by Ryan Troy two years ago, their rapid success was officially recognized when they were designated as the Official Ubuntu Forums.

This document aims to:

- Increase recognition of contributions in the forums with membership, which is ultimately used to approve Community Council members.
- Provide a clear delegation and codifications of the existing leadership in the forums and plan for handling these decisions in the future.
- Describe clear democratic and meritocratic processes for the appointment of leadership and staff positions in the forums.
- Remove several "single points of failure."
- Describe methods for both preventing and resolving any future inter-administrator or inter-staff conflicts within the forums.
- Recognize the hard work of the forums staff through recognition as an integral and *integrated* part of the forums community.
- Provide a straightforward process for top forums contributors to be recognized as full members in Ubuntu, with the right to vote on resolutions posed by the Community Council.
- Provide for a reporting process so that news, ideas and work done in the project by forums users will be communicated to the broader community and appropriately recognized.

Changes to Current Ubuntu Policy

The proposal includes both new policy and the codification of a few existing Ubuntu policies. These should be discussed with the Community Council and the forum staff. After it has been approved by the Community Council we will add it to the community governance page (*http://www.ubuntu .com/community/processes/governance*) in the Ubuntu website.

Note that the document is structured to describe NOT JUST the forums, but instead all the areas of the project which are large and independent enough to have their own dedicated leadership structures.

Team Councils

For active teams and subprojects with Ubuntu, the Ubuntu Community council delegates many of its responsibilities to "Team Councils." These councils act as proxies for the Community Council over a particular team or scope of activity within the Ubuntu community. These governance councils are ultimately responsible for the actions and activity within their team or scope and to resolve disputes and manage policies and procedures internal to their team and frequently appoint Ubuntu members on behalf of the Community Council.

The Ubuntu Forums Council (FC) is the team governance council for the official Ubuntu forums.

Forums Council Charter

The Forums Council is the group that is ultimately responsible for the governing of the forums and interfacing between the forums and the rest of the Ubuntu community and governance systems. It will:

- Consist of five (5) members. Membership should be public and published.
- Decisions will be made by a majority of voting Forums Council members when at least three and more than half of the total members have voted.
- FC members should be accessible by and responsive to the forums community (i.e., through a dedicated forum).
- Hold "meetings" regularly and visibly. Meetings can either be in IRC in the "ubuntu-meeting" channel or in a special, publicly visible area or subforum.
- Be appointed by the Ubuntu Community Council in consultation with the Forums Council, forums staff, and active contributors to the forums. Nominations would be open and public and would be considered and evaluated by the CC. Each candidate should prepare a wiki page summarizing their nomination and their contributions and including and referencing testimonials (e.g., something similar to what is prepared for Ubuntu membership). The CC commits to evaluating all nominations on the following criteria, listed in order of importance:
  — The nominees['] (*essential*) active status as an Ubuntu member.
  — The nominees['] support from *at least* one active forum staff member (essential).
  — Opinions and testimonials (positive and negative) from current members of the Forums Council;

- — Opinions and testimonials from current forums staff;
- — Opinions and testimonials from Ubuntu Members, Ubunteros, and other active participants in the forums;
- — Clear evidence of activity within the forums (quality, quantity and duration);

- Serve terms of two (2) years. FC members could serve multiple or repeated terms. Weight will be given to proved contributors and reelection of consistently active members should be both easy and common.
- Be formed, initially, of the current forums administrators (i.e., Ryan Troy [Ubuntu-Geek], John Dong [jdong], and Mike Braniff [KiwiNZ]).
- Have a chairman with a casting vote, appointed by the Community Council, initially to be Ryan Troy.

The FC would have a number of rights and responsibilities, and be ultimately responsible for the smooth operation of the forums. These include:

- Appointing or recalling administrators, moderators and forums staff or determining criteria by which they are appointed.
- Resolving disputes between forums staff and moderators as per the existing dispute resolution system and forums guidelines.
- With advice, feedback, and help from the forums staff, maintaining and enforcing the Forums Guidelines and associated infrastructure (e.g., the resolution center).
- Regularly and when possible (i.e., monthly), sending reports or representatives to CC members to weigh in on issues of membership and to update the council on the FC business.

Staff and Ubuntu Membership

Forums staff will be appointed by the Forums Council. Forums staff are expected to uphold and set an example that is consistent with the Code of Conduct.

Forums staff and participants have the option to become Ubuntu members. Current staff can apply for membership at an Ubuntu CC meeting. Their contributions as staff members and contributors on the forums should provide more than sufficient evidence of a sustained and significant contribution to the Ubuntu community.

Dispute Resolution

The FC will be responsible for maintaining forum guidelines and systems for internal conflict resolution (e.g., the forums resolution center).

Additionally, they should provide a documented method whereby any disagreements or conflicts *between* moderators can request a hearing by the FC.

In extreme situations, users and moderators who feel that they have not been given a fair hearing by the FC can appeal a decision to the CC. The CC considers the FC to be a greater authority on forums matters and in the majority of these cases, the CC will likely refer these issues back to the FC.

Any deadlock within the FC will can be referred to the Community Council for resolution.

The Ubuntu Forums Council has been hugely successful, and the expectations around its governance have never been questioned. The document helped keep everyone on the same page.

Nominating and Electing Council Members

With a firm foundation of how your Community Council will work and one that has been publicly documented and approved by the community, the next step is to populate the council with members. Earlier we discussed the attributes we are looking for in members (willing to listen, unbiased, objective, responsive, attentive to detail, etc.), but now let's talk about how we can find and motivate these people.

Forming a new council

When forming a new council, especially the first council in your community, you typically need to grandfather people in. In other words, the first set of members who govern the council are a handpicked group who you are confident will get the council up and running under the agreement you just codified.

All of your community members need to feel that they have the opportunity to be on the council, but you also want to ensure that you maintain a high level of quality among your council members. A common solution to this problem is to have an election in which your community can vote for those who govern them.

Unfortunately, the big misconception in community elections is that elections alone will sort the wheat from the chaff. In other words, many believe that if you have an open election, the community will settle on the highest-quality candidates for the council. This is often not the case.

Popularity contests do not form great governance bodies. Someone without the maturity and vision you need may have a lot of friends and influence and snag a place on the council. On the other hand, there may be a quiet and conscientious community member who is perfect for a position in the council but never gets noticed. In fact, the most qualified community members hardly ever put themselves forward for a governing council, because they are too wrapped up in doing their work for the community. Fortunately, governments found long ago an effective compromise between pure representative elections and top-down selection: a nomination process.

Pull together the members you know well, who you feel are the current de facto leaders of the community, and hold a meeting to nominate the appropriate people for a position on the council. The people who can participate in this discussion could be a founder, highly visible contributors, an existing council, or others with experience and insight into the community that you trust. This group should nominate a good range of people, and preferably more people than you have places for on the council. As an example, if you have five seats on the council, try to come up with seven or eight nominations. Each person should be an excellent candidate who satisfies the criteria we discussed earlier.

Of course, you should always ensure that before potential members are publicly nominated, you contact them to determine whether they actually want to be on the council. Many people want to have nothing to do with governance. As you talk up your goals, some will come around to realize that serving on the council complements their current ways of contributing and flexes their talents, but others really have no stomach for meetings or rule making, and should not be browbeaten into serving.

Assume that you'll be rejected the first time you approach each potential candidate. It's almost a given. After all:

- Most people are naturally modest and do not want to claim an honor. Even heroes who rescue people from burning buildings always give speeches afterward saying, "I'm not a hero."

- The people you want are busy and happy contributing to the community. They're afraid that joining the council will take time away from their regular contributions (and they're usually right), and they're also afraid that governance is relatively dull.

- Most people have never served on a board or council and don't know what it entails. They assume they don't have the competence to do so.

- All kinds of cruft around the image most people have of governments and leaders get in the way of their seeing the good things councils can do.

Anticipate all these reactions. They are legitimate, but you have counterarguments to offer. Try to meet in person with a candidate to listen to her views and have a candid exchange. If a face-to-face meeting is not possible, try to use speak via telephone. The general points you can make are:

- Your community has reached a point where the lack of governance (or in the case where a council is creating subcouncils, the relative lack of attention to one area) is preventing the members from doing what they want. The potential candidate is furthering her personal goals as well as the goals of the community by taking on the new tasks of governance.

- Power is not a bad thing. Whatever goals the contributor has, she can push them forward on a much greater scale by representing her needs on the council and making sure the community provides the resources for these tasks.

- Nobody is putting on a jacket with medals and ribbons; serving on a council is not equivalent to becoming a generalissimo. Other members of the community will still view the council members as ordinary folks whom they can complain to and have a beer with.

- Some of the greatest life lessons come from serving on governing bodies. Those who do it say afterward that they learned an immense amount about people, organizations, and the essential ways in which the wheels of life turn in terms of timing, finance, and so forth.

- A council term is limited, and before she knows it, she will be back in the rank and file doing the work she originally loved—but this time with a far deeper understanding of this work and how to make it successful.

- Everybody feels the same way at first. The very qualities that make them feel inadequate are precisely the ones that will make them good council members.

Most candidates, once you sincerely hear their viewpoints and offer your own, will come around and agree to serve. But as I mentioned, some are truly ill-suited to council work. If they remain convinced that they'll be bored, frustrated, or unproductive on your council, don't pressure them—just express appreciation for the work they're already doing. You can probably find a team handling some task that they'd like to work on, and over time they may work themselves through the community structure into a governance position.

Next, ask candidates to produce pages that act as a platform for their candidacy. This page should essentially persuade anyone reading it that he is perfect for the role. To make this as simple as possible, you should provide candidates with a template that they can fill out with their information. Here is a suggested template:

> Candidacy Document for <name>
> Date: <date>
> INTRODUCTION
> <some introductory text explaining who they are, summarizing their experience and what they can bring to the council>
> COMMUNITY EXPERIENCE
> Item of experience.
> Item of experience.
> TESTIMONIALS
> <here other members can add their support for the candidate>
> <name> <email> <reason for support for a position on the council>
> GOALS
> <what they'd like to accomplish in their council role>

Each candidacy template should be made available online in the same place so that your community members can review it. A wiki is a great solution.

You can then open up a vote. How you conduct this vote depends largely on how your community is structured. As an example, if you have the concept of membership, such as approved members or approved developers, it is recommended that you allow only those approved contributors to vote. This will give all legitimate members of the community a voice, while ensuring that the decision is made by those who actually know the community well enough to offer an informed opinion.

If your community is more loosely formed and just consists of anyone who joins a forum or mailing list, it is more suitable to nominate members from core contributors in the community.

Ubuntu Governance Example

So far in this chapter we have discussed the requirements for governance, created a Community Council, explored the requirements for council members, and chosen the council's members.

As we said way back in Chapter 1, stories are the vessels of great best practices, and with governance such an important part of community growth, I want to devote a good chunk of this chapter to an example of an open, transparent, and effective community that I have been involved in putting together: the Ubuntu community. This case study will give you a firm idea of how one large community has approached it, and the lessons learned.

In the Beginning...

In 2004, Mark Shuttleworth, a South African entrepreneur, founded the Ubuntu project. A longtime user, fan, and contributor to free software, he built his digital certificate company, Thawte, on a Free Software foundation. When he sold his company to VeriSign, he made what can only be described as a "rather large bucket of money."

After spending a year in Russia training for a quick trip into space as the first South African space tourist, Mark started laying plans for a new Linux distribution. At the time, distributions were nothing new: Red Hat, Mandrake, Debian, and others were already producing comprehensive operating systems that technical types such as myself were not only using, but were also trying to convince our reluctant friends and family to use.

Mark's vision was different. First, he wanted to build Ubuntu on the excellent foundation of the existing Debian distribution. To do this he hired some of the cream of the crop in the Debian community, and they set to work to build a powerful and easy-to-use operating system. His vision did not end there, though. Mark not only wanted to promote an open source operating system, he also wanted to have the operating system be openly governed. Mark knew the importance of community, and he knew the importance of transparency in a community.

At the time, Linux distributions were going through something of an evolution. Linux was beginning to enjoy real commercial interest from the widespread IT industry, and some of the traditional Linux distributors, such as Red Hat and SuSE, were seeing serious adoption. Unfortunately, with all of these business interests, power lunches, and monetization, there was a general feeling (at least as I remember it) that community was getting a little lost in the mix.

This was not exactly surprising. The traditional IT industry was built on an understanding that programmers are hired to build your software, and that product managers make the decisions required to direct those programmers and deliver your product.

Linux and open source were different: these companies had to understand that volunteers in bedrooms, basements, and universities had as much input in the direction and focus of that software as anyone else.

We now know that if these community members are welcomed and treated in a collaborative manner, a company can net a huge amount of unpaid development. The buzzwords *crowdsourcing* and *peer production* are widespread in the business world. Unfortunately, many of the companies jumping on the open source bandwagon back in 2004 failed to understand and embrace this community. Instead, they merely *tolerated* it as a politically correct nod to the wider open source community.

Ubuntu was different. Unlike other companies that wanted to keep governance control of the community in their own hands, Mark wanted Ubuntu to be a *pure* community. He was keen that there should be a community governing body and that everyone should be able to join that body based on hard work and commitment to the community.

It is this open community governance that attracted me to Canonical and made me want to become the Ubuntu community manager. I was attracted by the premise of a Linux distribution that combined a real, open, community governance infrastructure with the commercial support and funding of a company. If we could strike this balance, the world would be our oyster.

The Structure of the Ubuntu Community

Like many open source communities, the Ubuntu project is *not* a democracy, but a meritocracy. Contributors are judged in the Ubuntu community on the basis of a *significant and sustained contribution*. It is this simple rule of thumb that determines who takes a place in our community as well as our governance positions.

Today, the Ubuntu community is broken into three approximate layers of governance, shown in Figure 10-1.

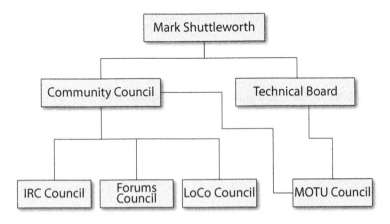

FIGURE 10-1. The Ubuntu community has a number of different groups that govern it, all driven by community members.

The community has been divided into four primary governing areas:

Mark Shuttleworth

As the founder and primary sponsor of Ubuntu, Mark is afforded the privilege of a tie breaking vote and of deciding what his employees at Canonical focus their work on. Although "Mark Shuttleworth" appears at the top of Figure 10-1, the Community Council and Technical Board do not report to him; this is purely to illustrate his tie-breaking privilege.

Community Council

This is the highest governing council in the community. It makes decisions about how the community is run, changes to processes, and other community-wide issues.

Technical Board

The Technical Board decides on technical process changes and technical policy decisions.

Team councils

These are specialist councils that govern specific parts of the community.

Let's now take each layer for a spin and explore how they fit together in the wider community. I will also kick off each assessment with the vital statistics of how that part of the community is structured.

Mark Shuttleworth

Reports to:	No one
Number of members:	1
Responsibilities:	Special role on Community Council and Technical Board

Mark Shuttleworth is the founder and primary sponsor of the Ubuntu project. He has poured millions of dollars of his own money into the project. In the wider community, Mark has two very distinctive privileges:

- He can assign Canonical employees to work on specific projects, specific feature goals, and specific bugs.

- He also has a tie breaking vote on the Technical Board and Community Council, should it be required.

Although the first point may be expected, as Mark is the founder and owner of Canonical Ltd., the second point may be a surprise. Tinfoil-hat-wearing conspiracy theorists could see this as a means of Canonical enforcing its will on the community. Certainly from my experience, this is really not the case.

Obviously every community functions best when it can reach broad consensus about a way forward. Collaborative discussion and decision making is always the desired approach in a volunteer. Unfortunately, it is not uncommon in the open source world for there to be many good arguments, and for arguments to divide communities rather than enrich them. The energy that is focused on these circular debates would always be better spent creating solutions to problems.

If there is a situation in which the community is deadlocked on a decision, with multiple valid arguments for a given position, Mark can use his casting vote to unblock it. Obviously this is not a decision that would be taken lightly, and at the time of this writing this casting vote has never been required since the formation of the project in 2004.

Community Council

Reports to:	No one
Number of members:	7
Responsibilities:	General community governance

The Community Council is the primary general governance council in the community. It has been present in the community since the inception of the Ubuntu project and has become a well-respected and instrumental part of the wider Ubuntu community.

The mandate of the Community Council is:

> The social structures and community processes of Ubuntu are supervised by the Ubuntu Community Council. It is the Community Council that approves the creation of a new Team or Project, and appointment of team leaders. In addition, the Community Council is the body responsible for the Code of Conduct and tasked with ensuring that maintainers and other community members follow its guidelines.

The way members are chosen is discussed in the section "Council or Board Member" on page 358.

Its responsibilities are:

- Maintaining the Ubuntu Code of Conduct, which describes the standards of behavior expected of Ubuntu maintainers and other community members.
- Arbitrating disputes under the Ubuntu Code of Conduct. This will happen if a member of the community has asked the Community Council to review the behavior of another member in terms of the Code of Conduct (a document that every Ubuntu member is expected to agree to that outlines basic levels of respectful collaboration).
- Team creation and appointment of team leaders.
- Creation of new structures and processes. A community member who wishes to create a new structure or process submits a proposal to the Community Council for discussion and approval. The Community Council determines lines of reporting and responsibility between different community structures.

The purpose of the Community Council is to provide a group of Ubuntu contributors who have experience working in a range of teams in the community. This group is available to hear any issues, conflicts, or requests that the community would like to raise and request a verdict on. Each council member is expected to vote with a +1 (meaning "yes") or a −1 (meaning "no"). A majority vote determines the decision of the Community Council.

Importantly, whenever the Community Council sits to decide on an issue, there must be a quorum: that is, a minimum number of members present to form a majority vote for the body.

The Community Council has decided on a range of issues over the years. Some examples of this include:

- The formation of new governance bodies, such as the Forums Council, IRC Council, and MOTU Council (a developer council).

- Approving and rejecting new members. This was later delegated to the Regional Membership Board (more on this later).

- Individual conflicts. Sometimes a member who feels a governance body has been inappropriate in judging a case escalates the issue to the Community Council (more on this later, too).

- The approval of new processes. One example is Monthly Team Reporting for approved teams, which asked teams in the community to provide summarized notes on their work every month.

For each of these issues the format is the same: the issue is raised with the council, it is discussed, and the council members have a vote. The majority vote concludes the decision of the Community Council.

An important consideration has been to make the Community Council as easily accessible and approachable to the community as possible. Any community member is welcome to raise an issue with the Community Council and have it discussed fairly and objectively.

This is how an item is put forward to the council:

- The community member adds the item to the Community Council Agenda, which is done by adding it to the Meeting Agenda page at *https://wiki.ubuntu.com/ CommunityCouncilAgenda*. Every Ubuntu community member is freely able to add items to the agenda.

- The Community Council meets twice a month to have an online meeting on IRC. Everyone is welcome to attend, and the meeting (at the time of this writing) happens in the #ubuntu-meeting channel on the Freenode (*http://freenode.net/*) IRC network. Meetings happen at 21:00 UTC on the first Tuesday of each month and 11:00 UTC on the third Tuesday of each month. The different times ensure that everywhere in the world has a reasonable chance in her local time zone to attend a meeting at least once a month.

- At each meeting, the list of agenda items on the *https://wiki.ubuntu.com/ CommunityCouncilAgenda* page are used as a source of discussion. Each item is discussed and a vote occurs. The majority vote is the concluded opinion of the Community Council.

This process has served the Ubuntu community well. It has provided a simple method in which any Ubuntu community member can raise an issue with the primary governing body of the community.

Technical Board

Reports to:	No one
Number of members:	4
Responsibilities:	Technical and process governance

The Ubuntu Technical Board has a somewhat unique and sometimes misunderstood role in the community. The Technical Board is intended to advise on the technical direction of Ubuntu and usually focuses on wide-reaching critical issues as opposed to the thousands of smaller technical decisions that are made every day in the community.

As with the Community Council, the Technical Board has a published mandate:

> The Ubuntu Technical Board is responsible for the technical direction that Ubuntu takes. The Technical Board makes final decisions over package selection, packaging policy, installation system and process, toolchain, kernel, X server, library versions and dependencies, and any other matter which requires technical supervision in Ubuntu.

There is also a set of published responsibilities for the board:

- The Ubuntu Packaging Policy, which describes the standards with which Ubuntu *packages must* comply. Each release of Ubuntu is associated with a specific version of the Package Policy. Ubuntu community members may propose updates and changes to the Package Policy.

> **NOTE**
>
> **Although I try to minimize technical discussions in this book, the concept of a *package* appears often enough to deserve a bit of background. Large projects such as Ubuntu are created by hundreds or thousands of teams working on software as different as word processors, graphing tools, games, scientific libraries, and device drivers. Each team produces one or more packages, in which form they distribute their software. One of the critical tasks of the Ubuntu project is to get these packages to work together. Some are more stable and trusted than others, so the packages are organized into different *repositories* to reflect such differences.**

- Ubuntu Release Feature Goals, which determine specific features that we aim to include in each release of Ubuntu. These are documented on the wiki pages for each release. Ubuntu community members may propose additional Feature Goals until that release is in Feature Freeze, after which Feature Goals will be deferred to the next release.

- Ubuntu Package Selection, the list of packages that will be installed in a Base or Desktop Ubuntu installation, as well as the list of packages that qualify for full support in the main repository as opposed to the universe repository. (The main repository is more selective and offers support for its packages.) You may propose packages for inclusion in the Base Install, the Desktop Install, or the main repository, where they will be immediately available to Ubuntu users.

Some readers may be wondering why the Ubuntu community has a separate Community Council and Technical Board, and feel it would make more sense to combine both into a single entity. The decision to have two governance bodies was deliberate.

The requirements for the governing members in the Community Council and the Technical Board are very different. Community Council members need to have a wide and expansive knowledge of the community, its processes, and its culture. It is entirely reasonable that these members have a more limited technical knowledge of Ubuntu: we don't expect them to be packaging or programming ninjas. Their expertise is based around general community awareness and decision making as opposed to technical expertise.

The Technical Board, on the other hand, has very demanding technical requirements for its members. Members should not only have a high level of technical expertise, but also have contextual knowledge of the entire distribution. As an example, we don't expect someone to be an expert in just the desktop, but also the entire underlying system, the toolchain, the bug database, and more. We call these developers *generalists*, and they are hugely valuable members of software-oriented communities such as Ubuntu.

In addition to having a strong technical knowledge, Technical Board members are expected to have a firm understanding of the processes and community infrastructure of the project; keep abreast of the technology and challenges on the horizon outside of Ubuntu; and show strong experience in software development, maintenance, and technical collaboration.

Ubuntu community members can engage with the Technical Board in much the same way as with the Community Council:

- Everyone is welcome to add items to the Technical Board Agenda page at *https://wiki .ubuntu.com/TechnicalBoardAgenda*.
- The board also meets regularly on IRC, and the community is also welcome to attend.
- Decisions are again made with a vote based around a quorum of Technical Board members attending the meeting.

The Technical Board has been hugely successful in providing governance and considered conclusions in some complex technical decisions. Some of these decisions have involved compelling technical issues, the ethics around software freedom, and other areas.

One example of a contentious topic was a proposal some time ago to have some advanced desktop effects technology switched on by default in Ubuntu. For this technology to work, it required the computer to have fully working 3D graphics hardware. Unfortunately, back in early 2007 some of the most common graphics hardware would work effectively only if a closed source, proprietary driver was installed. For the effects technology to be switched on, we would need to ship a closed source driver that could be installed if the hardware was present.

This caused enormous controversy inside and outside the Ubuntu community. Many were worried that the core ethic of Free Software would be compromised if the proposal went forward. For a while the atmosphere got a little tense, and some bloggers assumed the role of prophets of doom, spreading fear of a closed source Ubuntu: "human sacrifice, dogs and cats living together...mass hysteria!" (Sorry, I am an outrageous *Ghostbusters* fan.)

To handle this feisty topic, a joint meeting between the Ubuntu Technical Board and the Ubuntu Community Council was chaired. The issue was discussed, and the combined board united around a common conclusion: Ubuntu would not ship closed source drivers, but infrastructure would be built that would make it devilishly simple to install the drivers if required so that the desktop effects technology could be used. The solution was elegant, combining an unrelenting commitment to providing ordinary computer users with dazzling technology and securing the free software ethics that are at the heart of the project. The community wholeheartedly supported the decision and how it was concluded.

Team councils

Report to:	Community Council
Number of members:	Varies; typically 5
Responsibilities:	Specialist governance

When the Ubuntu community was born, the Community Council and the Technical Board were the only two governance bodies put in place. They smoothly handled their respective parts of community governance and were productive in that work. As the community grew, though, thousands of contributors joined the project, hundreds of teams were formed, and huge demand was placed on the Community Council and Technical Board. The Community Council in particular began to struggle under the workload, and meetings lasting upward of three hours were routinely organized to handle the sheer volume of requests. Something needed to change.

At the 2006 Ubuntu Developer Summit in Mountain View, California, it was decided to form a new layer of governance called team councils. A limited set of subcouncils would be set up in parts of the project where repeated requests for governance were made. These councils would then govern those areas of the community.

One such example was the Ubuntu LoCo Teams. This worldwide community of 200+ local Ubuntu user groups would get together to advocate Ubuntu, provide support, organize release parties, and more. As this part of the Ubuntu community continued to grow, its governance needs heightened. Decisions about hosting, team naming, documentation, events, team approvals, and more were required. So the Community Council decided to form a LoCo Council that would tend to these decisions.

The LoCo Council was officially appointed by the Community Council, and the new LoCo Council members were chosen based on their years of experience with Ubuntu LoCo Teams. The council went on to successfully govern the community.

Similar councils were set up for other parts of the Ubuntu community, including the IRC Council, Forums Council, and MOTU Council. In each case, the Community Council appoints the members, although for new members of existing councils these appointments are often based on recommendations from the existing council. We discuss how to set up councils such as these in more detail a little later in the chapter.

Membership

Inside the Ubuntu world it doesn't take long before you see references to "a member of our community" and the prospect of "joining the community." The concept of *membership* is something that varies tremendously across different communities. For some communities, membership is merely taking an interest in what active members are doing, whereas other communities have a more formalized style of membership that requires some kind of approval process.

In the Ubuntu community anyone is welcome to join and participate, and formalized membership is not required. This ensures that the community is open for people to join and dip their toes in. This is great for people new to Ubuntu, but we do have some more formalized membership roles for those who want to provide a more concrete level of contribution or those who want to contribute to critical parts of the system that require approval. These roles are:

Ubuntu member

This is a basic level of approved membership that indicates that a contributor has provided a reliable level of contribution. This role doesn't depend on the type of contribution: people can become members if they do packaging, development, translations, documentation, advocacy, or whatever else is recognized to be of value.

Developer

For those who need upload access to our primary software repositories, this role is required. Candidates must adhere to a more complex set of technical requirements.

Governor

This is a role that applies to anyone on a governance body in the community. This role requires a demonstration of the attributes of a great council member, discussed earlier in this chapter.

Each role has a different set of expectations and requirements. Let's now delve into each in more detail.

Ubuntu Member

This is the first level of formalized membership that someone would shoot for upon joining the project. This role essentially guarantees that the contributor has demonstrated effective participation in a large distributed community such as Ubuntu. Each prospective member must sign the Ubuntu Code of Conduct.

To clarify what this role means, a mandate was defined at the inception of the project:

> Membership in the Ubuntu community recognizes participants for a variety of contributions, from code to artwork, advocacy, translations and organizational skills. If you are active in the Forums, or submitting icons or sounds or artwork, then you are eligible for Membership, which gives you a say in the governance of the project.

One of the reasons we have the concept of an Ubuntu Member is to help the project identify reliable contributors. Anyone who is approved as a member is likely to understand the basics of what is involved in participating in a distributed project such as Ubuntu. Although this level of membership does not guarantee quality of work, it does provide a fairly reliable baseline for engagement: it shows that the contributor has a history of providing sustained contributions to a community. This in itself is useful for a range of purposes, such as soliciting input, voting, encouraging participation in other parts of the project, and mentoring new community members.

Users apply for membership through the following process:

1. The user must have a profile on Launchpad, where people engage in Ubuntu work such as packaging, translations, bug triage, and more.

2. An application document is created on the Ubuntu wiki. This application should include some standard items: a summary of contributions to Ubuntu, a link to the user's Launchpad profile, a complete description of contributions to Ubuntu, plans and ideas for Ubuntu in the future, and testimonials of other Ubuntu Members who support the application.

3. The user signs the Ubuntu Code of Conduct. This ensures that the contributor agrees to participate under positive rules of engagement in the community. The vast majority of reasonable and self-aware contributors automatically meet all of the criteria from the Code of Conduct.

4. The user then adds her application to the next Regional Membership Board meeting. There are three boards—Americas, Europe, and Asia—and each board votes on applications from their regions. As an example, an applicant in Paris applies to the European Membership Board.

5. The user must attend the meeting (which takes place online) where the board members review the application and ask any relevant questions. After a review, the board votes, and a majority vote is considered approval for membership. If the member is not approved, she is welcome to apply again at a later date.

Approved members also receive some privileges:

- An *@ubuntu.com* email alias that forwards to your real email address
- An ubuntu/member/your_nick hostname IRC cloak
- The right to print business cards with the Ubuntu logo
- Syndication on Planet Ubuntu of their blog
- An Ubuntu Member title at the Ubuntu Forums
- A free subscription to the *Linux Weekly News* website

The concept of Ubuntu membership proved to be hugely valuable, offering a reliable assessment for a person's commitment to Ubuntu and ability to contribute. This approach to membership could be applied easily to most communities.

Before I wrap up this section, I want to share an important note: despite Canonical investing millions of dollars each year in Ubuntu, this does not fast-track employees or step over any existing community processes. I am an example of this. When I joined Canonical as the Ubuntu community manager, I was expected to step before the Community Council, present my application, and apply for Ubuntu membership. Fortunately I got it. It could have been a little weird if I didn't!

MEMBERSHIP EXPLOSION? SCALE IT UP!

Traditionally, membership in the community was judged by the Ubuntu Community Council. As Ubuntu continued to grow in popularity and the community grew at a similarly frantic pace, the Community Council found itself overstretched in its ability to keep up with applications.

This is the reason the Regional Membership Boards were set up: they offered a more scalable solution to the sheer growth of the project.

Developer

Development is a critical part of Ubuntu. It is developers who take the thousands of open source applications and tools available online, package them, and make them available for easy installation and use on an Ubuntu system. These developers also fix bugs, deal with security issues, and ensure that these applications and tools integrate properly in the distribution.

Anyone is welcome to apply for a developer role in the Ubuntu community. There is no requirement to work at Canonical. In fact, many of the top-level developers who work on the most significant parts of Ubuntu are volunteers. Having this level of openness has been a huge boon for transparency in the Ubuntu project, but it has also required a carefully thought-out process for assessing developers, in order to maintain packages' standards of quality. These standards of quality are equally applied to all prospective developers, regardless of whether they work at Canonical.

I'll talk briefly about these developer roles as they exist at the time of this writing, but it should be noted that we are currently going through something of a change and adjusting the processes behind these roles. As such, I will discuss the current published processes to give you a good idea of an approach that has worked well since the beginning of the project. Just don't be surprised if you look into the Ubuntu community at a later date and the landscape is a little different.

Ubuntu is split into a number of different repositories. These are the servers that contain the collections of packages that form the Ubuntu system. There are a number of repositories, but two primary ones:

Main

> This is the primary, officially supported repository. All of the applications here are considered critical to Ubuntu. They receive security updates, and Canonical also supports them in its commercial support services. This repository contains everything that appears on the Ubuntu installation disk.

Universe

> This repository is the entire archive from Debian (which Ubuntu is based on) but with packages built against Ubuntu. In other words, this repository contains the same software as Debian, but tweaked and tested to make sure it will run on Ubuntu. These applications are unsupported: end users are responsible for checking on security updates themselves, and Canonical does not provide support for *universe* packages in its commercial support services.

Each of these repositories is matched to a specific developer role:

Main→ubuntu-core-dev

> Developers who have direct upload access to *main* are called *Ubuntu Core Developers*. These developers demonstrate extensive packaging ability across a wide range of areas in the Ubuntu system. To apply for this role, the developer must have produced a significant number of packages that have been reviewed by existing developers and demonstrated a consistent level of excellent work. The Ubuntu Technical Board is the governing body that makes decisions about who gets approved as an Ubuntu Core Developer.

Universe→ubuntu-motu

> Developers who want to build packages for *universe* are called *MOTU Developers*. MOTU is short for—wait for it—Masters of the Universe. Yes, the Ubuntu project loves He-Man.

Membership in MOTU is less stringent than for Ubuntu Core Developers, although a substantial competence is required. The process for applying for MOTU is to have a number of packages reviewed on the sponsorship queue (as discussed in "Reviewing new developers: In depth" on page 114) and then to put forward an application to the MOTU Council for approval.

Both of these roles require a consistent grade of quality. Having direct access to the *main* and *universe* repositories means that developers can have direct and lasting consequences on millions of Ubuntu users around the world.

WHY CHANGE?

Earlier in this section I informed you that we are currently changing the processes around how people join the Ubuntu community as developers. The reason for this is that we are streamlining the project to make it easier for people to get involved. This is intended to solve some problems with the current approach:

- Today we have two classifications of developer—Ubuntu Core Developers and MOTU Developers—that determine who works on which repository. We should instead have one classification of developer and determine which parts of Ubuntu the developer works on as permissions within his role.

- Right now, if you become a developer you get access to the full repository. We would like to provide access for contributors to work on specific parts of the archive.

- We are also adjusting some of the technical processes controlling how contributors participate.

These changes are ongoing.

Council or Board Member

The last type of membership role we will discuss here is that of a member on a governing body such as the Community Council, the Technical Board, or Forums Council. How did the Ubuntu community approach identifying suitable community members for these different governance bodies?

For most new councils, the primary council members are often handpicked to get the council off on a strong footing. This happened with the Community Council, Technical Board, and most of the team councils, such as the Forums Council, IRC Council, and MOTU Council. Typically, the first generation of these councils is picked by the highest governing body. As an example, the Community Council was formed by Mark Shuttleworth and the forefathers of Ubuntu. Later councils, such as the Forums Council, had their initial members nominated by the Community Council.

When the council term ends, a new generation of members can be nominated. In most of these cases existing members are welcome to stand again for nomination, and there is an open call for other contributors to propose themselves for membership in the body.

Escalation

Every community has conflicts and other problems, and I devote Chapter 11 to these issues. Before we get there, I want to discuss how the Ubuntu community handles the escalation of problems and conflict because this is a very clear responsibility that falls under the wing of governance.

The challenge here is simple: if there is a problem, how does someone get advice from an objective and more experienced third party? What then happens if the person with the issue feels that the objective third party was not objective at all? What happens next, and how is the issue escalated?

Our goal is to create an escalation path that starts at the most immediate decision-making body and then progressively pushes the issue farther up the chain if a satisfactory conclusion is not reached. The primary reason why escalation is important is that you don't want to trouble the senior levels of governance unless absolutely required.

Let's look at an example. The Ubuntu Forums community defines an escalation path that looks like Figure 10-2 (the process begins at the bottom of the diagram).

FIGURE 10-2. The Forums community has a number of escalation points so that the Forums Council does not get inundated with every issue.

Imagine that someone is frustrated that one of his discussion threads in the forum was deleted because it was considered offensive. This is how the escalation path works (correspond each step to the diagram in the figure):

1. Forums Thread

   The first place there is likely to be conflict is the main forum. The user will undoubtedly complain loudly, and other forum members will try to discuss the issue and calm the user down. If the contributor wants to escalate this further, the next stage is reached.

2. Forum Moderators

   This is a special part of the Ubuntu Forums where users can take complaints. On this level, the forum moderators, who have insight and administrative control in the day-to-day running of the forum, can comment on the decision made in the original forum. Hopefully at this level the insight of the moderators is considered suitable third-party input and the issue can be settled. If the user still considers the issue a problem or feels the moderators are not judging it fairly, it can be escalated further.

3. Forums Council

   The issue is now taken to the Forums Council. The council not only oversees the governance of the wider forums but is also there to judge the effectiveness of the moderators. At this level, the Forums Council members should assess the behavior of the moderators in addition to the issue itself. If the Forums Council considers the matter to be handled fairly and objectively by the moderators, the issue should be considered closed. If the user is still not happy, however, he can then escalate the issue to the final level.

4. Community Council

   At this point the user is effectively saying that the forum moderators and Forums Council are all doing a substandard job in assessing the problem. The Community Council should now assess the verdict of the Forums Council as well as the issue itself and pass a verdict. If at this point the user is still unhappy, he is going to remain unhappy. But four levels of governance, each embodying a wealth of experience and insight into the community, have now weighed in on the matter.

Expanding Governance

One of the most wonderful attributes of communities is their ability to surprise. From tiny acorns great trees grow, and the branches of community often spread far and wide.

We have seen this countless times, be it Ubuntu, Wikipedia, the Barack Obama campaign, or other communities you may have joined. When your community manages to captivate and develop mindshare, not only does the focus of the community grow but so does your membership. More of these people want to be a part of the journey that your community is on, and they often share the same passion and devotion to reaching the final destination as you do.

Although no one is going to quarrel with this growth, it can generate a headache: how on earth do we scale up our governance bodies to manage this larger group of people?

Fortunately (in terms of hard problems) or unfortunately (in terms of not many people joining your community), this is a problem that only some of you will need to face.

Knowing When It Is Time

In an ideal world we would not need to set up any governance in the first place, let alone set up additional subcouncils. Each additional level of governance that you add to your community is another step away from being a simple and nimble entity that is clear for everyone to understand. It gets a lot ickier when there are Community Councils, team councils, delegated bodies, and other such pomp and grandeur. Your community should set up this additional governance only if *absolutely necessary*.

Of course, many communities need multiple levels of councils, and we certainly discovered that in the Ubuntu community. Despite its seeming complexity, I know that every piece in the Ubuntu community is *absolutely necessary*, and that is our ethos here.

Additional governance is required only when existing governance bodies are not able to scale or cater to your community's requirements. Unfortunately, some communities don't quite get this right and decide to set up vanity councils: governing bodies that achieve nothing more than making the members of the new council feel special.

This can happen in the simplest of scenarios. As an example, imagine that the Tobe project that we discussed earlier really took off and became the hot new thing. If it is like any other successful community, a raft of additional resources will be created for the project. One typical example would be discussion forums. When the forums go online, we would likely see the same thing that has happened in other communities: a very passionate yet vocal community makes its home in the forums.

Although the Tobe Forums community may be small, the vocal few in the forums want to feel special: they want a governing council. In their eyes, governing councils bring all kinds of fun things: a sense of control, authority, and power across the wider project. Not only this, but they see a council as required for the community to be a *real* community.

Nonsense.

There is simply no reason for this council. The Tobe Community Council already exists as a place to resolve issues, and the wider Tobe community is still fairly small. By creating this council you will effectively double the risk of bureaucracy.

Here are some indicators of when it might be time to reopen this chapter, blow off the dust, and read how to build a council again, but this time a subcouncil:

Bottlenecks

Many councils face bottlenecks. These typically occur when the existing council is failing to organize meetings, a few people on the council are holding back their decisions, or there is too much work for the council to do. The first two issues should be solved by fixing your existing council. For the third issue, you may want to see whether the existing council can commit more time to the council. If not, another council may be required.

Specific knowledge required

When you form a large subcommunity in a specific area of your community, that subcommunity may require some specific knowledge that your general Community Council does not possess. When you see many issues occur that require this knowledge, a subcouncil may be required. One area that often calls for specific knowledge is conflict resolution in specific parts of the project. As an example, conflict in a developer community will require knowledge of both the people involved and the development tools and processes.

Separation of skills

When you have a general Community Council up and running, you may find that a number of requests fall into one specific category and that these requests need more focus and experience. An example is if you get lots of technical requests that require extensive knowledge. This may warrant the formation of a Technical Board.

Locale/language

If you have a large community forum around a specific language or locale and the people there are struggling to communicate with the main Community Council, a regional council or language-focused council may be required.

Each of these situations exceeds the time, knowledge, or skills of the existing governance body. The quantity of requests is the justification for the subcouncil: if you get only a few domain-specific requests that your Community Council struggles to deal with, a separate council may not be required, but if the council gets regular and repeated requests, it is worth considering.

There are many examples where the issues just described resulted in the formation of councils. One such example, mentioned earlier, was the formation of the Ubuntu Membership Boards. In terms of expertise, the Community Council was capable of handling each membership request, but the sheer volume made it unfeasible. These three subcouncils were formed to cover the Americas, Europe, and Asia, and took over the responsibility of reviewing Ubuntu membership requests.

Another example was the formation of the Forums Council, triggered by the overwhelming demand for governance and forums experience in the forums community. Similar considerations also spawned the Ubuntu MOTU Council, which governs the developer community that builds packages for parts of Ubuntu. The council was formed from existing

MOTU developers to provide a better level of knowledge for assessing new developer requests. All of these examples have ultimately been successful in governing their respective parts of the community.

Building the Subcouncil

Fortunately, once you have been through the process of building your main Community Council and have justified to yourself and your community that a subcouncil is required, forming this new subcouncil is relatively straightforward. All you need to do is repeat the steps earlier in this chapter that explained how to form a new council.

While following the process, you should take extra care to codify the council thoroughly. You should consult heavily with your community and expect a barrage of questions seeking to justify the new council.

Your community is going to be nervous about new governance, and you will likely notice a slight paranoia that some of their rights are going to vanish as they perceive the cold chains of bureaucracy clanking down hard on the community. If you've followed the careful thought processes I've described, such concerns are ridiculous.

We are all here to show bureaucracy who is boss, and ensure that it has no home in our communities. Make sure your community knows this. This will require ensuring that your codification is easy to read and understand, and regular reassurance to your community about the scope and responsibility of the new governance body.

When you have a broadly acceptable codification in place, the next step is to run it past the existing Community Council. You should expect the document to go back and forth with the council a few times before it is considered complete. When this is ready, you are all set to ask the Community Council to nominate members for the new council and optionally have an election with your community members to select from these nominees.

Escalation

With at least two councils in place, you should now ensure that your community is entirely clear on how each council works and also how they fit together. More specifically, your community needs to know how issues can be escalated from one council to another.

To do this, you should write an *issue escalation document* that illustrates clearly how an issue should flow through your governance structure. Here is an example of how this document could be applied to the Tobe community with its Community Council and Forums Council.

TOBE COMMUNITY FORUMS ISSUE ESCALATION

In the Tobe community, we have two governing bodies that are available to resolve and manage issues. These are:

- Tobe Community Council—This council is the highest-serving governing body in the Tobe community. It discusses and decides on general community issues, policies, and processes. This council is also the top-level platform to discuss conflict issues.

- Tobe Forums Council—The Forums Council governs the Tobe forums community and reports to the Tobe Community Council.

If you have a problem or concern, these governance structures are available to listen and pass judgment on the issue in question.

If you have a FORUMS issue, you should first add your issue to the Tobe Forums Council agenda by clicking [here]. Do not take your issue to the Tobe Community Council; you will be immediately asked to refer to the Tobe Forums Council first.

If you are dissatisfied with the service you have received from the Tobe Forums Council, you are welcome to escalate the issue to the Tobe Community Council. Please note that by doing this you are effectively stating the following:

- You believe that either the issue was not fairly and objectively considered by the Tobe Forums Council or that the council members do not possess the knowledge to effectively pass judgment on the issue in question.

- You are happy for the Tobe Community Council to perform an assessment of how effective the members of the Tobe Forums Council were in assessing the issue.

To escalate the issue, add an item to the Tobe Community Council Agenda by clicking [here].

We discuss how these escalation incidents are specifically addressed in Chapter 11.

Communicating Between Councils

When I originally discussed how to build a new council, I stressed just how important it is that you create communication channels for the council. This is an expected resource in each and every council that your community puts together. It allows the council to share ideas, deliberate on topics, and reach decisions.

Friends, the communication love doesn't end there, though. Now we must put our devious little minds to another opportunity: how can we help our multiple councils communicate with one another? The reason and inspiration behind this shared cross-council communication are those two magical words in community management: *best practice*.

If you have two councils that are formed (e.g., a Community Council and a Forums Council), you essentially have two groups of motivated, responsible, objective, and reliable people. Although each member on these councils should have a minimum level of suitability for the council based on the attributes that we discussed earlier in this chapter, there is oodles of potential for these council members to learn from one another and further improve and refine their governance abilities.

To do this, I recommend you set up an additional mailing list on which you ask every council member in your community to be a member. I know, I know, you are probably getting a little sick of setting up all of these mailing lists, and I am by no means encouraging *mailing list fetishism*, but this cross-council list will be a valuable resource. Another added benefit of this list is that it lets you address all of the governing members of your community in one place, which is helpful for sharing best practices.

Although it may seem a little less-than-transparent, I again recommend that this governance mailing list be a closed, members-only list with closed archives that only the current council members in your community can access. The reasons for this are the same reasons behind the recommendations for each council to have a private mailing list: for honest and frank conversation to flourish, they often need a context that is unmonitored.

Summary

In this chapter we have covered one of the most critical components in community management. Although governance has the ability to glaze eyes, it is a key ingredient in producing a healthy, vibrant, and accessible community.

Of course, governance is a large and complex subject, and the academic brigade has written many books on the topic. I have tried my damnedest to cover this sometimes-dusty topic as simply as possible and to give you an overview of the primary elements that are important in most communities. This chapter should give you a great head start in producing a governance system that is simple, unobtrusive, and fair to your entire community.

CHAPTER ELEVEN

Handling Conflict and Relationships

"The people to fear are not those who disagree with you,
but those who disagree with you and are too cowardly to let you
know."

—*Napoleon Bonaparte*

BACK IN 2007, I WAS PACKING MY SUITCASE TO HEAD TO A CONFERENCE IN EUROPE. Tired of
trying to cram everything into a tiny bag, I decided to check my email, where I had received
a somewhat concerned note from a member of a user group.

The group (which shall remain unnamed) had been experiencing some rather ugly conflict
between two members fighting for leadership. Both individuals felt they were the better choice
for leadership but were rather ironically demonstrating their clear lack of leadership experience
by having a public spat in the interests of securing power. The poor soul who sent me the
concerned email informed me that the situation was making the user group not a very fun
place to be. I responded, and in the interest of not missing my plane I returned to resolving
my own conflict between my underpants and travel bag.

A little while later, another email arrived about the same group, sharing similar concerns and
calling out one of the leaders for being unprofessional, bullish, and impolite to the members
of the group. While I was reading the email, another arrived. This one (replete with a flurry
of uppercase, highlighted, and boldface statements) defended the actions of the leader I had
originally read about. In contrast, this writer accused the other leader of corruption and

misconduct in the group. Somewhat concerned, I replied to each email to say I would be in touch but had to literally run out the door to get into the cab that would take me to the airport.

As I sat in the cab, I pondered how I was going to handle the situation. In between the barrage of opinion spurting from the cabbie's somewhat foul mouth about how the economy was on the brink of melting, I was somewhat preoccupied with trying to flesh out a solution to the complex situation that confronted me. (In retrospect, it seems that cabbie wasn't as much of a whack job as I first thought....)

Between getting in the cab, getting to the airport, and getting online, all of which took about 45 minutes, I had received another 6 emails from the same group, all from different people. Clearly something was very, very wrong there. Each email had a strong opinion. Some correspondents supported one leader or the other, but most were sick and tired of the arguments, shouting matches, and inability to listen. A community that was once rewarding and fun to be a part of had turned into a roller coaster with a chunk of track missing.

What happened next was the largest conflict resolution experience of my career to date. It resulted in a slew of meetings, soliciting feedback (which generated more than 60 emails in response over the course of a single day), and driving forward to a solution that sought to satisfy both of the proposed leaders and the wider community. We got there in the end, but it was a tense few weeks in an environment in which carefully chosen words, detailed next steps, and patience all took center stage.

The Nature of the Beast

Conflict is part and parcel of life. We see it every day on television; hear it every day on the radio; and read about it every day in our email, social networking websites, newspapers, magazines, and books. Most of the time, Louis Armstrong provides the soundtrack to our wonderful world, but every so often life gets a little edgy and our soundtrack is replaced with one from Slayer.

You should absolutely expect conflict in your community. No community to date has been unblemished by conflict, and its presence is no reflection on your community, its members, or its leaders. You could tirelessly spend each and every day making the tiniest of considerations and changes, refining your processes and governance to the nth degree, and ensuring that you are regularly checking in on the happiness of your members, and you will still find conflict lurking somewhere.

The reason is simple: people are people, and sometimes people just don't get on. You may have two people who have similar interests, similar backgrounds, and similar perspectives but just rub each other the wrong way. People are big bags of variables: different cultures, opinions, approaches, ideas, values, and more. When one big bag of variables doesn't match another equally big bag of variables, spats, arguments, and fuss ensue.

There is a science out there that explains how conflict occurs, but it is grounded in this plethora of variables, stimuli, nature-versus-nurture debates, and other elements. It is possible to devote your life to the topic: there is a sea of content about the psychology of conflict, anger management, cultural impact, expectations, and negotiation skills. Although you are welcome to submerge yourself in this academia, much of it will not be particularly useful when trying to figure out how to untwist the knickers of two people caught up in a fracas.

As a general rule, conflict is rare, and it doesn't need a lifetime of devotion to the library of academia. What it needs are straight, practical, hands-on approaches to dealing with common situations. With this in mind I wanted to include this chapter as a summary of the most important things to know when dealing with your community's conflict. It will give you the tools for handling the level of conflict you are likely to deal with.

The Structure of Strife

Let's kick off the chapter by exploring some of the high-level elements involved in conflict. The following are three fundamental ingredients that are often present in a conflict:

Confident/free-thinking personalities
> Typically the participants in the conflict are not exactly wallflowers. They are often strong personalities who are not afraid to speak up when they are unhappy.

Incompatible goals/values
> There are invariably one or more goals or values that the participants disagree on. Importantly, these are typically *perceived* goals and values. The reality is often very different, as we will explore later in this chapter.

Interaction
> The fact that two strong personalities disagree on goals or values does not in itself cause conflict; it is the manner in which these personalities interact that causes the sparks to fly. The source and nature of the interaction is often a key component in the conflict.

Conflict is a little like really bad food. There are many strong flavors out there (these are our personalities), and many of them have distinctive purposes (these are our goals/values). When the ingredients are in their boxes and bottles in your kitchen cupboard, they are innocent and innocuous. However, putting them together in the same dish can potentially create something that leaves an unpleasant taste in your mouth for a long time. On the other hand, strong flavors put together in the right way can complement one another and produce stunning outcomes and tastes that become memorable, long-lasting, and incredibly enjoyable.

Rather unsurprisingly, conflict does not make for healthy community. Conflict is the acid that slowly erodes community: it causes uncertainty that thrives in an uncomfortable and unpleasant environment. With a community generally populated with volunteers, it doesn't take a rocket scientist to understand how unappealing this kind of environment can be.

Although an irksome aspect of human behavior, conflict does offer us valuable insight. It helps us to identify the personalities in a community, it demonstrates a sense of passion in your members, and it shows very clearly that your community is alive and thriving as opposed to a lifeless husk. Conflict is always going to be present in a thriving community, and strangely it is one metric of success.

This reminds me of an incident that happened a few years back when I wrote a blog entry on *http://www.jonobacon.org/* and received an awfully mean-spirited and nasty comment: personal, full of vitriol, and entirely unnecessary. As soon as I read it I became very self-reflective and worried that the statement may have represented the views of more than that individual. In doing so, I entirely failed to balance the picture and consider the countless pleasant comments and wonderful email that I received. My mind zoned in on the negative.

In the midst of all of this, I logged on to discover a message from my friend Christian Schaller:

> Hey Jono. I saw that comment on your blog, you must be delighted!

When I asked in what possible dimension that comment would make me happy, Christian responded with:

> For someone to write that it means that they care what you think, so much so they felt the need to write it on your website. Congratulations!

In a strange and twisted way, Christian was right. When people care about something, it will often inspire them to take great lengths to protect it from something they disagree with. When this happens, conflict brews.

As a community leader, your community will look to you for guidance and advice when conflict rears its ugly head. You need to be prepared to step in and provide security and confidence. You need the skills to handle conflict in a way that is professional and reasoned, and subscribes to the underlying values of your community.

Conflict resolution in a volunteer community is very different from conflict resolution in a formal organization such as a company or a government agency. Community conflict often requires more sensitivity and restraint. The risk associated with putting a foot in the wrong place with community conflict resolution is that any party who is unhappy with your solution may well leave. If you have to deal with conflicts too often, you may end up losing many great members of your community. In more formal settings, the likelihood of employees leaving after conflict is much reduced, as they have to earn a living and put food on the table for their family.

The Calm Before the Storm

Conflict resolution is a skill that is heavily grounded in experience. Handling conflict teaches a new lesson every time, and these lessons help define an approach, a sensibility, and a method.

This experience has also been shown to develop one significant skill: the ability to detect and preempt conflict before it even happens.

Conflict does not just appear out of nowhere. A series of utterances and interactions occur, each one evidence of the brewing storm, before the conflict ultimately reaches the somewhat irksome plateau of a spat. If you can see and detect these indicators, you have the opportunity to step in before the going really gets rough.

Although every community is different, many of these warning signs are shared across all communities. Let's now take a spin through some of these indicators of a conflict on the horizon. As we explore these topics, we will end each discussion with a quick and dirty set of preventive bullet points that you can jot down to help avoid these issues in the first place.

Contentious Personalities

One of the most delightful attributes of community is its ability to energize and enable people. Without having any prior experience or reputation, many go on to develop expertise and respect by starting at the beginning and leveraging the opportunity of community to do amazing things. One underlying attribute that makes this possible is the openness involved in community: everyone in a volunteer community is welcome to join and participate. With such openness as the norm, the exceptions to the rule—when people who actually get rejected from a community—are usually those who perform gross misconduct that socially disappoints the wider community. Thankfully these kinds of incidents are rare.

If we draw a conceptual line that puts the ideal polite and engaged contributor on the far left of the line and the frustrating, imbecilic clod on the far right, there is a significant scale in between where the vast majority of your contributors will find their home. Those personalities who edge farther toward the right of that line are prime candidates for causing frustration and conflict. Let's explore this in more depth.

Profiling the polemical

In my time working with community I have experienced a range of personalities that have been controversial, disruptive, and at times outright infuriating. Within this realm, it is tempting to shun each figure as an undesirable member of your community and try to disengage from him in the hope that he will move on to annoy someone else.

In many cases, though, this is a crying shame. Some community members can appear irritating and troublesome at first, but when you give them the benefit of the doubt, you and they can often grow to work well together. This all boils down to understanding personality differences and the causes behind them.

When you deal with conflict, you are invariably dealing with cases in which someone just doesn't like someone else, largely due to personality differences. If you can understand and reconcile these differences, progress can be made. Let's first look at some of the reasons why people may appear vexing to others:

Age

Although many will deny it, age can dramatically affect how people engage in community. This can vary from methods of communication (younger people often shorten and codify their language, such as with "txtspeak" and "lolspeak") to different values, perspectives, opinions, and approaches. In many cases younger people are more trigger-happy, adventurous, and argumentative than older people, and this can be a prominent source of conflict. As many people get older, they become "set in their ways" and less likely to change and reflect on their views. Although this naturally does not affect everyone, it does apply to many.

Culture

With so many communities living online and garnering an international audience, culture can play a big role. This can affect temperament, preparedness, approach, and other elements. Culture can be a subtle contributor to conflict: often these differences are difficult to spot unless you are intimately familiar with both cultures. This is also a sensitive topic, as the acknowledgment of cultural differences can often be wrongly interpreted as racism. Tread carefully, Obi-Wan.

Opinions

It is interesting how some people just seem to have more opinions than others. These people can be both a blessing and a curse. If you put two of these opinion-laden folks together, things can get fiery quickly. The subtlety here is not in whether someone has an opinion but in how constructively that person can express it.

Experience

The level of each person's knowledge of the subject and the community itself can play a huge part in conflict issues. Sometimes those with more experience in the community expect those with less experience to know more, and consequently frustration builds. Not good.

The interesting commonality among all these attributes is that people can and have been known to mature in each area. Understanding this maturity can be the key to understanding your wider community and its personal development better. It can also be an important topic to communicate when things get contentious.

Community participation is a little like starting a new career. In the beginning, you make unintentional mistakes. Failing to see the mistakes, you need to have people point them out for you so that you can learn. The reason for these mistakes is not because you are stupid, but simply because you don't know the ropes yet. When you learn how things work, the mistakes usually decline consistently until they become rare blips in an otherwise perfect signal.

From a community leadership perspective, it is essential to understand the importance of allowing people to mature. You are going to come across some people who frustrate you. Some of these people will make every mistake in the book, and at times it will make you question your own faith in community ("How can we ever achieve our goals with people like this in the world?").

To really *feel* this growth in people, you need to experience it. After a few years of conscious awareness of how people mature, you are sure to see and experience examples of it happening in your community. For example, a guy joined a user group that I had formed and proceeded to break every possible rule, social convention, and principle in the group. He frustrated many, some of whom lit their torches and called for his ousting. Although there was little doubt that he was a frustrating force in an otherwise calm community, I had a hunch that he had the ability to change. I held strong, and I encouraged patience among my fellow community members; before long, we started to see improvement.

As the guy spent more time in the community he learned how it worked, began to take part in the culture as opposed to questioning it, and eventually became one of the most proficient and well-respected members. Today others look to him for advice and guidance; it just took him a little while to get there.

Sharing feedback about personality issues

When I studied at university one of my roommates had developed what can be politely described as an *odor issue*. Less politely, he smelled bloody awful; a unique bouquet of vinegar, onions, and pee all mixed together. Dip your bread in that oil, my friends. Although everyone knew of the funk that followed him around, no one wanted to tell him.

I felt awful for the guy, as I had the hunch he didn't know he smelled that way. One evening I sucked down some confidence and talked to him about it in a sensitive but honest way. He was stunned; he had absolutely no idea about the funk, but was committed to fixing it. He showered more often, amped up his deodorant, and cleaned his clothes more often and the problem went away. It was unpleasant to tell him the news, but it was the right thing to do.

There will be times when you are going to need to sit down with some of your community members and share some feedback that other people don't want to share. In many cases the recipients of your feedback will be as in the dark about their issues as my roommate was about his.

There are two examples I want to share that I think illustrate this pretty well.

In one of the communities I have worked with, there was a guy who we shall refer to as *Bob*. Bob was a committed and hard-working member of the community and contributed to many different areas, but primarily technical development. While he had grown a strong reputation as a technical expert in the community, he had also started to develop a reputation for being a bit difficult to work with.

This reputation stemmed from the very direct and almost aggressive way in which he responded to some of the changes that occurred in the project's policies and technologies.

When he first started responding in this way we presumed he was particularly frustrated by the issue in question, but when he responded in a similar way to *many, many* issues, he started developing a reputation for being a grumpy, miserable sod.

This was a shame. He was an awesome contributor and a really nice guy, and I had a hunch that he probably didn't realize he was doing this.

One day I called him and gently shared this feedback. He had no idea about the impression he was leaving, and was thankful to hear my news albeit concerned about his reputation being tarnished. I reassured him that I felt this was a completely recoverable situation and recommended he just reevaluate some elements of the way he shared his perspectives. I also offered to review some of his responses before he sent them. Within a few weeks the issue was resolved.

My second example was not driven by the frustration of others, but rather was something I observed in a community member's behavior.

While attending a series of discussion sessions at a technology event, I noticed that someone participating in the conversations seemed to have a fairly short-tempered way of expressing his opinions. He was also noticeably defensive when others challenged his opinions or suggestions, and this sometimes caused a slight tension in the room.

Although no one had complained to me about this, I noticed it and I had a sneaking suspicion he probably had no idea he was doing it. Again, I sat down and shared this feedback in a sensitive manner. As I had guessed, he was oblivious to the fact that he was responding and communicating in this way. During the next session after I shared this feedback, he was much calmer and less defensive, and the tension evaporated.

I learned some valuable lessons in these experiences. First, just because someone exhibits a personality trait (positive or less so) does not necessarily mean he is aware of it. Second, you should present this feedback as a friend rather than as a leader; the feedback should not feel like a performance review or a scolding. You should also present this feedback within the context that you would want the recipient to be aware of it so that he can respond and react to the issue if he wants to. Finally, always use either face-to-face or video/audio mediums (e.g., phone) to share this news; you want the recipient to hear the humanity in your voice as you share the feedback. Email and chat channels are not the right mediums for this kind of feedback.

Poisonous people

While some people are able to grow and mature, some outright bad apples may unfortunately join your community. Some of these people will be obvious (posting loud, obnoxious, or offensive comments), but some will be far subtler and more devious.

The latter are often known as *poisonous people*. These are the people who express dissatisfaction with your community or direction, and actively seek others to join their campaign of negativity.

These people are not only interested in expressing their own concerns, but also want to build a coup of counteropinion against your community.

Many of these poisonous people often operate under the radar. The conversations will typically happen in private with only one side of the perspective represented, but their actions will lead to substantial conflict that threatens the entire community. Try to be aware of who these people are. Typically their names will come up in conversations where it becomes clear they are expressing private concerns and negativity with multiple people. Expressing concern does not make people poisonous, but privately rallying support against the community without any discussion or debate of the issues in the common communication space *does* make them poisonous.

You should handle these known entities with caution: jarring moves in their direction can dial up the poison even further. You need to fight poisonous people not with words but with evidence. Disprove their comments with calm and reasoned commentary amply bolstered with third-party references and evidence. You can then let your community members make up their own minds.

TIPS FOR AVOIDING CONFLICT

- **Understand the factors that can affect how people conduct themselves in a community.**
- **If someone is causing conflict, assess how much you feel she could mature. If you have faith, encourage the detractors to share that faith.**
- **Identify poisonous people and watch them carefully. Give them additional attention to limit their damage: identify their concerns, discuss them, try to weed out any communication errors, and generally try to calm their concerns and worries.**

Barriers to Input

One of the most basic concepts in most volunteer communities is *openness*. For a volunteer community to thrive, openness is necessary to secure the impression that your community members can have a tangible impact on the direction and focus of the wider community. You always want your community to thrive on the opportunity to discuss, debate, and reason, and for their views to be listened to and acted on where appropriate. In other words, your community should always feel that their input is welcome. It may not be acted on, but it should be received in good faith.

As we discussed in Chapter 10, not all communities are created equal. Some are driven in a dictatorial fashion by specific people or by handpicked rock stars. Some communities are far more open, and some are leaderless and driven by consensus and action. It is important that the expectations around input are accurately communicated. If your community is pushing, as part of its core values, openness and the encouragement of input and contribution, you need to ensure that people can actually do that. If they can't, you are going to have some angry villagers on your hands.

So, before you respond to criticism, don't start from the assumption that it is unfounded. Take a good, hard look at your community and determine whether a problem really does exist. If it does, fix it. Reread this book and ensure that you are implementing all the tips scattered throughout regarding open engagement. And invite the critics to help, if they are at all competent and conciliatory.

Bickering can often occur in communities driven by a commercial sponsor. Regardless of how open your governance is and how well the sponsor's paid staff members engage the rest of the community, volunteers will always worry about having less input in the community than paid staff members. It's easy to see why: if a company puts your community at the center of its universe and throws some dollars at it, it is likely that it will have a vested interested in making its money work for it. This could *theoretically* affect the weight of participants' opinions about the community's direction.

> **NOTE**
>
> Folks, notice the nicely emphasized *theoretically* in the previous statement. The reason for this is that I was playing devil's advocate a little. Many communities have paid sponsors, and in my experience most sponsors respect the existing lines in the sand that the community has drawn and don't throw their commercial weight around. It is important not to automatically associate "paid sponsor" with "in charge of direction."

If your community has a paid sponsor, you need to go out of your way to ensure that the community members still feel they are able to contribute. If your community is open and transparent and has facilities to engage with community development, ensure that you celebrate those facilities and regularly remind your community that they will be treated no differently from those representing the commercial interest. If a community member is citing claims of unfairness due to this commercial sponsor, the only way you can achieve this is to build trust. To do this, I recommend that you get on the phone with this person, get all the issues out on the table, clarify areas of confusion and miscommunication, and build a schedule of regular communication to tend to and provide feedback on the issues that were raised. You don't need to always provide solutions, but you do need to have your ear to the ground and be sensitive to problems and issues.

If you are a community manager for a commercial sponsor, you may find yourself in the difficult spot of the sponsor demanding something that the community doesn't want. This is a complex and sensitive situation to manage, and you should tread carefully.

You should begin by determining exactly what the sponsor (who may well be your boss) wants and how it can achieve this with the least amount of disruption to community goodwill, governance, or processes. If the sponsor is determined to get this work done and is willing to step outside published governance, you should get an outline of the proposed work, submit it to the community, and ask the governing body (if it exists) to gather community feedback on the proposed plan and provide a summary of the community's feelings on it. If the sponsor chooses to ignore this opinion and go ahead, you need to make it very, very clear that it could significantly harm community relations.

Regardless of whether there is a commercial sponsor, the trick here is to pay attention when people feel they don't have input into decisions and/or direction. When there is a sense of lost control, people will often bottle it up and only discuss it with a few other friends who they feel will sympathize with them. These people are not poisonous, and there is no malice behind their actions; they just don't know where to turn and feel that they are not being listened to. In such circumstances, the issue can quickly blow out of proportion. If you get a whiff that something is not quite right, investigate it immediately and reassure the concerned parties that things have not changed and the community is still as volunteer-focused as it has ever been.

To reassure your community, you should remind them of the community-facing resources that encourage people to submit their ideas and views. In the Ubuntu community, we put the following in place to encourage an environment of openness and collaboration:

Mailing lists
> A range of public mailing lists are available, complete with publicly visible archives.

Brainstorm website
> This is a website in which people can submit ideas to be voted on. This offers a great list of items that are high-priority in the minds of the Ubuntu user community.

Public IRC channels
> This range of publicly accessible IRC chat channels is where Canonical staff members perform most of their work, and therefore have a virtual ear to the ground.

Sponsored developer participation
> Canonical also sponsors many community developers to the twice-annual Ubuntu Developer Summit. This encourages strong community participation.

These resources and their open and participatory nature should speak legions in the interest of welcoming your community's input and ideas. Although you should certainly remind your members of these open facilities, you should also go one step further. If you have a serious complaint on your hands from someone who feels that her input is not welcome, you should dig through these resources and find examples when the community has been involved in a productive change. Pointing to a public mailing list is one thing, but pointing to five productive conversations on that mailing list that illustrate your community's openness is much more valuable.

I have one final note about this particular cause of conflict. You should expect that some people will generate conflict simply because they offered input and their input was not acted on. As an example, someone may recommend that your community takes a particular direction, but for various reasons that direction is not taken and the original provider of the input gets agitated and makes claims that he is not being listened to. This is nothing more than griping.

You will always need to deal with these kinds of accusations: you simply can't please all the people all the time. In this scenario the solution is to again provide evidence that your community has engaged in input. But do be frank: tell the complainer that sometimes people don't get their way. Provide examples of how you have not gotten your way as a counter to him feeling isolated and singled out.

TIPS FOR AVOIDING CONFLICT

- **Ensure that there are very clear channels in which your community can engage.**
- **Ensure that feedback, opinions, and ideas *are* discussed, considered, and engaged with.**
- **If part of a commercial sponsor, always ensure that your staff members are publicly engaging and not hiding in private communication channels.**

Problems with Responsibility

Every community contains groups of people who have clear and perceived responsibilities. These folks are commonly seen as leaders who make decisions and the real movers and shakers who represent the wider community. These people with responsibility can include:

Governing members
Members of councils, boards, advisory groups, and more

Team leaders
People who run the many and varied teams your community may have in place

Community managers
People specifically given the responsibility to help advise the community and smooth out any bumps in how it works

Sponsored leaders
Prominent members of the community who fund significant chunks of it and possibly pay staff members to work with it

Each role brings an expectation around engagement. Your community will expect a certain degree of professionalism, responsibility, and responsiveness. When a member feels these attributes are compromised, up pops the big hairy eyeball that points at said leader. I don't like hairy eyeballs, and neither should you.

There are two primary causes of this conflict that happen far more in communities than they should, and both are interlinked.

The first is having too many eggs in one basket. This is when a single person has too much responsibility and control over a given part of the community. This can happen a lot with resource management. It is common to have one person as the single point of contact for administering mailing lists, accounts, forums, or other resources. This is all fine and dandy when that person can keep up with the maintenance requests, but when that falters, frustration follows closely after.

This ties into the second issue: responsiveness, a problem that has plagued every community. The reason is fairly obvious when you consider it: community leaders are typically highly motivated, fidgety people who have no problem keeping themselves occupied. Busy people tend to become really busy people, and it is not uncommon for them to take on a little too much. Too many responsibilities and not enough time is a recipe for further community frustration.

NOTE

Remember that you could be a bottleneck, too. If you find that your TODO list is spiraling out of control, it is likely you are a bottleneck. Check which items are blocking on you, and try to spread them out to more people.

If left untended, these issues can cause wider annoyance and even nastiness. This happened in a community in which I played a loose role a few years back. There was a single community member who maintained many of the resources the community used. This person always denied additional help and contributions and wanted to handle the resources himself. As time went on, he became increasingly difficult to get a hold of. Maintenance requests were largely ignored. Frustration set in and thus emerged accusations of ego, self-obsession, the willingness to put personal interests ahead of the community, and other irksome claims.

While at a conference, I was chatting to a friend of mine about these issues and he gave me a piece of advice that has stayed with me. He said:

> You know, I can understand the frustration people have with [BLANK], but the reason he has become unresponsive is not because of any malicious intent but purely because he just got busy. We are all guilty of this.

He wasn't wrong. Even though many were claiming this guy was fast becoming the son of the devil, such ramblings became overstated because (a) they were largely expressed in private cabals of people who all agreed and (b) they had never confronted [BLANK] with the issues and never got his side of the story. Movie fans may consider this all very reminiscent of the legend of the unseen Keyser Söze in *The Usual Suspects*: the legend was somewhat outstripping the reality.

The obvious solution to this problem is to avoid these bottleneck issues in the first place, but despite your best efforts, you are still likely to experience some conflict as a result of these issues. Your primary role here is to investigate both sides of the story, provide feedback from everyone involved, and make necessary changes that are in the interests of the community where required. Don't allow members of your community to become Keyser Söze: break down the issue, understand all sides, and bring balance to the discussion.

TIPS FOR AVOIDING CONFLICT

- **Try to avoid bottlenecks set up by specific community members. If you experience them, unblock them as soon as possible.**
- **Dissuade personal comments and remarks if bottlenecks appear.**
- **Always consider whether bottlenecks have a malicious undertone. If they don't, make that clear to detractors.**
- **Encourage public discussion of resource issues as opposed to private bickering sessions.**

Lack of Justice

The final topic we should cover as a common source of conflict is the feeling that previous conflict issues or problems were not handled in a manner that was expected.

Conflict resolution is seen by many as a means of those with influence delivering justice where it is genuinely required. When that justice is not exercised, a previously happy bunny can dramatically take on the guise of an extremely agitated and frustrated negativabunny. That's right, folks, I just said "negativabunny." Let's see how much Google Juice we can squeeze out of that word....

Claims of ineffective conflict resolution and injustice are concerns that call on you to commit a significant amount of your energy. While there are many causes for conflict, your community will depend on its leaders to unblock conflict and restore order. When this happens, all conflict feels temporary and manageable. If your community loses faith in its leader's ability to unblock and resolve these problems, it can feel as if the earth is shaking. It can make the community feel like a lawless state in which agitation and arguments reign supreme. This is obviously not a good position to be in.

One trait of a firm and clear governance structure is to allow assessments of the very people who assess and handle conflicts. As an example, if you have a forums community governed by a Forums Council, that council should deal with conflict and unrest. If that council fails to reach a desirable outcome, concerned community members can escalate the matter to the top-level Community Council that the Forums Council is subservient to.

The most important advice in avoiding this kind of criticism is always to engage in conflict resolution in a detailed and effective way. If this is a public conflict, you should regularly engage with the community to show you are helping to deal with the situation. If the conflict is private, those who claim that conflict was not resolved may simply be unaware that it was resolved. In many cases you can settle any concerns by dropping a quick email to the concerned members to let them know the situation was handled and resolved.

TIPS FOR AVOIDING CONFLICT

- **Always deal with conflict. Never leave issues languishing or unresolved.**
- **In public conflict, ensure that you are seen to be acting. Provide input, feedback, and reassurance in public communication channels. Justice must be done and it must be *seen* to be done.**
- **Always be responsive to concerns.**

PHYSICAL VIOLENCE: NEVER ACCEPTABLE

It goes without saying that violence is never acceptable in your community. While it is rare, you must be prepared to take a zero-tolerance view in case it does happen. If someone is violent to another member, make it clear that (a) the attacker must leave the community, (b) you will inform the authorities, and (c) the attacker will be able to rejoin the community after he has cooled down and demonstrated that he will never again resort to such behavior.

Informing the authorities—which includes the police as well as the leaders of institutions you're involved with, such as universities—is important for several reasons. First, violent people tend to escalate their behavior imperceptibly, and law enforcement can benefit from seeing patterns of escalating behavior so that they can ward off real danger. Second, you need to protect your community against legal retaliation, because violent people often turn around and invent charges against their victims.

Another subtle point is that you consider very carefully whether you should mention that violence is never tolerated. For many, the merest mention of the topic is so obvious that it can be interpreted as patronizing. This really depends on your community. For example, it is undoubtedly going to be more acceptable to mention this topic in an urban regeneration community as opposed to a local neighborhood knitting group.

The Conflict Resolution Process

Now that we have covered many of the warning signs and indicators of conflict, you will hopefully have an opportunity to step in and deal with the issue before it really flares up. Even if you don't manage to catch the warning signs and step in, you can apply a similar process to managing the actual conflict.

Of course, experts have proposed many, many different approaches to resolving conflict, and each situation is in itself unique. There is no cookie-cutter approach to dealing with conflict, and experience is the best judge of how to move forward to resolve issues.

What I am going to present here is a broad description of steps I generally use to deal with contentious issues. These steps map out the primary elements involved in conflict resolution, and you can build on them to form your own style.

Interestingly, while I was reading some of the many books about conflict resolution, I discovered a theory developed by Johnson & Johnson in 1994. I have been living and practicing this approach to conflict resolution for years without realizing it had a name. I was all set to call it *Bacon's Great Conflict Resolution Theory* when I discovered that those pesky Johnsons got in there first.

Regardless of who coined the theory, it is a practical, real, and directly usable approach for communities. Let's take a look at Johnson & Johnson's approach:

1. Collect data—Learn what the conflict is about, and develop an objective picture of all parties' perspectives.

2. Probe—Ask open questions, listen, and engage with all parties to get the full story.

3. Save face—Work toward a winning resolution for everyone, and try to avoid embarrassing either party while always remaining objective and unemotional.

4. Discover common interests—Finding common interests and alliances will help find points of commonality beneath the conflict.

5. Reinforce—Where both parties share a perspective and agree, reinforce those perspectives, and particularly try to use data to back it up.

6. Negotiate—Start simple, trying to get both parties to agree on simple solutions, and then continue to build toward the common goals of both parties involved.

7. Solidify adjustments—Review, summarize, and confirm the areas in which both parties agree.

Each step is performed one at a time. Naming and being conscious of these seven steps is useful for breaking down the process of conflict resolution. A little later we are going to walk through the resolution process and flesh out these steps, but before we do that, let's cover some general best-practice elements involved in the process.

The Role of a Facilitator

When conflict occurs, the person who steps in to straighten out the issue has a role similar to that of a judge or magistrate: to investigate the issue fairly and objectively and to reach a conclusion based on that fair and objective judgment. This is the role of the *facilitator* (also known as a *mediator*).

A facilitator can't be just anyone: she must secure the trust and confidence of the warring parties. The parties involved need to have faith that the facilitator is going to take a fair, reasoned, and thorough approach to the conflict.

The probability that the conflict will be resolved is hugely dependent on this faith. With this in mind, let's spend some time looking at the profile of a great facilitator. This can give you some food for thought for your own role as a facilitator.

Be objective

Objectivity is the foundation of all effective conflict resolution. As we discussed earlier, you need to build faith in the participants. To do this, you need to build faith in the wider community that you can act in an entirely objective fashion. This raises a difficult question, though: how do you demonstrate objectivity in your community yet still offer opinions and direction? To remain objective, do you need to never express your own opinion?

Not at all. Objectivity does not spring from remaining aloof and above the fray, but in the way you engage in discussions and topics. This is all about how you interact with the community. There are a few simple best practices that can help communicate your objectivity to the community:

Be honest
> There is no such thing as an objective but dishonest person. If your community doesn't trust you, they won't believe in your ability to be objective. As such, be honest at all times, privately and publicly.

Admit when you are wrong
> Sometimes you are going to get it wrong…in public. Instead of denying any mistakes or withering behind a wall of silence, put your head above the pulpit and admit when you get it wrong. This is an extension of being honest, and your community will respect you for it.

Don't wear the flame suit
> Every community has flame wars, that is, the arguments and disagreements that happen on mailing lists, websites, blogs, and elsewhere. Don't get involved. Participating in the flame wars causes you harm in two ways. First, it raises the temperature, because a well-respected community member has sought to weigh in, which drags the war out longer. Second, you don't want a reputation for taking part in online spats. Instead, you want a reputation for resolving them elegantly, and the place for elegance is not in a flame war.

Don't be afraid
> Another key component in building honesty with your community is to be honest and up-front when you disagree with someone. Every so often, you are going to need to grab someone by the virtual collar and let him know what a destructive force he is. Under the

premise that your conduct is fair and balanced and that the cause is reasonable, many community members will respect you for your frankness. Just be careful not to veer into outright bollocking.

Always remember that building confidence in your objectivity works only if you are genuinely...objective. Objectivity doesn't grow naturally in most people; you need to consciously consider it and work on it.

OBJECTIVITY AND ANNOYING PEOPLE

There are many ingredients that can risk or taint your objectivity. One of the most significant is trying to remain objective when dealing with someone you just don't like. Is it possible to be objective with someone who previously humiliated you personally on his blog?

It is, but it requires careful and conscious consideration to ensure that you keep on the straight and narrow and don't let personal animosity blur your ability to judge a situation fairly.

The solution to this is always to remember that the community is bigger than you, that guy, or anyone else. Your ability to resolve conflict is something that you are seeking to achieve for the community, and you need to keep its best interests at heart. That could mean engaging respectfully with someone you don't like, even someone who was disrespectful to you.

My dad is a magistrate for a small county court in Northern England. Every morning when he drives to the courthouse, he recites his oath of office to himself: "I, John Richardson Bacon, swear by Almighty God that I will well and truly serve our Sovereign Lady Queen Elizabeth the Second in the office of Justice of the Peace and I will do right by all manner of people after the laws and usages of this realm without fear or favor, affection or ill will." It keeps his mind focused and keeps him objective.

Be positive

Conflict is not fun for anyone involved. A conflict situation is a mishmash of different emotions from the different parties: anger, frustration, annoyance, self-reflection, embarrassment, and more. You should do your best to lighten the atmosphere.

Being positive breaks down into several stances. First, you should be positive about the ability to find a solution and an outcome. You need to give the participants in the conflict a positive impression that you can help, that you sympathize with their plight, and that you are going to help them to resolve the problems.

Second, you should be positive about the wider community and the values behind the project. As an example, whenever I have dealt with conflict situations in the Ubuntu community, I have started by reminding participants why we are all involved. This positivity not only reminds the participants of the important wider picture, but also highlights a connection among the members of the conflict.

Finally, there is huge value in just offering a generally positive and lighthearted approach to the situation. Having a generally positive demeanor, smiling, and using upbeat language and subtle humor are all great methods of lightening the slightly cloudy atmosphere. Of course, there is a balance to be struck here: don't turn your role as facilitator into that of a stand-up cabaret comedian, but a few subtle, amusing references here and there will ensure that everyone stays as positive as possible.

Be open

I am going to let you in on a little secret. The word *open* irritates me. Well, let me be clearer: the *overuse* of the word *open* irritates me, and in recent years the word seems to be more prevalent than a furball in an animal shelter.

When used within the context of conflict resolution, a valuable application of openness is to seek equality with all participants in the conflict and thus avoid cliques and in-jokes.

Some years back, I was observing a friend of mine dealing with a conflict situation who managed to violate this goal of equality and openness. He did this by engaging differently with one of the participants: he knew that person more personally and referred to various in-jokes and private references. Rather unsurprisingly, the other person (who was just as bemused about the in-jokes as I was) felt he never had a shot at an objective judgment. Don't make the same mistakes yourself.

Be organized when you put your feet firmly into the shoes of a facilitator. Make sure to schedule calls and meetings at times you can adhere to; under no circumstances should you simply skip meetings or stop responding to email. Timeliness is key.

KEEP RECORDS

Always document what happens during conflict resolution. Get permission to preserve emails and other communications from all parties. Write down notes from sessions. In this way, you can refer back to previous communications when people dispute the facts. Keeping records is also important because conflicts sometimes escalate to higher levels of the community, and members will want a history of what happened. Your conduct may even come under examination.

While it is important to keep records, don't be tempted to quote people out of context and use their words against them. This serves no purpose other than to make people feel cornered. The records are instead a useful resource for keeping track of the discussion as a whole.

Be clear

The most fundamental task when beginning conflict resolution is to communicate to all parties involved the expectations around your role as facilitator. The primary expectations that I communicate are the following:

Solutions are the goal

> I am here to find a solution. There may be open wounds and cuts and bruises from previous exchanges, but we all need to find agreement on how to move forward.

Evidence is central

> The process is going to concentrate on evidence as opposed to emotion. The facts and reality of a situation are the guiding force, and emotion, carping, complaining, and assumed perception are not going to have a place in the discussion. This does not prevent an aggrieved party from asking for discipline toward someone who has violated the community's standards regarding respect, tolerance for others, and basic etiquette.

Conduct must be under control

> All discussion must be polite and respectful. You will not accept disrespectful, threatening, or violent behavior.

Compromise is the modus operandi

> The goal here is to find a solution that satisfies the majority of considerations in the main parties, but this solution may not be 100% of what everyone—or even anyone—wants.

By framing the conversation with these expectations on all sides, you will help get the conflict resolution wheels on the runway and prepare for takeoff.

Resolving the Conflict

Earlier we talked about the seven-step Johnson & Johnson method for dealing with conflict resolution. Over the following pages, we are going to explore this process by breaking it into five parts:

1. Calm and reassure.
2. Get the facts.
3. Discuss.
4. Document.
5. Reflect and maintain.

These five parts will embody different steps of the Johnson & Johnson theory outlined earlier. In each part, we will discuss in detail the different considerations facing you. Each consideration is driven from countless conflict resolution incidents that I have been involved in over the years.

To make this content easier to understand, it is always good to apply the theory to a real scenario. As such, on the following pages I will be discussing a real incident that occurred between two very prominent members of a user group who were in fairly serious conflict over how to handle monetary donations to the group. Naturally I have changed the names to protect the innocent, but let me introduce you to the two characters:

"Lee"

> Lee was loud, at times obnoxious and slightly egotistical, but despite these traits clearly a sensitive guy. His commitment to the group was unwavering, and he was always coming up with ideas and creative methods of growing the group and doing exciting things. With this in mind, Lee was keen to set up a facility to handle money (bank account, accounting, tax returns, etc.) and a governance body to handle this facility.

"Alan"

> Alan was quieter than Lee, but never afraid to voice his opinion. Alan was the kind of guy who would bear grudges, but would not engage in confrontation. Alan took an immediate and visceral dislike to the idea of a money-handling facility. He was a firm believer in keeping the user group as simple as possible, and felt that Lee's idea would create an unnecessary and complicated bureaucracy.

We will call this example "the fantastical user group debacle" and refer to it in each of the five parts. All set, friends? Let's go....

Part 1: Calm and reassure

Before we begin the Johnson & Johnson items, the first step is to provide as much calm and reassurance as possible to the parties involved in the conflict. The goal here is to set the tone for the conversation so that it begins without aggression and shouting. If you are receiving an aggressive tone, you should first have a conversation with the person involved and make it clear that you are there to help, but you can't do anything until he calms down. Use reassuring and familiar language. For example, talk about "calm," "resolving," "peace," and "community." You absolutely cannot move forward effectively if an aggressive tone is used, because it will instantly deter the opposite side of the argument.

It is this very first step where you need to firmly assert your position as facilitator. You need to reassure the factions and seal your commitment to finding a solution, demonstrating absolute objectivity and focusing on evidence in the interest of finding a solution.

You need to strike a delicate tone here: sound reassuring and caring, but don't sound like a pushover. You need to ensure that both participants are clear that you will be firm and fair and that you will hear all sides of the story.

The fantastical user group debacle. Alan and Lee clearly disagreed on how to handle money in the user group. Although this was the current topic, the initial email I had received suggested this was merely the straw that broke the camel's back. It was becoming evident that the two just didn't like each other very much and saw the world very differently.

Both had exchanged testy words with each other, primarily over email, but they shared even more fervent words about each other with me. The language was very emotional: talk of "hating" each other, "refusing" certain ideas, and "demanding" various assurances.

To get this off on the right foot, I always prefer to discuss things on the phone. Both Alan and Lee were happy to talk, and I called both separately to begin the discussion.

It was important that these were individual phone calls. At the beginning of the calls, I received the expected vitriol toward the other, and I sought to calm them down first. I then made it clear that I was here to help, to offer an objective investigation into what had happened to cause this rift and to offer my input. With so much anger on display, I made it very clear that I had my own requirement before starting: a polite and reasoned tone. I stressed that aggression and bickering had no place in the discussion. Both agreed, and we were off to a good start.

My goal now was to help identify if there was a way these two passionate community members could straighten out their differences or at least work cohesively in the same volunteer environment.

Part 2: Get the facts

J&J Elements Covered:
Collect data
Probe

The goal of this phase is to assemble as much evidence about the situation as you can. The real focus and priority here is to find unequivocal evidence, that is, evidence of the situation that can be independently verified. Here we want to separate out emotion and get to the heart of what really happened.

You should first speak to those on both sides of the conflict and ask them to provide you with their stories. To engage in this discussion, you need to decide how to communicate with them. I highly recommend doing this on the phone or via Voice over IP (such as Skype) if possible. A phone conversation is far more interpersonal and allows both parties to communicate more quickly than over email or a chat medium such as IRC.

When you gather this initial story, you should expect a fairly significant amount of venting and emotion. Expect both parties to speak quickly, dart the focus around different issues, and keep remembering details and frustrations they had previously forgotten to mention in the conversation. While you have this conversation, bear a few things in mind:

Listen

Take your time and listen to the person carefully. Give her a chance to speak, get her frustrations off her chest, and provide you with as much data as possible.

Ask questions

Start by asking the person to start at the beginning, walk her through what happened, and ask lots of questions about each step in the timeline. If you are uncertain about something, don't be afraid to ask. Remember, you want to gather as much data as possible.

Don't offer opinion

Try your best to not offer an opinion or emotional reaction to what the person tells you. Even if you strongly agree or disagree with her sentiment, you should try to just gather the facts as best you can.

Make notes

Always have a pen and paper (or text editor) ready before you have the conversation. Note the timeline, the issues, and other elements of the story.

After this initial conversation, you should have a firm idea of the involved parties' primary problems and concerns. At the end of the conversation you should ask for one more thing: ask both parties independently to send you an email with as much evidence and details that illustrate their concerns as possible.

The next step is to reenact a childhood dream of mine that has been left dormant for years: to assume the investigative role of Columbo. That's right, folks, it's time to don the long mac, chomp on the somewhat dog-eared cigar, and begin hunting for additional third-party evidence. Here you want to augment the content submitted from the (naturally biased) participants of the conflict and find some other data that can help you figure out where things stand.

To do this, you need to know where to look. Some of these may apply to your community:

Public communication channels

Look for public discussion on mailing lists, in logged IRC channels, on social networking websites, and elsewhere.

Hooks

Earlier in the book, when we explored how to measure community, we talked about the hooks that can be used to extract meaningful data about your community. Think about which hooks could be useful to gather relevant data. As an example, if the conflict is surrounding a specific person screwing up bug reports, look into the bug tracker and make a note of the activity that occurred there.

Content

Take a look at blogs, blog comments, articles, and other written material that may be relevant to the topic. There may even be evidence lurking in podcasts, online videos, and elsewhere.

When you have gathered as much evidence as you can find, you now have to consider whether you need third-party opinions. If the conflict concerns the conduct of people in the community, or it affects the wider community or other public issues, you may want to gather some feedback.

There are two approaches to soliciting feedback, both of which have pros and cons. First, you could target certain people for their opinions on the issue. The benefit of this is that you can specifically target people who you know to be objective and unbiased on the issue. The downside is that you get a limited spread of knowledge that may not accurately reflect the situation.

The second approach is to place a call for more data from the general community. The pros of this approach are that it is open and inclusive to the wider community, but it does have problems: (a) it raises the profile of the problem, which is typically the opposite of what you want, and (b) it can bring out all manner of crazies.

I recommend you take the former approach, but ensure that you have a wide range of opinion and still maintain a strong sense of objectivity around the information that you receive.

ALWAYS MAINTAIN PRIVACY

When soliciting opinions about a conflict issue, you should do your best to obscure the identities of those from whom you solicit private opinions.

When you have solicited your evidence, input, and general feedback on the conflict, you will have enough material to begin forming a position on what has happened. Although you have to remember the possibility of bias in each piece of evidence and opinion, it is likely that you are beginning to get a broadly accurate idea of what has happened and what went wrong.

You now need to reconcile this evidence and input with the goals, values, and perspectives of the community. Have any of the actions of those involved fallen outside the culture of your community? Is there any evidence of personal benefit being put forward as the best interests of the community?

Now is the time to review the situation and adopt your unbiased perspective to draw a conclusion on what has happened. With almost every conflict situation, the fault will lie with both parties in different areas. You should note how each party could have handled the situation better, and if and when they acted outside the reasonable (and preferably documented) expectations of the community.

The fantastical user group debacle. Earlier I mentioned that I had initial phone calls with Alan and Lee to calm their frustrations. I used my phone calls partly to gather some initial feedback on what the primary issues were (the donation system being one of them) and their respective viewpoints.

Alan gave me a patchwork of his problems with Lee and Lee's perspective, a stream of consciousness that came flooding toward me in one big, disorganized mess of thoughts. I noted everything he said, and regularly repeated key problems that he outlined to ensure that we were both clear on what he was saying.

I then did the same for Lee. This time, an even more disorganized set of thoughts came flying in my general direction. Lee was less angry at Alan, but he was clearly frustrated with the situation and was growing impatient.

Because the environment that encased these issues was a user group, I started doing some third-party research. I looked into their mailing list, lingered on their IRC channel, and had a few private one-on-one conversations with people whom I knew to be objective in that community. As I received more evidence, a pattern was forming: Lee's requests were increasingly erratic, demanding, and personally driven. It seemed that Lee not only wanted a governed body to cover how money was handled, but he also wanted almost absolute control himself. Reports of Lee's demanding nature and self-perception of leadership was concerning other group members. Although it was clear he was not seeking to make money from the group, there was maybe a little too much desire for power in his plan. My hunch was that Lee's desire for power was an insecurity caused by the rift between him and Alan, another very prominent community member.

At this point in the process, I was faced with two challenges. First, there were the specific relationship problems between Lee and Alan, but there was also the wider concern in the community surrounding Lee's conduct and leadership efforts. My feeling was that if I could reduce the venom between Alan and Lee, this would (a) bring less of their personal anger to general community meetings, (b) drive toward a solution on the money-handling issue, and (c) inspire Lee to become more reasonable and less power-hungry.

Part 3: Discuss

J&J Elements Covered:
Save face
Discover common interests
Reinforce
Negotiate

The next step is to engage in a conversation with both parties that nudges them toward a conclusion. The goals of this part are to discuss the issues, hear all sides together, and then find solutions and consensus in areas where both sides agree. This is all about searching through the chaotic claims and memories for patterns where you can lay down an eventual consensus. By finding these patterns, you can make progress toward a general agreement and also build a more positive atmosphere around shared values as opposed to differing ones.

The first step is to schedule the discussion. If the conflict is between two specific people, the best medium for discussion is typically a conference call. This can happen on a range of online telephony services (such as Skype) or by using a conventional telephone conference call service. Many conventional handsets even support three-way conversations at no extra cost.

If the conflict is public and part of a team or group, schedule a public meeting. I have found the most suitable medium for this to be IRC. It allows people to share thoughts quickly so long as they can all get online at a specific time.

Your choice of medium is heavily dependent on what is comfortable for your community. The most important factor is that it is real-time: the discussion needs the immediate give and take of a meeting of minds. Email and forums are fine for discussing general issues of the conflict, but the resolution really needs to happen in real time.

The most important points about scheduling a public meeting are that it should (a) be in a neutral or, if suitable, public place and (b) at a time that is convenient for the primary stakeholders in the conflict. What you want to avoid is scheduling a meeting when one of the primary participants has to get out of bed at 3 a.m. to take part in the discussion. That person will invariably be a little grumpier than normal (shocking, I know!), and said grumpiness will infect the discussion and complicate matters.

> ### NOTE
> Face-to-face meetings for conflict resolution are sometimes possible, and while they are valuable in many instances, I generally recommend against them. Body language plays a huge role in face-to-face conflict resolution and can distract the participants from the issues as well as provide a more intimidating environment in which participants may struggle to find consensus.

Whether public or private, you should keep the length of the meeting to a set amount of time (one hour is usually advisable). There are a few reasons for this.

First, if you have an open-ended meeting, it will go on for a *long* time and some of the participants will grow tired of the meeting before others, causing frustration. Second, a set amount of time will keep everyone focused on the details and mitigate inane rambling, diatribes, and monologues, which are always common in these kinds of discussions. Finally, you need to think of your own sanity, too: dealing with a juicy three-hour chunk of conflict resolution can drive you potty. If you break down the discussion into manageable chunks, it will mean that the members of the discussion are always fresh and so are you.

With the meeting scheduled and everyone either on the line or in the channel, you can begin the discussion. Although there is no fixed formula for handling these contentious topics, we will now discuss a broad template that can get you started.

First, introduce the conversation. Say who you are and the role you are playing; state the purpose of your meeting; and reiterate the values, goals, and bigger picture of the community. Make it clear that you are here to help and will be taking an objective role in discussing all the issues involved.

Next, clarify the ground rules for the discussion. Make it clear that the discussion needs to remain polite and honest and that everyone should be driving toward a conclusion. Also make it clear that while everyone involved cannot fix the problems of the past, you can work together to produce a better future that avoids these issues. Reinforce that to achieve this better future it will require the commitment of everyone in the meeting to move toward a solution. Ask everyone to enter the discussion with an open mind to finding this solution.

Now it is time to get to the meat of the conflict resolution process. Friends, this is where the action really happens. Discuss the different issues openly and objectively, seek additional input, and focus on how you can make small agreements here and there. Remember that the goal here is to achieve lots of little victories.

Try to reframe the conversation away from what the participants disagree on and toward what they agree on. Cover each issue one at a time and slowly build more and more little agreements. When you reach a consensus on a specific topic, make it clear that you are making progress (but don't be tacky when celebrating this progress).

Throughout the meeting, take plenty of notes and be careful to jot down areas in which you reach consensus. These notes should preferably be public so that there can be agreement on the wording: the devil is always in the details. Make sure everyone understands the consensus, as sometimes subtle differences in interpretation can blow up later in the discussion. As such, when an agreement is made, repeat it and ensure that you get a clear consensus from everyone. The devil is in the details here, too: when you repeat what you understand as the agreed-upon view, one of the members of the discussion is likely to disagree with a certain choice of words or require clarification. As such, adjust your language until everyone is happy.

When you reach the end of your time slot, you should thank all of those involved for their contributions, express pride that you all made progress, and repeat the areas in which you reached consensus. If you didn't reach consensus on anything, indicate that you still made progress and that you are confident that more progress will be made in the next meeting. You should never end a meeting without scheduling the next one: this will ensure that the issue has a sense of continuity.

The fantastical user group debacle. To resolve the conflict between Alan and Lee, I scheduled a conference call to bring them together and discuss their different opinions. Fortunately, both were based in the same time zone, so I scheduled a call that was mutually convenient for them. Before the call began, I refreshed my memory of the evidence using the notes that I had gathered. My goal in the call was to find as much consensus as possible, particularly around the money-handling issue. While it was the group's decision as a whole about how they handle donations, I was keen to reduce the vitriol from the Lee and Alan relationship because this would then help the discussion with the rest of the group to be less emotional.

When the call began, I largely followed the steps I outlined on the previous few pages. I introduced myself and my involvement, made it clear that reasoned and polite discussion was required in the call, and started covering each issue one by one. I started with general attitudes toward funding resources in the group. The first piece of consensus we achieved was that the group did want to conduct activities that required equipment and therefore an outlay of money. This was a step forward: both Alan and Lee agreed that the need to handle money in some way was required.

The next part of the discussion was to cover typical activities requiring money. Was this a small amount of money for printing and CD duplication, or was it a larger expense for equipment and travel? Consensus struck again with agreement that costs would be for small to medium-size expenses, the most costly being a few nights in a hotel and a train ticket.

At this point in the discussion, there was a general atmosphere of agreement in the call. Both Alan and Lee were loosening up and more pleasant with each other, and the growing sense of agreement was having an impact. As the call progressed, we edged further and further toward agreement on a series of different issues. After a few more small steps forward, the time was up. I reiterated our progress and we all agreed to have a wider meeting on the money-handling topic with the community.

A week later, the community meeting kicked off, and I shared some of the agreements that Alan and Lee had formed. We then moved forward to discuss how donations would be handled, and the community agreed on PayPal. The next step was to discuss the crux of the issue: who would look after the money. Alan and Lee each expressed their perspectives in turn and other community members weighed in. A number of community members expressed concern over a full governance solution to handling money, and naturally Alan reiterated his views on the matter while Lee and some others provided their opposing views.

To find a middle ground, I proposed that instead of a full governing body to look after the money, Lee (who had been the primary champion of a money management facility in the group) would handle the funds but provide open accounting of the funds. I also recommended regular meetings with the group about how the money was being handled. Furthermore, I offered Lee the task of investigating what we would need to do to satisfy the local tax requirements.

The group unilaterally agreed. Bingo! This tentative and fragile agreement was the victory that we could build on to later reach a firmer sense of agreement and consensus. The next step was to document the extent of this agreement so that everyone would be (literally) on the same page.

Part 4: Document

J&J Elements Covered:
Solidify adjustments

As you proceed through your negotiations in the previous part, you should document each agreement in detail and ensure that both parties agree to what you have documented. It is this agreed-upon document that is going to form the basis of cooperation between the two parties in the future.

With this document, once again the devil is in the details. Ensure that you use precise, descriptive language and try not to use conflated or ambiguous words. This document should be unsexy but accurate: its purpose is not to enthuse or inspire, but to accurately describe the agreement in all of its boringly descriptive and unexciting glory.

As you build up this document, check in formally with each party to gain agreement on each addition. By the end of the discussions, when you have consensus on all major areas, the document should not be a surprise to anyone.

The fantastical user group debacle. In the case of our friends Alan and Lee, I spent a total of three calls with them fleshing out a conclusion to the conflict. In each call we made progress, and with each agreement I noted the precise results in a document we all shared. After each meeting, I emailed them with a summary of what we agreed and the total set of agreements. The act of documenting our progress and sharing it fostered a real sense of progress.

Part 5: Reflect and maintain

The final part of the conflict resolution process is twofold: to maintain progress on the agreed-upon outcomes and to encourage a general sense of personal development in the members of the conflict.

The former goal is an exercise in keeping your wheels on the road. Just because you have a set of written, agreed-upon outcomes doesn't mean anyone is going to stick with them. Don't hold the members' hands as they execute the outcomes, but check in every so often and ensure that everything is running smoothly. This can often be as simple as a quick email to each party to see how things are going. To ensure that you don't forget, it's often useful to put it in your calendar for a few weeks' time.

The second element is subtle yet important. In many cases of conflict, the participants often become very reflective at a later date. Many will review their actions and their conduct, and while they will remain resolute in some of their opinions, they may also express regret at how they handled certain situations.

These reflective lessons are valuable, and your community needs reinforcement when they happen. To see why, think back to when you have made your own reflections on your life. When someone has been by your side to cheer you on, it gives you much more determination to be consistent in the change. Because you are the person who helped get these two parties through the conflict, they will be looking to you for guidance and validation.

Offering this validation is something worth doing, but it must be done very carefully. There is a fine line between validating and patronizing. Help to validate them, but listen carefully to the feelings they express, and don't rush. Get it right, and not only have you unblocked the conflict but you have helped to improve someone's life inside and outside your community.

The fantastical user group debacle. After finishing the conflict negotiation with Alan, Lee, and the wider group, I stayed in regular touch with everyone, and I am still in touch with them today. I have chatted informally with them on IRC and on the phone—and while blowing the froth off a few cold ones—and have helped to reinforce their growth. While I've helped them, they have also helped me—a lot. The reason I picked their story for this example is no coincidence: it is their conflict that helped me to really understand the topic better—but more importantly, to understand them better. At its heart, conflict is about understanding people and helping them to understand each other, and by exploring and learning some of these approaches, sooner or later you will have your own Alan and Lee story to take lessons from.

Dealing with Burnout

So far in this chapter we have explored the importance of conflict, the different elements of the conflict resolution process, and how to step through it. The majority of this content can be applied when people fall out, get frustrated, get out of bed on the wrong side, and otherwise end up in the ditch. Unfortunately, there is one other element in life that specifically falls into the "not fun" category: *burnout*.

> **NOTE**
> Although I have always dreamed that when someone shouts, "Is there a doctor on the plane?" I can step up to the plate, unfortunately, I am not a doctor, and you should remember this as you read this section. My carefully scrawled and spellchecked words are no replacement for the opinion of a medical professional. If you are worried about burnout, see your doctor and get some advice.

Burnout is a problem that affects all walks of life, all people, and all professions. As such, it is a problem that affects all communities, and yours is no different. Burnout refers to long-term exhaustion that typically causes lack of interest and focus. Unfortunately, it can be devilishly difficult to spot and prevent in your community.

Burnout appears as a series of often subtle changes in personality, perspective, values, and behavior in the sufferer. As these changes progress, it can be difficult to identify that members are suffering from burnout. Unfortunately, burnout often is misdiagnosed as irrationality, short temperament, unusual and strange behavior, lack of tolerance, or for the ladies out there, accusations of "the wrong time of the month."

While it is difficult to identify categorically, fortunately there is some compelling research that was first published in the June/July 2006 issue of *Scientific American* in an article called "Burned Out." It presented the findings of two psychologists, Herbert Freudenberger and Gail North, and their *Burnout Cycle*. The cycle is composed of 12 phases that outline the progressively serious steps that are part of burnout.

These steps don't necessarily happen in a sequential order (it can vary from person to person), and some sufferers will skip some of the steps whereas others will dwell longer on them. These steps offer an interesting list of warning signs for potential burnout victims. Let's take a look at them:

1. A compulsion to prove oneself

   Often burnout is triggered by an obsessive commitment to prove yourself. This desire is founded in demonstrating to your colleagues and particularly yourself that you can knock the ball out of the park.

2. Working harder

   To knock the aforementioned ball out of the aforementioned park, hard work is needed. This is manifested in long days, longer nights, and an inability to switch off results.

3. Neglecting one's own needs

   In this stage, simple pleasures such as sleeping, eating, socializing with friends, and watching *Seinfeld* are seen as just that: pleasures, and as such, a distraction from work. (I am not sure if there is a proven connection between a lack of *Seinfeld* and burnout, but there should be.)

4. Displacement of conflicts

   In this stage, you don't really understand the problems that you have. If they lead to discomfort or even panic, the victim dismisses the impressions because they feel threatening.

5. Revision of values

   In this phase, the obsession and focus of work means that traditional values such as friends or hobbies are dismissed, rejected, and pushed aside. Here your only evaluation of success is being good at your job.

6. Denial of emerging problems

   In this phase, cynicism, intolerance, and aggression raise their ugly heads. Colleagues are dismissed as idiots. Your increasing problems are blamed on lack of time, incompetent coworkers, and unfair workloads.

7. Withdrawal

   You reduce your social interaction and contacts to a minimum and dial up your work to 11. You may start relieving the stress by boozing more often during the week or possibly even resorting to drugs. Whatever your choice of substance, you appear to be indulging in it a little more than usual—and dangerously so.

8. Obvious behavioral changes

   Your strange and erratic behavior is obvious to your friends, family, and colleagues. You are not yourself, and your nearest and dearest can see it a mile off.

9. Depersonalization

   At this point you feel like you offer no value to the world, and lack confidence in what you feel you could once do. Your life feels like one long series of mechanical and emotionless functions.

10. Inner emptiness

You feel an expressed sense of emptiness. You resort more to booze or drugs or possibly find relief in overeating, strange and exaggerated sexual behavior, or other activities.

11. Depression

    Here you feel hopeless, lost, and exhausted, and see little in the way of rays of light for the future.

12. Burnout syndrome

    At this, the most serious level, you feel suicidal and desperate for a way out. You are on the verge of mental and physical collapse and need medical support and attention.

Wow, by the end of reading that lot you may want to go and pet a small animal, watch *The Sound of Music*, or sniff a rose. It is pretty frightening stuff, and unfortunately it appears to be prevalent.

Some of you will have read the list and identified with many of these steps, whereas others of you will be identifying friends, family, or colleagues who may have exhibited some of the steps. I have met and known people who have exhibited almost all the behaviors described in these steps, and when serious burnout takes its grip, it can destroy families, careers, and many other aspects of life.

Detecting and Treating Burnout

With the risks evident in the list of symptoms, you are sure to be wondering what is the best approach to manage this risk. Is there a way to identify and react to burnout in your community?

This is something I have participated in during various discussion sessions at different conferences. Unfortunately, there is no recipe or secret formula for dealing with burnout in a community. The best solution is to subscribe to one simple philosophy that has helped people deal with complex life changes and decisions for years:

> I got your back, dude.

Although it may seem outrageously simple, the easiest and most applicable method is to first develop a nose for symptoms and to then extend a personal hand of friendship to the sufferer. Having that sense of companionship through a tough time can really help with burnout.

To detect the symptoms you should first read, reread, and then read again the 12 items in the Burnout Cycle. These items provide a core set of knowledge for understanding the nature of burnout. You should then keep a general eye out for these symptoms in your community. Specifically look for and be conscious of changes in behavior. If someone just "doesn't seem herself," she may be getting bitten by burnout. It is these changes in behavior that are the typical signs.

If you suspect that someone is getting burned out, just strike up a personal conversation and be entirely frank. Tell the person you noticed she has been a little different recently and that you are concerned. Ask her if she is OK, and ask if there is anything you can help with. In many cases the person will tell you what is on her mind, what is stressing her out, and any problems she appears to be having.

With overwork as a common cause of burnout, you should also ask how she is coping with her workload and if there is anything you can do to ease it. This offer of help in itself can be a stress reliever—it is a validation that someone is there to help her get through her TODO list.

Required rest and relaxation

One of the most effective methods of shackling up burnout is to get away from things and unwind. It is amazing how a small vacation can help someone decompress.

This happened to me when I felt I was burning out. I felt like I wasn't myself and could feel how stressed and anxious I was. To deal with this, I went to Ireland for a long weekend to visit a friend. It is incredible how those few days with a friendly face, getting out in the countryside, having a few drinks, and getting away from a computer helped.

If you suspect you or someone else is burning out, tell him to do the same and get away for a few days. He will almost certainly claim he can't or doesn't need to, but stand firm: it is for his own good, and he will thank you for it.

VOLUNTEERISM ESCAPES NOTHING

When on the subject of communities and stress, looks can be deceiving. Although most communities are firmly wedged in the volunteer category, that doesn't mean their participants don't develop, feel, and react to stress. The lack of compulsion behind volunteers' involvement and contribution does not mean volunteers who feel stress can just go and do something else. People grow attached to communities, their ethos, and their sense of family. The involvement may not be contractually required, but it is often emotionally required inside the mind of the contributor.

Work/Life Balance

At the center of the somewhat unpleasant universe that is burnout is the problem of balance. Although there is little concrete scientific evidence to determine who burnout is more likely to pick on, mere observational evidence suggests that technical folks, musicians, counselors, authors, and teachers have a higher than normal risk of reserving a place on the dreaded Burnout Cycle.

Balance is a surprisingly complicated goal for many to achieve, particularly if your community is an online, Internet-based community. Years ago it was easier to get balance: you simply switched off your computer and went and lived the parts of your life that didn't involve a mouse and a keyboard. As the Internet has steamed into our lives more and more, the amount of time in our lives that doesn't involve said mouse and keyboard is being reduced.

In addition to the familiar tools of the workplace, such as email, office suites, web browsers, and accounting packages, we now have social networking websites such as Facebook and MySpace; blogging sites such as Blogger and Wordpress.com; microblogging with Twitter and identi.ca; and online chat services such as Skype, Google GChat, MSN, Yahoo! IM, and AIM. Let's also not forget the entertainment on the Web: countless websites, animations, videos, and articles are all there to attract us to the computer. We can then seal the deal with the myriad other online facilities such as Internet banking, review websites, mapping tools, online shopping, games, and more.

It is easy to see how this merry band of pixelated distractions can take Ctrl, and it is not entirely unsurprising that someone could spend a whole day and most of an evening in front of a computer. This is itself not exactly healthy: computers are great, but everyone should spend some time away from them to decompress, get some fresh air, and energize other attributes of the human condition, such as going out, playing sports, spending time with friends, embracing a loved one, and other fun things that don't involve staring intently at a screen.

Addiction

The problem is that when the rest of your life is wrapped with window borders, you are only ever a click away from either work or other commitments, such as community. While we want to encourage our community members to throw themselves into our goals and enjoy every moment of it, it is important to ensure that in the process of doing so they don't ignore and neglect other parts of their lives.

Addiction has affected many online communities: there are contributors and members who spend every conceivable moment of their lives embedded in the community. This can be seen everywhere. I know of many people today who appear to be constantly online at all times of the day, always responsive to chat messages and queries and seemingly never away from their screens.

For many this is an agreeable choice that they can step away from when needed. Many people can wake up at 7 a.m., work all day, spend the entire evening in front of the computer in pursuits of their own, head to bed at 1 a.m. or 2 a.m., and spend a valuable six hours sleeping, only to wake up and repeat. That may be OK because these people can easily go away for a weekend, spend a few evenings doing something else, and go on vacation without getting jittery. For some, though, even spending one evening—let alone a whole weekend!—away from their familiar screen can seem like too much. In these cases we are seeing strong signs of *addiction*.

You should be very cautious of addiction: it is never healthy in anyone. Unfortunately, the nature of the addicted beast typically means these people are in a state of denial about their condition. Just as with alcohol, cigarettes, or gambling, claims of "I could stop if I wanted to" are often thrown in the general direction of naysayers, but these claims are rarely, if ever, tested.

The reason for your caution is that at some point an addicted member *will* burn out. It may take longer than expected, but when it does, it could have catastrophic results. Keep an eye on your community members and how much they are online: if it feels like too much, a quick and sensitive word in their ear can help them get away for a few days.

Handling Absence

One of the most challenging things to deal with in a community is when your community members leave. Of course, there are many reasons why people may leave, but they can be broadly divided into three categories:

Planned

> Planned absences are when a community member provides notice that she either will be away for a period of time or is leaving for good. This can include going on vacation, having children, taking some time away from the community to decompress, and so on.

Gradual

> Some community members will gradually reduce their involvement as time goes on without any notice or intent to give notice. This can often happen when people simply get busy with other things and their availability is reduced, as well as when a member doesn't enjoy the community as much as he did, yet doesn't want to commit to leaving.

Abrupt

> Sometimes a community member will just vanish. This can be caused by a new relationship (someone falls head over heels in love and vanishes for a while to live his life to the soundtrack of *Dirty Dancing*), a blowout with someone in the community, or an illness; unfortunately, sometimes people vanish for unknown reasons.

In your community you always want to strive to be able to plan for absence and identify ways to fill in the gaps where possible. As such, you should always encourage a culture in which your community members inform one another when they are going away for a while (or for good). You should also encourage a culture of leaders stepping down gracefully (this is something we have done in Ubuntu as part of our Code of Conduct, and it has worked well).

In cases when an absence is abrupt and unexpected, your first goal is to ensure that the community member is OK. Check in with him and see if there are any problems you can help to resolve. If it looks like he will be coming back, try to get an estimate of how long he will be gone and use this as a means to find someone to cover his work while he is away. If he doesn't plan to come back you should build some buzz to find a replacement for his role in the community.

Handling Bereavement

The death of a community member can be a challenging and difficult time. It can also be a surprisingly heartwarming time, as your community pulls together like a family to console and support one another.

In 2011, a member of the Ubuntu community died; he was called Andre. He was a prominent and active member of the Brazilian community and was a popular and well-loved friend to those who knew him. Unfortunately, Andre had been suffering from some health issues for some time, and many people didn't know about this as he kept these challenges to himself. He died the week of one of our Ubuntu Developer Summits.

I had not handled the death of a community member before. I made sure to mark his memory and his wonderful contributions to our community, but to also not tell people how they should grieve; I believe grief is a very personal journey. To find this balance I decided to hold a minute of silence in the closing ceremony of the summit and put up a big picture of Andre. Another member of the community also organized a book so that people could write their condolences and memories for Andre's family.

Although this was a sad time, the way the community came together to support one another, celebrate Andre's memory, and be there for one another as a family was a memorable and warming experience. My advice, if you need to handle a similar situation, is to be respectful in marking the memory of the member who passed while also being respectful of the different ways in which people grieve.

Summary

Throughout this chapter, we have explored some of the darker alleys of community leadership. While working with community is an unbridled pleasure and joy 90% of the time, the remaining 10% of life can be the most difficult and sensitive to deal with. This 10% can also bring the most stress to your table and is the most likely cause of uncertainty in how to move forward.

The most important thing to remember through all of this is that conflict and its associated resolution is not new. It is as old as the world itself, and countless generations of people just like you have learned how to deal with contentious issues before you. While the topics and advice covered in this chapter will get you off to a great start, you should do your best to find a mentor. Find someone who has been around these parts before, and ask her if she will advise you from time to time about where to go when faced with a fork in the road. Accept that the first few times you mediate, you'll make mistakes—and don't feel bad if the outcome is less successful than you had hoped.

Great community resolution is based on experience. The advice throughout this chapter, combined with the advice from a mentor and augmented with your own growing body of knowledge, will combine to help you handle these testing situations elegantly, and before long you will become the mentor to others.

Good luck!

CHAPTER TWELVE

Creating and Running Events

"The meeting of two personalities is like the contact of two
chemical substances; if there is any reaction, both are
transformed."

—*Carl Gustav Jung*

ON JULY 3, 2001, MY FRIEND LEE JORDAN AND I BOARDED THE TRAIN FROM
WOLVERHAMPTON TO LONDON. It was early, we had barely slept the previous night, and
we should have been grumpy. We were not, though. We were on our way to the Linux Expo
at the Olympia Exhibition Hall to run an exhibition stand for the KDE project, and we were
jazzed up.

We'd spent two weeks building up to the event, gathering t-shirts, posters, fliers,
demonstration machines, leaflets, customized name badges, and more. I was determined to
make sure that anyone and everyone who walked past our 6' × 4' booth would leave with a
memory. Of course, I hoped this memory would be of the incredible technology behind the
KDE desktop as opposed to the tired-looking, long-haired 22-year-old with a guitar pick on a
chain around his neck.

We got far more than we bargained for. The booth was well received and was in itself a learning
experience. We got to understand expectations around KDE far better, got to show off and
educate people about the project, and met a number of new contacts. In addition to this, we
met many members from elsewhere in the open source community. We also got to meet a
range of open source companies and publishers (in fact, it was at that show where I scored my

first writing gig). Finally, while at a social event at a nearby pub, I found myself in between Alan Cox and Jon "maddog" Hall, two legends in our community.

Afterward, tired and weary, Lee and I dragged ourselves back to Euston Station, boarded our train, and for the first time in three days, sat down and breathed.

My body was utterly exhausted, but my mind was exhilarated. I had just experienced a roller coaster of thrills. I had traveled to a place I was unfamiliar with. I represented a community I was proud of, met people I had only chatted with online, shook the hands of two of my open source heroes, and even managed to score the chance to get an article printed in a magazine. In the same way my very first encounter with community way back in Chapter 1 inspired me to explore it further, this, my first event, secured my desire to make my passion for community my career.

Building Family Values

Way back in the first chapter, I waxed lyrical about *belonging*. This is the magical substance that builds strong, enjoyable, and motivated communities. Communities that instill a sense of belonging in their members are, by definition, mature and capable. Those who belong feel productive and empowered, and they form the firm foundation of your community.

Although many of the workflow approaches we have covered in this book will build a sleek, efficient, and effective community, the impact of these approaches on belonging is primarily by association. When you have smooth processes and infrastructure in your community, it makes the community feel effortless, and it makes your community members feel productive. When they are productive and enjoy the fruits of their labor, a sense of belonging begins to develop.

Great communities are built on great relationships. When people *really* feel a sense of belonging they are enjoying not only being productive but also swimming in the tide of your community's personality. When you put productive people together in a room (real or virtual) and they feel a sense of *family*, your community will be inundated with belonging.

Family is the operative word here. Many of us traditionally feel it from our experiences with our parents and siblings, but we feel it elsewhere, too. Many will feel a sense of family in their local bars and restaurants, at their school or college, in coffee shops, and elsewhere. The sense of family exists when you not only feel a sense of belonging, but also share a very deep and personal connection with other people.

The difference between *belonging* and *family* is subtle yet important. It is entirely possible that people can feel a sense of belonging and yet have little in the way of a personal engagement with other community members. I have seen countless examples of members who enjoy an administrative role in a community, be it system administration, resource management, or something else. These members often enjoy the nuts and bolts of helping the community but rarely socialize or engage with their fellow members. They feel a sense of belonging because they know their contributions are respected by the wider community and that their work is important for the community to prosper.

As community leaders we should aim for belonging but strive for family. A key technique for achieving this is *events*.

Events

Most mornings my alarm goes off at 7:30 a.m. I wake up, grumble at the alarm, and then drag my sorry arse downstairs where I bow at the altar of the coffeemaker. Still waking up, I struggle to comprehend the coffee-making steps. I bumble through the process, spilling water everywhere, getting coffee grounds stuck to my bathrobe, and generally hating the world until I have finished chugging my thermos of wake-up juice that I clutch for dear life as I read my email.

My day then consists of the same approximate set of ingredients. I spend the morning on the phone with my team, colleagues, community members, and journalists. I then attack my inbox with a piercing determination, grab a sandwich for lunch, and spend the afternoon working on my objectives and initiatives. This, my friends, is my routine.

Your community has a routine, too. Every day your community members will engage in their own set of stock interactions with your community. This may be sending email, having conversations, producing things, or other activities. Whatever these actions may be, they will happen each and every day—neither different nor unexpected. So far in *The Art of Community*, the topics we have discussed have been the fodder that helps make this routine as enjoyable and productive as possible.

This is still, however, routine. It is healthy to break routine. For many, this means a vacation, visits from friends and family, and other time away from the community. If you want to break routine yet still have your community contributing, an excellent solution is to organize and run *events*.

Events are special, focused times in which a group of people do the same thing. This could be a large gathering such as a conference or a small online meeting. Regardless of what the event is, every event gathers together a group of people at a set time. This gathering of people can be hugely motivating for a community.

As we will discuss in more detail a little later, events don't have to be physical face-to-face meetings. They don't have to be large and formalized, and they don't have to be complex and expensive to organize. Events can be small, informal, and based online.

Whatever kind of event you organize, it can offer a range of benefits to your community:

Building family

Bringing people together, particularly in social settings, helps to build a sense of family. You want to have your community not only get on well in a productive sense, but also get on well as friends. We will discuss this more later.

Breaking the routine

All events break the routine. As an example, if you are an online, software-oriented community, a physical event such as a conference or summit will get you out of the house or office and meeting people and sharing conversations. In the same manner, an online meeting will also break the routine: it will bring people together for a shared discussion, which is often fun and exciting to be a part of.

Focusing the mind

Events provide an excellent opportunity to focus your members on given projects or targets. Many events focus on a particular date, release, or project. An example of this is the Ubuntu Developer Summit, which focuses on the next release of Ubuntu.

Identifying leaders

Organizing an event almost always inspires the leaders and strongest personalities in your community to bubble up to the surface. This is an excellent opportunity to note these leaders as you grow your community. Events also allow new people to shine: those who might not be programmers or master quilters—or whatever your community focuses on— can exercise other talents when organizing the event.

Taking the pulse

Events are a useful opportunity to get some insight into the goings-on of your community. This insight will most typically be shared in social events, such as casual meetings in the bar during the evenings of a conference.

These benefits all help not only to keep your community productive, but also to excite, focus, and energize them. Events are an excellent opportunity to really fire up your community, produce social bonds, and sow the seeds for long and rewarding contributions to your community. Events are not merely nice, optional variations of the norm; they should be a regular part of your community's growth.

Although all events used to fall into the same broad category of face-to-face meetings, the explosion of the Internet and digital connectivity has opened the door to a new breed of event that augments these traditional localized meetings.

As such, events can be divided into two broad categories: *physical* and *online* events. We will examine both areas in detail throughout this chapter, but let's first have a look at how to organize events in general.

Getting Organized

Events, particularly physical events, are big barrels of details. Everyone I have ever spoken to regarding event organization has always learned the hard way that being organized is the only way to ensure that all of your plans land on the ground running. Getting a detail wrong can undermine the entire event. For example, you may have a perfectly laid out conference but forget to get signs made with directions to the different rooms, so people struggle to find the location of the talks they are interested in.

Step 1: Identify Requirements

You need to choose which kind of event you would like to organize and then identify which steps are involved. We will defer discussion of these steps until a little later when we delve into the different needs for various physical and online events.

When you have an idea of these needs, write them down and flesh out an action plan for carrying out that specific component. As an example, if one of those items is accommodation, you should note each step involved in sourcing accommodation.

Step 2: Find Help

The next step is to find people to help you organize the event. This is particularly important for physical events. For smaller events, such as small sprints, you may not require much help, but for larger events, such as conferences and summits, you will definitely need help.

For physical events it helps to find people in your community who are happy to look after specific roles. Here are some of the role divisions that may apply to the events you run (not all will apply to every event):

Accommodation
  This person organizes the hotel options and reservations.

Sponsorship
  If you are seeking sponsorship for the event, you should have a single point of contact to deal with the sponsors.

Merchandise
  If you have t-shirts, lanyards, and other items that need to be arranged, this person organizes these.

Speaker liaison
  This person will work to find and schedule speakers. This person also manages the scheduling of speakers.

Special events and catering
   This person will arrange any catering requirements as well as social events, parties, and additional gatherings.

When you have these roles identified and filled, you should organize regular meetings where organizers update one another on their progress in organizing the event and discuss further work and any problems.

I recommend that you hold these meetings every two weeks at first, and in the two months leading up to the event, accelerate the meetings to be held weekly. I also recommend that you organize conference calls, if possible, to host the meetings, although an online chat medium will also work.

> **N O T E**
>
> Here I have listed only the roles that apply to physical events. Physical events are always much more complicated to organize than their online counterparts: there are a lot more components to figure out, and many of these components rely on outside parties, such as hotels, catering companies, equipment providers, and more. Although you can divide online event organization into roles, too, online events typically require far less work and can be organized by a single person.
>
> If you find that your event is too much to handle for a single person, though, do break it into roles in a similar way.

Step 3: Set Deadlines

This is what I consider the most valuable step of all in organizing your event. You should look at the range of components in your event planning and produce a set of deadlines that provide plenty of time to achieve those tasks.

Imagine you are organizing a conference. For each major task listed in the previous section, you should prepare a set of deadlines. As an example, these could be some deadlines for the process of opening up a call for papers, choosing proposals, and announcing the final decided list of speakers:

- February 23—Begin planning Call for Papers and put together website form for submissions.
- March 9—Open up the event's Call for Papers and publicize.
- April 13—Announce "One week left!" for the Call for Papers.
- April 20—Call for Papers closes. Announce.
- April 21—Begin reviewing submitted papers.

- April 27—Final list of papers decided. Notify all those who submitted papers of their success/rejection. Request confirmation of attendance. Begin developing the schedule.
- May 4—Announce the schedule.

When you set this collection of deadlines, you should ensure that your fellow organizers can see them, too. A great solution to this is to set up a shared calendar on a service such as Google Calendar and ensure that each organizer has access.

Step 4: Make Time

The world is becoming an increasingly busy place, and time is an ever-rarer resource. You are a busy person, too: you are involved in your community; you are working to improve, enrich, and inspire; and you have your own set of tasks and responsibilities to look after. With so much going on, making the commitment to run an event can be daunting. All of the event organizers I have spoken to about their first few events have always waxed lyrical about how much more time was required than they expected. You should ensure that you block out a good amount of time so that you can give your event the amount of care and feeding that it deserves.

GOOGLE AND EVENTS

Leslie Hawthorn leads the outreach side of Google's Open Source Programs Office, which focuses primarily on Google's student programs, the Google Summer of Code for university students, and the Google Highly Open Participation Contest for precollege students. Leslie has also been involved in the organization of many conferences, including the Ubuntu Developer Summits in 2006 and 2008, MeetBSD 2008 conference, GitTogether '08, LugRadio Live USA 2008, and DjangoCon 2008. Leslie's team has hosted more than 100 community events at the Google HQ over the past three years, and has worked with community members on hundreds of sponsorships for other community events during that time frame.

Leslie is intimately familiar with the problem of not allocating enough time for an event:

"My basic rule on timing is to assume everything, from writing up conference call notes to catering setup, will take at least two hours longer than I've planned and to build in that margin for error into the whole of the event plan. It's far better to have an extra few hours to brainstorm, have a coffee, and take stock than to run around fixing issues and leaving out details at the last minute. It makes for a much better experience for the event organizers, as well, as they can focus on the pleasure of interacting with and learning from the attendees instead of putting out fires."

When considering how much time to allocate to your event organization, you should not only determine the preparation time needed, but also how much time you have available when the event is *happening*.

The days that the event is running are an incredibly stressful time for an organizer, and many of the frustrations and difficulties are caused by the pressures of time constraints. Always try to factor in more time than you need: having everything ready and waiting is a lot more fun than running around like a headless chicken panicking about time. Leslie also has some words of wisdom on this topic:

"People generally underestimate the amount of time it will take to get things done, even when there are many hands to help with planning and execution. I've found this situation to be especially true the day of an event; folks often don't leave themselves enough time for setup and attendees are left standing around waiting for the party to really get started.

"Folks also tend to assume that a larger group of folks organizing logistics is better, but I've found this scenario only holds true when you have one or two charismatic folks giving direction to the rest of the organizing team. Without clear instruction, people tend to get distracted by less important details or talking with friends, and a great organizer knows both how to detect these lags early (and often) and how to politely refocus efforts on the task at hand.

"Also, your event managers need to remain available to direct traffic rather than jumping into the fray until the finishing touches are required; shifting focus from directing to doing can leave some folks unclear on what should happen next, particularly when they're in a brand-new location and are unfamiliar with how best to utilize the space or a venue's processes for setup, etc. When people aren't sure what to do, this leads to distraction for those team members who are focused on a particular task. As tempting as it is to jump in and help when managing an event, it's best to hold back and make sure the organizing team feels empowered to get things done and clearly understands what's expected of them."

Time is an important resource. Make sure you have plenty of it at your disposal, and it will put your event in good stead.

Organizing Physical Events

I don't have space to cover all the types of events you might want to hold, so I'll focus on the most popular and common events:

Sprints

> Common in the software development world, a sprint is when a number of (traditionally online-based) developers get together to work in the same physical location. The foundation of a sprint is merely to be in the same room working, but people naturally use the opportunity of being in the same location to have discussions, solve problems, and perform other activities.

Summits

> Summits are organized events in which the members have a series of discussion and debate sessions. Summits rarely have prepared presentations where someone speaks and the

audience listens. Summits are instead a series of discussion sessions that hopefully result in an outcome. We will talk more about summits a little later in this chapter.

Conferences

Conferences are composed of a series of presentations in which a speaker talks about a topic and the audience listens. Conferences are primarily useful for disseminating knowledge to others. Conferences are also a useful place to get people together for other events. Some communities deliberately collocate other events, such as sprints, at times and places near conferences that many people will be attending, in order to make it cheaper and easier for potential attendees to visit both.

Cons

Cons (usually short for conventions) are popular in the user community, particularly in story-related communities such as movies and comics. These events are focused on fans coming together to celebrate something (e.g., *Star Trek* fans coming together to discuss the show, showcase their outfits, and participate in other strange activities).

Release parties

Release parties celebrate the release of something. These parties are common in the software, movie, and gaming worlds. These parties are often social gatherings in pubs and restaurants and have real value in building community. Some release events are fuller and incorporate presentations, workshops, and other features.

Each type of event is composed of broadly the same ingredients: a group of people meeting at the same venue to do something. The way they differ is in the focus of the event, be it working together (sprint), discussing ideas (summit), sharing knowledge (conference), coming together to meet like minds (cons), or celebrating something (release parties).

It should also be noted that physical events are excellent opportunities for socializing with your community. With each event, there is invariably an adjoining set of social events and parties to get your community members to enjoy one another's company.

Common Attributes

Although it may seem like the different types of physical events are very dissimilar, they all share some common ingredients. Before we move on to look at the specifics of some of these events, I want to discuss a few of these shared ingredients that apply to *all* physical events. When you have a firm idea of how these ingredients will look, you will be 90% of the way to having your event ready.

NOTE

For each of the following elements, ensure that you document all the details on a website. Your event website is a critical component of your physical event, and visitors will expect it to be up-to-date.

It is also recommended that you have a private organizers' website that can act as a home for the many organizational details that develop as the different parts of the event are put together. Ensure that this information is there, too.

Location/venue

All physical events need a home. The first choice you need to make is the location. If you are organizing an event in which you expect your community to fund their own travel to attend, you should try to choose a location that is as convenient as possible for most of your members who are likely to attend. As an example, if most of your members are on the East Coast of the United States, hold it there. If most of your members are in Australia, hold it there.

Choosing a venue for your event depends heavily on the kind of event you are organizing. If you are holding a sprint, a small venue is likely to be suitable, such as a hotel meeting room. If you are organizing a large conference, you may need a larger and more complex venue.

In addition to choosing the size of the venue, you should consider some other, subtler elements:

Public transportation
> Can your attendees get there on public transportation, and can they get elsewhere in the area, too?

Distance from airport/train/bus stations
> Many of your attendees may be flying in from other countries or getting trains/buses to the event. You should try to aim for a venue that is a reasonable distance from those transport links. If people will incur a hefty taxi bill to get to the venue, you will get some frustrated attendees.

Distance from accommodations
> Many people who attend an event may be in a hotel. Is the venue within a reasonable distance? There are few things more frustrating than a venue with no nearby accommodation.

Proximity to eating/drinking establishments
> If you are holding an all-day event (as many of these events are), you should ensure that your attendees can easily get to local bars and restaurants. Ensure that the range here is as flexible as possible, too: are there vegetarian, vegan, and halal options? Many of your attendees will want to get together for some drinks and dinner. You should ensure that the bars and restaurants are within reasonable distance, and if not, ensure that public transportation can get people to them.

Cost

Venues range hugely in terms of cost. Here you should think imaginatively: consider some less obvious venues as suitable options. As an example, when we were organizing LugRadio Live in the United Kingdom, we considered options such as bars, music venues, and outdoor events. Unfortunately, desirable choices for many of the other items on this list tend to require a high-cost location, because that's the kind of location near airports, nice restaurants, and so on.

A subtle consideration when choosing a venue is how your audience will perceive it. As an example, if you run a business community, you may want to choose a venue that is more professionally oriented, such as a business center or hotel conference facility. If your community is more low-key, you will have more flexibility with venue choice.

When I was involved in organizing LugRadio Live, a loose, social, and informal event that was part of our LugRadio podcast, we discounted many venues due to the "feel." We were explicitly looking to achieve a social environment for the show, and many available places didn't fit, including university lecture theaters and hotel conference facilities. We instead chose student union bars, independent theaters, and football stadium facilities: the latter all immediately expressed a more social and fun feel than the former.

Another consideration is the venue's environmental impact on the mood of the event. When we organized the Ubuntu Developer Summit in Seville, Spain, the venue was in a large underground conference facility in a hotel. There were no windows, making the summit feel more constrained and causing people to tire earlier. The lack of windows meant attendees could not see daylight, and as such could not judge the time of day as the light changed.

THE COMMUNITY CASE BOOK

Contracts in the meeting and hospitality industry can be tricky and often contain hidden expenses or restrictions that may not be obvious to you at first.

—*Ilan Rabinovitch, on Contracts*

Read the full interview in Chapter 14.

Accommodation

For many physical events, people from out of town will attend. This will usually mean they need to stay in a hotel. Many will expect you to tell them about reasonable hotel options, so you should provide these on your event's website.

There are three tasks that you should work on in terms of accommodation:

Provide a range of options

Everyone has different budgets when it comes to hotels. Provide details for a range of room rates and quality.

Negotiate a special room rate

Call each hotel in the area and ask if they can organize a special room rate for you. Many hotels will provide a room rate if you ask your attendees to give the hotel the event name or a special code. One thing to be cautious of: some hotels want you to reserve a block of the hotel for the discounted rate. This is risky if this is your first conference. Whatever you do, do not put down an unaffordable deposit to reserve the rooms with the expectation that people will come. It is too risky.

Document your hotels

Put a travel page on your website that contains all the hotels people can stay at. List the hotels in order, starting with the one offering the largest discount on the nightly rate. Ensure that you include the full address of the hotel (with zip/postal code so that people can put it in their GPS units), as well as the telephone number.

You will probably find one or two hotels that are particularly accommodating (pun intended) to you and your event. Many of these hotels are hoping for repeat business in future years if the event becomes an annual fixture. These relationships can often blossom with positive effects on your event over the years. When we organized LugRadio Live, our regular hotels would go increasingly out of their way to provide a great service for us and our guests. Keep these hotel representatives in your circle of professional friends.

You should always pick primary hotels for your event. When traveling to an event from out of town and not knowing any of the natives, your attendees will want to be in a hotel with other attendees so that they can socialize in the hotel bar, share cabs, and coordinate other activities. These primary hotels at events become a social hub. As such, when deciding which hotels will carry this role, ensure that you check facilities such as bars, restaurants, and fitness centers.

BARGAIN HUNTER

When you ask for discounted room rates, it is likely the hotel will push back at first. Persevere. Tell them how important your event is, and tell them that you really want to recommend their hotel as "an" (not "the"; that would be lying) official hotel.

Keep asking and pushing for the discount. You have nothing to lose and lots to gain. If you get that discounted rate, it will make your event more affordable and allow more people to attend.

Equipment

Every event has equipment requirements. This can range from pens and paper to complex IT and networking facilities. You should ensure that you have a clear idea of your equipment needs and that you have a means of meeting them in time for the event.

Although seemingly a simple consideration, figuring out what you need to take to the event may be harder than you think. Imagine you are organizing a sprint. You may think of some of the obvious equipment requirements such as whiteboards, pens, networking equipment, cables, and power strips. There are many less obvious pieces of equipment, however, that you may not have thought of. This could include signs to show people where to go, adhesives such as Blu-Tack and tape, pins, lights, converter cables, speakers, notepads, whiteboard dry wipes, and more. These simple and easily forgotten parts can make a big difference!

To ensure that you don't forget anything, you should jot down your full equipment needs and consult with your community to see if there is anything you have forgotten. And like all your planning, the resultant list will be a useful reference point for future events.

Date/time

You should announce the date of your event at least four months before it happens. For events where you expect international visitors, I recommend you provide six or preferably eight months' advance notice so that there is enough time for visas to be organized. Don't let the wheels of government cause problems. International visas were a scourge on events for the first few years after the attacks of September 11, 2001, and can still get in the way of travel between some countries.

When picking a date for your event, you need to decide on two things:

How long
> How long will your event last? We will discuss this in more detail later when we cover specific types of events.

When
> Picking a time can be complicated. You need to ensure that your event does not conflict with events of similar interest, that the dates are suitable for the venue, and that they do not conflict with any holidays. You will never completely bypass every competing event and holiday, so use your best judgment.

One important tip that so many conferences and events still seem to get wrong: always put the date of your conference on the front page of your website. Don't bury the date three pages deep into the website. It will frustrate potential attendees and might suppress attendance.

Cost

One of the most difficult decisions to make for many events is whether to charge for entry, and if so, how much. Much of this discussion is entirely dependent on the type of event that you are running, its expected attendee demographics, and whether the event seeks to make a profit.

This was something we considered heavily for LugRadio Live. The event was very much intended to be a community event. It was never intended to make any profit. The only concern was covering the cost of the event (and much of this was reduced due to sponsorship, which we will discuss later).

One conscious decision for LugRadio Live was to make it affordable for everyone. We were not especially big fans (to say the least) of open source conferences for which community members were expected to pony up $800 to attend. We felt this produced a false economy: a conference in which significant portions of the demographic of open source members were unable to attend.

On the other hand, even though we had enough sponsorship to make the entrance to LugRadio Live free, we decided to charge a nominal fee (£5 at the door). The reason for the charge was subtle: if something is free, people will rarely commit to it. Even with a tiny cover charge, it would mean people who registered to attend would actually show up.

Registering attendance

For many events there should be a means for attendees to let you know in advance that they are going to attend.

Having this information is useful for a few reasons. By far the biggest worry in organizing an event is whether people are actually going to show up. This is typically less of a worry for invitation-only sprints, but a significant cause of nervous twitching when organizing a conference. It is always advisable to have a way for people to register their attendance so that you have an idea of where your numbers stand. Another benefit of knowing these numbers is that if you have an outright success on your hands and are likely to have many more people attending, you can make preparations to deal with the increased traffic at the event.

It is important to remember, though, that conference preregistration figures often don't reflect the final attendance, particularly for events that are free or where people can pay at the door. In these cases, where there is simply no justification for them to preregister, there needs to be a reason and a catalyst, such as limited availability or discounted ticket prices. In the eyes of a prospective attendee, simply saying, "It helps the organizers know how many people are coming" is not adequate justification for preregistering; justification needs to be something the attendee will feel is a personal benefit. This is where the cost of your event plays a large role. If you are charging $1,000 for a conference ticket and preregistration allows people to get a $400 discount on the ticket, you will see more preregistrations.

Although many formal events keep attendee lists private, or share the lists only with other attendees, many community events ask attendees to register publicly so that everyone can see who's coming. This provides a small incentive to register in advance: attendees can then encourage colleagues whom they want to meet to come.

Events have different approaches to registering attendance. For the majority of you reading this book, I am willing to bet that you are primarily organizing small summits and sprints for your community. In these cases, a wiki page is a perfect solution: simply ask your community members to add themselves to a page if they plan to attend.

For much larger conferences and sprints, you may want to use a conference management system or a custom website to handle the attendance registration process. You also may want to include an online payment process with your registration facility.

Catering

You need to decide whether you want to have food at your event. For a daytime event, this is most typically lunch and breaks. If it is an evening event, the catering is usually dinner and drinks.

Catering can make the cost of the event balloon, so you need to consider it carefully. An added complication is that many venues will restrict you to using only their on-site kitchen or a specific vendor. You should check this when investigating the venue. Such locked-in vendors usually lead to outrageously inflated costs, but you can't really blame the venue, because it has its own advantages in maintaining a relationship with a vendor who gets to know it well.

Expectations around catering vary. For a small, locally organized event, catering is not typically expected. If you are organizing a large professional conference, lunch will be expected, particularly if you are charging a significant entrance fee. Regardless of what you decide, it is highly recommended that you have drinks available: people get thirsty throughout the day, particularly if there is lots of discussion.

If you do decide to cater your event, a buffet-style format is recommended for both lunch and dinner options. It is easier to organize, promotes socializing (instead of people sitting at the same place at a dinner table all night), and is often cheaper.

IF YOU DON'T CATER...

...you should ensure that you provide details of local, reasonably priced food and drink providers. I always recommend providing a list of fast food restaurants as well as sit-down restaurants and bars. Again, the key is to provide a range of options that can suit as many tastes and budgets as possible.

Insurance/unions

One area that you should properly investigate when planning your event is the insurance needs and possible union requirements for your area. These issues vary tremendously around the world.

I experienced this firsthand when comparing the experience of organizing LugRadio Live in the United Kingdom and in San Francisco. The events were a world apart in terms of insurance and union requirements. The San Francisco event was a far more complicated affair with more rigorous and complex requirements than its UK counterpart.

With the laws and requirements varying so much around the world, it is difficult for me to give any concrete advice other than to ensure that you check these legal elements thoroughly. If you are unsure, ask the venue management for its advice.

> **NOTE**
> You should also make a point of looking into basic first aid facilities. If someone slices his hand open or passes out, you want to be able to react appropriately. Preferably you should have someone available on-site who knows first aid.

Organizing a Sprint

Sprints are events in which your community gathers together to work in the same physical location. Sprints rarely have any special timetabled content, such as talks or presentations, and their primary focus is more on getting people to work individually or on shared projects, taking advantage of the face-to-face time to have discussions and solve problems together where required.

The primary requirement for a sprint is to provide a working environment. This is dependent on the kind of work your community performs, but for most communities it's likely to be a conference room with tables and chairs where your community can sit together to work.

I have organized a number of sprints for different purposes, including specific team sprints for my own team and wider community sprints. You should always allow a sprint to be a sprint. Over the years I have seen many people organize sprints and instead try to turn them into more of a summit, replete with brainstorming sessions. I was one of them. When I used to organize sprints for my team, I would run them largely as minisummits, and we would discuss and flesh out plans for the coming cycle. At one wider team sprint I could not be there with my team, and they reported back that having the opportunity to just work, as opposed to brainstorm, was hugely productive. Since then I have been careful to ensure that sprints are primarily focused on working together. To achieve this, I reserve the mornings for brainstorming and the afternoons for sprinting.

Additional notes

Here are some additional notes that build on the topics I covered in general earlier:

Location/venue

Sprints are typically smaller events and require smaller venues. Bear in mind that the sprint is intended to be a working session, and therefore you may need facilities for this work, such as Internet access, plenty of power outlets, and tables and chairs. For a small sprint the venue can be informal and loose, with many communities sprinting in houses and apartments.

Accommodation

There are no special accommodation requirements for sprints.

Equipment

The equipment requirements depend on the type of work you will be doing. As an example, if you are doing software development, people should bring their own laptops, but you may want to provide blank media, commonly requested cables, power strips, USB storage devices, and so on.

Date/time

The length of the sprint should reflect how long you can reasonably expect people to be together. Do remember that people will need to book time off work to be there, and some may be away from their families and children. I recommend that a sprint range from three to five days. I do not recommend a sprint that lasts longer than a week.

Cost

To the best of your ability, sprints should be free. You should seek to cover your costs with sponsorship if your organization can't pony up the funds itself.

Registering attendance

You will want to get a firm idea of who is coming, but also make the sprint open so that anyone is welcome to attend. Specialist sprints will require specific invitations to the people whom you want to attend.

Catering

Many smaller sprints either provide a buffet lunch or defer lunch to nearby restaurants. You should have plenty of water and cups available, and preferably some sodas or coffee. Some caffeinated beverages are particularly important if you have a long sprint: people will rely on them to wake up in the mornings.

Insurance/unions

As always, check into the insurance requirements for the sprint. There are unlikely to be union issues.

Organizing a Summit

Summits are organized events in which your community gathers to discuss and debate a set of topics with the purpose of accomplishing a goal.

An example of this is the Ubuntu Developer Summit (UDS). During every release cycle, the Ubuntu community gathers together to discuss, debate, and design the next release of Ubuntu. The summit is broken into a number of tracks (community, desktop, server, mobile, quality assurance, etc.), each containing a number of sessions. Each session has a leader who focuses the discussion on the topic, and the attendees weigh in and discuss the best choices. By the end of the session, the expected outcome is a broad solution that can then be documented as a specification from which the community can work.

The UDS is a large and comprehensive summit that has been running for a number of years. It attracts more than 200 attendees, involving a huge range of sessions over multiple concurrent tracks, and remote participation. Organizing and running the event is a large and comprehensive undertaking, and it would require another book the size of *The Art of Community* to discuss all the details. I do, though, want to distill some of the key lessons learned from organizing the UDS that you can apply to your own summits.

Structure and scheduling

The primary goal of a summit is to ensure that people can discuss and debate topics to the point of producing a solution. For this you need to have a template for how many sessions will appear in your schedule. As an example, you might have the following schedule.

8:30 a.m.	Doors Open
9 a.m. – 10 a.m.	Session
10 a.m. – 11 a.m.	Session
11 a.m. – noon	Session
noon – 1 p.m.	Lunch
1 p.m. – 2 p.m.	Session
2 p.m. – 3 p.m.	Session
3 p.m. – 3:30 p.m.	Break
3:30 p.m. – 4:30 p.m.	Session
4:30 p.m. – 5:30 p.m.	Session
5:30 p.m. – 6 p.m.	Closing/Wrap-Up

This schedule is productive but not too taxing on your visitors. It provides six session blocks with breaks for lunch and other rest, ensuring that your attendees don't go for too long without a break, which is always recommended.

If you find that you are going to require more than six sessions on one day, you may want to consider multiple tracks—sessions running at the same time. As an example, at the last UDS there were seven concurrent tracks. Of course, there is an obvious downside to this approach: people can't be in two (or seven!) places at the same time. With this in mind, you need to ensure that the tracks are distinct and will attract different interests.

When having multiple tracks, you should account for a lot of time spent moving around.

Inside a session

For each session, ensure that the room is set up to encourage discussion. Chairs should be in circles or around tables, not facing front, which implies that only the session leader matters.

Each session should have two people serving specific roles:

Leader (also known as a facilitator)
> The leader is responsible for ensuring that the session is kept on-topic. Sessions can easily get sidetracked, so the leader must be prepared to bring discussion back. The leader should also ensure that everyone gets a chance to speak and that the session reaches a conclusion. Every session should result in a set of actions to implement the work that was discussed in the session.
>
> Be careful in your wording here. A *leader* is often assumed to have special expertise or authority. Some people prefer *facilitator* just because they don't like the presumption that the leader tells other people what to do.

Notetaker
> In the interests of referencing the session as well as transparency and openness for people who can't attend the summit, a person should take notes about what was discussed and the concluded actions. Some sessions find it useful to post notes on a bulletin board or easel. In any case, the session leader should not be the notetaker; each role requires full concentration and a different kind of thinking.

Always be conscious of community members who can't attend sessions. Your notes should help them feel a part of the session, but you may also want to consider options for remote participation. This could be as simple as a conference phone that people dial into or as complex as a video link. Twitter and/or identi.ca could be great options for this. Physical attendees could post messages of what is being discussed, and online attendees can then read and respond.

I have been involved with a variety of methods of remote participation. A conference phone to dial into is always a useful option: it is low maintenance and requires little conscious thought. A video link is more complex and more intrusive in the session because it relies on members of the session to operate the camera so that it points at the person who is speaking. Another possible option is an audio feed that streams onto the Internet. People can then respond to topics via an online chat service such as IRC, or even a microblogging service such as Twitter or identi.ca. You should evaluate your options and see what is doable with the resources and time that you have available.

Event-specific notes

Here are some additional notes that build on the topics I covered in general earlier:

Location/venue

Summits are typically small to medium-size events and often include multiple concurrent tracks that will need separate rooms. You may also want to provide a morning plenary presentation for all the guests, which will require a larger room. Bear in mind that the summit is intended to be a working session, and you may therefore need facilities such as Internet access, plenty of power outlets, and tables and chairs.

Accommodation

There are no special accommodation requirements for summits.

Equipment

Summits are generally entirely discussion-led, but you may need to supply an Internet connection, data projectors, whiteboards, writing pads, and pens and pencils.

Date/time

The length of the summit should reflect how long you can reasonably expect people to be together. Do remember that people will need to book time off work to be there, and some may be away from their families and children. I recommend that a summit range from three to five days. I do not recommend a summit that lasts longer than a week.

Cost

To the best of your ability, summits should be free (free events provide a lower barrier to participation and do not exclude those who can't afford the fee to get in). You should seek to cover your costs with sponsorship if your organization can't cover the funds itself.

Registering attendance

You will want to get a firm idea of who is coming, but also make the summit open so that anyone is welcome to attend. As such, it is recommended that you have an attendee list but also publicize the open nature of the event.

Catering

Many smaller summits either provide a buffet lunch or defer lunch to nearby restaurants. You should have plenty of water and cups available, and preferably some sodas or coffee. Some caffeinated beverages are particularly important if you have a long summit: people will rely on them to wake up in the mornings.

Insurance/unions

As always, check into the insurance and union requirements for the summit.

CASE STUDY: GOOGLE SUMMER OF CODE MENTOR SUMMIT

For some time Google has been running a program called Google Summer of Code, which provides funding for open source projects to develop new code, features, and initiatives. The program has been overwhelmingly successful. Hundreds of projects have benefited, and millions of dollars have left Google's ample wallet as part of the program.

Each year Google invites two individuals from each successful project involved in Google Summer of Code to its annual Mentor Summit at Google HQ. Leslie Hawthorn of Google reports:

"I'm particularly proud of the feedback we've received on the Summits, our attendees repeatedly telling us that the connections they make that weekend lead to collaborative development between projects. It's also an excellent opportunity for these seasoned Open Sourcerers to share best practices and not just around participating in Google Summer of Code; some of the most important knowledge-sharing that takes place at the Summits is when contributors finally get to meet face-to-face; exchange ideas; and form the social ties that cause patches to be reviewed and merged more quickly, requests for support answered rapidly, etc. The typical view of FLOSS (Free/Libre and Open Source Software) development is that everything takes place online, but that's only a part of the interactions that fuel Open Source; without these in-person meetings, establishing a reputation and securing the trust of one's fellow project members certainly occurs, but much more slowly. Bringing together these experts from each project helps everyone to build rapport rapidly, greasing the wheels of online activity through social bonds.

"We primarily organize the Summits by using our mailing lists and a wiki. Each participant is encouraged to propose sessions in advance of the unconference, with all suggestions collected on the wiki; the mailing list is primarily a vehicle for reminding folks to update our shared online resource. Once attendees arrive, we ask them to write out their ideas for session topics on large pieces of paper, which are then posted for all to review. Each attendee is given sticker dots so that she can +1 sessions, meaning adding a dot to the topic's poster signifies interest in attending a particular discussion. This system allows us to easily determine which sessions require the largest amount of space for participants, which is particularly handy when managing logistics for an unconference, as there's no set agenda in advance. The posters also give us all the opportunity to discern which ideas are most compelling—and which challenges are most daunting—within our community. By structuring the meeting as truly participant-driven, our attendees are guaranteed to get precisely what they need from their participation provided they put energy into the wider discussion.

"During sessions, we encourage everyone to take notes on the conference wiki to most widely share what they've learned. As is typical during any conference, there are many more sessions that attendees would like to go to than they actually are able to, so these notes allow folks to glean something from the discussions that took place and to know whom to follow up with later for additional exploration or collaboration. The good folks at Oregon State University's Open Source

Lab host this community wiki for us, which is globally readable so that everyone has the benefit of our collective experience. Several community members have volunteered to administer the wiki and are actively (re)organizing the content so it's most useful to would-be Google Summer of Code participants and anyone else looking to run a similar outreach program. See *http://gsoc-wiki.osuosl .org/index.php/Main_Page*."

Organizing an Unconference

Unconferences are a relatively new addition to the menagerie of commonly organized physical event types. In its goals, an unconference appears to be the same as a normal conference: a group of people gather in a venue to watch a series of talks and discussions. There is, though, one key difference: an unconference has its schedule created on the day of the event in an entirely free-form way. One example of an unconference is the Community Leadership Summit, an event which I organize each year to bring community leaders, managers, and organizers together. You can find more details about the event at *http://www .communityleadershipsummit.com*.

The history of unconferences traces back to O'Reilly's invitation-only geek event, FooCamp ("Friends of O'Reilly" camp). The real success and growth of unconferences has been exhibited by the BarCamp spin-off events.

BarCamp was originally a joke between Chris Messina and a couple of friends regarding some somewhat disgruntled people who had not been invited to O'Reilly's FooCamp. Curious as to why these people were complaining, Chris and friends decided to run an equivalent event, coining it BarCamp, as a nod to the (ironic in this case) foobar references in O'Reilly books. Chris explained to me how the event came about:

> We just thought it'd be fun to get a bunch of friends together and have an emergent (or "open space") event to offset FooCamp. The crazy thing is that we planned the whole thing in only six days. I was on Instant Messenger and email and calling people trying to get a venue: originally thinking of doing real camping in the mountains! When nothing panned out, Ross Mayfield from SocialText saw Andy Smith's call for a space, realized that we were just down the street, and offered up his new space down the road. Once we had a venue, everything fell into place.

Since these humble beginnings, there have been over 500 BarCamps in all the major inhabited continents. There have also been less-nerdy spin-off events, with one such example being WineCamp, a derivative of BarCamp in which a mix of nonprofits and technology fans camp out at a vineyard with no water or power. Chris noted that not having Internet access and power was actually a boon:

> On the second day of the camp, we went to a winery where we had WiFi and power and worked on producing all the ideas we'd brainstormed offline the previous day. It was seriously productive and hugely interdisciplinary. It's events like that that blur boundaries and encourage diversity that I think are the most rewarding to me.

Unconferences are an excellent way to host discussions that everyone has the opportunity to drive. They are, by definition, intrinsically open events. By allowing your guests to set the schedule on the same day, you are opening up the event to all manner of topics, even if attendees prepare a session before they arrive and volunteer it.

From my experience with unconferences, the free-form scheduling always uncovers unusual and intriguing topics. There will be topics proposed that you or a wider scheduling body would have never thought of, and this can make for some really interesting and fascinating discussion.

Fortunately, unconferences are devilishly simply to organize. In addition to the obvious resources, such as a venue and attendees, your primary consideration is a place where people can add their sessions to the agenda. Most unconferences feature a large whiteboard (or two whiteboards side-by-side) on which you write the conference grid. This is a box that shows the rooms along the top and the times down the side. This will result in a number of session slots in which people can write in their sessions. The whiteboard should be in a central location that's easy for people to check regularly.

NOTE

Normally with an unconference there'll be 100 or so attendees and quite a lot of talk tracks (say, 7), so each talk is expected to attract only 10 or 20 people; this means you need lots of small rooms, not one big one, and it means a talk is less intimidating for a speaker because talks normally end up being discussions anyway when there are only 6 of you.

Another consideration is to provide a wiki and other resources to wrap around the event. Even Chris Messina, one of the originators of this style of event, likes to keep things simple:

> [For BarCamp] we really relied on the wiki, the mailing list, blog posts, and photos posted to Flickr. In the early days, I'd say that made up 98% of the documentation. There was also word of mouth, of course—individuals became spreading vectors in and of their own right. The rules themselves were also fairly viral—I mean, we basically stated, along the lines of *Fight Club*, "If this is your first time at BarCamp, you must present!" We weren't draconian about it, but that was an important aspect of the event: no spectators.

Given the slightly unusual format of an unconference, it is recommended that you attend a few of these events before you organize your own.

Event-specific notes

Here are some additional notes that build on the topics I covered in general earlier:

Location/venue

Although many unconferences are called camps, a campsite is not typically required as a venue. Provide a number of breakout rooms in which to have the different sessions. These rooms will need to have tables and chairs.

Accommodation

Again, camping facilities are not typically required. If you do want the event to take place at a campsite, ensure that you have an area in which your attendees can pitch tents. Also ensure that there are toilet and washroom facilities. Some unconferences that take place in offices allow people to sleep on the office floor. If you do this, make sure you remind people to bring sleeping bags.

Equipment

The main equipment that you will need includes a large whiteboard and dry-erase markers that your attendees can use to contribute their sessions to the schedule.

Date/time

Unconferences are typically no longer than one or two days.

Cost

Costs vary between these events.

Registering attendance

Attendance registration at unconferences varies: some are open events with open attendance, and some are closed, invitation-only events.

Catering

Many unconferences either provide a buffet lunch or defer lunch to nearby restaurants. You should have plenty of water and cups available, and preferably some sodas or coffee. Some caffeinated beverages are particularly important if you have a long unconference: people will rely on them to wake up in the mornings.

Insurance/unions

As always, check into the insurance and union requirements for the venue.

Getting Sponsorship

Everyone reading this book is lucky, because community is one of the rare places in the world in which we can exist, build bridges, and reward victories without bowing to the filthy lucre. In our palm-lined oasis, money is rarely a consideration. Sometimes, though, it is.

The vast majority of physical events cost money. Venues need to be booked, equipment needs to be rented or purchased, and other costs need to be covered. Unless you are charging an entrance fee that covers costs or another party you know is feeling particularly generous, it is likely you are going to need to find sponsorship to cover these costs. Let's now take a little time to talk about what is involved in finding sponsorship.

Understanding Your Needs

Sponsorship is a somewhat hit-or-miss process. Although your community does good and valid work, what you are essentially doing here is asking someone for some free money. It doesn't matter if the party you are asking is a large company. Large companies still need to account for the purposes of their expenditures, and particularly when the economy is facing difficult times, justification has never been more important.

Fortunately, I have a surefire way to improve your chances of getting sponsored. This is a theory that has been designed, refined, tested, and further refined to present a cookie-cutter concept that can be applied perfectly to your community—a cookie cutter built from reason, experience, and perfected mathematical ingenuity:

> The less money you ask for, the more likely you are to get it.

Pretty stunning stuff, eh?

OK, back to the point. Consider yourself in the position of Chief Checkbook Holder for a large organization. If one community asks for $500 and another community asks for $5,000, which are you more likely to scrutinize? From which are you more likely to demand your money's worth in associated advertising and favors? Which are you more likely to say no to?

> **NOTE**
>
> **Although this theory can be applied in a general sense to most volunteer community events, if you are organizing a large conference event (particularly if the audience is composed of professionals), asking for more money can legitimize the event. Although true, you should tread carefully with this approach: get it wrong and you may get nothing.**
>
> **If you are considering asking for a significant sum of money, I recommend you speak to someone with event organization experience first and get that person's take before you click the Send button on your proposal to the sponsor.**

As such, you need to perform an exercise in cost cutting. You should first produce a big list of everything that is going to cost money, in either rental or purchase costs. This list should be accurate and complete. Everything from pens to the venue to expensive computing equipment should be on that list.

Your next step is to go through the list and turn it into a trimming exercise. The goal here is not to remove things you actually need, but instead to find ways to source those things without paying for them. I know I shouldn't need to say this, but people…stealing is not an option. If I get a letter from my attorney telling me that a community project leader is in prison for stealing 20 rack-mount servers and is pinning it on "the British dude who wrote *The Art of Community*," I am not going to be particularly happy.

What I am suggesting is that you try to source those things by borrowing, sharing, making, or otherwise gathering them. Follow the general theme of the book here: think outside the box. Inspire yourself to get as much of what you need as you can without merely going and paying for it.

When we started organizing LugRadio Live in England, we did a lot of this. We borrowed projectors from some friends, and the screens from others. We got donations of paper and pens from an office worker whose company had plenty of spare supplies to contribute; we produced the name badges, posters, and programs ourselves; we asked a conference to give us spare lanyards, as they didn't need them; we provided the audio equipment ourselves; and we used a cut-out potato and ink to stamp the hands of attendees (really). Although some of this may seem a little cheap, what many of you want to achieve is not a large business conference. We are a volunteer community, and it is OK to be a little rough around the edges. Rough around the edges and endearing are close bedfellows (no one has ever forgotten that potato stamp).

When you have been through your list and have a final tally of things you just have to rent or buy, calculate the cost of those elements. You now have a much lower figure to request sponsorship for, and you are much more likely to get it.

SWEAT VERSUS SPONSORSHIP

I hate to belabor the point, but after my previous diatribe about thinking outside the box to source what you need without having to ask for sponsorship, I know many of you will think, "Well, it's just going to be easier to ask for the sponsorship."

It is easier. I am not denying that. But being frugal with the mighty buck is not only a positive exercise in how to put together an event, but importantly, it is the *right thing to do* for your sponsor.

If you treat them with respect by asking only for exactly what you need, you will be sowing the seeds for a long and fruitful relationship.

Finding and Handling Sponsors

By now you have your sponsorship figure. The next step is to determine how many sponsors are likely to be able to cover it. Of course, anything to do with figures is difficult to provide concrete advice for, so take some of these words as general guidelines only.

If you need $2,000 or less, it is likely that you can find a single sponsor who can probably cover the full cost. Still, you may want to consider breaking the figure in half (e.g., $1,000 per sponsor) and therefore asking each sponsor for less. Remember the golden rule:

The less money you ask for, the more likely you are to get it.

When you have an idea of how much you want to ask from each sponsor, you can begin thinking of potential sponsors.

The best bets for potential sponsors are companies that are related to your community's activities. As an example, if you are an open source community, there is a raft of open source companies and wider IT companies with an interest in open source. Naturally, another indicator toward a potential "yes" on your sponsorship request is that the company has money. If the company is known to be struggling financially, save your energy and focus only on cash-positive organizations.

Determining potential sponsors can be a tricky road to navigate. The best way to do this is to run the idea of sponsorship by some people you know well in existing companies who are potential sponsors. They may be able to help you get up to the next rung in the ladder. Every time I have organized an event that needed sponsorship, this has been my first port of call.

Another approach is to meet someone involved in an existing event that is similar to your own and ask how that person handled sponsorship. Another useful technique is to look at the sponsorship lists for these other events. Often the primary sponsors are listed on the front page of the event website.

Setting expectations

When asking for sponsorship, it's important to remember that you are engaging in a business transaction. The organization giving you money expects something in return. Specifically what they expect varies tremendously between sponsors.

Some sponsors will expect almost nothing. A good example of this is a company called Bytemark Hosting, which has sponsored every year of LugRadio Live since it began. The company has provided venue sponsorship year after year, even back when no one knew the event or its expectations. Bytemark not only had faith in the event but was gracious in its expectations: all it wanted was an exhibition table.

On the other hand, some sponsors want the moon on a stick. Another (unnamed to protect the innocent) sponsor I have dealt with wanted branding scattered across the venue, weekly calls with its demanding marketing manager, regular branding mentions in the podcast that we did, control over the size and location of its booth, and other requests. The experience with that sponsor was, frankly, a huge headache that none of the event organizers needed, especially with so much else going on.

You need to set your own balance of what to offer and ensure that sponsorship requirements don't impinge on the values of the event. For LugRadio Live, we decided on a set of opportunities that we would present to sponsors in exchange for sponsorship, offers that we felt did not compromise the ethics or atmosphere of the show. These included:

- Sponsor logo printed on the back of the program
- Small sponsor logo printed on the back of the presenter and crew t-shirts
- Sponsor logo and link presented on the event website
- Exhibitor space at the event in a location where the most traffic flowed
- A thanks to the sponsor in the LugRadio live show in front of the event audience

In addition to this, we clarified with all sponsors that no editorial content or changes could be mandated by a sponsor. In other words, we would always have complete control of the content of the podcast, as before.

When you want to approach sponsorship, you need to have your own list of bullet points indicating what you can offer the sponsor. The ones I listed are a good starting point.

When you put together your list like the one just shown, be sure to clarify how sponsorship intersects with editorial privilege. For instance, a logo is obviously a form of advertising and simply indicates you made a deal for much-needed financial support. In contrast, some forms of sponsorship are a bit insidious. When a sponsor gets the right to deliver a keynote, you are pretending to offer your attendees useful information when all you're doing is delivering them up as a captive audience for marketing.

The pitch

Now that you have your sponsorship figure and your set of bullet points to indicate what you will offer, you need to put together your pitch. It should be a short document that outlines the event, what you need sponsorship for, and what you can offer the sponsor.

The length of this pitch should reflect the amount of money you are asking for and the complexity of the event. If you are organizing a large conference with 2,000 expected attendees and are asking for $50,000, you should sharpen your pencil and prepare a comprehensive, detailed, multipage sponsorship request.

I am willing to bet that 98% of you reading this are not in that position and are instead asking for a fraction of that amount for an event with no more than a few hundred attendees. As such, your pitch can be much more straightforward and can fit into a one- or two-page document or a single email to the sponsor.

In your pitch, you should include the following details:

Key information about the event
The name of the event, where it is located, the date(s) that it is happening, and the number of expected attendees. You should also do your best to describe your attendees' interests; sponsors want to know that their company logos will be seen by people who could become customers.

Purpose
Why the event is important and unique.

Requested figure
The required sponsorship amount and the date by which you need it.

Reason for sponsorship
What the sponsorship money will cover. Be honest here; don't say that $500 is going to cover way more than it can reasonably cover.

What the event provides

The set of bullet points indicating what you can provide in exchange for the money.

Contact details

Your name, email address, and a daytime and evening phone number.

Your pitch should be straight to the point, respectful, frank, and complete with all of the details just shown. When you have your list of sponsors and contact people, you should send off your pitch and cross your fingers.

> **NOTE**
>
> **Whatever you do when emailing sponsors, don't email multiple sponsors at the same time. In other words, don't send an email with a CC list as long as your arm. It is cheap and disrespectful to your sponsors.**
>
> **Each potential sponsor that you send your pitch to should get an email directed specifically to that contact, personally addressed to the contact (e.g., "Dear Alan").**

Handling the Money

If you manage to source an agreed level of sponsorship from a company or two, congratulations! The next step is to know how to deal with the money.

If you are dealing with a small sponsor, the transfer of the money will likely be quick and efficient. Some sponsors may just cut you a check or perform a bank transfer. Other sponsors may have more complex requirements and request invoices, purchase orders, or other paperwork.

When you agree to the sponsorship amount and conditions, you should ensure that you are entirely clear on how this process works. The reason for this is twofold. First, satisfying these requirements may take time, and you want to ensure that this time is factored into your plans. What you don't want to do is get into a situation in which you have ordered a lot of equipment and resources and have not yet received the sponsorship money to pay for it. That happens way more than it should, so be cautious of it.

The second reason is that sponsorship can open up a rabbit warren of other headaches. As an example, consider this trail of dependencies:

1. To get the sponsorship money, the sponsor requires a bank account to transfer the money to.

2. To set up a bank account, you may need to be a registered organization in your country. This will require certain community members to be signatories on the account. And this in turn may require some kind of community assessment of who takes on these responsibilities.

3. To be a registered organization, you will need to file your taxes. This will require a formal paper trail. You will also need a regular reassessment of how well the members who are representing this organization are functioning.

None of this work is enjoyable. It is a painful bureaucratic necessity for accepting sponsorship money. You should ensure that you are entirely clear on the ramifications for accepting the money from sponsors and what is involved. Keep it as simple as possible.

AVOID HEADACHES: INVOICE DIRECTLY

A great approach that can avoid the problems of managing money is to never handle money in the first place and simply have the sponsors invoiced. As an example, if you need to spend $500 to hire a venue, just ask the venue to bill the sponsor. This means the money never passes through your hands.

If you would like to pursue this approach, you should obviously ask whether the sponsor is happy to do this. Some sponsors are simply not set up for this method of dealing with events.

You should also ask the venue. Some venues will not invoice people other than the primary contact for the event.

Case Study: The Ubuntu Developer Summit

So far we have explored a few different types of physical events and the core organizational elements that go into them. While many readers of the first edition of this book found this content useful, a lot of people asked me to share more about how we organize our Ubuntu Developer Summits. For the uninitiated, the UDS events are uniquely focused on getting attendees into a collaborative environment to discuss, debate, and plan the next version of Ubuntu. We have run a UDS every six months since the beginning of the project (Ubuntu releases every six months), and with each event we have iterated and improved on what went before and now have the event down to something of a science.

Unlike other similar events, we have worked hard to squeeze every ounce of productivity out of attendees. Everything from the structure of the schedule, to the stewardship of the sessions, note-taking facilities, and room layout has been tweaked and improved to make the event as efficient as possible.

I am now going to take a detailed spin through how we put together a UDS as of the time of this writing. If you are interested in organizing a face-to-face event for your community to decide on plans, much of these lessons learned should be useful to you. The UDS is a large and comprehensive event, but this approach can also apply to smaller events; just pick and choose what you feel will work well for your event. Grab a coffee and a slice of pizza, and get ready to step behind the scenes of a UDS.

The Ethos of the UDS

The UDS is the most important event in the Ubuntu calendar. It happens at the beginning of a new six-month Ubuntu release cycle, and the goal of the event is to bring together the cream of the crop in the Ubuntu community to discuss, debate, and lay down plans for what we are going to do for the next release of Ubuntu.

Importantly, the UDS is not a conference. It is very much a work summit; a collection of meetings in which attendees have the luxury of being together in the same room (most of us communicate and collaborate online), and there is a firm expectation that the week will result in a concrete set of plans for what we will do in the next release of Ubuntu.

While the UDS has certainly grown over the years, the ethos and goals of the event have not. These goals are:

A get-things-done environment
> We always want the UDS to be an environment which, while hectic and exhausting, gives our attendees a great sense of accomplishment when the event is completed. We have actively built an atmosphere in which we judge success based on concrete output.

Firm output
> How many of you have been to a conference or event and didn't feel like you got a lot done, other than networking? At each UDS we work hard so that everyone leaves the event with concrete plans and goals for the next release. To many attendees no output means no success in a session.

Optimized for collaboration
> While *optimized for collaboration* sounds like a horrible buzz phrase, we really have tried to ensure that every session at each UDS is fine-tuned to help people inside and outside the room participate as effectively as possible.

Open to all
> The UDS has always been an event. While Canonical (the commercial sponsor of Ubuntu) has always driven the content of each UDS and sent many staff and community members, we have always encouraged open participation from the public. Importantly, a core part of this ethos is in welcoming remote participants who can take part online.

Awesome work and play
> While the UDS is an intense and hectic work environment, we have also worked hard to make it an inherently social event, and to help reconnect and create new social bonds among our community members. Our goal is that our attendees leave with a strong sense of accomplishment of the work they achieved as well as with a full complement of new friends and colleagues.

While we run each UDS every six months, we have never rested in assuming that the current formula is perfect. Quite the opposite; we almost get close to a "It ain't broke, so why are we trying to fix it?" atmosphere at times. But after each event, we always conduct a survey to gather feedback on the event, assess how well it went, perform a stakeholder review, and make appropriate changes where it makes sense.

How It Works

The UDS has a fairly simple structure for attendees. The event lasts a week, from Monday to Friday, and each day is broken into a series of (approximately) one-hour sessions. The venue has 14 meeting rooms available, and thus 14 sessions can occur at any one time. With so many types of discussions split across so many sessions, we have a series of *tracks* that represent different themes of discussion. Examples of tracks include *Desktop, Server, Community, Kernel*, and *Design*. Each track has a track lead who coordinates the sessions for her respective track.

Throughout the venue, we have TV screens displaying the schedule and the attendees choose which session they want to attend at the beginning of each time slot. Each session covers a specific topic and the attendees discuss plans for that topic. As an example, a session may be how to *grow the number of Ubuntu translators* and the attendees will share and discuss ideas for how to accomplish this goal. Then, near the end of the session, the session leader will jot down a set of work items that the attendees agreed to.

That is the basic gist of how a UDS works. Let's now delve into the details of how the event is put together, along with many of the subtle decisions we have made over the years that have helped the event become what it is today. Believe me, folks, you have no idea how much blood, sweat, and tears have gone into this damn event; I hope you can all get some value from reading about how it has evolved.

The Organizational Team

The UDS has become a significant event with many different organizational attributes as well as a number of stakeholders. Over the years one of the important lessons we have learned is to make sure we have a clear idea of who is looking after different parts of the event and who is responsible for getting input from different stakeholders who have needs that must be met at the event. Before we take a look at how the organizational team is divided up, let's look at who these stakeholders are.

The UDS is almost entirely funded by Canonical, the commercial sponsor behind Ubuntu. As such, some members of Canonical have specific requirements that we must meet. In addition to this, there are other investors in the event as well as those who have a significant level of editorial influence and impact on the event. The following list is a broad approximation of these stakeholders (in no particular order):

CEO

Most of the requirements coming from the Canonical CEO are attuned to the efficiency and return on investment in the event. Fortunately, in terms of editorial direction, our CEO does not impose any unrealistic or unreasonable expectations.

Founder

Similarly for Canonical's founder and head of Product Strategy; his primary input is in ensuring that the event is a productive and worthwhile experience. Again, our founder rarely imposes any unrealistic or unreasonable expectations.

Director of Ubuntu engineering

The director of Ubuntu engineering typically has few requirements for the event other than ensuring that a core set of goals and requirements for the forthcoming release have good airtime and focus at the event.

Engineering managers

The Ubuntu engineering managers (I am part of this team) make up the bulk of the track leads at the event. Their primary requirements are to be able to schedule and deliver sessions effectively.

Community

Of course, there is the wider community who have a clear set of ideas and requests for how the UDS operates. While the community has no operational responsibility to deliver on these requirements (unlike the needs of the CEO, founder etc.), I still consider the community to be an important stakeholder as the event attracts many community attendees. Our community rarely has any specific requirements, but often presents many great and some not-so-great ideas.

Sponsors

Finally, with each UDS we have some sponsors who assume responsibility for specific parts of the event. These requirements are typically localized to the area they are sponsoring, and the UDS sponsorship opportunities provide suitable borders around what the sponsors can and can't expect to influence.

With a clear idea of the stakeholders involved, we can also segment the different types of organizational responsibility and assign these areas to specific people. In the case of the UDS, these are the different segments of work:

Venue

This is everything to do with the venue: requesting meeting space, liaising with the venue staff, communicating requirements to the venue, handling the caterers, ensuring that accessibility needs are met, reviewing the room layout, ensuring that the right number of tables/chairs are sourced, and so on.

Assets

These are all the materials you need to run the event. This includes organizing banners, badges, t-shirts, signs, sponsorship logos, and so on. This work also involves liaising with designers to produce the necessary artwork to go on these materials, and ensuring that the art is ready in time so that the materials can be produced in time for the event.

Scheduling and content

This involves coordinating the sessions, opening keynotes, wrap-up sessions, plenaries, group photos, and other schedule-related content. This job also involves ensuring that we have the schedule available for everyone to access, that track leads can schedule their content, and that changes can be made to the schedule.

Infrastructure

This is the networking, audio/video facilities, projection, and other machinery that allows attendees to get online, provide presentations, and meet other needs. Importantly for the UDS, this also includes ensuring that remote participants can take part in the sessions, so this involves streaming audio from all the rooms, providing online streams that people can connect to, and providing IRC channels for each room so that remote participants can communicate with the session.

Attendees

This is everything to do with getting attendees to the event and ensuring that they have what they need to participate. For the UDS this involves not only providing suitable travel details, but also ensuring that attendees have rooms and roomies, dealing with visas, handling last-minute travel snafus, and handling other logistical components.

Sponsorship

This involves finding companies to sponsor different parts of the UDS and effectively representing these sponsors at the event. This job also involves setting expectations effectively and handling sponsor requirements where appropriate.

For each area a member of the team is assigned to deliver on that specific area. That person's responsibility is to ensure that the stakeholder's needs are sufficiently met and that everything is in place for the event regarding that area. As an example, the person who is coordinating the infrastructure side of the event can reasonably assume the other areas are handled and just focus on the infrastructure component.

My responsibility in this mix is to manage these different pieces. I tend to liaise with each person assigned to these areas and help them to unblock issues and ensure that everything is on track. I also provide a decision-making function when stakeholders are either not interested or have no opinion in a given decision point.

Organizational cadence

As you can see, with such a major event to coordinate and a comprehensive organizational team to manage, the potential for something going arse-up is pretty significant. As such, we put together a regular cadence of discussions in the buildup to the event.

In the first month after the previous event we send out a survey to gather input and feedback on the event to help us guide our next event forward. When this survey is completed I review the content and formulate the results into a slide deck that I share with many of our key stakeholders. For each piece of feedback (and particularly for areas of concern or focus), I present some recommendations for improvements or changes.

Shortly after I send out the deck, I coordinate a call with these stakeholders to run through the deck and jot down requirements, decisions, or areas of discussion. The goal of this call is to swiftly gather feedback and keep the group focused on making decisions around the points raised. If this call is successful (that can be a big "if" sometimes), I will have a bullet-point list of changes or areas of renewed focus. I then share these finalized conclusions with the group.

At this point the venue coordinator either has picked out a new venue or is looking to source a venue. During the following few months there is not a lot to do in terms of UDS coordination; so we reconvene with a regular set of stakeholder calls with people more specific to the strategic direction of the event (in other words, this doesn't usually include the CEO and founder, but does involve the director of Ubuntu engineering, venue coordinator, and me). These calls happen every two weeks as we nail down further strategic changes to the event.

In the six weeks or so building up to the event, we start a weekly cadence of organizational calls. These calls typically involve most of the representatives of the areas discussed earlier (venue, assets, infrastructure, etc.). In these we start nailing down many of the organizational details of the event.

During this time, I work to keep an overview of the organizational process and try to unblock areas, particularly unclear requirements from stakeholders. Even outside of the regular cadence of meetings there is a regular stream of communication within the organizational team. The UDS is genuinely a team effort, and the culture of being able to assume that a given organizational lead had her respective area covered helps to make the entire team successful.

The Venue

The UDS is an unusual event for many different reasons. First, it is a heavily optimized collaborative event; second, it takes place every six months (which is unusual for an event of this size); and third, each UDS often takes place in a different location.

In my time working at Canonical, the UDS has taken me around the world. I have been to Budapest, Seville, Boston, Orlando, California, Prague, Barcelona, Brussels, Dallas, and elsewhere. Traditionally, the UDS would alternate between the United States and Europe. Alternating between these different countries was useful not only for growing my collection of souvenir refrigerator magnets; because the UDS is an open event, it enabled people in those regions to join us, thus diversifying the attendance at the event.

As the UDS has increased in size, though, choosing a venue has become more complex. Finding a venue that can house around 500 attendees and provide the facilities we need has edged the UDS into large-conference territory, and many such facilities are booked two years in advance. In addition to this, the UDS has become a far more complex event to organize with significant requirements, particularly in terms of infrastructure, audio/video, and assets. Five years ago, all we required was a projector and a few wireless access points. Today, we require a huge room filled with flight cases jammed with infrastructure.

Because of these complexities, the UDS tends to take place at previously visited venues these days. This allows us to book a venue before another conference gets in there first, and it provides a known target, which is particularly useful for the infrastructure and venue relations side of the organizational work.

I am now going to take a spin through some of the considerations we make when choosing a venue. These considerations apply for pretty much all venue sizes, so if you are organizing a smaller community conference, these should be useful pointers for you to think about.

Meeting room requirements

The UDS is a pretty big event. While around 500 attendees may not seem huge, the focus of the event is to get these attendees into a regular stream of diverse yet manageable sessions. Over the years part of the challenge involved determining the ideal number of concurrent sessions that we want running at the event. On the one hand, we want to provide plenty of space for people to have sessions, but on the other hand, we don't want empty rooms or rooms filled to overflowing.

Through trial and error, surveys, feedback, and a certain amount of alchemy, we have determined that we need around 10 rooms for the event. Some UDS events we have also aligned with another event (such as the Linaro Connect summit), and we have upgraded the concurrent room list to 14 rooms.

Fourteen rooms is not the end of the story, though. We also need a plenary room that is large enough to hold 500 attendees, and at least 4 rooms that we can use for scheduling private meetings. In addition, we typically need an office room, an audio/video crew setup room, and the usual facilities that go with these needs, such as restrooms, disabled access ramps, sufficient ventilation, air conditioning, and so on.

The private meeting rooms are simple to coordinate, and so is the plenary room; ensure that the latter can accommodate the number of attendees and have room for a main stage, as well as projector screens halfway up the room so that people at the back can see.

The meeting rooms are a little more complex, though, as some sessions will have very few participants, while others will be very popular; I have seen some sessions have only 2 people in them and others have over 100. As such, I always recommend that we find a range of meeting room sizes and that we try to ensure that most can seat at least 50 attendees (30–50 attendees seems to be the average size of a UDS session).

Social events are another consideration. At each UDS we typically have a meet-and-greet buffet on the Monday evening and a closing party on the Friday night. It is impractical to have these events in the plenary room as that would require setup and breakdown for the usual day-to-day plenary facilities. As such, our venue requirements also include a room where we can have a social function for around 500 guests.

This also gets more complex when you have sponsors who want to organize their own social events; typically they won't want all social events to take place in the same room each night. As such, a venue with multiple social event locations is a great find. Of course, you could host social events off-site, but organizing buses is a pain, and buses impact the social structure of the event; if the last bus leaves at 9:30 p.m. and you are having a great time, the event is cut off prematurely.

When you have an idea of your meeting room requirements you should consolidate these into a document that you can send to potential venues to see if they meet your needs.

Location

Location, location, location, baby! This is what toadying real estate agents tell us all the time, but exactly the same applies to choosing a great venue for your event.

Location choice is a delicate balance. On the one hand, you want to pick a fun, interesting, and desirable location, but on the other hand, you don't want your attendees to spend their time out and about, soaking up the location, and not actually participating in your event.

This choice is more complex for smaller events where you have a wider set of options available for venues. If you are hosting an event for 100 people and need 3 or 4 rooms, you can pretty much hold that event anywhere; there are plenty of venues that meet your needs. For an event such as a UDS with its extensive meeting room and space requirements, our options are considerably more limited.

The simple reality is that there just aren't that many venues that can support a UDS's requirements, and as such, it makes the location list a pretty straightforward choice between a limited set of options.

While I am not actively involved in the choice of venue or location for the UDS, I have worked with the team that is, and these are some of the considerations they make based on location:

Safety

> Safety is the first and primary consideration. You should always check to see if there is any political or civil unrest in the area where your event will take place, and check how safe the neighborhood is. The last thing you want is an incident occurring at the event and putting anyone in harm's way.

Travel

> Some locations are just intrinsically easier to get to. The UDS attracts people from all over the world, and many, many people must hop on a plane in order to attend. As such, good travel links, and importantly, ensuring that people can get there without too many flight connections, is an important attribute to check. More flight connections mean more uncomfortable travel and more opportunity for things to go wrong (canceled/delayed

flights). You should also assess how far the venue is from the local airport/train station/ bus link; if you are allowing people to expense their taxis to the venue, it all adds up.

Social opportunities

The social opportunities in the area are important to consider. Some locations can offer too few (e.g., we once had a UDS in the middle of a Belgian forest with nothing to do, and things started getting a little like *Lord of the Flies* after a few weeks), while others can offer too many (e.g., I am pretty sure there will never be a UDS in Las Vegas). From my experience, most people want a few decent dinner options within walking distance, a cheap bar nearby where they can socialize, and if possible, a convenience store to buy forgotten toothbrushes and deodorant.

Desirability

Picking an interesting location can often significantly increase the chances of people attending the event and tacking a few days before or after the event for some vacation time. I have seen this in past years when the UDS has taken place in Florida, Prague, and California.

Local opportunities

Another consideration, particularly for commercial investors in the community, is to identify local opportunities that can be connected to an event. A good example of this for a technology company would be to have an event near Silicon Valley in California; you could then use the event as a means to attract companies and representatives to meetings. This is something we sometimes consider for the UDS.

Of course, an important consideration in all of this is cost. With the UDS we know the venue costs will be significant due to the size of the event, and we also factor in the cost of the local amenities. As an example, Las Vegas and the San Francisco Bay Area are pretty expensive areas, but Eastern Europe is much cheaper.

Instead of looking for a clear-cut solution in each case, try to find a balance. You may find a venue that is inexpensive but in an area that doesn't offer much in terms of socializing, or you might find a venue that is more expensive but is convenient in terms of travel and offers lots of fun things to do. Try not to obsess over the small details, and instead pick the best option based on the attributes that are important to you.

Facilities

With the growth of the UDS, our facilities requirements have grown significantly, too. These include your requirements outside the core requirements of the event.

For the UDS, we have to ensure that the location provides what we need to hold the event as well as provides accommodation for our attendees. While we have sometimes provided bus services between area hotels and the UDS venue, this is a logistical challenge and so we tend to prefer to hold the UDS in a hotel that can also provide accommodation to attendees. This makes life a lot simpler.

In terms of accommodation, we ask attendees who are sponsored or who work for Canonical to share a room, and we have a reasonable idea of the number of double rooms that are required. We also try to ensure that there are good catering facilities at the hotel (for breakfast) and at the meeting venue (for lunch). In addition, we try to make sure we can offer other niceties such as Internet in the rooms, a gym, and a decent hotel bar that is not too expensive where people can socialize in the evenings.

Be a little cautious when booking blocks of hotel rooms. Most venues will ask you to block off a certain number of rooms (e.g., 100 rooms) and possibly pay a deposit. If you have a firm idea of how many people are attending (as we do with the UDS), it is safe to book that block. If you are unsure how many people will attend your event, be careful when estimating the number of rooms to block; many folks who say they will go will not show up.

While we have a firm idea of the required number of rooms for the UDS and we work to ensure that we get a good rate on them, we also try to ensure that people who are attending of their own accord can get a discounted rate. Talk with the hotel to see if these attendees can get a discounted rate; the hotel should be able to offer you something, particularly if you are already bringing a substantial chunk of business their way.

It is recommended that you produce a list of requirements that you can present to potential venues, particularly if you are booking both meeting space and hotel accommodations.

CREATING AN ACCESSIBLE EVENT

We have always worked hard to help the UDS to be as accessible as possible. Making an event accessible often requires some trial and error so that you learn which are the important accessibility requirements to put in place.

Of course, an obvious requirement is that the venue is handicap-accessible. Subtler items that can sometimes be forgotten include ensuring that your buses are wheelchair-accessible, ensuring that signs are large enough for those with vision problems to read, not creating signs that are unreadable for those with colorblindness, and ensuring that you provide other options for those with particular dietary requirements.

A great way to develop this experience is to reach out to attendees with accessibility needs and ask them for their feedback on what can be improved for each event; before long you will have a clear idea of what areas you need to focus on.

Assets

For every UDS a large number of assets need to be produced as part of the event. These assets are used to decorate the venue, provide useful information to attendees, and meet other needs. These assets include the following:

Hangable banners

We usually hang some large Ubuntu banners outside the venue to indicate where the event is, as well as in other parts of the venue (such as behind the registration desk). These are usually vinyl banners that don't include specific event information on them, so they can be used at multiple events.

Pop-up banners

We also have a series of pop-up banners that provide information specific to the event. These include banners with event-specific details such as the release name and logo, as well as banners for social and other events. These pop-up banners cannot be reused for future events due to their event-specific content.

Badges

Traditionally we used to just print badges with the name and IRC nickname of the attendee. These badges would be provided with an Ubuntu-branded lanyard to go around the attendee's neck. These days we use a more comprehensive foldable badge that includes other information, such as a map of the venue, key web addresses, social event start times and rooms, and other content. This foldable badge includes this information inside the folds, with the attendee's name and nickname appearing on the outside of the badge. While they are more expensive, we have found these badges to be really useful. Another, more recent change is getting lanyards made for each UDS so that we can include the sponsor's logo.

Signs

While an important asset, general signage can be created on-site with a printer. These are just basic signs that hang on meeting room doors and indicate session names and times, general information, new information, and more. A ream of paper, a printer, and a branding-compliant template are all you need to make the sign love happen.

T-shirts

We also produce a few different types of t-shirts for the event. First, we create a t-shirt design for each track lead. As an example, when I lead the Community track, my t-shirt has the usual event branding as well as "COMMUNITY" written on the back of the shirt (the other tracks have their track names on the back of their shirts). We give each track lead five t-shirts (one for each day). We also have a set of crew t-shirts made for community crew volunteers, and a set of t-shirts made for general distribution so that all attendees get to take a t-shirt home with them. For the former two (track leads and crew) we can get specific size requirements, but for the latter (general attendance t-shirts) we just make them available in a range of sizes. Be sure to get shirts that go up to XXL.

While these may seem fairly straightforward items to put together, remember that a chain of events needs to occur to produce these items. A design needs to be created and approved, the design needs to be sent to the producer, and the items need to be produced and then shipped to the venue. My advice is to get the design completed and approved ASAP; design requirements often get delayed and can cause headaches in terms of getting assets produced in time.

There are, of course, some other little bits and pieces you should have together for your event. These include things such as stationery for the registration desk, and any assets required by sponsors for the social events and other areas (such as signs next to sponsored coffee or lunch breaks). I recommend you create a list that you can refer to for each event so that you won't forget anything.

Finally, even if you don't need them, I recommend you place a few whiteboards next to the registration desk. These boards are useful for adding late-breaking information and changes to the event or sessions.

Infrastructure

Infrastructure is a critical part of each UDS. The infrastructure is a collection of tools and facilities that help our attendees work effectively. We can reasonably break this down into infrastructure required by on-site attendees as well as infrastructure required by remote participants.

For on-site attendees this includes things such as the event network (providing general access to the Internet), television screens displaying the schedule so that people can see which session to go to next, projection equipment in each meeting room, projection equipment in the main plenary room (and additional chained projectors so that people at the back can see, too), as well as local mirrors of some important Ubuntu archives so that the Internet is not getting hit constantly.

Another important piece of infrastructure that is provided are video recording facilities. We don't videotape every session (there are too many of them), but we do allow track leads to select which sessions must be videotaped, and our crew (which is composed of sponsored attendees who volunteer) ensures that the cameras are switched on and videotape these important sessions. Our A/V crew then encodes these session videos and puts them on YouTube so that the wider community can access them.

The flip side of the on-site infrastructure is the remote participation infrastructure. A core value we have always held at the UDS is that we should make it possible for attendees who can't attend physically to participate in the sessions. We achieve this by ensuring that every room has microphones at the front. The room is laid out in a special fishbowl layout (which we will discuss shortly) that helps to ensure that the main speakers are near the microphones. These microphones stream the audio from the room live out to the Internet and anyone is able to listen in on the session.

In addition to this, there is a projector in every room that displays a chat room that remote participants can communicate with. This provides an effective way to hear the conversation but to reply via a chat channel (we did try to do a two-way chat some time ago, but it didn't work out and just created a bunch of awkward silences).

> **NOTE**
>
> **If you have audio/video streaming from your meeting rooms, be sure to remind people to not have private conversations in there. We had a particularly amusing case a few years back when an attendee wandered into a room during a break at a UDS and had a blazing row with his wife while it was being streamed online. Fortunately, a member of the staff noticed this within a heartbeat and cut the feedback so that the attendee and his wife could argue in privacy.**

Room Layout

You would imagine that the layout of a meeting room is pretty straightforward, right? Well, it can be quite complex. As an example, how many chairs to do want in there? What sort of layout do you want—theater-style, classroom, or meeting? Do you want tables in there, and if so, what kind of tables? What other facilities do you want in there? How many projectors?

The room layout of a UDS is something we have iterated on significantly over the years, and I believe we have determined what is probably the most efficient layout possible. It looks like Figure 12-1.

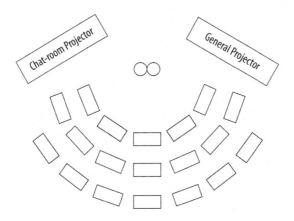

FIGURE 12-1. The UDS meeting room layout is designed to ensure that the primary participants are close to one another and to the projectors and microphones.

At the front of the room you can see two projector screens. The one on the left shows the chat room that is set up for that particular room. When remote participants look at the schedule and decide to join a session, they can join the chat room for that room and then communicate with the room. We always encourage session leaders and attendees in general to keep an eye open for contributions in the chat room, and this has generally worked pretty well.

The other projector is for general use. Many people plug their laptops into this projector to show web pages, create agendas, perform demos, or just show the current set of notes.

Between the projectors are two microphones (illustrated in the figure as the connected circles). These microphones point to different sides of the room, and pick up the general discussion in the room and stream this online for the remote participants.

Each square shown in the figure represents a chair in the room. This layout is called a *fishbowl* and is designed to get the primary participants in the meeting to sit closer together. The idea is simple: those people participating most in the session are encouraged to sit closer to the front of the room, and those who are mainly listening or occasionally participating are encouraged to sit near the back.

This format has a few distinct benefits:

Good for remote participants
> One of the most frustrating experiences for a remote participant is when he can't hear people in the room speaking because they are too far away from the microphones. The fishbowl approach, by definition, asks active speakers to sit closer to the front, which is closer to the microphones that stream the content to remote participants. This makes it much easier to hear what is going on.

Easy access to projectors
> Typically, active speakers in a session may want to use the projectors, either by referencing contributions from the chat room or by plugging their laptop into the general projector to show content or take notes. Sitting these active speakers closer to the front makes the projectors more conveniently available.

Less bending and twisting
> If you don't have a fishbowl layout and active speakers are scattered around the room, attendees may have to bend and twist their bodies to see who is speaking and to participate in the discussion. If these active speakers are at the front of the room they are closer to one another and everyone else just needs to face forward. This reduces the strain and pain that can build up when you are bending and twisting all day in sessions.

An important point about using the fishbowl is that you need to enforce it; if someone is actively participating, be sure to ask her to move to the front so that she can be part of the fishbowl. You should also try to keep some space open near the front so that participants in wheelchairs can be closer to the front of the fishbowl.

The Timetable

At the core of the UDS is the timetable; an intricate tapestry of meetings designed to debate, discuss, and disseminate information. Let's take a quick look at the different types of content that are on the schedule.

Opening keynotes

The first hour of the event, on Monday at 9 a.m., is devoted to the opening keynotes. During this hour we welcome people to the UDS and explain how it works, and a couple of visionary keynote speakers then take the stage to set the scene for the event.

I usually spend the first 15 minutes of this hour welcoming people and explaining how the event works. This is always a difficult presentation for me because many folks in the audience hear this presentation every six months and I don't want to bore them, but folks who are new to the UDS need the information being presented. I have found that keeping the presentation to 15 minutes prevents returning attendees from getting bored while providing new attendees the information they need to make the event successful.

My presentation touches on many things that you may want to cover at your own events:

- Welcome people to the event and explain how much of a thrill it is to have them there
- Briefly celebrate the new release and then focus people on the upcoming release and what we are working toward
- Revisit the ethos of Ubuntu and how we are all here to further our mission
- Introduce many of the different groups in the room by asking them to stand up and be acknowledged
- Explain the schedule, where to find it, and how it works
- Explain how a session works, how to run one, and how to get the most out of it
- Show how people take notes and jot down work items
- Cover the different social events going on throughout the week
- Remind people to keep an eye on their things and not to leave laptops in the rooms
- Ask people to not drink, eat, work, or play too much

After these introductory points I hand things over to the individual keynote speakers. At the UDS we always have at least one keynote speaker, and usually two. I typically allocate 20 minutes for each keynote speaker, but they always run the risk of going over that time limit. Be sure to provide a clock and remind your speakers to keep their presentations to 20 minutes. You should also sit in the front row and discreetly let them know when they need to wrap it up; you don't want to have the keynotes eat into the first set of discussion sessions.

Plenaries

The UDS used to follow a purely session-driven schedule. We would kick things off at 9 a.m., start running through the sessions, and then wrap up at 6 p.m. each day. While this was productive, it also gave us a problem: how do we augment these great discussions with information regarding what is going on in the community? There was always so much cool work going on, and we felt it could be awesome to have a way to share this work with the wider audience.

And thus plenaries were born. Each day at 2 p.m. we begin an hour of 15-minute plenary sessions that take place in the main auditorium where the kickoff session took place.

We invite everyone to participate in the plenaries; as such, they often consist of a mix of tech demos, summaries of in-process work, and sponsor presentations. Importantly, for the sponsor presentations we disallow marketing pitches; they have to be of genuine interest to the audience.

These plenary sessions get booked up incredibly quickly and have been very popular with UDS attendees. I recommend you have similar sessions at your events.

Lightning talks

Something we tried out a few years ago that has proven to be hugely popular is the *lightning talk*. These are very short (usually not longer than five minutes) talks that provide a quick spin around a topic, a short demo, or something else. Some of the most memorable moments at the UDS have been topics and demos shown in the lightning talks session.

We always host the lightning talks on Friday afternoon because people are usually pretty burned out at that point and it is easier to keep their attention with a collection of short talks.

The most important thing when running lightning talks is to stick to the time slot for each talk. You will want an energetic moderator who is not afraid to boot people off when their time is up. We usually have lightning talk speakers line up in a row next to the stage so that they can be ushered on one by one.

If you want to allow people to use slides, make sure you provide a projector with multiple inputs. This way, while someone is speaking, you can ask the next person to get her laptop plugged in and ready to go. You want to avoid wasting time setting up equipment.

Lightning talks are always really popular at the UDS and other events, and I recommend that you have such a session at your own events.

Sessions

Sessions are the meat and potatoes of a UDS. They provide a tremendous amount of face time for a community that is used to communicating online. Sessions have a very clear focus: discuss and debate a topic, and leave the room with a clear set of work items to move forward on the topic.

Each session has a leader who coordinates and manages the discussion in the room. It is the session leader's responsibility to ensure that the topic gets plenty of discussion, that everyone gets to participate (not just the loudest people), and that the session remains on topic and on track.

The quality of the sessions is heavily based on the ability of the session leaders to meet these responsibilities, and we work hard to help session leaders learn how to run a session as deftly as possible.

We recommend the following approach:

Introduce the topic
> Introduce the topic of the session and explain any backstory and context behind the session. Invite others to ask questions if they understand the focus of the session.

State the goal
> What do you want to get out of the session? We always want a clear articulation of work items for next steps, but what do you want the work items to accomplish?

Discuss the topic
> Always be on the lookout for people who are unable to get a word in but want to contribute, and also look out for people rambling off-topic and cut them short if required to keep the session focused. Encourage people in the room to take notes.

Define work items
> About 10 minutes before the end of the session, I always recommend that session leaders cut the conversation short and focus on documenting work items. This is when the session leader should explicitly ask those who contributed if they will be willing to volunteer to handle work items to achieve different parts of the goal. Be sure to document these work items.

If session leaders stick to this formula everyone should feel like they were included in the session, and you should have some concrete work items that you can focus on after the event.

Scheduling

With a good idea of how a UDS is structured, the final piece for us to discuss is how sessions are scheduled and put on the timetable that is displayed on the screens throughout the UDS.

I should warn you that the process we use is heavily customized for the UDS and does not use an off-the-shelf solution that you can replicate. Everything mentioned here does fall in the category of Free Software, though, and you can pull these pieces together. But even if you don't use these tools, an explanation of why we do it this way could be useful when putting together your own solution.

With most events, the scheduling component is separate from the project management component. Events are organized, some kind of conference system is used in which you can fill in a form to add a session, but then much of the work agreed on at the event is lost in a litany of notes and other random content. Often there is no implicit connection between the session and the work outlined in the session.

We built a system for the UDS that helps close this gap.

For each piece of work that we want to focus on in a new release we ask our community to file a blueprint. A blueprint (as discussed in "Structuring Your Projects" on page 281) is a web page that reflects the current status of a project. The blueprint also provides a means for people to subscribe to it to see when the project status changes.

We ask our attendees to file blueprints for all the projects they want to work on in the next cycle. Each blueprint can be targeted to an upcoming sprint. One of these sprint options is the next UDS.

When a blueprint is targeted for a sprint it is added to a queue of blueprints to be reviewed for inclusion in the next UDS. Blueprints we approve are automatically scheduled in a system called summit.ubuntu.com. This system is a custom-built scheduling system that reads in all the blueprints and schedules them on the right track based on how they were named (e.g., a blueprint that starts with "community" is added to the *community* track).

When someone subscribes to a blueprint, summit.ubuntu.com identifies that this person should be in the session. People can also mark themselves as *participation essential* for a blueprint. The summit.ubuntu.com system then builds a schedule based on when everyone can attend the session, prioritizing the sessions by those marked as *participation essential* for a given session. This approach ensures that we have a fully optimized schedule.

The scheduling system also includes a feature that prevents people from camping out in rooms and missing out on other sessions they may want to attend. We used to manually schedule the UDS and assign rooms to tracks; thus people who would be interested in a track would sometimes set up shop in a room and not leave. This would reduce the level of cross-pollination across different tracks. To help with this we added a feature to summit.ubuntu.com to not allow two sessions of the same track to follow on from each other in the same room. This means you will always need to leave the room to move to a session if you want to follow the same track, and it gets people to more actively assess different sessions.

THE UDS SPONSORSHIP PROCESS

To apply for sponsorship you must start by filing an application in the sponsorship system. Sponsorship is open to everyone. We also ask the Ubuntu Engineering Management team and certain developers at Canonical to make recommendations in the system. The outcome of this process often nets more than 120 names in the system. We usually sponsor around 60 people, so our goal is to whittle down the list to those who are likely to bring the most value to the UDS for the goals of that specific release.

That last bit—"that specific release"—is important. All UDS attendees bring value to the event, but given the limited number of people we can sponsor, it makes sense to bring in people who can provide valuable input to the goals and focus of the next release. This is not exclusive: we also prioritize some folks based on recurring value (e.g., governance members, some core-devs, etc.), but as a rule we focus on that given release, not on Ubuntu in general.

In our system we provide the ability for engineering managers and key staff members to vote on applications by assigning each one a number ranging from +3 (the applicant is considered essential for goals related to that release, and bringing huge input and value to sessions) to -3 (there are significant concerns or objections about that person attending, such as worries about not attending sessions, wasting time, being disruptive to other attendees, etc.).

Then points are applied based on the following:

- We give everyone who has never been to a UDS event 1 point. This is because we want to provide an opportunity for new folks to take part in this valuable experience in the Ubuntu community. We also give 1 point to anyone who is an Ubuntu Member, a core-dev, a MOTU member, or a member of a governance board. We preseed these scores because we consider the combination of new blood and acknowledged experience to be a good combination.

- We ask the Ubuntu Engineering Management team and key staff members to vote for people. They can give candidates a number ranging from +3 to -3, and if they don't know the candidate the score is left at 0. Rarely do people get negative scores; this typically occurs only in cases when someone is considered extremely disruptive, abusive, a time-waster, or has demonstrated wasteful or disruptive conduct at a previous UDS.

The scores are aggregated to form a final score (e.g., if two engineering managers provide a -1 and a +3 the final score will be +2). With this we then have a big list of sponsored attendees in aggregated score order from high to low.

At this point we have to perform some editorial input on the lower part of the group. As an example, candidates 45–55 may all have +2 scores, which gives us 10 slots, but then we might have 20 candidates with +2 scores. At this point I will assess the goals of the release and the needs of the engineering teams and shortlist this final 10 in the group to form the final 55 or so. I usually approve 55 out of the 60 at this point because there are always engineering managers who have late-breaking needs that must be satisfied, so I leave a buffer of 5 slots to accommodate these needs.

Finally, the list goes to Mark Shuttleworth who takes a final look and typically makes a few amendments (generally, people he wants to go who are not on the list) and then the list goes to Marianna, who sends out the invitations.

For every UDS there are those who are offered sponsorship but who cannot attend, so we also have a backup list of people with the next highest scores who we invite to take up the places of those people who can't join us.

As you can see it is a pretty fair system. It takes multiple levels of input from a variety of staff members and favors people if they have not been to a UDS before or if they have achieved membership, are governors, or are approved developers. I am sure some of you will take issue with the fact that this is all Canonical-driven, but remember, this is a Canonical-funded event; the UDS is not funded by a foundation or suchlike. In the future, however, I would like to invite the perspectives of some governors on sponsorship applications if that makes sense.

Organizing Online Events

In recent years the growth of the Internet has produced an increasingly interactive Web. Gone are the days of an Internet largely populated by static web pages. Today the Internet is the same thriving and growing library it ever was; it's just that now it is a library in which you can talk to the other visitors.

When we look back at the history of communities in which people worked together on the Internet, virtually all communication was handled in two environments: email or Usenet (groups in which you send email). Both of these media have always been slow. When you discuss a topic over email, it is entirely expected that a conversation can last days or even weeks, with hours in between each message.

Although email still dominates the world as a primary medium for general communication online, advances in real-time discussion facilities have made it possible to hold real-time meetings in which people converse with one another in the same time slot. This has raised the opportunity for online meetings in which multiple people can join and have a conversation.

Online events are something that I have used extensively throughout my work with Ubuntu, but it surprises me how little other communities have made use of them. In the Ubuntu community, they have been hugely useful and always netted upward of 300 attending each event.

If you have a geographically dispersed community, here are some of the types of online events that could be useful to run:

Tutorial weeks

These are special weeks in which a series of teaching and best-practice sessions are run to educate your community in how to do things. This has been used extensively in the Ubuntu community.

Release parties

Many communities have online release parties to celebrate the release of a new piece of software, initiative, or some other project. Instead of meeting in a bar or restaurant, these parties happen online in a chat room, and people sit at their computers and have a few drinks while having a good time with one another.

Focused activity days

These days are intended to bring the community together around a specific initiative. In the Ubuntu community, these events come in the form of Bug Days (designed to focus people on fixing bugs) and Docs Days (designed to focus people on improving the community documentation).

I have not included team meetings in this, as they are less special events and more an expected component in teams and governance bodies. Online events related to governance and conflict resolution were discussed earlier in the chapters devoted to those topics.

Common Attributes

Earlier, when we explored some of the organizational characteristics behind physical events, we discussed some common elements that apply to all events. This included accommodation, date/time, equipment, and so on. We are now going to do the same for online events. The following are the common considerations that apply to all online events.

Medium

The first and most important consideration is what medium you want to use to host the event. Each medium that you use will need to be in real time: it is the instant gratification of real-time communication that makes events feel like events.

These are some of the attributes that you should look for in a medium:

Appropriateness

Will the medium meet your needs? As an example, if you are running a training course for a few hundred people, a voice teleconference is inappropriate because only one person can talk at a time. However, you might deliver a talk and answer questions over a voice connection while accepting questions and allowing chat on a text medium.

Accessibility

You should ensure that all of your members can access the medium you choose. This depends a lot on your community. With this consideration, you need to determine not only whether your community has the technical facilities (e.g., computing power and Internet bandwidth) but also whether members are familiar with or able to learn how to access the medium.

Values

You should ensure that the chosen medium meets the values of your community. As an example, if you are part of an open source community that values software freedom, you should not choose a medium that is closed source.

Whatever your choice of medium, you should ensure that access to it is well documented and that your community is fully aware of where to find the documentation and how to connect.

Internet Relay Chat (IRC). Examples include:

- Freenode (*http://www.freenode.net/*)
- EFNet (*http://www.efnet.org/*)

Internet Relay Chat is a simple and efficient medium that is popular in the technical community. IRC is also open and transparent, and there are free clients for all operating systems. Another benefit of IRC is that it can host literally hundreds of participants at the same time, yet is low-bandwidth: it does not require a fast Internet connection. This is important if your community members may be using dial-up Internet access.

IRC has two downsides. First, it is text-only, and some may not find it quite so engaging. Second, it is largely unknown in nontechnical communities. As such, if you decide on IRC for a nontechnical event, you will have to tutor your community on how to use it.

I have found IRC to be an excellent medium for organizing events. I have used it for many Ubuntu-related events, such as the Ubuntu Open Week, Ubuntu Developer Week, LoCo Documentation Days, release parties, and more. While IRC is useful, I have always been conscious to remember that most members start out unfamiliar with IRC and how to use it. You should always ensure that there are nice, clear instructions (with screenshots) showing how to connect with IRC.

Voice over IP (VoIP). Examples include:

- Skype (*http://www.skype.com/*)
- Ekiga (*http://ekiga.org/*)

Online telephony such as Skype or a Session Initiation Protocol (SIP) client such as Ekiga is the equivalent of having a conference call. As such, the same benefits and limitations apply: you can't practically have more than 5–10 people in a conversation, but it does feel engaging. A downside of this medium is that it requires (a) a reasonably powerful Internet connection and (b) sound hardware and a microphone, which may not be as common as you would expect.

I have found VoIP to be useful for meetings, but not for general-purpose events due to the scaling issues. Another blocker for VoIP is that while Skype works great for many people, other clients require a significant amount of fiddling with firewalls and other networking mumbo jumbo to get them working. When you organize an event, the last thing you want is your attendees fighting with the tools they need to connect.

Virtual worlds. One example is:

- Second Life (*http://secondlife.com/*)

These 3D environments offer an interesting possibility for events. The largest and most popular is Second Life, which has literally thousands of people online.

Virtual worlds offer an interesting physicality to an event. Second Life, for example, has hosted many events inside its environment, including gatherings, concerns, book readings, presentations, and more. In a virtual world, you have a physical avatar that you can move around in the world. While there, you can text or voice-chat with other in-world avatars, buy and sell items, and create buildings and other things.

A particularly interesting feature with the voice chat in Second Life is spatial sound, in which the location of the sound in the stereo field changes based on where the person is. As an example, if you sit between two people in a discussion, the person on the left will come out of the left speaker more.

Virtual worlds do, however, require significant computing resources to use (high-powered graphics card and audio hardware, significant Internet bandwidth) and also a good knowledge of how to use the world, navigate, and communicate with people. Although clients such as Second Life seem like an exciting bridge between the real and the online world, you should ensure that they don't block accessibility for your community. If the majority of your community can use Second Life, great, but if many struggle to meet the requirements, choose a different medium.

Date/time

When choosing an event date and time, be conscious that you are potentially open to a worldwide audience. As such, you are faced with the complex task of picking a time that will suit most of your likely attendees.

Here you need to take a reasonable survey of where most of your attendees live in the world and what times are going to be suitable for the majority. You are never going to make everyone happy all the time, and some people will complain because they won't be able to attend.

A common approach I have used is to pick a time that is in the afternoon in Europe. As an example, with Ubuntu Open Week (a week of tutorial sessions), I ensure that each day there are only four or five hours of available sessions but that they are spread throughout the week during European afternoon hours. This ensures that the West Coast of the United States can get online early in the morning, while on the East Coast of the US it is midday, and in Asia and beyond it is later at night. This approach has helped our events to hit the most people within the worldwide spread of contributors that are involved in the Ubuntu community.

Another complexity in picking times is communicating the time. There are many ways of describing different times, such as Pacific Time, Central Time, Eastern Time, Greenwich Mean Time, and Central European Time. Daylight saving variations make it even more complicated. Fortunately, there is a solution to this in the form of Coordinated Universal Time and its ludicrously jumbled acronym, UTC.

When everyone uses UTC, people can calculate their local time zone offset based on the difference between UTC and their local zone. Although many people are still unaware of what UTC is, I highly recommend that you use it: it is becoming a more common reference as more communities have online events. When using UTC, it is recommended that you still add other time zones next to the statement, for example, "Our next meeting will take place at 9 p.m. UTC (10 p.m. London, 2 p.m. San Francisco, 5 p.m. New York)."

> **NOTE**
>
> **I highly recommend sending out a reminder two hours before the event via email, your website, Twitter, identi.ca, and so on, to remind people that the meeting is happening soon. This will help remind people of the time and reduce time zone confusion.**

Online Discussion Meetings

Communication within your community should always be your top priority. When the communication channels are open and conversation flows freely, your community gains momentum, progress is made, and your members will feel engaged.

Internal communication should seek to satisfy a range of needs that are involved in running a successful community. These needs are oriented around communicating progress on your goals, identifying direction, regular social connections, and day-to-day discussion.

Meetings are a key component in ensuring that your community is running effectively. They provide a number of opportunities:

Discuss progress
> With your strategic plan and road map in place, you can use meetings as an opportunity to communicate progress on OBJECTIVES, GOALS, and ACTIONS.

Discuss solutions
> Meetings are a chance to discuss the implementation of solutions and any problems that your community may have.

Assign tasks
> Meetings are useful for identifying what needs to be done and getting people to volunteer to work on specific tasks.

Resolve conflict
> Every community has conflict, and yours will be no different. Meetings are a useful place to air issues and resolve personal conflict. We discussed conflict resolution in detail in Chapter 11.

Within every community, a primary medium for regular communication should exist. Every community member should know they can come together with other members at an agreed place and at a regular interval to discuss and debate the issues that are before the community. This is the function of a regular meeting.

The first step in getting regular meetings up and running is to choose a location. There are various options available, such as IRC, conference calls, and more. I recommend IRC, though, as these meetings will be open and relatively easy to access, and the conversations can be logged. You should ensure that wherever you choose to hold your meeting, the meeting is open to all and the tools required to join the meeting are freely available.

Choosing a time

The next step is choosing a regularity and a time. Regularity is how many times you want the meeting to occur. This could be weekly, biweekly, monthly, or otherwise. Whatever you decide, choose that regularity and stick to it. Ensure that your regularity is bound to a day. As an example, your meeting could be "the first Monday of the month." Regularity is largely dependent on your community and how much discussion needs to occur. I recommend a minimum of one meeting a month and to increase the regularity if required.

Choosing a time is a complex task for international online communities. You should look at your primary set of contributors and where they are based, and ensure that you have your core contributors at meetings. Try to pick times that average out as suitable for the majority of contributors. This may involve some early mornings or late nights for some people to attend. If you have a truly global spread of contributors, you may also want to alternate meeting times so that the early mornings and late nights don't bite the same contributors every time. Some contributors will simply never be able to make the meetings due to the times. You should ensure that these people can access meeting notes or a log of the discussion.

Advertising the meeting

With these details in place, you should advertise the meeting clearly to your community. The most common place to do this is on a website. Make sure you have all the details clearly available. You should also specify the time zone of the meeting. A useful tip here is to use the UTC time zone, which is internationally recognized.

Here is an example of how you can make your meeting available:

> MyProject Monthly Meeting
> The MyProject Monthly Meeting is an opportunity for our community to come together to discuss progress, technical issues, problems, and other issues relevant to MyProject. Everyone is welcome to attend.
> WHEN: First Monday of every month
> TIME: 20.00 UTC – 21.00 UTC
> WHERE: #myproject IRC channel on irc.freenode.net

With the meeting text ready, it is time to ensure that your community knows that the meeting exists. You should publicize your meeting in the places where your existing community and prospective community are likely to find it.

The first and most obvious place is your website. Ensure that your meeting is prominently located: it should not be buried behind some obscure menu options. You should have a link to the meeting on the front page of your website, and it should be common knowledge where to find the page.

You should ensure that the URL to the meeting page does not change. This is particularly important if the meeting time and date are changing and if you are using the page as a place to put the agenda.

You also should announce and publicize the meeting in your community's primary communication channels. This could include your mailing list, in the topic of your IRC channel, and on blogs. The whole point of the meeting is to get your community together, so you should make every effort to ensure that the community knows about it.

When the meeting is complete, you should also publicize the results. Many of your members will be keen to see what was discussed and what the outcomes were. Publicizing meeting results also indicates to your members that important things take place there. This will help them decide whether they want to join the next meeting.

> **NOTE**
>
> **With guerrilla marketing, not only are you marketing something, but you also are encouraging your community to market the same thing in their own way. An example of this is asking your community to do the marketing on their websites or in the signature of their emails.**
>
> **This is a useful technique for publicizing important community features and events such as meetings. You should encourage your community to share in getting the word out there.**

Setting the agenda

Every regular meeting should have an agenda set. This can be set by those who organize the meeting, but a preferred approach is to allow your community to submit agenda items. This ensures that everyone is welcome to use the meeting as an opportunity to raise issues.

The method of soliciting agenda items is really up to you, but I recommend that people add their items to an existing agenda so that everyone can see the full agenda. This avoids duplication of agenda topics. A good method of doing this, and one used in the Ubuntu community, is to use a wiki. Put your meeting time and details on the wiki, and use the wiki page as a place for the community to add agenda items.

Running the meeting

It is essential that your meeting is run well. There are few things more frustrating than a well-organized community meeting with an agenda that fails to reach any conclusions, fails to keep to time, and fails to cover all the topics in the agenda. Your goal is to keep the meeting moving along, ensure that everyone gets their chance to speak, and ensure that outcomes are generated. The most important aim for any meeting is to generate *output*. At the end of your meeting, you want to ensure that there is something to show for it.

Now I want to share some best practices for chairing these kinds of meetings that will help you get the most out of your own meeting time:

Explain the structure

Kick off the meeting and issue a general welcome. Make it clear at the beginning of the meeting that everyone is welcome to contribute to the discussion. Next, explain how the meeting works: a series of agenda items will be raised and discussed, and then action items will be generated for each topic.

Keep your eye on the clock

Always keep a keen eye on the clock. If the meeting has a fixed length (usually an hour), keep to that time. This will mean determining how much time each agenda item has for discussion. This may also mean stopping the discussion on an agenda item to move onto the next topic.

Ensure speaking equality

Some people in your meeting will dominate the discussion, and some will be more reluctant to chip in. To ensure that everyone gets a say, you may need to prompt the quieter people and ask if they have any comments. Naturally you should do this only if they are likely to have a comment: don't just pick on people because they haven't said much.

Focus on outcomes

Always do your best to keep the discussion focused on finding outcomes and actions for moving forward. Every meeting has the potential to turn into a long discussion with no outcome or next steps. Always keep your mind focused on what needs to happen next to move the topic or goal along to the next stage.

There are pages and pages of content written in books about how to chair meetings well. Doing it effectively is very much a learning process, and it will take time for you to find your feet. I highly recommend sitting in on other, longer-established community meetings to learn how those chairs keep their meetings ticking along.

Organizing Online Tutorials

When I first joined Canonical as the Ubuntu community manager, I set myself a career-long goal of trying to understand how to bridge the gap between a user and contributor. Fundamentally, there is no difference between a user and contributor. Both are big bags of flesh and bones, but some people manage to get up and running as a contributor and some don't.

A key driver in my mind was education. While we had oodles of documentation, people really learn when they sit in the same room, sharing a computer and pointer, gesturing, and sharing knowledge. Although I could not get our entire community in the same room, I was keen to get as close to that educational nirvana as possible.

With this in mind, I developed the concept of the Ubuntu Open Week: a week of IRC tutorial sessions that teach attendees how to do something. The week includes sessions for a wide variety of hands-on topics such as how to file a bug, how to triage bugs, how to create patches, how to translate the messages displayed by applications, and more. Each session is delivered by a competent community member, and most of the sessions have included upward of 250 attendees. I am going to use my experiences with the Ubuntu Open Week as a basis to explain how to run your own online tutorial sessions.

Scheduling

To create the Ubuntu Open Week, we first decided when it should occur and how many days it should last. Traditionally I have run the event from Monday to Saturday so that those who cannot attend midweek can join for at least one day. Each day usually has between three and five sessions. With this schedule I knew how many session leaders I needed to find. It is up to you and your community to determine what kinds of sessions are scheduled.

Announce the completed schedule primarily within your internal community communication channels, such as mailing lists and chat channels, and on your website. You may also want to consider doing some external publicity to encourage new contributors.

Preparing for a session

Before you kick off your tutorial sessions, it is recommended that you ask your session leaders to prepare for the session. Even though each session lasts only an hour, that can feel like an awful lot of typing in the thick of things. As such, it is recommended that your session leaders prepare a script for a reasonable chunk of the session, with each item of discussion on a separate line. This script could look a little like this:

```
hi everyone!
welcome to my session about how to apply as an Ubuntu developer
in this session we are going to discuss the process of how you prepare, document and apply
for approval as an Ubuntu developer
. . .
```

Grammar fans may have noticed that the script lacks uppercase letters and punctuation. IRC as a medium tends to lack these attributes, and as such, looks more free-flowing and conversational. You want your session leaders to sound this way, and so it is recommended that they deliberately keep the script in lowercase letters.

Running a session

The way we have typically run the sessions in the Ubuntu Open Week is to have two IRC channels open at any one time:

#ubuntu-classroom

> This is the channel where the session leader delivers the tutorial content. It is expected that attendees do not speak in this channel while the session is in progress. If you do get excessive chatter, you may need to ask a channel administrator to mute the attendees.

#ubuntu-classroom-chat

> This channel is where people can discuss the session while it progresses, and ask questions.

Questions are an important part of a tutorial session, but questions could easily get lost in the flurry of discussion in the *#ubuntu-classroom-chat* channel. So we defined and published a convention for people to ask questions. The attendee simply prefixes a question with "QUESTION." As an example:

> QUESTION: How do you attach a patch to the sponsorship queue?

This convention makes it simple for questions to leap out within the mass of discussion in the channel.

> **NOTE**
>
> One of the excellent attributes that makes IRC so suitable for tutorial sessions is that the session can be logged easily. You should ensure that every session is logged and put somewhere on your website for people to access.
>
> Session logs are a great source of content. Many of the questions that are featured in the sessions could be source material for a FAQ, or the full tutorial session log could be expanded into a full HOWTO document. These are excellent tasks that some members in your community might be interested in performing.

Event-specific notes

Let's take a look at some additional notes for conducting tutorials online:

Medium

> IRC is the recommended medium for this type of event. IRC allows many people to join, is ideal for concurrently running a session and also allowing people to discuss it, and allows the session to be logged.

Date/time

> There are no additional considerations beyond the general notes that were discussed earlier.

Summary

In this chapter we have explored many of the fundamental attributes involved in putting together an event. I not only explained the importance of events in the wider scheme of community, but also explored the different types of events available, discussed the core elements involved, and provided a few examples of some events that you could organize.

The topic of event organization is huge. Countless books, papers, and courses have been created for it. As such, we have only scratched the surface of the science of running great events, and there is still much to learn. What this chapter has provided, though, is a firm foundation that will get you up and running to produce some useful and effective events for your community. Use this chapter as a starting point, run some events, learn from other people, learn from yourself, and continue to refine and perfect your events.

Every event needs at least two or three tries before it really finds its feet. This has been the case with every event that I have been involved in organizing. It takes time to really understand the event, the needs of your attendees, the organizational requirements, and the amount of time required to get everything ready.

Events can be the glue that connects your community together with its core ethos and reinvigorates and reinforces the reason why people are involved. Get it right, and you and your community have so much to gain. Good luck!

CHAPTER THIRTEEN

Hiring a Community Manager

"I like work: it fascinates me. I can sit and look at it for hours."

—Jerome K. Jerome

LIKE MANY FOLKS, I HAVE HAD THE GOOD FORTUNE AND OPPORTUNITY TO DO MY FAIR SHARE OF TRAVEL TO CONFERENCES AS PART OF MY WORK. As a result, I have been able to experience many of the conferences I once dreamed of attending, but there were still some I never quite had a chance to get to.

One such show was Ohio Linux Fest, a midsize community-run conference devoted to all things Linux and open source. I had always heard great things about the show from a member of my team and members of the community, but for some reason the Fates always conspired against me and I was busy every time the show was scheduled: I was either traveling, in meetings, on vacation, or otherwise unable to get out to Ohio.

Back in early 2008, though, I received an email about the show inviting me to speak. Knowing full well that something was going to get in the way at some point in the future, I slam-dunked the dates into my calendar with a little note next to them:

MAKE IT HAPPEN THIS TIME.

I responded to the email expressing interest, and the organizers kindly offered me the keynote speech. Somewhat flattered at the invitation, I happily accepted.

As time meandered on toward the show, I started working on the keynote and created a presentation that would eventually become the foundation for writing *The Art of Community*. It was that talk specifically that inspired much of the thinking behind the first two chapters of this book. I wrote my slides, carefully tweaking each word, and my presentation, rehearsing my endless stream of (often awful) jokes and ensuring that everything was as shiny and buffed as it could be.

The Fates cooperated this time, and when I got to Ohio and to the conference, I was instantly deluged with meetings, discussions, and other work that I needed to tend to. While hugely productive and useful, there was also a negative aspect to this barrage of activity: I didn't get a chance to see and mentally prepare for the room I was to deliver my keynote in. I knew the talk was going to pull a decent audience, but I didn't fully understand the sheer size of the room until I arrived, 20 minutes before my speech. It was enormous, and while speaking was by no means new to me, this was a new level. It was the first time I had been nervous about a speech in a long time.

Fortunately, the keynote went well and was well received by the audience. As I packed up my laptop and chatted with some of the audience members, one guy stood there quietly and waited for me to finish my conversations. As everyone left, he walked over and said:

> Nice to meet you, Mr. Bacon, thanks for the speech, but I really fucking need your help.

Somewhat stunned at the presence of an f-bomb in the opening line of a new conversation, I let the guy continue to explain that he had been tasked with finding a community manager for his company (a small independent software vendor), but was struggling. He had flown here from Canada desperate for help. Although the seriousness and extent of this poor guy's panic was rare, the confusion surrounding community management and how it fits into an organization is not.

It is becoming increasingly common for an organization that either has a community or is seeking to build one to hire someone to lead this work. Unfortunately, in many cases they have no idea of what specifics they want or who to look for. Many look to existing community managers for advice and guidance.

This book has focused on teaching a prospective community manager and community leader how to build and inspire a strong and productive community. However, this book has not explored how to bring such a role into an organization and help get that person up and running easily. This in itself presents its own set of challenges and opportunities, and these are the focus of this chapter.

Although this chapter may initially seem to be the stuff of managers tasked with hiring staff, it can also be of real value to (a) existing community managers who want to build a team and (b) community managers who are looking to understand the needs and expectations of their communities.

Why Community Building Has Become a Big Business

Community has become quite the buzzword in many business circles, particularly in IT. Its presence is felt more and more at conferences, in papers, on blogs, and across the current global sensation that is Twitter. Regardless of the medium, this explosion of interest in community has happened for three closely interlinked reasons.

Community is implicitly a positive word. It speaks of openness, participation, awareness, and an agreeable intention to engage in an environment driven by merit as well as caring for others. For open source companies, this is powerful inferred meaning that speaks well to their audience. As such, it makes entire sense for a company to light up its website like a Christmas tree with references to "community."

Second, for those interested in open source, community has become synonymous with "engagement in the open source space." Open source companies are fully aware that if they don't have an answer for their community relations strategy, they simply won't be taken seriously by a significant demographic of people. Whereas five years ago this demographic of people was often seen as strange, hygienically challenged, bespectacled nerds who lived in their mothers' basements, it is now well known that those with buying capacity and/or influence are placing importance in the community attributes of open source. These are *real* customers who have developed this value expectation due to the constantly reinforced open source mantra of participation, community, and technical quality. When the industry cradles open source and its associated values, the big cats in the ecosystem need to adjust to reflect that.

Finally, irksome economic times have resulted in very real consequences for small businesses. Executives have been forced to reassess how they can achieve their goals and ambitions with a more painful awareness of the bottom line. Multiple marketing and engineering people can be expensive—a lot more expensive than a community manager.

The accumulation of reasons for building community in a business environment has created a strong commercial justification for community and for those who can build it, along with a set of expectations around what these community builders can deliver.

AVOIDING THE HYPE

A problem befalls (a) those who seek to understand the scope of community and (b) those who communicate their expectations and experiences of building community.

In every industry, certain words that once had reasonably obvious illustrative attributes and consequences have subsequently become colloquial references. We have seen this extensively with trademarks: aspirin, the hoover, cellophane, thermos, and even heroin were all once trademarked to specific companies (Bayer, Hoover Company, DuPont, Thermos GmbH, and Friedrich Bayer & Co., respectively). Using hoover as an example, in England many people will refer to any brand of vacuum cleaner as a "hoover." At one point in time, though, "hoover" pointed to a very specific representation of focus, quality, and expectation in a vacuum cleaner, embodied in products from the Hoover Company. Since then, the trademark has been somewhat genericized in different parts of the world, and what some refer to as a "hoover" will often bear little resemblance to the virtues of Hoover Company vacuum cleaners.

Community managers face similar risks built on misguided expectations. With all of the buzz, focus, and excitement around community management flowing, some more public representatives of the role have been a little guilty of stepping over, hiding, and downplaying the very real day-to-day focus of this work in favor of academically pleasing social science. When the high-level representation of community managers overplays the very real "on the ground" focus of the role, the balance becomes unset and there is a risk of genericizing community management as "the theory of working with groups of similar interests" as opposed to connecting the term firmly with hands-on best practice in building real communities that do real, measurable work.

As you are looking to fill your community manager role, be aware of this hype and how it affects candidates. To avoid it, look for substance in the day-to-day interactions, achievements, and efforts in the candidate's work. If there is an overwhelming level of theory and social science in response to direct questions about this day-to-day work, alarm bells should trigger.

The Role of a Community Manager in the Corporation

In recent years the Internet has been ablaze with chatter over where community management should fit into an organization. Is *marketing* or *engineering* an apt destination for the reporting line? Do we expect our community managers and representatives to report to the director of marketing or the chief technical officer? More specifically, when you bring a community manager into your organization, which of these two teams do you feel can most effectively support and enable a community builder to actually build a great community?

I firmly believe that community management is a tale with both marketing and engineering story lines flowing through it. If one is missing, community can feel unbalanced, misrepresented, and ineffective. We should always seek to celebrate and market the opportunities and importance of community, but that means nothing if you are not willing to roll up your sleeves and build and reinforce the collaborative technical groundwork in your community.

Ultimately, your community manager should be well versed in the mechanics and technical/ social foundations of collaboration in open source communities and should be able to strategically structure and execute objectives that enable your community on the ground to do great work. You should ensure that your community manager has a close connection to your technical leaders, but also a close connection with your marketing department to help them articulate and express your community story.

THE COMMUNITY CASE BOOK

You must be open about your philosophies, your practices, and your plans. You must tell the community what they can get for free and what they will need to pay for. By integrity I mean that whatever business model you choose, it must be based on respect for the individual: respect for users and respect for customers.

—*Mårten Mickos, on Community and Business*

Read the full interview in Chapter 14.

Setting Expectations

Before you put pen to paper on a job description for your new community manager, it is important to get some expectations straight around the role. Community management is fundamentally complicated, and many organizations with mismanaged expectations have made some very costly mistakes in finding someone to effectively build their community. Unlike positions with a longer history in companies, where roles and expectations are clear, community management embodies a lot of ambiguity and can confound hiring managers.

Scope of the Role

Busy hiring managers who already have many other roles to fill often fail to recognize the importance of understanding a community, so their job description contains unreasonable expectations around the role. A mismatched job description means that when a candidate is found, he resultantly has something of a bumpy road in getting a grip on the role. If you are lucky and get a hardy candidate who is willing to take the knocks while the role is being fleshed out, you may come out all right in the end, but the adjustment is stressful for most candidates and wasteful for the company.

To understand the scope of the role, you need to first understand (a) what the scope of the community is and (b) what your expectations are for someone to work with that community to enable and extend it. Let's break these two separate points into a series of questions that you should answer before you craft the job description, beginning with the scope of the community itself:

- Who is in your community?
- How big is it?
- What kinds of skills and diversity are present in your community?
- How does the community interact and work with your company?

- What kind of governance infrastructure is in place?
- Who are the contentious people, and what are the contentious topics?

To determine the expectations around managing that community, we can approach the previous set of questions but assess where we see them trending in the future:

- How do you want to better understand who your community is?
- How would you like to grow the skills and diversity in your community? What are the primary skills and roles that you would like to focus on?
- How would you like to change, improve, and otherwise focus on how your community works with the company?
- What new and improved governance is required, and where should you focus your efforts first?
- How would you like to resolve and improve relations with the contentious people and topics in the community?

When you have answers to all of these questions, you should have a set of broad, high-level goals and ambitions that you would like to see your community manager focus on. You should now run these goals and ambitions past some other members of your organization to ensure that they are doable for a community manager candidate. As you receive feedback, you can refine this set of goals and expectations.

When you have hired your manager, you can use this set of goals and expectations to build a full strategy for the manager. We will discuss this a little later in this chapter.

Risk

One element you should be entirely clear about is the risk associated with bringing a community manager on board. Fundamentally, what you are doing is hiring someone who will become a public face and representative of not only the community, but also the company. If you get the right person with a strong commitment to both, you have the potential for a long and productive relationship. If you get the wrong person, your difficulties may be embarrassingly exposed to the world.

The primary risk here is that when someone represents your community, she acts as a delicate middleperson between the organization and the community. This person plays a careful role in balancing expectations and making it clear that she will represent the best interests of each to the other.

With this responsibility lies the risk of the community manager getting frustrated with both the organization and the community. If the agitation is sourced from the organization, the manager may decide to leave and potentially defame the organization to the community as revenge. On the other hand, if the source of the frustration is from the community, the manager may get burned out and generate problems internally that ultimately reflect back on both the community and the organization. We discussed the topic of burnout earlier in Chapter 11.

In summary, you need to be extremely careful about whom you hire into your community management role. You and your community manager are going to need to be able to understand these risks and be able to handle them in a professional and upstanding way. You need to find someone whom you implicitly trust and who is not going to put a personal agenda before the community.

Breaking Tradition

Another expectation to adopt is that community managers may well need to step outside the traditional boundaries of the business world. For a community manager to really build a rapport with the community, he needs to fundamentally be a member of that community and exhibit the culture of that community. That in itself can ruffle some feathers in the organization.

Much of this is based around seemingly unimportant elements that actually play a key role in community management. As an example, most volunteer communities are very casual places. People wear casual clothes, and you should expect your community manager to do this as well. You should expect your community manager to be vocal, loud, and opinionated. It is this over-the-top personality that will pump up the community and get them excited. You should expect stimulating and vivacious presentations at conferences, laptops covered in stickers, amusing and conversational interviews, and other elements. While I am not suggesting that you should demand these attributes from your community manager, don't be surprised if you get them.

In my own experience, I have brought a huge amount of my personality to my work. My communities know of my wacky sense of humor, my love of heavy metal, my loud and gag-laden presentations, and my up-front and frank discussions with community members. I am proud of this approach to my work, and other communities are likely to be the same. You should ensure that your hires are free enough to exercise individuality in this role.

Despite this, of course, there is a line. When you have the opportunity for vivacious and excitable representation in the role, there is an increased possibility of your community manager putting a foot down wrong, offending someone, stepping out of line, or otherwise embarrassing herself, the community, and the company.

Expect it. Every community manager steps over the line at some point, and you should expect it to happen within her first year on the job. When it does happen, use it as an opportunity to sit down with her and have a discussion about where the line is drawn and how to avoid problems in the future. A frank and open discussion will not only make it clear that the behavior was unacceptable, but also will ensure that your relationship with the community manager is built on a foundation of openness and frank discussion.

Control and Reporting

The final clear expectation you should have in your mind is where your community manager sits in the company. Earlier we talked about whether the role fulfills more of a marketing or engineering approach, and you should consider this carefully.

To make this decision, look back at the questions we discussed when talking about the scope of the role earlier in this chapter, and determine whether your community manager is going to be focusing more on your message about the community or the collaborative infrastructure, processes, and growth of the community. In other words, are you expecting your community manager to help talk about the community and company at conferences and to customers and journalists, or to actually help grow, build, refine, and optimize the nuts and bolts in the contributor community?

It is likely that the answer to this question will be "both," but consider which is the prevalent focus. As an example, if your community manager is primarily looking after a contributor community that produces an open source product, I heavily recommend that she reports to an engineering manager. If, however, you primarily expect the community manager to fly around the world to talk about and represent the community at conferences and tradeshows and to speak to the press, I recommend two things. First, have her report to your marketing department, and second, change her title from community manager to something else: she is representing the community, not managing it, and many people will expect the latter and be disappointed.

The ability to enact change

Hot on the heels of which part of the organization the community manager reports to is how much control and opportunity this person has to enact change. This is a complex but unfortunately common problem with many who have hired community managers: they succeed in bringing information about the community into the company, but lack the power and contacts to implement any of the change they recommend.

As an example, imagine your community manager recommends a series of improvements to an element of your community's technical workflow. These improvements may require technical changes or refinements in other parts of the organization, such as a specific engineering resource. If the community manager rolls up to that person's cubicle and plonks down a big list of required changes, it is unlikely those changes will be implemented anytime soon. That engineer has her own big ol' list of work to focus on, and any additions, such as these proposed refinements, are likely to be gently shaken down to the bottom of the TODO list.

To mitigate this blockage, you should ensure that your community manager has a degree of control over changes and refinements to parts of the organization upon which the community's work depends. While I am not expecting you to have engineering teams report to a community manager, make sure engineering managers make community changes and requirements a priority when gathering requirements in a new strategic plan or cycle.

Another excellent approach that has worked for me is to form a small ad hoc team with approval from the managers. This small team works together to solve problems that involve multiple teams in the organization. As an example, if you have an engineering problem that involves a source control system and a website, have one person who represents the source control system, one who represents the website, and your community manager. Form an agreement to work together on combined problems and get approval from the manager to regularly discuss the prioritization of these problems.

The Responsibilities of Community Engagement

Another important attribute to consider is how your organization expects to interact with the community after a community manager comes on board. In many, many organizations, once they proudly hire someone into an explicit community management role, other people in the organization assume that the community manager will carry out interaction with the community on behalf of the teams. As an example, if a software company has a department that builds a particular product, it may be assumed that any and all community growth and interaction with regard to that product will be performed by the community manager.

You need to determine whether your community manager will indeed perform this function in the organization or whether he will instead act as more of a consultant to help other people in the company work directly with the community. Whatever the decision, it needs to be clearly communicated across the organization and the community.

My recommendation is that your community manager should perform direct interaction with the community for some teams but act as a consultant for most community-facing teams. This way you will have a high quality of interaction in key places where it matters most, and can build a culture of community interaction in your organization. This approach is also far more scalable: having a single person act as the community representative will always end up blocking on that person.

Salary

Salary is a hugely complicated topic when it comes to hiring a community manager. The reason is fairly simple: the role is so new and unknown for many organizations that it is difficult to gather fair expectations around salaries and a market rate.

Unfortunately, many of the common resources HR departments tend to use to gather data provide mismatched and unrepresentative information to work from. As an example, you can do a search for "community manager" and find an average salary in many recruitment and job database websites, but in almost every case the search returns entirely unusable data.

The reason for this is that the term *community manager* points to all manner of different types of responsibilities in all manner of different types of organizations. I know "community managers" who work for tiny nonprofit charities and organizations and who look after a community of less than 30 people. I know of others who look after communities of hundreds of thousands of people with complex collaborative frameworks, technical workflow, and significant public focus and responsibility. These are not the same types of role and should not demand the same salary.

Another consideration is the "manager" part of "community manager." Many community managers don't actually manage anyone: the "manager" in their title points to their influence over the community. As an example, in my current role I manage a team of community managers who work on many different aspects of a community. So while part of my role firmly involves influencing a large and thriving community, I also have the formalized, traditional management responsibilities of a team inside an organization. This kind of management role should be reflected in the salary decision.

Unfortunately, I can offer limited advice on a suitable salary for your community management role. The decision requires a firm awareness of the market (the supply and demand) and deriving a figure at that point. I have previously advised companies about salaries, so feel free to contact me if you are unsure. Otherwise, take the pulse of your community as well as the wider marketplace, come to your own figure, and run it past a few other hiring managers who have hired community managers. This should help you find a compelling and fair figure for both your company and potential candidates.

Communicating Expectations to the Candidate

After resolving in your own organization the expectations we have covered over the past few pages, you should make them clear to potential candidates. Some of them should be expressed up front in the hiring process and as part of the interviews: the primary expectations around the role, what they will be working on, and what they will mainly spend their days doing. These expectations are the meat and potatoes of what will constitute the role.

There are some other, subtler expectations that may be involved in the role, though, and you should make these clear also. Many are rife with potential for causing trouble if they are not made clear from the get-go. So take a look at the following list of expectations and see whether they apply to the community management role you are looking to fill. If so, make them clear to candidates in the interview process.

Adjustments to the role
> The role of community manager in your organization will likely adjust, grow, and change on two levels. First, the expectations around how your community is managed will change as you learn more about the community, as your organization changes its focus, and as your company grows or shrinks. Second, the specific areas of focus and strategy that are covered in each strategic document will undoubtedly change. Your community manager needs to be flexible in both of these areas.

Unusual hours

Many communities span multiple countries, connected by the Internet. With this in mind, your community manager may have to keep some unusual hours. This is common when scheduling online meetings and events: to ensure that a chunk of the world can attend the meeting, it can often mean your community manager getting out of bed in the middle of the night to attend. You should ensure that she is willing to do this.

Travel

Many community roles involve extensive travel to conferences, sprints, and other events. Although many jump at this opportunity, others have families and partners to consider. Also remember that circumstances change: people get married, give birth, and want to get off the road. You should expect that while your candidate is happy to travel right now, that's likely to change in the future.

Public attention

Many community managers become public representatives of the community and the company, and you should make it clear if this is an expectation. If it is, the candidate should expect to have to answer tough questions sometimes in interviews, on panels, and elsewhere. If this is the case, you should make clear to him that he will be expected to fulfill this role, but you should also support him extensively in handling these issues.

Conflict resolution

Many community management roles involve dealing with conflict and contentious situations. Some people are uncomfortable with these expectations, and you should clarify them up front. More details on the specifics of conflict can be found in Chapter 11.

Technical knowledge

Some communities are very technical places. These communities often require a community manager with extensive technical experience in the workflow, infrastructure, and processes of a technical collaborative community. You should make these requirements clear to your candidate and set an expectation that these technical requirements are likely to increase as your community evolves, changes, and grows. The candidate will be expected to learn these new concepts and skills.

Presentation skills

Many community managers get out on the conference circuit and perform presentations about their work. You should check whether they are happy to do this. You should also research whether they are actually any good at presenting: sometimes no presentation is better than a horribly delivered presentation. As such, you may want to pass the presentation helmet to someone else.

You should get these issues on the table in the first interview. The expectations should be clear and up-front to avoid any uncertainty in the future, and you should preferably document them for future reference. Where you document them is up to you and your department: some may feel the contract is the most suitable place, whereas others may consider an addendum document for employment that sets clear but noncontractual requirements.

Managing Your Community Manager

When you have recruited someone to fill the community management role in your organization, the next step is to ensure that you get that person settled into the role easily and effectively. While there are plenty of books available for hiring people and having them settle in, I want to share some hints and tips with specific regard to community managers.

When I have hired people to join my team and manage a community, I have broken down the process into three primary areas:

Induction
> The first month is critical when someone joins your organization and, more specifically, your team. These are the topics involved in this very early part of the community manager's new employment in the organization.

Strategy
> This is how you define and build a set of agreed-upon objectives so that you and your community manager are entirely clear on where to focus her efforts.

Management and communications
> These are the weekly operational elements involved in managing your community manager.

Let's now take each area for a spin and explore some of the attributes involved. Let me state again that I am focusing only on elements that specifically apply to community managers. You should augment these words with the general best practices used when new employees enter your organization.

> **NOTE**
> As we work through each area, I will present the information from the perspective of the manager of a community manager. As such, much of this information will be of primary use either to readers who need to hire and manage a community manager or to community managers who are hiring a team. As I mentioned at the beginning of this chapter, though, if you are a current or prospective community manager, this content can help illustrate some of the expectations that your manager will have of you.

Induction

When your community manager first joins your organization, you will have to cover the usual set of induction-related items: setting up email addresses, accessing company resources, creating calendars, and other such activities. Although these are important, they are not of interest to us here. More important is the way your community manager exploits the induction period to define his reputation in the organization and the community.

Internal reputation

Reputation is critical for all community management. From the perspective of the company, a community manager is seen as an important entity who has knowledge, focus, and awareness of not only how the community members think but also how they work. Remember: many people simply don't understand how community works, and the community manager acts as a translation layer to help other parts of the organization understand how this seemingly random entity functions.

With this in mind, you should carefully consider how your community manager builds his reputation in the organization. This is important for a few reasons. Your community manager is going to need to know how to work with and interact with different parts of the organization, and vice versa. He will be faced with many different challenges and queries within the community, and many of these topics will need to be forwarded and integrated into other parts of the organization.

Another important reason to build these bridges is to help your organization understand what a community manager does. With the role still very new and unknown in the minds of many, some people will either not know what the purpose of the role is or misconstrue or simply hold a cynical idea of it ("Oh, community management—that's just hanging out with nerds and writing blog entries" is one verdict I once heard!).

It is important to clarify to everyone what the role involves and build a solid reputation for your community manager. It helps to schedule a set of introduction meetings or calls with other departments in your organization and make sure to involve your community manager in wider discussion and topics where appropriate.

Community reputation

Your community manager's reputation is critical with the community she is hired to work with. One of the very first tasks she should focus her efforts on is building a strong reputation with the community.

It is possible that this reputation already exists if you hired her out of an existing community. If not, you should ensure that she has the time and encouragement to get out there and get to know the community. This can involve a range of approaches:

Participation in communication channels
> The community manager should participate in communication channels such as mailing lists, forums, and other resources. This should not just involve reading, but responding and participating in discussion, too.

Blogging
> If the community is one that is likely to read blogs and online articles, your community manager should be actively writing about her work. This is an excellent platform on which

to build a medium for writing about her efforts, where she is working, and what achievements the community has made.

Travel

If your community needs to secure a reputation with the wider community in which your specific community fits, you may want to send your community manager off to some key events and encourage her to make some presentations. Travel is also an excellent opportunity to network and get to know important members of the community well.

To help your community manager build her reputation, I recommend you ask her to read other parts of the book, most specifically Chapter 7.

BE WARY OF TOO MUCH TRAVEL

I have an important tip when it comes to travel, based on a mistake made with many new community managers.

The recipe is often the same when a new community manager starts. He joins, there is a little bit of press and hype, and then the organization sends him around to every conceivable conference in the interest of building his reputation.

Although this is excellent for building relations with the community and beyond, it is very costly, both in terms of time and money. Aside from the obvious monetary costs and the effect on personal life, conference travel is going to seriously disrupt your community manager's ability keep up with email, have calls, and hold meetings. Regular and consistent participation in these more mundane activities is critical to getting the basic work of the community done.

So don't make your community manager travel too much. His primary value is on the ground working with your community: don't compromise that in the interest of presenting at conferences.

Strategy

From the very start of your community manager's term of service with your organization, you should have a strong focus and strategic priorities. A strategic document that outlines your community manager's responsibilities, split into objectives, goals, and success criteria as we did in Chapter 2, will communicate what your community manager should be working on and formalize your expectations.

A strategic plan is valuable to guide all your employees, of course, but it's particularly important for your community managers because there is simply so much scope in their work. A community is a huge, boiling pot of activity that can produce a potentially epic collection of information on which a community manager can focus. It is important, therefore, for you and your community manager to understand, prioritize, and focus on a selected set of objectives and goals.

When your community manager comes on board, show her the strategic plan you developed from Chapter 2, agree on a set of objectives, break them down into goals, and flesh out the strategic document into tasks for the community manager. The strategic plan will also help you track progress on that work as it proceeds.

Management and Communications

As with any other staff member, you will need to manage and check in regularly with your community manager. Although many of the common approaches for managing staff can be easily applied to a community manager as well, I'll note here a few specific considerations.

These considerations are primarily related to how your community manager works with other teams inside your organization and how he brings those teams community input. We can highlight two primary areas of focus:

Weekly engagements
> Each week, your community manager should work with different parts of your organization to determine what goals to work on and to quickly identify anything that stands in the way of those goals.

Community feedback
> Your community manager is an excellent funnel through which the community can channel feedback and opinion to the organization. You want to ensure that this is factored into your community manager's workflow.

Let's now take a look at both of these topics in more detail.

Weekly engagements

As soon as your community manager joins your organization, you should set up regular calls or meetings in which you cover the following:

Areas of focus
> Discuss the current topic and areas where the community manager should focus her attention. Ask her where she feels she should be focusing her efforts, then help and advise her on how to achieve these goals.

Strategic review
> I recommend that in each meeting you review your strategic document and the community manager's own goals that you drew from it, to track progress. This is an excellent opportunity to highlight any blocks or problems with progress and to ensure that you are in the loop.

Opportunities

Always explicitly discuss new opportunities and areas where you may want to consider focusing your efforts, either now or in the next strategic time frame.

Problems and concerns

You should always ask your community manager what issues, problems, concerns, and blocking factors are causing difficulties for his work. In many cases, relatively simple issues will be blocking work and initiatives, and you might be able to help solve this.

Community problems and concerns

You should also check in to see whether there are any problems with initiatives and work in the community itself. Are members of the community blocking this work? Are there concerns and problems in the community for which you can offer help to your community manager?

In addition to your personal meetings, determine what other parts of the organization should communicate with the community manager on a weekly basis. You may want to organize a team call that bridges several parts of your organization. By making your community manager a member of a wider team, you can ensure the flow of information between your product engineering teams and the community manager.

Finally, you should advise your community manager on who else she should check in with on a weekly basis. This may include marketing, senior management, other specific parts of the organization, or people who are working on specific projects that involve the community.

Community feedback

When your community manager joins you, do your best to ensure that she is able to get feedback from the community to key members of your organization. Community managers are always seen as primary contact points in communities, and you should expect them to receive input, opinion, concerns, worries, and other useful feedback from the community. You want to ensure that this feedback gets delivered to the right ears.

The easiest method of doing this is to make sure your community manager knows where feedback should go. When a new community manager joins an organization (particularly a large one with a complex hierarchy), this can be a complicated topic. It could be useful to directly provide her with a list of contacts to get in touch with when different topics of feedback come up. In addition to this, you should always ensure that she feels comfortable asking you to whom she should forward feedback if she is unsure.

Summary

Throughout this chapter we have explored many of the topics involved in hiring a community manager. We have covered how to set reasonable expectations, how to merge that role into your organization, and how to build a measurable strategy to keep you and your community manager on the same page. Even if you faithfully carry out these steps, you should still expect a certain amount of the unknown.

Community management is still a very new profession. As community management becomes a more common role in organizations, and as I hopefully put out further editions of *The Art of Community*, I look forward to solidifying this chapter with more and more advice. Fortunately, the information I have provided here should get you off to a great start. If you temper this chapter with your own experience and what your community manager tells you, you will get everyone off on the right foot.

CHAPTER FOURTEEN

Community Case Book

"Learning never exhausts the mind."

—*Leonardo da Vinci*

WHEN I STARTED WRITING THE FIRST EDITION OF *THE ART OF COMMUNITY*, MY PRIMARY GOAL WAS TO DISTILL AND PRESENT ONE MAN'S THESIS AND APPROACH TO COMMUNITY MANAGEMENT AND LEADERSHIP. The logic was simple: I have a pretty firm grasp of my own experiences, opinions, and approaches, and I could confidently articulate them.

As I continued writing the book, I found myself wanting to include some of the knowledge I was fortunate enough to glean from others. I included this content, cited it where relevant, and provided props to those who helped me to define and grow my career. While this knowledge was useful in augmenting the content of the book, I didn't have the space to tell the stories or feature those insights in greater detail.

When I started writing this second edition of the book I really wanted to include this additional content. There are so many inspirational and fascinating community stories going on right now in the world, and this chapter pulls together many of them.

Included here is a collection of interviews with various friends who have been doing great community work over the years. These stories are diverse and cover technology, music, business, and other areas, and I encourage you to read them all, even though it takes a bit of a time commitment. They tell the stories and perspectives of many community leaders who are at the forefront of change and innovation within their respective worlds.

Linus Torvalds, Linux

Linus Torvalds is the creator of the Linux kernel and arguably the forefather of the Linux movement. He has been the chief architect of the kernel for many years and today acts as the project's primary coordinator. In the year 2000, Linus was voted 17th in the *TIME 100*, TIME magazine's list of the top 100 most important people of the century; in 2004, TIME named him as one of the most influential people in the world, and in 2006, the magazine named him as one of the revolutionary heroes of the past 60 years.

Here we discuss how Linux started, and how Linus grew his community, defined a clear set of values, and structured his community to be successful, all wrapped inside his trademark honesty and frankness.

When Linux started, how did you get people interested in participating?

> Very early on, I wasn't even interested in people really participating; I wanted comments and suggestions for features people needed. It was my project, for my own use, and what I was interested in was not really so much help, as keeping my project alive by having others give ideas and keep me motivated.
>
> When people started sending patches, I initially often ended up rewriting them to suit me better.
>
> So I really didn't plan any of it, or work at trying to get people to participate. But once they started to engage in the project, I was very open to the issues they had, partly because I really had no plan of my own, so people sending me patches never interfered with some "bigger plan" of mine. Even when I rewrote the patches, the project was clearly pretty open.

What do you consider the important values in the Linux kernel community and in how people participate?

> Different people have different ideas about what's important, and that's OK. To me, a project is only as useful as its users find it, so to me what's important is code quality, and that we don't break users' environments. At the same time, I do it because it's fun and interesting, and that's the "value" I appreciate.
>
> To others, it's the whole "freedom" thing, and yet to others it's about making a living. And it's all OK, and I don't think the "important values" are what matters, but that open source allows people to work together despite having all these totally different ideas of what they want to do and even *why* they want to do it.

The Linux community has a very flat organizational structure and does not have countless governance bodies as seen in other large projects. Why do you feel Linux has not been tempted down this route?

> I really don't know. Personally, I don't like committees, and I absolutely abhor the groups with "commit privileges." But clearly they have worked for other projects, so maybe my personal dislike of them may be a bit odd. I don't like the politics that seem to often happen in those kinds of environments, and I believe that they also tend to make forks very acrimonious, because they tend to turn a technical disagreement into a social problem.
>
> The Linux model was always pretty distributed, even back before we used distributed tools. That may sound odd, because in some ways the original model of me doing tarballs and patches was *really* centralized, and I was the only one with "commit privileges." But while that was true at

one level, at another level it was true that a lot of other people simply had their own trees, and distributions all had theirs, and there was never any kind of "cabal" that controlled things. We all controlled our own trees, and the fact that I never paid anybody or acted in that kind of position meant that I couldn't force people to do what I wanted, and while I was in some respect a central figure, I didn't really have any power to tell people how they had to work.

And I still eschew trying to have some kind of "technical board" that decides what direction development should take. Or rather, I think it's healthy that there are *many* of those technical boards, all with their own agenda, and none of them "owns" the kernel. And I am still central, but I'm still central with no real power over anybody, just the trust of people that I don't do totally crazy things.

And it seems to be working. In the kernel community, we've had lots of forks, but they tend to be technical in nature. Not all of them work, and I'm not claiming that people are *happy* when their fork doesn't necessarily end up being used, and there is obviously always jockeying for position, etc., but on the whole I think it's still a pretty "healthy competition" rather than the kinds of ugly forks that some projects have had.

Knock wood.

You have seen Linux grow from a small project to a global contributor base. What were the main challenges in dealing with this growth?

Oh, we've had several times when we've had some really bad growing pains. It's seldom so much about the code not working as the flow of development not working, and something (often *somebody*) holding things up. And yes, that somebody has sometimes been me, and we've had to figure out how to change how we do things so that no single person ends up being that kind of bottleneck.

We seem to have succeeded pretty well, but it's not always been pretty. We change our code *all* the time, and each release tends to have a million lines of changes or so. But changing how you actually *do* something, that can be painful, and people will fight that tooth and nail. It's how we're wired up: we all get comfy with our way of doing something, and doing things another way is just irritating and inefficient.

So we've had issues over tools and code flow—back with the original tarballs and patches, then bitkeeper, and then it took *years* for people to really grow comfy with git.

How did you handle some of these challenges with this growth?

Very little of it was planned. Sure, we have had transitions that were actually explicitly planned and designed, but they tended to have been about the details—the big stuff was all pretty organic. We started doing something, it worked for a while, then it didn't scale anymore, we got into big and ugly fights, and we ended up trying some other approach. Very much a "trial and error" kind of model, where the approaches that work were kept, and the ones that cause friction and problems eventually get whittled away and changed.

And I really want to stress the "not a lot of planning" part. All our big changes came not because we foresaw some better way of doing things, but because our old ways of doing things got *so* painful that people started really disliking each other because things weren't working smoothly.

The kernel has garnered significant commercial interest. How have you balanced the interest of these companies with the values your community holds important?

I actually think the commercial interests have been very important to make sure that they balance the purely geek interests.

In other words, I think a lot of technical projects tend to easily bog down in technical issues, and only have technical users, and never become very good. And I think a lot of the reasons why Linux got successful was because we ended up also getting all these commercial interests (fairly small in the beginning, but it was a small project, so...) that actually counteracted some of the "by geeks, for geeks, nontechnical people need not apply" mentality that can otherwise often happen.

So the whole "technical versus business interests" thing I think has worked really, really well, and both bring a lot to the table. A company that lets *pure* business interests say what should be done will result in a bad product, but it's equally true that having pure technical issues at heart is also a bad approach.

And no, it's not that we actively tried to somehow "counteract" the business interests. Sure, we're technical people, and we distrust business people with their two-drink minimums at a rather visceral level, but I think having both has been very, very important.

What are the main lessons you have learned over the years about working with the community and what advice would you offer budding community leaders?

Don't try to "work the community." You can't. It's not about a project leader trying to take advantage of all those people lining up to help, because that's not what will happen. Instead, do the best you can, and help them do what they want. Then you may be able to occasionally guide them in particular directions when they trust you.

Mike Shinoda, Linkin Park

Mike Shinoda is the principal songwriter, rapper, keyboardist, vocalist, and rhythm guitarist of the rock band Linkin Park. Mike has been exploring many facets of community, technology, and collaboration in his work. He has been actively involved in growing a global Linkin Park community, coordinating community resources and media, ensuring that the band has a close connection with fans, and more.

Mike has also spoken extensively about social media and the role of large record companies in the modern music industry. Outside of Linkin Park, Mike also formed Fort Minor as a side project, is an active artist and painter, and has produced a number of albums.

How did Linkin Park grow a community of fans around the band back when you started out?

We started the band out of our apartments in Los Angeles. We were in college at the time, around 1998, and the Internet hadn't really caught on yet, as strange as that is to say. When we really started promoting our music, we were handing out cassette tapes. At our shows, we always hung out by the merchandise booth, to meet new fans. We would hand them our mailing list, which had options for snail mail and email; more than half the people didn't fill in an email address, because most people weren't really using it yet. It was a different time.

When we chose the name Linkin Park, we originally wanted to spell it "Lincoln Park"...but we also had the foresight to know the importance of getting a memorable domain. So we chose to spell it "Linkin" because *www.linkinpark.com* was available.

After that, we got on the road and we made sure to always super-serve the fans that chose to sign the mailing list. We sent them free tapes and stickers. When they ran out, we sent them more. And we packaged and shipped everything ourselves, right out of our drummer's apartment.

As the band has achieved wide success, how has the relationship with your community grown and changed?

Today, with a fan base as big and spread out as ours, the toughest part is keeping everyone informed and keeping our messages organized. We always have a TON of stuff going on. Aside from the obvious things like albums, singles, and tours, we have a Linkin Park documentary-style channel on YouTube, an online radio station, a charity called Music For Relief, side projects, art shows, clothing and merchandise...I feel like the list can go on forever. Notably, we also have a fan club called the LP Underground that has a nonstop universe of action going on all the time: Linkin Park "Summit" convention events (think LP Comic-Con), surprise chats with band members, exclusive music, and an episodic LPUTV channel which is updated a few times a month.

The key, for us, is to know what lanes to put all that information in. You can't blast all that info to the whole fan base (via Facebook or Twitter, for example) because most people will feel like they're getting spammed. And on the other end, there are people who can't get enough, no matter how much we've got going on.

With this success, how have you as musicians handled the sheer scale and growth of your community? Have you tried to maintain a personal connection with your fans despite the growth?

Today, an honest face-to-face is the most valuable thing. Back in 1999, on our first tour, we did meet-and-greets with fans before every show. We thanked them for coming, we signed stuff, and we took pictures. As the band grew, we constantly reminded ourselves to never let that go. On our tour last month, we signed for up to 100 people every night.

It also should be said that we know the value of a surprise. Especially one that lets the fans know we're listening. I'll often reply directly to comments on *mikeshinoda.com*, and I love to get into Q+As and debates with the fans online. We ask for suggestions on a lot of our online programs and our websites. I also randomly drop into the fan chat rooms unannounced. I'll chat for a few minutes with the 20 or so people that are in there, to give them special time; then I'll tweet that I'm in the chat and hundreds of other people will show up. That way, the ones who were there first get special time, and I still spend time with the larger group. I think it's important to do it on "my time." I don't really schedule these activities, because then I'll feel like it's "work." I only go in when I feel like I want to.

Linkin Park and Fort Minor have evolved in the digital and social networking age. How have you used these technologies to interact with and grow your community?

We were unbelievably lucky to have *Hybrid Theory* come out just as Napster and the MP3 really took off. We got to ride that last wave of big album sales with a hit—not many albums will ever receive a Diamond Award again. I think it taught us to be grateful for each moment, because everything can change so quickly. And it also taught us to watch technology, because music and tech go hand-in-hand.

Specifically, I think our philosophy has become one of championing new sites and technologies we believe in, and making ourselves available wherever the people are. We poll our fan base to find out what they're up to. We collect whatever data we are allowed to. We create separate online access points—and embrace all the different ways people choose to keep in touch with our band—so they can connect to us via whatever thing they like to use. Facebook gets the bigger updates, Twitter gets its own things, LPU gets lots of exclusive ones, and so on. Right now, we know a large percentage of our fans love video games, so we make a lot of efforts in that space.

Traditionally, music fans have just been shared consumers. Do you see opportunities for artists where fans can collaborate around content to support and grow awareness of the artist?

When we announced our fourth studio album, *A Thousand Suns*, we opened up a contest where fans could remix our new single, "The Catalyst"...but the catch was they hadn't heard the single yet. It hadn't been released. We gave them random tracks of the song—a drum loop here, a guitar there, a couple vocals that didn't quite line up—and let them guess at what it would sound like. And we announced that whoever we picked as the winner was going to get to write with the band, and their material was going to end up on the album, officially, everywhere in the world.

This idea was a huge risk for us. Fans could decide that the song was "supposed" to sound a certain way, or like a fan version more than ours! And what if the person who won ended up being terrible, and we were forced to put some of their awful material on our album? In the end, we decided to bite the bullet and go through with the experiment for the sake of doing something groundbreaking—and a little dangerous.

There were thousands of submissions. I think we heard all of them. A third of the entries actually submitted tracks where the parts didn't start on the same beat as our song; they were a quarter note early or late (on beat, but shifted), which sometimes sounded bad, but occasionally sounded cool.

Finally, we found an amazing submission by a guy from Poland named *NoBrain*. We instantly knew he was a good fit. The ways he was effecting the sounds in the remix felt as if he had already heard the album. His winning remix was featured on the B side of the single for "The Catalyst," and he wrote with us on a song called "When They Come For Me." Since he lived in Poland, and our timeline was tight, we wrote and recorded with him online, using Skype and an online recording community called Indaba.com. It was a home run.

We live today in a remix and YouTube culture. How do you see this culture from the perspective of an established artist and content producer, particularly in an increasingly paranoid record industry?

I like fan participation and community. That's all good. The main place I'd like to see a change, in general, is that moment when a fan decides to buy a song or album. For some reason, they still think they need to go to an online store like iTunes or Amazon. For Linkin Park, we offer the fans a lot of incentive to buy directly from us. We have exclusive packages that include limited and unique other stuff that you can't get anywhere else, like signed skate decks, limited edition tees, posters, and art books.

Even if someone just wants to buy the album and nothing extra, we give them more, for the same price! We might give them videos, extra songs, access to discounts on other merchandise, or concert ticket presales. I don't know why fans haven't realized they get a ton more value when they buy direct from us, but someday they will.

You have said in the past that you see no reason why an artist needs to sign to a big label. Do you feel there is an opportunity for a community of fans to provide the same support that a label would produce, and if so, how so?

An unestablished artist has very few reasons to go to a major label. I always tell upstart musicians to go it alone, try to learn everything they can, try to be as self-sufficient as is reasonable, and focus on building a fan base artist-to-fan. You'll get a better understanding of what you're doing, and you'll have the chance to build a substantial base organically. If you get some traction, you know you've got something that works. And look at it this way—who would the labels want to sign: a new artist who only has 100 fans online but a slick demo with a name-brand producer or manager, or a new artist who can sell 10,000 copies and a proven and organic connection with their fans? The latter situation will have labels beating down your door with better offers, and it will be up to you to decide whether or not to turn them down.

I suppose the only time that isn't true is when the artist simply wants to be a pop star, and is happy letting the label turn them into a profitable commodity in order to be famous. But in that case, I wouldn't call them an "artist," and they may not even be a "musician." I'm not very familiar with that mindset. To me, the real excitement comes from a true artist-fan connection. A movement. A culture. That's where the magic is.

If you work hard to improve your craft, and care deeply about the integrity of your art, I think you have a good shot. I believe if you make something good, success will follow. "Success" doesn't just mean money, by the way. Doing what you love to do—and being able to live a comfortable lifestyle while doing it—is a great gig.

Mårten Mickos, MySQL and Eucalyptus

Mårten Mickos was the CEO of MySQL AB, was senior vice president of the database group at Sun Microsystems, is a member of the board of Mozilla Messaging and RightScale, and Entrepreneur In Residence at Benchmark Capital. Currently he is CEO of Eucalyptus Systems, the company behind the Eucalyptus open source cloud infrastructure.

Mårten has been at the forefront of the open source business world and has been faced with the responsibility of balancing the corporate interests of an organization with the participatory interests of a community. This provides him with unique insight into how others in a similar position can face this equilibrium, too.

Where do you see the opportunity for companies to harness community?

Any company that has a broad customer or user base can harness community. I am not saying it is easy, but it can be done. Today, the concept of "community" stretches far beyond open source software.

Some examples: Local Motors engages with the community to design cars, BurdaStyle to design sowing patterns. *Star Wreck* is the most popular Finnish movie ever made. It was produced by a community of enthusiasts and distributed through free downloads all over the world. The TED conference has built up an amazing community of speakers and influencers who produce and share amazing talks.

The notion of a community and of an architecture of participation is so strong that it can apply even to closed source software. Microsoft may not understand the value of FOSS, but they have built an impressive developer community around Visual Studio.

You have been at the forefront of how companies and community fit together. What do you feel are the ground rules for ensuring that a company and community work well together?

Transparency and integrity. You must be open about your philosophies, your practices, and your plans. You must tell the community what they can get for free and what they will need to pay for. By integrity I mean that whatever business model you choose, it must be based on respect for the individual: respect for users and respect for customers.

People will accept many different models as long as they know they can trust you and that you have told them all the important aspects of your thinking.

Branding can be a sensitive topic. At MySQL, we had the same brand for the community stuff and the commercial stuff. Everything was just "MySQL." Around Red Hat it is different. You have Linux the project, Fedora the community distro, and Red Hat the paid-for enterprise product. Canonical uses "Ubuntu" both for nonpaid community software and paid-for offerings. Again, as with business models, many different approaches are OK, but you must be clear to your ecosystem how you will deal with naming and branding. Open source people can be quite particular with how they want software and related offerings to be named.

How do you balance the needs of company stakeholders and community stakeholders?

The key to this balancing act (and, I'd say, to any balancing act) is to be very clear on how the model works and what the goals are. As an open source software vendor, there is a reason you have a community. There is a reason you have paying customers. There is a reason you have investors (if you do). You need to go through the sometimes cumbersome thinking process of why exactly you are dealing with some group.

For instance, if you want a community so that you get help in finding and fixing bugs, you need to make it very easy for anyone to adopt your software, even at the expense of short-term revenue goals. Otherwise, you won't have a community. If you want a community so that you have a champion in every organization, you may take some other actions. If you want a community that may turn into paying customers (not that I personally believe much in that model), you will take some other actions. Your actions in this balancing act are a direct function of what your real goal is.

My point is that when properly analyzed, the "balancing act" isn't really a balancing act other than over a timescale. You have some goals you must achieve right now and other goals you will achieve later. The goals are not in conflict with each other—they just have different maturity times.

How do you ensure that the community's needs are not overlooked as a company grows and scales upward?

You need to be clear about your strategy, and you need to stick to it. There could, for some companies, be a temptation to go for short-term benefits in the hope that "the community won't notice." That won't really work. You must have a well-articulated strategy and stick to it.

Even as I say that, it still isn't easy. As an example, MySQL got criticism in 2007 and 2008 for changes we did to our business model. If you study those events closely, I think you will see that throughout this time, we improved what was available free of charge to our user community. The community got more than before.

But we also added more commercial features and offerings. Some saw this as a deviation from our stated business model. They felt that we had an obligation to not produce anything that was only for paying customers. The way we saw it, that was an extra—something we produced on top of whatever we would have been doing anyhow for the community. What we did for the free and open source software communities was bigger, stronger, and more valuable than before. So we felt we had provided the community with a net positive. We felt we were entitled to additionally build something for paying customers only.

Many agreed with us, but not all. For some, it boiled down to a difference in view of what an open source business model is allowed to be. We were convinced we took care of the needs of the community better than before. But the fact that we *also* produced commercial stuff became a contentious topic with some. I don't think there really is a generic solution to this dilemma. As an open source business leader, you just must be ready for situations where you cannot please all.

What do you look for in the perfect community manager?

This is a difficult question to answer, because "community manager" is such an elusive job title. You could say that everyone in the company needs to be community-focused, so there isn't a need for a specific community manager.

But if you do hire one, which I recommend, what should she or he do? In my view, the main role of a community manager is to ensure that the company's operations are open, community-friendly, and inviting of participation. The main role is about helping manage the company's day-to-day operations.

The community manager does NOT have to be a blogger and [tweeter] and social person in general. It doesn't hurt if she/he is, but this is not the main point. The person also doesn't have to attend every meet-up and FOSS event. The main point is turning the company inside out—making it an outward-focused organization that willingly, and I think I would say charmingly, engages with the world around it.

When that basic function of enabling public participation is in place, then the community manager can think of how to lead and guide the community members, how to invite them to take small or large responsibilities in the community, and how to communicate with the broad community.

Mike Linksvayer, Creative Commons

Creative Commons (*http://www.creativecommons.org*) has been a revolutionary force in enabling artists and content creators to share their work easily and effectively. The organization has created a set of licenses that make it simple to protect the content creator's rights while building a culture of sharing, remixing, and creating derivative works. I am a huge fan of Creative Commons and this book is licensed under a Creative Commons license.

Mike Linksvayer serves as vice president of Creative Commons. Mike originally joined Creative Commons as its chief technical officer in 2003 and then became vice president in 2007. Previously he cofounded Bitzi, an early open content/open data service.

You have been at Creative Commons for a long time now. How did the organization look when you joined?

I joined Creative Commons in April 2003, a few months after the first Creative Commons licenses were released. We were in the basement of the Stanford Law School, as that's where Lawrence Lessig was. Various people had been involved over the preceding year, but essentially there were three staff [members] just before I joined. There was a very loose community initially, based on the notoriety of Lessig and other founders and some friendly coverage in the usual (for the time) geek outlets such as Slashdot—more a variety of well-wishers than a community.

What kind of community did you set out to grow?

The other person Creative Commons hired in April 2003 was our first international coordinator, based in Berlin. One community that we set out to grow, initially via this position, was a network of legal scholars around the world, who could collectively figure out how Creative Commons licenses work with copyright law in various jurisdictions around the world. This is the main community that Creative Commons was and is intentional about growing. We also set out to grow connections with related communities—for example, open access, open education, open source—and mostly deliberately stayed away from trying to create Creative Commons subcommunities within these movements, and instead play a supporting role.

There always has been a mostly latent "Creative Commons community" of people who aren't tied to a Creative Commons affiliate institution, and may or may not be involved with other nearby movements, but for whatever reason see Creative Commons as one of their primary passions—which is fantastic, of course. Creative Commons the organization hasn't ever really set out to "organize" this largely latent community, mostly due to lack of bandwidth (admittedly this could seem shortsighted), and it isn't clear how this community ought to be cultivated—it is a very diverse set of people. I and some others see mobilizing this community (I'm actually more comfortable thinking about it as a movement) in some form as one of the biggest opportunities Creative Commons has in its next decade.

What approaches did you use to grow your community?

Regarding the international community of legal scholars we intentionally created, we gave them interesting, challenging, but highly delimited work—"porting" the Creative Commons license suite to their respective jurisdictions. (A "port" is usually both a linguistic translation and legal "translation" to reference local laws, drafting style, etc., where appropriate to hopefully make the ported licenses more understandable to the legal community in a given jurisdiction, but achieve the same effects to the extent possible.) This element of concrete work made it relatively easy to determine what kind of team (usually composed of people from one or more local institutions) could be part of the formal community—they had to bring certain legal expertise, interest, and capacity—and gave community members a strong sense of ownership and contribution.

How much growth have you seen in this work?

In the past eight years Creative Commons licenses have been ported to over 50 jurisdictions via this process and community. In a sense this is just another instance of work occurring in chunks amenable to work being done by lots of different people, but I think the subject matter and large size and duration of the chunks makes it fairly interesting. Although many of the affiliate projects have formed their own local communities that have given feedback on license drafts, the overall process is highly controlled by experts, and openness to attracting and up-leveling drive-by contributors [is] not much of a factor. This arrangement has been shown to not be competitive for building an encyclopedia, nor for most software and cultural projects, but perhaps should be evaluated if one thinks their project requires long-term commitment from a community with narrow and rare expertise.

Among the community involved in license porting, there has always been a desire to also do advocacy and outreach, and sometimes art projects and software development. This has occurred organically, but over the last year or so we've also formally recognized those activities as potential responsibilities of a Creative Commons affiliate. While producing interesting work, a community that only really needs a few lawyers in each country is self-limiting. The aforementioned activities need unlimited resources, including the involvement of many more lawyers, who are crucial in persuading institutions and governments to adopt Creative Commons tools as policy, for example. Probably over the next few years there will be many more institutions and people officially involved in the Creative Commons community, with impressive outreach and projects around the world as a result.

The Creative Commons philosophy, particularly a few years ago, was fairly alien to the normal culture of content licensing and distribution practiced by large record labels and studios. How did you communicate this message to your community?

Building a commons is still completely alien to "big content"; not even relevant, really. Giving up the ability to legally persecute fans and users is a bridge too far for those whose dominant interest is protecting and milking existing revenue streams for however many quarters their horizon is. If it takes destroying the Internet to do that, so be it. This has to change, but the change won't come from big content adopting Creative Commons licenses wholesale (though of course we appreciate when a progressive element does so for a project, and I'd be happy to be wrong), but through policy change that removes their ability to persecute fans. Have we reached "peak copyright" yet?

Communicating this to the Creative Commons community is not a challenge—they already knew how poorly aligned the interest and practice of big content and society are, and for many people this was a motivating factor for getting involved in Creative Commons.

So where do you see the primary challenge today?

The challenge has been figuring out where the commons can make a big difference, given the indifference to hostility of big content. The answer has [been] arrived at fairly organically, learning both from the broader community (e.g., FLOSS, Wikipedians, the Open Access movement) and from the Creative Commons affiliate community's work on institutional and government policy. The summary is that Creative Commons' sweet spots are community and mass collaboration projects, where legal freedoms are necessary for a project to scale, just like in FLOSS, and in publicly interested policy, where the policymaker might be a funder, an institution, or a government. In both of these cases, the appropriate Creative Commons license or public domain tool is a standard, well-understood and recognized instrument that can be made the legal basis of a project, or slotted into a broader policy intended to benefit the public, instead of engaging in expensive debate and reinvention—and there's a big community of experts eager to help, wherever one is in the world.

There is this passionate Creative Commons community out there, but how did you build a community that takes the Creative Commons ethos, and spreads it farther and advocates it to others?

Sharing, giving credit where due, valuing the common good, using technology to encourage such, not persecuting people who do those very natural things—things that one might recognize as "the Creative Commons ethos"—all precede Creative Commons. They're essentially human. Creative Commons created some practical tools that one can use to further those ends and a brand that denotes such an ethos at our particular juncture in history. People would've been spreading that ethos in the same contexts Creative Commons is now—one can see an explosion of experiments in open content licensing in the years just before Creative Commons launched. Hopefully, overall, Creative Commons has made those people more effective than they would've been without a fairly high-profile and well-resourced (but tiny in the scheme of things) license steward, that is, Creative Commons.

We did make an attempt in approximately 2005–2008 to provide a nexus for open movements to meet and collaborate, a subsidiary called iCommons (now a small independent charity) that ran a series of "iSummits." These turned out to be mostly useful for bringing the Creative Commons community together, so our next global gathering, which did not occur until September 2011, made no pretense of being anything other than a Creative Commons summit. There remains a huge opportunity to, at appropriate times, work together with other communities and movements with an overlapping ethos—more of that is happening, but slowly, and not under an umbrella brand.

Creative Commons is now a well-established organization and community. How do you keep your community passionate about Creative Commons and Free Culture?

Regarding the Creative Commons affiliate community (copyright and other experts mentioned earlier), carefully and collaboratively. Some of the core work by that community is changing: we're working on version 4.0 of the Creative Commons license suite now, which has the aim of being unambiguously global—porting as it has been done so far may end, or at least will be a special case. We have to build the diversity of the work of this community, and it has to be even more vital and challenging work; for example, Creative Commons adoption as policy, leveraging Creative Commons' reputation in nearby policy debates impactful to the commons, Creative Commons as a subject of legal, economic, and other research, and interfacing with

WIPO and other international institutions. We have to strive to make Creative Commons a truly international organization itself. What this means for governance, staffing, fundraising, the structure of relationships with affiliates and other organizations—we don't know yet, and [it] will probably always be evolving.

Regarding the broader community and potential movement, the flip answer is that we don't have to do anything. The passion is there, and Free Culture, Creative Commons, open education, etc., provide endless good news and opportunity for all interested—and occasionally we get a gift in the form of a ridiculously incorrect attack on Creative Commons from a big content executive—that fires everyone up. However, there's a lot that we do, the single most important one being serving as a great license steward, which includes everything from explaining and answering questions to advocacy to actually getting the licenses "right" so that they're the best tools for growing the commons. If our explanations of the licenses are confusing, or we have licenses that don't serve to build the commons, it puts a real damper on the ability of the community to advocate and spread Creative Commons, and their passion for doing so.

The 4.0 process is also going to be crucial for engaging the broader community, and be a determinant of how much passion and energy we see from them over the next decade. My highest aspiration would be for the 4.0 licenses to have received overwhelming input and buy-in from both the broadest set of "netizens" (if I may use a 1990s term) interested in the common good and policymakers, forming a standard for information and innovation policy and norms for a generation. Coming anywhere near that goal will require lots of community organizing!

Creative Commons is funded by donations. What approaches have you used to gather these donations?

So far the vast majority of our funding has come from US-based private foundations. Our main effort for community support (which I consider the [healthiest] form of funding, and should over time become the most important pillar) has consisted of an annual fall campaign, mostly conducted online—think a micro version of the Wikimedia fundraising campaigns that many readers might have seen. Creative Commons has a lot of learning and growth to do here. The main reason to cultivate the Creative Commons community is that doing [so] will be instrumental for accomplishing our mission; but it is true that we hope that a portion of the community has the means and feels our work is important enough to donate each year.

Tim O'Reilly, O'Reilly Media

Tim O'Reilly is the founder of O'Reilly Media, a diverse company with a goal to spread the knowledge of innovators. O'Reilly started doing this via the publication of books (*The Art of Community* is published by O'Reilly), many of which are the best-known books in the technology field. O'Reilly has since diversified into conferences (e.g., OSCON, Strata, TOC, Velocity, and Where), organizing the popular FooCamp gathering of leading minds in the industry, and has an investment division called O'Reilly AlphaTech Ventures (OATV).

Tim has also been seen as a thought leader on change and innovation in technology. He was a driver in the adoption of Web 2.0 and has been a proponent of social media, and particularly Twitter.

What is your social media story? How did you get started, and what attracted you?

My "social media story" begins long before Facebook or Twitter. When I organized my first conference, the Perl Conference, in 1997, it was because I recognized that there was a community online that would benefit from connecting in person. To this day, my best ever social media experience was the rush of being in the same place as people, who in many cases, had worked together online for years, but had never met in person, didn't even know what each other looked like, had never heard the sound of each other's voices. It's important to remember how primitive the Internet was, and how much of what we take for granted today didn't exist yet. There was wonderful community, but it was a community of code and comments, of IRC and mailing lists.

When I organized the Freeware Summit (later known as the Open Source Summit) in 1998, it was because I recognized that there were multiple communities like that, that their leaders had never met in person, and would benefit from talking about common problems and shaping a common story. And being a media company, we organized a press conference at the end of the day to get that story out. And sure enough, two months later, Linus Torvalds was on the cover of *Forbes*, with full-page pictures inside of Larry Wall, Richard Stallman, Brian Behlendorf, and others.

Social media is about community, about the stories that tie those communities together, and about tools to amplify the connections between them. I was doing that long before I got on Twitter or Facebook.

Which social media networks really captured your interest first?

It was Twitter that first pulled me in. I had signed up for Twitter and Facebook to try them out, but didn't stick around. But one day I checked back into Twitter, and by gum, I had 5,000 followers! I was embarrassed that I hadn't been giving them anything to follow, so I started to tweet actively. And because I'm an ideas guy, what I shared was links to what I was reading far more than what I was doing. That's a style of tweeting that *@jayrosen_nyu* christened "mindcasting." At the time, it was somewhat atypical, but it's since become one of the most common forms of tweeting.

How has your usage of Twitter changed and evolved over time?

Now that I have over 1.5 million followers, that's a kind of publishing platform. I follow about 800 people and try to pass on a lot of tweets from them via retweet, as a way of amplifying not just the ideas but other people who are good sources of them. I measure my tweeting success not just by how many people click on my links but also by how many followers I can add to someone who "gives good tweet." I was proud when someone created a graph of what they called "the @timoreilly bump" showing the spike in their followers. And of course, that's what I do as a book publisher and conference producer, too: find good stuff and try to amplify it.

But I also have a second private account that I use for what *@leisa* called "ambient intimacy." That's where I follow 20 or 30 people I really care about, and with whom I share personal details of my life. That's the original Twitter use case, and I find it really lovely.

But I religiously read and reply to my @ messages on my main Twitter account, because it allows anyone to reach me and vastly increases serendipity. And some of the folks I follow have figured out to DM me when they want to bring my attention to something they've posted, in hopes I'll retweet it.

Increasingly, I'm using Twitter and Google+ as a kind of one-two punch. For short links, Twitter is ideal. But if I want to share more of an opinion and engage with those who comment on my links, I post to G+, and then use Twitter to point to that post rather than to the original story.

Many new technologies have surfaced over the years, but why do you think social media in particular has been so successful?

The two greatest social media success stories to date, Facebook and Twitter, succeeded for very different reasons, in my opinion. Facebook found a natural market where people are trying to get to know other new people in a compressed time frame, and built an app that "just worked" for that target audience. Once it thoroughly dominated that niche, it spread from there.

Twitter's secret sauce was its minimal nature. And asymmetric following was its really great viral hook.

But in the end, social is everywhere. Wikipedia is social, for instance. In his wonderful new book, *Reinventing Discovery*, Michael Nielsen says something like "Wikipedia is not an encyclopedia. It is an online city whose principal export to the net is an online encyclopedia." And of course, this is true of open source development communities as well.

Social media has been known to be incredibly disruptive. What are the most memorable and inspiring social success stories that you have seen?

The Arab Spring is obviously the canonical example, but #ows (Occupy Wall Street) is happening right now as an example of the interplay between social media and real-world disruption.

How do you feel that social media has opened up opportunities for communities to prosper?

I'm not convinced that the current generation of social media sites have helped communities to prosper in the way that earlier technologies like mailing lists or even Usenet did. They create a social graph centered on the individual rather than the community. The development of tools to support communities is still an untapped opportunity.

Today social media seems to largely involve the exchange of messages. How do you think social media can evolve to further empower collaborative community beyond that of exchanging messages?

If you consider Twitter, Facebook, and Google+ to be the apogee of social media, yes, it is mainly about the exchange of messages. But what's really more interesting is collective work, or the production of collective value. And as I tried to make clear in my original advocacy about Web 2.0, "collective intelligence"—which is another face of social media—has been a driver of every major advance on the Web.

This idea of collaborative value creation is obviously central to something like Wikipedia, but it's also at work in Google. It is our collective activity of creating and linking to web pages that Google mines to create its search engine.

And of course, it's central to software development tools like Github.

I'm also fascinated by tools like Kickstarter, which allow for collaboration in funding of projects, and even Storify, which allows someone to build a more lasting product out of a stream of tweets.

With an increasingly social world, how do we balance visibility and privacy?

We balance visibility and privacy in the same way we've always done, with social norms. We don't keep people from peering into our homes at night by living in windowless buildings. We have lightweight privacy mechanisms like curtains, and we stigmatize (and penalize) people who peek through them.

Because of the breadcrumb trails we leave about ourselves online, and the power of data mining to assemble those trails into full loaves of bread, we've got to give up on the idea that privacy is based on secrecy. It's based on a society that knows when to avert its eyes.

Carolyn Mellor, X.commerce, PayPal, and eBay

Carolyn Mellor (*@carolynmellor*) is senior manager of the X.commerce developer community. She is responsible for working with the X.commerce community team to create and build community programs that will support and advocate the needs of developers and merchants working with X.commerce.

Carolyn has been in technology for 20 years and has held multiple technical management positions within eBay and PayPal; in addition to building a successful multilevel technical support organization she led a technical product team responsible for merchant and partner experience. Prior to PayPal, Carolyn spent five years managing internal and external technical support groups at UPS, and nine years leading an IT department and developing websites for a large automotive dealer group.

What are the goals at PayPal and eBay for working with the community?

We have several goals for working with the community. Of course, we want to have new developers join our community—interact with us and use our services. Our goals are around community registrations, activity on and off our website, participation in our events, and using our products. Our ultimate vision is to create a robust ecosystem around commerce that provides the support and opportunities for developers to turn their creative ideas into reality and generate revenue.

How have you structured the developer community, and how do you work with them?

Currently we are structured by business unit—we interact with the community based on which of our services they use. As we evolve, I think that we may change the structure as well as the interaction.

How do you manage this as a team?

Currently we have community managers for each one of our business units (e.g., eBay, PayPal, X.commerce, Magento); this allows the community managers to gain some level of product and service expertise so that they can engage with and support the community. We have our online communities structured this way as well as our programs; this allows for easy interaction between developers using the same services.

How did you structure your technology to ensure the community can use it easily and effectively?

Because of our organic growth and the fact that we have merged multiple communities together, we have structured our website by business unit so that developers interested in the products and services of that business can find everything they need. In the last few years, we have added more features and utilized them throughout all of our communities. We have chosen technology that can be updated quickly, has an engaged community, and is scalable for our needs.

You have a team working on these goals. How did you grow the team and what do they do?

I have grown my team in order to serve our different developer communities. Currently we have one community champion per service/business unit. The community management organization presently develops a global community engagement strategy and owns the objectives, priorities, schedules, and key results. We lead the effort to design and launch new community features in partnership with product management, engineering, and other cross-functional stakeholders.

How do you do this work?

We coordinate content creation through writing or facilitating blog posts, articles, newsletters, communication materials, and material for social media channels. In addition, we share community feedback with our internal product teams, so their feedback is incorporated into current and future road maps. We drive building, planning, and executing engagement programs to grow community acquisition and interaction. We do this by creating, managing, and growing the organization's presence through blogs, Twitter, Facebook, YouTube, and other strategically relevant online properties.

Our community champions are also responsible for customer support—answering questions however they come in (phone, email, Twitter) and managing/organizing moderation of any online feedback or Q&A forums. We utilize user measurement tools to provide reports on metrics, and continually seek ways in which to improve on those metrics through new initiatives.

How do you break down these different types of work?

Our overall community team consists of several teams: the evangelist group that educates developers on our products, the tools and docs team that generates tools for developers to interact with our services, the events and outreach team, which coordinates developer events, and our X.com ProductD/Product team that builds and supports our website.

What resources and facilities have you put in place to help the community collaborate together?

We have put in place the ability to collaborate online with functionality and recognition/rewards (via points and badging). We have also created developer councils that are held quarterly to ensure interaction with our product teams and the community. We have also facilitated yearly developer events for approximately 10 years—beginning with eBay DevCon and now with the Innovate Developer Conference.

You have organized a developer event. What were the goals with the event and how did you structure it to accomplish those goals?

We organize a large developer event yearly. This event, called the Innovate Developer Conference, was initially focused on PayPal and now includes all of our properties: eBay, PayPal,

X.commerce, and Magento. Our goals of the conference are attendance, education (measured through surveys), and, of course, a stage for product/program announcements. Events also tend to provide a goal for product teams to create features to launch at the event.

How have you balanced the commercial needs of PayPal and eBay with the needs of the community?

We are lucky; our organization sees the value of community. We see the value of connecting people together to create monetization opportunities, value, and products. We believe that the more people feel a part of and participate in the community, the more value they will bring to our business units. In fact, we do not require any info/login to use our tools/technologies. Only when you want to test/go live and participate in community features on the site are you required to register. We believe that the more people we get to use our products and engage with us, the better off we are as a business. We are only successful if our developers/merchants are successful, and we believe that the community enables both.

Ilan Rabinovitch, Southern California Linux Expo

Ilan Rabinovitch is a cofounder of the Southern California Linux Expo (SCALE) and the Texas Linux Fest, and is a frequent contributor to community-focused open source events and conferences. Ilan currently serves as president at LinuxFests.org, where he helps open source communities launch and operate their own events by providing fiscal sponsorship, planning support, and advice.

When not planning events and participating in open source communities, Ilan is employed as a system administrator usually focusing on large-scale web operations; recent clients include Edmunds.com and Ooyala.

With the success of these events Ilan has earned a reputation as one of the most competent event organizers in the open source community.

How did you get started in event organization?

SCALE, the Southern California Linux Expo, has its roots in the Los Angeles area Linux User Group community. Prior to starting SCALE, many of us were involved of a series of events known as "LUGFests" hosted by the Simi-Conejo Linux User Group in 2001 and 2002.

LUGs or Linux User Groups were very popular in Los Angeles at the time. We had about a dozen different user group meetings around the Southern California area that would meet weekly to discuss Linux and open source software. The LUGFests were one- and two-day events we held about once every six months to bring all of these user groups together.

The LUGFests were a great deal of fun; we held them at a venue provided by Nortel. One of our user group members, Orv Beach, was the IT director for the facility and arranged for us to use their cafeteria and conference rooms for the event. The event included presentations by local user group members, with some companies sending representatives to speak. We also had an exhibit in Nortel's cafeteria, where individuals demonstrated various open source applications and Linux distributions. A few of the early open source-focused companies such as VA Linux and LinuxCare sent representatives as well, but the focus was mostly on Linux users showing one another projects we were interested or involved in.

How did the LUGFests transition into SCALE?

Unfortunately, after four LUGFests, the dot-com bubble burst resulted in us losing the venue Nortel had previously been providing. Without a home and wanting to continue organizing an open source event in Southern California, we teamed up with a group of students at two local universities, UCLA and USC, to start SCALE.

When starting SCALE we came to a few realizations. The first was that unfortunately there were no companies in Southern California willing to donate space. This meant we would need to find ways to raise money and rent space. To finance the event we began allowing companies to rent exhibitor space for their products, alongside the open source projects and user groups who were exhibiting.

We also realized that we wanted a more varied group of attendees. While the LUGFests primarily focused on individual users and community members, we felt this new event was also a great opportunity to reach a wider audience. We wanted to help grow the open source community and provide educational programs for both existing and new users, while also giving us, the organizers, a chance to meet developers and community leaders that rarely came to Southern California Linux User Group meetings.

After the buildup, how did you start the first event?

We proudly launched our first event in November 2002, cosponsored by USC, with the slogan "We are bringing businesses, academic institutions and the Linux community together in a way that no other conference does!" At the end of the first event we knew we had filled a need for the local community. Attendees, speakers, and exhibitors alike were asking when and where we would reprise the event.

The first SCALE in November 2002 drew in 400 attendees, 6 presentation sessions, and an exhibit hall made up of 30 tabletop displays. We could not have had more than 10 volunteer team members planning the event, while today it takes a team of well over 40 volunteers to pull off the conference.

By our second event, we had nearly doubled in size, so we added a 2X to our name as a play on words. We had "SCALE"d to twice our original size. For a while we were able to hold true to our name, doubling or tripling in size annually.

How big is the event these days?

Our 10th annual event, SCALE 10x, was 10x our original size, other than possibly in our budget. The name stuck, though, and we continue to "SCALE" up where we can. Our February 2011 event drew over 1,800 attendees; SCALE 10x had 2,000 attendees. Our expo floor has grown from 3,840 square feet at our start to 16,000 square feet today. SCALE 10x had 100 exhibitors, nearly 100 speaker sessions, and 4 days of activities. This year we cohosted 15 community events at SCALE, outside of the main SCALE program. We had never planned for SCALE to be this large, but we are proud of what it has become.

How has the event changed and grown over the years?

While our mission remains the same, the rapid growth has changed us. SCALE is no longer just an event organized by a group of local volunteers; we now provide a home for at least eight other conferences organized by partners in the community. This has essentially allowed us to become an incubator for new events as well as offer more varied content to our attendees and community.

What kinds of events does this include?

Some examples of this have included an open source health-care track, DOHCS, which eventually spun off as its own separate conference; activity days for distributions such as openSUSE and Fedora; Ubucon; and others. This allows us to include more niche project- or community-specific content at SCALE, which might not be a good fit for the wider event.

In addition to all of the content we added, we have also lost some. For example, while local user groups used to make up a large portion of our exhibit hall, we now have very few that put together a presence at the event. When we first started each user group would pick a topic they wanted to demonstrate and staff a demo table with their members. At some point along the way, the local user group members realized they wanted to attend the event rather than work it, especially when the projects they previously demonstrated started to join us with their own booths. We still have one or two of these user groups participate on the expo floor, but it's down from the original 10 back in 2002, to around three or four depending on the year.

You all started off as new to event coordination. What were some of the early mistakes you made in retrospect?

When we started SCALE, and before that, the LUGFests, most of us had never organized an event before. We were mostly college or high school kids, and had no idea what we were getting ourselves into. Who knew 10 years later we would still be doing this?

The biggest mistake we made at the first SCALE was not being 100% transparent with the venue about our plans. As a result, we found ourselves in situations where we were overloading circuits with the power draw from our expo floor, or bargaining for bandwidth at the last minute. If you have found the right venue to partner with, their staff is on your side. No matter how unique your event is, their staff runs events year-round and likely has some insight they can offer. They want your event to be successful so that you will come back and work with them again, but they cannot help make that happen if they do not know the details of your program.

Speaking of venues, what do you look for in the perfect venue to host SCALE?

This has changed over the years, but at the moment the two most critical factors for us are location and physical space available. The SCALE team likes to stay with a given venue as long as we can, but when we move it is most frequently because we either found a more accessible location or need more space.

When SCALE moved close to the Los Angeles airport, the new location made it quite convenient for someone from out of town to travel to our event. As a result, our attendance nearly doubled and we started to draw in attendees from around the country rather than just Southern California.

Keep in mind that while having enough space is key, having too much space can also be a problem. You want to find a venue that fits your program. For example, in 2006 we moved from the Los Angeles Convention Center to a smaller hotel because we found that we were regularly lost in a sea of empty space, or crowded out by larger events. At a hotel we fit in better, and our needs were taken more seriously by the venue staff as we were a sizable business for them.

Aside from space, what other considerations do you have for a venue, and what advice do you have for our readers?

When we put together our annual request for proposals, other factors we keep in mind are:

Cost

> Unless your venue is donated, renting meeting space will likely be your largest expenditure. Make sure the venue fits your budget, and look for hidden costs. Even free venues may have associated costs, such as requiring you to use their audio/visual or catering services.

Layout

> Are your meeting rooms easy to find? How far are your meeting rooms from each other? It is important that it be easy to get between all of the rooms your event will use without getting lost. If flow is not right, your event can either feel empty or feel overcrowded.

Electrical power

> One lesson we learned at the first SCALE was that electrical power is a requirement that needs to be communicated clearly to a venue. We learned this the hard way, when one of our exhibitors turned on their rack of servers and tripped all of the breakers in the exhibit hall floor. If your venue is unsure of their circuit layout or how much power they can provide, insist that they hire a third-party vendor to help. Most hotels and conference centers know what their capabilities are, but you never know until you ask.

Bandwidth

> SCALE attendees will use as much bandwidth as we can provide. Whether it be to blog about the sessions they are in, contribute to a project in a hackathon/bug jam, or to download software they learn about in a session, they expect Internet service that works. Unfortunately, at many hotels or convention centers your attendees will likely be sharing an Internet connection with less bandwidth than they have at home. Internet connectivity can also be expensive. We frequently encounter venues that will charge thousands of dollars to provide a single Ethernet port, charge per wireless/wired device, etc. If Internet connectivity is important to your program, make sure to ask about these conditions up front and consider them as you plan your budgets.

Vendor requirements

> As a volunteer-run event, SCALE prefers to do much of our own setup, teardown, wiring, and other activities. Many venues have union or vendor requirements that would prevent us from performing these tasks ourselves. We tend to prefer venues that offer us the most flexibility in selection of vendors

Let's move on to discuss the schedule. How do you assess the submitted papers to ensure that you have an interesting range of presentations?

SCALE recruits most of our content through a call for proposals. As part of this call for proposals we define a range of tracks or topics we wish to see covered. This provides submitters visibility into which topics are most likely to be accepted, and identifies the target audiences we as a team would like to cater to each year.

At the end of our call for proposals, we have a program committee that reviews the submissions to select the sessions we feel would be the best fit for our conference. We work to ensure that this committee has a diverse background so that we have sufficient expertise to review each proposal. Some years we do better at this than others, as our team membership changes.

How do you then select the final schedule of presentations?

The selections generally occur in two phases. First, the team votes on each of the submitted sessions to identify which they would like to see part of SCALE. We then meet as a team either virtually or in person to discuss the top-ranking proposals for each of the audiences or topic tracks we created. This gives us a chance to ensure that we do not select 100 sessions on the same topic, as well as allowing individual committee members to advocate for a particular session or topic they feel was overlooked.

We believe there is room for improvement in this system, but so far it has served SCALE well.

What approaches have you used to attract the big names to come and speak at SCALE?

These days SCALE has built a reputation for itself that makes it significantly easier to attract speakers. But even now there are speakers who elude us. We tend to work with our past attendees, speakers, and exhibitors to request introductions to speakers we would like to invite, or to provide references if we need them.

Earlier in our history, we did not, however, have this advantage. To build our own reputation we partnered with the University of Southern California's (USC) computer science department. They allowed us to use their name in association with our event, and introduced us to their contacts, which gave us some credibility with both speakers and sponsors.

We are also lucky, however, in that our event focuses on the open source community, and that with few exceptions, participants in this community are easily reachable and open to being approached. Since they work in the open, it is often easy to know which individuals are experts in their field. Most speakers were happy to help or attend your event if their schedule allows them to do so.

What advice would you give an event organizer to attract some big names to speak at their event?

The short answer is, do not be shy: if you want someone to present at your event, contact them. The worst thing that can happen is that they can turn you down. In your communications make sure to include all of the pertinent information, such as date, location, number of expected attendees, and an overview of the event format or topic. This information will help them evaluate the event and determine if it is a good fit for their schedule.

How do you handle the finances for SCALE? How do you predict the costs for the event and cover these costs in a way that is affordable for the community to join?

From the start, the SCALE team wanted to keep the event affordable; after all, our roots were in free events such as the LUGFests. For this to be viable we build our budgets assuming our sponsorship packages will cover all of our overhead, with attendee registration fees only being intended to cover the costs of the items they receive.

At the start of the planning cycle, usually six to eight months out, we work with our individual team members to generate budgets that outline expenditures we either have to make or would like to make—everything from venue rentals [and] printing costs to staff lunches and attendee giveaways. We then use these budgets to identify rates for sponsorship packages and targets for the number of sponsors at each level.

We then check in regularly throughout the year to see if we are meeting our targets or not. In some years we have found targets were not met, so we had to cut perks such as attendee t-shirts; if we find ourselves leaning the other way we identify additional attendee programs we can offer or find good causes where we feel the funds would be helpful.

SCALE is seen as one of the best open source community events in the United States. How have you maintained the "community feel" of the event?

I believe the largest contribution to the "community feel" is that the event is organized by the community. New team members join every year to help with areas they feel they can improve. As a result, everyone who attends SCALE feels like they helped to make the event successful.

Another contributing factor is that we make a strong effort to avoid undue influence by sponsors in our presentation selections or programming. We never allow product pitches in our conference program; these are reserved for our exhibit hall. And even in the exhibit hall we make an effort to ensure both the community and commercial organizations are on equal footing.

At the start of each year, we allocate 50% of our exhibit space for use by nonprofit or community organizations, with the other 50% being designated for commercial use. There is no nonprofit zone: all of the groups are mixed in together. We then assign different team members to recruit commercial and nonprofit exhibitors, ensuring that both types of exhibitor are well represented.

This equal priority on both groups is key to our success. Commercial exhibitors pick up on the community vibe from their neighbors and tailor their demos and messaging accordingly, and the community exhibitors get just as much attention and foot traffic from attendees as our largest commercial [exhibitors].

Finally, we build our schedule to allow attendees time to mingle and interact outside of formal programming. SCALE includes 30-minute breaks between our sessions to allow attendees to socialize with each other, with speakers, and with exhibitors. Our attendees call this the hallway track, and tell us they often learn more during these breaks than they do during sessions.

What are the main things you have learned over the years about putting on a event the size of SCALE?

Remember why you started your event. As a community event, your goal is most likely to provide an enticing program for your contributors and/or users. Focus on them. They care most about content and activities. Build a program that you would personally want to attend and participate in. By focusing on the attendee experience, you will ensure they enjoy themselves and find the experience to be productive. They will then return year after year.

Event planning is hard work. Do not try to do it on your own. Unlike software projects, which release when ready, your event date will come whether you are ready or not. It is important to build a solid team of contributors with whom you can share the load and upon whom you can rely for support when you find yourself underwater.

Much like any other project, communication is key. Make sure you meet with your collaborators regularly and that everyone is clear on their roles and responsibilities, and then report back regularly on progress. Your colleagues will not know when you need help if they never hear from you about how your projects are coming and vice versa. Similarly, your venue or vendors will not know what you expect of them unless you effectively communicate your requirements. Meet with both groups early and often.

Finally, read everything carefully before you sign it. Contracts in the meeting and hospitality industry can be tricky and often contain hidden expenses or restrictions that may not be obvious to you at first. If you do not understand something, ask other meeting planners. There are many groups in this space that can provide you with advice. One such group is *http://www .meetingscommunity.org/*, which maintains forums and mailing lists where meeting planners can exchange ideas and ask questions.

Richard Esguerra, Humble Indie Bundle

The Humble Indie Bundle has been a unique force in presenting a collection of free games in which consumers are invited to contribute financially to support the project. The project has been hugely successful, earned impressive donations, and launched some fantastic games and the careers of their developers.

Richard works with game developers, nonprofits, and Humble Bundle customers to promote awesome, cross-platform video games and support vital causes. Every day he enjoys a healthy mix of email correspondence, social media interaction, and gameplay. The gaming community is notoriously tight, with creators and fans interacting quite closely, and every day brings an exciting new opportunity for Richard to develop the scene and catalyze changes in the overall industry.

Previously, Richard was an activist at the Electronic Frontier Foundation, advocating for free speech, privacy, and the spread of new business models for creators, where developing and interacting with online communities was of vital importance in the work of defending digital civil liberties.

What is the history of the Humble Indie Bundle? Where did the idea come from?

> The cofounders of the Humble Indie Bundle originally headed up an indie game studio called Wolfire Games, where they learned a lot about making games and the state of the industry. They had an indie game called Lugaru, and they wanted to find a way to promote it alongside the games made by their friends in the indie game community. They had assessed—as Cory Doctorow and others have said—that an independent creator's number one challenge is obscurity.

> As indie game developers and geeks themselves, they had observed various trends through sites like Reddit, Slashdot, Ars Technica, and so on. It was clear that the gaming communities didn't like DRM. Online sales that were package deals were very popular. Pay-what-you-want seemed to be somewhat hit-or-miss, but was almost always newsworthy. They were inspired by these various promotions and set out to combine all of the ideas into one, big, blowout Internet-melting event. That's essentially how the Humble Indie Bundle was born.

What kind of community did you set out to create?

While at Wolfire Games, the cofounders built a focused community of gamers and developers passionate about creating and contributing to the dream games that they've always wanted. When they moved forward with the Humble Indie Bundle, I think that the cofounders more or less set out to create a community—out of the much broader community of PC gamers—that would love and appreciate indie games. Now, the broader gaming world is starting to awaken to some of those ideas and take notice that indie games can be more adventurous than the typical mainstream hits.

How did you encourage people to purchase and thus support the project?

The Humble Indie Bundle was intended to be as compelling as possible by giving the gaming community an almost unprecedented good deal: pay-what-you-want for several awesome games, support indie game developers and worthwhile charities, and have complete control over how your purchase dollars are distributed. They designed the site to be easy to use, and the founders focused heavily on customer service, making sure that any potential customer would have few to no barriers to deciding to participate.

How did you track the success and growth of your community?

We publish live stats during every promotion, which lets everyone know how things are going. It's easy to see what the average price is, which platform's users (Windows, Mac, or Linux) are the most generous, and so on. In the past, Windows users have led the charge in terms of number of sales, but Linux users have been the most generous by far.

Customers can sign up to receive email announcements when a new bundle goes live, so that's been another way for us to know if gamers are excited about what we're doing. We also lurk and post on Reddit, which is one of our favorite online communities. A lot of the posts seem genuine, and the bad apples intent on derailing discussions seem to have less of an effect there.

What opportunities and challenges have you faced with your community since the project started?

Technical support is a pretty big challenge for each bundle. Games, like all software, can suffer from bugs or misconfigurations that require attention and know-how to fix. As our customer base has grown, so has the need to be available and responsive to our customers. At the same time, our community is also really instrumental for helping us do what we can to improve the state of the games, especially the Linux builds. When a user reports a bug and can give us good details about how to reproduce it, it gives the developer the best possible chance to squash that bug.

Have you seen people abusing the Humble Indie Bundle approach?

We've had to deal with individuals using the promotion in illegitimate ways: namely, buying bundles in bulk for a single cent, and attempting to use them in volume to win contests run by some of the folks we work with. We announced a change that requires a $1 minimum in order to be able to obtain the games through the Steam game distribution platform. (As a customer, you can still pay less than $1 and still receive the games as a direct download from us.) So far, we're happy to report that the community seems to be supporting us with this decision.

What kind of reaction have you had from the traditional gaming world to the project?

There has been a lot of enthusiasm from all corners of the PC gaming world. I think that there has always [been] a unique kind of respect for indie game developers, but without a coherent context, there hasn't always been a straightforward way to support and appreciate their work. Cave Story, for example, came out originally as a solo passion project of a Japanese developer named Pixel. It made a huge impression as a vivid throwback to platforming classics, but it was kind of a happy shock—the broader gaming world didn't know what else to do with their enthusiasm. The Humble Indie Bundle and other profile-raising projects run by indie developers are highlighting all the interesting creative work that's going on, and making it exciting and accessible to more gamers.

Game creators have responded strongly as well: we have productive, interesting conversations with developers and small studios every day. One of the most rewarding parts of doing bundles is seeing developers rewarded for taking a risk, following through with their vision, and developing a game independently.

Mark Bussler, Classic Game Room

Veteran filmmaker and game journalist Mark Bussler is the executive producer, director, and head writer for the Classic Game Room (CGR) video game review show and series of videos that debuted in 1999 and have aired on YouTube since February 2008. Classic Game Room now boasts a family of channels with over 315 million video views and hundreds of thousands of subscribers. Fans that enjoy Bussler's laid-back and entertaining look at modern and retro video games connect with the show through the CGR website (*www.ClassicGameRoom.com*) and social media outlets such as Facebook, Twitter, and YouTube.

Originally launched in 1999, Classic Game Room was the first classic video game review show on the Internet and developed a cult following before its cancellation in late 2000 due to lack of funding. During the years between the show's original cancellation and its relaunch on YouTube, Bussler produced and directed numerous feature documentaries for DVD, HDTV, and television. With his background, Bussler has grown an impressive online video community and he offers some fantastic insight to his work here.

What is the history of Classic Game Room? How did you get started?

Classic Game Room was started in 1999 as a low-budget TV show on the Internet. While it gained a small cult following, it was cancelled in late 2000 after we could not monetize it and were unable to get funding. I ended up producing documentaries for several years until late 2007 when I was ready for a change and the Internet was ready to monetize online video. Classic Game Room returned with new episodes in February 2008 on YouTube with advertisements to support the show and an audience flocking to YouTube.

Classic Game Room has developed quite a following. Was the original plan to create this fanbase?

Yes, it's essential to have a fan following if you plan on making a living as an artist. When you build a fanbase and work with the audience to create videos that they enjoy and that you enjoy making, there's always excitement about what's coming out next. The audience has always been very supportive and they've kept the show growing and changing.

Has the success of the show surprised you?

It's taken about four years of daily hard work on YouTube since 2008 and more than 12 years total to get Classic Game Room where it is now. If the show is considered successful then I think it's earned it! I am very happy that a lot of people enjoy it and care enough to watch every day and take input from my reviews but it's not surprising at this point. If anything, I think it should be even bigger, but I have a very long-term outlook with this.

What tools and facilities (e.g., forums/social media) have you used to help the Classic Game Room community keep in touch?

Up to now, YouTube has been the primary tool that allows viewers to keep up-to-date with new reviews and communicate with each other. We have forums on our website and have been making a stronger push into other social media outlets like Facebook and Twitter over the past year. What's amazing is the amount of time it takes to coordinate all of this and respond to people. Once you pass 25,000 followers it's nearly impossible to keep up as one person. It is a company effort now as several people all work to keep Classic Game Room's 200,000+ followers updated and communicating.

How can people in your community participate and contribute to Classic Game Room?

Communication through our own website at ClassicGameRoom.com is the best method to send a message because it goes directly to us. However, we have increased our Facebook and Twitter presence and find those to be valuable tools when connecting with fans. Viewers can also comment on videos or join our forums and I try to do daily Twitter updates. Sending us messages on YouTube or over Xbox and PS3 is the worst way because we can't manage or filter any of those messages.

Classic Game Room has been around for quite some time. How has the community for the show changed over that time?

The audience has definitely gotten more international and younger as the years have gone by, and I think this is an Internet trend in general. We've always had a very diverse audience that ranges from parents to college students and high school students who enjoy a wide variety of gaming eras.

How have you kept your community excited and interested in Classic Game Room over the years?

CGR mixes it up constantly and goes with the flow. Viewers will let you know what they want to see and what they've enjoyed or not enjoyed. That input is valuable. I also review games from the '70s up to the newest releases and try to cover a wide variety of styles that other shows might not. The basic formula hasn't changed. Classic Game Room is about having fun when playing games, whether it's for Atari 2600 or PlayStation 3. Our audience has always enjoyed that viewpoint and that's how I review. I also cover a lot of retro items that collectors and hobbyists enjoy hearing about, and thanks to eBay and rereleases that's always relevant.

Classic Game Room has used YouTube extensively for delivering content. What advice would you offer other communities for delivering great content and getting people to watch it?

> There's definitely an oversaturation of content on the Internet and on YouTube now, so it's harder than ever to get noticed and break out. I would recommend ignoring all "overnight successes"—you can't predict that or what will go viral; there's nothing to learn there. Growing a successful, sustainable show or blog is a lot of hard work and the tools are constantly changing. I'm not sure I have good advice other than networking with like-minded people, producing good content, using all of the tools available, and having a realistic business plan. Producing good content alone is not enough, that's for sure. You need to do it all, and that's a lot of work.

How do you financially support the creation of the show? Is it purely Google AdSense?

> In order to keep the reviews free for the viewer, Classic Game Room has been entirely ad-supported up to this point. Google has certainly found ways to monetize videos and website traffic, but like everything on the Internet, that is constantly changing and it's up to us to keep up. Using social media tools allows us to hear from fans and it's this relationship that keeps CGR growing, entertaining, and adaptable to change. If I hear of a cool new trend I'll do the exact opposite and just assume it won't work, so it's always a nice surprise if it does!

Mary Colvig, Mozilla

Mary Colvig is director of Contributor Engagement at Mozilla, maker of Firefox and one of the most successful open source projects in the world. Mary's focus is to empower and support Mozillians around the world—people who passionately support, champion, and contribute to Mozilla.

Mary has been involved with Mozilla since 2005 and has a lengthy background in PR and community marketing. She has been the driving force behind many community marketing efforts and is known to set the odd world record. Outside Mozilla, Mary is an active volunteer with the Leukemia and Lymphoma Society's Team-in-Training program and a board member for Hidden Villa, a nonprofit educational organization.

How did you get started working for Mozilla?

> It all started with a run. In 2005, I started training for my first Ironman through the Leukemia and Lymphoma Society as a volunteer fundraiser and met Rafael Ebron of the Mozilla Foundation. We quickly became running buddies and then colleagues when Mozilla started looking to bring on a new PR team. The chance to work with an organization with not only a product I love, but a mission and not-for-profit focus, was too great. It combined all my passions in one, and I ended up leading Mozilla's PR team.

> I beat Rafael at Ironman Canada 2005, but it didn't jeopardize my work with Mozilla, luckily. In 2006, I joined as a paid staff member to round out the marketing team of three.

Mozilla set out with a brave goal for Firefox. How did you start building your community?

> Our community traces its roots back to 1998 when Netscape created the Mozilla project, a free and open source project chartered to create the next-generation Internet suite for Netscape.

Within the first year of its creation the Mozilla project drew community members from around the world who helped not only to enhance functionality of the browser, but contribute to planning and overall management of the project and create a variety of new browsers.

The Mozilla community started to really gain momentum around the launch of Firefox 1.0.

The first steps we took in building a Firefox community were bringing in a few very talented volunteer engineers, Pierre Chanail, Mike Connor, Blake Ross, and others, to help us build a great product. No matter how passionate a community you have, if you don't have a product that makes a difference in users' lives, you're not going to achieve great success.

But even with a great product, we were stuck if people didn't know about it. At this point in time, more people had come online after the death of Netscape than had ever been online during the browser wars. However, most folks didn't know what a browser was or how to download an alternative browser, presenting a challenge for us.

How did you reach out to these folks?

In the summer of 2004, Blake Ross and Asa Dotzler started an effort to reach out to bloggers who were saying good things about Firefox and ask them to put up a "download Firefox" button on their site. We needed to distribute the work to make an impact with this campaign, so Blake and Asa blogged, asking for volunteer help in building a tool to manage this process. That was the beginning of Spread Firefox.

Spread Firefox became the engagement hub for Mozilla—the first large-scale community-based marketing effort the Web had ever seen. It grew to tens of thousands of members in just a few months and was the launch point for such campaigns as the New York Times Project, Firefox Flicks, and the Download Day campaign that set a Guinness Book record for most software downloads in a single day.

Mozilla has both a contributor and end-user community. What approaches have you used for growing both?

We consider everyone that chooses to use Firefox and Mozilla products as valuable members of our community. Whether or not end users realize it, choosing to use Firefox and share it with friends and family is critical to advancing our mission to create a thriving Web.

From a product standpoint, we make our users stakeholders. We encourage and enable users to customize Firefox and to take part in test driving and providing feedback on our products. This is everything from thousands of add-ons to a button built right into Firefox to provide direct feedback.

Our marketing efforts aren't traditional, either; we aim to build a personal rapport and create programs that allow users to show their support and feel a part of the overall Firefox community. This spans simple programs like our Affiliates buttons (website badges used to drive downloads), to collectively setting a Guinness World Record, to our Join Us membership program. We now have hundreds of millions of users and over 10 million direct relationships.

In terms of growing our contributor community, the principles are fairly similar in how we approach users. We work to have a compelling mission and live up to it everyday, build great products and technologies, provide opportunities for people to participate, and foster relationships.

How have you kept your community excited and interested in participating?

Foremost, it's critical that our mission and how we fulfill it has stayed relevant and compelling. We're one of the largest and most successful open source projects in the world and we've empowered millions of people to take control of their online experience, and we're continuing to evolve to keep shaping the future of the Web for the public good. This keeps people engaged.

This means expanding our scope, including Firefox for mobile, Identity and Apps, as well as initiatives around media and education. This provides volunteers and paid staff alike the chance to explore new opportunities and keep learning. At the same time, as Firefox adoption has grown, our community has had the chance to see their hard work end up in front of hundreds of millions of people. That's pretty compelling.

What glue have you used to keep your contributors together?

In addition to new products and initiatives, we've worked hard this year to get programs and infrastructure in place that support Mozillians. This includes creating a learning and development team that will support all Mozillians, building out a community directory to allow us to easily find one another, a Mozilla Reps program to better support advocacy activities and provide growth opportunities, and more.

Ultimately, we're a people-powered organization, so taking the time to foster relationships, socialize face-to-face, have fun, and see your work make an impact are just as important as any volunteer management structure.

Mozilla (the company) has grown significantly over the years. How have you balanced the relationship between company and community?

Here at Mozilla we don't see a delineation between the "company" and the "community"—we're all Mozillians. The Mozilla community comprises thousands of paid staff and volunteers working in concert to put millions of people in control of their online experience. This provides us a hybrid workforce of incredibly invested individuals—some paid and some not—that allow us to have [a] major impact on the Web. We work very hard to foster an inclusive community; each and every Mozillian should consider themselves a community manager. We all need to help on-ramp and support people trying to make an impact in our functional or regional areas. In turn, our company is here to support this overall community.

What challenges have you faced in this work?

Obviously, our rapid growth hasn't been without its bumps over the last years. Like any rapidly growing organization, we've had our growing pains. It's impossible to keep track of everything that is going on and this can be uncomfortable at times. As we've grown in number and we've taken on more ambitious projects, many of us have found ourselves in the position of having to narrow our focus, delegate, and make room for new people. This can be unnerving for anyone, whether you're a volunteer or paid staff. However, the influx of so many new people, skills, and intelligence will help us meet the new challenges that face us.

How have you handled the on-boarding of people who have come from outside traditional open source and web development communities?

The growing popularity and awareness of Firefox has drawn more and more people interested in making a difference on the Web. At the same time, the expanding scope of the Mozilla project has resulted in many more avenues for involvement and lower barriers to entry. It can be a challenge for any would-be contributor to make sense of all these opportunities and get started. We're finding we have a discoverability and on-boarding problem across all our functional areas that impacts potential volunteers from all backgrounds.

We're focusing efforts on identifying these contribution efforts, creating clear contribution paths and matching people in literally every functional area, from legal to coding to marketing to localization and more. Most of this can be fairly low-touch: being rigorous about documenting contribution opportunities and how-to guides, as well as revamping our main online touchpoints to find easy ways to get involved. However, most of us joined Mozilla based on a relationship or another Mozillian reaching out and providing a helping hand.

It's important to not lose sight of this, but [to] explore ways to make this more scalable, and it goes back to my point about each and every Mozillian needing to be a community manager. To increase our reach and touch, we launched our Mozilla Reps program which is essentially a field organization of experienced Mozillians charged with advocating for Mozilla, bringing in new contributors and mentoring them. We're also experimenting with new things like mentored first "bugs" and how we might leverage and host thousands of small events and meet-ups to introduce Mozilla. It should be easy for anyone to join Mozilla and make a difference!

Dries Buytaert, Drupal and Acquia

Dries Buytaert is the original creator and project lead for the Drupal open source web publishing and collaboration platform. Dries also serves as president of the Drupal Association, a nonprofit organization formed to help Drupal flourish.

He is also cofounder and chief technology officer of Acquia, a venture-backed software company that offers products and services for Drupal. In addition, he is a cofounder of Mollom, a web service that helps you identify content quality and, more importantly, helps you stop website spam. A native of Belgium, Dries holds a Ph.D. in computer science and engineering from Ghent University and a licentiate in computer science (MsC) from the University of Antwerp. In 2008, Dries was named one of the Best Young Tech Entrepreneurs by *BusinessWeek* and made *Technology Review*'s annual list of 35 Innovators Under 35.

What is the history of the Drupal project?

> I started work on Drupal in 2000. I had a need for a private message board and at the same time wanted to learn PHP and MySQL, two relatively new technologies at the time. Instead of using an existing message board, I decided to write my own, so I could learn about PHP and MySQL.
>
> Back then, Drupal didn't have a name as I was only using it on my sites; first my dorm room's intranet and later *http://drop.org*. Drop.org evolved from a message board into an experimental platform where I played with new technologies like RSS, RDF, "public diaries" (which later became blogs), user ratings, and more. As I added functionality, my message board system evolved into a content management system, or CMS.
>
> Furthermore, I started to use Drop.org to write and to highlight other trends on the Web. Slowly, Drop.org started to attract an audience of people interested in the future of the Web. Some

visitors would write to ask for the source code behind Drop.org. Other visitors would suggest new features for Drop.org.

How did your project transition into the Drupal we know and love today?

In January 2001, I decided to release the source code behind Drop.org as open source. I named it "Drupal," as a play on the word *druppel*, which is Dutch for "drop." I didn't have big plans for Drupal. I just wanted to share the code because people were interested. I expected maybe a dozen people would download and use it.

In the early days I focused, completely and utterly, on the aesthetics of Drupal's code. I spent days trying to do something better, with fewer lines of code, and more elegant than elsewhere. For that reason, I didn't care to maintain backward compatibility either. It felt is was the right thing to do.

What kind of community did you set out to create?

Early contributors to Drupal were developers. They fell in love with Drupal because it implemented state-of-the-art web technologies, and it did so [in a cleaner], more flexible, and more performant [way] than most other open source CMSes. I gave them free reign to implement their ideas in the best possible way, even if that negatively impacted Drupal's usability.

How did these developers start collaborating with you and with one another?

Initially, other developers would just email me patches. Then I set up a mailing list where we would exchange patches. When that stopped scaling, we decided to use CVS to exchange patches. Eventually, we built our own bug tracking and code sharing tools on Drupal.org.

Even today, the Drupal community is very developer-focused. I no longer think that is best for a tool like Drupal, and so for many years many of us have been actively recruiting designers, usability experts, [and] information architects to Drupal. The best communities are well-rounded.

How big is the Drupal community?

It wasn't until Drupal was four years old that I gave my first presentation about Drupal. To the best of my knowledge, that was really the first time that more than 20 Drupal contributors got together in person. It was a lot of fun, and made me decide to organize the first Drupal Conference in Antwerp, my hometown. Five years into Drupal, about 40 people showed up in Antwerp. More than 3,000 people attended DrupalCon Chicago in 2011, and each conference keeps on growing.

Our website, Drupal.org, gets more than 1 million unique visitors per month. Every month, thousands of people contribute to Drupal development on Drupal.org. Together, we've created over 12,000 modules that can be used to extend Drupal. About 1,000 people got patches accepted into Drupal 7 core. It is a legendary piece of work, by the community, for the community. We celebrated the release with 248 parties in 88 countries.

Do you feel that open source really empowered your community to grow like this?

Open source is the best way to build and distribute software. In some but not all cases, open source provides viable business models. An important reason why the Drupal community is so large is that we managed to create a large commercial ecosystem around Drupal. There are thousands of developers making a living with Drupal, and because of that they have a vested interest in helping to maintain and advance Drupal.

I don't see Drupal's growth stopping soon. First of all, the Web continues to expand. Second, in a world where websites become increasingly complex, it becomes less and less attractive to develop a website when you can assemble one by leveraging thousands of modules. Open source content management systems are disrupting the traditional content management industry and driving proprietary players to niche markets. All things combined, I think Drupal could easily grow into a billion-dollar industry over the [coming] years.

With a community as large as Drupal, how did you handle the scale as it grew?

At each step in our growth, we had to scale all aspects of the project; our tools, our methodologies, our infrastructure, our conferences, etc. Sometimes you can scale by automating things or by creating more efficiencies in how you work, but more often you have to scale by building a great team. You want to surround yourself with talented and passionate people, empower them, and transfer responsibilities to them. Then encourage them to do the same.

When Drupal was small, I wrote all the code, read all the support questions, and managed the infrastructure. Today, we have thousands of volunteers that contribute to different aspects of Drupal. I only review other people's code and barely code myself, and I don't think I can actually log in to our servers anymore. It's hard to let go of things that you are passionate about, but you have to if you're going to scale. This is true for everyone in the Drupal project, not just for me.

How did you govern and manage the community as it scaled up?

We govern the technical aspect from the project separately from the logistical aspects.

For the logistical aspects, I cofounded the Drupal Association. The Drupal Association currently employs more than five full-time staff [members]. They work with the larger Drupal community to maintain our server infrastructure, to organize several Drupal conferences each year, and more. The direction for the Drupal Association is set by its board of directors, of which I'm president. It is not always easy, but we elect the board of directors such that they represent the different aspects of our community. By doing so, we make sure that the Drupal Association serves the needs of the community, and not the other way around.

What makes the Drupal Association special is that it has no influence over the technical direction of Drupal. The Drupal community uses a do-ocracy model, meaning people work on what they want to work on, instead of being told what to work on. Decisions are usually made through consensus building and based on technical merit, trust, and respect. As the project lead, and with the help of my comaintainers, I help guide the community in strategic directions.

As a BDFL (benevolent dictator for life) I can veto certain decisions, or more importantly, I can make decisions when the community gets stuck. This happens, for example, when there are two competing implementations for a particular feature and the community can't agree on which proposed architecture is better.

How have you balanced the community relationship and investment from Acquia?

While Acquia may be the largest contributor to Drupal, it is still only one of many. Only a small percentage of all code contributions come from Acquia.

My priority is to help make sure that Drupal is successful. That happens to align well with my role at Acquia. Quite simply, Drupal has to be successful for Acquia to be successful. I believe this strongly enough that I would make decisions that negatively impact Acquia if it is the best decision for Drupal.

Before [I started] Acquia, Drupal was a hobby project. In other words, Acquia has allowed me to do more. I'm able to work on Drupal more than I would have if I'd continued Drupal as a hobby project. I also believe that my role at Acquia has only helped me do a better job as the project lead. Acquia has enabled me to get closer to end users of all kinds. I travel to more Drupal events and interact with more Drupal users and developers.

I love that, as a company, we can do well and can do good at the same time. A lot of the venture capital money we raised has flown back into the Drupal project or has been used to create awareness for Drupal. Everyone benefits from that.

James Spafford, Media Molecule

James started a 12-year career in the game industry as a game tester, but pursued his passion for online communities and landed roles in community management and content writing at MMO publisher NCsoft.

James joined MediaMolecule, creator of the hugely popular LittleBigPlanet games for the PlayStation 3, PSP, Vita, and other devices. The LittleBigPlanet franchise built a new community by providing gamers with the ability to create levels and content collaboratively and share it in an online gaming universe. This provided a fascinating and ground-breaking community case study.

After falling in love with LittleBigPlanet, James dived into the existing LittleBigPlanet community, building various LittleBigPlanet websites with a friend and former colleague. These grabbed the attention of some people at Media Molecule, who after a bit of nudging, gave them both jobs.

James lives on the Internet, and got a taste for community management and web content creation after founding his first fan site at the age of 16, later going on to cofound the cult editorial gaming site Idle Thumbs. He'd love to add that he's into mountain climbing, kayaking, and other exciting things, but in reality he spends most of his time either on a train to and from work, literally feeding his obsession with delicious food and drink, or on the Internet playing games.

When you were conceiving the LittleBigPlanet community, what goals and intentions did you set out to achieve?

I joined Media Molecule (Mm) shortly after LittleBigPlanet's launch, forming a small community team with my friend, Mm Designer Tom Kiss, so the community had already been conceived to a certain point. At the time, most communication about the game came from Media Molecule's own blog, as there were no official LBP destinations for reaching out to the players, other than some outdated marketing sites—Flash-based media-heavy sites with no customer interactivity.

As such, the community was quite spread out, and news seemed to come from many different sources. Our first steps were about [ensuring that] we had the basics of community covered: we reclaimed Littlebigplanet.com, and built a community-focused website for people to gather around—a place to get news, media, and support.

We also needed to make sure we had a voice in various social media places, like Twitter and Facebook, and also within the established fan communities, so we could talk to people where they were already hanging out.

With all this in place, we could write news, talk to players, hold contests, and also we were able to start addressing a bigger and steadily growing issue...

What issue was that?

LittleBigPlanet is all about being able to create your own things and share them with others. The aim was to bring creative people together, and to help people find great new things to play online.

Before the game launched, the team had little idea just how successful it was going to be, if anyone would participate at all...It turned out to be far more successful than they ever envisioned. Within six months over a million levels had been shared online. The systems designed to help people find the good stuff had only really been tested with hundreds of levels, not millions, so they needed some urgent attention.

We were able to help shape an improved set of in-game tools which we steadily built on and finally completely overhauled for LittleBigPlanet 2. Additionally, though, we developed another community destination to address the problem: LBP.me (*http://lbp.me*).

LBP.me takes all the creations made in LittleBigPlanet and serves them onto the Web. Every player and every level has a unique short URL, complete with useful info like screenshots and reviews, plus the ability to queue a level for play when you next turn on the game. LBP.me made sharing creations with others a lot easier, and combined with friend feeds, also available online, it serves as a vital tool to help you find the levels you actually want to play amongst the nearly 6 million levels now available.

How did you want to differentiate the LittleBigPlanet community from other online gaming communities?

One of the main things I specifically wanted to ensure was that the community had a spirit that reflected that of the game: one of collaboration and sharing.

Lots of online communities can be very competitive, especially between different fan sites and groups, and I wanted to try and have the spirit of sharing be the overwhelming feeling. We tried to always be as inclusive as possible, and work to make people feel like they were part of one big group of friends. I think we achieved that quite well; community sites hold interlinking contests, share resources, link to one another, and generally act friendly towards one another, so it feels like that worked for the most part. Of course, there are occasional feuds, but less so than any other community I've worked with, for sure.

A cute way we tried to encourage this at the start was by bringing back the web-ring, a forgotten feature of the Web, and something that every website used to belong to. We gave it a twist, though: the widget which you had to put onto your own site in order to be part of it would recommend another random site for people to visit, and the index of all the sites was always random. We didn't want any elitist top-sites lists, just sharing.

With such a diverse and often very young audience, how have you kept community conduct and the content produced clean, and how have you avoided porn, spam, and other inappropriate content?

We have an easy-to-use reporting tool in-game, reflected on the Web, too, that allows people to report inappropriate or offensive levels, and these are then moderated by teams based within the various Sony Computer Entertainment offices in each region around the world.

This system generally keeps naughty things out of sight; largely, though, we've found that people have a desire to contribute positively to the LittleBigPlanet. I think the game's charm works wonders on people; it's what embodies the spirit that I was so keen to have the community reflect.

What day-to-day work do you need to do as a community manager for a gaming community?

It can differ quite a bit depending on the game type, or if you are based at a publisher or at a developer, but in general it's probably not too different from any online community management. You are the conduit between the people playing and the people making the game. This means a lot of scouring on forums and social media to see what the mood is or if anything unusual is happening, and using those same channels of communication to let people know about cool events or issues they may encounter, etc. I talk to a lot of people, write content for the Web, plan events, etc.

As I'm based within the development team, it also means that some of my day can involve working on the game itself, and helping to devise the parts of the game that will have [an] impact on the community, or will hook into things we will build on the Web—for instance, designing the ratings and review systems for levels, or designing the in-game social systems.

I guess the main benefit of it being a [gaming] community over any other one is that I get to play the game [a lot]…and as our game is about allowing people to make other games, it never gets old!

Your community has scaled hugely, yet Media Molecule is a small studio. How have you coped with the scale?

Keeping Mm small has been a tough job all round, and we rely on our friends at Sony for lots of things, but we also get by with a little help from our friends, quite literally. In terms of development we outsource some things to friendly local companies, or other cool folk we are fans of. Community is no different, but our friends are key members of our community that we can rely on to talk to us regularly, and notify us if things are going wrong, if they have a cool thing that needs to be promoted, or if we missed something we need to do something about!

I would say that surrounding yourself with active and helpful people from the community is essential for any community manager, especially one on a small team. They're often quite obvious standout people who contribute a lot, or seem to post in every thread. Getting these people on your side is fairly easy as they are fans to begin with, and keeping them there is very beneficial. Plus, you get to make new friends, and possibly even new employees.

With LittleBigPlanet you can create content that is shared publicly. What challenges have you seen with how people perceive the ownership and the rights they have over such content, and how have you managed these expectations and challenges?

When someone creates something, [even] if a legal agreement means they lose ownership of it by uploading it to a server, they still perceive it as theirs; after all, they made it!

A real challenge we've faced there is in the moderation service that takes down naughty levels. With the current moderation system, there is no communication between a player and the moderator when their level is removed.

Whilst lots of people will know exactly why their creation is gone, because they obviously broke the rules, there are still cases where people do not understand what has happened to *their* level, and sadly won't be able to find out either, which can, quite understandably, result in hurt feelings.

Ideally, I'd much prefer a more open solution, where people can easily get feedback on why their creation has been censored, and be able to talk to a real person about their problems and to find out how to fix them.

What have been the main lessons learned throughout your experience of building the LittleBigPlanet community?

As a team we've learned a great deal about providing a service to people versus selling a game to people. Whilst LittleBigPlanet is a video game on a console, it's also a platform for people to Play, Create, and Share their own creations, and as such it needs to feature the same tools and services that any similar platform, such as YouTube or Flickr, might provide. LittleBigPlanet is also very similar to a massively multiplayer online (MMO) game in many aspects, and in an ideal world would carry the same level of ongoing support and service that is common in the MMO world: more two-way support for player issues, fast bug fixing, etc.

We've also learned lessons about how people relate to their creations, and share them. Once someone has spent 40 hours making something, they are going to be proud of it, and they will want to share it with people, and show off. They will want to share it with people who might not be able to see it if it just exists inside a game world. Getting these creations out of the game and onto the Web allows people to share far more easily, in places where they like to hang out with their non-LittleBigPlanet friends. For us, LBP.me was our solution, and we very much consider it an extended part of the game design itself.

We're always watching and learning, and iterating on our designs as the community evolves, so we can build a better and more enjoyable experience, and everything we have learned will be applied to our future projects.

Personally, I've learned that a simple game about playing, creating, and sharing can have some wonderful effects on people's lives, and that I'm very lucky to have worked with a community of lovely, creative people who seem to be able to blow my mind on an almost daily basis!

CHAPTER FIFTEEN

Onward and Upward

"**Focus on the journey, not the destination. Joy is found not in finishing an activity but in doing it.**"

—*Greg Anderson*

AND THIS, MY FRIENDS, BRINGS US TO THE END OF THE FIRST PART OF OUR JOURNEY. Way back in Chapter 1 we started with a bird's-eye view of community, and we have gradually zoomed in closer and closer to look at the day-to-day details. Throughout our journey, we have talked through the major topics in building a strong community.

When I conceived the content for this book, I was keen to put together a solid foundation to get the new community manager, leader, or organizer up and running as quickly as possible. I wanted to cover a diverse range of topics without bogging you down with impractical details and academic hand waving. With these goals in mind, I am proud of the outcome: I think *The Art of Community* provides the springboard to help you all build great communities.

This is only the beginning, though. The French critic and poet Paul Valery once said, "A poem is never finished, only abandoned," and the same can be said of this book.

Community management, leadership, and organization is a new and young science. There is still a long road ahead and many things to learn on the way. The first edition of *The Art of Community* was part one in an ongoing journey to document the art of building strong and effective communities. This second edition has brought a raft of updates and new content, but the content here is still a snapshot of knowledge that is begging to be extended and augmented as we explore the road ahead and discover more answers about this sometimes strange but always fascinating science.

As we close this edition, I want to share some other resources that can help you to continue on your journey.

Building Our Own Community

Since the first edition of *The Art of Community*, I have maintained a website for the book (*http://www.artofcommunityonline.org*), with updates, articles, and a place for you all to share your feedback.

The goal of the website is to not only provide a place to find out about the book, but also share interesting news, stories, articles, and feedback about topics related to community management and leadership. The website is highly social and you can share your comments, ideas, and thoughts throughout the different articles that are present on the site.

Social Media

You can also keep up-to-date with the community surrounding *The Art of Community* across a range of social media resources. Each resource is regularly updated with news about the book, interesting articles, reviews, and more. They also provide a great way to get in touch with me and discuss community management. This includes:

Twitter
  http://www.twitter.com/artofcommunity

Facebook
  http://www.facebook.com/artofcommunity

Google+
  https://plus.google.com/u/0/b/105128579377492328643/me/posts

If you want to keep up-to-date with me and my work, be sure to check out these resources:

Blog/home page
  http://www.jonobacon.org

Twitter
  http://www.twitter.com/jonobacon

Facebook
  http://www.facebook.com/jonobacon

Google+
  https://plus.google.com/u/0/114419073019603780828/posts

LinkedIn
  http://www.linkedin.com/pub/jono-bacon/0/32a/b61

Videos

I have also created a YouTube channel that is regularly updated with videos about community management, leadership, and other topics, including many of the topics covered in this book.

You can find the channel and subscribe to it at:

http://www.youtube.com/jonobacon

The Community Leadership Summit

As discussed earlier in the book, I wanted to write *The Art of Community* not only to provide one person's thesis on how to build and grow a productive and inspiring community, but also to use the book to trigger more discussion about community management ideas, best practices, and approaches. As I settled into the brutal writing schedule, I was excited about the book, but I still felt like something was missing. Seemingly being someone who prefers to replace sleep for heartburn, I decided there was one additional thing I wanted to work on: a central event and meeting place for community managers.

Like many community managers, I had traveled around the world, trudging from conference to conference to talk up my communities, but I had little opportunity to sit down with other community managers, including those from competing companies, to discuss our craft. Back then, community management was still very much in its infancy, so I assumed the attendance would be fairly small, and an intimate event could generate some really great discussion.

And thus the Community Leadership Summit was born. From its humble beginnings in 2009, the event has been run each year with over 200 attendees from a variety of different industries, projects, perspectives, and backgrounds coming together to share ideas and best practices. The event has even inspired other smaller, regional Community Leadership Summit events, too. Figure 15-1 is a group photo from the 2011 event.

FIGURE 15-1. This group photo shows many of the attendees from the 2011 Community Leadership Summit event.

The event is designed to bring together people like you and me to discuss, debate, and share our journey in learning how to build community.

How It Works

The Community Leadership Summit is a free event that usually takes place in Portland, Oregon (although this may have changed by the time you read this). The event is open to anyone who wants to participate, and it provides a combination of an open and scheduled agenda.

Most of the schedule is organized as an *unconference*; this means the schedule is open at the beginning of each day, and attendees can suggest topics and volunteer to run sessions. This approach to scheduling generates a much more diverse set of topics and content, and is much more reactive to areas of interest in community management and leadership. As an example, here are some topics from the last event:

- Top 10 Tips for Growing Your Community
- Mentoring: Recruiting New Community Members
- Offline Communities to Online Tribes
- Killer Collaboration
- The Zen of Conflict
- Fostering a Community As a Company of One
- Community and the Corporate Fortress
- Giving Props: Building Incentives and Recognition

Importantly, *everyone* is welcome to organize and run a session; an important part of the Community Leadership Summit ethos is that the event should be open to all and provide an environment where everyone can contribute interesting ideas and content.

This open schedule is also augmented with some scheduled sessions around areas of interest to community managers and leaders. This includes presentations and lightning talks; and we have even had a stand-up comedy routine in the past, too!

Finally, the Community Leadership Summit is a very social event. It is a great opportunity to meet other community managers and leaders between sessions, during breaks, and at the evening events that we organize.

Joining Us

If you would like to attend the next Community Leadership Summit, go to *http://www .communityleadershipsummit.com/* to find out when the next event will be held. You can also find plenty of information on the website about how the event works, how to suggest and propose content, who is attending, and other topics.

Although the event is free, we ask everyone to register at *http://www.communityleadershipsummit .com/register*. We do this just so that we know approximately how many attendees are joining us at the event.

Keeping in Touch

So, without further ado, it is time to close this book and go out there and build an incredible community. Good luck, and do let me know how you all get on. I am always excited to hear your stories, feedback, and ideas. You can get in touch with me at *jono@jonobacon.org*.

CONSULTANCY SERVICES

I also offer a range of consultancy services in community management, leadership, and growth. If you want to discuss your needs, feel free to email me at *jono@jonobacon.org*.

Numbers

3D environments, 455–456
5-A-Day campaign, 211, 213–214, 216

A

A Thousand Suns (album), 488
accommodations for events, 415–416
accomplishment, sense of, 126–127
accountability, 51, 313
Acquia, 513–516
action vs. theory, 17
Ad Hoc Peer Review, 114–116
addiction, 400–401
AdSense, Google, 65–66, 401
advertising, 65–66, 224
advocates vs. salespeople, 201–202
age, and member behavior, 372
alliances, 223–224
amateur press, 227–228
Anderson, Chris, xiv
announcement phase of buzz cycle, 214–216, 218, 222
anonymity, when gathering feedback, 264–265
appreciation, 127–128
Aq (Stuart Langridge), 21
ArduPilot Mega design, xi–xiv
assumptions, during brainstorming sessions, 54–55
At Home with Jono Bacon (live stream show), 233
audience, 135–136
author of this book, 522, 525
awareness, creating, 183–184

B

Bacon, Jono, 522, 525
badges, at events, 444
bandwidth, at events, 503
banners, at events, 444

BarCamp, 426, 427
Basinger, Mike, 311–313
belief
    evidenced by LugRadio community, 11–12
    importance of, 11
    instilled by Obama election, 12–13
belonging
    and threats on community, 9
    building into social economy, 5–8
    impact of workflow on, 406
    teams as units of, 33–34
    vs. family, 406–407
Betts, Andrew, 229
bikeshedding, 85–86
bit.ly service, 175
Blair, Tony, 199, 200
Bloch, Peter, 8
blogs
    and private information, 267
    community manager as contributor to, 477
    contact information on, 205
    disagreements on, 229–230
    history of, 228
    setting up, 208
blueprints, 281–282, 286, 451
bots, 153
bottlenecks
    causes of, 298, 379
    facing councils, 362
Bowling Alone (Putnam), 6
brainstorming, 53–56
broadcast appreciation approach, 128
broadcasting with social media
    contents of broadcasts, 172–173
    overview, 163
    using Twitter, 173–176
Buffy the Vampire Slayer forum, 35
bugs
    fixing, 261
    reporting, 149, 260
    tracking, 148–151, 149, 260

We'd like to hear your suggestions for improving our indexes. Send email to *index@oreilly.com*.

writing, 1
   (see also documentation)
   cultural differences in, 88–89
   inspirational, 95–96, 200–201
   mechanics of, 88
   mission statements, 48–49
   simple, clear language, 89–92
   tone, 86–94

X

X.commerce developer community, 498–500
X.org Foundation, 108
xFree86 project, 107–108
Xiaojiang Huang, xiii
Xubuntu community, 47–48

Y

YouTube, 231–232, 510

Z

Zazzle, 66
Zinsser, William, 90

Jono Bacon is an award-winning and leading community manager, author, and consultant. Currently the community manager for the worldwide Ubuntu community, Bacon is a regular keynote speaker. He has also authored four books and acted as a consultant to a range of technology companies. Bacon's blog (*http://www.jonobacon.org/*) is one of the most widely read open source blogs, and he writes regularly about community management.

COLOPHON

The cover fonts are Akzidenz Grotesk and Orator. The text font is Adobe's Meridien; the heading font is ITC Bailey.

Have it your way.

Get even more for your money.

Join the O'Reilly Community, and register the O'Reilly books you own. It's free, and you'll get:

- $4.99 ebook upgrade offer
- 40% upgrade offer on O'Reilly print books
- Membership discounts on books and events
- Free lifetime updates to ebooks and videos
- Multiple ebook formats, DRM FREE
- Participation in the O'Reilly community
- Newsletters
- Account management
- 100% Satisfaction Guarantee

Signing up is easy:

1. Go to: oreilly.com/go/register
2. Create an O'Reilly login.
3. Provide your address.
4. Register your books.

Note: English-language books only

To order books online:
oreilly.com/store

For questions about products or an order:
orders@oreilly.com

To sign up to get topic-specific email announcements and/or news about upcoming books, conferences, special offers, and new technologies:
elists@oreilly.com

For technical questions about book content:
booktech@oreilly.com

To submit new book proposals to our editors:
proposals@oreilly.com

O'Reilly books are available in multiple DRM-free ebook formats. For more information:
oreilly.com/ebooks

O'REILLY®

Spreading the knowledge of innovators oreilly.com

CPSIA information can be obtained
at www.ICGtesting.com
Printed in the USA
BVOW04s0328261016

466025BV00001B/1/P